SEXUALITY

SEXUALITY

A Reader

edited by Karen Lebacqz
with David Sinacore-Guinn

The Pilgrim Library of Ethics

THE PILGRIM PRESS, *Cleveland, Ohio*

The Pilgrim Press, Cleveland, Ohio 44115

Printed in the United States of America on acid-free paper.

04 03 02 01 00 99 5 4 3 2 1

Library of Congress Cataloging-in-Publication Data

Sexuality : a reader / edited by Karen Lebacqz with David Sinacore-Guinn.
p. cm.
Includes bibliographical references.
ISBN 0-8298-1210-5 (paper : alk. paper)
1. Sex. 2. Gender identity. 3. Man–woman relationships. 4. Sex (Psychology). 5. Sex role. I. Lebacqz, Karen, 1945– .
II. Sinacore-Guinn, David.
HQ21.S4754 1998
306.7—dc21 98-37851
CIP

Contents

THE RELATIONAL SELF

THE SOCIAL CONSTRUCTION OF SEXUALITY

SEXUAL VIOLENCE

THE PERSONAL IS POLITICAL

PART TWO
The Search for Ethical Guidance

Acknowledgments

I AM INDEBTED to several colleagues for their help, particularly Dr. Natalie Polzer, Dr. Kathryn Young, and Dr. Victor Hori of McGill University. Above all, thanks go to David Sinacore-Guinn for his very able assistance at every step of this process. It has been a collaborative venture from the beginning, although I take full responsibility for all errors of commission and omission.

Introduction: The Method behind the Madness

Karen Lebacqz

Not all young people are sexually active today, but their music presupposes a knowledge level and a familiarity with sexual terms and expressions that would shock some of their parents. It is my conviction that such lyrics do not serve young people well when it comes to understanding dimensions of sexuality or developing an adequate sexual ethic. It is also my conviction that we can do better and that the next generation need not repeat the mistakes of the past.

The design for this reader grew out of my efforts to put those convictions into practice by teaching sexual ethics to undergraduates at McGill University. Teaching in a university setting has its demands: multiple religious traditions must be represented and respected, Western philosophical reasoning and social sciences must be included, and the realities of college life must not be neglected. These demands convinced me that we needed an approach to the teaching of sexual ethics that I did not find readily available.

Many texts on sexual ethics work out of a single tradition, presenting Jewish or Christian or Western philosophical views of sexuality, for example. While their modesty of effort is to be commended, they do not present a sufficient range of material for good university teaching. Very few look at more than one tradition; those that do tend to have chapters on "Jewish attitudes," "Hindu views," and so on. They present traditions as parallel but not necessarily as having anything to teach each other. I am firmly of the conviction that all traditions can learn from each other, and I want a text that enables, and even requires, that mutual learning.

Another typical approach in college texts is the "hop, skip, and jump" tour of sexuality. Chapters are offered on topics such as singleness, homosexuality, marriage and divorce, pornography, and so on. This allows the reader to go to the precise topic of interest but fails to show how these topics are interrelated, how they are all shaped by culture, and how a coherent framework toward addressing them might be developed. College students want, need, and deserve a coherent approach that allows them to develop their own framework, respectful of their own traditions and family backgrounds, but with exposure to critical sources and challenges.

This book makes an effort to do just that. It is a collection, but a collection with a difference: it is meant to be read as a whole, not as a sourcebook from which one can simply pick and choose according to some topic of interest. It weaves sources and issues together, developing a framework as it goes. By the end, the reader will have encountered discussions of celibacy, singleness, partnered sex, marriage, divorce, the influence of media on sexuality, rape, the formation of male and female identity, lesbian, gay, bisexual, and heterosexual sexuality, and many other specific issues. The reader will have explored sexuality in Buddhist, Hindu, Islamic, Jewish, and Christian traditions, as well as in philosophical frameworks. But there are no sections on homosexuality, Jewish sexual ethics, or feminism; rather, insights from gay and lesbian writers, Jewish thinkers, and men and women have been woven into the text throughout.

This interweaving is meant to accomplish two things. First, it acknowledges that every voice, tradition, and era may have something to teach us about sexual ethics. Second, it allows the development of a perspective on sexuality that is coherent, even though it is formed of insights from the diversity of traditions, eras, and voices. In a postmodern world, we need not be stuck with ethical relativism. This is not a single-authored systematic analysis of sexual ethics, then, but it is also not simply a collection of scattered readings. It is like a patchwork quilt, where pieces of different texture and sometimes even of clashing color can nonetheless be formed into a whole picture that has a shape, structure, meaning, and perhaps even beauty. While no single view is advocated, and there are certainly differing views represented, the reader who completes this text should have developed resources for analyzing and criticizing messages about sexuality given through popular culture.

The text is in two parts. In part 1 we explore different dimensions of sexuality. Recognizing that college students are often dealing with changing bodies and raging hormones, the text begins with what is often our most unexamined assumption: that sex has to do with bodies. Starting with our *embodiment,* we work outward to examine how that body is part of a sexual *self,* how the sexual self connects to others in *relationship,* how we are shaped by our *culture,* and particularly in the West by links between *violence* and sexuality, and how what we think of as personal is therefore deeply *political.* Having taken this journey, we are ready to acknowledge that any adequate sexual ethic will have to be self-consciously political: it will have to attend to the realities of cultural shaping and of the distribution of power that so often determines not only what counts as acceptable behavior but even what counts as knowledge.

In part 2 we turn to exploring resources for the development of an adequate sexual ethic. We look at how *text, tradition, reason,* and *experience* might be appropriated as sources that tell us who we should be and how we should behave. Finally, we look at several *contemporary proposals* for how to frame a coherent and valid sexual ethic adequate to the political task of recognizing our historically formed, culturally conditioned, tradition-bound selves.

It will be readily apparent that what is offered here is only a small sampling from the myriad of things that have been written on sexuality and sexual ethics. Journals on sexuality abound. There is an entire *Encyclopedia of Homosexuality.* No text can reflect the actual richness of the discussion on sex. Difficult choices had to be made. I have included here some "classics" (e.g., Tachibana), some "contemporary classics" (e.g., Nelson, Wolf, *Humanae Vitae*), and also some discussions by less well known but provocative thinkers. Each of these selections was chosen with my purposes in mind. Authors were not consulted and the selections here will not necessarily reflect the fully developed thinking of any author. For example, the only piece of my own included here is more than ten years old and certainly does not adequately express my current perspectives. But it fills a particular niche in the development of the framework offered here, and that is why it was chosen.

It should also be clear that choosing a selection does not necessarily mean that I agree with the author's perspective. While I think we have something to learn from each of the selections here, and I hope that, taken together, they make a quilt worthy of our attention, I have deliberately chosen some provocative items with which I do not agree. Part of the task of ethics is learning to do critical analysis, and it is my expectation that readers of this text will bring to bear that analysis on every item here.

I made a concerted effort to include writings from five major religious traditions, but the resulting text is still heavily Western and Christian. Indeed, the very category of sexual ethics is a Western category. It reflects the history of Western culture and fits best the two religious traditions most closely associated with that culture—Judaism and Christianity. Western approaches to sexuality and sexual ethics do not always fit well with other religious traditions. There is no discussion of sexual ethics in most Buddhist texts. Buddhist ethics tends to focus on the development of attitude, character, and vision, on ways of being in the world and ways of perceiving the world. It is not oriented toward problem-solving or behavioral issues, as Western ethics tends to be. In spite of the inclusion of writings from other traditions, therefore, those traditions may not be well represented in a text whose overall framework remains Western. This is perhaps a place where we need to learn from the silences by attending to ways in which even the categories are foreign to many ways of thinking. Sexual ethics, like all ethics, is an ongoing conversation, and this collection is only one voice in the dialogue.

Part One
DIMENSIONS OF SEXUALITY

EMBODIMENT

[1]

The Moral Significance of Female Orgasm: Toward Sexual Ethics That Celebrates Women's Sexuality

Mary D. Pellauer

FOR A FEMINIST like me, there are many lovely puzzles in sexual ethics in the Western tradition. None, however, is so basic as the curious notions of women's sexuality. To correct these misbegotten notions, it is not enough just to criticize the errors. We must create more adequate accounts of female sexuality. As one small step in that project, in this essay I will explore one aspect of women's sexual experience—orgasm.

I do so for a set of interconnected reasons. For the last fifteen years I have been deeply involved in the movement against physical and sexual abuse. The feminist movement has asserted that sexual violence is not sex, and we have worked to make this new distinction persuasive. To get further with this project, we need to pay at least as much attention to our joys and delights as to our pains and disappointments. Otherwise we limit our own thriving.[1]

While orgasm is not a sufficient condition for good sex, it may be among the necessary ones. Thus the text below will describe some experiences of female orgasm, prospecting for *concepts* appropriate for this moral terrain.[2] I

SOURCE: From Mary D. Pellauer, "The Moral Significance of Female Orgasm," *Journal of Feminist Studies in Religion* 9, no. 1–2 (spring/fall 1993). Used by permission.

will suggest from this account a few themes to which we could usefully pay more attention. I invite my colleagues in feminist ethics to work this area further.

This invitation is not pro forma. I need help. I find this topic confusing—sometimes literally beyond words, sometimes just not fitting well with other ethical language. This may be due to my lack of skill or to problems inherent in this topic, or both. I have no qualms about admitting I need help; this area has been systematically overlooked and distorted in the previous centuries of sexual ethics. Female orgasm is problematic from the start. Before we look specifically at my account, we need to glance at some of the problems.

What Happens When We Think About Female Orgasm?

We find out it's not easy. Female orgasm is problematic in a surprising number of ways. These difficulties group themselves into three large sets: First, we cannot take the experience for granted. This is extremely odd, and the more we think about it, the odder it becomes. The issues about whether women experience orgasm soon coalesce into a second area, intellectual or conceptual problems. Third, some features of the experience itself make it difficult to communicate.

The Experiential Problems

Even sexually active women cannot take orgasms for granted. Faking orgasms is a topic we now find portrayed in popular movies like *When Harry Met Sally* or discussed in magazines on the supermarket stand.[3] Even in these decades after Masters and Johnson and the whole sex therapy industry spawned by their work, sexologists find many women unsure what orgasm really is.

Anorgasmia among women appears to be common in our society, though perhaps less common than it once was. Its exact extent, now or earlier, is not clear.[4] The best contemporary evidence about the extent women experience orgasms comes from the 1990 *Kinsey Institute New Report on Sex:*

> Approximately 10% of all women have never had an orgasm by any means (this is called total anorgasmia). Between 50 and 75% of women who have orgasms by other types of stimulation do not have orgasms when the only form of stimulation is penile thrusting during intercourse.[5]

"Orgasmic dysfunction" is now *defined* as the inability to reach orgasm while masturbating. This definition conceals an enormous range of problems in sexually active relationships.

Note that these 1990 Kinsey Institute figures are stated as blunt facts, unqualified by social group, culture, or historical period.[6] Indeed, for total anorgasmia, figures in the 10 percent range have been constant through the last two decades. For earlier in the century the classic Kinsey reports are indispensable. It is rarely noticed that to the "0–6" continuum of heterosexual-homosexual orientation, the Kinsey team added another category—type X. Type X appeared for the first time in *Sexual Behavior in the Human Female,* for this category was composed almost entirely of women. Individuals were rated X if they did "not respond erotically" to anybody, neither the other nor the same sex. From the description, I cannot tell whether the individuals of type X were anorgasmic or asexual altogether. The Kinsey team categorized 9 percent of the sample as anorgasmic, but also named 2 percent as asexual.[7]

Before Kinsey, numbers like these did not exist. Prescriptive literature of the Victorian period took female disinterest in sexuality for granted. Sexual anesthesia was expected. (The cleverness of Kinsey's strategy was to assume that women had orgasms, asking only how often and with whom.) We now know that this ideology was not so all-encompassing as historians once thought. Prior to the Victorian period, information is murkier yet, but sexual anesthesia was not assumed.[8]

Partial anorgasmia, or occasional sex-without-orgasm, is harder to count. Figures about the proportion of women's sexual experiences that include orgasm are not very precise. The 1990 Kinsey Institute *Report* tells us:

> About 23% of women have experienced their first orgasm by age 15 and 90% by age 35. These figures include orgasm from masturbation, a partner's manual and/or oral stimulation of the genitals, nocturnal dreams, fantasy, and other sources—not just intercourse.[9]

The diversity of women's experiences of sex in these dry numbers is fascinating. More importantly, it is fundamental to any discussion of female sexuality. Women cannot take orgasms for granted. Men apparently do so, at least for most of the life span. Female orgasm does not come "naturally." We have to *learn* it. While this may also be true of male orgasm, it is emphatically the case for women. What is learned may be learned askew, idiosyncratically, or may be biased by hidden assumptions. Many layers of interpretation swathe experiences of orgasm like veils or shawls—thus pressuring us toward the second layer of problems.

Interpretive Problems

Several issues arise. Some, easier to name than to overcome, arise from social pressure: What will people think? When I told several women I was writing about orgasm, the range of responses was intriguing. "So many women are so far from there—they can't talk about sexuality at all, not even the simplest and most basic parts," said one. (This is true.) Others were tired of the pressure to have orgasms or the immense relationship issues. A third group hinted that perhaps I thought I was better than other women. Still others were simply silent. A small group said, "Neat, I'll look forward to finding out what you have to say." Some ethicists may dismiss social pressure as negligible; I cannot. It created internal inhibitions and self-doubts about this work, a tidal pull through which I had to wade in order to persevere, not always clear why I was doing so.

Responses like these raised a myriad of questions about what orgasm means to women. What differences are important between women who find this topic energizing and those who find it wearisome? Between those willing to talk and those who are silent? Does having orgasms confer moral status? Can sex-without-orgasm still be good sex? Is orgasm a male-dominated standard for evaluating sex?

Whether we experience orgasm may be related to the conflict of interpretations. Earlier in this century, women who did not have vaginal orgasms were called frigid. By now almost everyone knows about the errors of the Freudian school, with its misbegotten notions of the women who had not made a successful transfer of sexual energies from the clitoris (childish) to the vagina (mature). Though the Kinsey team was critical of this understanding and emphatic about the need for more empirical data, it was the work of Masters and Johnson in their laboratories, and the many women who volunteered there, that corrected basic errors of this interpretation.[10]

Most recently, the discovery of sexual violence has shifted interpretations once again. Today we are much more likely to learn that abusive experiences, especially in childhood, are the prime reasons that otherwise healthy women have sexually dysfunctional experiences.[11] (And this is what we call them: "dysfunctions.") The studied disinterest in sexual violence that prevailed in the first two-thirds of the century has been overwhelmed by the detailed exploration of several kinds of sexual abuses.

However, it remains the case that women who have not been directly victimized by sexual abuses may still not experience orgasm. We also need, by and large, accurate information about female sexuality, personal sexual knowledge of the kind gained by masturbation, and if in a relationship, a partner informed (informable?) and willing to respond to the woman's specific needs. This is a complex combination of conditions.[12]

What it means to us, what differences between us are crucial—these issues encroach on others that are akin. An account is a created artifact, a second-order phenomenon. To recognize that sexuality is always already interpreted—even in the driest of scientific or medical tomes—is indispensable.[13]

To create an "account" means to describe in words, and written words at that.[14] Writing not only inscribes this description, fixing and distancing it, but it shapes these words by genre.

Until very recently, written accounts of sexuality were dominated by a few genres—medical/scientific and confessional/pornographic, in particular.[15] These genres may inflect women's accounts into line not only with sexist expectations but also with newly formed feminist expectations that may be shortsighted or too small. Much as I might wish for a new genre to realize the newness of accounting for female sexuality, I have no such exalted end here. Some commentators suggest that first-person descriptions of experience by ordinary women are a new genre, and I will employ this method here as the starting point for ethical reflection, together with comments on the problems of giving such an account.[16] Whether in the long run this practice will yield new methods in ethics, I cannot say.

Phenomenological Problems

Knots and snarls of other kinds also appear in the topic. If I persist despite the previous layers of problems (no small effort) and scrutinize my experiences, four specific features of orgasm as experienced also make an account problematic.

To begin with, orgasms are brief, even ephemeral; they are bursts of intense pleasure that may be overwhelming. Even if one has several, each is fairly short.[17] The fleeting nature of the experience makes it hard to capture; "overwhelming" is tricky both to live through and to describe.

Second, to describe an orgasm ordinarily means to remember it. This requires special skills or insight—memory, for instance, or a gift for words. Trying to describe one while it is occurring is odd (though one might try this, for instance, to heighten the pleasure of one's partner), but I usually find that words disappear or they reduce to expressive noises. When I try to remember an orgasm, it proves tricky to recall a specific one. They run together in my mind.

Even so, third, they are not all alike. Some are intense bursts, some are more diffuse. (So much so, in fact, that I can now wonder if the first problem is stated properly.) Some are better than others, and I am not sure if this is always a case of "more" (more pleasurable) or if there are qualitative differences. They group together in families, or perhaps arrange themselves on a continuum. Furthermore, while there are things I can do to ensure that I experience an orgasm, I am not in control of the kind of orgasm I experience on any given occasion. If I notice that I am forgetting the more diffuse ones, I cannot plan to have one in order to explore its details.

Fourth, how do I know that the experiences of other women are like mine? Women do not often talk about orgasms. Indeed, they are so very personal that we may suspect that we are not experiencing the same thing. "Did the earth move?" asks a character in a Hemingway novel. Well, maybe not. Should it? I have felt shaken, almost shivered apart, but I have never felt the earth move. If another woman says it is like a hiccup (another image I cannot relate to), are we different in some fundamental way? Are there correlations between these chasms or nuances of experiences and other factors, such as social class, culture, race or ethnic background, sexual orientation, religion? We don't know exactly.

That there may be such correlations leads me to name at least the clear limits, right at the start, of this sample of one. I am predominantly heterosexual, a "1" on the Kinsey scale.[18] I have a doctoral degree. I am white by "race," though beige and pink in fact. Today I have a lot of money by our culture's standards, though I remember what it was like to be poor. Both class and education correlate with specific strands of sexual experience in our society, though perhaps more so for men than for women. And in Kinsey's sample and some other studies since, for women (but not for men), we must add religion.[19] I am Lutheran by denominational heritage and ongoing choice, though denomination is too crude a measure for the real differences among women. It is important that I heard in confirmation (1958–60) that God created human sexuality and declared it to be "very good," a cause for celebration, though subject to sin. (I was later surprised to find that all Lutherans did not learn this in confirmation, indeed, that very few did.) That is a lot of limits.[20]

These limits may be insurmountable hazards. Alerted to them, however, we can guard against universalizing any particular instance without serious checking with the varieties of women's experiences. I acknowledge these limits; indeed, I embrace them. They are the roots of my standpoint in the world. If we do not tell the truth as it appears to us from our many standpoints, we have no hope either of broadening our range of vision or of finding any similarities between us. My experience is not enough, to be sure, but it is enough to begin.

My account will be conspicuously heterosexual. It is safer in this homophobic and heterosexist society for a heterosexual account to take public form. It is also relatively safe for me to describe my sexual experiences because I am in a long and stable marriage. If I were a lesbian, and/or if I were single, it could be extremely dangerous to do what I will do here. If I were African American, Asian, Native American, Hispanic, or Jewish, I would risk setting off racism. This is tragic. It is straightforwardly unjust. It strikes at the heart of our ability to assess the moral significance of female orgasm. It means that the best discussions of these issues may never occur in public. Male ethicists may never hear them. I may not either. (Safety is not morally neutral.)

Some readers may be thinking: With such an array of problems, why bother? I too might grow weary just at this point, but I don't. Problems can also be sources of curiosity and creativity, provided we linger with them, mull over them. I experience a curious exhilaration about these problematic layers, each one multiple: Why are there so many? It would be enough to have one set. (It certainly would be enough to have the problems of whether we are experiencing orgasm.)

The presence of three distinguishable layers of problems leads me to speculate that female orgasm is *overdetermined as problematic.* I begin to suspect that female orgasm is very important indeed. What stirs in our orgasms, that there should be so many obstacles around them? And this lures me on: the prospect of pleasure, rejoicing, delight. Whether absent or present, what does pleasure mean? Is it essential or accidental? Is it ethically significant, even foundational? To get at those issues, we must look closely at the experience.

Stalking the Big O

At the risk of being overprecise, I find six important elements in my experiences of orgasm. I do not claim them as normative, but as suggestive, provocative, intriguing. They are worth lingering over.

1. *Being Here-and-Now.* There are no recipes for lovemaking to orgasm (except this one). It is not capable of being routinized. What gave me a delicious tingle yesterday may be ho-hum blah today, and vice versa. Yesterday's slow and languorous time may be today's urgency and snap changes, or vice versa. Yesterday's silly mood may be today's solemnity or earnestness. Every time I must enter fully and freshly into just what is here-and-now, the precise sensations that occur in the blending of our bodies.

   And this is difficult. Any number of distractions can endanger full awareness—muscle cramps, odd mental associations, ill health, differences in timing. (We can also add pain, unpleasantness, aversion to certain behaviors, numbing out, flashbacks.) Cracker crumbs in the sheets, for instance, left there by a child reading, can become boulders when all the nerve endings are firing. At other times, oddly, the focused human spirit can shut out everything but the luminous glow of the other's skin/self, magnetically pulling me away from the rest of the universe so completely that nothing else can get in, not even those same cracker crumbs. Which will be the case on any specific occasion, is impossible to foretell.

Concentrating, focusing—these are "mental" abilities that are as much a part of sex as any purely physical abilities. Being fully present, where is the language for this? Meditation is the closest analogue I know; this comparison is surprisingly apt, for both are disciplines of being here-and-now, of letting go. This is to be receptive in a way that is not the opposite of sometimes insisting or demanding. Forcing or faking are the enemies of this state.

2. *Varieties of Sensations.* So, what is it like? I descend into our skins, attention riding the places where we touch, following the curve of this back under my fingertips and palms, following the electric trail of these hands on my planes, the sweated prairies of our torsos pressed into each other, the moisture of the inside velvet of this mouth joining with mine, the blessed smells of sweat rising as incense, the rises of flesh where little hairs entice me to run and play like a child in the woods. We mingle and mesh. Hands are electric. The passage of palms and fingertips over my skin leaves lightning trails of incandescence behind to mark where they move. In early states it is all surface.

At some point this glowing heat intensifies, shifting inward and downward inside me. But what these feelings gain in intensity, they lose in clarity. The middle is often confusing. I often do not know exactly what I want or need at this time. This stage does not supply me or my partner with clear guidance about how to satisfy these deep undercurrents. Sometimes I flail around. But in the farther reaches of this phase, I would do anything to make this last forever. (I think this is what the sexologists call the "plateau phase.") There is something greedy and isolated in this experience, especially in the last moments. I am both completely focused on my partner's touches and yet somehow the other almost disappears, leaving me riding this flesh.[21]

There is a directionality here. I seek to go further, riding the edges of the eruption to tip into the volcano. To stop here is frustrating, incomplete; it leaves me with a sense that it is not over, that there is more. Yet it is not automatic that I will go over the edge to this something else.

If I am lucky, I do go over the edge. Tremors center in my pelvis, vibrating me like a violin string. As I am shaken from the hips outward, my bones turn to lava, languorous liquid fire, heated jelly in the pelvis and thighs, magma coursing molten down.

Sometimes it is not this strong or vibrant. If I try to replicate yesterday's experience, I am frustrated. If I expect magma to course down my legs, a spasm of calm surprises me, like a cool ripple in a pond, more a release from tension than shaking in a vast hand.[22] All I can do is to remain open to the flaring guidance I receive from the impulses and feelings as they arise, little beaconlights summoning me forward.

Though there is pleasure in plenty here, pleasure alone does not do justice to this experience. Pleasure has been present all along the way. There is more. But this language suggests that the difference between orgasm and what precedes it is only quantitative. This is mistaken. It is also a difference in quality. To elucidate this change in quality, I add another element.

3. *Ecstasy.* At the moment/eternity of orgasm itself, I melt into existence and it melts into me. I am most fully embodied in this explosion of nerves and also broken open into the cosmos. I am rent open; I am cleaved/joined not only to my partner, but to everything, everything-as-my-beloved (or vice versa), who has also become me.[23] The puny walls of my tiny separate personhood either drop so that I-you-he-she-we-they-it are one *or* they build up so thoroughly that all/me is one.[24] Either way of stating it calls out for its opposite: paradoxland.

An alternate reading of this quasi-mystical dimension: My partner's skin is an icon of the universe. I am enraptured, captivated, mesmerized, by the planes of this back, arms, navel plain, thighs, the globes of this rear end blending gracious curves into thighs and back, and by my own as well. I fall/slide into them, and they turn into the universe. When I am in this state, reverently and greedily cherishing these gracious plains of flesh, whole-self-as-caress, I want to cherish every plane in the world with this same tenderness—the wood of the bedside table, the walls of the room, the grass of the yard outside, the iron bars of the back fence, the gnarled bark of trees, all call out to me to caress them in this same tender mood, not to intrude upon them my sexuality, but to cherish them as I cherish our skin/self.

Orgasm is sui generis. It is paradoxical. Ecstasy is what is at stake here.[25] *Ek-stasis,* standing outside the self, is the closest word for this state. At the same time, it is the most definite incarnation I know outside of childbirth, for in it I am most completely bound to the stimulation of my body. Thus, immanence and transcendence meet here, another paradox. The experience is peculiar/wondrous in other ways as well. To everyday consciousness, the dissolving of ego's boundaries, nonseparateness, may always look like nonexistence. It scares me. It also makes me thrive. Now I know the full range of my capacities and my ownmost being. It is a limit-experience.[26]

4. *Vulnerability.* As our relationship deepened and improved, as we learned together about female orgasm, I became heartshatteringly threatened by

the goodness of this experience, this ecstatic union with my beloved. Some of that was intrinsic to the paradoxes above, but not all. It slowly became apparent that my partner eagerly and persistently sought *my* pleasure. My ecstasy excited and touched him; he was eager for my orgasm. This was daunting, especially if I grew impatient. On the occasions when I felt that I would never get it off, and that it was time to quit, he would not.

That my pleasure was important to him, this was hard to accept, to let in. That he would refuse his own release till I had mine, that he was willing to persist in trying to bring my release/ecstasy, that he reveled in it: This shook me very deeply. It was so very unexpected. My surprise about this says more about me than it does about him. I did not expect to be loved. I did not expect him to have the capacity to put me before himself. I expected only to be secondary.[27]

There is an ambiguity here. Some partners and some circumstances might make his stance oppressive. Some may consider the pursuit of orgasm to be a distortion of sexuality, another instance of male goals and male will overriding female choices. I can only report that I did not and do not experience it this way. I experience it as grace, an instance of his vulnerability-to-me reaching out to meet my vulnerability-to-him.[28]

5. *Power.* Perhaps it could easily become domination, because there is power in this transaction. Indeed, sometimes I balk at this ecstatic explosion precisely because of the power. Sex with him is a living icon of the power in his body, making me tingle along every nerve at his touch, making me rouse urgently toward him. That is because I love him and he turns me on. There is a dialectic here of his power meeting mine, that is, he has this power because I respond to him and this response is mine. But I only "know" that, in a kind of distanced way. I do not experience it, I have to reason it out. When his hands glide along my skin, I experience it as the power of his hands and not the power of my response. He may experience it as the power of my response, but I do not. And possibly I cannot, because what is "really" happening here is the power of the connectedness between us. The tingle is neither in his hands nor in my skin, but only at the interface between them. Separated, there is no tingle, no power. Our nonrelational language makes it difficult to say this and sometimes difficult to perceive it. (And "interface" is not a very sexy word.)

But, as we touch, mingle, play together in our bed, I experience these connections occurring as *his power,* the more so the closer I approach to orgasm. Therefore, I experience an orgasm and all the impelling feelings before it as his power over me. This frightens me. I must open myself up to his power over me in order to receive this ecstasy, and this is not easy. It depends upon trust that is built up in many elements of our relationship—the mutuality growing, the confidence in reliability, the sense that this person will not hurt me on purpose, our abilities to forgive each other.

6. *Nothing Above Can Be Taken for Granted.* All of this is complicated by the fact that I do not experience this tingling/burning/melting every time we touch, nor even continuously during our lovemaking. Indeed, most of our touch is warm, nurturing, nonsexual touch. Only sometimes do these sparks flare.

   Part of the difficulty of making love is right there. Either of us can be mistaken about whether the other is turned on by something we are doing. It requires communicating about which is which, and what we want. I have to say what I want. I am not always good at that; sometimes I am a coward, yes, but sometimes I literally do not know. Sometimes the effort of concentration does not seem worth it. And on those occasions, not always, but often, no orgasm.

   On the other hand, sex-without-orgasm is not nothing. Besides the pleasure inhering in every stage before orgasm, there is also warmth, comfort, intimacy, the experience of belonging in an embrace. I would not trade these non-orgasmic goods of sexuality even for ecstasy.

Flirting with the Edges of Sexual Ethics

So, what does it mean? There is too much here for one essay to tidy up all the loose ends, and I affirm that.[29] I intend to conclude this essay only in the minimal sense of ending it. I find it hard to draw conclusions in the sense of coming to rest in a particular insight. (This may be inevitable since I have stressed the boundarylessness of orgasm.) I have been tempted to start several new essays at this point. I suspect this is because concentrating on female sexuality is potentially system-generating, that is, it points us toward a different way of life as well as a different way of thought, or several.

This leads into a first set of concluding comments. *We need a multiplicity in feminist sexual ethics that can at least match the multiplicity of women's sexual experiences.* Ethical reflection on female orgasm could go in many different directions, and these differences enrich rather than threaten our work. I invite my colleagues to give more attention to several clustered themes.

The power issues are familiar. Though feminist ethics has done more to illuminate mutuality than any other kind of ethics, we have hardly exhausted the topic. Considering trust, vulnerability, and openness may be key for moving the discussion another notch.[30]

Some readers may wish to raise issues about the sacred. Some empirical studies since the Kinsey reports stress that religion continues to make a difference in whether women experience orgasm. If this is so, it raises a host of intriguing questions. Further, if I am right that ecstasy is a limit-experience, then religious issues are inherent in orgasm. Whether, and if so how, specifically Christian ethics or theology may be related to female orgasm is an open question.

Historical and social topics, touched briefly in the section on anorgasmia, are worth pursuing. The historical character of sexuality is strongly resisted in our culture. That we are malleable in our most intimate places, our muscles and cells, leads me to paradox again. (This might explain body-mind dualism without falling into it.) We could also use some serious interpretation of the fact that sexuality is learned (rather than "natural") and what difference this makes to ethics.

Warmth, comfort, touch, intimacy, the nonorgasmic goods of sexuality, could all bear much more reflection. How we might talk about a sense of belonging that could be distinguished from patriarchal ownership (belonging with versus belonging to) could be crucial. Obviously I have laid aside desire, imagination/fantasy, and masturbation-to-orgasm—all extremely important topics for female sexuality.

Though my darling is an important background presence here, I have bracketed all questions about the sexual experiences of men. Having women comment about male sexuality would at least be a refreshing change from the prior centuries. I believe that we can do this empathetically and insightfully, because otherwise what would be the point?

If I had many more pages, I would reflect on the changing boundaries about sexual matters in our society and the need to dance between the polarities of uniting and differentiating. I would want to work out the ways that experiences of good sex ground the movement against sexual abuses, since hostility and domination do not mix with any of the six elements of orgasm.

Issues about writing may also be important. How do I communicate the bursting delight, the delicious melting-into-existence of good sex? The language of so much academic prose is dreary, boring, and distanced. These qualities contradict the experience. I do not mean only that we need more passion in sexual ethics, but we need the whole range of emotional expressiveness. Besides being passionate and intense, good sex can also be fun, humorous, and lighthearted. I'd like to encourage my colleagues to try out various tones of voice—rushing breathlessness, lyrical modes, perplexity, tenderness, frustration. It would be good if we thought more seriously about genre as well as about concealing and revealing in nonfiction. Issues about writing are in part issues about language. So we need to open space for a second set of comments.

What Ethical Language Fits?

When I consider the language of ethics and my experiences of orgasm, I am confused. Little of it seems relevant to the specific character of ecstatic union. Even if we begin with simple, basic ethical terms, something goes awry.

Consider "should." It is instructive to notice what happens if we ask: "Should women have orgasms?" or more precisely, "Should women have orgasms when we have sex?" In several ways this question is odd. Consider, for instance, its parallel, "Should men have orgasms?" or "Should men have orgasms when they have sex?" In almost all cases (before advanced age or specific dysfunctions such as retarded ejaculation), if a man is having sex, he is having an orgasm.[31] Most men cannot imagine having sex regularly, let alone for years, without orgasms.

Just as peculiar is what happens when we try to answer the question. The consequences of saying *either* no or yes are odd. Though at first glance, I want to say, "yes of course," this does not accomplish much in the way of healing. Indeed, it may be actively harmful for anorgasmic women. "Should" can deepen women's problems rather than transform them.[32] On the other hand, saying no commits us to enshrining women in deprivation: clearly unacceptable.

These same problems arise for other varieties of ethical language: orgasm is not a duty or an obligation. (This line of thinking may be what creates faking.) I have problems asserting that it is a right, though the consequences of arguing that it is not a right are unacceptable. It is not a virtue; it neither produces virtue nor proceeds from virtue. (On the other hand, female orgasm is emphatically not a vice.) It is not a privilege or a luxury. It is a good, and a very high-level good at that, but a peculiar one. It is not an achievement, however much I have worked hard.

The language that feels closest for me may raise other feminists' hackles—the theological language of gift or grace, the surprisingly unmerited, gratuitous gift. The heterosexuality of my account creates some of these problems. It may suggest that our orgasms are at men's disposal; out of the abundant generosity of their hearts, they provide them for us. Such thoughts of course do extreme damage to the mutuality of the experiences I have with my beloved. We both had to learn; we both had to work hard; nonetheless, there is a gratuitousness to the fact that orgasms resulted. It was more like good fortune, luck, chance, or accident. Chance and luck have disappeared from ethics altogether, let alone sexual ethics. I invite my colleagues in ethics to meditate on the dangers and possibilities of chance for women's sexuality.[33]

In one sense, whether orgasm is a gift from a partner is beside the point. Orgasm is a gift I receive *from my own body.* My very flesh has this capacity to burst me open to existence, to melt me down into a state in which my connections to the rest of the universe are not only felt, but felt as extremely pleasurable, as joyous.[34] But to this foundational celebration of female embodiment and the fragile chanciness of good relationship, I must add the vagaries of culture: available accurate information, both physiological and experiential; the new trust and courage of many women willing to explore and report on our sexuality as we live it; the writers, publishers, and feminist booksellers who make knowledge accessible (at a price); the rape crisis centers, women's shelters, therapists, and other healing agents who make personal/social change possible (sometimes at no price, sometimes at very high prices).

It is peculiar that so few ethical discussions of sexuality take up female orgasm, let alone its problematic character or its importance to flourishing. Much more emphasis and lingering philosophical care has been spent on desire.[35] This may be one of the distinguishing marks of patriarchy in sexual ethics: Men are able to take pleasure for granted in sex. Or perhaps they translate pleasure into desire (as in "she wants it" or "I want it"). The progress from desire to pleasure to ecstasy is precisely what women cannot take for granted in our society.

The Western tradition has been quick to talk about the need for spirit or mind to rule the body with its imperious passions. We have been less apt to talk at length about the gifts body gives to the spirit. Perhaps they have been taken for granted by the men who have always known *ek-stasis* and its releases, with or without that of their partners in bed. Perhaps they have always been able to explore these pleasures more freely than women.

We do not have a language fully empowered and inflected with women's sexual experiences. The time has more than come to talk publicly about the body as women experience it, to see what new concepts would await us there, and to incorporate—that is, take into all our bodies, those of groups as well as of individuals—the insights we need in order to be gentler on ourselves, each other, people far away, and also on the very planet's skin. Body does have gifts to give, and what helps us to experience more of life as cherishable, this can only be a help to our choices in daily life.

What we linger over tells us what is important to us. Indeed, I suggest that *lingering* is part of the ethical language we need. Along with lingering, I have found myself using other terms that are not usually on the tip of the ethicist's tongue: Inviting. Safety. Diversity. Healing.[36] Let's linger a while more on the constructive possibilities of female orgasm.

The Moral Significance of Ecstasy

This experience makes me wonder many things: Why do we think we are really "separate" from each other anyway? Do men experience orgasm as melting union? If women could take orgasms for granted, what exactly would be the consequences? Or, should men take orgasms less for granted? Do they need to have less sex so that they can value it more deeply?[37]

The mystical character of my description may be what is most striking. What does it mean? Is it normative? And what does "normative" mean in this context? (1) Does it mean that it is a source of values and norms, standards by which I evaluate the rest of life? (2) Does it mean that all women "should" experience orgasm as I do? That the norms and values I find here extend beyond my skin out into the universe? I am reluctant to conclude that it is normative in this second sense, for several reasons.

First, I am mystically inclined in general. This may be true of many women, but not all. Like social location, personal idiosyncracies like this may tempt us into universalizing what cannot bear this moral weight.[38]

Second, some women explicitly resist giving orgasm any "meaning," let alone the expansive sense of ecstatic union in my account. "Sex is just—sex," they say, sometimes with a shrug. Or "an orgasm is an orgasm is an orgasm."[39]

Third, the most important moral questions here are precisely about these differences. How do we deal with persons whose experience is different from our own? Do we shut them out or shut them up? I invite my colleagues with different experiences of orgasm to describe what it is like for them, to dissent, to add nuances, or to start over in a different place. (Like safety, invitation is not morally neutral, especially in sexual matters.) That we listen respectfully and attentively for the differences is very important.

There may be still other reasons to resist assigning too much ethical weight to ecstatic union. Everyday consciousness in our society, even my feminist consciousness, resists living with the paradoxes of ecstasy. *Paradoxes are hard to live with.* They feel in the first instance like contradictions. To tell a paradox apart from a contradiction is not easy. Therefore to dwell on them is potentially crazy-making. (And too many nuances risks losing the ability to communicate with the woman on the street.) In the second instance (that is, after thinking about it), some of the paradoxes result from the limits of language. We just can't say it right, the words make it sound like a muddle. Falling silent, as many women do, may be an appropriate response when language does not provide concepts that fit experience. (There is no way around the problems of language. We must go through them.)

Several other serious puzzles arise when we linger over female orgasm. If women experience more sexual pleasure, do we become more demanding outside of bed as well (and vice versa)? Does good sex make us more capable of valuing excellence in other realms of life? Is making love a means of grace? Is it insightful to speak of our sexual pleasure as "the advent of non-sense that multiplies sense," granted to women "provided it isn't discussed"?[40] Can all these be right at once? How does this immanent/transcendent joy relate to others?

A good sexual experience is a source of worth and value to the participant(s). To touch and be touched in ways that produce sweet delights affirms, magnifies, intensifies, and redoubles the deep value of our existence. Ecstasy spills over onto the world outside the bed, not accidentally but intrinsically. It awakens rejoicing, but more: wonder and reverence, the poignant astonishment that we are here, that we live, that anything at all is here, that life can enfold such bursting joy. What if more of life were like this? In my experience, female orgasm is so rich, so abundant in meaning that it is supersaturated with it. It is superabundant, a treasure trove. Women wondering, women marveling: Is this different from Socrates' besotted *thaumazein?* Or from the reverence and awe that are its counterpart in Israel and the Christian theological tradition? Or for that matter, from the laughter of Aphrodite?

After reading a version of this essay, my darling said, "Too much *schlag,*" thinking of Viennese pastries mounded with whipped cream. And as with any diet overdosing on one rich element, this very superabundance signals that we can overdo it. Though this cannot be an ethics of scarcity, nonetheless we must be able to look at scarcity and surplus together, to hold one in each hand, so to speak. Ethics differentiates. To forget anorgasmia while we are talking about the significance of orgasm is to falsify women's sexuality.

I am reluctant to conclude more about female orgasm until we are more sure about how to encompass graciously the diversity of women's sexual experiences. The fact that women cannot take orgasm for granted while having sex is among the most important aspects of this topic. Most certainly this points us toward the strange and distorted twists of sexuality under patriarchal conditions. But more than that, it may offer unlooked for grounds of hope in reconstructing sexual ethics on a new basis. Questioning what is taken for granted by previous models is typical of paradigm shifts.[41] Not being able to take ecstasy for granted opens a space for inquiry, an expanded vision. Women's experiences of sex-without-orgasm may therefore be as crucial as orgasm for a developed feminist sexual ethics. Both provide loci for examining a whole range of intertwined and complex goods in sexuality that have not been explored.

We need to follow the trails of our joy with the same persistent adventurousness with which we have explored the pains of sexual abuses. We need to explore this terrain in a mood that can acknowledge the disappointments without letting go of delight—balancing them, so to speak, one in each hand. (This may return us to the language of rights.) Ethics is certainly fueled by the insistent No to wrongs and injustices. But we need equally lavish insistence on the Yeses, the visions and joys that lure us toward them.

Celebrating women's sexuality is key to good sexual ethics, feminist or not. Such a celebration requires a many-meaninged, many-valued, many-voiced complexity that can rejoice in the fact that we are many and not one. Appreciating that sexuality is multivocal and multivalent is not usual in sexual ethics. We are right now in a transition state. We need many more voices raised to describe, to speculate, to linger over the meaning of our delights.

Notes

This essay springs from my joy in the company of Beverly Wildung Harrison as a colleague in ethics. When I was a graduate student in this field in the late sixties and early seventies, there were so few women in ethics that I nearly memorized her early articles. My pleasure in her as a colleague deepened in the six years I taught at Union Theological Seminary in New York. In those years I occasionally taught two courses with her and others: Ministry in Feminist Perspective and Feminist Ethics (so far as I know the first course with that title). I cannot count the ways I am indebted to her even when I am disagreeing.

Many conversations with other women have contributed to this essay. Special thanks over the years to Christine Gudorf, Sarah Bentley, and the members of the Mudflower Collective; more recently to Sherry Harbaugh, Janet Larson, Karen Bloomquist, Patricia Jung, Adele Resmer, Anita Hill, Daryl Koehn, John Ballew, Elizabeth Bettenhausen, DeAne Lagerquist, Susan Thistlethwaite, Margie Mayman-Park, and Anne Gilson, who all read drafts of this essay.

1. Audre Lorde's classic essay, "Uses of the Erotic: The Erotic as Power," in *Sister Outsider: Essays and Speeches* (Trumansburg, N.Y.: Crossing Press, 1984), 53–59, touched off some of this discussion more than a decade ago. Carter Heyward's *Touching Our Strength: The Erotic as Power and the Love of God* (San Francisco: HarperSanFrancisco, 1989) mines this vein for feminist rheology.
2. Just as I did in "Moral Callousness and Moral Sensitivity: Violence against Women," in *Women's Consciousness, Women's Conscience: A Reader in Feminist Ethics,* ed. Barbara Andolsen, Christine Gudorf, and Mary Pellauer (Minneapolis: Winston Press, 1985).
3. See, for instance, Susan Jacoby, "When Women Lie about Sex," *New Woman,* December 1991, 32–34, or Lesley Dormen, "Honey, You're a Great Lover . . . *Not!" Ladies' Home Journal,* July 1992, 70–75. Faking orgasms is a moral issue unique to women and may be uniquely illuminating for the moral structures of women's experience under Western patriarchy.

4. To do justice to anorgasmia requires a whole essay in itself; though I prefer to call it sex-without-orgasm. I believe we need to look at three different groups of experiences of sex-without-orgasm: aversive sexual experiences (consenting encounters that include serious turnoffs), pre-orgasmic experiences, and experiences in which the woman, for whatever reasons, chooses not to have an orgasm.
5. June M. Reinisch with Ruth Beasley, *The Kinsey Institute New Report on Sex: What You Must Know to be Sexually Literate* (New York: St. Martin's Press, 1990), 203.
6. The *Kinsey Institute New Report on Sex* has no references for race or ethnic groups anywhere in the text, nor any comments on this silence. The original Kinsey team in the 1940s was explicit about excluding two groups of women: 915 white females who had served prison sentences, and the 934 members of the "non-white sample." See Alfred C. Kinsey, Wardell B. Pomeroy, Clyde B. Martin, and Paul H. Gebhard, *Sexual Behavior in the Human Female* (Philadelphia: W. B. Saunders and Co., 1953), 22. Shere Hite's questionnaire did not ask its respondents any questions about race and was sent to groups with overwhelmingly white audiences. See *The Hite Report: A Nationwide Study of Female Sexuality* (New York: Dell, 1976), 39, 23–24. Masters and Johnson employed an all-white sample from the upper middle class. See William H. Masters and Virginia B. Johnson, *Human Sexual Response* (New York: Bantam, 1966), chap. 2, "The Research Population," 9–23. For a good analysis of these and other flaws in sexology, see Janice Irvine, *Disorder of Desire: Sex and Gender in Modern American Sexology* (Philadelphia: Temple University Press, 1990).
7. For data on anorgasmia from the early 1970s, see Helen Kaplan, *The New Sex Therapy* (New York: Brunner/Mazel, 1974), or Lonnie Barbach, *For Yourself: The Fulfillment of Female Sexuality* (Garden City, N.Y.: Doubleday, 1975). For the basic description of Type X, see Kinsey et al., *Sexual Behavior in the Human Female,* 472; for the percentages, see 513, 512, where some were described as also not erotically responding to masturbation, sexual fantasies, or dreams. On the other hand, they also said "it is doubtful whether there is ever a complete lack of [orgasmic] capacity" (373). "Inhibitions" were cited as the primary reason for not reaching orgasm (see 374, 329).
8. See Nancy Cott, "Passionlessness: An Interpretation of Victorian Sexual Ideology, 1790–1850," in *A Heritage of Her Own: Toward a New Social History of American Women,* ed. Nancy Cott and Elizabeth Pleck (New York: Simon and Schuster, 1979); and James Mahood and Kristine Wanburg, eds., *Clelia D. Mosher: The Mosher Survey* (New York: Ayer Company Publishers, 1980). For pre-Victorian medical manuals that discussed women's orgasms, as well as the changes in the mid-1800s, see John S. Haller Jr. and Robin M. Haller, *The Physician and Sexuality in Victorian America* (Champaign: University of Illinois Press, 1974). A good survey of sexuality in U.S. history is John D'Emilio and B. Estelle Freedman, *Intimate Matters: A History of Sexuality in America* (New York: Harper & Row, 1988). A recent work on the earlier centuries is Thomas

Laqueur, *Making Sex: Body and Gender from the Greeks to Freud* (Cambridge: Harvard University Press, 1990).

9. Reinisch, 85. Those last three words were a veiled critique of the original Kinsey team's preoccupation with orgasm during coitus. As Kinsey said, "There has, of course, been widespread interest in discovering what proportion of the coitus of the average female does lead to orgasm, and in discovering some of the factors which account for such *success or failure in coitus"* (374, emphasis mine). After lengthy cautions about the many variables that make it difficult "to calculate what percentage of the copulations in any particular sample lead to orgasm," *Sexual Behavior in the Human Female* said that "the average (median) female in the sample had reached orgasm in something between 70 and 77 percent of her marital coitus" (375) and in about 40 percent of the unmarried coitus (330). The highly visible charts in the chapter on marital coitus differentiated only between women who "never" experienced orgasm and those who did "plus or minus always." This makes me wonder about spurious precision. If it is true that half to three-quarters of women in the United States cannot experience orgasm from intercourse alone, then these numbers are highly questionable. Other methods were called "pre-coital petting techniques" by the Kinsey team.
10. The *big* qualifier in *Human Sexual Response* was that women reach orgasm "with effective stimulation" (see 4 and following).
11. See the review of the evidence in the appendices in Wendy Maltz and Beverly Holman, *Incest and Sexuality: A Guide to Understanding and Healing* (Lexington: Lexington Books, 1987).
12. While the proportion of U.S. women who masturbate has grown over the last fifty years, it still does not reach the same level as among men. "Among the thousands of people interviewed by Kinsey during the 1940s and 1950s, 94 percent of males and 40 percent of females reported having masturbated to orgasm. More recent studies report that about the same percentage of males masturbate but that the percentage of females has increased to around 70 percent (or more, depending on the study)," says Reinisch, 95.
13. Irvine, *Disorders of Desire,* is the most comprehensive commentary on the politics of interpretation among sexologists. See also Carol Vance, "Gender Systems, Ideology and Sex Research," in *Powers of Desire: The Politics of Sexuality,* ed. Ann Snitow, Christine Stansell, and Sharon Thompson (New York: Monthly Review Press, 1983), 371–84.
14. Not that writing is the primary element in sexuality; far from it. Nor is writing the primary mode of doing ethics, sexual or otherwise. Problems arise when we identify writing as a privileged entrée into female sexuality, as French feminist Helene Cixous entices women to do: "To write. An act which will only 'realize' the decensored relation of woman to her sexuality, to her womanly being, giving her access to her native strength; it will give her back her goods, her pleasures, her organs, her immense bodily territories which have been kept under seal." Or again, "And why don't you write! Write! Writing is for you, you are for

you; your body is yours, take it." This lovely French intellectualism is not a good guide to sexuality. Cixous does not exhort women to build houses, quilt, or any other kind of physical activity (not even exercise) to gain access to our sexuality. These comments can be found in "The Laugh of the Medusa," in *New French Feminisms,* ed. Elaine Marks and Isabelle de Courtivron (Amherst: University of Massachusetts Press), 250, 246.

15. Mariana Valverde, *Sex, Power, and Pleasure* (Philadelphia: New Society Publishers, 1987), draws attention to the hazards of these two genres for feminist reflections. Thus she omits the novel, therapeutic/instructional manuals, and theological or ethical work. Still, Valverde's work has much to recommend it, including a chapter on "pleasure and ethics." I agree that a feminist ethics aims not to provide rules or recipes but "to provide women with the intellectual skills to reason about their particular situation, paying close attention to the interconnections between the sexual and non-sexual aspects of our lives" (185), though what women lack is not skills but *concepts.*
16. Barbara Ehrenreich, Elizabeth Hess, and Gloria Jacobs, *Re-Making Love: The Feminization of Sex* (New York: Doubleday, 1986), 78–81.
17. "A few seconds," says *Human Sexual Response,* 6. Even the longer experience Masters and Johnson called "status orgasmus" lasted only 20 to 60 seconds (131).
18. The 0–6 scale has been frequently criticized, but it remains useful. It has been complicated by using several overlapping scales rather than one. See Eli Coleman, "Assessment of Sexual Orientation," *Journal of Homosexuality* 14, no. 1 (1987): 9–24.
19. For the lack of correlations between women's experiences of orgasm and factors of education or class, see 520–21, 529, of *Sexual Behavior in the Human Female.* In contrast, they found religion "definitely and consistently" affected women's orgasms. They differentiated religion by large groups (Protestant, Catholic, Jew) and within these by intensity (religiously devout, moderately devout, and inactive). For married women, they concluded: "In nearly every age group, and in nearly all the samples that we have from Protestant, Catholic and Jewish females, smaller percentages of the more devout and larger percentages of the inactive groups had responded to orgasm after marriage. Similarly, the median frequencies of orgasm for those who were responding at all were, in most instances, lower for those who were devout and higher for those who were religiously inactive" (529). For single women, see 515–16 and 521–22.
20. These pale, however, by comparison with the fact that I grew up in an abusive home. My mother was a battered woman, and I was incestuously abused by my father. The incest I experienced colors much of my adult experiences of sexuality. It gave me concepts before I was ready for them—shame, secrecy, aversion, flinching, flashbacks. I am forced to place these ideas next to more usual ones: attraction, pleasure, joy. I spent more than a decade healing from these wounds. (The literature on healing after sexual abuses has grown large. For a good guide to "how" in a case like mine, see Ellen Bass and Laura Davis, *The Courage to*

Heal: A Guide for Women Survivors of Child Sexual Abuse [New York: HarperCollins, 1988]).

21. Extreme bodily states may all have this isolating quality. Serious pain, for instance, is also difficult to communicate. See Elaine Scary, *The Body in Pain: The Making and Unmaking of the World* (New York: Oxford University Press, 1985).
22. For other descriptions of women's orgasms, especially their varieties, see Sheila Kitzinger, *Woman's Experience of Sex: The Fact and Feelings of Female Sexuality at Every Stage of Life* (New York: Penguin Books, 1983); Shere Hite, *The Hite Report.* Though fiction is outside my boundaries here, see also Louise Thornton, Jan Sturtevant, and Amber Coverdale Sumrall, eds., *Touching Fire: Erotic Writings by Women* (New York: Carroll and Graf, 1989); Michelle Slung, ed., *Slow Hand: Women Writing Erotica* (New York: HarperCollins, 1992); Margaret Reynolds, ed., *Erotica: Women's Writings from Sappho to Margaret Atwood* (New York: Fawcett, 1990).
23. This melting union is where I would begin a critique of Masters and Johnson, churlish as this may seem when we owe so much knowledge of female orgasm to them. Their descriptions of orgasm are limited to sensations; any sense of unity with the partner disappears, as do any other wider feelings (such as love). This may have been because so much of their work was based on masturbation, or because of other assumptions. For an analysis of a "materialism" Masters and Johnson shared with Kinsey, see Paul Robinson, *The Modernization of Sex: Havelock Ellis, Alfred Kinsey, William Masters and Virginia Johnson* (New York: Harper & Row, 1976, 1989). Robinson suggests that Kinsey made "a decision to evaluate sexual experience strictly in terms of orgasms, and orgasms themselves strictly in terms of numbers. This meant he took no statistical note of how orgasms differed from one another in intensity or in the emotional values associated with them [and] . . . he distrusted those who imputed that the physical reality of sex was somehow trivial when compared to its psychology. 'Such thinking,' he wrote, 'easily becomes mystical' " (57). Obviously, I have become mystical.
24. This language of union may lead readers to assume that I am describing intercourse, a literal uniting of bodies by putting the penis inside the vagina. I have been careful not to describe how ecstasy is reached, not only because I am not writing an instructional manual, but also in order to leave this question open. If the empirical studies cited in the first section are to be trusted, most women (including me) do not experience orgasm as a result of intercourse alone.
25. Ecstasy language appears more often these days. See, for instance, Margot Anand, *The Art of Sexual Ecstasy: The Path of Sacred Sexuality for Western Lovers* (Los Angeles: Jeremy P. Tarcher, 1989), though she contrasts ecstasy with "ordinary genital orgasm" (3); or Linda Murray, "Sexual Ecstasy," *New Woman,* April 1992, 57–59. (The headers for this essay say that "there is an erotic pleasure greater than orgasm" and that women can go "beyond ecstasy.")
26. I have formulated "limit-experience" by analogy to "limit-question." Steven

Toulmin, *The Place of Reason in Ethics* (Chicago: University of Chicago Press, 1987).

27. Readers may be jarred by the sudden appearance of male pronouns here. Perhaps an experiential account cannot avoid some references to the gender of one's partner, and my partner is male. But homophobia/heterosexism is not to be swept aside by this bare assertion, which evades the moral onus of the charge. In fact, I have written elements 1–3 *deliberately* in inclusive language because I believe these three dimensions are the *same* regardless of the gender of a woman's partner. Elements 4 and 5, on the other hand, are written differently because gender is essential to differences of vulnerability and power in our society.

   To illuminate these differences, I invite the reader to try a thought-experiment. Change the pronouns in this account to explore what difference they make: "My ecstasy excited and touched her; she was eager for my orgasm . . . on the occasions when I felt I would never get it off, and that it was time to quit, she would not. That my pleasure was important to her, this was hard to accept, to let in. That she would refuse her own release until I had mine, that she was willing to persist in trying to bring my release/ecstasy, that she reveled in it: This shook me very deeply. It was so very unexpected. My surprise about this says more about me than it does about her. I did not expect to be loved. I did not expect her to have the capacity to put me before herself. I expected only to be secondary." For me, there are significant differences between these lines and those in the body of the text. They shift in moral status for two reasons: (1) They change in genre from nonfiction to fiction. This is a technical issue about writing, and whether it is large or small depends on the relationship of truth-telling to genre. (For instance, how does fiction tell the truth?) (2) His maleness was the fundamental reason that I expected to be secondary in our sexual relationship. This is a large social issue that has nothing to do with expertise or technical questions. Since this is not an essay about homophobia, I invite readers to explore for themselves whether changing the pronouns changes the moral structure of the argument, both here and in element 5, and to reflect on why.

28. I have learned from Karen Lebacqz to highlight vulnerability in thinking about sexuality. See "Appropriate Vulnerability: A Sexual Ethic for Singles" in *After the Revolution: Sexual Ethics and the Church* (Chicago: The Christian Century, 1989).

29. As I have said in another context, tidiness is not useful for feminist reflection, at least not right now. See Mary Pellauer and Susan Thistlethwaite, "A Conversation on Healing and Grace," in *Lift Every Voice: Christian Theology from the Underside,* ed. Mary Potter-Engel and Susan Thistlethwaite (San Francisco: HarperCollins, 1990).

30. Jessica Benjamin, *The Bonds of Love: Psychoanalysis, Feminism and the Problem of Domination* (New York: Pantheon, 1988), suggests the primal necessity of recognition for both mutuality and female desire.

31. English has amazingly strong street language to disapprove of a woman who arouses a man but does not satisfy him. We have *no* comparable language for the reverse.
32. This is why many sex therapists avoid or even attack ethical language. For example, Barbach says "this confusion between sexuality and morality has been another source of conflict for many women" *(For Yourself,* 20, but see similar comments on 6, 8, 9, 16, 21, 88, 92).
33. Martha Nussbaum, *The Fragility of Goodness: Luck and Ethics in Greek Tragedy and Philosophy* (New York: Cambridge University Press, 1986), may open a space for thinking about fortune and ethics.
34. In another sense, of course, I do receive this gift from my partner, and I cannot separate this fact from the rest of our relationship. That my beloved lingers over my pleasure until it culminates in ecstasy tells me vividly that I am his beloved, that I am truly valued by him as I value him. This ecstatic union overflows into the rest of our relationship, as we circle around the well of abundance in the center of our love, dipping in and out of it.
35. For instance, Roger Scruton's *Sexual Desire: A Moral Philosophy of the Erotic* (New York: Free Press, 1986) contains only passing references to orgasm, though he is not alone in that.
36. There may be many others as well. In addition to references elsewhere, other useful published sources include Sarah Lucia Hoagland, *Lesbian Ethics: Toward New Value* (Palo Alto, Calif.: Institute of Lesbian Studies, 1988); Katie G. Cannon, *Black Womanist Ethics* (Atlanta: Scholars Press, 1988); Beverly Wildung Harrison, *Making the Connections: Essays in Feminist Social Ethics,* ed. Carol S. Robb (Boston: Beacon Press, 1985); Eve Browning Cole and Susan Coultrap-McQuin, eds., *Explorations in Feminist Ethics: Theory and Practice* (Bloomington: Indiana University Press, 1992); Claudia Card, ed., *Feminist Ethics* (Lawrence: University of Kansas Press, 1991); Susan E. Davies and Eleanor H. Haney, eds., *Redefining Sexual Ethics: A Sourcebook of Essays, Stories and Poems* (Cleveland: Pilgrim Press, 1991).
37. Kinsey, and many sexologists after him, seem to think "more is better." We may have many reasons to question this.
38. Even all mystical experiences are not the same. I have them in many other areas of life besides orgasm, in nature or in worship, but most vividly in public transportation, historical sites, and large crowds. I am not primarily a sexual mystic, nor a nature mystic, but a social mystic. These differences, once again, are important. (I learned these distinctions from a presentation by Naomi Goldenberg at the AAR more than a decade ago.)
39. Betty Dodson, *Sex for One: The Joy of Selfloving* (New York: Crown, 1987), 87. This point is partly to oppose any notion that the way a woman reaches orgasm makes any moral (or other) difference. Ehrenreich, Hess, and Jacobs go further: "Sex should have no ultimate meaning other than pleasure, and no great mystery except how to achieve it," and it is obnoxious to have "every pleasure and sensation burdened with 'meaning'" *(Re-Making Love,* 194–95, 205). On the

other hand, they note that "the consumer culture offers the ultimately meaningless version of sexual revolution" (205). (I agree.) The Kinsey team defined orgasm as "an explosive discharge of muscular tension at the peak of sexual response," akin to a sneeze; they were ascetic about claims that it was more (*Sexual Behavior in the Human Female,* 627 ff.).

40. For others' reflections on these questions, see respectively Dorothy Dinnerstein, *The Mermaid and the Minotaur: Sexual Arrangement and Human Malaise* (New York: Harper & Row, 1976), esp. 73–75; Audre Lorde, "Uses of the Erotic: The Erotic as Power"; Rebecca Parker, "Making Love as a Means of Grace: Women's Reflections," *Open Hands* 3, no. 3 (winter 1988): 8–12 (thanks to Anita Hill for drawing my attention to this essay); Julia Kristeva, "Oscillation between Power and Denial: An Interview with Xaviere Gauthier," in *New French Feminisms,* 165–66.
41. Thomas Kuhn, *The Structure of Scientific Revolutions* (Chicago: University of Chicago Press, 1970).

[2]

Embracing Masculinity

James B. Nelson

Body Theology and Male Genitals

What are the spiritual meanings of the male genitals? The question seldom has been asked, particularly in Christian conversation and literature. There are predictable and important questions about the appropriateness of even considering the issue. Before we go further, we must attend to them.

First, some will simply find the question distasteful. Anti-body feelings nurtured by centuries of sexual dualism are strong indeed. And the genitals are the supreme test. Discomfort over seriously considering the body to be of spiritual significance becomes repulsion when the focus is the genitals. The reaction is predictable, but deeply regrettable. God has created us good in all our parts, and an incarnationalist faith bids us celebrate *all* of the body as vehicle of divine presence and meaning.

Can the sexual feelings, functions, and meanings of our genitals be important modes of revelation? Admittedly, the thought has been far from commonplace in Christian theology. Yet a broader view is needed. The distinguished historian of religion Mircea Eliade saw our human sexual experience

---

SOURCE: James B. Nelson, *The Intimate Connection: Male Sexuality, Masculine Spirituality* (Louisville, Ky.: Westminster John Knox Press, 1988).

as an "autonomous mode of cognition." It is, he believed, a fundamental way of knowing reality immediately and directly. Eliade went so far as to declare that sexuality's "primary and perhaps supreme valency is the cosmological function. . . . Except in the modern world, sexuality has everywhere and always been a hierophany, and the sexual act an integral action and therefore also a means of knowledge."[1] Sexuality thus is a pathway into the mystery of the cosmos. As a hierophany it is a manifestation of the sacred, revealing to us what is beyond our conscious rational apprehension. True, this is a bold claim that goes against the accepted view. Centuries of dualism have taught us that the body (especially in its sexual dimensions) reveals nothing of the spirit. But a holistic spirituality demands that we make this bold claim.

Even if this is granted, however, some will object that such a focus for the masculinity question will simply invite back all the distortions of genitalized masculinity. I am sympathetic with this concern. Such distortions are prevalent in men's experience, and they are serious. Let us name them once more. There is the genitalization of sexual feeling, the Pinocchio-like experience of life in the one organ while the rest of the body feels lifeless and deprived of eros. The consequences are manifold, and we have already examined some of them. There is the one-sided phallic interpretation of reality, which overvalues the linear, the vertical, and the hard while undervaluing the cyclical, the horizontal, and the soft. Again, the results in men's one-sided shaping of their world are enormous. Also, there are the ways in which the penis becomes associated with violent and detached meanings, as its slang names amply suggest—cock, prick, tool, rod, and even a gun with its bullets. Such meanings do not readily suggest the genitals as graciously integrated into the body of love. And there are body-affirming feminists, men as well as women, who will resist the thought of any kind of male genital affirmation precisely because they are so keenly aware of the wounds caused by phallic violence. Attention of any kind given to the penis might suggest just another thinly disguised form of masculinist oppression. These suspicions, sadly enough, are understandable.

Where are we left? One option seems to be the firm discipline of the genitals. If my penis seems to have a mind of its own, I must deprive it of that freedom. I will be its master and keep it from running amok. The trouble with servants and slaves, however, is that they seldom know their place. They are treated as machines, whose only purpose is to perform the functions determined by their masters. But either as slave or as machine, that part of me will be dead. I will have deprived it of its right to live *except* as slave or machine. This puts me right back into the dualism of control: the higher over the lower, master over servant. The spirit or mind with its higher capacities for thought and virtue must control the body, especially the penis, with its physical appetites.

Even though many Christians seem to hold a different theological theory about the body in all of its parts—good because made by God, and a temple of the Holy Spirit—a simple test proposed by H. A. Williams suggests another reality.[2] Suppose that in church on Sunday morning this lesson from Paul is read: "I appeal to you therefore, . . . by the mercies of God, to present your bodies as a living sacrifice, holy and acceptable to God, which is your spiritual worship" (Rom. 12:1). What prospects come into our imaginations as response to this exhortation? Does it conjure up images of physical pleasure and ecstasy? "Not at all," says Williams. "The prospect conjured up is the dreary duty of controlling the body, or if the body is recalcitrant of forcing it, negatively, not to do this, that, or the other, and positively to energize itself in the performance of this or the other kind of good works. But whether understood negatively or positively the exhortation is taken automatically as a call to the joyless task of disciplining the body and oppressing it by imposing upon it an alien will, treating it in short as a dead object to be pushed around."[3] If that is true of our actual functioning attitudes toward the body as a whole (regardless of the theological notions we might have in our heads), how much truer it probably is of our genitals.

However, the master-slave discipline of the genitals will not work. They are finally treated not as a vital part of us but as something denied the right to live except as slave machines. Nor will it work to ignore our genitals or consign them to hell as beyond redemption. It will not work because that which is consigned to hell just will not lie down. While Williams is speaking of bodies in general, his words are just as true of our genitals in particular: "Being in hell, the place of the undead, they are always somehow planning and threatening their revenge, and they may in the end catapult us into nuclear catastrophe. . . . The body deprived of *eros* inevitably becomes the champion of *thanatos*. Better to die completely than to fester in hell."[4] Indeed, hell is the place of the dead who will not accept their death.

The alternative, however, is not to give our genitals the freedom of their demands. That was the solution for some people in the "sexual revolution" of recent decades: if in the past we have oppressed our bodies and genitals, let us now give the slaves their freedom. But subjecting our genitals to oppression has made them subject to compulsions, and compulsions do not satisfy. They give only fleeting, momentary relief. Compulsions of genital instinct just replace compulsions of the head, but there still is no fulfillment. We still remain divided. Only the balance of power has changed. What we need is truly the resurrection of the body in all its parts. We do not need the crazy behavior of the slave let loose for the evening.

Still, we cannot insist on utter clarity or purity in our experience. Williams's words are wise: "For in experience compulsion and resurrection are often mixed up together. Indeed the experience of resurrection often grows from what was originally an experience of compulsion. If we are perfectionists or purists here we shall find ourselves cut off from all experience of love."[5] Sometimes illusion is the midwife of reality, and paralysis from the fear of illusion may mean that reality will forever escape us.

In recent years a number of feminist women have fruitfully explored the spiritual meanings of their own female body experiences—the nature of their breasts and genitals, their experiences of menstruation and birthing. We men traditionally have identified women with their biology and neglected our own. It is time that we inquire about ourselves.

Phallus

In his suggestive book *Phallos: Sacred Image of the Masculine,* Eugene Monick explores the psychic and religious dimensions of the male experience of his phallus, his erect penis.[6] Every male, he asserts, directly knows the meanings of erection: strength, hardness, determination, sinew, straightforwardness, penetration. Because erection is not fully under a man's conscious control, because the penis seems to decide on its own when, where, and with whom it wants erection and action, the phallus seems to be an appropriate metaphor for the masculine unconscious.

From time immemorial it has fascinated men. Numerous ancient expressions of phallic art and worship are well known, from the common representations on ancient Greek pottery, to the huge erection of the Cerne giant (carved in the first century B.C. by the Celts into a chalk hill in Dorset, England), to the modern-day Hindu cult of Shiva, where the phallus is an image of divinity.[7] Beyond such outward evidences of religious veneration, men of every time and place have known a religious quality to their phallic experience. To adapt Rudolf Otto's words, it is the *mysterium tremendum.* Such encounters with the numinous produces responses of fascination, awe, energy, and a sense of the "wholly other."[8] Through the phallus, men sense a resurrection, the capacity of the male member to return to life again and again after depletion. An erection makes a boy feel like a man and makes a man feel alive. It brings the assurance and substantiation of masculine strength.

Yet, as with other experiences of the holy, males feel ambivalent about the phallus. Erections must be hidden from general view. They are an embarrassment when they occur publicly. Men joke about erections with each other but cannot speak seriously. The secret is exposed only with another person in intimacy or when a male permits himself to experience his potency alone. If the mystery is exposed publicly, somehow the sacred has been profaned.

Furthermore, there is a double-sidedness to the phallic experience. One dimension is the *earthy* phallus.[9] This is the erection perceived as sweaty, hairy, throbbing, wet, animal sexuality. In some measure it is Bly's Iron John maleness. Men who have rejected this may be nice and gentle, but they seem to lack life-giving energy. Their keys remain hidden under the queen's pillow—indeed, with the cooperation of the king, for the powers of social order always distrust the earthy phallus. And there is reason for distrust, because there can be an ugly, brutal side to the earthy phallus that uses others for gratification when this part of a man's sexuality does not find balance with other sides. Yet without positive presence of earthy energy a man is bland. There is gentleness without strength, peacefulness without vitality, tranquility without vibrancy.

Men also experience the *solar* phallus.[10] Solar (from the sun) means enlightenment. A man's erect penis represents to him all that stands tall. It is proud. The solar experience of erection puts a man in touch with the excitement of strenuous achievement. It is the Jacob's ladder and the mountain climb, which rise above the earthy and the earthly. It is the satisfaction of straining to go farther intellectually, physically, and socially. Solar phallus is transcendence. It is the church steeples and skyscrapers that men are inclined to build. Solar phallus represents what most men would like to have noted in their obituaries. In Carl Jung's thinking, solar phallus is the very substance of masculinity. It is, he believed, *logos,* which transforms thought into word, just as eros (which he called feminine) transforms feeling into relatedness. I believe Jung misled us with his bifurcations of masculine and feminine principles, unfortunately grounding them in common gender stereotypes. Nevertheless, logos is an important part of the male experience both represented and invited by the solar phallus.

As with the earthy phallus, there is a shadow side to the experience of the solar phallus, too. It is the patriarchal oppression of those who do not "measure up." It is proving one's worth through institutional accomplishments. It is the illusion of strength and power that comes from position. It is the use of technical knowledge to dominate. It is political power which defends its ideological purity at virtually any price and then prides itself on standing tall in the saddle. It is addiction to the notion that bigger is better. The distortions of solar phallus are legion. Yet without its integrated positive energy, a man lacks direction and movement. Without the urge to extend himself, he is content with the mediocre. Without the experience of the wholly other, life loses its self-transcendence.

Thus far I have agreed in broad outline with Monick's significant analysis:

the importance of both the earthy and the solar phallus, their integration, and the dangers of their shadow sides. Here, however, Monick stops. He believes that phallus, the erect penis, is *the* sacred image of the masculine. That seems to be enough. But it is not. Left there, I fear we are left with priapism.

In Roman mythology Priapus, son of Dionysus and Aphrodite, was the god of fertility. His usual representations were marked both by grotesque ugliness and an enormous erection. In human sexual disorders, priapism is the painful clinical condition of an erection that will not go down. Priapus and priapism are symbolic of the idolatry of the half-truth. Phallus, the erection, indeed is a vital part of the male's experience of his sexual organs. Hence, it is usually a vital part of his spirituality. But it is only part. Were it the whole thing, his sexuality and his spirituality would be painful and bizarre, both to himself and to others. That this in fact is too frequently the case is difficult to deny. Our phallic experience gives vital energy, both earthy and solar. But we also need the affirmative experience of the *penis.*

Penis

In our daily lives, almost all men are genitally soft by far the greater share of the time. Genitally speaking, penis rather than phallus is our awareness, insofar as we are aware at all. (For economy in words, I will use "penis" for the organ in its flaccid, unaroused state.) We are genitally limp most of our waking moments, and while erections come frequently during sleep we are seldom aware of them.

Psychically, the experiences of phallus and of penis seem very different. An erection during waking hours claims my attention. Frequently I choose not to act upon its aroused urgency, and sometimes in embarrassment I hide its evidence. But its claims on my psychic awareness have an undeniable phallic imperiousness. The penis is different. Most of the time I am unaware of it. It is just there, part of me, functioning in my occasional need to urinate, but most often invisible from my conscious awareness, much as an internal organ. But when I am conscious of it in dressing or undressing, I am aware of its difference from phallus. Penis is considerably smaller. It is wrinkled. There is even something comical about the contrast (as a man's wife or lover occasionally might tell him). It has a relaxed humility. In its external existence it seems vulnerable, and with the testicles it needs jockstrap protection during the body's vigorous athletics.

In spite of the quantitative dominance of penis time, men tend to undervalue penis and overvalue phallus. Part of that, indeed, simply stems from conscious awareness. When the phallus is present, it demands our attention.

The penis does not. Part of the difference, however, is a matter of intentional valuation. We have been taught and have learned to value phallic meanings in patriarchy: bigger is better (in bodily height, in paychecks, in the size of one's corporation or farm); hardness is superior to softness (in one's muscles, in one's facts, in one's foreign policy positions); upness is better than downness (in one's career path, in one's computer, in one's approach to life's problems). In "a man's world," small, soft, and down pale beside big, hard, and up.

Penis is undervalued, also, because we so commonly identify male energy and true masculinity with the vitality of young manhood. Infant males and little boys have frequent erections, but true phallus—the heroic sword raised on high—is the property of young manhood. As age comes upon a man, hardness changes and modifies. It is less apparent, less urgent, less the signature of his body. Phallus bears intimations of life and vigor, while penis bears intimations of mortality. Fearing mortality, men tend to reject the qualities of penis and project them upon women who are then seen to be small, soft, and vulnerable, qualities inferior to the phallic standard. Wrinkles, so typical of penis, are not permitted in women if they are to retain their womanly attraction.[11]

But the undervaluing of penis and the overvaluing of phallus take their toll. The price is paid by all who suffer because of patriarchy, for this spiritual body dynamic, while hardly the sole cause of such oppression, surely contributes to it. But oppressors themselves are also oppressed in the process. So what is the price paid by men? One cost we must look at is the deprivation of a significant kind of masculine spiritual energy and power.

The history of Western spirituality reveals two traditional paths to the presence of God: the Via Positiva and the Via Negativa, the positive way and the negative way.[12] The former is a way of affirmation, of thanksgiving, of ecstasy. It is the way of light, the way of being filled by the sacred fullness and rising to the divine height. The Via Negativa is a way of emptying and being emptied. It is the way of darkness. It is sinking into nothingness and into the sacred depths. In spirituality, each way needs the other for balance and completion. The overdevelopment of one to the detriment of the other brings distortion. I believe that in the male experience the Via Positiva has profound associations with the phallus, while the Via Negativa correspondingly is connected to the penis. And in most men it is the latter which remains underrecognized, underclaimed, underaffirmed.

Consider some aspects of the Via Negativa as expressed by a great Christian mystic who knew this way, Meister Eckhart (1260–1327). It is quiet, not active: "Nothing in all creation is so like God as stillness." It is the darkness more than the light: "The ground of the soul is dark." It appears to be less rather than more: "God is not found in the soul by adding anything but by a process of subtraction." It is a deep sinking and a letting go: "We are to sink eternally from letting go to letting go into God." It is the abandoning of focus and attention: "One should love God mindlessly, without mind or mental activities or images or representations." It is the paradox of nothingness embracing something: "God is a being beyond being and a nothingness beyond being. . . . God is nothingness. And yet God is something."[13]

All such modes of the Via Negativa are a man's experiences of his penis, not his phallus. Think of sinking and emptying. The penis is empty of the engorging blood that brings hard excitement to the phallus. Its flaccidity is a letting go of all urgency. It has nowhere to go. It just is. It just hangs and sinks between the legs.

Sinking, emptying, is a way of spirituality.[14] It means trusting God that we do not need to *do,* that our *being* is enough. It means yielding to our tears that keep coming and coming once they begin. It means trusting ourselves to the darkness of sleep, so like the darkness of death. It means abandoning our own achievements and resting in the depths of meaning we do not create. Men often resist these things. But sinking and emptying are as necessary to the spirit's rhythms as they are to the genitals'. Without periods of genital rest, a man lacks phallic capacity. Without times of retreat to the desert, there is no energy for greening.

Or consider darkness, another theme of the Negativa. It seems related to the cosmic womb of our origins, and it has its own energy. Rainer Maria Rilke writes, "You darkness, that I come from/I love you more than all the fires that fence in the world . . . and it is possible a great energy is moving near me/I have faith in nights."[15] But most men are less at home in the darkness than in the light. We are heirs of the Enlightenment, a male-oriented rational movement that sought to shed light on everything. Our psyches seem to link darkness with death, and fear of death is characteristic of the patriarchal society. Starhawk, speaking of the holiness of darkness, maintains that the dark is "all that we are afraid of, all that we don't want to see—fear, anger, sex, grief, death, the unknown."[16]

The penis, in contrast to the phallus, is a creature of the dark. It is resting. Asleep. Usually we are unaware of its presence. But we are conscious of the presence of phallus, just as we are aware of the presence of light. Taught to prize light and fear the dark, we have also been taught to prize the phallic virtues and to fear the meanings of penis. Its quiescence seems symbolic of death, its limpness the reminder of male-dreaded impotence, and fears of death and impotence are the cause of much destruction. But without the darkness there is no growth, no mystery, no receptivity, no deep creativity. Without the gentle dark, light becomes harsh.

Masculine Energy: Beyond Androgyny

For a variety of reasons, men have come to believe that phallus is the emblem of masculinity, the signature of true maleness. But this is only partly true, and partial truths taken as the whole truth become both demonic and self-destructive. A man's penis is as genuinely his reality as is his phallus, and just as important to his male humanity. Spiritually, the Via Negativa is as vital to him as the Via Positiva. It may also be the case that men's overvaluation of phallus, and the undervaluation of penis, is one important reason for our confusions about gender identities and the notion of androgyny.

The concept of androgyny has been commonplace for some years.[17] Most simply put, it denotes the integration within a single person of traits traditionally identified by gender stereotypes as masculine and as feminine. Thus, androgynous people characterize themselves both as strongly self-reliant, assertive, and independent, and as strongly understanding, affectionate, and compassionate. Androgyny is an appealing alternative to the oppressiveness of gender role stereotypes. It goes beyond the false dualism of the belief that there are certain inherent personality traits of the male and of the female. It moves us beyond oppressive gender expectations into the possibility of a more genuinely human liberation for each and for all.

The concept seems appealing theologically. Nicolas Berdiaev, the Russian philosopher-theologian, pressed the idea in 1914, long before its currency in social psychology. There is, he declared, a fundamental androgyny of the human being created in the image of God, an androgyny that the gender roles of the world have not destroyed. "In fact, 'in the beginning' it is neither man nor woman who bears the divine similitude. In the beginning it is only the androgyne . . . who bears it. The differentiation of the sexes is a consequence of the fall of Adam." Now, estranged from our essence, we have a compelling desire to recover our lost unity through recovery of the lost principle. "It is by means of this femininity that the male-human can once again be integrated to the androgynous source of his nature, just as it is through this masculine principle that the female-human can be . . . integrated to her lost androgynous source. . . . Ultimately it is in God that the lover meets with the beloved, because it is in God that personality is rooted. And the personality in God, in its original state, is androgynous."[18]

Berdiaev was ahead of his time. Most later male theologians of this century have not seriously raised the androgynous theme but rather have emphasized the need of gender complementarity. Karl Barth is typical.[19] He believes that our humanity, created in the image of God, is "fellow-humanity." We are incomplete by ourselves. Men and women come into their fullness only in intimate relation to persons of the opposite sex. Barth's position rests on the assumption that by nature the personalities and qualities of the two sexes are essentially different and that each needs the other for completion. There is no androgyny. Barth draws a clear conclusion from this concerning homosexuality: it is perversion and idolatry. One who seeks same-sex union is narcissistically seeking the self. It is a quest for self-satisfaction and self-sufficiency, but such aims can never be realized because the two sexes are fundamentally necessary for each other. While I find Barth's emphasis on the *social* nature of our true humanity commendable, his notion of gender complementarity is deeply flawed. It rests on the uncritical use of gender stereotypes, and it particularly oppresses gays and lesbians, all who are female (because those stereotypes do), and all who are single (among the latter, Jesus included). The notion of gender complementarity is a giant step backward from androgyny.

Androgyny is an ancient theme, prevalent in classical mythology. In Christian thought it was present far earlier than Berdiaev. Yet I believe his was the first clear statement of the essential androgyny of *both* sexes. Earlier versions, blatantly patriarchal, found only the male androgynous. Woman was made necessary as a differentiated sexual being only because man had lost his state of perfection and needed her feminine principle for his human completion. She, however, remained half human.

Nevertheless, androgyny as a theological concept, even in Berdiaev's promising way, runs into some of the same problems as are present in current social psychology. One problem is both definitional and practical. Does the concept mean that both "feminine" and "masculine" characteristics somehow essentially (by nature or by God's design) exist together in every individual, and thus they should be developed and expressed? This seems to be the most common understanding. In the psychological literature sometimes it is labeled "monoandrogynism," to distinguish it from variations of the theme. But this can be oppressive in its own way. Now each person has two sets of gender traits to learn and incorporate instead of one. Now everyone is expected to acquire thoroughly both "instrumental/agentic" ("masculine") and "expressive/nurturant" ("feminine") characteristics in equal amounts, a standard that would seem to double the pressure that people traditionally have felt.

Even more basically, another problem is that androgyny is based on the assumption that there are, indeed, two distinct and primordial sets of personality characteristics—one "masculine," the other "feminine." Even if we assume that each sex is capable of developing both sets of traits, the definition itself perpetuates the very problem it had hoped to overcome. It still locates one constellation of qualities essentially and dominantly in men and the other constellation essentially and dominantly in women. Jung's psychological thought exemplifies this, as do those who draw upon him, for example, in speaking of the male's need to develop "his latent feminine side." In fact, there is a built-in obsolescence to this concept. For if each sex stopped adhering only to its primary characteristics, and if the two gender stereotypes subsequently became less distinct from each other, androgyny in the current sense would lose its meaning.

One way out of the conceptual difficulty is simply to envision the complete transcendence of gender-role traits (sometimes called the "polyandrogynous" possibility). Here, personality traits are seen as having no connection at all with biological sex. Each individual is viewed as different from every other individual, for each has unique interests and capacities. In many ways this vision is promising. It frees individuals to be who they uniquely are. However, there remains a problem. The notion of gender-role transcendence, while it honors uniqueness, does not hold up any vision of inclusiveness or relative balance in personal qualities. A given individual could still be as one-sided as ever, even though the rigid linkage between certain traits and one's biological sex had been severed.

Nevertheless, an important question still remains. Is there anything *distinctive* to the experience of one's own biological sex that grounds us in the development of a more whole personality, a personhood richer than its specific gender stereotype? More particularly, is there anything in the male body experience that enables him to transcend the traditional cultural images of masculinity?

If that is the case, it is difficult to see why the call to more inclusive personhood would be fundamentally oppressive. If as a man I were called upon to acquire feminine qualities *in addition to my natural masculinity*, that would be one thing. I might be capable of doing that, but it would feel much like learning a second language as an adult, adding another linguistic capability to my native tongue. Even if through years of study and practice I become somewhat proficient, my second language would always be that—a second language, added on, requiring additional effort. My strong inclination would always be to see the world primarily through the images of the language of my birth. On the other hand, were I "naturally bilingual"—born into a bilingual family and society, schooled in the images of both from my earliest days—the inclusiveness of languages would not feel like a burden. It would feel natural.

My illustration admittedly suffers, because languages are thoroughly social inventions and learnings. Our bodies are not. While they have many social, learned meanings attached to them, they also have a biological givenness. My point, however, is this: We have been given "bilingual bodies." Even if one language has been developed more than the other, the second language is not foreign to us. It is not something we need to add on. It is just as originally part of us as the language with which, by accident of circumstances, we have become most familiar.

It is time to move beyond the usual meanings of androgyny. The vision for men is not to develop "feminine" energies (or for women to develop "masculine" energies). Rather, the vision for men is the fullest development of our *masculine* energies. But the issue is *fullness.* We are not talking only of phallic qualities. Penis is vulnerable, soft, receptive. Penis represents and invites the spirituality of the Via Negativa. But a penis is not "feminine"—it is as authentically masculine as is phallus. It bears qualities rooted in the fullness of the male's sexual experience, in the fullness of his body affirmation. So we who are men are simply invited to develop the masculine more richly. To speak this way is not to play word games. Linguistic sleight-of-hand tricks are abstractions. Incarnational reflection does not thrive on abstractions, but tries to represent bodily realities honestly.

Finally, it is important to recognize that each dimension of the male genital experience involves the other. Each of us experiences only one body, though in our experience there is the conjunction of apparent opposites. Paradoxically, the opposites are only apparently so. Each is implied by and contained within the other. Penis is always potentially phallus. The soft receptivity of penis implies relationality. But phallus is aroused as the genital aspects of relationship are anticipated or fantasized. So, also, the hard energy of phallus literally bears the signs of gentleness. The lover is amazed at the velvety texture and softness of the head of the man's rock-hard erection. Men know the vulnerability of their testicles and shield them from harm even during arousal and lovemaking. Indeed, male vulnerability is most present exactly at the spot where colloquial language locates male courage: "He has balls."[20]

Such is the marvelous conjunction of apparent opposites in the male's sexual body, a wholeness inviting him to richness of personhood. It is at the same time the bodily experienced invitation to richness of spirituality through the apparent opposites of Via Positiva and Via Negativa. Such is the golden ball of legend, representing connectedness and radiant energy.

Power and Size

One of the central issues in spirituality is *power.*[21] It is evident whenever personal beings are present to each other. Men's lives—and the lives of all those affected by patriarchy—have been dominated by one particular perception of power. It is *unilateral* power. It is also called zero-sum power, or the power of a closed energy system, inasmuch as it carries with it the assumption that there is only a limited quantity of power available, so that the more one person gets the less is available to the other. Unilateral power is nonmutual and nonrelational. Its purpose is to produce the largest possible effect on another, while being least affected by the other. Its ideal is control.

"In this view," writes Bernard Loomer, "our size or stature is measured by the strength of our unilateral power. Our sense of self-value is correlative to our place on the scale of inequality."[22] But the sense of self one has in this understanding is nonrelational, self-contained. It is the traditional masculine ideal of the Lone Ranger. The aim is to move toward maximum self-sufficiency. Dependency on others is weakness. But this kind of power, in reducing mutuality, produces estrangement among people. We are deadened to our interdependence and to the mystery of each other. This is unmodified phallic power.

Christianity has often embraced this view of power in its views of God. At such times it has seen God as omniscient, omnipotent, and controlling the world by divine fiat. This theology was built upon the same sexual dualism that split spirit from body. Spirit was seen as eternal, complete, and changeless, while body was temporal, incomplete, and changeable. God had unilateral power. "He" was perfect in his completeness and unaffected by those "below."

At the same time Christian theology embraced this unilateral understanding of power as applied to God, it had problems. The gospel message was quite clear that among people this was "worldly" power. Because such power was one-way and controlling, it seemed to be the antithesis of love. When Jesus renounced the power of the world, it was this kind of power he forsook. Thus, in Christianity a view of love as similarly one-way arose. It was the traditional interpretation of agape—a one-way divine love, a concern for the other with no concern for oneself. It was this kind of love that Christians were told to emulate. A one-sided love became the compensation for a one-sided power. One extreme was designed to offset a contrary extreme. The loss of eros and the goodness of the erotic, the confusion of selfishness with self-love—such were the prices exacted by unilateral power and unilateral love.

There is, however, another understanding of power. "This is the ability both to produce and to undergo an effect. It is the capacity both to influence others and to be influenced by others."[23] This is *relational* power. It is generative power, the power of an open energy system. Instead of a fixed, limited amount, the assumption is that shared power can generate more power. People are enhanced by this kind of power, mystery is affirmed, interdependence is celebrated. This, however, is not the power represented by the penis, but by the whole of the genitals and the whole of the body.

These distinctions concerning power bear on the problem of androgyny. Traditional androgyny begins with a combinationist assumption. It takes a fixed notion of the masculine (the active agent), a fixed notion of the feminine (the receiving, nurturing one) and tries to combine them in one person. However, in regard to power, both understandings of gender roles are deficient. The "feminine" principle has been under attack because it suggests a neurotic dependence on others and lack of sufficient autonomy. The "masculine" has been under attack because it suggests the urge to dominate others without being at the same time influenced by them. The point is that both are faulty. Adding one to another to achieve a balance is not the solution. Rather, the solution is understanding that both are definitions marred by fear and insecurity. The "feminine" fears self-dependence, while the "masculine" fears interdependence. Such fear is born of insecurity. It is the absence of authentic power.

Just as wholeness for either a man or a woman is not some combination of the masculine and the feminine, so also authentic relational power is not a neat combination of the active and the receptive. Relational power understands that the capacity to absorb the influence of another without losing the self's own center is as truly a quality of power as is the strength of exerting influence on another.

Loomer calls this kind of strength "size," the capacity to become large enough to make room for another within the self without losing the self's own integrity or freedom. "The world of the individual who can be influenced by another without losing his or her identity or freedom is larger than the world of the individual who fears being influenced. . . . The stature of the individual who can let another exist in his or her own creative freedom is larger than the size of the individual who insists that others must conform to his own purposes and understandings."[24]

Sexual experience always involves power. The experience of phallus without penis is unilateral power. The colloquial male ideal of the phallus is "two feet long, made of steel, and lasts all night." Phallus can handle multiple orgasms (or partners) without being reduced to flaccidity. The phallic perception of woman is as the receptacle for phallic power and emission. The ideal: affect without being affected.

In contrast, the man who affirms his whole sexuality knows that both phallus and penis are one. They are different but interdependent qualities of one male reality. Each at the same time is the other. In spite of the myth of phallic unaffectedness, men know that they are not made of steel, nor do they last all night. Phallus not only delivers effect but is also very much affected. In intercourse it is changed, transformed into penis. "Transformed" is a good word. Sometimes we use the language of death and resurrection about the male genital experience, but it is time to reassess that imagery. It can be highly misleading, even destructive. Yet I fear that the image is fairly common in the male psyche. It suggests that phallus is alive and then, when spent, dies. Penis, then, is the death from which phallus is raised once again. But this interpretation implies a very unilateral understanding of power. Only the phallus has power, the penis does not. Further, the suggestion is that, at least in the heterosexual experience, the woman is somehow associated with the "reducing" the phallus to flaccidity. Thus once again we make, even if unconsciously, the connection between woman and passivity. Now the woman somehow is responsible for the man's passivity, his loss of power and agency. But with the language of death and resurrection the psychic connections become more vicious. Now the phallus dies, and the connection is established between the woman and death. And death is assumed to be the enemy.

But when the phallus becomes penis it does not die. There is simply a change to another form of its life. When the phallus becomes penis it does not lose its power, except when that power is understood unilaterally. Rather, the penis has a different kind of power. It is now the man's genital sexuality expressing its capacity to absorb change. What was once hard and imperious is now soft and gentle. In both dimensions the man is experiencing his masculine power, and both are aspects of relational power. True power is mutuality, making claims and absorbing influence. It is different from the "mutuality" of external relatedness, which trades in force, compromise, and accommodation. It understands the paradox that the greatest influence often consists in being influenced, in enabling another to make the largest impact on oneself.

When a man so understands his sexuality he better understands true power, and when he understands power he better understands his sexuality. The same is true of size, for size and power are intimately related. However, "the wisdom of the world" about male genital size measures quality precisely in terms of quantity. Bigger is better. The masculinist fantasy says not only "made of steel" but also "two feet long." It does not matter that sexologists and sexual therapists tell us that the actual size of the male organ is quite irrelevant to effective sexual functioning and the quality of lovemaking—irrelevant except for one thing: too large an organ causes problems. Still, myth and fantasy persist. Pubescent boys still measure themselves and each other. The record holders are honored in the neighborhood gang. And, as noted earlier, Freud continues to be debunked in his contention that penis envy is a persistent phenomenon of the woman's unconscious; rather, it persists in the surreptitious, glancing comparisons made in the men's locker room.

In contrast to such worldly wisdom about size as quantitative, consider Loomer's description:

> By *size* I mean the stature of a person's soul, the range and depth or his [or her] love, his [or her] capacity for relationships. I mean the volume of life you can take into your being and still maintain your integrity and individuality, the intensity and variety of outlook you can entertain in the unity of your being without feeling defensive or insecure. I mean the strength of your spirit to encourage others to become freer in the development of their diversity and uniqueness. I mean the power to sustain more complex and enriching tensions. I mean the magnanimity of concern to provide conditions that enable others to increase in stature.[25]

When a man understands this meaning of size, his genital sexuality is less anxiously, more graciously celebrated. And when that is true, he also better understands the true meaning of size as criterion of genuine power.

If the themes of death and resurrection can be misleading when applied to penis and phallus, surely they have valid and profound meanings for our sexual and bodily lives more generally. The resurrection of the body in our experience means that mind and body no longer make war on each other, each trying to control or dominate the other. Now I can feel that I *am* my body, and that does not in any way contradict the fact that I am my mind or spirit. Death separates. Resurrection and life reunite. To be raised to life is to discover that I am one person. Body and mind are no longer felt to be distinct.

We usually have such an experience now and then. Most likely it is temporary, soon forgotten, for we have lived much of our lives with dualistic self-understandings and dualistic perceptions of reality at large. So body and mind fall apart again, each competing with the other for the prize of being me. Death sets in once more. But resurrections occur, and in those moments I know myself to be one. When that happens, the experience of oneness with myself brings with it the strong sense of connectedness with the rest of the world. I feel connected to—more than separated from—the people, creatures, and things among whom I live. They have their own identities, yet they also become part of me and I of them. My resurrection is the world's resurrection as I know that world.[26] The same applies to a man's genital perception. Resurrection occurs when penis and phallus are one, neither competing for the honor of being the man. When that happens there is true power—and authentic size.

Notes

1. Mircea Eliade, *Images and Symbols* (New York: Sheed & Ward, 1969), 9. Cf. Eugene Monick, *Phallos: Sacred Image of the Masculine* (Toronto: Inner City Books, 1987), 34.
2. H. A. Williams, *True Resurrection* (New York: Harper & Row, 1972).
3. Ibid., 32–33.

4. Ibid., 33.
5. Ibid., 39.
6. Monick, *Phallos.* I acknowledge my particular indebtedness to his insights in the following paragraphs.
7. Mark Strage, *The Durable Fig Leaf* (New York: William Morrow & Co., 1980), chs. 1 and 5; also Monick, ch. 2.
8. Rudolf Otto, *The Idea of the Holy,* trans. John W. Harvey (London: Oxford University Press, 1923). Cf. Monick, 26.
9. Monick calls this the "clithonic phallos"; see 94–96.
10. Cf. Monick, 48–49.
11. I am indebted to the Rev. Kenneth W. Taylor for these projection insights and also for pressing me to reflect more about the affirmation of genital softness.
12. See Matthew Fox, *Western Spirituality: Historical Roots, Ecumenical Routes* (Notre Dame, Ind.: Fides/Claretian, 1979); also Fox's *Original Blessing,* op. cit., ch. 1, note 17.
13. Quotations from Eckhart are taken from Fox, *Original Blessing,* 132–33, 137, and 139.
14. See Robert A. Raines's beautiful meditation on sinking, in *A Faithing Oak: Meditations from the Mountain* (New York: Crossroad, 1982), 9–10.
15. Rainer Maria Rilke, *Selected Poems of Rainer Maria Rilke,* trans. Robert Bly (New York: Harper & Row, 1981), 21.
16. Starhawk, *Dreaming the Dark: Magic, Sex, and Politics* (Boston: Beacon Press, 1982), xiv.
17. See my fuller discussion of androgyny in *Embodiment* (Minneapolis: Augsburg Publishing House, 1978), 98–101. While I still endorse much of that discussion, I am now inclined to move beyond the concept. A useful summary of the social-psychological literature on androgyny is found in Susan A. Basow, op. cit., ch. 1, note 13, chs. 1 and 13.
18. Nicolas Berdiaev's thought on androgyny is found mainly in his work *The Meaning of Creativeness* (1914). I am quoting the summary by Philip Sherrard in *Christianity and Eros* (London: SPCK, 1976), 61–62.
19. See Karl Barth, *Church Dogmatics,* III/4 (Edinburgh: T. & T. Clark, 1961), esp. 166.
20. Monick, op. cit., 50.
21. In these reflections on power I have been particularly influenced by Bernard Loomer, "Two Kinds of Power," *Criterion* 15, no. 1 (winter 1976).
22. Ibid., 14.
23. Ibid., 19.
24. Ibid., 21.
25. Bernard Loomer, "S-I-Z-E," *Criterion* 13, no. 3 (spring 1974), 21.
26. See Williams, *True Resurrection,* 33.

[3]

In Pursuit of the Perfect Penis: The Medicalization of Male Sexuality

Leonore Tiefer

SEXUAL VIRILITY—the ability to fulfill the conjugal duty, the ability to procreate, sexual power, potency—is everywhere a requirement of the male role, and thus "impotence" is everywhere a matter of concern. Although the term has been used for centuries to refer specifically to partial or complete loss of erectile ability, the first definition in most dictionaries never mentions sex but refers to a general loss of vigor, strength, or power. Sex therapists, concerned about these demeaning connotations, have written about the stigmatizing impact of the label: "The word *impotent* is used to describe the man who does not get an erection, not just his penis. If a man is told by his doctor that he is impotent, and the man turns to his partner and says he is impotent, they are saying a lot more than that the penis cannot become erect" (Kelley, 1981, p. 126). Yet a recent survey of the psychological literature found that the frequency of articles with the term *impotence* in the title has increased dramatically since 1970. In contrast, *frigidity,* a term with equally pejorative connotations and comparable frequency of use from 1940 to 1970, has almost totally disappeared from the literature (Elliott, 1985).

SOURCE: From Leonore Tiefer, "In Pursuit of the Perfect Penis: The Medicalization of Male Sexuality," in *Sex Is Not a Natural Act and Other Essays* (Boulder, Colo.: Westview Press, 1994). Used by permission.

In this chapter I would like to show how the persistence and increased use of the stigmatizing and stress-inducing label of *impotent* reflects a significant moment in the social construction of male sexuality. The factors that create this moment include the increasing importance of lifelong sexual activity in personal life, the insatiability of mass media for appropriate sexual topics, the expansionist needs of specialty medicine and new medical technology, and the highly demanding male sexual script. I will show how these factors interact to produce a medicalization of male sexuality and sexual impotence that limits many men even as it offers new options and hope to others. Let me begin with a discussion of men's sexuality and then discuss what medicine has recently had to offer it.

Male Sexuality

Sexual competence is part—some would say the *central* part—of contemporary masculinity. This is true whether we are discussing the traditional man, the modern man, or even the "new" man:

> What so stokes male sexuality that clinicians are impressed by the force of it? Not libido, but rather the curious phenomenon by which sexuality consolidates and confirms gender. . . . An impotent man always feels that his masculinity, and not just his sexuality, is threatened. In men, gender appears to "lean" on sexuality . . . the need for sexual performance is so great. . . . In women, gender identity and self-worth can be consolidated by other means. (Person, 1980, pp. 619, 626)

John Gagnon and William Simon (1973) explained how, during adolescent masturbation, genital sexuality (i.e., erection and orgasm) acquires nonsexual motives—such as the desire for power, achievement, and peer approval—that have already become important during preadolescent gender role training. "The capacity for erection," they wrote, "is an important sign element of masculinity and control" (Gagnon and Simon, 1973, p. 62) without which a man is not a man. Allan Gross (1978) argued that by adulthood few men can accept other successful aspects of masculinity in lieu of adequate sexual performance.

Masculine sexuality assumes the ability for potent function, but the performances that earn acceptance and status often occur far from the bedroom. Observing behavior in a Yorkshire woolen mill, British sociologist Dennis Marsden described how working-class men engage in an endless performance of sexual stories, jokes, and routines: "As a topic on which most men could support a conversation and as a source of jokes, sexual talk and gesture were inexhaustible. In the machine noise a gesture suggestive of masturbation, intercourse, or homosexuality was enough to raise a conventional smile and re-establish a bond over distances too great for talking" (Marsden, quoted in Tolson, 1977, p. 60). Andrew Tolson argued that this type of ritualized sexual exchange validates working men's bond of masculinity in a situation that otherwise emasculates them and illustrates the enduring homosocial function of heterosexuality that develops from the adolescent experience (Gagnon and Simon, 1973).

Psychologically, then, male sexual performance may have as much or more to do with male gender role confirmation and homosocial status as with pleasure, intimacy, or tension release. This assessment may explain why men express so many rules concerning proper sexual performance: Their agenda relates not merely to personal or couple satisfaction but to acting "like a man" during intercourse in order to qualify for the title elsewhere, where it *really* counts.

I have drawn on the writings of several authorities to compile an outline of ten sexual beliefs to which many men subscribe (Doyle, 1983; Zilbergeld, 1978; LoPiccolo, 1978; LoPiccolo, 1985): (1) Men's sexual apparatus and needs are simple and straightforward, unlike women's; (2) most men are ready, willing, and eager for as much sex as they can get; (3) most men's sexual experiences approximate ecstatic explosiveness (the standard by which individual men compare their own experience, thus becoming disappointed over suspicions that they are not doing as well as others); (4) it is the responsibility of the man to teach and lead his partner to experience pleasure and orgasm(s); (5) sexual prowess is a serious, task-oriented business, no place for experimentation, unpredictability, or play; (6) women prefer intercourse, particularly "hard-driving" intercourse, to other sexual activities; (7) all really good and normal sex must end in intercourse; (8) any physical contact other than a light touch is meant as an invitation to foreplay and intercourse; (9) it is the responsibility of the man to satisfy both his partner and himself; (10) sexual prowess is never permanently earned; each time it must be reproven.

Many of these demands directly require—and all of them indirectly require—an erection. James Nelson (1985) pointed out that male sexuality is dominated by a genital focus in several ways: Sexuality is isolated from the rest of life as a unique experience with particular technical performance requirements; the subjective meaning for the man arises from genital sensations first practiced and familiar in adolescent masturbation and directly transferred without thought to the interpersonal situation; and the psychological meaning primarily depends on the confirmation of virility that comes from proper erection and ejaculation.

It is no surprise, then, that any difficulty in getting the penis to do what it "ought" can become a source of profound humiliation and despair, both in terms of the immediate blow to self-esteem and in terms of the eventual destruction of masculine reputation that is assumed will follow. Two contemporary observers expressed men's fears of impotence in these terms:

> Few sexual problems are as devastating to a man as his inability to achieve or sustain an erection long enough for successful sexual intercourse. For many men the idea of not being able to "get it up" is a fate worse than death. (Doyle, 1983, p. 205)
>
> What's the worst thing that can happen? I asked myself. The worst thing that can happen is that I take one of these hip, beautiful, liberated women to bed and I can't get it up. I can't get it up! You hear me? She tells a few of her friends. Soon around every corner there's someone laughing at my failure. (Parent, 1977, p. 15)

Biomedical Approaches to Male Sexual Problems

Within the past decade, both professional and popular discussions about male sexuality have emphasized physical causes and treatments for sexual problems. There is greater awareness and acceptance within the medical profession of clinical and research work on sexuality, and sexually dissatisfied men are increasingly willing to discuss their problems with physicians (Bancroft, 1982). The professional literature on erection problems has focused on methods of differentiating between organic and nonorganic causes (LoPiccolo, 1985). Recent reviews survey endocrine, neurologic, medication-related, urologic, surgery-related, congenital, and vascular causes and contrast them with psychological and relationship causes (Krane, Siroky, and Goldstein, 1983).

Although the physiological contributions to adequate sexual functioning can be theoretically specified in some detail, there are as yet few diagnostic tests that enable specific identification of different types of pathophysiological contributions. Moreover, there are few medical treatments available for medically caused erectile disorders aside from changing medications (particularly in the case of hypertension) or correcting an underlying disease process. The most widely used medical approach is an extreme one: surgical implantation of a device into the penis to permit intromission. This is the penile prosthesis.[1]

The history of these devices is relatively short (Melman, 1978). Following unsuccessful attempts with bone and cartilage, the earliest synthetic implant (1948) consisted of a plastic tube placed in the middle of the penis of a patient who had had his urethra removed for other reasons. Today, several different manufacturers produce slightly different versions of two general types of implant.

One type is the "inflatable" prosthesis. Inflatable silicone cylinders are placed in the *corpora cavernosa* of the penis, the cylindrical bodies of erectile tissue that normally fill with blood during erection. The cylinders are connected to a pump placed in the scrotum that is connected to a small, saline-filled reservoir placed in the abdomen. Arnold Melman (1978) described how the prosthesis works: "When the patient desires a tumescent phallus, the bulb is squeezed five or six times and fluid is forced from the reservoir into the cylinder chambers. When a flaccid penis is wanted, a deflation valve is pressed and the fluid returns to the reservoir" (p. 278). The other type of prosthesis consists of a pair of semirigid rods, now made of silicone, with either bendable silver cores or hinges to allow concealment of the erection by bending the penis down or up against the body when the man is dressed.

Because these devices have been implanted primarily by private practitioners, the only way to estimate the number of implant operations conducted to date is from manufacturers' sales figures. However, many devices are sold that are not used. A French urologist estimated that 5,000 patients were given penile implants in 1977 alone (Subrini, 1980). It seems reasonable to guess that by the mid-1980s hundreds of thousands of men had received implants.

Needless to say, many articles have been written stressing the need to carefully evaluate men who might be candidates for the procedures. Surgeons are concerned to exclude

> patients at risk of becoming psychotic or suicidal, developing chronic psychogenic pain, or initiating inappropriate malpractice suits. . . . A second important concern has been to rule out patients whose erectile dysfunction is psychogenic and could be cured without surgery . . . although several urologists have reported high patient satisfaction when carefully selected patients with psychogenic dysfunction received penile prostheses. (Schover and von Eschenbach, 1985, p. 58)

Postimplant follow-up studies have typically been conducted by surgeons interested in operative complications and global measures of patient satisfaction (Sotile, 1979). Past reports have encouraged the belief that the devices function mechanically, that men and their partners are able to adjust to them without difficulty, and that the prostheses result in satisfactory sexual function and sensation. But recent papers challenge these simple conclusions. One review of the postoperative follow-up literature was so critical of methodological weaknesses (brief follow-up periods, rare interviews with patients' sexual partners, few objective data or even cross-validation of subjective questions about sexual functioning, among others) that the authors could not summarize the results in any meaningful way (Collins and Kinder, 1984). Another recent summary criticized the implants' effectiveness:

> First, recent reports indicate that the percentage of surgical and mechanical complications from such prosthetic implants is much higher than might be considered acceptable. Second, despite claims to the contrary by some surgeons, it appears likely that whatever degree of naturally occurring erection a man is capable of will be disrupted, and perhaps eliminated by the surgical procedures and scarring involved in prosthetic implants. Finally, it has been my experience that, although patients are typically rather eager to have a prosthesis implanted and report being very happy with it at short-term surgical follow-up, longer term behavioral assessment indicates poor sexual adjustment in some cases. (LoPiccolo, 1985, p. 222)

Three recent urological papers report high rates of postoperative infection and mechanical failure of the inflatable prosthesis, both of which necessitate removal of the device (Apte, Gregory, and Purcell, 1984; Joseph, Bruskewitz, and Benson, 1984; Fallon, Rosenberg, and Culp, 1984). The first paper reported that 43 percent of patients required at least one repeat surgery; the second found that 47 percent of 88 devices implanted since 1977 had malfunctioned; and the third reported that 48 percent of 95 patients had their prostheses malfunction in one way or another since 1977.

In perhaps the only paper reporting on the effectiveness of penile implants in gay men, a therapist who had worked with three such patients indicated that "the implants were less successful with homosexuals than with heterosexuals because there tends to be much more direct penile contact in gay sexuality than in heterosexual sexuality. The person with the implant is aware of the difference, not his partner" (Paff, 1985, p. 15). One of the patients had to have the implant removed because of a mechanical malfunction.

Public Information about Penile Prostheses

Public sexual information is dominated by health and medical science in both language and substance. Newspapers present "new" discoveries. Magazines have "experts" with advanced health degrees outline "new" norms and ways to achieve them. Television and radio talk-show guests, also health-degreed "experts," promote their latest books or therapeutic approaches as "resources" are flashed on the screen or mentioned by the host. Sexuality is presented as a life problem—like buying a house, having a good relationship, dealing with career choices—and the "modern" approach is to be rational, orderly, careful, thorough, up-to-date, and in tune with the latest expert pronouncements.

The public accepts the assumption that scientific discoveries help enable people to manage and control their own lives and welcomes new biomedical developments in areas perceived to be matters of health and illness. Sexual physiology has a tangibility that "love" and "lust" lack and thus seems more suitable to people as a language for public discourse. When biomedicine, health, and physiology are considered the appropriate sexual discourse, scientists and health-care providers are the appropriate authorities.

The media have presented information about penile prostheses in the same straightforward, rational, scientific, informative way as they have presented other "news" about sexuality. An early article in the *New York Times* (Brody, 1979), for example, presented the findings of a urological paper that had appeared in the *Journal of the American Medical Association* the day before. But not only was the science discussed, the article also gave the address of the prosthesis manufacturer as well as typical financial cost, length of hospital stay, and insurance coverage. A *JAMA* editorial criticizing the study's inattention to the patients' sexual partners was mentioned in the final two paragraphs.

An article in the April 1985 issue of *Vogue* exclusively discussed the new medical and surgical approaches to impotence under a typically simple and optimistic title, "Curing Impotence: The Prognosis Is Good." The article mentioned the financial cost of the devices as well as an in-development "electrostimulatory device to be inserted in the anus before intercourse and controlled by a ring or wristwatch-like switch so that patients can signal appropriate nerves to produce an erection" (Hixson 1985, p. 406). The style of the writing was technical and mechanical and so simple and cheerful that it was hardly amazing to read: "While psychological impotence problems probably also require psychological treatment, the doctors feel that successful electronic intercourse may provide the confidence needed by some men" (p. 406).

Literature for patients has been developed by the major prosthesis manufacturers and is available at patient education centers, in doctors' waiting rooms, and through self-help groups such as Impotents Anonymous. A typical booklet is seven pages of high-quality glossy paper with photographs of healthy young couples sitting in a garden, watching a beautiful sunset, or sitting by the ocean (Brooks and Brooks, 1984). Entitled *Overcoming Impotence,* the text reads, "Impotence is a widespread problem that affects many millions of men. It can occur at any age and at any point in a man's sexual life. The myth of impotence as an 'old man's disease' has finally been shattered. Impotence is a problem of men but also affects couples and families. Now, as a result of recent medical advances, impotence need no longer cause frustration, embarrassment and tension. New solutions are now available for an age-old problem."

In the second section, on causes of impotence, the booklet reads as follows: "The causes can be either physical or psychological. For many years, it was believed that 90 percent of impotent men had a psychological cause for their problem; but as a result of recent medical research, it is now known that at least half of the men suffering from impotence can actually trace its origin to a physical problem." After a lengthy discussion of the methods used to distinguish between physical and psychological impotence, the booklet continues in its relentlessly upbeat way: "For the majority of men who are physically impotent and for those who are psychologically impotent and do not respond to counseling, a penile implant offers the only complete, reliable solution. It offers new hope for a return to satisfactory sexual activity and for the disappearance of the anxieties and frustrations of impotence."

This conclusion, of course, seems to provide a straightforward technological solution to a technical problem. No mention is made of individual differences in adjusting to the prosthesis or even the fact that adjustment will be necessary at all. The mechanical solution itself will solve the problem; the person becomes irrelevant.

Other patient information booklets are similar: informative about the device and reassuring about the outcome. In addition to lengthy and detailed discussion of specific physical causes of impotence, there is a brief mention of psychogenic impotence. One booklet says: "Another group of patients have some type of mental barrier [*sic*] or problem. This latter group may account for as high as 50% of the people with impotence, but only a small number of these people are candidates for a penile implant" (Medical Engineering Corporation, 1983). Is it any wonder that men who "fail" the physical tests and are diagnosed as having psychogenic impotence cannot understand why they should be deprived of the device?

Urologists have begun in recent years to specialize in the diagnosis and surgical treatment of impotence. A quarterly publication from a prosthesis manufacturer "for surgeons practicing prosthetic urology" devoted a front page to the subject "Impotence Clinics: Investments in the Future" (American Medical Systems, 1984). Newspaper advertisements appear from groups of urologists with names such as "Potency Plus" (a group in California). Another group (also in California), which calls itself "Potential," advertises, "Impotence. . . . There could be a medical reason and a medical solution." An ad in a New York newspaper is headlined "Potent Solution to Sexual Problem."

Another source of publicity about the physical causes and treatments for erectile difficulties has come from the Impotence Institute of America, an organization founded by a man who has described how his own search ended happily with an implanted penile prosthesis. Although the subhead on the not-for-profit institute's stationery is "Bringing a 'total-care' concept to overcoming impotence," the ten men on the board of directors are all urologists.

In 1982 the institute created two consumer-oriented groups, Impotents Anonymous (IA) and I-Anon, based on the Alcoholics Anonymous model (both the institute's founder and his wife had formerly been members of Al-Anon). Recent correspondence from the institute indicates there are now seventy chapters of IA operating and another twenty planned. A 1984 news article about IA, "Organization Helps Couples with Impotence as Problem," repeated the now familiar information that "until five years ago most physicians believed that up to 95% of all erectile impotence stemmed from psychological problems, [but that] medical experts now agree that about half of all impotence is caused by physical disorders." The IA brochure cites the same numbers.

Let us turn now to a critique of the biomedical approach to male sexuality, beginning with this question of organic and psychogenic etiology.

Critique of the Biomedical Approach

The frequent claim that psychogenic impotence has been oversold and organic causes are far more common than previously realized has captivated the media and legitimated increased medical involvement in sexuality. An *International Journal of Andrology* editorial summarizes the shift:

> Medical fashions come and go and the treatment of erectile impotence is no exception. In the 20s and 30s, physicians and surgeons looked for physical causes and tried out methods of treatment, most of which now seem absurd. Since that time there has been a widely held view that 90–95% of cases of impotence are psychologically determined. Where this figure came from was never clear [some sources cite Havelock Ellis], but it has entered into medical folklore. In the past five years or so, the pendulum has been swinging back. Physical causes and methods of treatment are receiving increasing attention. (Bancroft, 1982, p. 353)

In the Center for Male Sexual Dysfunction in the Department of Urology at Beth Israel Medical Center, New York City, more than 800 men have been seen since 1981 for erectile problems (I began working there in 1983). Very few who, on the basis of a simple history and physical, could be unambiguously declared "psychogenic" were immediately referred for sex therapy; the remainder underwent a complete medical and psychological workup. Over 90 percent of these patients believed that their problems were completely or preponderantly physical in origin; yet we have found that only about 45 percent of patients have exclusively or predominantly medically caused erectile problems and 55 percent have exclusively or predominantly psychologically caused problems. This approximately fifty-fifty split is, in fact, what is often cited by the mass media. But most of our patients (more than 75 percent) are referred by their primary physicians because of their likely medical etiology and their need for a comprehensive workup.

A Chicago group found that 43 percent of the men coming to a urology clinic for impotence evaluation had at least partly an organic basis for their problems, whereas only 11 percent of the men coming to a psychiatry department sex clinic had organic contributing factors (Segraves et al., 1981). A review of all patients seen at the Johns Hopkins Sexual Behaviors Consultation Unit between 1972 and 1981 showed 105 men over fifty years old with a primary complaint of erectile dysfunction. Even in this age group, only 30 percent could be assigned an organic etiology (Wise, Rabins, and Gahnsley, 1984). After listing sixty-six possible physical causes of secondary impotence, Masters and Johnson (1970, pp. 184–185) reported that only seven of their 213 cases (3 percent) had an organic etiology.

Obviously, one cannot describe the actual rate of occurrence of any particular problem (e.g., "organic impotence") without describing the population from which the sample comes. The urology departments' findings that approximately half of the patients seen for erectile problems have a medical cause *cannot* be generalized to other groups (e.g., men in general practitioners' waiting rooms reading prosthesis manufacturers' literature, men watching a TV program about impotence) without further normative data collection. It is important to emphasize that even men with diabetes, a known cause of peripheral neural and vascular difficulties that could result in impotence, are as often potent as not (Schiavi, Fisher, Quadland, and Glover, 1984; Fairburn, McCulloch, and Wu, 1982), and impotence in a diabetic cannot be predicted from the duration of the diabetes or the presence of other physical complications.

An even more serious criticism of the biomedical trend is the common tendency to contrapose organic and psychogenic causes of impotence as mutually exclusive phenomena. Joseph LoPiccolo (1985) wrote, "Conceptually, most of the research suffers from the flaw of attempting to categorize the patients into discrete, nonoverlapping categories of organic or psychogenic erectile failure. Yet, many cases, and perhaps the majority of cases, involve both organic and psychogenic erectile factors in the genesis of erectile failure" (p. 221). Sally Schumacher and Charles Lloyd (1981), in a review of 102 cases seen at two different medical school centers, concluded, "All patients reported psychological distress associated with their impotence [including] inhibitions, shame, avoidance, insecurity, inadequacy, guilt, hostility, fear of intimacy" (p. 46). A urologic review of 388 cases concluded, "There are wholly organic bases and also totally psychological causes for impotency; yet the two generally coexist. It is most probable that in all cases of organic impotency a psychologic overlay develops" (Finkle and Finkle, 1984, p. 25).

The explanation, I believe, is not so much that all cases involve a mixture of factors but that all cases involve psychological factors in some degree. The director of a New York sexuality clinic summed up her impressions similarly: "We have found in our work . . . that, where organic determinants are diagnosed, inevitably there will also be psychological factors involved, either as co-determinants of the erectile dysfunction or as reactive to it. . . . A man's emotional reaction to his erectile failures may be such that it serves to maintain the erectile problem even when the initial physiological causes are resolved" (Schreiner-Engel, 1981, p. 116).

The consequences of this implication are particularly serious given that, as LoPiccolo (1985) noted, "many physicians currently will perform surgery to implant a penile prosthesis if any organic abnormality is found" (p. 221). The effect of psychological factors is to make the dysfunction look worse than the medical problem alone would warrant. Altering the man's devastated attitudes will improve the picture, whatever else is going on.

Michael Perelman (1984) referred to "the omnipresent psychogenic component existing in any potency problem regardless of the degree of organicity" (p. 181) to describe his successful use of cognitive-behavioral psychotherapy to treat men diagnosed with organic impotence. He reminded his readers that physical sexual function has a psychosomatic complexity that is not only poorly understood but may have the "ability to successfully compensate for its own deficits" (p. 181). Thus the search for *the* etiology that characterizes so much of the biomedical approach to male sexual problems seems to have less to do with the nature of sexuality than with the nature of the medical enterprise.

The Allure of Medicalized Sexuality

Men are drawn to a technological solution such as the penile prosthesis for a variety of personal reasons that ultimately rest on the inflexible central place of sexual potency in the male sexual script. Those who assume that "normal" men must always be interested in sex and who believe that male sexuality is a simple system wherein interest leads easily and directly to erection (Zilbergeld, 1978) are baffled by any erectile difficulties. Their belief that "their penis is an instrument immune from everyday problems, anxieties and fears" (Doyle, 1983, p. 207) conditions them to deny the contribution of psychological or interpersonal factors to male sexual responsiveness. This denial, in turn, results from fundamental male gender role prescriptions for self-reliance and emotional control (Brannon, 1976).

Medicalized discourse offers an explanation of impotence that removes control over, and therefore responsibility and blame for, sexual failure from the man and places it on his physiology. Talcott Parsons (1951) originally argued that an organic diagnosis confers a particular social role, the "sick role," which has three aspects: (1) the individual is not held responsible for his or her condition; (2) illnesses are legitimate bases for exemption from normal social responsibilities; and (3) the exemptions are contingent on the sick person recognizing that sickness is undesirable and seeking appropriate (medical) help. A medical explanation for erectile difficulties relieves men of blame and thus permits them to maintain some masculine self-esteem even in the presence of impotence. According to Masters and Johnson,

> Understandably, for many years the pattern of the human male has been to blame sexual dysfunction on specific physical distresses. Every sexually inadequate male lunges toward any potential physical excuse for sexual malfunction. A cast for a leg or a sling for an arm provides socially acceptable evidence of physical dysfunction of these extremities. Unfortunately, the psychosocial causes of perpetual penile flaccidity cannot be explained or excused by devices for mechanical support. (Masters and Johnson, 1970, pp. 187–188)

Perhaps in 1970 "devices for mechanical support" of the penis were not widely available, but now, ironically, impotent men have precisely the type of medical vindication that Masters and Johnson suggested would provide the *most* effective deflection of the "blame" men feel for their inability to perform sexually.

Men's willingness to accept a self-protective, self-handicapping attribution (i.e., an illness label) for "failure" has been demonstrated in studies of excuse-making (Snyder, Ford, and Hunt, 1985). Reduced personal responsibility is most sought in those situations in which performance is related to self-esteem (Snyder and Smith, 1982). It may be that the frequent use of physical excuses for failure in athletic performance provides a model for men to use in sexuality. Medical treatments not only offer tangible evidence of nonblameworthiness but also allow men to avoid psychological treatments such as marital or sex therapy, which threaten embarrassing self-disclosure and admissions of weakness men find aversive (Peplau and Gordon, 1985).

The final allure of a technological solution such as the penile prosthesis is its promise of permanent freedom from worry. One of Masters and Johnson's (1970) major insights was their description of the self-conscious self-monitor-ing that men with erectile difficulties develop in sexual situations. "Performance anxiety" and "spectatoring," their two immediate causes of sexual impotence, generate a self-perpetuating cycle that undermines a man's confidence about the future even as he recovers from individual episodes. Technology seems to offer a simple and permanent solution to the problem of lost or threatened confidence, as doctors cited from *Vogue* to the *Journal of Urology* have noted.

The Rising Importance of Sexuality in Personal Life

Even though we live in a time when the definition of masculinity is moving away from reliance on physical validation (Pleck, 1976), there seems to be no apparent reduction in the male sexual focus on physical performance. Part of the explanation for this lack of change must rest with the increasing importance of sexuality in contemporary relationships. Recent sociocultural analyses have suggested that sexual satisfaction grows in importance to the individual and couple as other sources of personal fulfillment and connection with others wither. Edmund White (1980) wrote,

> I would say that with the collapse of other social values (those of religion, patriotism, the family, and so on), sex has been forced to take up the slack, to become our sole mode of transcendence and our only touchstone of authenticity. . . . In our present isolation we have few ways besides sex to feel connected with each other. (p. 282)

German sexologist Gunter Schmidt concluded,

> People are being deprived more and more of opportunities to feel they are worth something to others, to experience what they are doing as something of significance, and to know that they are indispensable to the lives of their families or at least a few friends. The experience of powerlessness, dependency, inner vacuum left behind sucks in any experiences which make one at least temporarily aware of one's own importance. . . . A particularly important mode of compensation for narcissistic deprivation is the couple relationship, or, more precisely, the emotions it can mobilize, such as falling in love and sexual desire and satisfaction. (Schmidt, 1983b, pp. 4–5)

The increasing pressure on intimate relationships to provide psychological support and gratification comes at the same time that traditional reasons for these relationships (i.e., economics and raising families) are declining. Both trends place pressure on compatibility and companionship to maintain relationships. Given that men have been raised "not to be emotionally sensitive to others or emotionally expressive or self-revealing" (Pleck, 1981, p. 140), much modern relationship success would seem to depend on sexual fulfillment. Although some contemporary research indicates that marriages and gay relationships can be rated successful despite the presence of sexual problems (Frank, Anderson, and Rubinstein, 1978; Bell and Weinberg, 1978), popular surveys suggest that the public believes sexual satisfaction to be essential to relationship success.

The importance of sexuality also increases because of its use by consumption-oriented capitalism (Altman, 1982). The promise of increased sexual attractiveness is used to sell products to people of all ages. Commercial sexual meeting places are popular in both gay and heterosexual culture, and a whole system of therapists, books, workshops, and magazines sells advice on improving sexual performance and enjoyment. Restraint and repression are inappropriate in a consumer culture in which the emphasis is on immediate gratification.

The expectation that sexuality will provide ever-increasing rewards and personal meaning has also been a theme of the contemporary women's movement, and women's changing attitudes have affected many men, particularly widowed and divorced men returning to the sexual "market." Within the past decade, sexual advice manuals have completely changed their tone regarding the roles of men and women in sexual relations (Weinberg, Swensson, and Hammersmith, 1983). Women are advised to take more responsibility for their own pleasure, to possess sexual knowledge and self-knowledge, and to expect that improved sexual functioning will pay off in other aspects of life. Removing responsibility from the man for being the sexual teacher and leader reduces the definition of sexual masculinity to having excellent technique and equipment to meet the "new woman" on her "new" level.

Finally, the new importance of sexual performance has no upper age limit.

> The sexual myth most rampant in our culture today is the concept that the aging process per se will in time discourage or deny erective security to the older age-group male. As has been described previously, the aging male may be slower to erect and may even reach the plateau phase without full erective return, but the facility and ability to attain erection, presuming general good health and no psychogenic blocking, continues unopposed as a natural sequence well into the 80-year age group. (Masters and Johnson, 1970, p. 326)

Sex is a natural act, Masters and Johnson said over and over again, and there is no "natural" reason for ability to decline or disappear as one ages. Erectile difficulties become "problems" that can be corrected with suitable treatment, and aging provides no escape from the male sexual role.

The Medicalization of Impotence: Part of the Problem or Part of the Solution?

The increasing use of the term *impotence* that Mark Elliott (1985) reported can now be seen as part of a medicalization process of sexuality. Physicians view the medical system as a method for distributing technical expertise in the interest of improved health (Ehrenreich and Ehrenreich, 1978). Their economic interests, spurred by the profit orientation of medical technology manufacturers, lie in expanding the number and type of services they offer to more and more patients. Specialists in particular have dramatically increased their incomes and prestige during the postwar era by developing high-reimbursement relationships with hospitals and insurance companies (Starr, 1982). In the sexual sphere, all these goals are served by labeling impotence a biomedical disorder that is common in men of all ages and best served by thorough evaluation and appropriate medical treatment when any evidence of organic disorder is identified.

There are many apparent advantages for men in the medicalization of male sexuality. As discussed earlier, men view physical explanations for their problems as less stigmatizing and are better able to maintain their sense of masculinity and self-esteem when their problems are designated as physical. Accepting medicine as a source of authority and help reassures men who feel that they are under immense pressure from role expectations but who are unable to consult with or confide in either other men or women because of pride, competitiveness, or defensiveness. That "inhibited sexual excitement . . . in males, partial or complete failure to attain or maintain erection until completion of the [*sic*] sexual act," is a genuine disorder (APA, 1980, p. 279) legitimates an important aspect of life that physicians previously dismissed or made jokes about. And, as I have said, permanent mechanical solutions to sexual performance worries are seen as a gift from heaven; one simple operation erases a source of anxiety dating from adolescence about failing as a man.

The disadvantages to medicalizing male sexuality, however, are numerous and subtle. (My discussion here is informed by Catherine Riessman's 1983 analysis of the medicalization of many female roles and conditions.) First, dependence on medical remedies for impotence has led to the escalating use of treatments that may have unpredictable long-term effects. Iatrogenic ("doctor-caused") consequences of new technology and pharmacology are not uncommon and seem most worrisome when medical treatments are offered to men with no demonstrable organic disease. Second, the use of medical language mystifies human experience, increasing the public's dependence on professionals and experts. If sexuality becomes fundamentally a matter of vasocongestion and myotonia (as in Masters and Johnson's famous claim, 1966, p. 7), personal experience requires expert interpretation and explanation. Third, medicalization spreads the moral neutrality of medicine and science over sexuality, and people no longer ask whether men "should" have erections. If the presence of erections is healthy and their absence (in whole or part) is pathological, then healthy behavior is correct behavior and vice versa. This view again increases the public's dependence on health authorities to define norms and standards for conduct.

The primary disadvantage of medicalization is that it denies, obscures, and ignores the social causes of whatever problem is under study. Impotence becomes the problem of an individual man. This effect seems particularly pertinent in the case of male sexuality, an area in which the social demands of the male sexual role are so related to the meaning of erectile function and dysfunction. Recall the list of men's beliefs about sexuality, the evaluative criteria of conduct and performance. Being a man depends on sexual adequacy, which depends on potency. A rigid, reliable erection is necessary for full compliance with the script. The medicalization of male sexuality helps a man conform to the script rather than analyzing where the script comes from or challenging it. In addition, "Medicine attracts public resources out of proportion to its capacity for health enhancement, because it often categorizes problems fundamentally social in origin as biological or personal deficits, and in so doing smothers the impulse for social change which could offer the only serious resolution" (Stark and Flitcraft, quoted in Riessman, 1983, p. 4). Research and technology are directed only toward better and better solutions. Yet the demands of the script are so formidable, and the pressures from the sociocultural changes I have outlined so likely to increase, that no technical solution will ever work—certainly not for everyone.

Preventive Medicine: Changing the Male Sexual Script

Men will remain vulnerable to the expansion of the clinical domain so long as masculinity rests heavily on a particular type of physical function. As more research uncovers subtle physiological correlates of genital functioning, more men will be "at risk" for impotence. Fluctuations of physical and emotional state will become cues for impending impotence in any man with, for example, diabetes, hypertension, or a history of prescription medication usage.

One of the less well understood features of sex therapy is that it "treats" erectile dysfunction by changing the individual man's sexual script. Sex therapists have described the process as follows:

> This approach is primarily educational—you are not curing an illness but learning new and more satisfactory ways of getting on with each other. (Bancroft, 1989, p. 537)
>
> Our thesis is that the rules and concepts we learn [about male sexuality] are destructive and a very inadequate preparation for a satisfying and pleasurable sex life. . . . Having a better sex life is in large measure dependent upon your willingness to examine how the male sexual mythology has trapped you. (Zilbergeld, 1978, p. 9)

Sexuality can be transformed from a rigid standard for masculine adequacy to a way of being, a way of communicating, a hobby, a way of being in one's body—and *being* one's body—that does not impose control but rather affirms pleasure, movement, sensation, cooperation, playfulness, relating. Masculine confidence cannot be purchased because there can never be perfect potency. Chasing its illusion may line a few pockets, but for most men it will only exchange one set of anxieties and limitations for another.

Note

1. . . . By 1994 the penile prosthesis, although still in widespread use, was a less popular treatment than the technique of self-injection of medication into the penis. . . .

Editor's note: The bibliographic references for this article have been omitted. The interested reader should refer to the original text, *Sex Is Not a Natural Act and Other Essays* (Boulder, Colo.: Westview Press, 1994).

[4]

Women and the Knife: Cosmetic Surgery and the Colonization of Women's Bodies

Kathryn Pauly Morgan

CONSIDER THE FOLLOWING PASSAGES:

If you want to wear a Maidenform Viking Queen bra like Madonna, be warned: A body like this doesn't just happen. . . . Madonna's kind of fitness training takes time. The rock star *whose muscled body was recently on tour* spends a minimum of three hours a day working out. ("Madonna Passionate about Fitness" 1990; italics added)

A lot of the contestants [in the Miss America Pageant] do not owe their beauty to their Maker but to their Re-Maker. Miss Florida's nose came courtesy of her surgeon. So did Miss Alaska's. And Miss Oregon's breasts came from the manufacturers of silicone. (Goodman 1989)

Jacobs [a plastic surgeon in Manhattan] constantly answers the call for cleavage. "Women need it for their holiday ball gowns." ("Cosmetic Surgery for the Holidays" 1985)

We hadn't seen or heard from each other for 28 years. . . . Then he suggested it would be nice if we could meet. I was very nervous about it. How much had I

SOURCE: From Kathryn Pauly Morgan, "Women and the Knife: Cosmetic Surgery and the Colonization of Women's Bodies," in *Living with Contradictions: Controversies in Feminist Social Ethics,* ed. Alison M. Jagger (Boulder, Colo.: Westview Press, 1994). Used by permission.

> changed? I wanted a facelift, tummy tuck and liposuction, all in one week. (A woman, age forty-nine, being interviewed for an article on "older couples" falling in love; "Falling in Love Again" 1990)
>
> "It's hard to say why one person will have cosmetic surgery done and another won't consider it, but generally I think people who go for surgery are more aggressive, they are the doers of the world. It's like makeup. You see some women who might be greatly improved by wearing make-up, but they're, I don't know, granola-heads or something, and they just refuse." (Dr. Ronald Levine, director of plastic surgery education at the University of Toronto and vice-chairman of the plastic surgery section of the Ontario Medical Association; "The Quest to Be a Perfect 10" 1990)
>
> Another comparable limitation [of the women's liberation movement] is a tendency to reject certain good things only in order to punish men. . . . There is no reason why a women's liberation activist should not try to look pretty and attractive. (Markovic 1976)

Now [think about] the needles and . . . the knives. [Think] carefully. [Think] for a long time. *Imagine them cutting into your skin.* Imagine that you have been given [cosmetic] surgery as a gift from your loved one who read a persuasive and engaging press release from Drs. John and Jim Williams that ends by saying, "The next morning the limo will chauffeur your loved one back home again, with a gift of beauty that will last a lifetime" (Williams, 1990). Imagine the beauty that you have been promised. . . .

. . . We need a feminist analysis to understand why actual, live women are reduced and reduce themselves to "potential women" and choose to participate in anatomizing and fetishizing their bodies as they buy "contoured bodies," "restored youth," and "permanent beauty." In the face of a growing market and demand for surgical interventions in women's bodies that can and do result in infection, bleeding, embolisms, pulmonary edema, facial nerve injury, unfavorable scar formation, skin loss, blindness, crippling, and death, our silence becomes a culpable one. . . .

. . . Not only is elective cosmetic surgery moving out of the domain of the sleazy, the suspicious, the secretively deviant, or the pathologically narcissistic, *it is becoming the norm.* This shift is leading to a predictable inversion of the domains of the deviant and the pathological, so that women who contemplate *not using* cosmetic surgery will increasingly be stigmatized and seen as deviant. . . .

. . . Cosmetic surgery entails the ultimate envelopment of the lived temporal *reality* of the human subject by technologically created appearances that are then regarded as "the real." Youthful appearance triumphs over aged reality.

I. "Just the Facts in America, Ma'am"

As of 1990, the most frequently performed kind of cosmetic surgery is liposuction, which involves sucking fat cells out from underneath our skin with a vacuum device. This is viewed as the most suitable procedure for removing specific bulges around the hips, thighs, belly, buttocks, or chin. It is most appropriately done on thin people who want to get rid of certain bulges, and surgeons guarantee that even if there is weight gain, the bulges won't reappear since the fat cells have been permanently removed. At least twelve deaths are known to have resulted from complications such as hemorrhages and embolisms. "All we know is there was a complication and that complication was death," said the partner of Toni Sullivan, age forty-three ("hardworking mother of two teenage children" says the press; "Woman, 43, Dies after Cosmetic Surgery" 1989). Cost: $1,000–$7,500.

The second most frequently performed kind of cosmetic surgery is breast augmentation, which involves an implant, usually of silicone. Often the silicone implant hardens over time and must be removed surgically. Over one million women in the United States are known to have had breast augmentation surgery. Two recent studies have shown that breast implants block X rays and cast a shadow on surrounding tissue, making mammograms difficult to interpret, and that there appears to be a much higher incidence of cancerous lumps in "augmented women" ("Implants Hide Tumors in Breasts, Study Says" 1988). Cost: $1,500–$3,000.

"Facelift" is a kind of umbrella term that covers several sorts of procedures. In a recent Toronto case, Dale Curtis "decided to get a facelift for her fortieth birthday. . . . Bederman used liposuction on the jowls and neck, removed the skin and fat from her upper and lower lids and tightened up the muscles in the neck and cheeks. . . . 'She was supposed to get a forehead lift but she chickened out,' Bederman says" ("Changing Faces" 1989). Clients are now being advised to begin their facelifts in their early forties and are also told that they will need subsequent facelifts every five to fifteen years. Cost: $2,500–$10,500.

"Nips" and "tucks" are cute, camouflaging labels used to refer to surgical reduction performed on any of the following areas of the body: hips, buttocks, thighs, belly, and breasts. They involve cutting out wedges of skin and fat and sewing up the two sides. These are major surgical procedures that cannot be performed in outpatient clinics because of the need for anesthesia and the severity of possible postoperative complications. Hence, they require access to costly operating rooms and services in hospitals or clinics. Cost: $3,000–$7,000.

The number of "rhinoplasties," or nose jobs, has risen by 34 percent since

1981. Some clients are coming in for second and third nose jobs. Nose jobs involve either the inserting of a piece of bone taken from elsewhere in the body or the whittling down of the nose. Various styles of noses go in and out of fashion, and various cosmetic surgeons describe the noses they create in terms of their own surnames, such as "the Diamond nose" or "the Goldman nose" ("Cosmetic Surgery for the Holidays" 1985). Cost: $2,000–$3,000.

More recent types of cosmetic surgery, such as the use of skin-expanders and suction lipectomy, involve inserting tools, probes, and balloons *under* the skin either for purposes of expansion or reduction (Hirshson 1987).

Lest one think that women (who represent between 60 and 70 percent of all cosmetic surgery patients) choose only one of these procedures, heed the words of Dr. Michael Jon Bederman of the Centre for Cosmetic Surgery in Toronto:

> We see working girls, dental technicians, middle-class women who are unhappy with their looks or are aging prematurely. And we see executives—both male and female. . . . Where before someone would have a tummy tuck and not have anything else done for a year, frequently we will do liposuction and tummy tuck and then the next day a facelift, upper and lower lids, rhinoplasty *and other things.* The recovery time is the same whether a person has one procedure or *the works,* generally about two weeks. ("Changing Faces" 1989; italics added)

In principle, there is no area of the body that is not accessible to the interventions and metamorphoses performed by cosmetic surgeons intent on creating twentieth century versions of "femina perfecta."

II. From Artifice to Artifact: The Creation of Robo Woman?

. . .

[Today, what] is designated "the natural" functions primarily as a frontier rather than as a barrier. While genetics, human sexuality, reproductive outcome, and death were previously regarded as open to variation primarily in evolutionary terms, they are now seen by biotechnologists as domains of creation and control. Cosmetic surgeons claim a role here too. For them, human bodies are the locus of challenge. As one plastic surgeon remarks:

> Patients sometimes misunderstand the nature of cosmetic surgery. It's not a shortcut for diet or exercise. *It's a way to override the genetic code.* ("Retouching Nature's Way," 1990; italics added)

. . . [Practices of coercion and domination are often camouflaged by practical rhetoric and supporting theories that appear to be benevolent, therapeutic, and voluntaristic. Previously, for example, colonizing was often done in the name of bringing "civilization" through culture and morals to "primitive, barbaric people," but contemporary colonizers mask their exploitation of "raw materials and human labor" in the name of "development."]

The beauty culture is coming to be dominated by a variety of experts, and consumers of youth and beauty are likely to find themselves dependent not only on cosmetic surgeons but on anesthetics, nurses, aestheticians, nail technicians, manicurists, dietitians, hairstylists, cosmetologists, masseuses, aroma therapists, trainers, pedicurists, electrolysists, pharmacologists, and dermatologists. All these experts provide services that can be bought; all these experts are perceived as administering and transforming the human body into an increasingly artificial and ever more perfect object. . . .

. . . For virtually all women as women, success is defined in terms of interlocking patterns of compulsion: compulsory attractiveness, compulsory motherhood, and compulsory heterosexuality, patterns that determine the legitimate limits of attraction and motherhood.[1] Rather than aspiring to self-determined and woman-centered ideals of health or integrity, women's attractiveness is defined as attractive-to-men; women's eroticism is defined as either nonexistent, pathological, or peripheral when it is not directed to phallic goals; and motherhood is defined in terms of legally sanctioned and constrained reproductive service to particular men and to institutions such as the nation, the race, the owner, and the class—institutions that are, more often than not, male-dominated. Biotechnology is now making beauty, fertility, the appearance of heterosexuality through surgery, and the appearance of youthfulness accessible to virtually all women who can afford that technology—and growing numbers of women are making other sacrifices in their lives in order to buy access to the technical expertise.

In Western industrialized societies, women have also become increasingly socialized into an acceptance of technical knives. We know about knives that can heal: the knife that saves the life of a baby in distress, the knife that cuts out the cancerous growths in our breasts, the knife that straightens our spines, the knife that liberates our arthritic fingers so that we may once again gesture, once again touch, once again hold. But we also know about other knives: the knife that cuts off our toes so that our feet will fit into elegant shoes, the knife that cuts out ribs to fit our bodies into corsets, the knife that slices through our labia in episiotomies and other forms of genital mutilation, the knife that cuts into our abdomens to remove our ovaries to cure our "deviant tendencies" (Barker-Benfield 1976), the knife that removes our breasts in prophylactic or unnecessary radical mastectomies, the knife that cuts out our "useless bag" (the womb) if we're the wrong color and poor or if we've "outlived our fertility," the knife that makes the "bikini cut" across our pregnant bellies to facilitate the cesarean section that will allow the obstetrician to go on holiday. We know these knives well.

And now we are coming to know the knives and needles of the cosmetic surgeons—the knives that promise to sculpt our bodies, to restore our youth, to create beauty out of what was ugly and ordinary. What kind of knives are these? Magic knives. Magic knives in a patriarchal context. Magic knives in a Eurocentric context. Magic knives in a white supremacist context. What do they mean? I am afraid of these knives.

III. Listening to the Women

In order to give a feminist reading of any ethical situation we must listen to the women's own reasons for their actions (Sherwin, 1984–85 and 1989). It is only once we have listened to the voices of women who have elected to undergo cosmetic surgery that we can try to assess the extent to which the conditions for genuine choice have been met and look at the consequences of these choices for the position of women. Here are some of those voices:

Voice 1 (*a woman looking forward to attending a prestigious charity ball*): "There will be a lot of new faces at the Brazilian Ball" ("Changing Faces" 1989). [Class/status symbol]

Voice 2: "You can keep yourself trim. . . . But you have no control over the way you wrinkle, or the fat on your hips, or the skin of your lower abdomen. If you are hereditarily predestined to stretch out or wrinkle in your face, you will. If your parents had puffy eyelids and saggy jowls, you're going to have puffy eyelids and saggy jowls" ("Changing Faces" 1989). [Regaining a sense of control; liberation from parents; transcending hereditary predestination]

Voice 3: "Now we want a nose that makes a statement, with tip definition and a strong bridge line" ("Changing Faces," 1989). [Domination; strength]

Voice 4: "I decided to get a facelift for my fortieth birthday after ten years of living and working in the tropics had taken its toll" ("Changing Faces" 1989). [Gift to the self; erasure of a decade of hard work and exposure]

Voice 5: "I've gotten my breasts augmented. I can use it as a tax write-off" ("Changing Faces" 1989). [Professional advancement; economic benefits]

Voice 6: "I'm a teacher and kids let schoolteachers know how we look and they aren't nice about it. A teacher who looks like an old bat or has a big nose will get a nickname" ("Retouching Nature's Way: Is Cosmetic Surgery Worth It?" 1990). [Avoidance of cruelty; avoidance of ageist bias]

Voice 7: "I'll admit to a boob job." (Susan Akin, Miss America of 1986, quoted in Goodman, 1989). [Prestige; status; competitive accomplishments in beauty contest]

Voice 8: (*forty-five-year-old grandmother and proprietor of a business*): "In my business, the customers expect you to look as good as they do" (Hirschson 1987). [Business asset; economic gain; possible denial of grandmother status]

Voice 9: "People in business see something like this as showing an overall aggressiveness and go-forwardness. *The trend is to, you know, be all that you can be*" ("Cosmetic Surgery for the Holidays" 1985). [Success; personal fulfillment]

Voice 10 (paraphrase): "I do it to fight holiday depression" ("Cosmetic Surgery for the Holidays" 1985). [Emotional control; happiness]

Voice 11: "I came to see Dr. X for the holiday season. I have important business parties, and the man I'm trying to get to marry me is coming in from Paris" ("Cosmetic Surgery for the Holidays" 1985). [Economic gain; heterosexual affiliation]

Women have traditionally regarded (and been taught to regard) their bodies, particularly if they are young, beautiful, and fertile, *as a locus of power* to be enhanced through artifice and, now, through artifact. In 1792, in *A Vindication of the Rights of Women,* Mary Wollstonecraft remarked: "Taught from infancy that beauty is woman's scepter, the mind shapes itself to the body and roaming round its gilt cage, only seeks to adorn its prison." How ironic that the mother of the creator of *Frankenstein* should be the source of that quote. We need to ask ourselves whether today, involved as we are in the modern inversion of "our bodies shaping themselves to our minds," we are creating a new species of woman-monster with new artifactual bodies that function as prisons or whether cosmetic surgery for women does represent a potentially liberating field of choice.

When Snow White's stepmother asks the mirror, "Who is fairest of all?" she is not asking simply an empirical question. In wanting to continue to be "the fairest of all," she is striving, in a clearly competitive context, for a prize, for a position, for power. The affirmation of her beauty brings with it privileged heterosexual affiliation, privileged access to forms of power unavailable to the plain, the ugly, the aged, and the barren.

The Voices are seductive—they speak the language of gaining access to transcendence, achievement, liberation, and power. And they speak to a kind of reality. First, electing to undergo the surgery necessary to create youth and beauty artificially not only appears to but often actually does give a woman a sense of identity that, to some extent, she has chosen herself. Second, it offers her the potential to raise her status both socially and economically by increasing her opportunities for heterosexual affiliation (especially with white men). Third, by committing herself to the pursuit of beauty, a woman integrates her life with a consistent set of values and choices that bring her widespread approval and a resulting sense of increased self-esteem. Fourth, the pursuit of beauty often gives a woman access to a range of individuals who administer to her body in a caring way, an experience often sadly lacking in the day-to-day lives of many women. As a result, a woman's pursuit of beauty through transformation is often associated with lived experiences of self-creation, self-fulfillment, self-transcendence, and being cared for. The power of these experiences must not be underestimated.

While I acknowledge that these choices can confer a kind of integrity on a woman's life, I also believe that they are likely to embroil her in a set of interrelated contradictions. I refer to these as "Paradoxes of Choice."

IV. Three Paradoxes of Choice

In exploring these paradoxes, I appropriate Foucault's analysis of the diffusion of power in order to understand forms of power that are potentially more personally invasive than are more obvious, publicly identifiable aspects of power. In the chapter "Docile Bodies" in *Discipline and Punish,* Foucault (1979, 136–37) highlights three features of what he calls disciplinary power:

1. The *scale* of the control. In disciplinary power the body is treated individually and in a coercive way because the body itself is the *active* and hence apparently free body that is being controlled through movements, gestures, attitudes, and degrees of rapidity.
2. The *object* of the control, which involves meticulous control over the efficiency of movements and forces.
3. The *modality* of the control, which involves constant, uninterrupted coercion.

Foucault argues that the outcome of disciplinary power is the docile body, a body "that may be subjected, used, transformed, and improved" (Foucault 1979, 136). Foucault is discussing this model of power in the context of prisons and armies, but we can adapt the central insights of this notion to see how women's bodies are entering "a machinery of power that explores it, breaks it down, and rearranges it" through a recognizably political metamorphosis of embodiment (Foucault 1979, 138).[2] What is important about this notion in relation to cosmetic surgery is the extent to which it makes it possible to speak about the diffusion of power throughout Western industrialized cultures that are increasingly committed to a technological beauty imperative. It also makes it possible to refer to a set of experts—cosmetic surgeons—whose explicit power mandate is to explore, break down, and rearrange women's bodies.

Paradox One: The Choice of Conformity—Understanding the Number 10

While the technology of cosmetic surgery could clearly be used to create and celebrate idiosyncrasy, eccentricity, and uniqueness, it is obvious that this is not how it is presently being used. Cosmetic surgeons report that legions of women appear in their offices demanding "Bo Derek" breasts ("Cosmetic Surgery for the Holidays" 1985). Jewish women demand reductions of their noses so as to be able to "pass" as one of their Aryan sisters who form the dominant ethnic group (Lakoff and Scherr, 1984). Adolescent Asian girls who bring in pictures of Elizabeth Taylor and of Japanese movie actresses (whose faces have already been reconstructed) demand the "Westernizing" of their own eyes and the creation of higher noses in hopes of better job and marital prospects ("New Bodies for Sale" 1985). Black women buy toxic bleaching agents in hopes of attaining lighter skin. What is being created in all of these instances is not simply beautiful bodies and faces but white, Western, Anglo-Saxon bodies in a racist, anti-Semitic context.

More often than not, what appear at first glance to be instances of choice turn out to be instances of conformity. The women who undergo cosmetic surgery in order to compete in various beauty pageants are clearly choosing to conform. So is the woman who wanted to undergo a facelift, tummy tuck, and liposuction all in one week, in order to win heterosexual approval *from a man she had not seen in twenty-eight years* and whose individual preferences she could not possibly know. In some ways, it does not matter who the particular judges are. Actual men—brothers, fathers, male lovers, male beauty "experts"—and hypothetical men live in the aesthetic imaginations of women. Whether they are male employers, prospective male spouses, male judges in the beauty pageants, or male-identified women, these modern day Parises are generic and live sometimes ghostly but powerful lives in the reflective awareness of women (Berger, 1972). A woman's makeup, dress, gestures, voice, degree of cleanliness, degree of muscularity, odors, degree of hirsuteness, vocabulary, hands, feet, skin, hair, and vulva can all be evaluated, regulated, and disciplined in the light of the hypothetical often-white male viewer and the male viewer present in the assessing gaze of other women (Haug, 1987). Men's appreciation and approval of achieved femininity becomes all the more invasive when it resides in the incisions, stitches, staples, and scar tissue of women's bodies as women choose to conform. And . . . women's public conformity to the norms of beauty often signals a deeper conformity to the norms of compulsory heterosexuality along with an awareness of the violence that can result from violating those norms. Hence the first paradox: that what looks like an optimal situation of reflection, deliberation, and self-creating choice often signals conformity at a deeper level.

Paradox Two: Liberation into Colonization

As argued above, a woman's desire to create a permanently beautiful and youthful appearance that is not vulnerable to the threats of externally applied cosmetic artifice or to the aging process of the body must be understood as a deeply significant existential project. It deliberately involves the exploitation and transformation of the most intimately experienced domain of immanence, the body, in the name of transcendence: transcendence of hereditary predestination, of lived time, of one's given "limitations." What I see as particularly alarming in this project is that what comes to have primary significance is not the real given existing woman but her body viewed as a "primitive entity" that is seen only as potential, as a kind of raw material to be exploited in terms of appearance, eroticism, nurturance, and fertility as defined by the colonizing culture.[3]

But for whom is this exploitation and transformation taking place? Who exercises the power here? Sometimes the power is explicit. It is exercised by brothers, fathers, male lovers, male engineering students who taunt and harass their female counterparts, and by male cosmetic surgeons who offer "free advice" in social gatherings to women whose "deformities" and "severe problems" can all be cured through their healing needles and knives. And the colonizing power is transmitted through and by those women whose own bodies and disciplinary practices demonstrate the efficacy of "taking care of herself" in these culturally defined feminine ways. Sometimes, however, the power may be so diffused as to dominate the consciousness of a given woman with no other subject needing to be present. . . .

. . .

In electing to undergo cosmetic surgery, women appear to be protesting against the constraints of the "given" in their embodied lives and seeking liberation from those constraints. But I believe they are in danger of retreating and becoming more vulnerable, at that very level of embodiment, to those colonizing forms of power that may have motivated the protest in the first place. Moreover, in seeking independence, they can become even more dependent on male assessment and on the services of all those experts they initially bought to render them independent.

Here we see a second paradox bound up with choice: that the rhetoric is that of liberation and care, of "making the most of yourself," but the reality is often the transformation of oneself as a woman for the eye, the hand, and the approval of the Other—the lover, the taunting students, the customers, the employers, the social peers. And the Other is almost always affected by the dominant culture, which is male-supremacist, racist, ageist, heterosexist, anti-Semitic, ableist and class-biased.[4]

Paradox Three: Coerced Voluntariness and the Technological Imperative

Where is the coercion? At first glance, women who choose to undergo cosmetic surgery often seem to represent a paradigm case of the rational chooser. Drawn increasingly from wider and wider economic groups, these women clearly make a choice, often at significant economic cost to the rest of their life, to pay the large sums of money demanded by cosmetic surgeons (since American health insurance plans do not cover this elective cosmetic surgery).

Furthermore, they are often highly critical consumers of these services, demanding extensive consultation, information regarding the risks and benefits of various surgical procedures, and professional guarantees of expertise. Generally they are relatively young and in good health. Thus, in some important sense, they epitomize relatively invulnerable free agents making a decision under virtually optimal conditions.

Moreover, on the surface, women who undergo cosmetic surgery choose a set of procedures that are, by definition, "elective." This term is used, quite straightforwardly, to distinguish cosmetic surgery from surgical intervention for reconstructive or health-related reasons (e.g., following massive burns, cancer-related forms of mutilation, etc.). The term also appears to distinguish cosmetic surgery from apparently involuntary and more pathologically transforming forms of intervention in the bodies of young girls in the form of, for example, foot-binding or extensive genital mutilation.[5] But I believe that this does not exhaust the meaning of the term "elective" and that the term performs a seductive role in facilitating the ideological camouflage of the *absence of choice.* Similarly, I believe that the word "cosmetic" serves an ideological function in hiding the fact that the changes are *noncosmetic:* they involve lengthy periods of pain, are permanent, and result in irreversibly alienating metamorphoses such as the appearance of youth on an aging body.

. . . There are two important ideological, choice-diminishing dynamics at work that affect women's choices in the area of . . . cosmetic surgery. The first of these is the *pressure to achieve perfection through technology.* The second . . . is the *double-pathologizing of women's bodies.* The history of Western science and Western medical practice is not altogether a positive one for women. As voluminous documentation has shown, cell biologists, endocrinologists, anatomists, sociobiologists, gynecologists, obstetricians, psychiatrists, surgeons, and other scientists have assumed, hypothesized, or "demonstrated" that women's bodies are generally inferior, deformed, imperfect, and/or infantile. . . .

[Now, women are being pressured to see plainness or being ugly as a form of pathology. Consequently, there is strong pressure] to be beautiful in relation to the allegedly voluntary nature of "electing" to undergo cosmetic surgery. It is clear that pressure to use this technology is on the increase. Cosmetic surgeons report on the wide range of clients who buy their services, pitch their advertising to a large audience through the use of the media, and encourage women to think, metaphorically, in terms of the seemingly trivial "nips" and "tucks" that will transform their lives. As cosmetic surgery becomes increasingly normalized through the concept of the female "make-over" that is translated into columns and articles in the print media or made into nationwide television shows directed at female viewers, as the "success stories" are invited on to talk shows along with their "makers," and as surgically transformed women win the Miss America pageants, women who refuse to submit to the knives and to the needles, to the anesthetics and the bandages, will come to be seen as deviant in one way or another. Women who refuse to use these technologies are already becoming stigmatized as "unliberated," "not caring about their appearance" (a sign of disturbed gender identity and low self-esteem according to various health-care professionals), as "refusing to be all that they could be" or as "granola-heads."

And as more and more success comes to those who do "care about themselves" in this technological fashion, more coercive dimensions enter the scene. In the past, only those women who were perceived to be *naturally* beautiful (or rendered beautiful through relatively conservative superficial artifice) had access to forms of power and economic social mobility closed off to women regarded as plain or ugly or old. But now womanly beauty is becoming technologically achievable, a commodity for which each and every woman can, in principle, sacrifice if she is to survive and succeed in the world, particularly in industrialized Western countries. Now technology is making obligatory the appearance of youth and the reality of "beauty" for every woman who can afford it. Natural destiny is being supplanted by technologically grounded coercion, and the coercion is camouflaged by the language of choice, fulfillment, and liberation.

Similarly, we find the dynamic of the double-pathologizing of the normal and of the ordinary at work here. In the technical and popular literature on cosmetic surgery, what have previously been described as *normal* variations of female bodily shapes or described in the relatively innocuous language of "problem areas," are increasingly being described as "deformities," "ugly protrusions," "inadequate breasts," and "unsightly concentrations of fat cells"—a litany of descriptions designed to intensify feelings of disgust, shame, and relief at the possibility of recourse for these "deformities." Cosmetic surgery promises virtually all women the creation of beautiful, youthful-appearing bodies. As a consequence, more and more women will be labeled "ugly" and "old" in relation to this more select population of surgically created beautiful faces and bodies that have been contoured and augmented, lifted and tucked into a state of achieved feminine excellence. I suspect that the naturally "given," so to speak, will increasingly come to be seen as the technologically "primitive"; the "ordinary" will come to be perceived and evaluated as the "ugly." Here, then, is the *third paradox:* that the technological beauty imperative and the pathological inversion of the normal are coercing more and more women to "choose" cosmetic surgery.

V. Are There Any Politically Correct Feminist Responses to Cosmetic Surgery?

Attempting to answer this question is rather like venturing forth into political quicksand. Nevertheless, I will discuss two very different sorts of responses that strike me as having certain plausibility: the response of refusal and the response of appropriation.[6] I regard both of these as utopian in nature.

The Response of Refusal

In her witty and subversive parable *The Life and Loves of a She-Devil,* Fay Weldon puts the following thoughts into the mind of the cosmetic surgeon whose services have been bought by the protagonist, "Miss Hunter," for her own plans for revenge:

> He was her Pygmalion, but she would not depend upon him, or admire him, or be grateful. He was accustomed to being loved by the women of his own construction. A soft sigh of adoration would follow him down the corridors as he paced them, visiting here, blessing there, promising a future, regretting a past: cushioning his footfall, and his image of himself. But no soft breathings came from Miss Hunter. [He adds, ominously,] . . . he would bring her to it. (Weldon 1983, 215–16)

But Miss Hunter continues to refuse, and so will many feminist women. The response of refusal can be recognizably feminist at both an individual and a collective level. It results from understanding the nature of the risks involved—those having to do with the surgical procedures and those related to a potential loss of embodied personal integrity in a patriarchal context. And it results from understanding the conceptual shifts involved in the political technologizing of women's bodies and contextualizing them so that their oppressive consequences are evident precisely as they open up more "choices" to women. "Understanding" and "contextualizing" here mean seeing clearly the ideological biases that frame the material and cultural world in which cosmetic surgeons practice, a world that contains racist, anti-Semitic, eugenicist, and ageist dimensions of oppression, forms of oppression to which current practices in cosmetic surgery often contribute.

The response of refusal also speaks to the collective power of women as consumers to affect market conditions. If refusal is practiced on a large scale, cosmetic surgeons who are busy producing new faces for the "holiday season" and new bellies for the "winter trips to the Caribbean" will find few buyers of their services. Cosmetic surgeons who consider themselves body designers and regard women's skin as a kind of magical fabric to be draped, cut, layered, and designer-labeled, may have to forgo the esthetician's ambitions that occasion the remark that "the sculpting of human flesh can never be an exact art" (Silver 1989). They may, instead, (re)turn their expertise to the victims in the intensive care burn unit and to the crippled limbs and joints of arthritic women. This might well have the consequence of (re)converting those surgeons into healers.

Although it may be relatively easy for some individual women to refuse cosmetic surgery even when they have access to the means, one deep, morally significant facet of the response of refusal is to try to understand and to care about individual women who do choose to undergo cosmetic surgery. It may well be that one explanation for why a woman is willing to subject herself to surgical procedures, anesthetics, postoperative drugs, predicted and lengthy pain, and possible "side effects" that might include her own death is that her access to other forms of power and empowerment are or appear to be so limited that cosmetic surgery is the primary domain in which she can experience some semblance of self-determination. . . . Choosing an artificial and technologically designed creation of youthful beauty may not only be necessary to an individual woman's material, economic, and social survival. It may also be the way that she is able to choose, to elect a kind of subjective transcendence against a backdrop of constraint, limitation, and immanence. . . .

As a feminist response, individual and collective refusal may not be easy. As Bartky, I, and others have tried to argue, it is crucial to understand the central role that socially sanctioned and socially constructed femininity plays in a male supremacist, heterosexist society. And it is essential not to underestimate the gender-constituting and identity-confirming role that femininity plays in bringing woman-as-subject into existence while simultaneously creating her as patriarchally defined object (Bartky 1988; Morgan 1986). In these circumstances, refusal may be akin to a kind of death, to a kind of renunciation of the only kind of life-conferring choices and competencies to which a woman may have access. And, under those circumstances, it may not be possible for her to register her resistance in the form of refusal. The best one can hope for is a heightened sense of the nature of the multiple double-binds and compromises that permeate the lives of virtually all women and are accentuated by the cosmetic surgery culture. As a final comment, it is worth remarking that although the response of refusal has a kind of purity to recommend it, it is unlikely to have much impact in the current ideological and cultural climate. . . .

The Response of Appropriation

. . . Rather than viewing the womanly/technologized body as a site of political refusal, the response of appropriation views it as the site for feminist action through transformation, appropriation, parody, and protest. This response grows out of that historical and often radical feminist tradition that regards deliberate mimicry, alternative valorization, hyperbolic appropriation, street theater, counterguerrilla tactics, destabilization, and redeployment as legitimate feminist politics. Here I am proposing a version of what Judith Butler regards as "Femininity Politics" and what she calls "Gender Performatives." . . .

. . .

Rather than agreeing that participation in cosmetic surgery and its ruling ideology will necessarily result in further colonization and victimization of women, this feminist strategy advocates appropriating the expertise and technology for feminist ends. One advantage of the response of appropriation is that it does not recommend involvement in forms of technology that clearly have disabling and dire outcomes for the deeper feminist project of engaging "in the historical, political, and theoretical process of constituting ourselves as subjects as well as objects of history" (Hartsock 1990, 170).[7] Women who are increasingly immobilized bodily through physical weakness, passivity, withdrawal, and domestic sequestration in situations of hysteria, agoraphobia, and anorexia cannot possibly engage in radical gender performatives of an active public sort or in other acts by which the feminist subject is robustly constituted. In contrast, healthy women who have a feminist understanding of cosmetic surgery are in a situation to deploy cosmetic surgery in the name of its feminist potential for parody and protest.

. . . As Butler correctly observes, parody "by itself is not subversive" (139) since it always runs the risk of becoming "domesticated and recirculated as instruments of cultural hegemony." She then goes on to ask, in relation to gender identity and sexuality, what words or performances would

> compel a reconsideration of the *place* and stability of the masculine and the feminine? And what kind of gender performance will enact and reveal the performativity of gender itself in a way that destabilizes the naturalized categories of identity and desire? (Butler 1990, 139)

We might, in parallel fashion, ask what sorts of performances would sufficiently destabilize the norms of femininity, what sorts of performances will sufficiently expose the truth of the slogan "Beauty is always made, not born." In response I suggest two performance-oriented forms of revolt.

The first form of revolt involves revalorizing the domain of the "ugly" and all that is associated with it. Although one might argue that the notion of the "ugly" is parasitic on that of "beauty," this is not entirely true since the ugly is also contrasted with the plain and the ordinary, so that we are not even at the outset constrained by binary oppositions. The ugly, even in a beauty-oriented culture, has always held its own fascination, its own particular kind of splendor. Feminists can use that and explore it in ways that might be integrated with a revalorization of being old, thus simultaneously attacking the ageist dimension of the reigning ideology. Rather than being the "culturally enmired subjects" of Butler's analysis, women might constitute themselves as culturally liberated subjects through public participation in Ms. Ugly Canada/America/Universe/Cosmos pageants *and use the technology of cosmetic surgery to do so.*

Contemplating this form of revolt as a kind of imaginary model of political action is one thing; actually altering our bodies is another matter altogether. And the reader may well share the sentiments of one reviewer of this paper who asked: "Having oneself surgically mutilated in order to prove a point? Isn't this going too far?" I don't know the answer to that question. If we cringe from contemplating this alternative, this may, in fact, testify (so to speak) to the hold that the beauty imperative has on our imagination and our bodies. If we recoil from *this* lived alteration of the contours of our bodies and regard it as "mutilation," then so, too, ought we to shirk from contemplation of the cosmetic surgeons who de-skin and alter the contours of women's bodies so that we become more and more like athletic or emaciated (depending on what's in vogue) mannequins with large breasts in the shop windows of modern patriarchal culture. In what sense are these not equivalent mutilations?

What this feminist performative would require would be not only genuine celebration of but *actual* participation in the fleshly mutations needed to produce what the culture constitutes as "ugly" so as to destabilize the "beautiful" and expose its technologically and culturally constitutive origin and its political consequences. Bleaching one's hair white and applying wrinkle-inducing "wrinkle creams," having one's face and breasts surgically pulled down (rather than lifted), and having wrinkles sewn and carved into one's skin might also be seen as destabilizing actions with respect to aging. And analogous actions might be taken to undermine the "lighter is better" aspect of racist norms of feminine appearance as they affect women of color.

A second performative form of revolt could involve exploring the commodification aspect of cosmetic surgery. One might, for example, envision a set of "Beautiful Body Boutique" franchises, responsive to the particular "needs" of a given community. Here one could advertise and sell a whole range of bodily contours; a variety of metric containers of freeze-dried fat cells for fat implantation and transplant; "body configuration" software for computers; sewing kits of needles, knives, and painkillers; and "skin-Velcro" that could be matched to fit and drape the consumer's body; variously sized sets of magnetically attachable breasts complete with discrete nipple pumps; and other inflation devices carefully modulated according to bodily aroma and state of arousal. Parallel to the current marketing strategies for cosmetic breast surgeries, commercial protest booths, complete with "before and after" surgical makeover displays for penises, entitled "The Penis You Were Always Meant to Have," could be set up at various medical conventions and health fairs; demonstrations could take place outside the clinics, hotels, and spas of particularly eminent cosmetic surgeons—the possibilities here are endless. Again, if this ghoulish array offends, angers, or shocks the reader, this may well be an indication of the extent to which the ideology of compulsory beauty has anesthetized our sensibility in the reverse direction, resulting in the domesticating of the procedures and products of the cosmetic surgery industry.

In appropriating these forms of revolt, women might well accomplish the following: acquire expertise (either in fact or in symbolic form) of cosmetic surgery to challenge the coercive norms of youth and beauty, undermine the power dynamic built into the dependence on surgical experts who define themselves as aestheticians of women's bodies, demonstrate the radical maleability of the cultural commodification of women's bodies, and make publicly explicit the political role that technology can play in the construction of the feminine in women's flesh.

Conclusion

I have characterized both these feminist forms of response as utopian in nature. What I mean by "utopian" is that these responses are unlikely to occur on a large scale even though they may have a kind of ideal desirability. In any culture that defines femininity in terms of submission to men, that makes the achievement of femininity (however culturally specific) in appearance, gesture, movement, voice, bodily contours, aspirations, values, and political behavior obligatory of any woman who will be allowed to be loved or hired or promoted or elected or simply allowed to live, and in any culture that increasingly requires women to purchase femininity through submission to cosmetic surgeons and their magic knives, refusal and revolt exact a high price. I live in such a culture.

Notes

Many thanks to the members of the Canadian Society for Women in Philosophy for their critical feedback, especially my commentator, Karen Weisbaum, who pointed out how strongly visualist the cosmetic surgery culture is. I am particularly grateful to Sarah Lucia Hoagland, keynote speaker at the 1990 C-SWIP conference, who remarked at my session, "I think this is all wrong." Her comment sent me back to the text to rethink it in a serious way. . . .

1. I say "virtually all women" because there is now a nascent literature on the subject of fat oppression and body image as it affects lesbians. For a perceptive article on this subject, see Dworkin (1989). I am, of course, not suggesting that compulsory heterosexuality and obligatory maternity affect all women equally. Clearly women who are regarded as "deviant" in some respect or other—because they are lesbian or women with disabilities or "too old" or poor or of the "wrong race"—are under enormous pressure from the dominant culture *not* to bear children, but this, too, is an aspect of patriarchal pronatalism.
2. I view this as a recognizably *political* metamorphosis because forensic cosmetic surgeons and social archaeologists will be needed to determine the actual age and earlier appearance of women in cases where identification is called for on the basis of existing carnal data. See Griffin's (1978) poignant description in "The Anatomy Lesson" for a reconstruction of the life and circumstances of a dead mother from just such carnal evidence. As we more and more profoundly artifactualize our own bodies, we become more sophisticated archaeological repositories and records that both signify and symbolize our culture.
3. I intend to use "given" here in a relative and political sense. I don't believe that the notion that biology is somehow "given" and culture is just "added on" is a tenable one. I believe that we are intimately and inextricably encultured and embodied, so that a reductionist move in either direction is doomed to failure. For a persuasive analysis of this thesis, see Lowe (1982) and Haraway (1978, 1989). For a variety of political analyses of the "given" as primitive, see Marge Piercy's poem "Right to Life" (1980), Morgan (1989), and Murphy (1984).
4. The extent to which ableist bias is at work in this area was brought home to me by two quotations cited by a woman with a disability. She discusses two guests on a television show. One was "a poised, intelligent young women who'd been rejected as a contestant for the Miss Toronto title. She is a paraplegic. The organizers' excuse for disqualifying her: 'We couldn't fit the choreography around

you.' Another guest was a former executive of the Miss Universe contest. He declared, 'Her participation in a beauty contest would be like having a blind man compete in a shooting match'" (Matthews 1985).

5. It is important here to guard against facile and ethnocentric assumptions about beauty rituals and mutilation. See Lakoff and Scherr (1984) for an analysis of the relativity of these labels and for important insights about the fact that use of the term "mutilation" almost always signals a distancing from and reinforcement of a sense of cultural superiority in the speaker who uses it to denounce what other cultures do in contrast to "our culture."
6. One possible feminist response (that, thankfully, appears to go in *and* out of vogue) is that of feminist fascism, which insists on a certain particular and quite narrow range of embodiment and appearance as the only range that is politically correct for a feminist. Often feminist fascism sanctions the use of informal but very powerful feminist "embodiment police," who feel entitled to identify and denounce various deviations from this normative range. I find this feminist political stance incompatible with any movement I would regard as liberatory for women and here I admit that I side with feminist liberals who say that "the presumption must be on the side of freedom" (Warren, 1985) and see that as the lesser of two evils.
7. In recommending various forms of appropriation of the practices and dominant ideology surrounding cosmetic surgery, I think it important to distinguish this set of disciplinary practices from those forms of simultaneous Retreat-and-Protest that Susan Bordo (1989, 20) so insightfully discusses in "The Body and the Reproduction of Femininity": hysteria, agoraphobia, and anorexia. What cosmetic surgery shares with these gestures is what Bordo remarks upon, namely, the fact that they may be "viewed as a surface on which conventional constructions of femininity are exposed starkly to view, through their inscription in extreme or hyperliteral form." What is different, I suggest, is that although submitting to the procedures of cosmetic surgery involves pain, risks, undesirable side effects, and living with a heightened form of patriarchal anxiety, it is also fairly clear that, most of the time, the pain and risks are relatively short-term. Furthermore, the outcome often appears to be one that generally enhances women's confidence, confers a sense of well-being, contributes to a greater comfortableness in the public domain, and affirms the individual woman as self-determining and risk-taking individual. All these outcomes are significantly different from what Bordo describes as the "languages of horrible suffering" (Bordo 1989, 20) expressed by women experiencing hysteria, agoraphobia, and anorexia.

References

Barker-Benfield, G. J. 1976. *The Horrors of the Half-known Life.* New York: Harper and Row.

Bartky, Sandra Lee. 1988. "Foucault, Femininity, and the Modernization of Patriarchal Power." In *Femininity and Foucault: Reflections of Resistance.* Irene Diamond and Lee Quinby, eds. Boston: Northeastern University Press.

Berger, John. 1972. *Ways of Seeing.* New York: Penguin Books.

Bordo, Susan R. 1989. "The Body and the Reproduction of Femininity: A Feminist Appropriation of Foucault." In *Gender/Body/Knowledge: Feminist Reconstructions of Being and Knowing.* Alison Jagger and Susan Bordo, eds. New Brunswick, N.J.: Rutgers University Press.

Brown, Beverley, and Parveen Adams. 1979. "The Feminine Body and Feminist Politics." *MIF* 3:35–50.

Butler, Judith. 1990. *Gender Trouble: Feminism and the Subversion of Identity.* New York: Routledge.

Changing Faces. 1989. *Toronto Star.* May 25.

Cosmetic surgery for the holidays. 1985. *Sheboygan Press.* New York Times News Service.

Falling in love again. 1990. *Toronto Star.* July 23.

Foucault, Michel. 1979. *Discipline and Punish: The Birth of the Prison.* Alan Sheridan, trans. New York: Pantheon.

Goodman, Ellen. 1989. "A Plastic Pageant." *Boston Globe.* September 19.

Hartsock, Nancy. 1990. "Foucault on Power: A Theory for Women?" In *Feminism/Postmodernism.* Linda Nicholson, ed. New York: Routledge.

Haug, Frigga, ed. 1987. *Female Sexualization: A Collective Work of Memory.* Erica Carter, trans. London: Verso.

Hirshson, Paul. 1987. "New Wrinkles in Plastic Surgery: An Update on the Search for Perfection." *Boston Globe Sunday Magazine.* May 24.

"Implants Hide Tumors in Breasts, Study Says." 1988. *Toronto Star.* July 29. Summarized from article in *Journal of the American Medical Association,* July 8, 1988.

Lakoff, Robin Tolmach, and Raquel Scherr. 1984. *Face Value: The Politics of Beauty.* Boston: Routledge and Kegan Paul.

"Madonna Passionate about Fitness." 1990. *Toronto Star.* August 16.

Markovic, Mihailo. 1976. "Women's Liberation and Human Emancipation." In *Women and Philosophy: Toward a Theory of Liberation.* Carol Gould and Marx Wartofsky, eds. New York: Capricorn Books.

Matthews, Gwyneth Ferguson. 1985. "Mirror, Mirror: Self-Image and Disabled Women." *Women and Disability: Resources for Feminist Research* 14(1): 47–50.

Morgan, Kathryn Pauly. 1986. "Romantic Love, Altruism and Self-Respect: An Analysis of Simone de Beauvoir." *Hypatia* 1(1): 117–148.

"New Bodies for Sale." 1985. *Newsweek.* May 27.

The Quest to Be a Perfect 10." 1990. *Toronto Star.* February 1.

"Retouching Nature's Way: Is Cosmetic Surgery Worth It?" 1990. *Toronto Star.* February 1.

Sherwin, Susan. 1984–85. "A Feminist Approach to Ethics." *Dalhousie Review.* 64(4): 704–13.

———. 1989. "Feminist and Medical Ethics: Two Different Approaches to Contextual Ethics." *Hypatia* 4(2): 57–72.

Silver, Harold. 1989. "Liposuction Isn't for Everybody." *Toronto Star.* October 20.
Warren, Virginia. 1989. "Feminist Directions in Medical Ethics." *Hypatia* 4(2): 73–87.
Weldon, Fay. 1983. *The Life and Loves of a She-devil.* London: Coronet Books; New York: Pantheon Books.
Williams, John, M.D., and Jim Williams. 1990. "Say It with Liposuction." From a press release; reported in *Harper's* (August).
"Woman, 43, Dies after Cosmetic Surgery." 1989. *Toronto Star.* July 7.

OUR BODIES, OUR SELVES

[5]

The Jewish Self

Eugene B. Borowitz

Five Premises for Jewish Duty

Like all humankind (the *benei noah),* Jewish selves (the *benei yisrael)* have a grounding personal relationship with God; but where the *benei noah* relate to God as part of a universal covenant, the *benei yisrael* have a particular, ethnic Covenant with God. Being a Jew may then be described in this metaphor as having an individuality that is elementally structured by participation in the Jewish people's historical relationship with God. In the ideal Jewish self one can detect no depth, no matter how intensely one searches, where the old liberal rift between general self and particular Jew still occurs. Jewish selfhood arises as ethnic existentiality while remaining an individuality dignified by autonomy; in this case autonomy is properly exercised in terms of its ultimate situation in the Jewish people's corporate, historic relationship with God.

In contrast to contemporary privatistic notions of selfhood, the Jewish self, responding to God in Covenant, acknowledges its essential historicity and sociality. One did not begin the Covenant and one remains its conduit only as part of the ongoing people of Israel. Here, tradition and ethnicity

Source: From Eugene B. Borowitz, "The Jewish Self," in *Contemporary Jewish Ethics and Morality: A Reader*, ed. Elliott N. Dorff and Louis E. Newman (New York: Oxford University Press, 1995). Used by permission.

round out the universal solidarity of humankind which this particularity grounds in its myth of the Noahide covenant. With heritage and folk essential to Jewishness, with the Jewish service of God directed to historic continuity lasting until messianic days, the Covenanted self knows that Jewish existence must be structured. Yet as long as we honor each Jew's selfhood with a contextually delimited measure of autonomy, this need for communal forms cannot lead us back to law as a required, corporately determined regimen. Instead, we must think in terms of a *self-discipline* that, because of the sociality of the Jewish self, becomes communally focused and shaped. The result is a dialectical autonomy, a life of freedom-exercised-in-Covenant. It differs so from older non-Orthodox theories of folk discipline—Zionism or Kaplanian ethnicity—or personal freedom—Cohenian ethical monotheism or Buberian relationship—that I wish to analyze in some detail its five major themes.

First, the Jewish self lives personally and primarily in involvement with the one God of the universe. Whereas the biblical-rabbinic Jew was almost entirely theocentric, the contemporary Jewish self claims a more active role in the relationship with God. In the days of buoyant liberalism this self-assertion overreached to the point of diminishing God's active role, sometimes countenancing supplanting God with humanity writ large. Postmodernity begins with a more realistic view of our human capacities and a determination not to confuse the junior with the senior partner. Knowing who calls and keeps us as allies endows each self with a value it could never give itself even by extraordinary achievement. To believe we bestow meaning on ourselves by our deeds inevitably destroys us, for no one can successfully keep filling up the relentless now of personhood with estimable accomplishment. When we live in covenantal closeness with God—asked only to be God's helpmeet, not God's equal in goodness—we acquire unique dignity and power and can hope to remain whole even when burdened by the world's injustice and our own heavy sins.

This consciousness of ongoing intimacy with God precedes, undergirds, and interfuses all the Jewish self's other relationships. It ties us to God's other partners for more than pragmatic or utilitarian reasons and gives us an ineradicable stake in humanity's welfare and destiny. It binds us with particular intensity to other Jews with whom we share a special dedication to God.

Yet the Covenant that affirms us also subjects us to judgment in terms of the quality learned through our personal involvement with God. What we do as persons, lovers, friends, citizens, humans, Jews, must live up to it or be found wanting. Wherever the Jewish self sees faithfulness to God imperiled, covenanthood requires it to be critical as well as supportive, perhaps even temporarily withdrawing from others in order to remain true to what once made them close. This applies with particular force to the people of the

Covenant. Pledged to live most intensively with God, this people and its communities must always stand under special scrutiny even as they also deserve our special love.

Community, Tradition, and Messianic Hope

Second, a Jewish relationship with God inextricably binds selfhood and ethnicity, with its multiple ties of land, language, history, traditions, fate, and faith. By this folk rootedness covenantal Jewish identity negates the illusion that one can be loyal to humanity as a whole but not to any single people, and it rescues the messianic hope from being so abstract as to be inhuman. Ethnic particularity commits the Jewish self to the spirituality of sanctifying history through gritty social and political struggles. Internally as well, each Jew becomes implicated in this people's never-ending struggle to hallow grim social circumstances or the temptations of affluence and show itself another faithful Covenant generation.

Nowhere can Jews hope to better fulfill the multilayered responsibilities enjoined on them by the Covenant than in the land of Israel organized as a politically sovereign, self-determining nation, the State of Israel. Every Jewish self must face the covenantal challenge of the desirability of moving there to join the Jewish people in working out its uniquely full response to God's demand that we sanctify social existence. Jews who do not find themselves able to fulfill this behest must nonetheless live by a particularly intense tie to the land of Israel and measure their Diaspora fulfillment of the ethnic obligations of Jewish selfhood by the standard of the State of Israel's Covenant accomplishments.

Ethnicity also has a certain normative force. As the Jewish self ponders a decision, it must attend seriously to the attitudes and practices of other Jews in this matter. They share the same Covenant, serve the same God, and reflect the same folk experience and aspiration. Often, what Jews have been told to do and what they now value will commend itself as covenantal wisdom. When the Jewish self has some ambivalence about its accepted path, loyalty to the folk will often cause the Jewish self to sacrifice personal predilection for folk unity. That most easily takes place when a community standard makes possible common ethnic activity—for example, a folk, not a personal, Jewish calendar—or makes demands that hardly can be called onerous or defiling—for example, kiddush over wine or grape juice and not the whiskey or spring water one might prefer. For the Jewish self, then, Covenant means Covenant-with-all-other-Jews, past and present.

For all the inalienable ethnicity of the Jewish self, it surrenders nothing of its individual personhood. In a given matter, the Covenant people may be inattentive to its present duty to God or, in a given situation, an individual Jew of certain talents and limitations may find it covenantally more responsible to go an individual way. Now covenanted selfhood requires conscientious self-examination in the light of community standards to determine whether this dissent of the Jewish self is willfulness or an idiosyncratic sensitivity to God. I shall return to this theme later in this chapter.

Third, against the common self's concentration on immediacy, the Covenant renders the Jewish self radically historical. Our Jewish relationship with God did not begin with this generation, and its working out in Jewish lives has been going on for millennia. Social circumstances and Jewish self-perception have changed greatly in this time yet the Jews we encounter in our old books sound very much like us. Different social circumstances aside, the underlying relationship between God and the people of Israel has remained substantially the same. For one thing, the same religious moments decisively shape our Covenant sensibility—Exodus, Sinai, settlement, Temple, exile, return, destruction of the Second Temple, Diaspora, the rise of the rabbis, medieval triumph and trial, which we extend by emancipation, Holocaust, and Third Commonwealth. We too live by Jewish memory. For another thing, reading our classic texts inevitably points up the constancy of human nature with its swings between folly and saintliness. Jews then behaved very much as Jews do today. Hence, much of what they did as their covenant duty will likely still lay a living claim on us. For the Jewish self, then, Covenant means Covenant-with-prior-Jewish-generations.

Many modern Jewish thinkers deprecated the idea of such a spiritual continuity. They thought our vastly increased general knowledge made us more religiously advanced than our forebears and optimistically taught that each generation knew God's will better than the prior one, a notion they called progressive revelation. Postmodern thinkers, such as myself, reverse the hierarchy. On most critical religious issues, no one writing today can hope to command the respect the authors of the Bible rightly continue to elicit. Moreover, since their life of Covenant was comparatively fresh, strong, and steadfast, where ours is often uncertain, weak, and faltering, we should substantially rely on their delineation of proper covenantal existence. The biblical and rabbinic texts have every Jewish right to exert a higher criticism of the lives of each new generation of Jews, so classic Jewish learning must ground Jewish selfhood as firmly as does personal religious experience.

In one critical religious respect, however, we stand apart from prior generations: our conviction that we must exercise considerable self-determination. If some respect for Jewish individuality had not always characterized Jewish spirituality, we would be astonished at the luxuriant display of change and innovation we find in Jewish religious expression over the centuries. Our radically transformed social and intellectual situation elicits a corollary reinterpretation of Covenant obligation. In particular, our sense of linkage with God prompts us to identify spiritual maturity with the responsible exercise of agency. Hence, we find it necessary to take initiative in untraditional fashion in order to be true to what our Jewish self discovers in Covenant. Here, too, our sacred books make their authority felt by challenging us to ask whether our deviance has grown out of covenantal faithfulness or trendy impulse.

Fourth, though the Jewish self lives the present out of the past, it necessarily orients itself to the future. All the generations of Jews who have ever been, including us, seek the culmination of the covenant in the days of the Messiah. The glories of the Jewish past and the rewards of the Jewish present cannot nearly vindicate Israel's millennial service of God as will that era of universal peace, justice, love, and knowledge of God. A Jewishness satisfied merely to meet the needs of the present but not radically to project covenantal existence into the far future betrays the hopes of the centuries of dedication that made our spirituality possible. The Jewish self, by contrast, will substantially gauge the covenantal worthiness of acts by their contribution to our continuing redemptive purpose. For the Jewish self, then, Covenant means Covenant-with-Jews-yet-to-be, especially the Messiah.

I can provide a personal analogy to the manner in which a vision of the far future limits the self in the immediate exercise of its freedom: the attainment of personal integrity. One can hope to accomplish that only over the years, for though the self constantly reconstitutes itself in the present, it also persists through time. Living detached from previous experience and with minimal concern for the future denies the chronological character of creatureliness and ignores our most creative individual challenge, to shape an entire life into humane coherence. The responsible self will cultivate the forms, habits, and institutions indispensable to long-range fulfillment. And when, in our frailty or indecisiveness, our autonomy falters before life's demands, we can hope these structures will carry our fragile self through the dark times with integrity unimpaired. All this is true of every human being but, I suggest, more intensively so for the Jewish self, whose integrity involves messianic steadfastness to God as part of the Covenant between God and the Jewish people.

Nonetheless, our covenantal future-directedness may also compel us to break with an old, once valuable but now empty Jewish practice. For Jewish selfhood also requires us to assure the Jewish future by making our way to it through the presently appropriate covenantal act. Even then, the awesome endurance of Jewish traditions will dialectically confront us with its question as to the staying power of the innovation we find so necessary.

The Compelling Selfhood of the Jewish Self

Fifth, yet despite the others with whom it is so intimately intertwined—God and the Jewish people, present, past, and future—it is as a single soul in its full individuality that the Jewish self exists in Covenant. I can illustrate my meaning best by using myself as an example. I must not hide from the fact that it is I, personally, who am making all these assertions. I believe God has objective reality—but I also do not know how anyone today can objectively make that assertion. I likewise believe that what I have been saying about Judaism is true regardless of my accepting it or not, that it would still be true and make rightful claims upon Jews even were I to come to deny all or any part of it. I proclaim the truth of the covenant between God and the Jewish people, but I know I can only speak from my own premises and perspective even as other people must do from theirs. None of us can escape from radical finitude to a conceptual realm of unconditional truth. The self, free and self-determining, must then be given its independent due even though, as a Jewish self, its autonomy will be exercised in covenantal context. At any given moment it is ultimately I who must determine what to make of God's demands and Israel's practice, tradition, and aspiration as I, personally, seek to live the life of Torah in covenantal faithfulness. For the Jewish self, then, Covenant means Covenant-with-one's-self.

Before I turn to the issue of how Jewish selfhood could lead to a new sense of corporate Jewish duty, I want to say something about the gap between the ideal of the Jewish self and the realities of being an individual Jew. I have been describing more a spiritual goal than a present condition, my version of what Rosenzweig called our need to move from the periphery of Jewish living back to its center. By the standards of this ideal, fragmentariness and alienation characterize most Jewish lives today; our lives commonly reflect more the brokenness of humanhood in our civilization than any integrating Jewish vision. This diagnosis leads to a therapeutic goal: bringing Jews to the greater wholeness of Jewish selfhood, a reconstruction of Jewish life that begins with helping individual Jews find greater personal integration, one that ineluctably involves them in community as with God. This constitutes the obverse of Kaplan's emphasis on changing our pattern of Jewish community organization so as to foster a healthy Jewish life.

How might this ideal, so individualistically based, bring a critical mass of Jews to communal patterns of covenantal observance? It cannot be created by a contemporary version of heteronomous law as long as we continue to accept the personal and spiritual validity of self-determination. But if Jews could confront their Judaism as Jewish selves and not as autonomous persons-in-general, I contend that they would find Jewish law and lore the single best source of guidance as to how they ought to live. Rooted in Israel's corporate faithfulness to God, they would want their lives substantially structured by their people's understanding of how its past, present, and future should shape daily existence. But as autonomous Jewish selves, they would personally establish the validity of every *halakhic* and communal prescription by their own conscientious deliberation. We would then judge their Jewish authenticity less by the extent of their observance than by the genuineness of their efforts to ground their lives, especially their actions, in Israel's ongoing Covenant with God. The more fully they integrate their Jewish selves, the more fully will every act of theirs demonstrate their Jewishness.

With autonomy then an integral part of Jewishness, some subjectivity will inevitably enter our Jewish practice, leading to a greatly expanded range of covenantally acceptable ways of living as an authentic Jew. Moreover, our simultaneous responsibilities—to self, to God, to the Jewish past, present, and future, and to humankind as a whole (through our continuing participation in the covenant of Noah)—will frequently clash with one another, leading to different views as to which should have greater weight. For these reasons I avidly espouse Jewish pluralism in thought and action. In our contemporary cultural situation I am more anxious about the corporate than the personal aspect of Jewish selfhood and therefore eagerly await the day when enough Jewish selves choose to live in ways sufficiently similar that we can create common patterns among us. A communal lifestyle, richly personal yet Jewishly grounded, would be the Jewish self's equivalent of *halakhah*.

Does my call for a community openness so tolerant of individuality destroy our character as a distinct people? Has not autonomy escaped from its covenantal containment and again manifested its anarchic and therefore ultimately un-Jewish character?

I cannot deny the risks involved in the path I am suggesting, but any theory that makes democracy a spiritual principle of our Judaism will face something of the same risks—and I do not believe any large number of Jews today will accept a nondemocratic theory of Jewish duty. Moreover, the act of passing substantial power from the rabbis to the community has, for all its weakening of community discipline, also produced unique human benefit. The demand that everyone in our community tolerate other Jews' radically differing views has produced a harmony among us unprecedented in Jewish history; our contemporary distress at Jewish interreligious conflict testifies to our ideals and to our distance from the Jewish past, when surly antagonism often reigned among us. Though covenantally contextual individualism will surely amplify Jewish diversity and threaten communal solidarity, there will never be any question about its directly authorizing and commending Jewish democracy.

An Odd but Instructive Case

I can make my meaning clearer by providing some concrete examples of how I apply this standard (though I acknowledge that others might utilize the same theory to reach other conclusions). I begin with a somewhat unusual matter: how an Orthodox Jew should face the issues created by the medical treatment of dwarfism. The *halakhah* imposes no special disabilities upon Jewish dwarfs, and while the condition is troublesome to those who have it and often a heavy burden for their relatives, it does not constitute a threat to life deserving of exceptional *halakhic* consideration. Some *halakhic* urgency for the treatment of dwarfism arises from the greater than usual difficulty dwarfs have in conceiving children.

The special *halakhic* difficulty once raised by dwarfism arose from the hormone with which it was treated. Before it had been synthesized, the hormone had to be collected from human corpses, bringing the laws of respect for the corpse into conflict with the desirability of curing a non-life-threatening condition. Various decisors discussed how the incisions should be made in the corpses so as to create the least disfigurement, wishing to be as respectful as possible while fulfilling the law's higher concern with a significant human need.

The non-Orthodox Jewish self would think about this issue in somewhat different fashion. A corpse, the physical remains of the self, surely deserves respectful treatment. Indeed, with lessening concern for the dead—fewer people saying kaddish and visiting graves—Jews need to be reminded that we do not know disembodied persons. However, when one thinks primarily in terms of selfhood, there will be little doubt that the needs of a living person override respect for a corpse. One can surely be a Jewish self as a dwarf, yet the selfsame psychosomatic view of the self that authorizes honoring corpses makes us appreciate the trials of dwarfism. Hence I would rule with little hesitation that the suffering of the dwarf, not respect for the corpse, would be our primary Covenantal concern here.

Fortunately, we find little difference in the practical outcome of applying Orthodox and Covenantal procedures. But, hypothetically, had rigorous *poskim* imposed such stringent conditions on cutting into the corpse as to have impeded the collection of the hormone, I would have demurred. I do not believe our tradition implies, our community wants, or God requires our giving the corpse such precedence over the living—and in this theoretical solution I could not accept the *halakhah*.

The classic cases of the *agunah* (deserted wife) and *mamzer* ("bastard") trouble us very much more than does dwarfism because they can create a radical distinction between what the *halakhah* can allow and what non-Orthodox Jews perceive as our Jewish duty. If required, observant Jews will repress whatever stirrings of autonomous rebellion they may feel in these cases so as to faithfully follow God's law. The Jewish self I have described will far more likely react indignantly at the inability of Jewish legal authorities to respond to what they too know to be clear-cut human and Jewish values. To maintain proper legal procedure an *agunah* can be debarred from remarrying and establishing a fully ramified Jewish home. Or, in consequence of a parental sin, someone ruled a *mamzer* cannot contract a marriage with a kosher Jew. These disabilities contravene some of our most primary covenantal responsibilities. The Jewish pain attached to them intensifies when we think of the Holocaust. Is there much in our hierarchy of Jewish duty that takes priority today over contracting a Jewish marriage and creating a Jewish family?

The covenantal trauma created by these laws cannot be assuaged by mitigation, by suggesting that compassionate decisors will limit the number affected or that accepting the few unresolved cases will allow us to maintain familial unity among Jews. In fact, Orthodox decisors continue to declare some people *agunot* and *mamzerim* and apply the consequent Jewish legal disabilities to them. As I understand the range of my obligations under the Covenant, I do not believe God wants some Jews to relate to other Jews by categorizing and treating them as *agunot* and *mamzerim.* Thus I will abet Jews seeking to fulfill their covenantal responsibilities outside these laws. As a pluralist, I oppose any suggestion by the non-Orthodox that Orthodox Jews should be asked to compromise their understanding of God's law for the sake of communal unity. I do, however, find it troubling that while the *halakhah* has kept some laws such as "an eye for an eye" in force but practically inoperable, contemporary *poskim* have not yet demonstrated such creativity in this area.

The issue of women's rights in traditional Jewish marriage and divorce law disturbs Jews like me far more because, committed so fundamentally to the concept of personhood, I consider women's equality a critical matter for contemporary Judaism. Again the mitigations do not persuade. But I cannot usefully say more. Non-Orthodox Jewish women have reminded us that they must be allowed to speak for themselves and they increasingly do so to those who will listen.

[6]

Claiming Power-in-Relation: Exploring the Ethics of Connection

Mary Grey

Introduction

A basic insight of feminist studies is that women often describe their experience using the terms *relatedness* and *interconnection.* Mutuality and solidarity are preferred ways of operating for the feminist movement. Feminist theologian Carter Heyward—in some ways a pioneer of relational theology—based her understanding of God on the idea of "power-in-relation." Claiming power-in-relation is making God present in the world, she wrote.[1] Where there is no relation, God is not. What is more, "connectedness" and "radical relatedness" are more illuminating images by which to understand our way of being in the world and our experience of Divine presence than a philosophy based on individualism and separation.

In this paper, I will test this idea as a basis for feminist ethics. That is, does using an image like power-in-relation, or, as I prefer to call it, a "metaphysic of connection,"[2] or interconnectedness, present a liberating ethic for women or trap us further into destructive, oppressive patterns of relating? My first question is how the experience of bonding and solidarity has actually worked

Source: From Mary Grey, "Claiming Power-in-Relation: Exploring the Ethics of Connection," *Journal of Feminist Studies in Religion* 7, no. 18 (1991). Used by permission.

in feminist networks: if it has not worked, what obstacles have been encountered? Second, I present an alternative model to that of individualism—a metaphysic of connectedness. Third, I explore this as both *revelatory paradigm and moral imperative.* The conclusion develops practical ways in which this model might offer new hope in conflictual situations.

The "Honeymoon" Days of Sisterhood

The early stages of the women's movement were the halcyon days of solidarity: "sisterhood is powerful" and the "cosmic covenant of women" (Mary Daly) were frequent inspiration for bonding. As Judith Plaskow put it in a recent paper:

> The dream we had in the heady, early days of the feminist movement, that the bonds of sisterhood would annul or eradicate traditional divisions of religion, race and class, and that we could formulate an analysis of women's situation and a program for action that would embrace *all* women was based not on engagement with the particularity of women's experience, but on a wave of a magic wand that made difference invisible.[3]

Although bonding-in-solidarity was felt to be the way towards eradicating structural oppression—the declared feminist agenda—this very bonding seemed to disguise divisiveness at many levels. Despite utopic visions of freedom and of a nonviolent world in harmony with the environment, despite the recovery of women's stories, lost from history, there is an apparent loss of faith, a disillusionment, in the actual effectiveness of bonding. Even the recovery of the stories has in some ways added to this. I see the following as key areas of difficulty:

- Poor women are separated from middle- and upper-class women by structures of poverty and class.
- Jewish women find it painful or even impossible to dialogue with Christians where it is not acknowledged that Christian theology developed at the cost of blaming the Jewish faith for the death of Christ, and, in the feminist case, for the death of the Goddess and the rise of God the Father.
- Black women find it almost impossible to dialogue with white women because of the history of white women's collusion in their oppression. This collusion has a history but also modern expressions.[4]
- Differences in sexual orientation impede dialogue. Heterosexual women barely grasp the contempt and the marginalization from which lesbian women suffer—and in which heterosexual women may collude. But

lesbian women may fail to appreciate the lack of freedom and the degree of manipulation in which heterosexual women are often trapped. Marriage can often prevent genuine women's friendship.
- Single women and elderly women are marginalized by suffocating "coupledom" or exclusive focus on youth.

All these obstacles are connected to some degree with the way women have been socialized to understand our own selves. Because women have internalized an ethic of self-denial and have been socialized into (frequently) demeaning forms of dependency and service, the range and nature of the bonding groups essential for the liberating or therapeutic process has been unappreciated. Many different forms of internalizing the "victim" or "self-denying" ethic exist, but because the oppressive social norms that cause these remain largely unchanged—especially in Church circles, there being no equal opportunities commission for the Church!—simply identifying this dynamic does not change it. A woman's sense of self can be so negative that, despite the bonding of the women's movement, loss of self-esteem can reoccur at different phases and crises of the life cycle. (Anita Spencer's book *Seasons* is very helpful for charting the tasks and pitfalls a woman faces at different developmental stages.)[5]

The problem is that our bonding occurs in a society whose very structures of consciousness are damaged. That the man/woman relationship suffers from damaged mutuality is clear. But there are wider chasms than this. The long exploitation of the planet which recurs in different insidious forms—the *Recurring Silent Spring,* as a recent book put it[6]—shows that the misuse of nature follows from seeing her through the prism of a machine to be manipulated, controlled, dominated as inert matter, separate from us. The fact that women have shared in similar exploitation tends to hide the fact that women, too, have colluded in the exploitation of nature. This in turn has destroyed a sense of community between Western women and women living in communities still respecting nature's rhythms.

A final factor must be added to this dismal catalog of obstacles to bonding. When I encounter the courage of Third World women in the face of oppression, I confront a suffering whose extent I can barely fathom. In the face of the vibrant faith springing from such a situation, how can I speak of dialogue? What forms of connection are appropriate here?

But if feminist theology is about a spiritual *vision*—which I believe to be a united factor—we are engaged in a journey or process toward a more authentic dialogue. This first phase has revealed the many pitfalls. Seeing ourselves as an integral part of oppressive structures we must acknowledge the truth that Rosemary Ruether has offered: "Women are not the great innocents of history!" This is the truth Martha Quest stumbled on at the end of a long journey to self-affirmation. In *The Four-Gated City,* the final volume of Doris Lessing's five-volume saga *The Children of Violence,* Martha was hit by the revelation "I *am* what the human race is. I am 'The Germans are the mirror and catalyst of Europe'; also 'The dirty Hun, filthy Nazi.' "[7]

We all participate in the basic energy or thrust of the world for positive or destructive ends. So, in seeking the vision that can ground women's solidarity more effectively we must reckon with the extent to which the very structures and processes of knowing, perceiving, and feeling are wounded by ethics of domination and cultural superiority, by the language of binary oppositions, and by the way all structures of our human interaction have become locked into the absolutizing of the "individualistic I," the "enclosed I" for whom full mutuality is impossible. But the very fact that our differences and tensions have now been thrown into such sharp relief does not detract from the original insights of sisterhood and solidarity. Far from it: it is this tireless digging away for the root causes of oppression which has exposed these painful conflicts. I argue not that connectedness is a futile dream but that the contemporary ethical model which encourages the development of the individual, motivated by self-interest, success-seeking, achievement-oriented, seeking mastery without counting the cost, must be replaced by an ethics of connection, interdependence, and the interrelatedness of all things.

A Metaphysic of Connection

The term *the connected self* was first used by Catherine Keller.[8] In an article on the ethics of inseparability Keller repeats the discovery of the woman Shug, a character from Alice Walker's *The Color Purple:*

> She say, My first step from the old white man was trees. Then air. Then birds. Then other people. But one day when I was sitting quiet and feeling like a motherless child, which I was, it come to me: the feeling of being part of everything, not separate at all. I knew that if I cut a tree, my arm would bleed.[9]

Women experience many such "epiphanies of connection." The history of women's spiritualities is discovering the many ways in which connectedness has been a strength.

In a "metaphysic of connection," the interdependence and interconnection of all things are seen on the widest possible scale. It is not simply that all *people* interconnect but that all living things are organically interconnected. This prevents *personal* relations from being romantically idealized and sees the basic energy, movement, and becoming of every organism in the world to be relational.

This way of seeing things derives in part from what is known as process thought, which views God and world as mutually involved in a process of becoming. Process thought deals not in macro- but in micro-units, tiny pulsations of being, or units of becoming. So it is easier to see how each pulsation organically influences something else—in the way that an explosion reverberates across a valley, influencing every living organism in that valley. On a small scale, think of a single shot in a film sequence: what appears to be a single shot is actually composed of a series of photographs—separate, but organically cohering in the whole. On a large scale, think of the nuclear experiments on the Pacific islands: air, water, soil were all affected. Pregnant women gave birth to deformed babies. And the whole tragedy interrelates with the weapons industry and the power-balance of East-West politics.

To think organically affects how we see interrelational dependencies and also affects our self-understanding. Not only do we *not* separate body/soul/mind/heart/erotic feeling from a holistic self-image, but we do not define ourselves as persons over against other persons. Organic, nondualist thinking demands that much as starting point. The self can be seen as a nondualist process of *many selves,* of becoming a self-in-relation, a connected self. I become in relation to you. We are part of each other. What is more, our mutual becoming happens in and through environmental influences, our situatedness in crowded cities or green fields, being limited by space-time dimensions which either encourage or block our growth. There is a mutual vulnerability between ourselves and that part of the cosmos in which *we* happen to be situated. Thus *interconnectedness* is both a new revelatory paradigm and a moral imperative.

Two objections will have already sprung to mind. I have just described how relatedness appears to have caused insoluble problems for the feminist movement. And, secondly, hasn't contemporary psychology of women clearly told us that women are primed developmentally to relate, and that this is proving to be our undoing? Because we hold relationship so dear, because we define ourselves almost totally in relational terms, and invest so much of ourselves in relationship, we submit to unjust and demeaning forms both at home and at work. Despite the significant achievements of *some* women in *some* situations, the secretary is still forced into the mold of the boss's wife or mistress, mothers still define themselves in relation to husband and children, and women are twice as likely as men to suffer from depressive illnesses or even commit suicide as a result of negatively experiencing relational involvements.[10] Furthermore, this depression caused by a loss of sense of self and sense of life's meaning can be experienced at *all* stages of the life cycle. Nor does it help to assume that *in itself* the pattern of heterosexual relating is the cause. Lesbian relationships too can break up through violence, leaving a woman devastated, where woman-identified relationship was assumed to be mutually self-affirming to the two involved.[11]

This seems to suggest that epiphanies of connection or interconnectedness spell utter disaster. In their recent psychological and sociological research, Jean Baker Miller, Nancy Chodorow, and Carol Gilligan have all pointed out the dangers to women of the development of empathic and relating skills. Jean Baker Miller warns of the danger of "fluid ego boundaries" and of a mediated sense of self.[12] Nancy Chodorow shows how the relational situation develops very differently for the young boy and girl. From the boy's great need for *differentiation* from his mother comes the male need to be *separate.*[13] Thus separation/connection becomes the male/female polarity. The male need to preserve individualization and identity through distance from the female world succeeds because women acquiesce in placing their relational/empathic skills in the service of male achievement. In serving masculine needs women live out relationality in dependent forms. The capitalist world added to this the stereotype of the traveling hero: pirate, explorer, absentee marketing executive, dependent on the stable woman tending the hearth. Odysseus wanders while Penelope weaves. Men's absence from the home has been socially sanctioned—women's has had to be justified. How, then, can interconnection be a revelatory paradigm?

Connectedness as Revelatory Paradigm

My argument is that connectedness and interdependence are deeper realities than separation and "the enclosed I." The problem is to understand and *enable* differentiation, pluralism, and diversity—whether religious, racial, or sexual—in such a way that the experience of one ethnic or faith group does not hold an exclusive position. If it is possible to establish that all human desire as well as the yearning of the whole of creation is for deep, meaningful, and just relation, insofar as epiphanies of connection can be discerned, I argue that these point to a profounder explanation of the "truth of the universe."

Facing the philosophical challenge here, one must ask whether there ever could be a discernible "truth of the universe." Immanuel Kant argued that ultimacy will always escape us. We content ourselves with artificially structuring what we "see" as "real." We can never penetrate the model we use to reality itself. What guarantee could there be that the model of connectedness or just relating, "the power that drives to justice and makes it" as Carter Heyward put it, has any claim to ultimacy as the fundamental energy of the universe?

Here I think a solution is offered in Carol Gilligan's call to discern the "different voice."[14] Gilligan refers here to an ethics of care which issues from women's experience, which she contrasts with an ethics based on rights and fairness, developed by her late colleague, Lawrence Kohlberg. Ethics of care, attention or responsibility spring from the experience of *trying to be faithful to relation or connection,* where this is known to be the bedrock of existence. It issues from touching a wellspring where tenderness, a passionate caring for the entirety of the relational nexus presents itself as ultimate. This is the experience of many groups in society who struggle to articulate a profundity of meaning which always eludes articulation and categorization. This profundity of meaning highlights something more significant than a reactionary, essentialist identification of women as society's nurturers and caregivers.

Cassandra, prophet and princess of Troy, "saw" another truth but was condemned by Apollo never to be believed when articulating what she saw. We normally encounter Cassandra through the patriarchal interpretation of Aeschylus; but more recently, feminist rewriting of the myth has appeared.[15] Christa Wolf, in her novel *Cassandra,* shows Cassandra reflecting, "Why did I want the gift of prophecy, come what may? To speak with *my voice: the ultimate.* I did not want anything different."[16] Dare I suggest that, with the paradigm of interrelatedness, we approach a degree of ultimacy, and that the reason it eludes articulation and conceptualization is that relational truth—like all truth—is forced to express itself through the inadequate, distorted vehicle of language? That is, one can speak in "another voice," but *never* totally authentically, because the language does not exist. The language of relationality—like the language of grace—is the most vulnerable one of all. It is defined by a double dynamic: giving/receiving, feeling/thinking. But—and here is the pitfall—it wants to maintain itself even in the absence of response. As Janet Morley so beautifully put it in her book of psalms:

> And though there is no one to hold me
> Yet I will hold my heart open.[17]

To return once more to Christa Wolf's Cassandra: as she nears death her visual powers increase but her ability to express herself decreases. Words leave her and only images are left: "The last thing in my life will be a picture, not a word. Words die before pictures."[18] To speak relational truth, is to speak as Cassandra did, with angst, to struggle against falling back into the use of the conventional "we," which is not the "we" of pure relation. Christa Wolf calls this an "addiction to agreement" (*ubereinstimmungsucht*): this means losing an authentic voice in order to win facile approval, in order to avoid "rocking the boat."

Secondly, interconnectedness can claim to be a revelatory paradigm because this is the means, above all, through which Divine power-in-relation is mediated. *Power* in this context means the relational drive and energy which *both* empowers human becoming and ecological growth and is the locus of Divine presence in the universe. *Divine presence* is used here both in the sense of ultimacy, the Sacredness of Being, and the process of coming to know and experience this (the drive to connect). Seeking to co-create in forming more just patterns of relating, new forms of mutuality, is both actively making God incarnate, and becoming not *passive* but *receptive* to the ways in which God is already active as energizing presence.

This does not necessitate returning to an Aristotelian/Kantian split between underlying reality and outward manifestations. Nor does it mean trying to prove the case simply by reiterating—without reasoned analysis—the power of the image of connectedness (which was a recent, unjustified criticism of *Weaving the Visions,* Carol P. Christ and Judith Plaskow's recent collection of articles developing the significance of mutuality and relatedness for feminist religious thought).[19]

From many angles it can be seen that "connection" is no abstract principle, but an energizing way of living and experiencing. A metaphysic of connection is a historical process. It is both a personal and communal process. As Keller, following Whitehead, wrote, "My process of 'being myself' is my origination from my possession of the world."[20] *Selving* means becoming a self; the word is taken from Gerard Manley Hopkins's poem "As Kingfishers Catch Fire":

Each mortal thing does one thing and the same:
Deals out that being indoors each one dwells;
Selves—goes itself; *myself* it speaks and spells
Crying What I do is me; for that I came.[21]

Just as I gather the world into me, so I too am gathered into world-becoming, with my whole relational nexus. Thus it is possible to discern moments in history when men and women, through the language, imagery, and ethics of interconnectedness, worked with the relational grain of existence in a positive way. But what cannot be ignored are the appalling tragedies that occur when "right relation" is trampled on, militarily, from the massacres of the Chinese warlords to the Holocaust, and socially, when the respected institution of the family masks incest, child abuse, and violence against women. In these instances human agency grasps fundamental energy for destructive purposes. Historical decisions that transform the relational scene (like the creation of apartheid in South Africa) mean that certain possibilities are lost or destroyed. Certain aspects of God have died.

This is where memory as a tool is relevant. Each culture and religion has symbols in which its history is remembered and made creatively present. For

Christianity the cross is the symbol of God's participation in the historical process of building just relation. It is also the symbol of the impaling of women—and other subjugated groups—on the cross of patriarchy. Could it also be the guarantee that the cumulative loss, the pain, the death of each small child is held as part of the process of building right relation *now?* What is remembered must be *re-membered* (Mary Daly's emphasis), integrated into the process of claiming relational power now and into the future. Hence the stress on "empowering memory."

But whereas memory reclaims strengths of lost foremothers and sisters, it also opens up festering wounds, as the present predicament acquires a history and an almost fated inevitability—like the long history of slavery, viewed globally. It is not what is remembered, but what cannot be forgotten, that causes anguish. The particularities of suffering threaten to overwhelm the overall commitment to relation. For Cassandra to preserve her authentic voice, Achilles must always be the "raging beast," Hecuba the colluding woman, the Greeks are always the alien others. How, then, is the metaphysic of connection as paradigm of ultimacy to be reconciled with a moral imperative to maximize connectedness?

Maximizing Connectedness–Connection as Moral Imperative

Maximizing connectedness is a multilevel endeavor. It begins with redefining the self. If we see ourselves, not as the absolute "I" over against the world, but as connected, in relation, the first thing that happens is a sense of freedom. We are set free from the burden of the past by our refusal to accept domination, poverty, and discrimination as our only options. If what I name as "myself" is in fact a fluid unity of many self-moments, there are many more creative possibilities and choices for future becoming. I can choose direction. I can learn and unlearn from entrapped moments of my life without denying or undervaluing the historical roots of a particular oppression. I do not play out a prearranged script. Being connected does not spell death to the self's free determination and creativity, but is the framework for making these concrete. Although becoming freer means being able to choose for maximal relational potential, it also means understanding realistically that choice and power to change are heavily dependent on economic circumstance. Even in the worst circumstances women's relational strengths have potential. A friend, a British criminologist, interviewing women in prison tells me of the strengths female bonding can provide for female prisoners whose self-esteem is low. Yet these very strengths are found threatening by prison authorities, who seek to undermine them.

The second task is to reassess the attachment/separation dynamic in one's life. Not *all* attachment is connection in the sense I use it. Not *all* separation is destructive. Many women entering middle adulthood experience a 'connected aloneness' which is comparable with religious contemplation and even to the mystical experience. (It could even be said that in a *spirituality of connectedness* lies the contemplative vocation.) But do we have the right to walk out of unhealthy dependency relationships? This cannot mean abandoning the elderly, infants, or handicapped—even when this burden of care is yet another obstacle to women's autonomous agency. To me the only answer is that we have to become what Heyward calls "mutually messianic," redeemers of each other, with the ability to sustain broken relation—even our own—on personal and political levels. Yet care and connection as moral imperatives should not dictate the sacrifice of one sector of the populace for another.

The next two tasks reveal a more hopeful dimension. For the third task is that of self-development within the context of the environment's process towards healing. Within a lifestyle where all things are connected it will be illogical to use health remedies, beauty techniques, food, clothes, or household aids which improve our sense of well-being at the expense of the environment. We are embarked on a common journey. With this in mind, the natural world itself can be experienced as "redeeming strength" (a theme which I explore elsewhere).[22] The healing strength of nature is one of the dimensions to be reclaimed from women's history.

Finally, claiming relational energy as moral imperative invites women to use hitherto hidden strengths as redemptive tools. "Embodied theology" really does mean acting boldly, but in a holistic and not a manipulative manner. Both Carter Heyward and Rita Brock have shown how claiming erotic bodily energy as sacred power can mean reverencing each other, touching each other—our selves, our lives, our political priorities—in liberating ways.[23] Struggling to break the dualistic split between rationality and emotion means daring to articulate the discoveries of feeling-knowing, the strength of a knowledge rooted in bodily experience. Only thus will the long exploitation of women's bodies and the body-denying ascetic spiritualities of many faiths begin to be overcome.

Conclusion

How then does the moral imperative to "maximize connectedness" move us beyond the impasses described at the beginning of this paper? To whom and with whom are we in relation? First and foremost, a metaphysic of connection means discovering our own authentic voices. This happens *in relation* to the group in which I am historically and culturally rooted. This means that women of privilege—for whom it has not been a great problem to discover a voice—have the responsibility to empower other groups of women, with whom we are as a political group *in relation,* to discover, own, celebrate, and mourn a story in all its particularity. *Differentiation* not *assimilation* must ground right relation. What this connectedness may mean for a privileged group of women is that the only form of relation possible is to listen, to learn, and to begin a journey of conversion as response to the lessons of history. The joy of a spiritual vision is the faith in its power to heal wounds. But this vision must be rooted in respect for the context of a group's experience (for example, the experience of Muslim women in Britain since the publication of Salman Rushdie's book); it must be attuned to the possibilities of the moment. The time may not be ripe for forgiveness. Authentic dialogue may not be an option. But a metaphysic of connection seeks always to discover *deeper sources of connection:* in our being human, in our being women, in our shared responsibility for the planet. Even in recognizing the sin of broken relation and assuming its burden we bring the energy for just relation into the political scene.

IN THE BEGINNING IS THE RELATION
IN THE END — THE HEALING
BUT IN THE PRESENT — THE ENERGIZING OF CREATION
FOR JUSTICE

Notes

1. Carter Heyward, *The Redemption of God: A Theology of Mutual Relation* (Washington, D.C.: University Press of America, 1982).
2. This phrase was first used—to my knowledge—by Catherine Keller, in *From a Broken Web: Separation, Sexism and Self* (Boston: Beacon Press, 1986).
3. Judith Plaskow, "Feminist Anti-Judaism and the Christian God" (paper delivered at the conference of European women in Theological Research, Frankfurt, September 1989), 2.
4. See, for example, Rhoda Reddock's work on slavery in the Caribbean. Reddock shows that white slaveowners prevented slaves from marrying and having children; it was "more profitable to get a good price" for the slave than to spend money on rearing slaves' children. Reddock's work is cited by Catherine Halkes, . . . *En Alles Zal Herschapen Worden* (And All Shall Be Re-Created: Thoughts over the Wholeness of Creation, in the Tension between Nature and Culture) (Baarn: Ten Have, 1989; English translation, London: SPCK, 1991), 57. For contemporary corollaries see the autobiographical work by Maya

Angelou, *I Know Why the Caged Bird Sings* (London: Virago, 1984). In her essay "Beyond the Peacock: The Reconstruction of Flannery O'Connor" (in *In Search of Our Mothers' Gardens* [London: The Women's Press, 1982]), Alice Walker explores the differences that define the lives of two women writers from the same region, one white, one black.

5. Anita Spencer, *Seasons: Women's Search for Self through Life's Stages* (Paramus, N.J.: Paulist Press, 1982).
6. H. Patricia Hynes, *The Recurring Silent Spring* (New York: Pergamon Press, Athene series, 1989).
7. Doris Lessing, *The Children of Violence: Martha Quest, A Proper Marriage, A Ripple in the Storm, Landlocked, The Four-Gated City.* All published by Collins, Grafton paperbacks. Quote from *The Four-Gated City,* 539. See also Carol P. Christ, "Explorations with Doris Lessing in Quest of the Four-Gated City," in *Women and Religion,* ed. Judith Plaskow and Joan Arnold Romero (Missoula, Mont.: American Academy of Religion and Scholars Press, 1974), 153 ff.
8. Catherine Keller, *From a Broken Web.* See also "Feminism and the Ethic of Inseparability" in *Women's Consciousness, Women's Conscience,* ed. Barbara Andolsen, Christine E. Gudorf, and Mary D. Pellauer (San Francisco: Harper and Row, 1985), 251–64.
9. Shug, in *The Color Purple* by Alice Walker, quoted by Keller, "Feminism and the Ethic of Inseparability," 251.
10. For documentation on the incidence of depression in women, see the papers of the Stone Center for Developmental Studies, Wellesley College; the research of Marcia Guttentag quoted in Maggie Scarf, "The More Sorrowful Sex," *Psychology Today* 12, no. 11 (1979).
11. See Lynn Segal, "The Beast in Man," *New Statesman and Society,* 8 September 1989.
12. Jean Baker Miller, *Toward a New Psychology of Women* (Boston: Beacon, 1978).
13. Nancy Chodorow, *The Reproduction of Mothering: Psychoanalysis and the Psychology of Gender* (Berkeley: University of California Press, 1978).
14. Carol Gilligan, *In a Different Voice* (Cambridge: Harvard University Press, 1982).
15. See, for example, Marion Zimmer Bradley, *The Firebrand* (London: Michael Joseph, 1988).
16. Christa Wolf, *Cassandra,* trans. Jan Van Heurck (London: Virago, 1984), 4. For a reflection on Wolf's Cassandra, see Petra Von Morstein, "A Message from Cassandra—Experience and Knowledge: Dichotomy and Unity," in *Feminist Perspectives: Philosophical Essays on Method and Morals,* ed. Lorraine Code, Sheila Mullett, and Christine Overall (Toronto: University of Toronto Press, 1988), 46–63.
17. Janet Morley, *All Desires Known* (London: MOW and WIT, 1988), 51.
18. Wolf, *Cassandra,* 21.
19. Carol P. Christ and Judith Plaskow, eds., *Weaving the Visions: New Patterns in Feminist Spirituality* (San Francisco: Harper and Row, 1989). For a review, see

Carol LeMasters, "Unhealthy Pluriformity," *The Woman's Review of Books* 7:1 (October 1989): 15–16.

20. Alfred North Whitehead, *Process and Reality: An Essay in Cosmology*, corrected edition, ed. Griffin and Sherburne (New York: Macmillan, 1978), 22.
21. Gerard Manley Hopkins, *Poems* (New York: Oxford University Press, 1948), 98.
22. Mary Grey, *Redeeming the Dream: Feminism, Redemption and Christianity* (London: SPCK, 1989; Mystic, Conn.: Twenty-third Publications, 1990). See ch. 3, "Women and Nature: A Redeeming Connectedness."
23. Carter Heyward, "Touching Our Strength: The Erotic as Power and the Love of God" (paper delivered at the Groningen University Congress, *Vrouwen over Grenzen,* Groningen, April 1989); Rita Nakashima Brock, *Journeys by Heart: A Christology of Erotic Power* (New York: Crossroad, 1988).

[7]

Celibacy, Chastity

Shundo Tachibana

. . .

THE LIFE OF CELIBACY, which is usually expressed by the term Brahmacariya, was inherited by Buddhism from Brahmanism with a slight modification both in the terminology and the idea, or it may be better to say that Buddhism organized an order of Brahmacārins of its own according to traditions which were current when it arose, and its own principles. According to the Dharmasûtras which deal with the domestic and social laws of ancient India based upon existing traditions, and date roughly from 500 to 200 B.C.,[1] boys belonging to the three upper classes, which classification was at that time well established, were to be initiated through the ceremony of Upanayana as students in the eighth year at the earliest and in the twenty-fourth at the latest from their conceptions. The students who were thus initiated were called Dvija or "twice-born," or Brahmacārins, "those who live a life of celibacy," and their life is Brahmacariya or "a life of celibacy." They were called "twice-born," because, besides their natural birth, they attained their spiritual birth by means of the Upanayana or initiation. They were then placed under the charge of teachers for periods from twelve to forty-eight

SOURCE: From Shundo Tachibana, "Celibacy, Chastity," in *The Ethics of Buddhism* (Surrey, England: Curzon Press, 1992). Used by permission.

years, the former period being considered to be necessary for the complete study of one of the four Vedas. Their chief duties were to study the Vedas, to beg food, to observe strict celibacy, and to live a simple self-restrained life. Day after day they had to recite the Vedas, and to kindle the sacred fire or feed it with fuel, or they might be instructed in the duties of a householder. With the exception of some rules with regard to substances of food, stuffs and colors of clothing, hairdressing, demeanor in public and behavior towards their spiritual teachers, penance for the breach of rules, and some other rules of minor importance, both Brahman and Buddhist students have many rules in common. If we were not engaged in discussing only the subject of celibacy, we should have a great deal to say about them. It is, therefore, not too much to say that Buddhism in connection with the life of a Brahmacārin owes much to Brahmanism, as it does in some other respects, or that both Brahmanism and Buddhism established rules according to the current traditions, or that indebtedness is reciprocal; all these may possibly be the case.

Now let us turn to our subject. According to ancient Indian customs, those belonging to the three upper classes had to pass through the four Āśramaṇas or orders of life: that of the Brahmacārin or Vedic student, that of the Gṛihastha or householder, that of the Vānaprastha (or Vaikhānasa) or hermit, and that of the Sanyāsin (or Bhikṣu) or ascetic. Of these four orders, the first and the fourth were compulsory, while the two middle were optional. In other words, everybody belonging to these classes so far as he was not an outcast for some reason had to pass a period of from twelve to forty-eight years as a student under the strict care of a spiritual teacher; and when this time came to an end, he could enter the life of one of the three other orders. (a) He might return home and perform the duties as the master of a house and the father of a family; or (b) he might become a hermit retiring into the woods, living on wild vegetables, flowers, fruits, and roots, wearing clothes made of skins or bark of trees, and practicing austerities, sometimes being accompanied by his wife in the case of one who entered this life after he had finished a householder's life; or (c) he might enter into the life of an ascetic immediately after finishing the order of a student, if he considered himself sufficiently purified by his studentship; but in the majority of cases, students at the completion of their term became householders, and after living a householder's life for some years and being blessed with male children, left home to spend their remaining years in celibacy, purity, and holiness. The life of an ancient Brahman therefore generally speaking was begun in celibacy, which with an interruption of a householder's life was resumed in the life of an ascetic. The Brahman Brahmacārin corresponds to the Buddhist Sāmaṇera, and the Brahman Sanyāsin or Bhikṣu to the Buddhist Bhikkhu, if a Brahman passed at once from studentship to the ascetic life, without any intervention of the householder's life. The name Bhikṣu, corresponding to the Pāli Bhikkhu, which is used in some Dharmasūtras[2] in the same meaning as the word Sanyāsin, reminds us of a close connection between the two. The difference between Brahman and Buddhist celibate lives was that in the former it was compulsory for everybody at the beginning and at the end of his life, while in the middle part of it celibacy was optional; while in the latter celibacy is compulsory only for those who have voluntarily joined the monkhood. As to the other Buddhists or lay people, they are not obliged to observe celibacy, except when they keep the eight precepts on the Uposatha days which come two or three times every lunar month or on some other special occasions. Those who have joined the monkhood are required to observe strict celibacy through life, first as Sāmaṇeras or novices, and later as Bhikkhus or fully qualified monks.

The term Brahmacariya is used in Brahmanism and in Buddhism in nearly the same sense, but not always. Buddhism gives it a peculiar meaning. Putting aside the case of Brahmanism, we shall examine in what senses this term is used in Buddhism. Among several different senses given to it, the following two seem to be the most remarkable. In the first place, it means complete celibacy or total abstinence from sexual intercourse, a vow which the Buddhist monk has to observe through life, and the layman only when he observes the eight precepts on the Uposatha days or on some other special occasions. Unlike the Brahman whose celibate life is interrupted by the life of a householder, the Buddhist monk has to be a celibate all through his life. The breach of this vow is the first of the four most serious offences (Pārājikā), the punishment for it being perpetual expulsion from the monkhood. In the Pātimokkha or code of monkish laws, we find twenty-one laws enacted concerning sexual intercourse. Brahmanism and Buddhism both give the same interpretation to celibacy or single life, though its performance, as we have repeatedly said, is different. In the second place, it means "a life of perfect holiness or purity" led by those who have entered the Four Paths. This is religious life in its perfect sense; and it seems that this sense is peculiar to Buddhism, as the performance of this culture is peculiar to it. It begins with the practice of self-control or what we may call the preparatory practice of purification in the Four Paths: keeping watch over the senses, being moderate in eating, being vigilant, thoughtful, and conscious.[3] This practice brings praise to the monk Nanda, half brother of the Buddha, for he is commended by the Buddha as skilled in it. The observance of the precepts cannot be overlooked. The precepts in the Pātimokkha are said to be the first part of, and in conformity with, the Brahmacariya or "life of holiness." If any one is firm and stable in observing them, and exercises himself in them, taking all upon himself, he will destroy the three bonds: the heresy of individuality, doubt, and erroneous religious practices and rites; and thereby he will enter the First Path. He will then destroy these three bonds and attenuate the three roots of evil, lust, hatred, and ignorance; and thereby enter the Second Path. He will next destroy the five bonds belonging to the lower parts, the heresy of individuality, doubt, erroneous religious practices and rites, lust after life in the Kāma-world, ill-will; and thereby enter the Third Path. Then lastly he will put an end to all the passions, and live, having for himself understood, realized, and attained in this very life to the emancipation of mind and of insight which is free from passion. Arahatship or Nibbāna, which is the final goal of Buddhist culture or Brahmacariya, is thus reached. Brahmacariya has as its chief end Nibbāna or Arahatship (A. i. 50, 168; iv. 77; S. ii. 278–9; 284). The expression *Vusitaṁ brahmacariyaṁ,* which we meet with so often, is another name for the accomplishment of Arahatship.

Brahmacariya therefore covers the whole of the religious life of the Buddhist monk, beginning with the observance of the precepts and ending with the attainment of Nibbāna. It is sometimes shown as the complete practice of the Eightfold Noble Path. The destruction of the three roots of evil is the perfection of Brahmacariya (S. v. 7–8, 16), because when these three roots of evil are entirely uprooted, the person will be perfectly purified. This is the goal, the *summum bonum* of the Buddhist culture. The practicer of Brahmacariya always has this single object before him. He performs it not for the purpose of being reborn in the heavenly world, or for obtaining celestial long life, celestial appearance, celestial pleasure, celestial reputation, or celestial authority. None of these has anything to do with the fulfilment of Brahmacariya (A. i. 115). Sometimes the object is stated as the destruction of five avarices (A. iii. 272), of seven bonds (A. iv. 7), of seven inclinations (A. iv. 9), or of suffering and pain (A. ii. 26; S. ii. 24–5); the abandonment of desire (S. v. 272); or freedom from lust (S. iv. 27); or the realization of the Four Noble Truths (A. iv. 383; S. iv. 51); or simply of the Noble Truth concerning suffering (S. iv. 138, 253; v. 6–7, 272). All of these different expressions, however, refer to one and the same thing, that is, the destruction of mental evil and the attainment of mental enlightenment.

As is clear from the above quotations, Brahmacariya, so far as Pāli Buddhism is concerned, covers the whole of the religious life, from keeping the precepts to obtaining Arahatship. It is the religious life in its truest sense, though the term is sometimes used loosely to denote the religious or rather celibate life of a Brahman,[4] or the life of an ordinary monk who has not yet entered the holy Paths;[5] consequently it seems to have no connection with ordinary celibate life, as in Brahman laws. But in further researches we find that celibacy is not absolutely disregarded in Brahmacariya or life of purification. Mention is often made in the Buddhist literature about "Brahmacariya which is complete in all its parts and perfectly pure,"[6] or of "Brahmacariya which is not broken, not interrupted, not variegated, free from any spot, perfect and pure."[7] No doubt Brahmacariya means the whole religious life, and not merely the celibate life of the monk. But the Buddha often referred in his discourses on Brahmacariya to the question of celibacy. Among ten sorts of obstacles, he mentions association with a woman as an obstacle to Brahmacariya (A. v. 134). Once while traveling with his disciples he saw a great fire burning. Pointing to it, he asked them which would be better for a person of loose morals, to embrace that great mass of blazing fire or to embrace a beautiful young woman. The disciples naturally answered that the latter would be the better, because the former would be hard and painful. The Buddha, however, denied it and said that the former would be better, because it might cause his death or give him as great pain as death itself, but it would not send him to hell after death, as the latter might possibly do. This sermon reminds us of Jesus preaching on sin when he said: "It is better for thee to enter into life halt or maimed, rather than having two hands or two feet to be cast into everlasting fire."[8] It is noteworthy that in both cases the moral is the same. In another place the Buddha says: "A Samaṇa or Brāhman, who declares himself to be a person of perfect Brahmacariya, may not enjoy sexual intercourse with a woman; but this is not enough to warrant such a declaration, for (a) if he allows a woman to rub his body with oil or perfume, to give him a bath and shampoo him, and enjoys and longs for it; (b) if he laughs, sports, or amuses himself with a woman; (c) if he looks into, watches with expectation, the eye of a woman who does the same in return; (d) if he listens through a wall or fence to the noise of a woman who is laughing, reciting, singing, or weeping; (e) if he remembers that he has formerly laughed, talked, and sported together with a woman; (f) if he sees a householder or a householder's son in possession of five sorts of pleasure, and being attended (by a woman); (g) or if he practices Brahmacariya desiring to join a certain class of celestial beings, saying 'Through this morality, religious practice, austerity, or through Brahmacariya, I shall be a certain celestial being, I shall be one of the celestial beings'; such Brahmacariya cannot be called unbroken, uninterrupted, unvaried, unadulterated, perfect and pure Brahmacariya."[9] So it is quite clear that though mere celibacy is not all that Brahmacariya means, it is an important element of it.

Whatever meanings the term Brahmacariya may convey, celibacy is an important part of it, and it is to be strictly observed through life by any monk or novice who has joined the Buddhist brotherhood. The punishment for its breach, as we have stated, is expulsion, the severest punishment for a monk, only comparable to excommunication in the ancient Christian Church, or to being made an outcast in the ancient Brahman community. The Buddha established such an institution, partly because, as in other cases of similar nature, he was influenced by the state of things in his days. Ancient Indians, extremely given to debauchery as they were, were on the other hand stringently austere in the matter of sexual enjoyment, and of eating and drinking as well. The Buddha condemned debauchery on the one hand, but at the same time he disapproved of the severe austerity then practiced. He recommended celibacy only to those who voluntarily took up a life of homelessness and who aspired after a higher nobler life through religious practice. Celibacy is the sacrifice of the greatest sensual pleasure, and can be attained only through powerful self-restraint. The monks are said to live a celibate life "for the sake of restraint of the five organs of sensation, abandonment of evils, freedom from human passions, and destruction (of the craving for existence)."[10]

Why is celibacy regarded so highly in Buddhism? What is its morality? it may be asked. In the first place pleasures which are enjoyed through the sense-organs are always regarded in Buddhism as mean and detestable, and the greatest of these perhaps is pleasure obtained from sexual relation whether physical or mental. This is the basest pleasure, so those who conquer it may be looked upon as noble respectable persons. It was certainly this psychology that produced the high esteem of persons of self-restraint. Reproductive instinct with appetite is the most powerful instinct that human beings are naturally endowed with. Great strength is needed to restrain it, and therefore those who do so are looked upon as persons of great strength. Great strength, whether physical or mental, is an indication of great personality. A man who controls sexual enjoyment is therefore a noble and strong man. Ancient religions as a general rule regarded the renunciation of sexual pleasure as one of the most praiseworthy human actions. Whether this renunciation was ascribed to the self-control of a religious man or to the power of a merciful God or gods who are supposed to act upon him as the result of his devotion, they esteemed him very highly. Reproductive instinct was symbolized or idolized in many ancient religions; but at the same time total abstinence from it was applauded in many of them; and this symbolization and absolute suppression often went on at the same time among the same religious people and in the same nation. The ancient Indians were extremely addicted to debauchery on the one hand, but on the other they regarded its absolute suppression as the end of high religious culture; or some mystic power was expected to come out of it. The Buddha in his inaugurating sermon referred to this when he said: "These two extremes, O monks, are not to be practiced by one who has given up the world. What are the two? The one, devotion to lusts and pleasures, base, sensual, vulgar, ignoble, and useless, and the other, devotion to self-mortification, painful, ignoble, and useless. By avoiding these two extremes, O monks, the Tathāgata has gained perfect knowledge of the middle path, which produces insight and knowledge, and conduces to tranquillity, to transcendent knowledge, to complete enlightenment, to Nibbāna. What is this middle path, O monks? It is the Noble Eightfold Path."[11]

He was disgusted with the sensual indulgence which was going on in India at that time, but on the other hand he could not approve of the severe austere life, which was taken up by some religious people, probably as a reaction from the sort of life which we have mentioned first, and which still remains even today in some degree. Hence his declaration of following the middle path between the two extremes, as is very well known to everybody. In spite of this, however, he could not keep from inclining—especially as the founder of a religion of strict self-control—to follow the rigorous side of his moral culture. His middle way, by which he intends to show us the mean between the two extremes, indulging exuberant pleasure and leading the severe ascetic life of self-mortification, is still tinged with the color of asceticism,[12] though of a mild nature. The absolute suppression of the reproductive instinct throughout life is thus made one of the main conditions of the Buddhist discipline. Certainly the Buddha in establishing this institution of celibate life, and his disciples in following it, do not crave after reputation for greatness or nobility of character. "This celibate life is not led, O monks," says the Buddha, "either on purpose to deceive people, or on purpose to be talked of by people, or for the profit of gain, respect, and praise, or for the sake of being gossipped about, or to secure popular recognition."[13] In this connection we may say this much: The Buddha established this rule partly in conformity with the ideas which were current in his days; because this was a common practice among the Brahmans and other religious men. To cut off the strongest human bond, or to suppress the meanest human desire, is the most significant preliminary to a course of religious life where vigorous mental struggle is needed. This will put an end to affection, passion, lust, infatuation, mental distraction or perturbation, etc., which may be expected to come out of sexual relation, and are fatally detrimental to higher mental culture. And this suppression will be a reliable testimony to its attainment.

In the second place, single life is more convenient for the accomplishment of a task which will engage anyone through life. The maintenance of a family is a heavy burden, under the load of which few people are able to stand and devote themselves to their life's work. Many shipwrecks of mankind are due to this overload. Even if the issue is not so grave, still much of human inertness is ascribable to this cause. In the field of spiritual works this burden is especially felt, and it is natural that those who have spiritual inclinations should take up a life of homelessness. Here the practice of celibacy will have double meaning, deliverance from worldliness, on the one hand, if not from the sensual indulgence of the world, and the adoption of a life of homelessness on the other.

The Buddha, who had spent his youth in luxury and indulgence in some measure, according to the general custom of noble people in his days, having seen the harmfulness of such a life to individuals and society at large, established an order of monks who would give up family life of their own accord and make efforts for personal deliverance and social enlightenment. It ought to be borne in mind that this is compulsory for those who have joined the brotherhood of their own free will, and as for the rest, they are entitled to call themselves Buddhists if they lead a life of chastity so far as sexual relation is concerned.

Chastity is a virtue included in the five precepts which are incumbent upon all lay Buddhists to keep. The continency of the married is considered as important as the single life of the unmarried. The unchaste life of the married man is absolutely repudiated as unbecoming for a Buddhist. In describing the chaste life of the ancient Brahman, which is vividly contrasted with that of the Brahman of the Buddha's days, he says as follows: "The Brahmans did not marry a woman belonging to another caste, nor did they buy a wife; they chose living together in mutual love after having come together. . . . They praised chastity and virtue, rectitude, mildness, penance, tenderness, compassion, and patience."[14] Or we may mention the following verse as a warning against a husband's faithlessness: "Let the wise man avoid an unchaste life as a burning heap of coals; not being able to live a life of chastity,[15] let him not transgress with another man's wife."[16]

About the mutual duties of husband and wife we find good moral teaching in the Siṅgālovādasuttanta.[17] In the first place, about the duties of a husband towards his wife, the Buddha says: "The husband ought to minister to his wife as western direction through the five ways: by honor, by respect, by chastity, by the abandonment of supreme authority, by the gift of ornaments." And about the duties of a wife to her husband he says: "The wife being regarded as the western direction through these five ways, sympathizes with her husband through five ways: she arranges his business well, she treats his attendants with kindness, she is devoted to him, she protects what has been accumulated, and she is skillful and diligent in all his works or duties."[18] The Buddha says nothing here about love between husband and wife; perhaps taking it as natural he thinks it unnecessary to say anything about it. Perhaps he means to say that the husband must not only love his wife, but also honor and respect her, and be courteous and faithful to her, and hand over authority to her. The wife on her side must be faithful to her husband, hospitable to her own and his relatives, and help him in conducting his business. Thus in the Buddhist home the wife is the queen. While the husband works away from home, the wife rules the home, all domestic business being laid upon her shoulders. About the duties of a man as the master of a family, the Buddha says: "Waiting on mother and father, protecting child and wife, and being engaged in a quiet calling, this is the highest blessing."[19] The domestic relations and blissful conditions in the Buddhist home are depicted in this simple verse. If a man is dutiful to his parents, and faithful and affectionate to his wife and child, and protects them, the family life which these people lead among themselves will be a very peaceful and happy one; there will be nothing more to be desired. And the village or the clan which these families compose will be very pleasant to live in.

The Buddha once delivered a sermon for Sujātā,[20] Sudatta's daughter-in-law, who being proud of her birth and beauty, was not obedient to her husband and parents-in-law. In the course of the sermon he mentioned seven sorts of wives: a murderer-like wife, a thief-like one, a master-like one, a mother-like one, a sister-like one, a friend-like one, and a servant-like one. He asked Sujātā what sort of wife she wished to be. Being softened in her heart by his sermon, she replied that she would be a servant-like wife. This does not mean that a servant-like wife is the Buddha's ideal wife. Her wish to be a servant-like wife was only an expression of her mind, which was humbled as the result of the preaching. The Buddha again says[21] that husband and wife, both of whom observe the five precepts or perform the ten meritorious deeds, are a god and goddess, and those who do not observe them, or do not perform them, are a couple of vile persons.

The most pathetic episodes that we find in the Buddhist literature in this connection, however, are those of Maddī,[22] wife of Vessantara, and of Ummadantī,[23] especially that of the latter. Ummadantī was the beautiful daughter of a rich townsman living in the capital of the Sibi country. The king, a Bodhisattva or a previous incarnation of the Buddha, wishing to marry her, sent for some Brahmans and told them to observe her future. Enchanted by her splendid beauty, they spoke unfavorably of her to the king. The king therefore gave up the intention of marrying her, and she married an officer in the king's service. Later, while driving through the town on a festival day, the king happened to see her, and fell into passionate love with her. This fact soon came to the notice of the husband, who out of loyalty, because the story tells us that he thought the king would die out of disappointment if he could not get her for his wife (Jāt. v. 217), proposed to the king to offer his wife to be queen. The king, though indeed vehemently infatuated with the beauty of the woman, was still able to discriminate virtue and vice in this connection, and owing to his strong attachment to the path of virtue, he refused to accept this unusual offer; and when he was pressed by the officer repeatedly, he reasoned with him in the following words: "One who by exceeding his attachment to my person does not heed even his own life is my friend, dearer to me than my kinsmen. His wife I am bound to respect as a friend's. You do not well, therefore, enticing me to a sinful action. . . . How can happiness be expected for him who commits a wicked action, though unwitnessed? . . . I should dare throw myself on a sharp sword or into a fire with blazing flames, but I shall not be able to offend against righteousness, which I have always observed, and to which I owe my royal bliss. . . . The virtuous do not like for themselves a pleasure procured at the expense of others whom they have distressed by bringing them into disrepute and the like. . . . If I should lack the power of ruling my own self, say, into what condition would I bring this people who long for protection from my side? Thus considering and regardful of the good of my subjects, my own righteousness, and my spotless fame, I do not allow myself to submit to my passion."[24] Finally the officer was dissuaded, and ceased to press the king to accept his wife, with which the dramatic story comes to an end. The respect for another's chastity and the idea of righteousness made the king, who was sick with love, rightly refuse to accept this offer.

Scanty as the materials are for proving the Buddha's attitude towards the questions which we have dealt with above, it is beyond doubt that he regards the continency of the married as important as any other teacher does. The question how the Buddha regards womanhood in general we may discuss later on. An interesting and at the same time difficult question will be: Does the Buddha approve of polygamy, which was a common practice in India and China in the Buddha's days? Brahmanism approves of it. According to the ancient Brahman codes of laws[25] the Brahman is entitled to marry three wives, the Kṣatriya two, and the Vaiśya and the Śūdra each one. Confucianism also approves of it, allowing the feudal prince to marry nine wives including the chief one.[26] We find it very hard to understand the Buddha's ideas about this, from lack of discourses dealing fully with this subject. But we infer, though not conclusively, from fragmentary sayings appearing here and there, that the Buddha approves of monogamy, but not of polygamy. It is true that on several occasions cases of polygamy and even of polyandry are mentioned as existing in society at that time, but only as instances of wantonness and lewdness. Even the harems of kings, which were so common in ancient

India, are often mentioned as seats of intrigue.[27] In the Aṅguttara (i. 137) we find the wanton life of a householder with four wives depicted. He lives in a comfortable house furnished and decorated. He is attended by four women, who serve and comfort him in every possible way. The description is naturally directed towards the mental and bodily suffering and pain which the householder experiences, and the wretchedness of this sort of life is emphatically described. In two other places of the same Nikāya (iv. 210, 214) we read that the householder Ugga, a Vesāli-man, whom the Buddha praises as a person with eight wonders, had four wives around him previous to his conversion. He gave them all up at the moment of his conversion, which he declares a wonder. In the Kunāla-jātaka, princess Kaṅhā marries the five princes of King Paṇḍu. Being not satisfied with them, she sins with her humpbacked crippled attendant. The five princes, knowing the faithlessness of the princess, give her up, and go into the forest to lead a retired life there.[28] The harem of a king is often mentioned. The queen, who is commonly expressed by the term *aggamahesī* or "chief consort of a king," seems to have been their leader. Pasenadi, the king of Kosala,[29] Udena, the king of Vaṁsas,[30] etc., seem each to have had a group of this sort of woman. Among legendary kings, Sudassana[31] is said to have had 84,000 wives; the harems of Prince Sīlavā,[32] King Brahmadatta,[33] King Kalābu of Kāsi[34] are also mentioned. We have called them harems, but their real nature and position being rather dubious, whether in the case of an actual king or a legendary one, we cannot be too strict in moral criticism in connection with them. In many cases it seems that a harem is simply mentioned as a necessary accompaniment of a king. We certainly cannot deny their existence, and it is true that we never hear of any king who abolished this system as a result of his conversion into Buddhism; but their coexistence with Buddhist faith will not do any discredit to it. On the other hand, we hear the Buddha preaching about the mutual duties of husband and wife to a young man Sigāla, as we have already quoted. Now a husband is told to honor and respect his wife; to be courteous and faithful to her; to hand over authority to her; and to provide her with ornaments. We can be assured of conjugal harmony existing in such a union. How can a husband who is faithful in observing these duties be other than a monogamist? The wife is said to be the best friend that one has.[35] Satisfaction with a single wife is always mentioned as a praiseworthy moral virtue.[36] "Let him not share a wife with another,"[37] says the Buddha. Thus polygamy as well as polyandry is rejected as mean and vicious. In mentioning the virtuous married life of the ancient Brahmans, the Buddha says that they did not marry a woman belonging to another caste, that they did not buy a wife, and that they chose living together in mutual love after having come together.[38] In describing the blissful condition of family life he mentions waiting on mother and father, protecting child and wife, and a quiet calling.[39] In these descriptions we can recollect only the happy union of a single man and a single woman. Though the authorities are rather fragmentary and scanty, we believe that what the Buddha always had in his mind was strict monogamy.

Notes

1. A. A. Macdonell, *A History of Sanskrit Literature,* 36, 258.
2. Ga. III. 2; Ba. 11, 12.
3. A. i. 166.
4. A. iii. 224; iv. 35, 136–37.
5. E.g., A. iii. 90, 96.
6. A. iii. 4; iv. 361.
7. A. iv. 54.
8. Mat. xviii. 8; Mk. ix. 45.
9. A. iv. 54–5.
10. A. ii. 26; It. 35, 36.
11. S. v. 421.
12. The Pāli term expressing asceticism is Tapo, which means "burning" or "consuming by heat." It may therefore be understood to mean zeal, earnestness, feverish exertion, like burning fire; torture, torment, or mortification, as if it is caused by burning fire, or something which burns evils; and it is in this last sense that the Buddhist Tapo is generally interpreted. Asceticism, so far as Buddhism is concerned, is merely self-control. Paramatthajotikā, II. 1, p. 145.
13. A. ii. 26; It. 35, 36.
14. Sn. 289–82.
15. I.e., a life of celibacy or single life.
16. Sn. 395.
17. D. iii. 180–93.
18. SBB. iv. 181–82.
19. Sn. 262.
20. A. iv. 91–4.
21. A. ii. 57, 59.
22. Jāt. vi. 479–593; Jātakamālā, 51–67.
23. Jāt. v. 209–27; Jātakamālā, 80–87.
24. These quotations are all taken from the translation of the Jātakamālā, SBB. i, pp. 120–28.
25. Va. I. 24; Manu III. 13; but according to Manu III. 23, the Brahman may marry six wives, the Kṣatriya four, the Vaiśya and the Śūdra each one; and according to the Institutes of Vishṇu, XXIV. 1–4, the Brahman four, the Kṣatriya three, the Vaiśya two, and the Śūdra one.

26. SBE. xvi. 183 ff. note. Both the Brahman and the Chinese are under the necessity of obtaining male descendants. "A Brahman needs his wife in obtaining offspring"; A. iii. 228.
27. Jāt. i. 262; ii. 125, 206; iii. 13, 168.
28. Jāt. v. 425–27.
29. Jāt. i. 381; ii. 206.
30. Com. on Dh. i. 162 ff.
31. Jāt. i. 392; D. ii. 187.
32. Jāt. i. 262.
33. Jāt. ii. 125; iii. 168.
34. Jāt. iii. 40.
35. S. i. 37.
36. Sakadārena santuṭṭho.
37. Jāt. vi. 286–87.
38. Sn. 290.
39. Sn. 262.

The Relational Self

[8]

Appropriate Vulnerability: A Sexual Ethic for Singles

Karen Lebacqz

ALL OF US SPEND our first years single. Most of us spend our last years single. As adults, we are single by circumstance or by deliberate choice. Given these simple facts, it is surprising how little attention and how precious little support the churches have given to singleness (except for the monastic tradition, with its very particular demands and charisms). The scriptural witness on singleness is virtually ignored, despite the fact that Jesus never married and Paul preferred singleness. Throughout history, churches have simply assumed that marriage is the norm for Christians.

Single sexuality, when it is discussed at all, falls under the category of "premarital sex." Churches clearly expect that those who are single will get married and that those who have been married and are now single through divorce or widowhood will simply disappear into the closet until they marry again. The slogan recently adopted by the United Methodist Church might stand as a summary of the traditional Christian view of sexuality: "celibacy in singleness, fidelity in marriage."

A new ethic for single sexuality is needed, for the tradition that requires

SOURCE: From Karen Lebacqz, "Appropriate Vulnerability: A Sexual Ethic for Singles," *Christian Century*, May 6, 1987.

celibacy in singleness is not adequate. This situation does not mean that anything goes or that the church has nothing to offer by way of a positive ethic for single people. The task is to thread our way between two views of sexuality: the "Old Testament" or "thou shalt not" approach exemplified by much of church tradition, and the "New Testament" or "thou shalt" approach evident in much of our current culture.

The "Old Testament" or legalistic approach to single sexuality is well summed up in a delightful limerick by Joseph Fletcher (in *Moral Responsibility: Situation Ethics at Work* [Westminster, 1967], p. 88):

> There was a young lady name Wilde
> Who kept herself quite undefiled
>   by thinking of Jesus
>   and social diseases
> And the fear of having a child.

The "thou shalt not" ethic was characterized by fear—fear of pregnancy and venereal disease—and by a series of "don'ts": don't have sex, don't take pleasure in it (at least, not if you are a woman), and don't talk about it. As the limerick suggests, sexual involvement was regarded as "defiling." "Bad girls" and "good girls" were defined according to their willingness to be sexual or not. There was no discussion of the sexuality of divorced or widowed men and women, and gay men and lesbian women simply stayed in the closet.

With the advent of the so-called "sexual revolution" and the birth control pill, fear of pregnancy was gone. After the "thou shalt not" of Christian tradition, we encountered the "thou shalt" of contemporary culture. Here, "love" was all that counted. Women were "liberated" and virginity was redefined as "bad." Now people talked about sex all the time, with everyone. Far from being defiling, sexual involvement was regarded as mandatory. Sex was supposed to be pleasurable, and "how-to" manuals abounded. Finally, everyone knew how—but had forgotten why. In short, fear was replaced by pressure—pressure to engage in sex, to do it right, to enjoy it, and to let the world know how much and how well you were doing it.

The result is a clash often internalized into a "Catch 22." In the wonderfully perceptive comic strip *Cathy,* Cathy Guisewite captures the confusion of many. As the almost-but-not-quite-liberated "Cathy" is getting dressed to go out on a date, she reflects: "I'm wearing the 'heirloom lace' of my grandmother's generation . . . with the conscience of my mother's generation . . . coping with the morals of my generation. . . . No matter what I do tonight, I'm going to offend myself."

Neither the legalistic approach of earlier Christian morality nor the permissive approach of contemporary culture provides a satisfactory sexual ethic for singles. And without a good sexual ethic for singles, there cannot be a good sexual ethic for couples either.

Can we construct a positive, Christian sexual ethic for single people? I think so. Let us begin with Christian tradition, which affirms that sex is a gift from God. It is to be used within the boundaries of God's purposes. As part of God's creation, sex is good. Like all of creation, however, it is tainted by the fall, and therefore becomes distorted in human history. It needs redemption. Such redemption is achieved by using sexuality in accordance with God's purposes and through God's grace.

The two redeeming purposes of sexuality have always been understood as procreation and union. With these purposes in mind, Christian tradition maintained that marriage was the proper context for sex, since it was the proper context for raising children and for achieving a true union. Catholics have tended to stress procreation as the primary purpose while Protestants have stressed union, but both agree on the fundamental purposes of sexual expression.

This tradition has had enormous practical implications for singles. The tradition condemns all genital sexual expression outside marriage, on the assumption that it violates the procreative and unitive purposes of sexuality. Nongenital sexual expression is also suspect, because it is thought to lead inexorably to genital expression. Given such a view of sexuality, it is difficult for single people to claim their sexuality or to develop a positive ethic for that sexuality.

Standards within both Catholic and Protestant traditions have recently loosened, but there has been no fundamental challenge to this basic paradigm. Today, some Catholics and most Protestants accept "preceremonial" sex between responsible and committed adults. (Paul Ramsey argues that this is marriage in the moral sense. See his "On Taking Sexual Responsibility Seriously Enough," in Gibson Winter, ed., *Social Ethics* [Harper & Row, 1968], p. 45 ff.) Both traditions have moved toward affirming union as primary, while still upholding the importance of procreation. The meaning of the two fundamental purposes has been expanded by replacing the term "procreative" with "creative" and the term "unitive" with "integrative." (See Catholic Theological Society of America, *Human Sexuality: New Directions in American Catholic Thought* [Paulist Press, 1977], p. 86.) Thus, there is some acceptance of non-marital sexual expression, provided it is in the context of deep interpersonal commitment.

But however important such revisions may be, they do not really accept sexuality outside marriage. Single sexuality is still difficult to claim. Neither Catholic nor Protestant tradition provides a totally satisfactory explanation of why sexuality should be fully expressed only in marriage or in a "preceremonial" relationship that will eventuate in marriage. Both traditions still uphold marriage as the ideal, but give no satisfactory reasons for that ideal.

I accept part of the *method* that has led to the traditional interpretation, but wish to offer an additional insight into the nature of sexuality that might provide a fuller appreciation of the ethical context in which sexuality is expressed. I agree with the traditional understanding that sex is a gift from God to be used within the confines of God's purposes. However, I would add to the traditional purposes of union and procreation another God-given purpose of sexuality that I believe opens up a different understanding of human sexuality and of a sexual ethic for singles (as well as couples).

Sexuality has to do with vulnerability. Eros, the desire for another, the passion that accompanies the wish for sexual expression, makes one vulnerable. It creates possibilities for great joy but also for great suffering. To desire another, to feel passion, is to be vulnerable, capable of being wounded.

There is evidence in Scripture for this view of sexuality. Consider the Song of Songs (the "holy of holies"), which displays in glowing detail the immense passion and vulnerability of lovers. This is not married or "preceremonial" sexuality, nor are children the justification for the sexual encounter. It is passion pure and simple. And it is graphic sex. The Stoic fear of passion is not biblical. From the Song of Songs we can recover the importance of sexual desire as part of God's creation.

It is equally important to recover the creation stories in Genesis. These are so often the grounds for our interpretation of what God intends human sexuality to be. It is from these stories that we take the phrase "be fruitful and multiply" and turn it into a mandate for procreation. It is from these stories that we hear the deep call for union between sexual partners: "This at last is bone of my bones and flesh of my flesh . . . and the two shall become one flesh."

Without denying the importance of these phrases and their traditional interpretation, I would stress another passage—one that has been ignored but is crucial for completing the picture. The very last line in the creation story in Genesis 2 reads: "And the man and his wife were both naked, and they felt no shame" (Gen. 2:25). In ancient Hebrew, "nakedness" was a metaphor for vulnerability, and "feeling no shame" was a metaphor for appropriateness. (On this topic I am indebted to the work of Stephen Breck Reid of Pacific School of Religion.) We can therefore retranslate the passage as follows: "And the man and his wife experienced appropriate vulnerability." As the summation and closure of the creation story, the verse tells us that the net result of sexual encounter—the purpose of the creation of man and woman as sexual beings who unite with one another to form "one flesh"—is that there be appropriate vulnerability.

Vulnerability may be the precondition for both union and procreation: without a willingness to be vulnerable, to be exposed, to be wounded, there can be no union. To be "known," as Scripture so often describes the sexual encounter, is to be vulnerable, exposed, open.

Sexuality is therefore a form of vulnerability and is to be valued as such. Sex, eros, passion are antidotes to the human sin of wanting to be in control or to have power over another. "Appropriate vulnerability" may describe the basic intention for human life—which may be experienced in part through the gift of sexuality.

If this is so, then a new approach to sexual ethics follows. If humans are intended to have appropriate vulnerability, then the desire to have power or control over another is a hardening of the heart against vulnerability. When Adam and Eve chose power, they lost their appropriate vulnerability and were set against each other in their sexuality. Loss of vulnerability is paradigmatic of the fall. Jesus shows us the way to redemption by choosing not power but vulnerability and relationship.

The implications for a sexual ethic are profound. Any exercise of sexuality that violates appropriate vulnerability is wrong. This includes violations of the partner's vulnerability and violations of one's own vulnerability. Rape is wrong not only because it violates the vulnerability of the one raped, but also because the rapist guards his own power and refuses to be vulnerable.

Similarly, seduction is wrong, for the seducer guards her or his own vulnerability and uses sex as a weapon to gain power over another. Any sexual encounter that hurts another, so that she or he either guards against vulnerability in the future or is unduly vulnerable in the future, violates the "appropriate vulnerability" which is part of the true meaning and purpose of our God-given sexuality. Prostitution and promiscuity are also generally wrong. In each there tends to be either a shutting down of eros or a form of masochism in which the vulnerability is not equal and therefore not appropriate. Sex is not "just for fun" or for play or for physical release, for showing off, or for any of a host of other human emotions and expressions that are often attached to sexuality. It is for the appropriate expression of vulnerability, and to the extent that that expression is missing, the sexual expression is not proper.

Nothing in what has been said so far suggests that the only appropriate expressions of vulnerability are in marriage. Premarital and postmarital sexuality might express appropriate vulnerability. Gay and lesbian unions, long condemned by the church because of their failure to be procreative, might also express appropriate vulnerability. At the same time, some sexual expression within marriage might not be an appropriate expression of vulnerability—for example, spousal rape or unloving sexual encounter. We must beware of the deceptions through which we reduce or deny vulnerability in sexuality—both the "swinging singles" image and notions of sexual "duty" in marriage deny appropriate vulnerability.

But what about singleness specifically? Is there any need for a special sexual ethic for single people? Precisely because sexuality involves vulnerability, it needs protective structures, A few years ago, the United Church of Christ proposed a "principle of proportionality" for single sexuality. According to this principle, the level of sexual expression should be commensurate with the level of commitment in the relationship. While I have some problems with this principle, it does have the merit of suggesting that the vulnerability involved in sexual encounter requires protection. The more sexual involvement there is to be, the more there needs to be a context that protects and safeguards that vulnerability. As Stanley Hauerwas puts it, "genuine love is so capable of destruction that we need a structure to sustain us" *(A Community of Character: Toward a Constructive Christian Social Ethic* [University of Notre Dame Press, 1981], p. 181).

Traditionally, monogamous marriage has been understood to provide that needed context. Whatever the actual pitfalls and failures of marriage in practice, certainly in theory the commitment of a stable and monogamous marriage provides a supportive context for vulnerable expressions of the self. Marriage at its best ensures that the vulnerability of sexuality is private and that our failures remain protected in a mutually vulnerable and committed relationship.

Singleness carries no such protections. It is an unsafe environment for the expression of vulnerability. No covenant of fidelity ensures that my vulnerability will not lead to my being hurt, foolish, exposed, wounded. In short, in singleness the vulnerability that naturally accompanies sexuality is also coupled with a vulnerability of context. Thus, singleness is a politically more explosive arena for the expression of vulnerability in sex because it lacks the protections of marriage. It heightens vulnerability.

An adequate sexual ethic for singles must therefore attend to what is needed for appropriate vulnerability in sexuality. Attention must be paid to the structural elements in the particular situation that heighten or protect vulnerability. For example, a sexual ethic for singles might take one form for those who are very young and another for those who are older. The protections of age and experience may make it sensible to permit sexual encounter for those who are older and single, while restricting it for the very young. Unequal vulnerability is not appropriate. In a culture, therefore, where men tend to have more power than women and women are more vulnerable than men, great care will be needed to provide an adequate context for the expression of sexuality.

We need a theology of vulnerability. Until such a theology is forthcoming, we can only struggle toward a proper sexual ethic. Single people will have to explore their own vulnerability to find its appropriate expression in sexuality. Neither the "thou shalt not" of traditional prohibitions nor the "thou shalt" of contemporary culture provides an adequate sexual ethic for singles. "Celibacy in singleness" is not the answer. An appreciation of the link between sexuality and vulnerability is the precondition for an adequate sexual ethic.

[9]

Making Love as a Means of Grace: Women's Reflections

Rebecca Parker

SEXUAL INTIMACY CAN SERVE as a resource for healing and transformation in our lives. Through it, we can experience a restored sense of intrinsic joy in being, elemental goodness, personal power to affect and be affected, intimate connection with all of life, and creative potency. When it functions this way in our lives, making love is a means of grace.

This is not to say that sexuality is the only means of grace available to us or that it automatically solves life's problems. On the one hand, there are other important means of grace—the world itself, the arts, friendship, rituals, meaningful work—to name a few. On the other hand, there are times when sex is not a rewarding or appropriate part of our lives.

The goodness of sexuality can be marred, denied, or even destroyed by any number of means. The use of sex in an act of overpowering or coercing another, sexual abuse of children by adults, intimacy outside one's committed relationship for the sake of punishing one's committed partner, addiction to sexual intimacy as the exclusive source of one's sense of worth, sexual intimacy as a ritual reinforcement of domination and submission (as in traditional

---

SOURCE: From Rebecca Parker, "Making Love as a Means of Grace: Women's Reflections," *Open Hands* 3, no. 3 (winter 1988). Used by permission.

"Christian" marriage)—these are examples of ways in which sexuality's goodness is denied or destroyed.

At some stages in life sexual activity is by choice, circumstance, or age not part of our lives. Childhood and early youth at best have other joys. We may find we must decide to limit our sexual activity to protect ours or another's health. Or our sexual experiences may have been so traumatic that we find abstinence to be the most healing choice, itself a means of grace. Furthermore, even our best sexual encounters may be fraught with human foibles or failures—we are blocked by fears and past hurts, insecurities, embarrassment, lack of confidence in our ability to give or receive pleasure, physical limitations, illness.

Sex is not the be all and end all of life. Other pressing issues of life—both sorrows and joys—sometimes rightly take precedence in our attention. We discover we can live without sex, or without good sex. We don't need it in the same way we need food, sleep, and shelter. We need it more like the ways in which we need community, opportunities to learn, art, a vocation. But, within its proper perspective, when it is not being abused or used as a tool of abuse, when circumstances are right and it is one part of our lives offering its own measure of joy—sex can be a means of grace not only "within the bounds of marriage," or even "within the bounds of committed relationship," but in many forms.

"For this is the meaning of desire, that wanting leads us to the sacred," writes Susan Griffin.[1] She is one, among several women writers, whose self-described positive sexual experiences form a body of literature that illuminates how making love can be a means of grace. Since so much of the writing and visual material available to us reflects views of sexuality formed in the context of patriarchal, heterosexist culture, it is important to turn to voices and visions from "outside" the dominant culture. Here, as one way to expand on the theme of making love as a means of grace, are reflections on some of the writings of women—lesbian, bisexual, and heterosexual—who have described their most positive sexual experiences.

Audre Lorde in her article "Uses of the Erotic" speaks of erotic experience as "the nurturer is nursemaid of all our deepest knowledge."[2] In her understanding, erotically satisfying experiences are ones in which sensual pleasure and creative power merge in a holistic experience of joy. Sexual intimacy can be an erotic experience, so can "building a bookcase, writing a poem, examining an idea."[3] One characteristic of women's positive experiences of the erotic is a reluctance to isolate such experiences singularly to sexual activity. Rather, erotic joy, as known in the best experiences of sexual enjoyment, becomes the touchstone of life. Erotic joy reveals the ultimate possibilities of life, and through experiences of erotic joy the rest of life is judged. In Lorde's view, the heights of sexual happiness become the foundation for ethics, "once we begin to demand from ourselves and from our life-pursuits that they feel in accordance with that joy which we know ourselves to be capable of."[4]

She goes on to say,

> When we begin to live . . . in touch with the power of the erotic within ourselves, and allowing that power to inform and illuminate our actions upon the world around us, then we begin to be responsible to ourselves in the deepest sense . . . we begin to give up, of necessity being satisfied with suffering and self negation, and with the numbness which so often seems like their only alternative in our society. Our acts against oppression become integral with self-motivated and empowered from within.[5]

This view of the erotic as the inner source of knowledge about fullness of life contrasts dramatically with the traditional Christian view of eros as destructive energy that leads to disobedience to God. Rather, sexuality is viewed as a source of insight and guidance into the way of life—carnal knowledge is not the fall, it is the wellspring of right living, a resource for sustaining the vision of what is just and good, as well as a constant source of refreshment of the desire for abundant life.

How might sexuality function in this capacity as "nursemaid of all our deepest knowledge"?

For one thing, sexual intimacy can give us a profound sense of our communion with all of life, our connectedness in contrast to our loneliness or alienation. Theologian Carter Heyward sees loneliness as the creation of patriarchal culture and theology. We are saved when we are restored to a sense of intimacy with all of life.

> We are untouched and untouching until we realize our intimacy; until we know a fundamental bond between our innermost senses of who we are. Intimacy is the deepest quality of relation, the realization of ourselves, generically, as *humanity*—people with something in common—rather than as alien pieces of flesh and blood playing our separate parts in a absurd drama of loneliness.[6]

In lovemaking we can have a sense of boundaries falling away between the self and the world. Sexual ecstasy may involve a sense of feeling as if the whole of life were flowing through one's body, or as if one were smelling, touching, tasting, and breathing the universe, or as if the self and the world were indistinguishable from one another. This boundless communion through the breakdown of a sense of boundaried selfhood is the very thing about sexuality that theologians such as Augustine, Bonhoeffer, and Fuchs have found so offensive—to them the breakdown of a sense of limit signals abandonment of

God. But it may in fact be the restoration of a healed sense of intimate connection to life. A woman describes a sexual experience:

> New life was felt in her, newer even than the earth's gracious giving, a hopeful stirring deep in her center. They were part of all life around them, and all of the alive natural facets of the world glowed and glistened between them. The sweet smell of their bodies came up with a warm rush of breeze and they breathed deeply of themselves and the earth and were filled with an effortless joy.[7]

Susan Griffin's description of making love moves close to a form of mystical enlightenment:

> And if I let myself love, let myself touch, enter my own pleasure and longing, enter the body of another, the darkness, let the dark parts of my body speak, tongue into mouth, in the body's language, as I enter, a part of me I believed was real begins to die. I descend into matter, I know I am at the heart of myself, I cry out in ecstasy. For in love, we surrender our uniqueness and become world.[8]

Describing this experience of sexual happiness as a merging with all of life, women use language similar to the language of mystical ecstasy. Images of profound stillness, whirling dervish ecstasy, and brilliant light are employed to describe sexual pleasure or orgasm:

> She felt it come up from the base of her spine. It was as though a door opened and allowed all of life to surge through her. The spinning sensation rose up and flooded her whole body, pushing at the boundaries of who she thought she was . . . pressing . . . pressing . . . pressing. . . . Finally, unable to hold the energy back any longer, she let it explode through every cell in her body, cleansing her with light and pulsating out into the room.[9]

Or,

> I am filled with light inside you. I have no boundary, the light has extinguished my skin, I am perished in light, light filling you. shining through you.[10]

This altered state of consciousness described by women during experiences of sexual intimacy carries with it not only unbounded joy—an expansion of the self into a field of light—but also matchless peace and life-renewing power:

> She felt what she could only describe as her spirit spinning somewhere with his. It was as if they were both floating outside time and space in a peacefulness that didn't exist on earth.[11]

> I know I am entranced at those times, gone into another dimension . . . the silver rays connecting between us fill me with strength, confidence, affirmation,

> joy, and some esthetic quality of beauty that is like another way of seeing, like being in another place.[12]

> And then we are free, floating outside our contours in emptiness. A stillness, a perfect stasis opens beneath us. Peace.[13]

In contrast to this empowering, intense sense of immediate joy, mystical connection, and communion that is refreshing and healing, positive sexual experience is also described by women as an experience that heightens a sense of personal presence and power, and initiates one into a clearer sense of strong selfhood. As a writer of feminist spirituality, Starhawk emphasizes this aspect of sexual intimacy:

> in sex we merge, give way, become one with another, allow ourselves to be caressed, pleasured, enfolded, allow our sense of separation to dissolve. But in sex we also feel our impact on another, we see our own faces reflected in another's eyes, feel ourselves confirmed, and sense our power, as separate human beings, to make another feel.[14]

We as human beings feel ourselves felt. We know we are here—not invisible. We feel our power to give joy to another. We know our presence is a blessing to the world. We feel the joy the presence of a lover gives us. We know soul to be the power of presence.

> Let me feel, more intensely, your full power and presence. Bathe me with the pleasure of your company. The mind's delight, my heart's delight. You, my soul met love, my bone's history, my eyes remembrance, my ear's companion, my tongue's perfect dialog partner. The life in you, so radiant, so deep, so there. You entice, excite, overwhelm me with joy and happiness, apple of my eye, ecstatic friend.[15]

Sexual intimacy imparts to us a knowledge of ourselves as a powerful presence, and love as enjoyment of the presence of power of another. As such, making love is a means of moving beyond a sense of ourself as passive. It saves us from the sin of feeling that we are helpless and empty, which leads to the horrible despair of believing we have no being. Theologian Daniel Day Williams says, "Inauthentic existence is the fall from inner self-determination. . . . Sin is . . . unbelief in ourselves."[16]

But making love can strengthen our sense of acting and being acted upon, restoring us to the balance that is the foundation of all ethical responsibility. Beverly Harrison asserts that personal well-being and healthy community depend on this kind of knowledge of ourselves. She says: "All of us . . . literally call forth each other in relationship, and our power of being and capacity to act emerges through our sensuous interaction in relation."[17]

Daniel Day Williams expresses a similar sensibility:

> The power to act is a condition of love: but it follows that the capacity to be acted upon, to be moved by another, is also required; for to act in love is to respond, and to have one's actions shaped by the other.[18]

Sexual intimacy, at its best, teaches us this truth about ourselves—that joy is grounded in relational power. Thus it frees us from the sin of pride (wanting to be completely in control) and the terror of despair (feeling ourselves to be completely powerless).

Finally, it should be observed that women describe a strong connection between sexual pleasure and creativity. This is in dramatic contrast to the predominant public image of sexual expression as a form of violence and destruction. Though in people's experience intimacy may be closely tied to love of life and the desire to bring life into being, public images often associate sex with destruction of life: the penis is spoken of as a weapon and sometimes shown used as one. Language about sexual intimacy is a language of war: people are conquered. Images that present sex as a joyful, creative act are largely absent from the public sphere.

The association of sexual joy and creativity is felt by some in specific connection with their power to give birth. A woman describes a sexual fantasy in which she simultaneously gives birth and is made love to by her partner.[19] A pregnant woman exclaims, "I feel so sexy—so, I don't know, ripe, fertile, full of energy, alive."[20] Another woman describes the birth of her daughter as an experience in which she felt overwhelmed with a mystical sense of connectedness to all of life, a whole body feeling of insight and ecstasy.[21] But the deeply felt tie between sexuality and creativity is not confined in women's experience to pregnancy and childbirth. Other experiences in which personal strength is harnessed to bring forth life are felt to have erotic overtones. Wherever passion, energy, joy, personal power, and creativity emerge and converge, the experience can be felt as erotic.

Creativity in every aspect of living requires an inner sense of "power to bring forth." One essence of sexual energy in human beings is this sense of "power to bring forth." Starhawk defines the erotic as "power from within."[22] This power is carried within the body of every human being. Our fundamental bodily experience is that sexuality is bonded to the power of life. Sexual energy is life-giving energy. We know that giving life to ourselves, to another, to a work of imagination or research, or a political cause—all forms of giving life to life—are bonded to sexual energy. Our sexual energy expands throughout life the more we choose to create out of the power within us. Our sexual body tells us we have the power to bring forth life. In this way, again, carnal knowledge saves us rather than damns us. It undergirds a sense of ourselves as people with the power, right, and responsibility to bring forth life. As a means of grace, it invites us to center our lives on the joy of creating.

Audre Lorde writes:

> In touch with the erotic, I become less willing to accept powerlessness, or those other supplied states of being which are not native to me, such as resignation, despair, self-effacement, depression, self denial.[23]

The zest for passionate, exuberant, creative living can be tasted and seen and thus restored and sustained through our sexual pleasure.

In sum, women's self-described positive sexual experiences disclose four sensibilities about our deepest being. The self we come to know in our best sexual encounters is first, a self that is intimately connected with all of life. It is not a discreet, self-contained entity, but a center of feeling flooded by the whole world. Secondly, the self we come to know has power to deeply affect another. It has the power of presence. It does not leave the world undisturbed but can activate profound pleasure in another by its very being. Thirdly, the self we come to know has the power to bring forth life. It is creative, originative, nurturing, and sustaining. Finally, the self we come to know takes joy in sheer being, in its own life and in the life it senses all around. Being itself is joyful, and being itself is a complex integration of breadth, created by receptivity to a vast field, and intensity, created by the power to move another and to bring forth life. In sexual intimacy we can experience ourselves as having power—the power of receptivity and action combined, the power of feeling and doing, being moved and moving. We feel the force of our soul, the reality of our powerful presence in the world, and we feel it with joy.

Sexual knowledge of this nature, knowledge bequeathed to us through our bodies, is gracious and saving knowledge. It releases us from a false sense of separation and alienation from the world. It baptizes us into the whole creation and tells us we are good. It explains our freedom to us—our power to bring forth life from within our very being—and gives us a standard for judging what is worthwhile. It restores to us a sense of the balance of power—we are neither totally passive nor totally in control. And in some moments, making love gives us a sense of complete peace through the experience of immediate joy.

Making love is not the be-all and the end-all of life. It rarely approaches perfection and isn't the most important thing we do. But it is far from the root of all sin. On the contrary, it can be life's most delightful means of grace. As such, it should be held in honor among all people, and no church should legislate against its potential for undergirding all that is right, good, and joyful in our lives.

Notes

1. Susan Griffin, *Pornography and Silence* (New York: Harper and Row, Colophon Books, 1982), 262.
2. Audre Lorde, *Sister Outsider* (Trumansburg, N.Y.: The Crossing Press, 1984), 56.
3. Ibid.
4. Ibid.
5. Ibid., 58.
6. Carter Heyward, *The Redemption of God* (Lanham, Md.: University Press of America, 1982), xviii.
7. Suzanne Miller, in Lonnie Barbach, ed., *Erotic Interludes: Tales Told by Women* (Garden City, N.Y.: Doubleday, 1986), 173.
8. Griffin, *Pornography and Silence,* 260.
9. Udana Power, in Barbach, *Erotic Interludes,* 21.
10. Susan Griffin, *Made from This Earth* (New York: Harper and Row, 1982), 226.
11. Power, in Barbach, *Erotic Interludes,* 29.
12. Judy Grahn, *Another Mother Tongue* (Boston: Beacon Press, 1984), 240.
13. Sandy Boucher, in Barbach, *Erotic Interludes,* 215.
14. Starhawk, *Dreaming the Dark* (Boston: Beacon Press, 1982), 138.
15. From a woman's personal journal.
16. Daniel Day Williams, *The Spirit and the Forms of Love* (New York: Harper and Row, 1968), 150–51.
17. Beverly Harrison, "Human Sexuality and Mutuality," in Judith L. Weidman (San Francisco: Harper and Row, 1984), 148–49.
18. Williams, *The Spirit and the Forms of Love,* 117.
19. Power, in Barbach, *Erotic Interludes,* 20–21.
20. Personal conversation, fall 1986.
21. Mary Brown, sermon, Wallingford United Methodist Church, Seattle.
22. Starhawk, *Dreaming the Dark,* 138.
23. Lorde, *Sister Outsider,* 58.

[10]

Sexuality and Marital Relations

Rachel Biale

Sexuality poses a great problem for all traditional societies. On the one hand the sexual drive is vital for the creation of a family and a social structure. On the other hand it poses a great danger to those very institutions. Sexual temptation and sexual incompatibility are the strongest forces which threaten family stability and marital harmony. Adultery, prostitution, incest, and homosexuality are problems which trouble every culture and society, as is the possibility of the dissolution of marriage through divorce or abandonment.

All Western religious traditions walk a tightrope between legitimation of sexuality and ascetic denial of the libidinal drive. The rabbis recognized this very tension in statements such as "Let us be thankful to our forefathers, for if they had not sinned we would not have come into this world" (Avodah Zarah 5a). Judaism achieves its balance primarily through the legitimation of sexuality in the confines of marriage, which is the primary instrument for harnessing the "constructive" side of the sexual impulse and restraining its "anarchic" aspect. Within marriage the Halakhah permits a fairly wide range of legitimate sexual expression, but it also regiments rather tightly the frequency and appropriate times for sexual activity through the laws of *niddah,* which proscribe sexual contact during and following menstruation, and through the laws of *onah,* which prescribe "the times for performing the conjugal duty."[1]

The laws that regulate sexuality are primarily addressed to men. Men are commanded to marry, to procreate, and to perform their conjugal duties at regular times. The main commandment that applies to women is observing the laws of *niddah,* the laws of the menstruant. Other than the general obligation not to consistently and unreasonably refuse sexual relations with the husband, women do not really have "sexual obligations" in marriage. They are not commanded to marry, and they are explicitly exempted from the duty of procreation. Conjugal relations are an obligation of a husband toward a wife, not vice versa.

The imbalance in sexual obligations between men and women is due to the differentiated view of male and female sexuality in the rabbinical sources. Male sexuality is seen by the rabbis as the greater threat to familial and social structures. Male sexuality is active and egocentric, and always in danger of "running wild." It must be restrained through the controls of marriage, procreative duties, responsibility toward the woman, and a powerful taboo on male homosexuality and masturbation.[2]

Female sexuality is seen very differently. This reflects as much social convention as it does the fact that our sources do not relay women's feelings and experiences firsthand, but men's perceptions and conjectures regarding women's sexuality. Women are portrayed as sexually introverted and passive, in contradistinction to the male sexual impulse which the rabbis, as men, experience as active and extroverted: "A man's sexual impulse is out in the open," and Rashi adds: "his erection stands out and he embarrasses himself in front of his fellows" (Ketubot 64b and Rashi's commentary). The notion is that though her sexuality is hidden, a woman's sexual impulse is as powerful as a man's obvious eroticism; perhaps her passion is even greater than that of a man.[3]

The paradox of women's intense sexual desires and their sexual passivity, whether innate or socially imposed, is seen by the rabbis as a great hardship. Indeed that, according to the rabbis, is "the curse of Eve," a curse on the first woman and all women after her:

> And to the woman He said,
> "I will make most severe
> Your pangs in childbearing;
> In pain shall you bear children.
> Yet your desire shall be for your husband
> And he shall rule over you." (Gen. 3:16)

The first part of Eve's punishment may be parallel to the first part of the curse of Adam: he is punished in his labor of tilling the soil, and she in hers, the labor of childbirth.[4] If indeed the eating of the forbidden fruit from the tree of knowledge involved some kind of sexual awakening, symbolized in the Genesis account (Gen. 2:25; 3:7) by the new shame over nakedness, then this is punishment in kind (*middah ke-neged middah*). The transgression involved the discovery of sexuality and the punishment makes its consequences painful.

The second part of the curse on Eve is not as plain, yet it is that part which we need to understand in order to study the place of female sexuality in and of itself, divorced from procreation. What is the precise nature of *teshukatekh,* "your desire"? Does the punishment consist in a general condition of the man's lording over the woman, or is this dominance directly related to the woman's desire?

The medieval biblical commentators varied in their interpretations of this second part of Eve's curse. The commentaries of Rashi, Ibn Ezra, and Nachmanides (Ramban) illustrate the variety in interpretation.

> "And your desire shall be for your husband"—[desire] for sexual intercourse. Yet you will not have the boldness to demand it [from him] with your own words. Rather "he shall lord over you"—all will come from him and not from you. (Rashi on Gen. 3:16)

Rashi defines desire very specifically as the desire for lovemaking (*tashmish*) and interprets the dominance of the man as specifically sexual as well. The woman's punishment is that she is unable to act to fulfill her desire; she does not have the boldness to initiate sex or ask for it. Her husband "shall lord over" her in matters of sex, "all will come from him"—all initiative will come from him, not from the woman.

Ibn Ezra interprets this part of the curse differently:

> "*Teshukatekh*"—your obedience. And the meaning is: you will obey whatever he commands you, for you are in his domain to do what he wishes. (Ibn Ezra on Gen. 3:16)

Ibn Ezra goes against the plain meaning of the word *teshukah,* interpreting the phrase perhaps as an abbreviated one meaning "your desire shall be subject to your husband's desire." However he arrived at it, Ibn Ezra understood the husband's dominance to be general, including all aspects of family life. In the total subjugation to the husband's will lies the woman's curse.

Nachmanides proposes another interpretation:

> The correct interpretation appears to me to be that He punished her in that her desire for her husband would be exceedingly great [so] that she would not be

> deterred by the pain of pregnancy or because he keeps her as a maidservant. Now, it is not customary for a servant to desire to acquire a master over himself, rather his desire is to flee from him. Thus her punishment is measure for measure [*middah ke-neged middah*]; she gave to her husband and he ate at her command and He punished her that she should no longer command him, but instead he should command her, entirely at his will. (Nachmanides [Ramban] on Gen. 3:16)

Nachmanides interprets desire, *teshukah,* like Rashi, as sexual desire, "exceedingly great" desire. But unlike Rashi, who sees the punishment in the man's monopoly over initiation of sex, Nachmanides sees the punishment in the woman's general subordination to the man. It is precisely because her sexual desire for the man is so great, in Nachmanides' view, that the woman accepts her status as a servant, contrary to human nature which drives a servant to flee his master rather than seek him. Nachmanides' view fuses the interpretation of "desire" as specifically sexual desire with the understanding of the man's dominance as a reference to all aspects of husband-wife relations. Nachmanides also links the first part of the curse, the pain of childbearing, with the sexual desire addressed in the second part. Like her husband's domination, the pain of labor is a curse which the woman accepts as a consequence of her sexual desire for her husband.

Both Rashi and Nachmanides and perhaps even Ibn Ezra (though he is not explicit) see the woman as caught in a bind between sexuality and subservience. Whether because she cannot initiate sex, or because she "pays" for her sexual desire with total obedience, the woman's curse is bound up with her sexuality. What are the legal implications of this curse?

> Rabbi Joshua ben Levi further stated: It is a man's duty to pay a visit to his wife when he starts on a journey; for it is said; "And you shall know that your tent is in peace" (Job 5:24). Is this deduced from here? Surely it is deduced from the following: "And your desire shall be to your husband" teaches that a woman yearns for her husband when he sets out on a journey. (Yevamot 62b)

It is a man's obligation to have sexual relations with his wife (the euphemistic "pay a visit") before departing from his house. Interestingly, the preferred proof-text for this principle is not the verse "And you shall know that your tent is in peace," which could easily be construed as a command, but the passage "And your desire shall be for your husband," which is neither an imperative nor addressed to a man. There is a point behind this preference for the text which appears less appropriate for deducing a commandment. The point is to link the woman's curse, her desire for sex and inability to initiate it, with the man's legal obligation to "pay her a visit," that is, to initiate sex at a time when he knows she desires it. It appears that the man's duty is to compensate for the woman's curse by initiating sex: this is the duty called *onah.* The curse which brings inhibition of sexual impulse is not to be perpetuated by the husband; rather, it is his duty to counteract it by initiating sex to meet the desires of his wife.

The curse on Eve may be understood as a symbolic formulation of the rabbis' view of female sexuality. Women were thought to have powerful sexual drives but to be temperamentally inhibited in initiating sex. Men do not share this inhibition and thus are commanded to initiate sex on their wives' behalf. Genesis 3:16, the curse on Eve, furnishes the reason for the commandment of *onah* but there is also a biblical legal source for this duty.

> [7]When a man sells his daughter as a slave, she shall not be freed as male slaves are. [8]If she proves to be displeasing to her master, who designated her for himself, he must let her be redeemed; he shall not have the right to sell her to outsiders, since he broke faith with her. [9]And if he designated her for his son, he shall deal with her as is the practice with free maidens. [10]If he marries another, he must not withhold from this one her food, her clothing, or her conjugal rights. [11]If he fails her in these three ways, she shall be freed, without payment. (Ex. 21:7–11)

In the context of a discussion of the laws pertaining to Israelite slaves (Ex. 21:1–11), this passage delineates the status and rights of a female sold into slavery. From this passage which gives the female slave three basic rights—food, clothing, and conjugal rights—the minimal rights of a free married woman are deduced. If these are the rights of a bondwoman, certainly they are also the rights of a free woman. The term for conjugal rights is *onatah* (i.e., her *onah*). The biblical text assumes that the meaning of *onah* is self-evident since it is not elaborated. Yet to the rabbis it is not self-evident, and they furnish several explanations of its meaning and origin.

The term *onah* is given two etymologies in the Talmud. The first one derives the term from the word meaning "season" or "period." Thus *onah* defines the frequency of sexual relations that a woman is entitled to by law. The second etymology derives the meaning of *onah* from the word *innui,* which means "causing pain or suffering." In this interpretation, denying a married woman her sexual rights would cause her pain and suffering. The requirement of *onah* protects the woman from the pain of sexual deprivation. While the first etymology is probably the correct one philologically, the laws of *onah* reflect both elements: they define the required frequency of sex and direct the husband to ensure that his wife gains pleasure from it.[5]

Another talmudic passage goes beyond the simple explanation and etymology of *onah.* In a midrashic interpretation of the three terms describing the bondwoman's basic rights—"*she'erah, kesutah ve-onatah*"—Ketubot 47b–48a attempts to expand our understanding of the qualitative nature of a husband's obligations toward his wife:

> Said Raba: The following Tanna is of the opinion that maintenance [*she'erah*] is a Pentateuchal duty. For it was taught: *She'erah* refers to maintenance for so it is said in Scripture: "Who also eat the *she'er* of my people." Her raiment [*kesutah*] is to be understood according to its ordinary meaning [i.e., clothing]. *Onatah* refers to the time for conjugal duty prescribed in the Torah, for so it is said in Scripture: "If thou shalt afflict [*te'aneh*] my daughters."
>
> Rabbi Eleazar said: "*She'erah*" refers to the prescribed times for conjugal duty for so it is said in Scripture: "None of you shall approach any that is his near of kin [*she'er besaro*] to uncover their nakedness." "Her raiment" [is to be taken] according to its literal meaning. "*Onatah*" refers to maintenance, for so it is said in Scripture: "And he afflicted [*innah*] thee and suffered thee to hunger."
>
> Rabbi Eliezer ben Jacob interpreted: [The expressions] "*She'erah kesutah*" [imply]: Provide her with raiment according to her age, viz. that a man shall not provide his old wife [with the raiment] of a young one, nor his young wife with that of an old one. [The expressions] "*kesutah veonatah*" [imply]: Provide her with raiment according to the season of the year, viz. that he shall not give her new raiment in summer nor worn-out raiment in the winter. Rabbi Joseph taught: "Her flesh" [*she'erah*] implies close bodily contact, viz. that he must not treat her in the manner of the Persians who perform their conjugal duties in their clothes. This provides support for [the ruling of] Rav Huna who laid down that a husband who said: "I will not [perform conjugal duties] unless she wears her clothes and I mine," must divorce her and also give her her *ketubah* payment. (Ketubot 47b–48a)

This passage brings as many possible interpretations of the three key words, *she'erah, kesutah,* and *onatah,* as one might imagine. Briefly summarized the variants are:

1. The Tanna (not identified by name): *she'erah* = her food; *kesutah* = her clothing; *onatah* = her conjugal rights
2. Rabbi Eleazar: *she'erah* = her conjugal rights; *kesutah* = her clothing (literal meaning); *onatah* = maintenance (i.e., food)
3. Rabbi Eliezer ben Jacob: *she'erah kesutah* (the two words form one idiom) = clothing appropriate to her age; *kesutah ve-onatah* (the two words form one idiom) = clothing appropriate to the season
4. Rabbi Joseph: *she'erah* = her flesh: it refers to physical contact during the performance of the duty of sexual relations (*onah*).

Rabbi Eliezer ben Jacob's interpretation of the three words as two idioms indicating clothes appropriate to the age and season is not intended to replace the mainstream interpretation of the three words as food, clothing, and conjugal rights. Rather, it seeks to expand our understanding of one of the rights by using the other words as if they were a commentary on the middle word, *kesutah.* The point of this expansion of the word for clothing is to indicate that the essential right for clothing includes the assumption that they will be provided in appropriate ways to meet the wife's needs as they vary with age and season.

The same principle of interpretation is used to expand the meaning of *onah,* conjugal rights. Rabbi Joseph applies the word *she'er,* which can mean meat or flesh, to the word *onah.* "Her flesh [*she'erah*] implies bodily contact" during intercourse. The word *she'er* sheds light on the quality of the conjugal rights assured in *onah;* conjugal rights are to be performed in intimate bodily contact. A man may neither perform his conjugal duties in his clothes nor require his wife to be clothed. If he demands that "she wear her clothes and I mine," he must divorce her for he has violated his obligations in marriage.

Nachmanides in his commentary on Exodus 21:11 goes even further, arguing that all three terms refer to conjugal rights, and leaving the rights of a woman to food and clothes to be based on a rabbinic ruling, not on this biblical passage:

> So therefore, *she'erah* [means] bodily closeness, and *kesutah* [means] her bed covers as it says "It is the only covering he has, what else would he sleep in?" (Ex. 22:26); *onah* [means] that he come to her at the time for lovemaking . . . , we shall interpret "He shall not diminish her flesh [*she'erah*]" to mean: he shall not deprive her of her flesh, that is to say, the flesh which is appropriate for her which is the flesh of her husband who with her becomes one flesh (Gen. 2:24). And the point of the passage in Exodus is that if he takes another he shall not diminish the closeness of flesh, the covers of her bed and her times of lovemaking following the "rule for daughters." And the reason is lest the other one be sitting on an opulent bed where they "become one flesh" while with the first one he sleeps as if she were a concubine, by chance and on the ground like a man coming to a prostitute. And therefore the scripture prevents him from this and thus the rabbis said "*she'erah* implies close bodily contact, viz. that he must not treat her in the manner of the Persians who perform their conjugal duties in their clothes." And this is the correct interpretation because usually the scriptures refer to intercourse [*mishkav*] in euphemisms and brevity, and therefore discuss these matters with allusions: *she'erah kesutah ve-onatah* refer to the three matters pertinent to the union of a man with his wife. And let this be the clear basis for the Halakhah and let the woman's food and clothing be based on the rabbis' rulings. (Nachmanides [Ramban] on Ex. 21:11)

According to Nachmanides Exodus 21:11 establishes the quality of *onah,* mandating physical intimacy, appropriate surroundings, and regularity.

But before we examine further the quality of the sexual relations which a woman is entitled to by the virtue of her *onah,* let us consider the basic mishnaic definition of *onah* which uses quantity as a defining yardstick: The passage which prescribes the frequency of *onah* appears in the context of a discussion of exceptions to the rule regarding *onah:*

> Mishnah: If a man forbade himself by vow to have intercourse with his wife Bet Shammai ruled: [she must consent to the deprivation for] two weeks; Bet Hillel ruled: [only for] one week.
>
> Students may go away to study the Torah, without the permission [of their wives for a period of] thirty days; laborers [only for] one week.
>
> The times for conjugal duty prescribed in the Torah are: for men of independence, every day; for laborers, twice a week; for ass-drivers, once a week; for camel-drivers, once in thirty days; for sailors, once in six months. These are the rulings of Rabbi Eliezer.

There is a disagreement between Bet Hillel and Bet Shammai concerning the maximum period of deprivation from *onah* that a woman may be subject to; Bet Hillel hold one week, Bet Shammai two. Though Bet Hillel and Bet Shammai differ in the length of time they allow for abstention and in their reasoning, the actual practical difference which results is not great. Both allow only a very limited period of abstention to fulfill a vow.

One acceptable reason for depriving a wife of her conjugal rights is the study of Torah. Students who are professionally dedicated to the study of the law may depart without their wives' permission, thus depriving them of their rights of *onah.* This passage states that they may only depart for the duration of one month, but another tradition holds that they may go away for up to three years. Though the latter tradition is accepted as Halakhah there is strong opposition to it. The opposing sentiments are recorded in statements and anecdotes which follow our passage in Ketubot (61b–62b) telling about students who went away to study for long periods with tragic consequences, such as their death or their wives' "losing the powers of procreation."[6] Laborers may only go away for one week to study because for them study of the law is not a full-fledged professional commitment, but only a short-term involvement in performing the *mitzvah* of Torah study. Subsequent discussion in the Talmud develops this principle further, ruling that a man may go away for a brief period, in other circumstances where the purpose of his journey is performing a *mitzvah.*

Now that we have understood the exceptions, let us return to the general rule regarding *onah.* The Mishnah provides a basic timetable for the frequency of sexual relations. This timetable is adjusted according to a man's profession so that he should be able to practice his trade and also fulfill his marital obligation. Thus a camel driver who must travel in caravans for long periods is only obligated to perform the duty of *onah* once every month and sailors only once every six months. An ass driver who goes on shorter trips from town to town must return home once a week to perform his duty of *onah.* Laborers are obligated to perform their duty twice a week: their work is taxing and might require them to stay away from home a few nights every week. The *Shulhan Arukh* actually makes a clear distinction between laborers who work in their own town and perform their duty of *onah* twice a week, and those who work in a different town and are obligated in the *mitzvah* only once a week (Orah Hayyim 240:1). Students of the Torah are obligated to perform their marital duty once a week, and the preference is for performing it on Friday night. Who are the *tayalim* (men of independent means) whose duty of *onah* is every night? "Said Rabin: they are like the decadent residents of Eretz Yisrael who wallow in food and drink and are therefore robust and have great strength for sex" (Ketubot 62b).

The fact that the duty of *onah* is linked to a man's profession reflects two assumptions in the rabbinical worldview. First, it reflects the great importance of the duty of *onah,* for it is necessary to restrict it in order to permit a man to practice his trade. The "ideal situation" from the woman's point of view is one where the man is not hampered by the demands of work, and performs the duty of *onah* every day. The second assumption is that a man is expected to have one trade all his life. In fact a man is defined by his trade. When a woman chooses to marry a camel driver she knowingly chooses not only a certain class and defined socioeconomic expectations, but also a certain kind of sex life.

In addition to the regular times prescribed by Rabbi Eliezer for *onah,* the Talmud adds other times when a man should initiate sexual relations with his wife: before he goes away, since "a woman yearns for her husband when he sets out on a journey" (Yevamot 62b), and "near her menstruation" (Pesahim 72b), because the woman knows that she is about to enter a period of abstention and thus desires sex.[7] The importance of the woman's desire is recognized in the requirement of keeping the duty of *onah* during pregnancy as well. Since during pregnancy there is no possibility of further procreation, and a man may also assume that the normal sexual relationship is subdued, the Halakhah prescribes the duty of *onah* with a pregnant wife as well. As against later popular notions which held sex to be detrimental especially toward the end of the pregnancy, the rabbis held that "during the first three months intercourse is hard on the mother and on the fetus, during the middle three it is hard on the mother and good for the fetus, and during the last three, good for both" (Niddah 31a).

Given the precise definition of the "times of *onah*" in the Mishnah and the Talmud, a fundamental question arises: are these times intended as a maximum or a minimum? In other words, is, let us say, twice a week for laborers the most often one may have sex and is more frequent intercourse thus a violation of the law? Or, conversely, is twice a week the minimum that a laborer owes his wife, but if both she and he wish they may have sex more often?

The Talmud already reflects a tension between these two possible interpretations of the prescriptions of *onah.* On the one hand there is the attitude exemplified by Raba's statement "it is a man's duty to please his wife with a good deed" beyond the requirements of "the periodic visit" (Pesahim 72b). In other words the times prescribed in the Mishnah set the minimal obligation and going beyond the "prescribed times" when the wife indicates her desire is an integral part of the *mitzvah* of *onah.* On the other hand a more ascetic attitude crops up in a pronouncement like "let not students of the law [scholars] be with their wives too frequently like roosters" (Berakhot 22a). This attitude tends to view the times prescribed in the Mishnah as a maximum: not as a binding legal limitation, but rather as a statement of what is decent and proper for men of spiritual and moral worth.

The conflict between the latter, ascetic view, and the former, more permissive view of sexuality intended for the woman's pleasure continues and sharpens in the post-talmudic development of the Halakhah. The most elaborate and forceful defense of the view of *onah* as a minimalist standard is Abraham ben David's work, *Ba'alei Ha-Nefesh.* Abraham ben David of Posquieres (Rabad) lived in France in the twelfth century and composed *Ba'alei Ha-Nefesh* as a guide for the pious life. He devoted a whole chapter, "Sha'ar Ha-Kedushah," to sexuality and marital conduct.

> The *onot* [plural of *onah*] set by the rabbis were determined in general, as they estimated the woman's notion of what she would be satisfied with according to her husband's ability and pleasure. If, however, he sees that she is asking him for that act and that she has a need for it, seeing this as she attracts his attention by adorning herself in front of him, then he is commanded to please her in this matter of *mitzvah.* (Abraham ben David, *Ba'alei Ha-Nefesh,* "Sha'ar Ha-Kedushah")

According to Rabad, the times for *onah* prescribed in the Talmud are only a general estimate; they are to be construed as the minimum standard for frequency of sex, the rabbis' guess of what women wanted. The obligation of *onah* includes the requirement that the husband be responsive to his wife when she tries to hint at her desire. Rabad's assumption that she would do that indirectly "by adorning herself in front of him" parallels what we have seen Rashi argue in his interpretation of the curse of Eve: when she desires sex a woman hints at it, not possessing the boldness to ask for it directly. It is the husband's obligation to counter her timidity by acting "to please her in this matter of *mitzvah*" when she signals her inclination.

As against the attitude of Rabad, both the *Tur* and the *Shulhan Arukh* open the discussion of the conduct of sexual relations with a similar statement: "If a man is married, let him not be with his wife too frequently, but only at the frequency prescribed according to the law of *onah* in the Torah" (*Shulhan Arukh,* Orah Hayyim 240:1; and *Tur,* Orah Hayyim 240 and Even Ha-Ezer 25). Karo, however, does instruct a man to be attuned to his wife's sexual needs during other times: on the night of the immersion in the *mikveh,* before departing for a journey (unless the journey is for performing a *mitzvah,* in which case the man is exempt!), and "when his wife is nursing and he recognizes that she is trying to seduce him and attract him by adorning herself in front of him so that he should pay attention to her." The nursing mother can easily be ignored by her husband, similarly to the pregnant woman. Because of her involvement with her infant as well as, perhaps, the effect of the postpartum recovery, a husband may assume that his wife is "asexual" during this period. Karo mandates that if she indicates her sexual interest the husband must be sensitive and responsive.

If we examine the representative opinions of Rabad and Karo on the prescriptions on *onah* we will find that the conflict between "minimum" and "maximum" is perhaps not as sharp and simple as it seems. Both Rabad and Karo emphasize the husband's obligation to be attuned and responsive to his wife's needs. They seem to have similar views of female sexual needs as legitimate, present throughout the life cycle, and in need of protection. Both start with the same assumption, that the laws of *onah* come to correct the natural imbalance between men and women in sexual temperament and power. The difference between the two lies in their view of male sexuality. Both of them regard the male sexual impulse as one which would be better controlled and restrained than given full satisfaction. However, Rabad so emphasizes the need to respond to the woman's sexual desires that he is willing to "ignore" the somewhat negative "side effect" of increased sexual activity for the man. Karo focuses more of his concern on restraining the man's sexual desire and fulfillment. Thus in order not to encourage scholars to spend too much time with their wives "like roosters," he defines the prescriptions of *onah* as a maximum. He seems to assume that going beyond these prescriptions would generally be a way of satisfying the man's (illegitimate) needs, while as a rule the woman is satisfied with the prescribed frequency.

We find the same concern for women's sexual needs in the writings of a contemporary halakhic authority, Moshe Feinstein. Feinstein holds that the sexual needs of contemporary women are greater than those of their predecessors because the general environment is more imbued with sexuality and temptation. Therefore he rules that the times prescribed by the Halakhah for scholars should be increased in his own day in order to meet the increased needs of contemporary women. He does not interpret the Mishnah's prescription as a strict maximum, and thus does not see great halakhic problems in increasing it. Rather, he sees it historically, as a reasonable estimate for its own time of what is proper between husband and wife:

> As to the innovation of recent authorities in our day, that students of the law [scholars] should perform the duty of *onah* twice a week: I too support this view. Furthermore, let me add that the main point of the *mitzvah* of *onah* is [suiting it to] what the woman desires and wants. Because of the promiscuity of this generation and the jealousy for another woman's lot a woman feels desire and erotic passion more often than once a week. Therefore, her husband is obligated in this respect because of the very essence of the duty of *onah*. Even if the husband does not perceive his wife's desire, one should attribute that to her embarrassment and her modesty, since it is because of these that the rabbis legislated set times. Therefore, the later authorities have ruled correctly that one should counsel and even obligate scholars to perform *onah* twice a week. (Moshe Feinstein, *Responsa Iggrot Moshe,* Even Ha-Ezer 3:28)[8]

Feinstein rules for increasing the frequency of *onah* in order to meet the increased sexual needs of contemporary women.

When we turn to the second aspect of the duty of *onah,* the quality of the sexual act, we find a parallel tension between the desire to restrain and curtail sexuality, and the wish to leave a certain freedom to husband and wife in intimate matters. While the Halakhah leaves considerable latitude for personal proclivities, the ascetic tendency remains a powerful psychological inhibition.

Let us examine the sources for the principle that the man's obligation in *onah* is to please and satisfy his wife.

> If a man is newly married, he shall not join the army nor is he to be pestered at home; he shall be left free of all obligations for one year to cheer the wife he has taken. (Deut. 24:5)[9]

A new marriage is one of the circumstances justifying an exemption from army service. The reason cited by the biblical text is to give the man the opportunity to cheer or rejoice with his wife. The biblical text does not distinguish between the man's joy and his wife's pleasure. Rashi, on the other hand, is very insistent on the distinction. The point of the biblical legislation, according to his interpretation, is that the man should bring joy and sexual pleasure to his wife:

> "And he shall cheer his wife"—as the translation of Onkelos [the Aramaic translation] has it: he shall cheer his wife. And whosoever translates "he shall rejoice

> with his wife" is wrong, translating *ve-samach* instead of *ve-simach.* (Rashi on Deut. 24:5)

Ve-samach means "and he shall rejoice"; the text, however, has *ve-simach,* which means "and he shall cause [someone else] to rejoice." Rashi makes it clear that the point is for the husband to bring pleasure to his wife; his own pleasure is only a consequence, not a motivation. So it is with the obligation of *onah:* a husband is to initiate sex in order to bring pleasure to his wife. His enjoyment of sex is merely a welcome "side effect."

Sefer Mitzvot Katan, a medieval popular compilation of *mitzvot,* makes the direct link between the Deuteronomic legislation and the commandment of *onah* in Exodus:

> "To cheer his wife"—as it is written "and he shall cheer his wife whom he has taken." The negative [*mitzvah*] is "Her *onah* shall he not diminish" (Ex. 21:11). And behold how great is this positive *mitzvah*. . . . even when his wife is pregnant it is a *mitzvah* to bring her joy in this manner if he feels she is desirous. (*Sefer Mitzvot Katan,* Positive Commandments No. 285)

Deuteronomy 24:5 and Exodus 21:11 are complementary aspects of *onah:* the former requires that the purpose of *onah* be the sexual pleasure of the woman; the latter prohibits diminishing the prescribed rights.

A man then fulfills two obligations when he initiates sex and intercourse: procreation and *onah.* What is conspicuously missing is his own sexual pleasure as a motivation. Rabad, in his chapter on sexuality in *Ba'alei Ha-Nefesh,* recounts four purposes, or intentions [*kavanot*], which make sex legitimate and desirable:

> These are the four *kavanot* for which that act is appropriate:
>
> The first one is for procreation (and it is the most befitting) and the *mitzvah* of *onah* which he is commanded not to subtract from.
>
> The second one is for the constitution of the fetus for our rabbis have said: The first three months it is hard on the woman and the fetus, the middle three it is hard on the woman and good for the fetus, the last—good for both of them. And this *kavanah* is also deduced from the *kavanah* of procreation.
>
> The third *kavanah* . . . [is that] she desires him, and he recognizes that she is trying to seduce him and that she adorns herself in front of him in order that he notice her. And all the more so, when he embarks on a journey, certainly, she desires him then. There is reward paid for this *mitzvah* which is the *mitzvah* of *onah.*
>
> The fourth is that he intends to restrain himself through it, so that he does not desire something prohibited when he sees that his passion increases and he is desiring that thing and is in danger of becoming ill. In this there is also

reward, but not as much as in the first, because he could have ruled his passion and curbed his desire. (Rabad, *Ba'alei Ha-Nefesh.* Sha'ar Ha-Kedushah)

Briefly summarized, the appropriate motivations for sex are:

1. Procreation and the prescribed times for *onah*
2. Improving the health of the fetus
3. *Onah* beyond the prescribed frequency
4. Restraining the man's passion and directing it to a woman permitted to him, as well as preventing illness due to unreleased sexual impulse.

The man's own desires and sexual needs are last on Rabad's list of acceptable *kavanot.* Even when the man's desires are taken into account, as in the fourth *kavanah,* it is not his sexual pleasure which Rabad accepts, but the prevention of sinful thoughts and physical hazard. As for the man's desires, Rabad counsels "he could have ruled his passion and curbed his desire."

It would be erroneous to conclude that male sexual desires were totally ignored. Rather, they were assumed to be an ever-present motivation for sex that did not need to be anchored in law. It was the woman's sexual needs that had to be formulated into law to ensure their fulfillment. Male sexuality had to be controlled and limited by the legal system, by harnessing it to ulterior ends: procreation and *onah.*

. . .

Notes

1. For general works on sexuality in Jewish law and tradition, see Roland Gittelsohn, *Love, Sex, and Marriage: A Jewish View* (New York, 1976); Robert Gordis, *Love and Sex: A Modern Jewish Perspective* (New York, 1978), as well as his *Sex and the Family in Jewish Tradition* (New York, 1967). See also Maurice Lamm, *The Jewish Way in Love and Marriage* (San Francisco, 1980). For a wealth of material on sexuality in the view of the Rabbis see Louis Epstein, *Sex Laws and Customs in Judaism* (New York, 1967). A good many of the pronouncements on sexuality in the Talmud and the Midrash (including some of the more daring and surprising ones) have been collected in the Hebrew anthology by Shlomo Shva, *Ahavah Doheket et Ha-Basar* (Tel Aviv, 1979).
2. On masturbation and touching of the genitals by men, see the statement "in the case of a man the hand that reaches below the belly button should be chopped off" (Niddah 13a).
3. The tension between the strength and covertness of female sexuality is expressed by another passage in the Talmud which forbids a court order to supply a woman with wine (as part of a *ketubah* settlement). Wine is dangerous

because it loosens the restraint and releases the hidden sexual impulse: "Rabbi Eliezer said: We do not order a woman to be supplied with wine since wine accustoms a person to desire sexual intercourse. For we have learned: one glass is beneficial for a woman, two glasses are a disgrace [*nivul*], three—she demands sex with her mouth, four—she demands even a donkey in the market and has no restraints.

"Raba said: all of that [is the case] if her husband is not with her, but if her husband is with her—it is permitted" (Ketubot 65a).

4. There are innumerable traditional and scholarly commentaries on the two Genesis stories. I recently found a new insight in an article by Meir Shalev ("Bible Now" [Hebrew], *Ha-Aretz* daily newspaper, May 21, 1983) in which he points out the fact that in the second story Adam and Eve are punished with the very same things which are their blessings in the first story, namely, taking dominion over the earth for Adam and procreation for Eve.
5. For the talmudic discussion of the nature of the affliction, *innui,* in sexual relations, see Ketubot 48a and Yoma 77a. For a good discussion of *onah* and, especially, the quality of the marital relationship, see David M. Feldman, *Marital Relations, Birth Control, and Abortion in Jewish Law* (New York, 1974), chaps. 4 and 5.
6. This issue should be understood as part of a larger one, the conflict between marriage and Torah study. This conflict is epitomized by the talmudic discussion of whether a man should study first or marry first, and the phrase "With a millstone around his neck how can he study Torah?" (Kiddushin 29b). There are also a number of stories illustrating this tension, most famous among them the stories about Akiva and his wife Rachel. Most of these stories have been collected in David Zimmerman's book *Eight Love Stories in the Midrash and the Talmud* (Hebrew) (Tel Aviv, 1981).
7. There is also a rule about initiating sex on the night after the immersion in the *mikveh:* Jerusalem Talmud Tractate Ta'anit 1:6 (it does not appear as an explicit *halakhah* in the Babylonian Talmud) and *Tur* and *Shulhan Arukh,* Even Ha-Ezer 76.
8. One of the first authorities to rule this way due to the sexual mores of his time was Yonah Landsofer (Prague, end of the seventeenth century) in his responsa *Me'il Tzedakah.*
9. My translation.

THE SOCIAL CONSTRUCTION OF SEXUALITY

[11]

Women's Sex Talk and Men's Sex Talk: Different Worlds

June Crawford, Susan Kippax, and Catherine Waldby

. . .

Introduction

This article addresses the issue of sexual communication and negotiation between men and women by analyzing their memories and accounts of sexual encounters. It is especially concerned with the conversations men have with women, and women with men, during a sexual encounter, and with the ways in which such talk, particularly that pertaining to "negotiation," is shaped by (as well as being constitutive of) gender and heterosexual relations.

The term "negotiation," as we use it in this chapter, refers to the interpersonal communication which takes place during a sexual encounter in order

SOURCE: From June Crawford, Susan Kippax, and Catherine Waldby, "Women's Sex Talk and Men's Sex Talk: Different Worlds," *Feminism and Psychology* 4, no. 4 (1994).

to influence what happens in that encounter in terms of the needs and desires of the two people involved. It is plain that negotiation is absent from some heterosexual encounters, for example rape (Bart and O'Brien, 1985), and it is widely accepted that communication between heterosexual partners is problematic (Cline et al., 1990; Cochran and Mays, 1990; Wight, 1992).

Communication does, however, take place and negotiation may occur. This article focuses on how heterosexual men and women communicate sexual interest and negotiate sexual likes or dislikes, and on the ways in which they initiate sexual contact and sustain sexual encounters. It focuses on the intersubjective nature of communication and on the ways in which shared meanings both facilitate and hinder negotiation.

Heterosexual practice is an area where it is particularly important to recognize that men and women inhabit somewhat different worlds. From birth, anatomy places men and women in different sexual worlds where differing points of view or frameworks for understanding sexuality are constituted. This renders communication difficult, and social and educational practices build upon and reinforce the separation of these sexual worlds. Not only is there a difference, but as feminist analyses of heterosexual practice have demonstrated, this difference is marked by power imbalance. The dominant version of heterosexual relations is a male-dominated one. Nowhere is this difference more obvious and nowhere more problematic than in the sexual relations of heterosexuals (Gavey, 1992; Gilfoyle et al., 1992; Hollway, 1984; Pateman, 1988; Wilkinson and Kitzinger, 1993).

There are many illustrations of the ways in which this power differential is experienced as a clash of understandings and meanings. One such illustration comes from AIDS preventive education campaigns which urge women to be more assertive (Commonwealth Department of Community Services and Health, 1988). As much of our earlier research has shown (Kippax et al., 1990; Waldby et al., 1990, 1993a, 1993b), such education campaigns position women as passive and weak, and in need of assertiveness training, but also, somewhat paradoxically, as agents responsible for safe sex and thus liable to infect men. Men and women appropriate safe sex messages within frameworks of taken-for-granted understandings that enshrine the power imbalance of gender difference. In this research, condom use is understood with reference to competing discourses—of sexual safety and risk, and gender relations. In the former condoms signify safety, in the latter condoms signify infidelity, lack of trust, promiscuity, an absence of love, a lack of commitment. (See also Holland et al., 1991; Thomson and Holland, 1994.)

It would, however, be a mistake to assume that the understandings that men and women bring to any sexual encounter and the conversations that take place are determined by the circulating hegemonic discourses of heterosexual and gender relations. Sexual communication and negotiation occur within an interpersonal context where meanings are called forth with reference to the unfolding joint actions of self and other (sexual partner) and with reference to the taken-for-granted and hegemonic discourses which govern heterosexual relations. Meanings are constructed and reconstructed intersubjectively, that is, with reference to the occasioned meanings as well as with reference to broader social meanings.

Intersubjectivity

The theoretical basis for our work comes from social constructionism (Harré, 1983: Shotter, 1984) and from a feminist theory of socialization which is closely related to it (Haug, 1987). Following Mead (1934), Shotter argues that intersubjectivity is constituted in interaction, in conversational moments (Shotter, 1993).

Mead (1934) grounded his notion of intersubjectivity in gestural communication. It is connected closely with the body and founded in cooperative action. Human communication is, for Mead, the basis of consciousness. Without human interaction, there is no human consciousness. Intersubjectivity precedes subjectivity; humans can only understand themselves and others in terms of how others respond to and interact with them.

Intersubjectivity is the space within which human beings make sense of their experience. It is the recognition of the other (others) as human like oneself and the knowledge that others recognize one in a similar way (Benjamin, 1988). It is knowing what it is like to be female, working class, poor, a member of a party or church, etc.; a knowing grounded in doing (Vico, 1968). It follows from this that although there are common understandings shared very widely within a given culture at a given time, there are also understandings shared by women which are different from those of men; by the working class as distinct from the middle class; by the sexually naive and the sexually experienced; and so on. In discussing heterosexuality, the question of gendered intersubjectivity is particularly salient, as is the question of sexual experience.

Intersubjectivity points to a sharing of meanings, the "taken-for-granted" that emerges from interpersonal interaction and from interpersonal communication. This "taken-for-granted" sense, this common (in the sense of shared) sense is grounded in experience and forms the basis of what is understood as "normal" as opposed to "deviant," and of what is expected or appropriate; it forms the basis of human moral judgments and evaluation. The relation of these understandings to the dominant and hegemonic discourses is complex—they may be identical and interchangeable; only partially congruent; or incongruent with the dominant discourses.

Intersubjectivity and Power

There are, as noted earlier, not only differences between men's and women's understandings of heterosexual relations and sexual practice but these differences are marked by power inequalities. Male discourses are hegemonic. The domination of male culture over female, through such things as media representations of heterosexual relations, and media and other cultural representations of women, ensures that women see themselves to some extent through men's eyes.

There are asymmetries of understandings, sometimes congruent with asymmetries of power. In the sphere of heterosexual relations, women may share men's understandings more completely than men share understandings with women. Women know—or think they know—how men feel. Women have no discourses with which to speak about female sexuality and female desire. As noted by Gilfoyle et al. (1992: 224), "the 'discourses' available in the contemporary Western language community within which we speak about sex are geared to articulating men's interests and accounts of sexuality."

Sexual communication and talk occurs with reference to the particularity of the sexual occasion; the occasioned meanings which emerge within such encounters are produced with reference to the dominant discourses, and are shaped and transformed with reference to them. How such modification and transformation occurs is central to an understanding of "sex talk" and sexual negotiation.

Sexual communication between a man and woman may be fully shared and the overlap between the man's and woman's understandings complete. Such congruence may occur in at least two ways: meanings may have been contested and over time a shared understanding reached in which case negotiation is no longer necessary; or the woman may unquestioningly accept the hegemonic and male view of heterosexual relations, in which case the sharing is illusory and negotiation deemed unnecessary. In the case of partial congruence, if the overlap in shared meanings is sufficient, negotiation may occur. Different gendered, occasioned meanings may coexist. Given the power differential, however, it is likely that the man's understanding of the sexual encounter is privileged and that his wishes prevail. If there is no congruence of meaning, then the man's behavior is unintelligible to the woman, and the woman's to the man. Negotiation in such cases is impossible.

This article argues that in Western culture the construction of common meanings with reference to heterosexual practice, meanings common to men and women, is especially difficult. As children, we learn about many things from adults, but with respect to sexual practice, there is great secrecy. The context in which sexuality is embedded, the choreography of sex and what counts as "normal" or "expected" or "taken-for-granted" remain unclear. The ways in which heterosexuals attempt to resolve this lack of clarity through talk and action, and the ways they attempt to make their sexual practice intelligible to themselves and others are the foci of this article. In particular, we are interested in the ways in which the discourses are revealed at the level of the interpersonal encounter, and how mismatches of meanings are either negotiated with reference to discourse or go unrecognized.

Method

The data in this article come from group discussions of men and women. The procedure for eliciting the male and female data differed. The women's data are from two groups of four women and one group of five women in the age range 30–50 years. The women's groups were memory work groups (Kippax et al., 1988; Crawford et al., 1992). These groups were conducted prior to the men's group.

In memory work, group members meet on a number of occasions over a period of six to eight weeks. Prior to each meeting, each group member writes a memory of a specific episode in response to a cue or "trigger." There are a number of rules for writing memories, one being to write in the third person from the point of view of an onlooker. Some of the cues used with reference to the memories discussed here were "looking," "being picked up," "romance," and "initiating sex."

The number of sessions in the women's groups varied from three to five. Each session was between two and three hours in duration. The data included the written memories and the transcripts of the discussions of the group. The content of these discussions included elaborations of the memories, identification of similarities and differences, new memories which flowed from the discussion, and general discussion of heterosexuality.

The men's group was planned as a memory-work group to gather data which would illuminate and complement the data from the women's groups. In the event it was not possible to form a men's memory-work group as the men did not feel comfortable organizing their group discussions in this way.

So instead, the men's data derive from focus group discussions (which were run with a male facilitator/participant) of four men aged from 21 to 42 years. Their brief was to discuss heterosexual experiences and, as far as possible, to focus on particular events such as early sexual experience, "picking up," being refused sex (which did result in one written memory), and having a woman initiate sex. The group met on four occasions, each lasting about two hours.

Despite differences in procedure, we believe that data from these groups of men and of women provide the basis for meaningful analysis. The data discussed in this article come from a larger pool of data (interviews with 74 male and 109 female students and 19 group discussions with men and women) and the material reported here both informed and was informed by the ongoing analyses of the larger data set.

Analysis

The data include information based on people's memories (reconstructions) of specific events, and the discussion of these events within the group. The data are examined at both a textual and a thematic level in order to examine the processes by which people come to understand their world. Clichés, what is taken for granted, contradictions, absences, conflict, and emotion surrounding the memory episodes, and discussions of them, are examined.

While the analysis also includes a consideration of the discourses of heterosexuality identified by Hollway (1984), it is not itself focused on an analysis of discourse, but rather on a consideration of the texts as accounts (Harré, 1983; Shotter, 1984) or constructions (Haug, 1987) of lived experience. These constructions of occasioned meanings are analysed to reveal the ways in which dominant discourses are referred to or appropriated in order to make experience intelligible.

An important focus of analysis is what is common across the accounts and memories. It is here that social processes, processes which are common to men and women, are uncovered. The ways in which untutored/early experiences are described reveal common understandings about heterosexual relationships which were important both at the time the experience occurred, and now at the time of describing it. Particular attention is also paid to memories relating to the beginnings of sexuality, on the assumption that it is these which form the basis for what occurs later.

The data are also examined in order to explore differences between men's and women's understandings. The focus on common themes, common understandings, and on processes which are social overcomes to a large extent problems arising out of the fact that the men's and women's groups carried out their tasks in different ways.

Results and Discussion

Intersubjectivity Lacking

In examining the data, we found many episodes where shared meanings were lacking or almost totally absent. These episodes illustrate many features of what Hollway (1984) called the "male sex drive" discourse, which refers to the very widely held view in our society that men have a strong sex drive which is largely uncontrollable. The sociobiological myth that in the animal kingdom the male has an imperative to pursue and procreate, and the female role is to be acquiescent and receptive, illustrates such hegemonic meaning. This is a discourse which easily accommodates Irigaray's argument (1985) that women's bodies are commodities for exchange between men. Female desire is absent from the male sex drive discourse.

A number of common social practices are sites in which elements of the male sex drive discourse, and the notion of woman as object, serve to render negotiation unintelligible.

Picking up/being picked up. In a previous article (Kippax et al., 1990), we noted that early memories from women illustrated the operation of an economy of exchange between men where women's bodies are the commodity (Irigaray, 1985). Women did not directly describe their encounters in these terms, but the theme emerged clearly in our analysis of the data, particularly the men's accounts.

In the men's discussion of their early sexual experiences, stories of a girl being handed over or offered by a male peer (or occasionally by another girl) recurred several times. Ian describes an experience which occurred when he was 14 years old. He and two friends "picked up" three girls at the beach:

> It was broad daylight. I really wanted to be with the girl that went with one of my friends. I was left with this fat thing, and as they wandered away my friend turned to me and said "She wants you to finger her" and I thought "Oh, hell — RUDE!" . . . she literally grabbed my hand and pushed it down her pants.

He clearly understands (both now and then) the situation as one where the woman is an object. She is procured by his friend, and "second best." He refers to her as a "thing."

A memory from one of the women is similar in situation to Ian's, though it happened at night rather than in broad daylight. Helen, aged 16, is at a beach concert with two female companions. They are "picked up" by three lifesavers. Two of her friends and two of the men disappear into the darkness, leaving her with Ken. This was a memory written (in the third person) in response to the cue "being picked up."

> Helen wasn't quite sure how it had happened . . . she felt quite uncomfortable, apprehensive, but also curious about what might happen. Ken was told that he could go with Helen . . . He didn't seem too pleased about it . . . Helen felt very embarrassed, she didn't know what to do . . . she didn't say much—the others told Ken that Helen liked him but this only seemed to make things worse . . .

> Helen felt that Ken believed that he had been allocated a totally unattractive social misfit.

There is more than a situational similarity between these two stories. In neither case does the woman say anything. Her wishes, likes, are conveyed to the man by another person. In the story told by the woman, she feels powerless, uncertain, and very much aware that he does not want her. In both memories, the man involved is expected to take the active role. He is subject to expectations that he should "do something"; she is subject to expectations that she should go along with whatever the something might be. In Ian's case, he would "lose face" if he did not cooperate. In Ken's case, he does not actually do anything (the memory continues with a description of how he fell asleep). Neither in Ian's description of the episode, nor in the responses of the other members of the group where it was recounted, was there any mention of how the girl might have felt. The way Ian recounts his memory invites the judgment that the girl is "forward," but in all probability she was just as much aware of her "second-best" status as Helen was. Her behavior may have been designed to compensate either Ian or herself for her lack of attraction for him.

Although the man and the woman involved in each of these episodes have been placed in a difficult situation by "the others," no sympathy is generated between them. It would be unintelligible within this social practice for Helen to convey to Ken that she understood his feelings. In both episodes, the woman must accept her status as object. She has no voice; her desires are voiced by others.

These episodes were by no means unusual. In several of the episodes discussed by the group of men a woman was "handed over" by another man or boy, and occasionally by another woman. She was spoken of as an object, sometimes in response to the feeling that she was strange or alien as in Ian's report.

Putting pressure on/being pressured. The male sex drive discourse is more directly involved in episodes where pressure is exerted. As Holland et al. (1991) found in their research on sexual negotiation, pressure is a very common theme in the way young women understand heterosexual experience. A memory from early adolescence illustrates pressure exerted on young women through social relations. Ann is constrained by the social practice of "going to the movies." She titled the memory "My Brother's Best Friend's Brother Is My Enemy." Ann was 15:

> Craig was her brother's best friend's brother . . . he invited her to the movies . . . they sat in the back row of the stalls. As soon as the movies started he grabbed her hand with his clammy one and placed it on his trousers through which she could feel a huge erection. She tried to pull her hand away but he held it pressed

> there very tightly for a moment before letting go, simultaneously slobbering in her ear, and trying to kiss her on the mouth. She felt intensely embarrassed and disgusted—he really repelled her physically. But she couldn't make a big scene—slap his face or get up and walk out because of the social relationship.

The man's desire is conveyed to her by his behavior, his erect penis is sufficient evidence of his arousal, and he has only to make her aware of this in order to engender in her some feeling of obligation. In such situations, women are not accorded respect, the men have no obligation to them; women's desire or lack of it is irrelevant.

In this example, Ann does not speak. Other women's memories of early experiences described situations where the man failed to listen to what they were saying. They say "no" or "stop" and "he didn't seem to hear her." In some cases, the woman has to be very forceful, either physically running away or pushing him away physically. In others, the woman is able to force the man to recognize that she really means it by "starting to cry," when her tears seem to shock him into the realization that he is dealing with a human being rather than an object.

In the following memory (written in response to "come and see my etchings") the woman reported that she had initially refused to go to the man's hotel room, and only went on the understanding that he needed a cup of coffee before he would be sober enough to drive her home:

> . . . There was no mention of coffee. He almost immediately turned off the light and started to try to make love to her . . . She said very firmly that she was not going to do this. He swore at her, calling her a prick tease, cunt, fucking bitch, and was really quite nasty . . . she left.

These two memories are illustrative of an absence of shared meaning—in the sense of occasioned meaning. In the last memory, for example, the woman believes that the man clearly understands that she is unwilling to have sex with him. This meaning is not shared by him; he acts as if he has not heard or does not comprehend. There were many examples in the women's stories which included phrases like "he didn't seem to hear her," "he just carried on as if she hadn't said anything."

In the absence of shared occasioned meaning, men and women play out scenes dictated by the male sex drive discourse. The parts to be played by the actors in the scene are set and no negotiation is possible. Not only is there no negotiation, there is in a very important sense no possibility for negotiation.

Doing what comes naturally. Some of the examples given by Gavey (1992) show very clearly that many women have experienced situations which may be understood in terms of a lack of intersubjectivity; where, for example, meanings about the difference between consensual and coerced sexual relations are not shared. The following story from Martin illustrates how men view such situations. Martin described an incident at a teenage party when he was 17 years old. He was with a girl who had "picked him up" at the beach, then rang him the next day and invited him to the party:

> . . . it was dark, it was very dark. There were about seven people on a bed. The others [on the bed] weren't really doing it—but somehow I remember just laying on top of her on this guy's parents' bed—and for some reason—I just unzipped the old fly and pulled her panties to one side and went uh uh uh a couple of times and that was sort of it—she really didn't say anything. I don't think she even knew—oh yes she did because the next day she said "I don't think we should do that again."

Martin described this as the first time he had "really done it." Note how the situation is described in naturalistic terms, it is not a shocking incident—how could it be with seven other people there? The story was received by the other men in the discussion group with laughter, approbation even. It was no special occasion, there was no need to explain anything, it was just "nature taking its course."

The assumption is that the woman was as willing as the man was, her consent was taken for granted. It is regarded as sufficient justification that she had "picked him up" and that she had invited him to the party. Her attempt to inform him later that she was not altogether a willing participant did not change his view of the event—he had almost forgotten this detail. Once again, there is little or no appreciation of how the situation may have appeared from the woman's point of view.

In the absence of occasioned shared meaning, both men and women turn to prevailing discourses. These, in general, privilege the male understanding of sexuality and heterosexual relations, and the female voice is barely heard. Indeed in two or three of these accounts, specifically in the accounts of Ian (see earlier) and Peter (see later) and to some extent those of Ann (see earlier), women's actions are positioned to legitimate male sexuality. Justifications are offered for not hearing or ignoring the women's voice; women are eager for sex. Negotiation is rendered impossible.

Incomplete Intersubjectivity

In the previous episodes, the woman was denied a voice for a number of reasons. The following examples are those where some degree of negotiation may have been possible, but anxiety, uncertainty, or inexperience on the part of one or both parties hinders the development of a more complete shared understanding.

Asking/being asked. We begin with two descriptions of experiences of loss of virginity from the women's data. In both cases, the woman decides that it is time to "do it."

Carole is 16. She has "made her choice" of a man, anxious to get this "awkward first time over and done with." She forms a relationship with a young man, and after several days she began to wonder why he was not suggesting a night together.

> Finally "Do you want to come home with me tonight?" Silently she hoped he would not spend too much time on foreplay, she wanted him inside her—and then it was over. She had expected pain, a little blood maybe, but nothing. It was almost too easy. He seemed pleased while she was rather disappointed. Not such a big deal she thought as she cycled home.

Here is an episode where negotiation may have been possible. She felt constrained to wait until he asked her, not sure of herself, thinking that perhaps she was not attractive to him. During the sexual encounter, although she has hopes, feelings, she remains silent. She could have discussed with him what she wanted and how she wanted it, but her inexperience made it difficult. The minimal communication involved ("Do you want to come home with me tonight?") could have been a point where she articulated something about what she wanted to happen, but she did not do so.

Other memories from women were also unromantic. Though deciding to "do it" their decision stems from pressure applied by the man, usually in the context of a relationship, such as the following story from Wendy, when aged 18:

> She tried "but I'm a virgin" but he replied "So am I, what's that got to do with it?" . . . She just had to say she didn't want to—it sounded a bit weak . . . every day for two weeks they met, drank port, gradually he wore down her resistance—when she finally allowed him in it was all a bit of an anti-climax and he seemed to take it for granted.

The shared meaning of the sexual encounter is partial; it is a matter of if and when not how and why, and what he will provide in return.

In Wendy's memory and others like it, the gaps in the shared occasioned meaning are filled by reference to the "have/hold" discourse as described by Hollway (1984). In this discourse, there is an ongoing relationship with expectations of fidelity and commitment. This is clearly seen in Wendy's memory: this is no one-night stand. She has given the man the "precious gift" of her virginity and he does not seem to appreciate it. From his point of view, as Pateman (1988) notes, once a committed relationship is set up, the woman's body is deemed available on demand.

Nevertheless, some negotiation is possible. In Wendy's case negotiation about contraception was part of the process, in Carole's she gets what she wants, although she is disappointed.

An example from the men's group touches on issues concerned with technique, discussed at length elsewhere (Waldby et al., 1993a). Male sexual technique refers to an aspect of the discourse surrounding heterosexual relationships which leave no room for the man to be anything other than an "expert." He is expected to know how to "go about it." He is expected to be the initiator, to know how to satisfy himself (and, by implication, the woman). He is permitted, like Martin, to learn "on the job," but may become anxious if he is not "ready for it."

Peter related an incident where a woman asked him to penetrate her:

> She lays on top of me and just out of the blue she says "Screw me." I freaked! I got up and I said "What time's your mum coming home?" I really didn't know what to do next, just how to go about it—it just didn't feel right.

Again, there is little if any negotiation. The fact that the woman asked the man to do something indicated that negotiation was possible. Peter covered up his anxiety and/or embarrassment by changing the subject. He did not talk to the woman about his feelings or hers. He not only "didn't know what to do" in terms of physical enactment, he also did not know how to handle the situation socially. Although in this encounter the woman is not an object, indeed she is assertive, she is still not accorded the status of an autonomous human being with desires of her own, or even someone to whom he could express his anxiety, and the fact that it "didn't feel right."

These episodes illustrate partial intersubjectivity. In the case of "loss of virginity," the men concerned are either unaware of the woman's inexperience or are unaware of its importance. In Peter's case, he and the woman misread each other's readiness for penetrative sex.

The presence of talk in these episodes, even though it did not lead to effective negotiation or communication, opens up possibilities for engendering increased levels of understanding. The talk in these episodes is not unintelligible, rather it is limited. Peter did not act as if he did not hear the woman; he heard her, and consciously distracted her from what she desired, by redefining the situation as one where intimacy was no longer appropriate. His strategy reveals that he understands her as a person who, like himself, will be inhibited by the possibility of her parents' return. What he does not understand is that her desire may have been strong, overwhelming even, and in need of satisfaction.

Shared Meanings: Possibilities

Although, in the cases of Peter and Ian, communication was unsuccessful when a woman was the initiator of sex, we found in our previous work (Kippax et al., 1990) that, in some cases, there was occasioned shared meaning. Some of the stories from women, where they were the initiators, seemed to offer some promise. Other stories where talk and understanding took place came from men.

Episodes where women initiate the sexual encounter often take place within Hollway's (1984) "permissive" discourse, where the woman is allowed to desire sex, although only in terms of what is ostensibly a male model of sex, where sex is equated with penetration (Hollway, 1989). One such episode is described by Jeanette:

> She really fancied him, so after a large number of strong alcoholic drinks she put her hand on his knee and said "I really want to fuck you" and he said "Me too."

In the permissive discourse, the needs and behaviors of men and of women are assumed to be equal. Women are permitted or even expected to express their own desires. She expresses her desire in these terms: "I'd like to go to bed with you" or "I'd like to fuck you."

The data indicate that such occasioned and shared meaning may be facilitated if the encounter is casual, a one-night stand or takes place on holiday; that is, outside the pressures of heterosexual relations. In such encounters, the negotiation is typically about whether to have sex or not; not what kind of sex.

There are also data which indicate that at the beginning of a relationship possibilities exist for the woman and man to negotiate. There was one description from the women's groups where successful early sexual experience was described in positive terms. Jacqui was 14:

> He was 17, and he and I both learned about sex together. It was pretty innocent. It was caring, a long relationship.

Possibilities for good early experiences with the opposite sex do exist; sometimes intimacy develops alongside the sex, sometimes intimacy precedes it as in the following male account:

> . . . one night early in our relationship, we walked from the city to X, a long walk. We talked to each other backwards and forwards about memories related to sex, starting with young very early memories, and it was amazing the effect of this, like we didn't discuss them, just told about a minute each. Then longer and more involved as we got to adolescence, and I realize now that little bits she

> would tell me about when she was very young . . . touching . . . and then I touched her that way when we were making love later and it was like, not "Tell me what you like" but like "I know about you and I love you."

The intimate talk between the man and the woman established a bond between them, such that the physical communication was built out of a sure knowledge, each of the other.

One reason why such encounters appear to be the exception is that men seem to feel an obligation for commitment if they relate to their female partner as a person. She may be content with a one-night stand, but would prefer it to be with someone to whom she can relate person-to-person as well as body-to-body. Men seem to relate to women on a person-to-person level only within some kind of ongoing relationship. Even in the previous example, the man seems to value the experience largely because it increased her (and possibly his) physical pleasure, not completely understanding that for the woman this may have been because of feelings of emotional closeness, arising out of being seen by him, and hence of being able to see herself, as a person.

Conclusions

By focusing the data collection and analysis at the interpersonal level, the study illustrates the ways in which occasioned shared meanings called forth in joint action may be overridden by hegemonic discourses.

In many of these situations, the experiences were not positive for either the man or the woman, but the man accepts no responsibility for what happens. The first story, that of Ian where he was left with an unattractive girl, is one of acting out of social obligation, but it is not obligation to the woman, rather it is obligation to peers or peer expectations.

Women also describe their sexual experiences in terms that appear to be characterized by social obligation, but here the social obligation is to the man or in the case of Ann's story at the movies, to her brother. The "obligation," the expectations, derive from prevailing hegemonic discourses of heterosexual relations and sexuality, particularly the "sex drive" and "have–hold" discourses. When occasioned shared meaning is absent, or when intersubjective understanding is only partial and the meanings called forth from the episode clash, the hegemonic discourses prevail.

These encounters are played out within the power relationships of dominance and subordination that exist in our society. The nature of these relationships ensures that when there are mismatches or misunderstandings it is the man's worldview which prevails; intersubjectivity is overridden. When intersubjectivity is partial or overridden, then negotiation falters or becomes unintelligible.

Women are unable to negotiate about sexual practice as long as they are regarded by men and hence to some extent by themselves as objects, as extensions of male desire, not as autonomous human beings in their own right. For men, negotiation seems to be irrelevant in many of their sexual encounters. In relating to a woman as an object, a man fails to interpret her actions, emotions, even her words as he would do in other situations. Men thus avoid negotiation because it may expose their anxiety and challenge their status as "experts." They are unwilling to risk being refused sex, as this is a challenge to their masculinity. This avoidance is largely at an unconscious, unquestioning level. They also quite consciously avoid negotiation because they fear being "trapped" by commitment if they begin to relate to the woman as a person.

Sexual Experience

The findings indicate that when two people are sexually inexperienced they are more likely than those sexually experienced to bring to their heterosexual encounter shared meanings which are largely determined by hegemonic notions about heterosexual practice. In addition, they may bring meanings which are not shared by men and women, but have been derived from largely informal same-sex interactions—talk, innuendo, jokes, stories—and, as we point out later, a knowledge (sometimes limited) of their own bodies. The meanings will almost certainly be modified by what takes place during the encounter. But it is not automatically the case that these meanings will be altered in a reciprocal fashion.

On the other hand, the findings also indicate that casual sexual episodes between sexually experienced men and women may provide the best space for the meeting of occasioned meanings. In turn this suggests, somewhat paradoxically, that the intimacy of long-term relationships may produce either an illusion of intersubjectivity or genuine intersubjectivity. In the latter case the very close correspondence or congruence between the meanings shared by both parties, as for example within a couple relationship of long standing, may render negotiation unnecessary. A particular sexual encounter then takes place against a background of many shared experiences, each partner "knowing" (usually fairly accurately) how the other feels. Negotiation about what happens on that occasion may take place, but more generally sex may occur out of habit, almost automatically, with every move more or less predictable to both parties.

On the other hand, when the shared meanings are largely at the broader social or cultural level, negotiation may also be nonexistent. In this case, too, sexual encounters may take place against a background of shared experiences, but what is shared is frustration, disappointment, humiliation, and coercion. This is because the shared meanings do not derive from the joint action and talk of the partners. They come from notions of what is "natural," biological, or instinctive. While the woman may have some expectation (possibly vague) that talk involving negotiation is appropriate, she soon becomes aware that she is seen by the man as an object, not as an agent, and negotiation is unintelligible. The absence or partial nature of intersubjective meanings is evidenced by the nonreciprocal nature of the understandings.

Intersubjectivity and the Body

There is another aspect of intersubjectivity that we have not addressed directly; that which is to do with the body. Although a central aspect of Mead's notion of intersubjectivity, the importance of the body, and of bodily response and bodily sensation as mediators of intersubjectivity, has often been overlooked. Such sensations take on particular significance in the area of sexuality.

Women experience heterosexual sex at the hands of men, and men at the hands of women. So heterosexual sex involves the tension between seeing the other as both like oneself and different from oneself, exploring both what is the same and what is different in the other. In recognizing difference, one is also conscious of sameness, and thus sexual difference both elicits and places boundaries upon intersubjectivity. Bodily difference contributes to lack of intersubjectivity. As our data indicate, the bodily reactions of the other were often seen as alien, mysterious, or unexpected. For example, the young girl in the movies did not expect the boy to have an erection, just as he was totally unaware that she would not be sexually excited by his placing her hand on it. When occasioned meanings are not shared, the basis for developing shared meanings which arises out of recognition of the other as being like oneself is less secure. Unexpected bodily reactions underline difference rather than engendering recognition.

Heterosexual encounters in this sense are very different from homosexual ones. Further, the conviction that one knows how the other feels cannot be held as strongly by heterosexuals as by homosexual men or lesbians. Heterosexual men and women are uncertain of the other's desires and wants. It is possible that sexual excitement and sexual tension are heightened by this very sense of difference, and the sense of danger that is engendered by uncertainty.

Intersubjectivity arises out of joint action and both builds and is built from shared meanings. In the area of heterosexual relations, inequalities of power, which are related to asymmetries of intersubjectivity, ensure the privileging of male heterosexuality: phallocentrism in a literal, as well as a metaphorical, sense. Sexually inexperienced heterosexuals rely on hegemonic understandings to a large extent, and joint action at the interpersonal level tends to reproduce such understandings.

Yet in sexual enactment, the conviction that one is able to know how the other feels in both the emotional or the physical sense is extremely strong. Indeed much of the pleasure of sexual engagement is related to coming to know how the other feels. Sex, in a very important sense, may provide a very firm basis for intersubjectivity.

A discourse of sex as pleasure, separating pleasure from procreation, and acknowledging women as active, desiring, and sexually assertive subjects, not necessarily centered around the erect penis, will challenge and confront established power structures. What is needed is a new mythology, one which speaks about mutual exploration, communication, discovery, and pleasuring one another, where penetration is not an end unto itself, but one of many possibilities for erotic enjoyment in heterosexual relationships.

References

Bart, Pauline, and O'Brien, Patricia (1985). *Stopping Rape: Successful Survival Strategies.* New York: Pergamon.

Benjamin, Jessica (1988). *The Bonds of Love: Psychoanalysis, Feminism, and the Problem of Domination.* New York: Pantheon Books.

Cline, Rebecca J. W., Freeman, Kim E., and Johnson, Sarah J. (1990). "Talk among Sexual Partners about AIDS: Factors Differentiating Those Who Talk from Those Who Do Not." *Communication Research* 17:792–808.

Cochran, S. D. and Mays, V. M. (1990). "Sex, Lies and HIV." *New England Journal of Medicine* 322:774–75.

Commonwealth Department of Community Services and Health (1988). *AIDS: A Time to Care, a Time to Act.* Canberra: Australian Government Printing Service.

Crawford, June, Kippax, Susan, Onyx, Jenny, Gault, Una, and Benton, Pam (1992). *Emotion and Gender: Constructing Meaning from Memories.* London: Sage.

Gavey, Nicola (1992). "Technologies and Effects of Heterosexual Coercion," in C. Kitzinger, S. Wilkinson and R. Perkins (eds.), *Special Issue on 'Heterosexuality', Feminism & Psychology* 2(3): 325–51.

Gilfoyle, Jackie, Wilson, Jonathan, and Brown (1992). "Sex, Organs, and Audiotape: A Discourse Analytic Approach to Talking about Heterosexual Sex and Relationships." *Feminism & Psychology* 2(2): 209–30.

Harré, Rom (1983). *Personal Being.* Oxford: Blackwell.

Haug, Frigga (1987). *Female Sexualization.* London: Verso.

Holland, Janet, Ramazanoglu, Caroline, Sharpe, Sue, and Thomson, Rachel (1991).

Pressured Pleasure: Young Women and the Negotiation of Sexual Boundaries. Women, Risk and AIDS Project, Paper No. 7. London: The Tufnell Press.

Hollway, Wendy (1984). "Gender Differences and the Production of Subjectivity," in Julian Henriques, Wendy Hollway, Cathy Urwin, Couze Venn, and Valerie Walkerdine (eds.), *Changing the Subject,* pp. 227–63. London: Methuen.

Hollway, Wendy (1989). *Subjectivity and Method in Psychology: Gender, Meaning, and Science.* London: Sage.

Irigaray, Luce (1985). *This Sex Which Is Not One.* Ithaca, N.Y.: Cornell University Press.

Kippax, Susan, Crawford, June, Benton, Pam, Gault, Una, and Noesjirwan, Jenny (1988). "Constructing Emotion: Weaving Meaning from Memories." *British Journal of Social Psychology* 27:19–33.

Kippax, Susan, Crawford, June, Waldby, Cathy, and Benton, Pam (1990). "Women Negotiating Heterosex: Implications for AIDS Prevention." *Women's Studies International Forum* 13:533–42.

Mead, George Herbert (1934). *Mind, Self, and Society from the Standpoint of a Social Behaviourist.* Chicago: Chicago University Press.

Pateman, Carol (1988). *The Sexual Contract.* Cambridge: Polity Press.

Shotter, John (1984). *Social Accountability and Selfhood.* Oxford: Blackwell.

Shotter, John (1993). *Cultural Politics of Everyday Life: Social Constructionism, Rhetoric, and Knowing of the Third Kind.* Buckingham: Open University Press.

Thomson, Rachel, and Holland, Janet (1994). "Young Women and Safer (Hetero)-sex: Context, Constraints and Struggles," in S. Wilkinson and C. Kitzinger (eds.), *Women and Health: Feminist Perspectives.* London: Taylor and Francis.

Vico, G. (1968). *The New Science of Giambattista Vico,* trans. Thomas Goddard Bergin and Max Harold Fisch. Ithaca, N.Y.: Cornell University Press.

Waldby, Cathy, Kippax, Susan, and Crawford, June (1990). "Theory in the Bedroom: A Report from the Macquarie University AIDS and Heterosexuality Project." *Australian Journal of Social Issues* 25:177–85.

Waldby, Cathy, Kippax, Susan, and Crawford, June (1993a). "Heterosexual Men and Safe Sex Practice: A Research Note." *Sociology of Health and Illness* 15(2): 246–56.

Waldby, Cathy, Kippax, Susan, and Crawford, June (1993b). "Cordon Sanitaire: Clean and Unclean Women in the Discourse of Young Men," in P. Aggleton, P. Davies and G. Hart (eds.), *AIDS: Facing the Second Decade,* pp. 29–39. London: The Falmer Press.

Wight, D. (1992). "Impediments to Safer Heterosexual Sex: A Review of Research with Young People." *AIDS Care* 4(l): 11–12.

Wilkinson, S., and Kitzinger, C., eds. (1993). *Heterosexuality: A "Feminism & Psychology" Reader.* London: Sage.

[12]

Pleasure and Performance: Male Sexuality

Christopher T. Kilmartin

Few areas of human behavior are as fraught with emotion as sexuality. Dealing with oneself as a sexual person often involves a wide array of experiences, including pleasure, mystery, wonder, lust, love, anxiety, guilt, repression, and confusion. During socialization, males (and females) receive quite a few messages about sexual feelings, sexual relationships, differences between male and female sexuality, sexual preference, seduction, intimacy, and sexual communication. Many of these messages are highly value laden. Some involve misinformation, half-truths, or unhealthy ways of thinking about the self. All of them influence the shaping of biological sexual tendencies into sexual behaviors and feelings, as well as the place in the total personality that is given to sexuality.

Masculine socialization experiences pervade every area of experience, and sexuality is no exception. The traditional male gender role contains many prescriptions for sexual behavior and experiencing, and these are embedded in the larger context of masculine values. Being a "real man" has often included expectations for certain ways of being a sexual man.

. . .

Source: From Christopher T. Kilmartin, *The Masculine Self* (Indianapolis: Macmillan/Maxwell, 1994).

Sexuality and Physical Development

A boy discovers his penis very early in life. Compared with the girl's vagina and clitoris, the penis is more external and visible. It is easily accessible to the boy's hands, and he finds that touching his penis produces very pleasurable sensations. It is not surprising that boys tend to begin masturbating earlier in life than girls, and that males tend to masturbate more frequently than females throughout life (Hunt, 1974; Kinsey, Pomeroy, Martin, & Gebhard, 1953). The stronger social prohibition of sexual expression for females in Western cultures may also contribute to this difference.

Since the boy's genitals are so obvious to him and touching them is so pleasurable, there is a tendency in males to focus sexual feelings solely on the penis. In contrast, girls' sexuality may be experienced as more diffuse, internal, and mysterious (Nelson, 1988). This "genitalization" of sex may dissuade males from developing a sensuality—an appreciation of pleasurable sensations in other parts of the body. Adult heterosexual women frequently complain that their male partners are only interested in the "main event" (intercourse), and that they do not value caressing, intimate conversation, or other forms of sensuality.

When a boy reaches puberty, his genitals increase in size, and he begins to experience very strong sexual feelings. Erections occur frequently and without warning, sometimes at the most inappropriate times. Occasionally, the boy wakes up to find that he has ejaculated in his sleep (a nocturnal emission, or "wet dream"). These events may give the boy a sense that he has no control over his penis. It seems to have a "mind of its own." Although he is obviously aware that it is a part of him, he may also experience his penis as somewhat extrinsic to the self. The large number of slang terms for male genitalia may be a cultural reflection of the male sense that a penis has its own identity and personality.

Sexuality and Masculinity

While the physical sex differences just described contribute to the distinct quality of male sexuality, they probably pale in comparison to the social forces that shape sexual expression in the male. Sexuality is central to gender identity, and thus we find prescriptions for sexual experiencing deeply embedded in traditional masculine forms.

Brannon's (1976) description of the four themes of traditional masculinity . . . provides a useful framework for understanding masculine sexual demands in the context of general male gender-role demands:

1. Antifemininity ("No Sissy Stuff"): The avoidance of "feminine" behaviors, interests, and personality traits

Sexually, women are seen as gentle, sensual, tender, submissive, passive, relationship oriented, and sexually desirous toward males. In order to define the self as masculine, the male may feel pulled toward expressing his sexuality with the opposites of these qualities.

Heterosexual men find themselves in somewhat of a quandary when they try to relate to women sexually. On the one hand, they have been raised to be separate from women. On the other hand, they naturally feel drawn toward women. Intimacy is threatening for many men because it involves connecting, being vulnerable, and sharing power, all of which have been labeled feminine.

Men employ a few typical strategies to deal with this contradiction between naturally occurring desires for intimacy and role demands for separation. First, they may learn to equate sex with intimacy. In fact, one euphemism for intercourse is "being intimate with" someone. However, sex and intimacy are not the same thing, and physical intimacy is not the same as psychological intimacy. True intimacy involves letting someone in to some of the most private parts of the self. While some of these parts may be physical, it is certainly possible to be sexual with someone in a very impersonal or detached way. Likewise, it is possible to be intimate without being sexual, through shared communication and experience.

Equating sex with intimacy creates a number of problems for men and women. While women tend to see sex in the context of psychological closeness and affection, many men experience sex in a more isolated way, as a physical release or an adventure (Blumstein & Schwartz, 1983). The antifemininity norm inhibits men from establishing true intimacy, which is considered a basic human need (Jourard, 1971). Women may feel deprived in their intimacy needs and become frustrated with male partners who seem overly focused on sex.

Some men encounter a different problem: the sense that love and sex are contradictory. Raised to believe that "good girls" do not have sexual feelings, men may degrade women who express their sexuality. The sexual "double standard" is alive and well. Women who engage in frequent sex with multiple partners are called "sluts" or described with the pejorative term "promiscuous," but men who engage in the same behaviors are "studs" or heroes.

Men who embrace the double standard fall victim to what has been termed the Madonna/whore complex: they cannot love someone if they are sexual with her, and they cannot be sexual with someone if they love her. Sexual expression is relegated to "one-night stands," short-term affairs, or perhaps hiring prostitutes. Most men prefer to have sex and love together (Pietropinto & Simenauer, 1977), but some find this to be impossible. They must separate sex from other aspects of relationships (Gross, 1992) in order to define themselves as masculine (Fasteau, 1974). Many studies have shown that men are much more comfortable than women with viewing sex as a physical activity that is relatively unconnected to relationships (Carroll, Volk, & Hyde, 1985).

2. Status and achievement ("The Big Wheel"): The masculine expectation for success and power

This norm is expressed in a set of demands for sexual competence, conquest, and performance. Traditional men view the sexual arena as one in which they can prove their masculinity by being successful competitors.

For many men, "success" is an outcome, not a process. The traditional masculine emphasis has been on getting something *done,* rather than on *the experience* of doing something. Masculine achievements are, by definition, things that have happened in the past that contribute to the sense of masculine identity. They are also *quantifiable:* Masculine success means "putting up numbers." Carrying this orientation over into sexual behaviors has often created problems for traditional men and those around them.

Sexual success can be described in a number of ways. First, it can be defined as "scoring"—having sex with as many partners as possible. This goal-oriented attitude toward sex focuses the man on the good feelings that come from having "conquered" someone and leads to a focus away from enjoying the sexual experience. Some men even want to hurry sex so that they can go and tell their friends about having "scored" and thus gain admiration and respect. The sexual partner, however, is a victim of disrespect. She (or he) is seen as merely an avenue to achievement and status (Gross, 1992) for the "playboy." This mentality dehumanizes the sexual partner.

Another way to succeed is through sexual performance, which is defined as being able to produce erections at will and repeated orgasms in one's partner, as well as having sexual stamina. Of course, "real men" are also described as having huge penises (another quantification). In fact, the penis is sometimes described as "his manhood." The message is that having less of a penis means being less of a man. Worse yet are equations of the penis with personhood: "He put *himself* inside her," or the parental admonition, "Don't play with *yourself.*" The masculine norms for performance, size, and stamina are summarized in what Zilbergeld (1992) calls "the fantasy model of sex . . . , it's two feet long, hard as steel, always ready, and will knock your socks off" (p. 37).

These masculine demands are impossible to fulfill for most men. First, despite numerous attempts, nobody has created a penis enlargement technique. . . . Despite reassurances from women and sexuality experts that genital size bears no relationship to sexual pleasure, many a man feels inadequate about the size of his penis (Nelson, 1988). Statements like, "It's not the size of the wand, it's the magic in the magician" or "It's not the size of the ship, it's the motion of the ocean" provide little comfort to these men.

Second, penile erection is affected by a variety of factors besides sexual arousal. Among these are hormonal fluctuation, fatigue, anxiety, drug use, distraction, or physiological problems (Luria, Friedman, & Rose, 1987). Very few men have not had at least an occasional transient erectile problem (Zilbergeld, 1992). Because of the social connection between sexual performance and masculinity, these experiences can lead to confusion, anxiety, self-doubt, or depression.

Third, men do not "give" women orgasms. Women experience orgasms, sometimes with the man's help. If the man takes responsibility for the woman's orgasm, he may be risking his masculine self-esteem on a process over which he has little control. Many men ask, "Did you come?" and "How many times?", not out of concern for their partners, but in order to validate their masculinity through success and quantification. Many women report having faked orgasms in order to soothe the man's worries about his masculinity (Basow, 1986).

Fourth, sexual interest wanes on occasion. Many who equate manliness with ubiquitous sexual impulse may feel inadequate at these times. In fact, a surprising number of men report having faked orgasms in order to maintain a facade of perpetual masculine arousal (Levine & Barbach, 1984). The popularly held belief that men have biologically stronger sex drives than women is not supported by any available scientific evidence (Byrne, 1977).

The performance orientation toward sex also downplays the pleasure orientation for the man. Zilbergeld (1992) points out that fictional accounts of sex nearly always emphasize male *action* and female *feeling:* his performance and her pleasure. Zilbergeld notes that, with regard to male characters in novels, "it is rarely clear what he feels and experiences. It's as if his feelings and pleasure are beside the point" (p. 49).

The image that emerges from this view is of the man as a sexual machine with his penis as the main component of that machine. Some slang terms for penis ("tool," "rod") convey this connotation. Of course, the man has to know how to run the machine, and there is a tendency for men to see sex as a set of technical skills rather than as a human connection. Gross (1992) notes that "sex manuals" reflect this orientation. Success involves mastering sexual technique.

3. Inexpressiveness and independence ("The Sturdy Oak"): The maintaining of emotional control and self-reliance

In nearly every arena of male gender-role behavior, men are expected to know what to do without being told. It is considered unmanly to be unsure of oneself or to ask someone else for help. Many adolescent boys receive relatively little information about sex from parents or the school (Petrie, 1986). Thus, they rely on the peer group, a source notorious for an atmosphere of boasting, lying, and transmitting misinformation, for education around this very important topic. In order to be accepted by his peers, the boy must act like he is "getting it" (from females, of course) and that he knows what to do sexually. In other words, he must display an aura of competence and knowledge while he often feels incompetent and ignorant.

The gender-role demand for inexpression encourages men to approach sexuality as if it were a job to do rather than a pleasurable encounter. Sexuality is a highly emotional and self-expressive area of human experience, but men who are oversocialized into their gender role feel compelled to approach it in a machinelike way. Zilbergeld (1992) reports that an astonishing number of men say that they do not enjoy sex.

For many men, sex is the only area of experience where they can express some positive feeling and desire for emotional attachment to another person. When sex and connectedness are compartmentalized, any feelings of tender emotion or attachment become associated with sex. As Nelson (1988) puts it, "If a man feels intense emotion, sex seems called for" (p. 40). But it is clearly possible and also desirable to be emotional and connected to people in nonsexual ways. The association between emotion and sexuality, together with the cultural prescription for the sexual objectification of women, makes it very difficult for some men to relate to women as friends or coworkers. . . . These factors are related to a variety of social problems such as sexual assault and harassment. . . .

The sexualization of feelings of attachment causes considerable consternation when men begin to feel close to other men. Because a woman's connectedness is not defined as exclusively sexual, she may feel quite comfortable in touching, sharing feelings, or even sleeping in the same bed with another woman. Men's relationships with each other, however, are often limited by the threat of feeling too close. . . . The fear of same-sex attraction is termed *homophobia.* Increasingly, homophobia is being identified as related to a variety of social issues (Blumenfeld, 1992).

4. Adventurousness and aggression ("Give 'em Hell"): The expectation to be daring, fearless, and self-assertive

This masculine norm encourages men to view sexuality as yet another area in which to exercise dominance and control. "Real men" want to get down to the business of intercourse. Fasteau (1974) notes that "for most men, courting and seduction are nuisances" (p. 32). Feelings and communication are "sissy stuff" (Zilbergeld, 1992). At the extreme, there are implications here for coercive sexuality. . . . The cultural myth, portrayed in movie after movie and novel after novel, is that women are reluctant participants in sex and that they respond to "forceful" men.

Traditional gender roles dictate that men take every sexual initiative. Farrell (1986) describes the following social message to the male: "Be prepared to risk rejection about 150 times between eye contact and sexual contact. Start all 150 over again with each girl" (p. 126). Because men are expected to be tough and strong, rejection is not supposed to hurt. While the sexual initiator has a kind of power, the ability to reject is also powerful. Neither role in the sexual script seems very comfortable: She must wait somewhat passively for him to approach, signaling her availability without being "too forward"; he must gather his courage and risk his masculinity despite his anxiety and feelings of inadequacy.

The pressure of being responsible for all sexual initiative may lead a man into a variety of dysfunctional and harmful behaviors. Treating women as sex objects and inferiors is one way to defend against the pain of rejection. If a man reduces a woman to a less than human status, he can more easily attribute her disinterest to stupidity or deny that, being nothing more than a "piece of ass," she has little power over his feelings. There may also be the tendency to deny the emotional component of sex or to develop anger and resentment toward women in general (Farrell, 1982).

If the man is "successful" at living up to the masculine ideal of promiscuity, then he is *really* taking risks. The very real threats of AIDS and other sexually transmitted diseases are more serious than ever, and unwanted pregnancies also present as much of a possibility as they ever did. Once again, being a "real man" is hazardous to one's health. "Studs" don't spend their time taking precautions to avoid disease or pregnancy, talking to partners about sexual histories and birth control, or turning down sex because it is risky to be promiscuous.

In conclusion, sex has traditionally been a major way for men to demonstrate their masculinity. Male gender-role values require men to be sure of themselves sexually, to be perpetually ready to perform, to retain a genital focus and goal orientation, to separate sex from love, and to obtain as many partners as possible. On the one hand, males are encouraged to freely express and enjoy their sexuality. In another sense, however, male sexuality may often be fraught with high anxiety, emotional constrictedness, and a strong sense of inadequacy.

References

Basow, S. 1986. *Gender Stereotypes: Traditions and Alternatives.* 2d ed. Monterey, Calif.: Brooks/Cole.

Blumenfeld, W. J. *Homophobia: How We All Pay the Price.* Boston: Beacon Press.

Blumstein, P., and P. Schwartz. 1983. *American Couples.* New York: William Morrow.

Brannon, R. 1976. "The Male Sex Role: Our Culture's Blueprint of Manhood, and What It's Done for Us lately," in *The Forty-nine Percent Majority.* D. David and R. Brannon, eds. Reading, Mass.: Addison-Wesley.

Byrne, D. 1977. "Social Psychology and the Study of Sexual Behavior." *Personality and Social Psychology Bulletin* 3: 3–30.

Carroll, J. L., K. D. Volk, and J. S. Hyde. 1985. "Differences between Males and Females in Motives for Engaging in Sexual Intercourse." *Archives of Sexual Behavior* 14: 131–39.

Farrell, W. 1982. "Risking Sexual Rejection: Women's Last Frontier?" *Ms.,* 100.

Farrell, W. 1986. *Why Men Are the Way They Are: The Male–Female Dynamic.* New York: McGraw-Hill.

Fasteau, M. F. 1974. *The Male Machine.* New York: McGraw-Hill.

Gross, A. E. 1992. "The Male Role and Heterosexual Behavior." In *Men's Lives,* 2d ed. M. A. Kimmel and M. S. Messner, eds. New York: Macmillan.

Hunt, M. 1974. *Sexual Behavior in the 1970's.* Chicago: Playboy Press.

Jourard, S. M. 1971. *The Transparent Self.* New York: Van Nostrand.

Kinsey, A. C., W. B. Pomeroy, C. E. Martin, and P. H. Gebhard. 1953. *Sexual Behavior in the Human Female.* Philadelphia: W. B. Saunders.

Levine, L., and L. Barbach. 1984. *The Intimate Male.* New York: Doubleday.

Luria, Z., S. Friedman, and M. D. Rose. 1987. *Human Sexuality.* New York: Wiley.

Nelson, J. B. 1988. *The Intimate Connection: Male Sexuality, Masculine Spirituality.* Philadelphia: Westminster.

Petrie, R. 1986. Personal communication.

Pietropinto, A., and J. Simenauer. 1977. *Beyond the Male Myth: What Women Want to Know about Men's Sexuality.* New York: Times Books.

Zilbergeld, B. 1992. *The New Male Sexuality.* New York: Bantam.

[13]

Capitalism and Gay Identity

John D'Emilio

For gay men and lesbians, the 1970s were years of significant achievement. Gay liberation and women's liberation changed the sexual landscape of the nation. Hundreds of thousands of gay women and men came out and openly affirmed same-sex eroticism. We won repeal of sodomy laws in half the states, a partial lifting of the exclusion of lesbians and gay men from federal employment, civil rights protection in a few dozen cities, the inclusion of gay rights in the platform of the Democratic Party, and the elimination of homosexuality from the psychiatric profession's list of mental illnesses. The gay male subculture expanded and became increasingly visible in large cities, and lesbian feminists pioneered in building alternative institutions and an alternative culture that attempted to embody a liberatory vision of the future.

In the 1980s, however, with the resurgence of an active right wing, gay men and lesbians face the future warily. Our victories appear tenuous and fragile; the relative freedom of the past few years seems too recent to be permanent. In some parts of the lesbian and gay male community, a feeling of doom is growing: analogies with McCarthy's America, when "sexual perverts" were a special target of the Right, and with Nazi Germany, where gays were

Source: From John D'Emilio, "Capitalism and Gay Identity," in *Making Trouble: Essays on Gay History, Politics, and the University* (New York: Routledge, 1992).

shipped to concentration camps, surface with increasing frequency. Everywhere there is the sense that new strategies are in order if we want to preserve our gains and move ahead.

I believe that a new, more accurate theory of gay history must be part of this political enterprise. When the gay liberation movement began at the end of the 1960s, gay men and lesbians had no history that we could use to fashion our goals and strategy. In the ensuing years, in building a movement without a knowledge of our history, we instead invented a mythology. This mythical history drew on personal experience, which we read backward in time. For instance, most lesbians and gay men in the 1960s first discovered their homosexual desires in isolation, unaware of others, and without resources for naming and understanding what they felt. From this experience, we constructed a myth of silence, invisibility, and isolation as the essential characteristics of gay life in the past as well as the present. Moreover, because we faced so many oppressive laws, public policies, and cultural beliefs, we projected this into an image of the abysmal past: until gay liberation, lesbians and gay men were always the victims of systematic, undifferentiated, terrible oppression.

These myths have limited our political perspective. They have contributed, for instance, to an overreliance on a strategy of coming out—if every gay man and lesbian in America came out, gay oppression would end—and have allowed us to ignore the institutionalized ways in which homophobia and heterosexism are reproduced. They have encouraged, at times, an incapacitating despair, especially at moments like the present: How can we unravel a gay oppression so pervasive and unchanging?

There is another historical myth that enjoys nearly universal acceptance in the gay movement, the myth of the "eternal homosexual." The argument runs something like this: gay men and lesbians always were and always will be. We are everywhere; not just now, but throughout history, in all societies and all periods. This myth served a positive political function in the first years of gay liberation. In the early 1970s, when we battled an ideology that either denied our existence or defined us as psychopathic individuals or freaks of nature, it was empowering to assert that "we are everywhere." But in recent years it has confined us as surely as the most homophobic medical theories, and locked our movement in place.

Here I wish to challenge this myth. I want to argue that gay men and lesbians have *not* always existed. Instead, they are a product of history, and have come into existence in a specific historical era. Their emergence is associated with the relations of capitalism; it has been the historical development of capitalism—more specifically, its free labor system—that has allowed large numbers of men and women in the late twentieth century to call themselves gay, to see themselves as part of a community of similar men and women, and to organize politically on the basis of that identity.[1] Finally, I want to suggest some political lessons we can draw from this view of history.

What, then, are the relationships between the free labor system of capitalism and homosexuality? First, let me review some features of capitalism. Under capitalism, workers are "free" laborers in two ways. We have the freedom to look for a job. We own our ability to work and have the freedom to sell our labor power for wages to anyone willing to buy it. We are also freed from the ownership of anything except our labor power. Most of us do not own the land or the tools that produce what we need, but rather have to work for a living in order to survive. So, if we are free to sell our labor power in the positive sense, we are also freed, in the negative sense, from any other alternative. This dialectic—the constant interplay between exploitation and some measure of autonomy—informs all of the history of those who have lived under capitalism.

As capital—money used to make more money—expands, so does this system of free labor. Capital expands in several ways. Usually it expands in the same place, transforming small firms into larger ones, but it also expands by taking over new areas of production: the weaving of cloth, for instance, or the baking of bread. Finally, capital expands geographically. In the United States, capitalism initially took root in the Northeast, at a time when slavery was the dominant system in the South and when noncapitalist Native American societies occupied the western half of the continent. During the nineteenth century, capital spread from the Atlantic to the Pacific, and in the twentieth, U.S. capital has penetrated almost every part of the world.

The expansion of capital and the spread of wage labor have effected a profound transformation in the structure and functions of the nuclear family, the ideology of family life, and the meaning of heterosexual relations. It is these changes in the family that are most directly linked to the appearance of a collective gay life.

The white colonists in seventeenth-century New England established villages structured around a household economy, composed of family units that were basically self-sufficient, independent, and patriarchal. Men, women, and children farmed land owned by the male head of household. Although there was a division of labor between men and women, the family was truly an interdependent unit of production: the survival of each member depended on the cooperation of all. The home was a workplace where women processed raw farm products into food for daily consumption, where they made clothing, soap, and candles, and where husbands, wives, and children worked together to produce the goods they consumed.

By the nineteenth century, this system of household production was in decline. In the Northeast, as merchant capitalists invested the money accumulated through trade in the production of goods, wage labor became more common. Men and women were drawn out of the largely self-sufficient household economy of the colonial era into a capitalist system of free labor. For women in the nineteenth century, working for wages rarely lasted beyond marriage; for men, it became a permanent condition.

The family was thus no longer an independent unit of production. But although no longer independent, the family was still interdependent. Because capitalism had not expanded very far, because it had not yet taken over—or socialized—the production of consumer goods, women still performed necessary productive labor in the home. Many families no longer produced grain, but wives still baked into bread the flour they bought with their husbands' wages; or, when they purchased yarn or cloth, they still made clothing for their families. By the mid-1800s, capitalism had destroyed the economic self-sufficiency of many families, but not the mutual dependence of the members.

This transition away from the household family-based economy to a fully developed capitalist free labor economy occurred very slowly, over almost two centuries. As late as 1920, 50 percent of the U.S. population lived in communities of fewer than 2,500 people. The vast majority of blacks in the early twentieth century lived outside the free labor economy, in a system of sharecropping and tenancy that rested on the family. Not only did independent farming as a way of life still exist for millions of Americans, but even in towns and small cities women continued to grow and process food, make clothing, and engage in other kinds of domestic production.

But for those people who felt the brunt of these changes, the family took on new significance as an affective unit, an institution that produced not goods but emotional satisfaction and happiness. By the 1920s among the white middle class, the ideology surrounding the family described it as the means through which men and women formed satisfying, mutually enhancing relationships and created an environment that nurtured children. The family became the setting for a "personal life," sharply distinguished and disconnected from the public world of work and production.[2]

The meaning of heterosexual relations also changed. In colonial New England, the birthrate averaged over seven children per woman of childbearing age. Men and women needed the labor of children. Producing offspring was as necessary for survival as producing grain. Sex was harnessed to procreation. The Puritans did not celebrate heterosexuality but rather marriage; they condemned *all* sexual expression outside the marriage bond and did not differentiate sharply between sodomy and heterosexual fornication.

By the 1970s, however, the birthrate had dropped to under two. With the exception of the post–World War II baby boom, the decline has been continuous for two centuries, paralleling the spread of capitalist relations of production. It occurred even when access to contraceptive devices and abortion was systematically curtailed. The decline has included every segment of the population—urban and rural families, blacks and whites, ethnics and WASPs, the middle class and the working class.

As wage labor spread and production became socialized, then, it became possible to release sexuality from the "imperative" to procreate. Ideologically, heterosexual expression came to be a means of establishing intimacy, promoting happiness, and experiencing pleasure. In divesting the household of its economic independence and fostering the separation of sexuality from procreation, capitalism has created conditions that allow some men and women to organize a personal life around their erotic/emotional attraction to their own sex. It has made possible the formation of urban communities of lesbians and gay men and, more recently, of a politics based on a sexual identity.

Evidence from colonial New England court records and church sermons indicates that male and female homosexual behavior existed in the seventeenth century. Homosexual *behavior*, however, is different from homosexual *identity*. There was, quite simply, no "social space" in the colonial system of production that allowed men and women to be gay. Survival was structured around participation in a nuclear family. There were certain homosexual acts—sodomy among men, "lewdness" among women—in which individuals engaged, but family was so pervasive that colonial society lacked even the category of homosexual or lesbian to describe a person. It is quite possible that some men and women experienced a stronger attraction to their own sex than to the opposite sex—in fact, some colonial court cases refer to men who persisted in their "unnatural" attractions—but one could not fashion out of that preference a way of life. Colonial Massachusetts even had laws prohibiting unmarried adults from living outside family units.[3]

By the second half of the nineteenth century, this situation was noticeably changing as the capitalist system of free labor took hold. Only when *individuals* began to make their living through wage labor, instead of as parts of an interdependent family unit, was it possible for homosexual desire to coalesce into a personal identity—an identity based on the ability to remain outside the heterosexual family and to construct a personal life based on attraction to one's own sex. By the end of the century, a class of men and women existed who recognized their erotic interest in their own sex, saw it as a trait that set them apart from the majority, and sought others like themselves. These early gay lives came from a wide social spectrum: civil servants and business executives, department store clerks and college professors, factory operatives, ministers, lawyers, cooks, domestics, hoboes, and the idle rich: men and women, black and white, immigrant and native born.

In this period, gay men and lesbians began to invent ways of meeting each other and sustaining a group life. Already, in the early twentieth century, large cities contained male homosexual bars. Gay men staked out cruising areas, such as Riverside Drive in New York City and Lafayette Park in Washington. In St. Louis and the nation's capital, annual drag balls brought together large numbers of black gay men. Public bathhouses and YMCAs became gathering spots for male homosexuals. Lesbians formed literary societies and private social clubs. Some working-class women "passed" as men to obtain better paying jobs and lived with other women—lesbian couples who appeared to the world as husband and wife. Among the faculties of women's colleges, in the settlement houses, and in the professional associations and clubs that women formed one could find lifelong intimate relationships supported by a web of lesbian friends. By the 1920s and 1930s, large cities such as New York and Chicago contained lesbian bars. These patterns of living could evolve because capitalism allowed individuals to survive beyond the confines of the family.[4]

Simultaneously, ideological definitions of homosexual behavior changed. Doctors developed theories about homosexuality, describing it as a condition, something that was inherent in a person, a part of his or her "nature." These theories did not represent scientific breakthroughs, elucidations of previously undiscovered areas of knowledge; rather, they were an ideological response to a new way of organizing one's personal life. The popularization of the medical model, in turn, affected the consciousness of the women and men who experienced homosexual desire, so that they came to define themselves through their erotic life.[5]

These new forms of gay identity and patterns of group life also reflected the differentiation of people according to gender, race, and class that is so pervasive in capitalist societies. Among whites, for instance, gay men have traditionally been more visible than lesbians. This partly stems from the division between the public male sphere and the private female sphere. Streets, parks, and bars, especially at night, were "male space." Yet the greater visibility of white gay men also reflected their larger numbers. The Kinsey studies of the 1940s and 1950s found significantly more men than women with predominantly homosexual histories, a situation caused, I would argue, by the fact that capitalism had drawn far more men than women into the labor force, and at higher wages. Men could more easily construct a personal life independent of attachments to the opposite sex, whereas women were more likely to remain economically dependent on men. Kinsey also found a strong positive correlation between years of schooling and lesbian activity. College-educated white women, far more able than their working-class sisters to support themselves, could survive more easily without intimate relationships with men.[6]

Among working-class immigrants in the early twentieth century, closely knit kin networks and an ethic of family solidarity placed constraints on individual autonomy that made gayness a difficult option to pursue. In contrast, for reasons not altogether clear, urban black communities appeared relatively tolerant of homosexuality. The popularity in the 1920s and 1930s of songs with lesbian and gay male themes—"B.D. Woman," "Prove It on Me," "Sissy Man," "Fairey Blues"—suggests an openness about homosexual expression at odds with the mores of whites. Among men in the rural West in the 1940s, Kinsey found extensive incidence of homosexual behavior, but, in contrast with the men in large cities, little consciousness of gay identity. Thus even as capitalism exerted a homogenizing influence by gradually transforming more individuals into wage laborers and separating them from traditional communities, different groups of people were also affected in different ways.[7]

The decisions of particular men and women to act on their erotic/emotional preference for the same sex, along with the new consciousness that this preference made them different, led to the formation of an urban subculture of gay men and lesbians. Yet at least through the 1930s this subculture remained rudimentary, unstable, and difficult to find. How, then, did the complex, well-developed gay community emerge that existed by the time the gay liberation movement exploded? The answer is to be found during World War II, a time when the cumulative changes of several decades coalesced into a qualitatively new shape.

The war severely disrupted traditional patterns of gender relations and sexuality, and temporarily created a new erotic situation conducive to homosexual expression. It plucked millions of young men and women, whose sexual identities were just forming, out of their homes, out of towns and small cities, out of the heterosexual environment of the family, and dropped them into sex-segregated situations—as GIs, as WACs and WAVES, in same-sex rooming houses for women workers who relocated to seek employment. The war freed millions of men and women from the settings where heterosexuality was normally imposed. For men and women already gay, it provided an opportunity to meet people like themselves. Others could become gay because of the temporary freedom to explore sexuality that the war provided.[8]

Lisa Ben, for instance, came out during the war. She left the small California town where she was raised, came to Los Angeles to find work, and lived in a women's boarding house. There she met for the first time lesbians who took her to gay bars and introduced her to other gay women. Donald Vining was a young man with lots of homosexual desire and few gay experiences. He moved to New York City during the war and worked at a large YMCA. His diary reveals numerous erotic adventures with soldiers, sailors, marines, and civilians at the Y where he worked, as well as at the men's residence club where he lived, and in parks, bars, and movie theaters. Many GIs stayed in port cities like New York, at YMCAs like the one where Vining worked. In his oral histories of gay men in San Francisco, focusing on the 1940s, Allan Bérubé has found that the war years were critical in the formation of a gay male *community* in the city. Places as different as San Jose, Denver, and Kansas City had their first gay bars in the 1940s. Even severe repression could have positive side effects. Pat Bond, a lesbian from Davenport, Iowa, joined the WACs during the 1940s. Caught in a purge of hundreds of lesbians from the WACs in the Pacific, she did not return to Iowa. She stayed in San Francisco and became part of a community of lesbians. How many other women and men had comparable experiences? How many other cities saw a rapid growth of lesbian and gay male communities?[9]

The gay men and women of the 1940s were pioneers. Their decisions to act on their desires formed the underpinnings of an urban subculture of gay men and lesbians. Throughout the 1950s and 1960s, the gay subculture grew and stabilized so that people coming out then could more easily find other gay women and men than in the past. Newspapers and magazines published articles describing gay male life. Literally hundreds of novels with lesbian themes were published.[10] Psychoanalysts complained about the new ease with which their gay male patients found sexual partners. And the gay subculture was not just to be found in the largest cities. Lesbian and gay male bars existed in places like Worcester, Massachusetts, and Buffalo, New York; in Columbia, South Carolina, and Des Moines, Iowa. Gay life in the 1950s and 1960s became a nationwide phenomenon. By the time of the Stonewall Riots in New York City in 1969—the event that ignited the gay liberation movement—our situation was hardly one of silence, invisibility, and isolation. A massive, grassroots liberation movement could form almost overnight precisely because communities of lesbians and gay men existed.

Although gay community was a precondition for a mass movement, the oppression of lesbians and gay men was the force that propelled the movement into existence. As the subculture expanded and grew more visible in the post–World War II era, oppression by the state intensified, becoming more systematic and inclusive. The Right scapegoated "sexual perverts" during the McCarthy era. Eisenhower imposed a total ban on the employment of gay women and men by the federal government and government contractors. Purges of lesbians and homosexuals from the military rose sharply. The FBI instituted widespread surveillance of gay meeting places and of lesbian and gay organizations, such as the Daughters of Bilitis and the Mattachine Society. The Post Office placed tracers on the correspondence of gay men and passed evidence of homosexual activity on to employers. Urban vice squads invaded private homes, made sweeps of lesbian and gay male bars, entrapped gay men in public places, and fomented local witch-hunts. The danger involved in being gay rose even as the possibilities of being gay were enhanced. Gay liberation was a response to this contradiction.

Although lesbians and gay men won significant victories in the 1970s and opened up some safe social space in which to exist, we can hardly claim to have dealt a fatal blow to heterosexism and homophobia. One could even argue that the enforcement of gay oppression has merely changed locales, shifting somewhat from the state to the arena of extralegal violence in the form of increasingly open physical attacks on lesbians and gay men. And, as our movements have grown, they have generated a backlash that threatens to wipe out our gains. Significantly, this New Right opposition has taken shape as a "pro-family" movement. How is it that capitalism, whose structure made possible the emergence of a gay identity and the creation of urban gay communities, appears unable to accept gay men and lesbians in its midst? Why do heterosexism and homophobia appear so resistant to assault?

The answers, I think, can be found in the contradictory relationship of capitalism to the family. On the one hand, as I argued earlier, capitalism has gradually undermined the material basis of the nuclear family by taking away the economic functions that cemented the ties between family members. As more adults have been drawn into the free labor system, and as capital has expanded its sphere until it produces as commodities most goods and services we need for our survival, the forces that propelled men and women into families and kept them there have weakened. On the other hand, the ideology of capitalist society has enshrined the family as the source of love, affection, and emotional security, the place where our need for stable, intimate human relationships is satisfied.

This elevation of the nuclear family to preeminence in the sphere of personal life is not accidental. Every society needs structures for reproduction and childbearing, but the possibilities are not limited to the nuclear family. Yet the privatized family fits well with capitalist relations of production. Capitalism has socialized production while maintaining that the products of socialized labor belong to the owners of private property. In many ways, childrearing has also been progressively socialized over the last two centuries, with schools, the media, peer groups, and employers taking over functions that once belonged to parents. Nevertheless, capitalist society maintains that reproduction and childrearing are private tasks, that children "belong" to parents, who exercise the rights of ownership. Ideologically, capitalism drives people into heterosexual families: each generation comes of age having internalized a heterosexist model of intimacy and personal relationships. Materially, capitalism weakens the bonds that once kept families together so that their members experience a growing instability in the place they have come to expect happiness and emotional security. Thus, while capitalism has knocked the material foundation away from family life, lesbians, gay men, and heterosexual feminists have become the scapegoats for the social instability of the system.

This analysis, if persuasive, has implications for us today. It can affect our perception of our identity, our formulation of political goals, and our decisions about strategy.

I have argued that lesbian and gay identity and communities are historically created, the result of a process of capitalist development that has spanned many generations. A corollary of this argument is that we are *not* a fixed social minority composed for all time of a certain percentage of the population. *There are more of us* than one hundred years ago, more of us than forty years ago. And there may very well be more gay mem and lesbians in the future. Claims made by gays and nongays that sexual orientation is fixed at an early age, that large numbers of visible gay men and lesbians in society, the media, and the schools will have no influence on the sexual identities of the young, are wrong. Capitalism has created the material conditions for homosexual desire to express itself as a central component of some individuals' lives; now, our political movements are changing consciousness, creating the ideological conditions that make it easier for people to make that choice.

To be sure, this argument confirms the worst fears and most rabid rhetoric of our political opponents. But our response must be to challenge the underlying belief that homosexual relations are bad, a poor second choice. We must not slip into the opportunistic defense that society need not worry about tolerating us, since only homosexuals become homosexuals. At best, a minority group analysis and a civil rights strategy pertain to those of us who already are gay. It leaves today's youth—tomorrow's lesbians and gay men—to internalize heterosexist models that it can take a lifetime to expunge.

I have also argued that capitalism has led to the separation of sexuality from procreation. Human sexual desire need no longer be harnessed to reproductive imperatives, to procreation; its expression has increasingly entered the realm of choice. Lesbians and homosexuals most clearly embody the potential of this split, since our gay relationships stand entirely outside a procreative framework. The acceptance of our erotic choices ultimately depends on the degree to which society is willing to affirm sexual expression as a form of play, positive and life-enhancing. Our movement may have begun as the struggle of a "minority," but what we should now be trying to "liberate" is an aspect of the personal lives of all people—sexual expression.[11]

Finally, I have suggested that the relationship between capitalism and the family is fundamentally contradictory. On the one hand, capitalism continually weakens the material foundation of family life, making it possible for individuals to live outside the family, and for a lesbian and gay male identity to develop. On the other, it needs to push men and women into families, at least long enough to reproduce the next generation of workers. The elevation of the family to ideological preeminence guarantees that capitalist society will reproduce not just children, but heterosexism and homophobia. In the most profound sense, capitalism is the problem.[12]

How do we avoid remaining the scapegoats, the political victims of the social instability that capitalism generates? How can we take this contradictory relationship and use it to move toward liberation?

Gay men and lesbians exist on social terrain beyond the boundaries of the heterosexual nuclear family. Our communities have formed in that social space. Our survival and liberation depend on our ability to defend and expand that terrain, not just for ourselves but for everyone. That means, in part, support for issues that broaden the opportunities for living outside traditional heterosexual family units: issues like the availability of abortion and the ratification of the Equal Rights Amendment, affirmative action for people of color and for women, publicly funded day care and other essential social services, decent welfare payments, full employment, the rights of young people—in other words, programs and issues that provide a material basis for personal autonomy.

The rights of young people are especially critical. The acceptance of children as dependents, as belonging to parents, is so deeply ingrained that we can scarcely imagine what it would mean to treat them as autonomous human beings, particularly in the realm of sexual expression and choice. Yet until that happens, gay liberation will remain out of our reach.

But personal autonomy is only half the story. The instability of families and the sense of impermanence and insecurity that people are now experiencing in their personal relationships are real social problems that need to be addressed. We need political solutions for these difficulties of personal life. These solutions should not come in the form of a radical version of the pro-family position, of some left-wing proposals to strengthen the family. Socialists do not generally respond to the exploitation and economic inequality of industrial capitalism by calling for a return to the family farm and handicraft production. We recognize that the vastly increased productivity that capitalism has made possible by socializing production is one of its progressive features. Similarly, we should not be trying to turn back the clock to some mythic age of the happy family.

We do need, however, structures and programs that will help to dissolve the boundaries that isolate the family, particularly those that privatize child-rearing. We need community- or worker-controlled day care, housing where privacy and community coexist, neighborhood institutions—from medical clinics to performance centers—that enlarge the social unit where each of us has a secure place. As we create structures beyond the nuclear family that provide a sense of belonging, the family will wane in significance. Less and less will it seem to make or break our emotional security.

In this respect gay men and lesbians are well situated to play a special role. Already excluded from families as most of us are, we have had to create, for our survival, networks of support that do not depend on the bonds of blood or the license of the state, but that are freely chosen and nurtured. The building of an "affectional community" must be as much a part of our political movement as are campaigns for civil rights. In this way we may prefigure the shape of personal relationships in a society grounded in equality and justice rather than exploitation and oppression, a society where autonomy and security do not preclude each other but coexist.

Notes

This essay is a revised version of a lecture given before several audiences in 1979 and 1980. I am grateful to the following groups for giving me a forum in which to talk and get feedback: the Baltimore Gay Alliance, the San Francisco Lesbian and Gay History Project, the organizers of Gay Awareness Week 1980 at San Jose State University and the University of California at Irvine, and the coordinators of the Student Affairs Lectures at the University of California at Irvine.

Lisa Duggan, Estelle Freedman, Jonathan Katz, Carole Vance, Paula Webster, Bert Hansen, Ann Snitow, Christine Stansell, and Sharon Thompson provided helpful criticisms of an earlier draft. I especially want to thank Allan Bérubé and Jonathan Katz for generously sharing with me their own research, and Amber Hollibaugh for many exciting hours of nonstop conversation about Marxism and sexuality.

1. I do not mean to suggest that no one has ever proposed that gay identity is a product of historical change. See, for instance, Mary McIntosh, "The Homosexual Role," *Social Problems* 16 (1968): 182–92; Jeffrey Weeks, *Coming Out: Homosexual Politics in Britain* (New York: Quartet Books, 1977). It is also implied in Michel Foucault, *The History of Sexuality*, vol. 1: *An Introduction*, trans. Robert Hurley (New York: Pantheon, 1978). However, this does represent a minority viewpoint and the works cited above have not specified how it is that capitalism as a system of production has allowed for the emergence of a gay male and lesbian identity. As an example of the "eternal homosexual" thesis, see John Boswell, *Christianity, Social Tolerance, and Homosexuality* (Chicago: University of Chicago Press, 1980), where "gay people" remains an unchanging social category through fifteen centuries of Mediterranean and Western European history.
2. See Eli Zaretsky, *Capitalism, the Family, and Personal Life* (New York: Harper

and Row, 1976); and Paula Fass, *The Damned and the Beautiful: American Youth in the 1920s* (New York: Oxford University Press, 1977).

3. Robert F. Oaks, "'Things Fearful to Name': Sodomy and Buggery in Seventeenth Century New England," *Journal of Social History* 12 (1978): 268–81; J. R. Roberts, "The Case of Sarah Norman and Mary Hammond," *Sinister Wisdom* 24 (1980): 57–62; and Jonathan Katz, *Gay American History* (New York: Crowell, 1976), 16–24, 568–71.
4. For the period from 1870 to 1940 see the documents in Katz, *Gay American History,* and idem, *Gay/Lesbian Almanac* (New York: Crowell, 1983). Other sources include Allan Bérubé, "Lesbians and Gay Men in Early San Francisco: Notes Toward a Social History of Lesbians and Gay Men in America," unpublished paper, 1979; Vern Bullough and Bonnie Bullough, "Lesbianism in the 1920s and 1930s: A Newfound Study," *Signs* 2 (summer 1977): 895–904.
5. On the medical model see Weeks, *Coming Out,* pp. 23–32. The impact of the medical model on the consciousness of men and women can be seen in Louis Hyde, ed., *Rat and the Devil: The Journal Letters of F. O. Matthiessen and Russell Cheney* (Hamden, Conn.: Archon, 1978), 47, and in the story of Lucille Hart in Katz, *Gay American History,* 258–79. Radclyffe Hall's classic novel about lesbianism, *The Well of Loneliness,* published in 1928, was perhaps one of the most important vehicles for the popularization of the medical model.
6. See Alfred Kinsey et al., *Sexual Behavior in the Human Male* (Philadelphia: W. B. Saunders, 1948), and *Sexual Behavior in the Human Female* (Philadelphia: W. B. Saunders, 1953).
7. On black music, see "AC/DC Blues: Gay Jazz Reissues," Stash Records, ST–106 (1977), and Chris Albertson, *Bessie* (New York: Stein and Day, 1974); on the persistence of kin networks in white ethnic communities see Judith Smith, "Our Own Kind: Family and Community Networks in Providence," in *A Heritage of Her Own,* ed. Nancy F. Cott and Elizabeth H. Pleck (New York: Simon and Schuster, 1979), 393–411; on differences between rural and urban male homoeroticism see Kinsey et al., *Sexual Behavior in the Human Male,* 455–57, 630–31.
8. The argument and the information in this and the following paragraphs come from my book *Sexual Politics, Sexual Communities: The Making of a Homosexual Minority in the United States, 1940–1970* (Chicago: University of Chicago Press, 1983). I have also developed it with reference to San Francisco in "Gay Politics, Gay Community: San Francisco's Experience," *Socialist Review* 55 (January–February 1981): 77–104.
9. Donald Vining, *A Gay Diary, 1933–1946* (New York: Pepys Press, 1979); "Pat Bond," in Nancy Adair and Casey Adair, *Word Is Out* (New York: New Glide Publications, 1978), 55–65; and Allan Bérubé, "Marching to a Different Drummer: Coming Out During World War II," a slide/talk presented at the annual meeting of the American Historical Association, December 1981, Los Angeles. A shorter version of Bérubé's presentation can be found in *The Advocate,* October 15, 1981, 20–24.

10. On lesbian novels see *The Ladder,* March 1958, 18; February 1960, 14–15; April 1961, 12–13; February 1962, 6–11; January 1963, 6–13; February 1964, 12–19; February 1965, 19–23; March 1966, 22–26; and April 1967, 8–13. *The Ladder* was the magazine published by the Daughters of Bilitis.
11. This especially needs to be emphasized today. The 1980 annual conference of the National Organization for Women, for instance, passed a lesbian rights resolution that defined the issue as one of "discrimination based on affectional/sexual preference/orientation," and explicitly disassociated the issue from other questions of sexuality such as pornography, sadomasochism, public sex, and pederasty.
12. I do not mean to suggest that homophobia is "caused" by capitalism, or is to be found only in capitalist societies. Severe sanctions against homoeroticism can be found in European feudal society and in contemporary socialist countries. But my focus in this essay has been the emergence of a gay identity under capitalism, and the mechanisms specific to capitalism that made this possible and that reproduce homophobia as well.

[14]

Sexism in the Early *Saṅgha:* Its Social Basis and Philosophical Dissolution

Sandra A. Wawrytko

> Female mendicants at the end of the twentieth century find themselves literally in a No Man's Land, seeking to gain their spiritual footing. Exploration of women's spiritual potential is an adventure in vaguely charted territory, on a path which transcends territoriality . . . if we proceed with positive motivation, our potential for effecting good in the world is greater than at any previous point in history.[1]

THE PRECEDING QUOTATION succinctly summarizes both the pressing problem facing modern Buddhists that I wish to address, and the strong incentives that exist to correct it. Simply put, the problem is a seething sexism within Buddhism that is as old—and deep-seated—as the *vinayic* inequities that constricted *bhikṣuṇī* behavior with a significantly larger number of precepts than their male counterparts, the *bhikṣuṇī*.[2]

SOURCE: From Sandra A. Wawrytko, "Sexism in the Early *Saṅgha:* Its Social Basis and Philosophical Dissolution," in *Buddhist Behavioral Codes and the Modern World,* ed. Charles Weihsun Fu and Sandra A. Wawrytko (Westwood, Conn.: Greenwood Publishing, 1994).

The motivation to correct all such discrimination, both latent and manifest, is purely *upāyic,* namely, to prevent the unconscionable waste of human potential that is the consequence of sexism. Buddhists should observe the warning inherent in the precariously perched position of today's Catholic Church, which is crumbling under the weight of its own sexist policies by continuing to exclude women from the priestly ranks at the same time that the pool of male applicants is diminishing sharply.[3] It is particularly appropriate that the *vinaya* be the first point of contact, since it is in this realm that the discrimination was first introduced. Equally significant is the spirit with which these rules were applied—what was once viewed as a means to the end of Buddhism's social survival must now be reassessed in terms of their potential for alienating the female half of the world's population, along with feminist supporters of the male gender. In this reassessment we have the full support of Buddhist tradition, as well as of Buddhism's founder. Thus, in his parting words to his disciples the Buddha explicitly sanctioned modifications of the rules, which had themselves evolved out of cases of concrete necessity.[4]

Several key points need to be considered in assessing the extent to which sexism has existed in the past and continues to exist within the *Saṅgha,* as well as the prospects for exorcising its negative effects in the future:

1. In terms of the available evidence, has the institution of the *Saṅgha* practiced discrimination based purely on gender considerations, thereby artificially limiting the development of female members? The answer undoubtedly must be affirmative. However it is of the utmost importance to reveal the underlying cultural context of pre-Buddhist India, the Brahmanical backdrop against which the Buddha articulated his radical worldview, to grasp fully the significance of this sexism and its influence on later Buddhist developments.

2. In terms of the same available evidence, most especially as contained in the *Cullavaga,* did the Buddha himself either actively support or passively sanction this discrimination? Here the record is more mixed. To answer this query we must consider the issue of textual integrity, as well as speculating on the degree to which the early Buddhist movement felt forced to adapt itself to the limited, sexist perceptions of its environment to ensure its survival as a viable movement.

3. Is the philosophy underlying Buddhism, as mirrored in the organizational structure of the *Saṅgha* and the *vinaya,* unavoidably sexist in nature? Does it suffer from an irrevocably "androcentric" bias, such that it never has and never can give equal hearing to the spiritual needs and experiences of women, as has been argued by some alienated feminists?—I will argue to the contrary, and point the way to a philosophically grounded dissolution or dissolving of sexism within Buddhism in the present day.

Our discussion begins with an exploration of the historical context of Buddhism's rise in India vis-à-vis the evolution of the *vinaya.* The reasons for the gender-based variations of the scope and content of the *vinaya* also will be addressed. Subsequent modifications of the *vinaya* in accordance with shifting cultural conditions will then be discussed. We will conclude with a consideration of the evolution of the *Saṅgha* in terms of prevailing social conditions.

Gynophobia: The Historical Context of the Rise of Buddhism

> If ever there has been a silent minority among Buddhist practitioners, it is the nuns.[5]

Although Śākyamuni Buddha preached a way of liberation patterned after his own awakening and rethinking of reality, the budding sect of Buddhism was not able to liberate itself completely from the confines of its own social and cultural context. Certain accommodations had to be made out of consideration for the sensibilities of the Indian audience in the design and structuring of the *Saṅgha.* These included restrictions on the practice of Buddhist women, mirroring the sexist climate of the times. Pre-Buddhist Indian culture had evidenced markedly misogynist tendencies from its formative period, as reflected in ancient texts.[6] This was due largely to the originally patriarchal, militaristic character of the culture, which emphasized the male warrior ideals to the exclusion of "womanish weakness." Often this denigration of women revealed itself as gynophobia—a deep-seated fear of women and their stereotypically conceived "natural power," such that they were perceived as a threat to the control of the male priestly caste and its dominant role in society.

From earliest times in all cultures women bore a dual identity for men as nurturing Mother, source of life as primeval womb, and Destroyer, the agent of death who forces us back into the "womb" of Earth. She that giveth also taketh away. This ambivalence is rooted in the fear of the power of sexuality with which women were associated in terms of both libidinous instincts and their procreative consequences. The uncontrollable force of human sexuality, with its potential for turning social order into chaos, likewise was projected onto woman as a group, each individual woman becoming an agent of this primal constructive/destructive energy.[7]

Within the Indian cultural context, the long-standing suspicion toward women centered on the perils they were assumed to pose to the proper performance of the all-important Brahmanical rituals, man's requisite participation in the magical sustenance of the cosmos. Thus we see "a characteristic trait of women in Indian folklore: they betray *everyone,* but they can also be helpful to everyone."[8] One such stereotypical example can be found in the various myths concerning the seduction and betrayal of Śiva, the Lord of Yoga, by his divinely chosen consort Pārvatī. The story underscores the desideratum of controlled sexuality; Śiva personifies male ambivalence toward sexuality in his original state of ascetic aloofness which must be penetrated by Pārvatī in order to unleash his seething store of erotic potential for the good of the cosmos. However, the "appropriate" woman as partner was relegated to the role of an *anima* figure or *śakti,* eternally dependent upon and ultimately evolved from the male. This male ideal of womanhood stood in sharp contrast to woman as an independent, self-subsisting individual possessed of power in her own right.[9]

Even in her circumscribed form, the "ideal" woman was inherently untrustworthy, as the mythical accounts repeatedly warned. The high level of male possessiveness—combined with fear of betrayal—that pervaded the culture is typified by the following verse from the Tamil classic of Jainism, the *Naladinannurru* (The Four Hundred Quatrains) comparing "the beauty of a faithful wife" to a scroll comprehended by its reader, a generous man's wealth, and a warrior's sharp sword.[10] Note the consistency in the analogical thinking here that portrays the woman as a passive object, resource, or tool to be wielded by the man, in effect reducing her to a mere extension of himself. She must combine both the beauty that is the source of her seductive potential and the faithfulness that tames that same destructive power if she is to be included among a man's "treasures."[11]

These stereotypical images were carried into early Buddhist literature. A pervasive ambivalence toward women surfaces in their classification under two general categories: their dependent roles as wives/helpmates, and simultaneously potential seductresses and adulteresses, or their feared independence as demonesses, capable of destroying both the efficacy of the sacrifice and the sacrificer. The wife of the Buddha and the numerous female attendants of his royal lifestyle fall into the former category, hence the necessity for his renunciation of the householder's life. The latter category is represented by the daughters of Māra—Desire, Pleasure, and Passion—who are said to have tempted the Buddha as part of their father's plot to thwart his enlightenment. At the root of both roles lies the male's fear of woman's devouring sexual potency, the power that both tempts and possibly terminates masculine power.

The identical formula of female perfidy is repeated in the *Jātaka* tales, a relatively late addition to the Buddhist canon. Similarly, the thought of an independent women, such as a *bhikṣuṇī,* unrestrained by a male master (father or husband) was psychologically associated with the feared demonesses who undermined spiritual practice. Thus, the husbandless woman heads the list of "ten sorts of individuals who are despised and condemned in the world, thought shameful, looked down upon, held blameworthy, treated with contumely, not loved," as described in the *Milidanpañhā.*[12]

This misogynist cultural baggage inherited from the pre-Buddhist mind-set helps to explain the misguided assumption of some Buddhist practitioners that a woman needs to seek rebirth as a man in order to achieve awakening. Such an assumption reflects the earlier Indian belief that birth as a woman was indicative of bad *karma,* a punishment for past misdeeds, consistent with the denigrated position of women in the Brahmanical social structure. Moreover, it has been argued that this assumption, however erroneous, does not bar women as a group from enlightenment: "Even if they [women] must appear as a male in their last birth, not only *can* women achieve Buddhahood, they certainly *will,* as will all men and other living creatures."[13] Effectively excluded from direct access to enlightenment and enlightenmental practice by this bias, Buddhist women were forced into roles of dependency on males for religious development, as institutionalized in the male-dominated *Saṅgha* system.

Not all woman quietly acquiesced to discrimination. Many accomplished practitioners addressed the misconceptions and sought to expose their inconsistency with Buddhist doctrine. For example, in the *Vimalakīrti Sūtra* a female bodhisattva is advised to seek reincarnation as a male to fulfill her practice. She, however, retorts, "I have been here twelve years and have looked for the innate characteristics of the female sex and haven't been able to find them. How can I change them?" She then transforms her questioner into a woman.[14] Jñanacandra, an incarnation of Tārā and follower of the Buddha, similarly was urged to seek return as a male by a group of monks. She pointed out the erroneous basis of this recommendation, replying: "There is no such distinction as 'male' and 'female' . . . and therefore attachment to the idea of 'male' and 'female' is quite worthless. Weak-minded worldlings have always been deluded by this." She then reaffirmed her commitment to work for the enlightenment of all sentient beings in female form.[15] A similar exchange is recorded between the nun Mo-shan Liao-jan and the monk Kuan-ch'i.[16]

Clearly, as these women practitioners were well aware, sexism as the practice of gender-based discrimination is inconsistent with Buddhist principles, as are forms of discrimination. Shohei Ichimura has cogently argued that the Budda was motivated in his teachings by a rejection of the Brahmanical worldview, and most especially the caste system, which was antithetical to the republican policy characteristic of his native Śākyan society.[17] A parallel can be drawn between the socially sanctioned and culturally ingrained prejudices of the caste system and institutionalized sexism. The sermons of the Buddha emphasize that the Four Noble Truths are accessible to all, without restrictions.

Unfortunately, as in many world religions, the Buddha's disciples were unable to sustain the sweeping vision of their teacher. The ways in which the *Saṅgha* dealt with the dual social problems of gender and racially grounded discrimination were separate and distinctly unequal. For example, considerably more attention was paid in the Buddhist literature to a refutation of the artificial distinctions of caste than to those associated with gender. In the end, Buddhism was unable to eradicate either form of discrimination within Indian society prior to its eradication/absorption by later religious trends. It remained for Mahatma Gandhi to resurrect these trends centuries later in his eclectic campaign of social and political reform.[18]

However, Buddhism's egalitarian values were not completely subverted and its impact on ancient Indian society was demonstrably supportive of feminist goals. For example, in contrast to the reigning Brahmanical tradition that had effectively excluded all but high caste males from pursuit of *moksa,* the egalitarian spirituality of Buddhism opened a new "career choice" to women beyond the roles of wife and mother. Women in early Buddhism were actively involved in terms of preaching, providing financial support, and volunteering time. The Buddhist institution of marriage likewise set forth the ideal of equality between spouses, including the wife's active participation in planning the future of offspring. Buddhist widows had the freedom either to enter the *Saṅgha* after the deaths of their husbands or remarry. They also were able to dispose of their own property and bodies without the need for male supervision. This stood in sharp contrast to the practice of *sati,* the self-immolation of women on the funeral pyres of their deceased husbands or today's involuntary immolation of unwanted wives, obvious violations of the Buddhist principle of *ahiṃsa.*

The socially liberating effect of Buddhism can be attributed in large part to its devaluation of marriage, that is, its displacement of marriage as the focal point of human life by the celibate lifestyle. For Buddhists the marital tie represented not a divinely sanctioned sacred ceremony, but simply a social contract in an admittedly lesser or merely preparatory lifestyle. This liberated women from the constricting confines of social destiny and the control of dominant males. The tenets of Buddhism legitimize the self-reliance of the single woman—whether unmarried, divorced, or widowed—without the need of being paired with a man to realize complete fulfillment. Thus, it has been said that the presence of Buddhist influences on various countries historically resulted in a higher status for women.[19]

With the removal of the impediment of marriage, women also were freed from four of the five conditions cited in the *sūtras* as manifestations of *dukkha* specific to the female gender—pregnancy, childbirth, the necessity of abandoning one's family to go to the husband's family, and the obligation to serve males. Only the biologically based *dukkha* of menstruation remained for the female practitioner.[20] As Peter Harvey notes, the abandonment of one's family and indentured service to one's husband are neither universal nor inevitable accompaniments of a married lifestyle, but simply the expectations inherent in a sexist social structure.[21] The same is of course true of the expectation that women are obligated to serve men. The liberating effect of breaking out of the subordinate role of a traditional Indian wife is reflected in a verse written by a Buddhist nun in which she exults over her freedom from "kitchen drudgery" and a husband who considered her an object of low rank. In contrast, her life as a nun allows for the comparative leisure of pursuing Buddhist practice.[22] The powerful attraction Buddhism must have held for women in early Indian society is clearly evident here. Even the ascetic restrictions of a nun represented a life of luxurious ease, both physically and psychologically, when compared to the demeaning harshness of her pre-Buddhist role as a drudge to an unappreciative spouse.

. . .

The *Vinaya* in Flux: Dissolving Sexist Attitudes

> From the Buddhist point of view, the objective is not merely to avoid male domination, but to avoid being dominated by preconceptions altogether.[23] For all its commitment to inclusiveness at the doctrinal level, institutional Buddhism was not able to (or saw no reason to) challenge prevailing attitudes about gender roles in society.[24]

As we approach the end of the twentieth century, we find that as a result of feminist consciousness-raising and changes in social structure, it is no longer *upāyic* to practice sexism as a concession to wider social pressures. In fact, we must beware of any such compromises, as well as of reactionary tendencies. Is Buddhism ready to meet this new challenge? Can Buddhists boldly forge a new Middle Way between the manifest sexism of the past and what amount to separatist religious movements championed by estranged women practitioners?

It is difficult for us to assess today whether the end, survival of the budding *Saṅgha,* truly justified the means of artificial restrictions placed on women practitioners to assuage the fears of an unenlightened community as well as of the Buddha's own disciples. What is clear is that the restrictions of the past, enshrined in the eight rules for nuns, have outlived their usefulness. In a world where women are recognized as autonomous beings—socially, politically, and economically—there is no longer any need or justification for the artificial imposition of male guidance. Under the present circumstances, such guidance is at best perceived as an unwarranted paternalism and at worst an interference likely to promote resentment.

Our sole task is to assess present circumstances and priorities that will serve the same *upāyic* intent that seems to have motivated the policies of the past. Simply stated, in what ways must the *vinaya* be modified in order to continue to make Buddhism viable here and now? What socially appropriate modifications can be expeditiously made in the *vinaya* as a means to the original end of guiding the behavior of "a balanced, integrated Buddhist practitioner"?[25] How can *vinaya* fulfill its original meaning of "that by which one is led out (from suffering)," so as to serve "not so much as prohibitions as aids to spiritual training that require those observing them to be ever mindful."[26]

Vindication for socially sanctioned adjustments to *vinaya* comes from one of its most notable distinguishing characteristics as established by the Buddha—its inherent flexibility. The evolution of the code parallels the practice of case law, as reflected in the *vinaya* texts which annotate the rules in terms of the specific situation that elicited their promulgation. Furthermore, the application of said rules is further defined within this context, delineating the limits inherent in its application in terms of test cases and legitimate exceptions to the rule. Further guidance comes from the principle that "every action ruled by the *vinaya* is based on doing as little harm as possible and as much benefit as possible for oneself and others."[27] Yet there is no doubt that women are daily harmed by the restrictions and prejudices inculcated by sexism—and harmed most especially in terms of the untimely obstruction of their spiritual potential.

Charges of "androcentrism," male-centeredness, in Buddhist doctrine have become fairly common among women who feel increasingly excluded from the very core of Buddhist life. The frequency of the charges is in part due to the fact that they contain a grain of truth. Historically, Buddhist practice has given preference to male perceptions, as evidenced in the preceding discussions. Thus, Diana Paul declares, "Buddhism is an overwhelmingly male-created institution dominated by a patriarchal power structure [in which] . . . the feminine is frequently associated with the secular, powerless, profane and imperfect."[28] Similarly it has been argued:

> Chinese Buddhism remained shaped by men as the primary participants, by their imagination and their language. It never allowed women's experience and language to have anything like an equal influence on its expressive forms. Thus, it never could become "androgynous"—a religion in which the imaginations and experiences of men *and* women, which might be expected to differ, could both enrich the tradition.[29]

A footnote to this passage goes on to extend the charge of androcentrism to Buddhism in general. Overlooking for the time being the dubious references to gender-specific imagination and language, which would immerse us in the endless debates about nature versus nurture in shaping human behavior, it seems at the very least odd to accuse Ch'an of all sects of androcentrism. The "face before your parents were born" or "original nature" is by definition devoid of social demarcations, including gender.

But precisely how is androcentrism—the nonegalitarian bias in favor of men and to the detriment of women—to be exorcised from Buddhism? Are some proposed cures as dangerous as the original disease? The danger inherent in many analyses of rightly outraged feminists is that they have the effect of undermining the very message of the Buddha, the Awakened One. They lead irrevocably to the conclusion that Buddhism is not committed to universal enlightenment, as the Buddha originally vowed, but rather operates at half capacity, serving only half of the human population. Taken to an extreme, this view may drive women to sever all ties with institutional Buddhism, as irretrievably sexist and male-dominated, thereby shutting them off from the enlightenment potential of the tradition. At the same time, those women who decide to pursue their own gender-specific enlightenment will have effectively shut themselves off from and disavowed half of the population, namely men. In both cases true enlightenment is belied by the continued wallowing in gender distinctions so inappropriately applied to spirituality. We all would then have been driven back to the *Saṁsāric* cant, so alien to Buddhist philosophy, that "anatomy is destiny."

> As long as a man or a woman takes thought of the fact that he is a man or she is a woman, just so long does Māra have power to tempt, but if a person takes thought of this no longer, then does Māra depart sad and dejected and the lute falls from his hand. Insight into the Dhamma wipes away all distinctions of sex.[30]

The problem dissolves because sexism is not inherent in the *Saṅgha* as philosophically considered, but rather is confined to the sexist and distinctly unenlightened attitudes of those who cling uncritically to the past. Ironically, such individuals represent the very constrictions against which Siddhārtha rebeled on his way to becoming the Awakened One. In emulating the Buddha we too must awaken to the distortions accompanying fixations on gender, whether dictated by a male or female bias. The inconsistency of sexism within the *Saṅgha* will thereby be exposed, and its perpetuation will be seen as both philosophically groundless and pragmatically indefensible.

. . .

Notes

1. Bhikṣuṇī Karma Lekshe Tsomo, Preface to *Sakyadhita: Daughters of the Buddha* (Ithaca, N.Y.: Snow Lion Publications, 1988), 13.
2. The exact number of rules varies according to sects; however, all are consistent in requiring more of women, circumscribing their lives more rigidly. Overall, the rules by which a *bhikṣuṇī* is bound by represents approximately a 30 percent increase over those for a *bhikṣu.* The numbers for women and men, respectively, as cited by Peter Harvey, are 311/227 in Southern Buddhism's Theravādin sects, 366/258 in the Mūla-Sarvāstivadin sect of Northern Buddhism, and 348/250 in the Dharmaguptaka sect of Eastern Buddhism; *An Introduction to Buddhism: Teachings, History and Practices* (New York: Cambridge University Press, 1991), 225. Presumably the distinction is based on the assumption that they have a greater need for externally "guided" discipline and a correspondingly lower level of innate resources.
3. For example, pressured by Vatican sources, a panel of U.S. Catholic bishops recently issued an eighty-one page pastoral letter, "Called to Be One in Christ," capitulating to conservative forces seeking to perpetuate the discrimination of the past. Although the bishops condemn "the sin of sexism," they also uphold the position of Pope John Paul II restricting the priesthood to males: "This constant practice constitutes a tradition which witnesses to the mind of Christ and is therefore, normative." "Bishops Back Male-Only Priesthood," *Los Angeles Times,* April 9, 1992, A26. More recently, in May of 1994, the pope has reiterated the official stance barring women from the priesthood.
4. Jampa Tsedroen, "Living by the *Vinaya* in the West," in Lekshe Tsomo, 204.
5. Karma Lekshe Tsomo, 18.
6. The common Indo-European roots of Indian and Greek culture demonstrate misogyny as a shared cultural trait in these respective cultures. See Eva C. Keuls, *The Reign of the Phallus: Sexual Politics in Ancient Athens* (New York: Harper & Row, 1985).
7. For a cross-cultural examination of the psychological implications of this deep-seated ambivalence, see Erich Neumann, *The Great Mother: An Analysis of the Archetype,* trans. Ralph Manheim (Princeton, N.J.: Princeton University Press, 1963).
8. Wendy Doniger O'Flaherty, *Tales of Sex and Violence: Folklore, Sacrifice, and Danger in the Jaiminiya Brahmana* (Chicago: University of Chicago Press, 1985), 93.
9. For a detailed exposition of the paradoxical nature of sexuality in Hinduism, see Stella Kramrisch, *The Presence of Śiva* (Princeton, N.J.: Princeton University Press, 1981).
10. *Naladinannurru,* 386, as quoted in *Sources of Indian Tradition,* Vol. I (New York: Columbia University, 1958), 69.
11. This gynophobia continued well beyond the time of the Buddha, as demonstrated by the following poems by the Sanskrit master of the Gupta period, Bhartrihari (died 651). In one poem woman is accused of clouding the "clear bright flame of man's discernment" with "lamp-black eyes," clearly associating

the female sex with a darkness that compromises the light of the male. In another piece a woman is eulogized for her physical beauty as various parts of her anatomy (eyes, teeth, face, and skin) are compared to the beauties of Nature. However, in an ironic twist, the softness of these features is bitterly contrasted with her inner soul "carved from flint." *Poems from the Sanskrit,* trans. John Brough (Baltimore, Md.: Viking Penguin, 1968), 56, 57.

12. As quoted by Heng Ching, in Karma Lekshe Tsomo, 91.
13. Karma Lekshe Tsomo, 83.
14. Diana Paul, *Women in Buddhism* (Lancaster: Miller, 1980), 169–71.
15. *Taranatha: The Origin of Tara Tantra,* trans. David Templemen (Dharamsala: Library of Tibetan works and Archives, 1981), 11–12.
16. *Ching-te ch'uan-teng lu; Chūan 11, Taisho shinshu daizokyo* 51, p. 289a.1ff, as cited by Miriam L. Levering, "Lin-chi (Rinzai) Ch'an and Gender: The Rhetoric of Equality and the Rhetoric of Heroism," in *Buddhism, Sexuality and Gender,* ed. José Ignacio Cabezón (Albany, N.Y.: SUNY Press, 1992), 151–52.
17. See Shohei Ichimura, "Buddhist Dharma and Natural Law: Toward a Trans-Cultural, Universal Ethics," in *Buddhist Ethics and Modern Society: An International Symposium,* ed. Charles Wei-hsun Fu and Sandra A. Wawrytko (New York: Greenwood Press, 1991), 394–96.
18. Note that women played a very active role in Gandhi's campaigns, while his philosophy considered sexuality a wasteful channeling of productive energy.
19. See Harvey, who cites evidence from Burma, Thailand, Sri Lanka, Tibet, and China, 214–15.
20. *Samyutta Nikaya,* IV, 239. It is noteworthy that the "curse" of menstruation is also a necessary accompaniment of the woman's reproductive powers. The frequent devaluation of that natural process in many cultures thus is consistent with the fear aroused in men by this and other "woman's mysteries." See Sandra Harding, *Women's Mysteries* (New York: Bantam, 1971).
21. Harvey, 215.
22. Therigata, *Psalms of Early Buddhists,* trans. C. A. Rhys Davids (London: Pali Text Society, 1964), 250, as quoted by Tsultrim Aillione in her Introduction to *Women of Wisdom* (London: Routledge & Keagan Paul, 1984), 8–9. An alternative, conspicuously less self-deprecating translation of this same verse recently has been made by Susan Murcott and John Tarrant in which the woman rejoices over her freedom from cooking utensils and husband, from the cycle of birth and rebirth, that previously encumbered her. "The Therigatha" (Selections), *Kahawai,* I, 3 (1979), 1–14.
23. Karma Lekshe Tsomo, 63.
24. Alan Sponberg, "Attitudes toward Women and the Feminine in Early Buddhism," in Cabezón, 3–36, and Denise Lardner Carmody, *Women and World Religions* (Nashville, Tenn.: Abingdon, 1979), 18.
25. Sylvia Wetzel, "The Function and Meaning of Vows," in Karma Lekshe Tsomo, 75.
26. Harvey, 224.
27. Jampa Tsedroen, "Living by the *Vinaya* in the West," in Karma Lekshe Tsomo, 202.

28. Diana Paul, in her introduction to *Women in Buddhism,* as quoted by Lenore Friedman in *Meetings with Remarkable Women: Buddhist Teachers in America* (Boston: Shambhala, 1987), 13.
29. Levering, 151.
30. Marie Beuzeville Byles, *Footprints of Gautama the Buddha: Being the Story of the Buddha His Disciples Knew Describing Portions of His Ministerial Life* (Madras, India: Theosophical Publishing House, 1967), 84.

Bibliography

Allione, Tsultrim. *Women of Wisdom.* London: Routledge & Keagan Paul, 1984.

Besserman, Perle, and Manfred Steger. *Crazy Clouds: Zen Radicals, Rebels & Reformers.* Boston: Shambhala, 1991.

Byles, Marie Beuzeville. *Footprints of Gautama the Buddha: Being the Story of the Buddha His Disciples Knew Describing Portions of His Ministerial Life.* Madras, India: Theosophical Publishing House, 1967.

Cabezón, José Ignacio, ed. *Buddhism, Sexuality, and Gender.* Albany, New York: SUNY Press, 1992.

Carmody, Denise Lardner. *Women and World Religions.* Nashville, Tenn.: Abingdon, 1979.

Friedman, Lenore. *Meetings with Remarkable Women: Buddhist Teachers in America.* Boston: Shambhala, 1987.

Harvey, Peter. *An Introduction to Buddhism: Teachings, History and Practices.* New York: Cambridge University Press, 1991.

Ichimura, Shohei. "Buddhist Dharma and Natural Law: Toward a Trans-Cultural, Universal Ethics." In *Buddhist Ethics and Modern Society: An International Symposium.* Ed. Charles Wei-hsun Fu and Sandra A. Wawrytko. New York: Greenwood Press, 1991.

King, Sallie B., trans. *Passionate Journey: The Spiritual Autobiography of Satomi Myōdō.* Boston: Shambhala, 1987.

Kramrisch, Stella. *The Presence of Śiva.* Princeton, N.J.: Princeton University Press, 1981.

O'Flaherty, Wendy Doniger. *Tales of Sex and Violence: Folklore, Sacrifice, and Danger in the Jaiminiya Brahmana.* Chicago: University of Chicago Press, 1985.

Sources of Indian Tradition. New York: Columbia University, 1958.

Templemen, David, trans. *Taranatha: The Origin of Tara Tantra.* Dharamsala: Library of Tibetan Works and Archives, 1981.

Tsomo, Bhikṣuṇī Karma Lekshe, ed. *Sakyadhita: Daughters of the Buddha.* Ithaca, N.Y.: Snow Lion Publications, 1988.

Wawrytko, Sandra A. "Women and Religion in Post-modern Japan: The Call for a New Yakami." *Explorations: Journal for Adventurous Thought,* vol. XII, no. 3 (spring 1994).

Wayman, Alex, and Hideko Wayman, trans. *The Lion's Roar of Queen Śrimala.* New York: Columbia University Press, 1974.

SEXUAL VIOLENCE

[15]

Tamar: The Royal Rape of Wisdom

Phyllis Trible

2 Samuel 13:1–22

From the book of Samuel comes the story of a family enmeshed in royal rape. Brother violates sister. He is a prince to whom belong power, prestige, and unrestrained lust. She is a princess to whom belong wisdom, courage, and unrelieved suffering. Children of one father, they have not the same care of each other. Indeed, the brother cares not at all.

Though part of a narrative about King David and his court, this tale of terror stands on its own.[1] Within a well-ordered design the plot moves from obstacles and plans to the crime and its aftermath. Three episodes (A, B, C) lead to the rape (D) and three follow from it (B', C', A'). Our task is to explore the artistry and meaning of this literary unit as we attend to its single female character.[2]

Before the Crime, 13:1–9c[3]

In preparation for the crime, episode one presents the characters and their circumstances; episode two reports a scheme devised for the prince by his advi-

---

sor; and episode three enlists the authority of the king. Circular structures organize these first two units while the third builds on a chain of command and response.

A. *Introduction: Characters and Circumstances, 13:1–3.* The story commences with a transitional phrase, "And it came to pass after this." Behind lie the sordid deeds of David to secure Bathsheba, the redeeming birth of his son Solomon, and a decisive victory over the Ammonites. The king has enjoyed success in all things public and private. But now the narrator leaves these exploits. To be sure, David alone survives from the preceding scenes, yet in a subordinate role. He is a member of the supporting cast.

Following the transitional phrase, a ring composition introduces the characters around a description of circumstances (13:1–3).[4] Within this structure, circular patterns reflect the whole. At the beginning come three children of David.[5] First named is Absalom, the third son, whose presence hovers over the entire tale, though he himself appears only near the end. Last is Amnon, the firstborn, whose desire initiates the action. Between these two males stands the female who relates to each of them and also has her own identity. Sister to Absalom and object of desire to Amnon, this beautiful woman is Tamar. The circular arrangement of the verse centers upon her:

To Absalom, son of David,
  a sister beautiful, with the name Tamar,
and desired her Amnon, son of David.
(13:1)

Two males surround a female. As the story unfolds, they move between protecting and polluting, supporting and seducing, comforting and capturing her. Further, these sons of David compete with each other through the beautiful woman.

For a time, the narrator puts Absalom aside to develop the latter half of the circle, "And desired her Amnon, son of David."[6] The information leads to the center of the episode, a description of circumstances that bode trouble (13:2). "So tormented was Amnon that he made himself ill on account of Tamar his sister" (13:2a, RSV). Although first linked to the crown prince solely as object of desire, Tamar receives here the designation "his sister." The word relating her to Absalom also binds her to Amnon. The storyteller has chosen to stress familial ties, for such intimacy exacerbates the coming tragedy.[7]

This sibling connection, however, is not the reason for Amnon's frustration and illness. His passion is pain "because a virgin was she, and it was impossible in the eyes of Amnon to do to her anything" (13:2b). Full of lust, the prince is impotent; full of sight, he lacks insight. As a virgin, Tamar is protected property, inaccessible to males, including her brother. Yet the ominous phrase, "it was impossible . . . to do to her anything," not only underscores his frustration but also foreshadows the disaster of its release.[8] Explicating the meaning of Amnon's desire, lust-sickness and violent yearning enclose the virgin:

> So tormented was Amnon that he made himself ill
> on account of Tamar his sister,
>
> for a virgin was she,
>
> and it was impossible in the eyes of Amnon
> to do to her anything.
>
> (13:2)

If in the first circle (13:1) the two brothers surrounding Tamar contrast helping and harming her, in the second circle one brother signifies total danger. In fact, the inhibition of violence leads to its opposite. Though Amnon finds it "impossible to do to her anything," a perspective and a plan come from someone else. Jonadab is that person.

As the conclusion to episode one, the introduction of Jonadab completes a ring composition:

> To Amnon a friend with the name Jonadab,
> son of Shimeah, brother of David.
> Jonadab was a very crafty man.
>
> (13:3)

At the beginning of the unit (13:1a), a prepositional phrase followed by a noun joined two people: "to *(lĕ)* Absalom . . . a sister." Then came her personal identity: "with the name Tamar." Now at the end is a parallel structure: "To *(lĕ)* Amnon a friend with the name Jonadab." Attached to the name is the identification, "son of Shimeah, brother of David." Jonadab is a cousin in the royal family. Like the king's sons, he relates explicitly to David and thus acquires a status never granted Tamar the daughter. Moreover, a juxtaposition of adjectives shows Jonadab's advantage over Tamar. Although she is "beautiful (*yph*)," Jonadab is "very crafty (*ḥkm*)."[9] His entrance gives Amnon the friend he needs to surmount the impossible. This pair contrasts with Tamar and Absalom. At the same time, the parallelism falters, for Tamar alone is the object and potential victim of lust. In the beginning, two brothers surround her; in the middle, sickness and contemplated violence entrap her; in the end, the very crafty Jonadab surpasses her. Truly, episode one portends disaster for Tamar.

B. *Jonadab and Amnon, 13:4–5.* From narrated discourse the story moves to a conversation between Jonadab and Amnon. Commencing with questions and closing with instructions, the crafty friend envelops the lustful prince in solicitude and advice. First, he provokes an explanation of Amnon's condition.[10]

> Why are you so haggard, son of the king,
>   morning after morning?
> Will you not tell me?
>
> (13:4, RSV)

Focusing upon royal as well as familial status, the vocative, "son of the king," heightens incongruity. Surely the heir apparent need not be weak, thin, haggard, or impoverished.[11]

Jonadab's approach succeeds, for Amnon answers forthrightly. "Tamar, sister-of Absalom, my-brother, I desire" (13:4). Syntax and vocabulary yield a well-constructed sentence of six Hebrew words. Tamar, the object of the verb, comes first, for she is his obsession. The remaining words are striking in their alliteration. Each begins with the letter *aleph,* giving the impression, perhaps, of halting sighs. Yet only at the end does Amnon reveal his yearning. "I (*ʾanî*)," he says emphatically, "desire (*ʾhb*)." Hence, the beginning and end of this sentence match the report that "her name was Tamar and desired (*ʾhb*) her Amnon, son of David" (13:1). Narrator and character seem to tell the same tale.

But the middle words of the confession alter this continuity: "sister-of Absalom, my-brother." For the first time, fraternal language enters to indicate friction between the royal sons. The designation, "sister-of Absalom," supports this tension while deflecting Tamar's kinship to Amnon (cf. 13:2). The entire phrase implies a different obstacle from the narrated explanation. According to Amnon, Absalom, not virginity, stands between the object and his desire. If this male can be removed, the female becomes accessible. "Tamar, sister-of Absalom, my-brother, *I* desire," says Amnon to Jonadab. In this speech-event converge the four characters whom the storyteller has juxtaposed (cf. 13:1, 3). Again, their pairing is uneven. Absalom and Tamar are the objects of discourse; Jonadab and Amnon plot against them.

"And Jonadab said to him [Amnon], 'Lie upon your bed and act ill'" (13:5). In Hebrew the first verb and object share the same root (*škb*), thereby introducing a key word: "Lie upon your lying-place." The second imperative, "act ill," exploits Amnon's condition. Though he has made himself genuinely sick (*ḥlh*) on account of Tamar (13:2), Jonadab recommends that he feign illness (*ḥlh*) to provoke a paternal visit.[12] In addition, he tells Amnon what to say.

When your father comes to see you,
then you say to him,
"Let come Tamar my sister
and let her feed me food
and let her do before my eyes the food
so that I may see
and eat from her hand."

(13:5b)

With attention to detail, the plan emerges. Amnon should use the coming (*bôʾ*) of his father to request the coming (*bôʾ*) of *his* sister, not Absalom's sister. To claim kinship with Tamar this time averts suspicion (cf. 13:4). Moreover, her visit should be lengthy. Not only would she, like a nurse, give Amnon food, but also, like a maid, she would prepare the food before his eyes, thus feeding the lust of sight. The phrase, "let her do (*ʿśh*) before my eyes the food," recalls the impossibility "in the eyes of Amnon to do (*ʿśh*) to her anything" (13:2). While the feeding and preparing of food occur in reverse order, the consequences come in proper sequence: "that I may see and eat from her hand."[13] The lack of an object for the verb *see* poses shrewd ambiguity.[14] Though David must be made to think that Amnon wants to see the food being prepared, the reader knows that he wants to see Tamar. Further, to "eat from her hand" would bring her within grasp.

Jonadab is indeed cunning.[15] Having elicited from Amnon a confession that seeks license, he schemes to gratify the prince. The skills of a counselor he employs to promote illness. He would use the father to overcome the obstacle of the brother and secure the sister. Around Amnon, then, his speeches weave a net of friendship that ensnares Tamar, Absalom, and David. With its own ring structure, this second episode bears emphatically the message of the first: Tamar is trapped.

C. *David and His Children, 13:6–9c.* From description (episode one) and advice (episode two), the story moves to action. In episode three, circular patterns yield to linear progressions that, nevertheless, begin and end at Amnon's house. The verbs *coming* (*bôʾ;* 13:6), *sending* (*šlḥ;* 13:7), and *going (hlk;* 13:7, 8) signal the movement of plot and place. Unlike the preceding episodes, this one mixes narrated and direct discourse. Storyteller and characters unite to continue the tale.

The scheme of Jonadab pivots on David. "Amnon lay down *(škb)* and acted ill and the king came to see him" (13:6a). Breaking with the vocabulary of Jonadab to identify David as monarch rather than father, the narrator accents authority without power. The king bows to the prince. So Amnon speaks, appropriating the words of Jonadab.[16]

> Let come Tamar my sister.
> Let her make bread *(lbb)* before my eyes,
> a couple of cakes,
> that I may eat *(brh)* from her hand.
> (13:6b)

A special verb for making bread *(lbb)* appears here. It suggests in Hebrew a play upon the word *heart,* and the pun fits the occasion.[17] Tamar preparing the desired bread will herself be the desire of Amnon's heart. Feasting upon her with his eyes, his lust will reach out to eat from her hand.

The son's request becomes the king's order. Immediately David sends (*šlḥ*) word to Tamar at the house. Though "the king" visited Amnon, "David" dispatches a message to Tamar. No familial language relates father and daughter—only two commands that impel disaster (13:7). First, "Go to the house of Amnon your brother." The fraternal reference would seem to guarantee safety. Second, "Make for him the food." The imperative *make* or *do* (*ʿśh*) hints that it is no longer impossible for Amnon to do (*ʿśh*) anything to his virgin sister (cf. 13:2, 5). Unwittingly, David has sealed Tamar's fate.[18]

From Jonadab to Amnon to David to Tamar the story develops, with increasing speed and varying nuances, from advice to request to command to obedience.[19] With Tamar, the parade of characters stops, and the chain of action holds. Direct discourse ceases. The narrator heightens suspense by concentrating upon the young woman. "So Tamar went (*hlk*) to the house of Amnon her brother" (13:8a, RSV). A parenthetical observation intervenes to continue an ironic play on the verb *lie (škb;* cf. 13:5, 6). "Now he was lying down" (13:8b). Amnon's supine position becomes a posture of power devastating for Tamar. So the attention returns to her. Six verbs, in sets of threes, detail her activities. They focus on Amnon's eyes:

> She took the dough
> and she kneaded it
> and she made bread *(lbb)*
> *before his eyes;*
> and she baked the bread (*lbbt*)[20]
> and she took the pan
> and she served
> before him.
> (13:8c–9b)

In obeying David, Tamar has become the object of sight. Amnon, the narrator, and the readers behold her. Voyeurism prevails.[21] Yet Amnon himself wants more than illicit sight; he desires forbidden flesh. Abruptly, he "refuses to eat" (13:9c). All that his lust demands he must have, and refusal is his way to fulfillment. The prince has duped the king; the princess must suffer the consequences. Thus the story moves to its center.

The Crime: Amnon and Tamar, 13:9d–18

In this central unit,[22] form and content yield a flawed chiasmus that embodies irreparable damage for the characters. Amnon's commands and various responses to them mark the beginning and the end.[23] Within the *inclusio* Amnon and Tamar are the sole participants. In the first half come his command and her response, followed by a conversation between the two. In the corresponding section of the second half, their conversation collapses into his command and her response.[24] The rape itself constitutes the center of the chiasmus.[25] This design verifies the message of the preceding circular patterns:[26] Tamar is entrapped for rape.

a Amnon's command to the servants and their response (13:9de)
  b Amnon's command to Tamar and her response (13:10–11a)
    c Conversation between Amnon and Tamar (13:11b–14a)
      d Rape (13:14b–15b)
    c'–b' Conversation between Amnon and Tamar:
        Amnon's command to Tamar and her response (13: 15c–16)
a' Amnon's command to a servant and his response (13:17–18)

(a) "Go out (*yṣ*ʾ), every man, from me," orders Amnon (13:9d). His command is obeyed in identical language. "And they went out (*yṣ*ʾ) every man, from him" (13:9e). Though all witnesses apparently leave, the narrator remains to see evil unfold and record its aftermath for the reader.[27] Amnon's power to banish all has its limits.

(b) Alone with Tamar, the prince addresses her for the first time but fails to use her name. "Bring the food (*bryh*) to the bedroom that I may eat from your hand" (13:10a).[28] What his eyes have possessed, his hand seeks to hold. Moving Tamar into the bedroom of the house (13:8) reinforces the planned intimacy.

The princess who once obeyed the king is the sister heeding Amnon's instructions. She ministers to a sick and deceiving brother. Not a word does she speak. Three main verbs describe her actions: take, bring, and give. The first verb parallels earlier deeds. "Tamar took (*lqḥ*) the bread," even as she had taken (*lqḥ*) the dough and then the pan (13:8). Parenthetically, this bread is the desired food (*lbbt*) "which she had made" (*ʿśh;* 13:10b). As she has "done" (*ʿśh*) the bread before the eyes of Amnon, so it becomes possible for him to "do" (*ʿśh*) something to her (cf. 13:2). "Tamar took the bread which she had made." If the verb *take* alludes to her past actions, the verb *bring* responds to present orders: "She brought [the bread] to Amnon her brother to his bedroom" (13:10c).[29] The third action, in the privacy of the bedroom, leads her directly to Amnon. "She gave to him to eat" (13:11a). The time for violence is at hand.

(c) "He grabbed hold *(ḥzq)* of her" (13:11b).[30] Quick and forceful action precedes a crude invitation for rape. "Come, lie (*škb*) with me, my sister" (13:11c, RSV).[31] Through a series of orders, all of them obeyed, Amnon has manipulated the occasion to feed his lust. This time, however, the royal command meets objection. In the presence of a rapist, Tamar panics not. In fact, she claims her voice. Unlike Amnon's brisk commands, her deliberations slow the movement of the plot, though they are unable to divert it.[32] If Amnon used the vocative to seduce her, she returns it to summon him to sense:[33]

> No (*ʾal*), my brother.
> (13:12a, RSV)

Negatives persist:

> Do not (*ʾal*) violate (*ʿnh*) me,
> for (*kî*) it is not (*lōʾ*) done thus in Israel.
> (13:12bc, RSV)

Her appeal is to the custom of their people, not to divine law or inner feelings. Repeating the key verb *do,* the last negative accents the point:

> Do not (*ʾal*) do (*ʿśh*) this foolish thing.[34]
> (13:12d, RSV)

Turning from prohibition, Tamar pursues the folly of Amnon's demand. Carefully she weighs the consequences in a rhetorical question about herself and a projected description of her brother:

> I (*ʿanî*), where would I carry my shame?
> You (*ʿattāh*), you would be like one of
> the fools in Israel.
> (13: 13ab)

Unrestrained, Amnon's desire means disaster for them both. Hence, Tamar seeks an alternative. The solution lies with David, the highest human authority in the realm. Referring to him as monarch, Tamar sets distance between father and daughter:

> Now speak to the king,
> for (*kî*) he will not keep me from you.
> (13:13c, RSV)

Her words are honest and poignant; they acknowledge female servitude. Tamar knows Amnon can have her but pleads that he do it properly.[35] Though Jonadab advised Amnon to seek David's help, how different was that counsel. Over against Jonadab stands Tamar. Wisdom opposes craftiness. In light of her words, not only Amnon but also Jonadab is a fool. Yet in this story victory belongs to the fools.

Precisely now, when Tamar speaks for the first time, the narrator hints at her powerlessness by avoiding her name. Repeatedly, the introductions to direct speeches of male characters use their proper names: Jonadab said, Amnon said, David said, and Absalom said. Such a pattern occurs even where the pronoun *he* would suffice (e.g., 13:6c, 10, 15c). By contrast, the name Tamar never prefaces her speeches, here or later (13:16a); only the pronoun *she* obtains. This subtle difference suggests the plight of the female. Without her name, she lacks power. Nonetheless, she speaks reason and wisdom.[36]

The words of Tamar fall on deaf ears. "He did not want to hear her voice" (13:14a). Passionately, Amnon has desired to see and touch her, for with these senses he has made of her what he wills. But to hear her voice is another matter; it disturbs the fantasies that eyes and hands have fashioned. To hear might mean repentance. So Amnon chooses to close out her voice, even leaving his refusal for the narrator to report. Amnon cares not at all for his sister. He acts against her will to pursue his lust.[37]

(d) Rape is the center of the chiasmus. Quickly, though with emphasis, the deed unfolds. Third-person narration distances the terror while reporting it. "He was stronger than she; thus he raped her and laid her" (13:14b). All three verbs come from the preceding section.[38] The one who "grabbed (*ḥzq*) hold of her" (13:11) is truly "stronger (*ḥzq*) than she." "Do not violate (*ʿnh*) me," she had pleaded (13:12); so "he raped (*ʿnh*) her." "Lie (*škb*) with me," he had ordered (13:11); now "he lay (*škb*)" not, however, with her because the Hebrew omits the preposition to stress his brutality. "He laid her."[39] If the repetitions of verbs confirm the predictability of Amnon's act, the direct object *her* underscores cruelty beyond the expected. The deed is done.

Violence in turn discloses hatred, the underside of lust. With profound insight, the storyteller interprets the terror of the act.

a b c
Then-hated-her Amnon a-hatred great indeed (*meʾod*).

c' b' a'
Truly (*kî*) great(er) the-hatred which he-hated-her
than-the-desire which he-desired-her.

(13:15ab)

Through a chiasmus of repeated words, the first two lines of this artfully constructed sentence focus hatred upon Tamar.[40] In the first line hate surrounds her (and Amnon too!), and in the second it attacks her through end-stress. Four times the verb and its cognate noun assault the victim. Structure and vocabulary secure hatred, and yet the sentence does not end. As a parallel in form to the second line, the third provides comparison and contrast. In using the word *desire* (*ʾhb*) to describe Amnon's feelings for Tamar (13:1, 4), this line shows that all along the desire was lust, not love. Having gratified itself, lust deepens into hatred. With all ambiguity eliminated, the two occurrences of the word *desire* yield to the four of *hate.*[41]

> Then Amnon hated her a great hatred indeed.
> Truly, greater was the hatred with which he hated her
> than the desire with which he desired her.
> (13:15ab)

Lust fulfilled escalates its attack on the victim. The crime is despicable; the aftermath, ominous.

c'-b'. A final conversation between Amnon and Tamar merges into command and response. Collapse of form and shrinkage of content show irreparable damage to the characters. Whereas preceding the crime four Hebrew words expressed Amnon's desire, "Come, lie with-me, my-sister" (13:11c), now two imperatives relay his revulsion, "Get-up; go" (13:15c). No longer does he call her sister or seek intimacy with her.[42] Instead, the imperative *go* (*hlk*) echoes derisively the command that first brought Tamar to his house, when David instructed her to go (*hlk;* 13:7).

This abused woman will no more heed Amnon's order of dismissal than she consented to his demand for rape. Nor does she allow anger to cloud her vision. If before the deed she sought justice, how much more after it! Though shorter this time, her words are equally firm.

They begin with the negative, "No (*ʾal*)." Unlike her earlier speech (13:12), the fraternal vocative is missing.[43] From Tamar's side, as from Amnon's, kinship language has ceased. "No," she said to him, "because sending me away is a greater evil than the other which you have done (*ʿśh*) to me" (13:16a).[44] If the narrator interprets that the hatred is greater than (*gĕdôlāh mē*) the desire, Tamar understands that the expulsion is greater than (*gĕdôlāh mē*) the rape. In sending her away, Amnon increases the violence he has inflicted upon her. He condemns her to a lifelong sentence of desolation (cf. 13:20b).

Tamar knows that rape dismissed is crime exacerbated. Yet she speaks to a foolish and hateful man who cares not at all for truth and justice, especially when embodied it stands in his presence. Before the crime, "he did not wish (*ʾbh*) to hear (*šmʿ*) her voice (13:14a); after the tragedy, he remains incorrigible. Hence comes the narrator's refrain, "But he was not willing (*ʾbh*) to listen (*šmʿ*) to her" (13:16b). The words of this wise woman he spurns a second time.[45] She speaks no more.

a'. The conclusion of the chiasmus expands upon its opening.[46] Amnon orders "the young man attending him, 'Send out this from me to the outside and bolt the door after her'" (13:17). At the start, Amnon wanted the servants out and Tamar in (13:9de); at the close, he wants the servant in and Tamar out.[47] Although his two orders correspond, the Hebrew verbs differ. The imperative expelling Tamar (*šlḥ*) mocks her own words rather than reverting to Amnon's earlier vocabulary (*yṣʾ;* 13:9de). "Sending (*šlḥ*) me away," she said, "is a greater evil than the other which you have done (*ʿśh*) to me." Amnon is capable of that evil. "Send (*šlḥ*) this away" (13:17b), he commands, speaking not to but about the woman who stands in his presence. She has become for him solely a disposable object. Furthermore, contrary to many translations,[48] he does not say, "Send away this woman from me." The Hebrew has only the demonstrative *this.* For Amnon, Tamar is a thing, a "this" he wants thrown out. She is trash. The one he desired before his eyes, his hatred wants outside, with the door bolted after her.

Yet his command receives delayed attention (cf. 13:9de). "Bolt the door after her" (*ʾaḥăreyāh;* 13:17c, RSV) leads to a narrative interlude beginning, "Now upon her" (*wĕʾālêhā;* 13:18a). While Amnon turns away from Tamar, the storyteller looks at her. Once again, she is the center of attention and once again without her name. "Now upon her was a long robe with sleeves, for thus were the virgin daughters of the king clad of old."[49] Sadly, what the robe proclaims Tamar is no longer. Filial and royal language has never attended this daughter of the king, and now the word *virgin* applies no more. Tamar is victim of a shame that her clothes cannot hide (cf. Gen. 2:25; 3:7).

Having placed the destroyed woman before our eyes, the narrator returns to the servant's response. At first glance, he appears to carry out the order precisely (cf. 13:9de). "He put her outside, the one attending him, and he bolted the door after her" (13:18b). Nuances show, however, that Amnon's power is waning. The description of Tamar has already broken the continuity between command and response. Moreover, when the servant does obey, Amnon ironically imprisons himself behind a locked door while releasing the proof of his crime. Further, though the imperative, "send out (*šlḥ*)," mocked Tamar's words (13:17), the storyteller halts the mocking. For the first time ever, narrated discourse fails to employ Amnon's vocabulary in reporting obedience to his command. Instead, the verb, "he put her outside" (*yṣʾ*), matches the first occasion (13:9de) when the servants were sent out. These subtleties in the form and content imply that Amnon is a fool in Israel. Surely the responses to his last words recall Tamar's prediction (13:13a).

After the Crime, 13:19–22

With the rape concluded, the plot moves to the aftermath: a meeting between Tamar and Absalom, a report on David, and a concluding description of characters and circumstances. These three episodes correspond, though with notable differences, to the three episodes before the crime. The first two units parallel in content and order the two immediately preceding the crime. The third episode returns to the opening verse of the story, thereby completing an overall ring composition (i.e., A, B, C, D, B', C', A').[50]

B'. *Tamar and Absalom, 13:19–20.* Before the crime a conversation between Jonadab and Amnon, centering upon Tamar, culminated in an appeal to David, the authority figure. Now, after the crime, a meeting between Tamar and Absalom, centering upon Amnon, matches this conversation. The meeting consists of narrated descriptions of Tamar (13:19 and 20c) encircling Absalom's words to her (13:20ab). The storyteller restores her name but removes her speech so that she continues to be powerless. In fact, she is the picture of desolation.

Tamar took ashes upon her head
  and the long robe that was upon her she tore.
She put her hand upon her head,
  and she went out; as she went, she wept.
(13:19)[51]

Taking ashes upon her head employs the same verb (*lqḥ*) that marked Tamar's ministrations to Amnon: she took the dough, she took the pan, and she took the bread (13:8, 9, 10). Action intent upon restoring life to her sick brother becomes her own movement toward living death.[52] Further, tearing (*qrʿ*) her long robe symbolizes the violence done to a virgin princess. Rape has torn (*ʿnh*) her (13:14). The hand she puts upon her head is the hand from which Amnon feigned to eat as he grabbed hold of his sister (13:5, 6, 10, 11). A woman of mourning, Tamar goes away weeping.[53] Tears have replaced her voice of wisdom.

Through five separate occurrences, the verb describing her departure here, "she went away (*hlk*)," forms a circle for her actions in the story. The first word addressed to her, the word that altered her life forever, is the imperative, "Go." "And David sent to Tamar at the house, saying, 'Go (*hlk*) to the house of Amnon your brother'" (13:7). In the indicative, this verb characterizes her obedience: "Tamar went (*hlk*) to the house of Amnon her brother" (13:8). The central use of the verb, with a special meaning, belongs to Tamar. Trying to reason with Amnon, she asked, "And I, where would I carry (go with, *hlk*) my shame?" (13:13). The desolation implied in her question finds confirmation in the final appearances of the verb, which parallel the first two. Matching David's imperative is Amnon's last word to Tamar, "Go" (*hlk;* 13:15). To be sure, unlike the first occasion, she resists the order, but the outcome is inevitable. "She went away (*hlk*); as she went (*hlk*), she wept" (13:19d). For emphasis, the ending repeats the verb, joining it to her cry of pain. As this rhetorical circle closes, Tamar's actions cease.

Immediately Absalom speaks. His words form the center of the episode. While the presence of this prince has hovered over the story from the start (13:1), only now does he himself emerge. Continuing to stress kinship ties, the narrator introduces him as the brother of Tamar. Absalom appropriates the theme in addressing her.

> And Absalom her brother said to her,
> "Was Amnon your brother with you?
> Now, my sister be quiet your brother is he.
> Do not take to your heart this deed."
> (13:20ab)

Absalom's counsel surrounds his sister with the brother who has raped her, thereby repeating the circular structure that has ensnared Tamar from the beginning. Yet the narrator suggests a change. Standing over Amnon her brother is Absalom her brother. To him is the power of speech with layers of meaning. On the surface, his words appear to countenance the rape, only delicately alluded to at that. In the name of family loyalty, Absalom would silence Tamar, minimize the crime, and excuse Amnon.[54] But the interlocking structures and substance of the entire story indicate a different reading. In contrast to each of the other male characters, Absalom is the advocate of Tamar.

First, as advisor, he is to her what Jonadab was to Amnon. In urging Amnon to "act ill," Jonadab counseled pretense for a specific time and purpose. When he spoke of letting Tamar do the food so that Amnon could eat from her hand, his language cloaked a scheme for manipulation, seduction, and rape. With their own nuances, Absalom's advice to Tamar may also conceal a plan for revenge. "Be quiet . . . do not take to heart" counsels pretense for a time and purpose.[55] Absalom explicitly introduces this speech with the adverb *ʿattah,* "now" or "for the time being" (cf. NJV). As Amnon's pretense deceived David, so Tamar's pretense will deceive Amnon. Further, rather than minimizing the crime, euphemisms such as "with you" or "this deed" underscore its horror. They cover the unspeakable, even as Jonadab's innocent vocabulary promoted rape. Clearly, Absalom counters Jonadab, though as advisor the brother cannot redeem for Tamar what she has lost.

Second, Absalom opposes Amnon. "Absalom her brother said to her, 'Was

Amnon your brother with you?' . . . Your brother is he." Fraternal language recalls the tension present in the opening verse of the story where Absalom and Amnon surrounded Tamar (13:1). Although Amnon seduced and polluted Tamar, Absalom supports and protects her. In sentences that are grammatically parallel, both brothers address her as "my sister," yet with different intents. For Amnon, lust shapes the speech, "Come, lie with me, my sister" (13:11). For Absalom, tenderness dictates the counsel, "For the present, my sister, be quiet." Moreover, far from condoning Amnon's act, Absalom plots revenge.[56] Brother opposes brother through their sister Tamar.

Third, Absalom counters David. By using David to overcome the obstacle of Absalom, Jonadab and Amnon weakened the king's authority. Now Absalom speaks to Tamar on his own authority without appeal to David. His position in the design of the story also indicates that he supplants the king. If just before the crime David determined the action, just after it Absalom takes charge. Speaking at the center of this episode, he, not the king, orders the life of Tamar. Indeed, as the only character to talk after the crime, he holds the power, and this power he will use on behalf of Tamar. Thus, Absalom stands apart from the other male characters, even though he cannot reverse the desolation of his sister.

Like the beginning (13:19), the ending of this episode stresses the ruin of Tamar. She lives in death.

> So Tamar dwelt, and she was desolate,
> in the house of Absalom her brother.
> (13:20c, RSV)

In the first house (13:7a), she was a beautiful virgin (13:1, 2). In the house of her brother Amnon (13:7b, 8), she became a violated thing (13:14, 17). In the house of her brother Absalom (13:20c), she is a desolate sister.[57] When used of people elsewhere in scripture, the verb *be desolate* (*šmm*) connotes being destroyed by an enemy (Lam. 1:16) or being torn to pieces by an animal (Lam. 3:11).[58] Raped, despised, and rejected by a man, Tamar is a woman of sorrows and acquainted with grief. She is cut off from the land of the living, stricken for the sins of her brother; yet she herself has done no violence and there is no deceit in her mouth. No matter what Absalom may plan for the future, the narrator understands the endless suffering of her present.

> So Tamar dwelt, and she was desolate,
> in the house of Absalom her brother.

In this description the storyteller continues to stress the fraternal bond. The repetition of the phrase, "Absalom her brother," matches the narrated introduction to his speech, "And Absalom her brother said to her" (13:20a).

These words form a circle around the circle made by Absalom's use of the phrase "Amnon your brother" (13:20b). At the center of the two circles is Absalom's vocative, "my sister." It contrasts with Amnon's earlier use of the designation (13:11). If the brother Amnon has ensnared Tamar his sister, the brother Absalom surrounds them both to crush Amnon and comfort Tamar.[59] Form and content show that Absalom not only counters but overcomes Amnon.

C'. *David and His Children, 13:21.* Unlike the earlier conversation between Jonadab and Amnon, the meeting between Tamar and Absalom fails to culminate in an appeal to David. Even so, the second episode of the aftermath does turn to David through observations by the narrator. "When the king David heard all these deeds, he was very angry."[60] Inversion of the usual order of a Hebrew sentence, to place subject before verb, emphasizes the contrast between David and Absalom. Use of both title and name, "the king David," reinforces the dissimilarity. The royal rather than familial designation connotes power, yet power that forfeits responsibility. Though the brother Absalom has hinted at a plan, the king David has neither speech nor plan.

The received text says only that the king was "very angry." A Qumran manuscript adds, "for he loved him because his firstborn was he." The explanation suggests opposite interpretations. Is David angry at Amnon for what he has done, or is David angry about what has happened to Amnon? In other words, does the father's love for his firstborn condone or denounce the crime? The Greek Bible removes the ambiguity: "And he [David] did not rebuke Amnon his son because he loved him, since his firstborn was he."[61] David's anger signifies complete sympathy for Amnon and total disregard for Tamar. How appropriate that the story never refers to David and Tamar as father and daughter! The father identifies with the son; the adulterer supports the rapist; male has joined male to deny justice for the female.[62] After all, in these days there is a king in Israel, and royalty does the right in its own eyes.[63] Truly, however, David the king does not do well to be angry (cf. Jon. 4:4, 9).

A'. *Conclusion: Characters and Circumstances, 13:22.* With the narrator still in charge, the last verse of the story returns to the first, thereby completing the overall *inclusio.*

Absalom did not speak *(dbr)* with Amnon
  either evil or good,
but Absalom hated Amnon on account of the deed *(dbr)*
  that he raped Tamar his sister.
(13:22)[64]

At the very beginning, Absalom and Amnon, identified as sons of David, appeared in parallel positions surrounding Tamar. Tellingly, Absalom's name came first, though the story moved with Amnon.

> To Absalom, son of David,
> a sister beautiful, with the name Tamar,
> and desired her Amnon, son of David.
> (13:1)

Here, at the end (13:22), while David's name has appropriately disappeared, the three central characters remain. No longer parallel, the brothers meet as subject and object. Absalom does not speak with Amnon, who has refused to hear the words of Tamar.[65] Absalom hates (*śnʾ*) Amnon, who hates (*śnʾ*) Tamar (13:15b). The fulfillment of Amnon's lust has replaced desire (*ʾhb*) with increasing hatred, indeed a hatred turned upon Amnon himself.[66] His brother Absalom, a greater obstacle than ever (cf. 13:4), holds the power.[67] Foreboding silence cloaks fraternal hatred.

Tamar's position has also changed. No longer surrounded by two brothers (cf. 13:20) nor desired by Amnon, she appears outside the structure of their relationship. As in the opening verse of the story, she is called the sister of Absalom, and yet this time no adjective of beauty modifies the noun. Instead, a verb of violence acts upon its object to defile; the sororal identification but underscores the horror of the deed. The beautiful virgin encircled (13:1–2) has become the raped sister isolated (13:22). Her plight is the reason for silence and hatred, and thus it is fitting that the end-stress of the story belongs to Tamar:

> but Absalom hated Amnon on account of the deed
> that he raped *Tamar his sister.*

Responses to the Crime

From Absalom and the Narrator. With its menace and foreboding silence, the conclusion of this story implies a sequel.[68] Absalom waits two years (13:23–39). Then, having persuaded his father to let Amnon visit at Baal Hazor,[69] Absalom orders him killed while Amnon was "merry with wine" (13:28, RSV). And it was done.[70] None other than the crafty Jonadab explains the murder to David: "For by the command of Absalom this has been determined from the day he [Amnon] raped (*ʿnh*) his sister Tamar" (13:32, RSV).[71] Absalom flees. David mourns, though we cannot be sure if the object of his grief is Amnon the murdered or Absalom the fugitive.[72] We can be sure that it is not Tamar the violated.

After three years, Absalom returns to Jerusalem, but David refuses for a time to see him (14:1–33). Reporting these events, the narrator includes this description: "Now in all Israel there was no one so much to be praised for his beauty (*yph*) as Absalom; from the sole of his foot to the crown of his head there was no blemish in him" (14:25, RSV). *Beauty* is the same word once used for Tamar. Brother and sister were a handsome pair in Israel, but now the sister dwells desolate. The narrator has more to say on the subject, switching from Absalom to his offspring. "There were born to Absalom three sons and one daughter; her name was Tamar" (14:27, RSV). Strikingly, the anonymity of all the sons highlights the name of the lone female child. In her Absalom has created a living memorial for his sister. A further note enhances the poignancy of his act. Tamar, the daughter of Absalom, "became a woman beautiful (*yph*) to behold." From aunt to niece have passed name and beauty so that rape and desolation have not the final word in the story of Tamar.

From the Readers. Absalom remembers; the narrator records; and we the readers respond.[73] If we cannot sanction the violent revenge Absalom exacted, we can appropriate the compassion he shows for his sister. Such appropriation leads to ironic reflections on a passage in Proverbs. As a textbook for young men,[74] Proverbs often exploits women for its own purposes. The foreign female symbolizes the wicked woman from whom Dame Wisdom[75] can protect the male.[76] Just such a contrast prevails when a teacher exhorts a young man:

> Say to wisdom, "My sister are you,"
>   and call insight an intimate friend
> to preserve you from the loose woman,
>   from the adventurer with her smooth words.
> (Prov. 7:4–5, RSV)

Only here does Proverbs designate wisdom as "sister."[77] The familial term resonates with our story because Amnon does call wisdom his sister.[78] Yet at this point ironies commence. "Come, lie with me, my sister," Amnon demanded, perverting the epithet to serve his lust. Tamar replied with wisdom:

> No, my brother.
> Do not violate me,
>   for it is not done thus in Israel.
> Do not do this foolish thing.
> (13:12, RSV)

Even after he raped her, she continued to speak wise words:

> No, because sending me away is a greater evil
>   than the other which you have done to me.
> (13:16)

Obedient to the first line of the proverb, Amnon did say to Tamar the wise woman, "My sister are you." His embrace, however, produced a royal rape of wisdom. In light of his action, the parallel line heightens the contrast: "Call insight an intimate friend (or kinsman)." This advice Amnon skewed. For his intimate friend he chose the crafty Jonadab, who offered the plan that would gratify the lustful sight of the prince. Thus, iniquity, not insight, came from this kinsman.

Saying to wisdom, "My sister are you," and calling on an intimate friend for insight, Amnon was truly preserved "from the loose woman, from the adventurer with her smooth words." Yet she was never his temptation. His evil was his own lust, and from it others needed protection. Hence, Amnon's behavior exposes the misogynous assumption of this proverb to inspire a different perspective. Moreover, compassion for Tamar requires a new vision. If sister wisdom can protect a young man from the loose woman, who will protect sister wisdom from the loose man, symbolized not by a foreigner but by her very own brother? Who will preserve sister wisdom from the adventurer, the rapist with his smooth words, lecherous eyes, and grasping hands? In answering the question, Israel is found wanting—and *so are we.*

Notes

1. With perhaps a few additional passages, 2 Samuel 9–20 and 1 Kings 1–2 constitute the larger narrative. On the historical issues, see, most recently, John Van Seters, *In Search of History* (New Haven and London: Yale University Press, 1983), 277–91. For bibliographies through 1978, see D. M. Gunn, *The Story of King David,* JSOT Supp. 6 (Sheffield: JSOT Press, 1978), 142–53; Charles Conroy, *Absalom Absalom! Narrative and Language in 2 Sam 13–20* (Rome: Biblical Institute Press, 1978), 155–73. Within this larger narrative, Conroy establishes 2 Samuel 13–20 as an originally independent unit (pp. 1–6, 86–114), a view accepted by P. Kyle McCarter Jr., "'Plots, True or False': The Succession Narrative as Court Apologetic," *Int* 35 (1981): 362–63; cf. Peter R. Ackroyd, who designates 2 Samuel 13–19 as the unit in "The Succession Narrative (so-called)," *Int* 35 (1981): 385–86. R. A. Carlson isolates 2 Samuel 13–14 as a unit; see *David, the Chosen King: A Traditio-Historical Approach to the Second Book of Samuel* (Stockholm: Almqvist & Wiksell, 1964), 163–67. To this section belongs our story, which is itself a unit.
2. Recent literary studies include George Ridout, "The Rape of Tamar: A Rhetorical Analysis of 2 Sam 13:1–22," in *Rhetorical Criticism,* ed. Jared J. Jackson and Martin Kessler (Pittsburgh: Pickwick Press, 1974), 75–84; Conroy, *Absalom Absalom!,* 17–39; J. P. Fokkelman, *King David,* vol. 1, *Narrative Art and Poetry in the Books of Samuel* (Assen, The Netherlands: Van Gorcum, 1981),

99–114. Kiyoshi K. Sacon, "A Study of the Literary Structure of 'The Succession Narrative,'" in *Studies in the Period of David and Solomon and Other Essays*, ed. Tomoo Ishida (Winona Lake, Ind.: Eisenbrauns, 1982), 27–54. Available to me only in a brief English abstract is the work of S. Bar-Efrat, *Literary Modes and Methods in the Biblical Narrative, in view of II Sam. 10–20; I Kings 1–2* (in Hebrew); but see his article, "Some Observations on the Analysis of Structure in Biblical Narrative," *VT* 30 (1980): especially 162–63. In contrast, not opposition, to these studies, I employ a feminist perspective so that hermeneutical emphases differ even when literary observations concur.

3. Wherever they are not identified in this essay, chapter and verse citations come from the book of 2 Samuel.
4. By including 13:4 in this first episode, Ridout misses the ring structure and also breaks the direct discourse of 13:4–5; see "The Rape of Tamar," 81.
5. Though none of the three children has appeared before, the names of the sons occur in the family chronicle (2 Sam. 3:2–3). On the matrilinear rivalry of Amnon and Absalom, see Jon D. Levenson and Baruch Halpern, "The Political Import of David's Marriages," *JBL* 99 (1980): 507–18. The daughter Tamar is truly a new character. Half sister of one brother and full sister of the other, she lacks a place in the list of David's offspring. The omission resonates with our story. While the language of father and son persists, the language of father and daughter never occurs.
6. Contrary to translations that identify Amnon's yearning (*ʾhb*) as love (e.g., RSV, NEB, and NAB), I have chosen the ambiguous word *desire* to let the plot dis close the precise meaning (cf. NJV).
7. On the importance of relational epithets, see Ridout, "The Rape of Tamar," 75–78; also Robert Alter, *The Art of Biblical Narrative* (New York: Basic Books, 1981), 180.
8. For negative meanings of the phrase, "to do . . . anything," see Gen. 22:12 and Jer. 39:12.
9. On the morally neutral quality of "crafty" *(ḥkm),* see R. N. Whybray, *The Succession Narrative* (Naperville, Ill.: Alec R. Allenson, 1968), 58; idem, *The Intellectual Tradition in the Old Testament* (Berlin: Walter de Gruyter, 1974), 89–93.
10. *Contra* Conroy, *Absalom Absalom!,* 28, Jonadab's question is not necessarily "an admission of ignorance," perhaps already "insinuating a pejorative judgment on the quality of this shrewdness." As a skilled counselor, Jonadab observes Amnon's condition and then invites the prince to discuss his problem.
11. These are all connotations of the adjective *dal.*
12. See Harry Hagan, "Deception as Motif and Theme in 2 Sm 9–20; 1 Kgs 1–2," *Biblica* 60 (1979): 308–10.
13. Note the chiastic arrangement of the sequence feeding/preparing//seeing/eating.
14. *Contra* Burke O. Long, "Wounded Beginnings: David and Two Sons," in *Images of Man and God,* ed. Burke O. Long (Sheffield: Almond Press, 1981),

28, 116 n. 20. The verb *see* (*rʾh*) also plays on the perspective that Jonadab gives Amnon as well as on the forthcoming visit of David to see (*rʾh*) this sick man (13:6).

15. For further evaluation of Jonadab, see Fokkelman, *King David,* 109.
16. A comparison of Jonadab's words (13:5b) with Amnon's version (13:6b) discloses the following: (a) The opening lines are identical. (b) Jonadab uses the neutral words *lḥm* and *bryh* for bread and food, while Amnon switches to a special term (*lbbt*) suggesting an erotic pun (see below). (c) The phrase "before my eyes" appears in both speeches to play upon the narrator's statement that "it seemed impossible in the eyes of Amnon to do to her anything" (13:2). (d) Though Jonadab proposed two petitions, feeding and preparing the food, Amnon cites one, the making of bread. (e) Similarly, Amnon modifies the results desired. While Jonadab spoke of seeing and eating (*ʾkl*) "from her hand," Amnon omits the seeing, uses a different verb for eating (*brh*), but retains the phrase "from her hand." Such stylistic variations delineate the characters.
17. See Conroy, *Absalom Absalom!,* 29f, especially note 43; Fokkelman, *King David,* 105–6; cf. Hans Wilhelm Hertzberg, *I & II Samuel,* OTL (Philadelphia: Westminster Press, 1964), 323.
18. Two of Amnon's telling phrases David omits: "before my [his] eyes"; "that I [he] may eat from her [your] hand." Further, though Amnon has requested the bread (*lbbt*) his heart desires, the bread (*bryh*) David orders reverts to the vocabulary of Jonadab. Hence, David avoids these dangerous words but retains the ominous verb *make* or *do* (*ʿśh*) that the narrator introduced (13:2), Jonadab appropriated (13:5b), and Amnon embraced (13:6b).
19. On the importance of command and response, see Conroy, *Absalom Absalom!,* 19, 37–38.
20. Note that the narrator views the occasion through the eyes of Amnon to designate the bread as special food (*lbbt*), the desire of his heart, rather than as the standard nourishment that Jonadab and David have specified.
21. See Long, "Wounded Beginnings," 28.
22. This central unit is the D section in the overall composition; see the schema given in the second paragraph of this chapter.
23. Though parallel in form, these sections diverge in length and content. Longer than the beginning (13:9de), the ending (13:17–19) contains a parenthetical note from the narrator (13:18a) that separates direct command and response.
24. Note that the structural collapse follows the rape. Thus defects in structure mark the injury to the characters themselves; rape violates the orderly patterns of life.
25. While the surrounding sections mix direct and narrated discourse, only the latter reports the rape, thereby distancing it.
26. See the comments on 13:1–3 above.
27. On the narrator's role in the story, see Conroy, *Absalom Absalom!,* 22–26; cf. Whybray, *The Succession Narrative,* 15–16. On the omniscience and in-

obtrusiveness of the biblical narrator, see Alter, *The Art of Biblical Narrative,* 183–85.

28. Shrewdly, Amnon switches to the neutral word for food (*bryh* instead of *lbbt*) as he speaks to the woman his appetite craves.
29. The epithet "her brother" underscores the familial theme that permeates the story.
30. On *ḥzq,* cf. Judg. 19:25, 29. . . .
31. In Hebrew each of these four short words ends with the same vowel sound (*î*) to yield emphatic assonance (cf. 13:4). They also play with earlier vocabulary. "Come (*bôʾî*)": As much as any other, this word (*bôʾ*) has moved the story to its center. Following the plans of Jonadab, David came to Amnon to hear the request, "Let Tamar my sister come" (13:5, 6). "Lie (*šikbî*)": Used three times to describe the position of Amnon (13:5, 6, 8), this verb (*škb*) assumes now a different meaning. The sick son lying down is the lustful brother seeking to lie with his sister. "Lie with me (*ʾimmî*)": The pronoun *me* recalls the emphasis with which Amnon confessed his selfish longings to Jonadab. "I (*ʾănî*)," he stressed, "desire" (13:4). "Come, lie with me, my sister (*ʾăḥôtî*)": The vocative calls forth conflicting associations. In the love poetry of Israel, "my sister" is an address of respect and endearment (cf. SS 4:9, 10, 12; 5:1–2), but on the lips of Amnon it is betrayal and seduction (cf. 13:5, 6). Appetite parades as affection; entrapment as endearment.
32. On the technique of contrastive dialogue, see Alter, *The Art of Biblical Narrative,* 72–74. Unlike Alter, I do not see Tamar's lengthy speech as a "kind of panicked catalogue."
33. Conroy finds here a concentric sentence structure; see *Absalom Absalom!,* 31:
    A Emphatic prohibition: No, my brother; do not violate me.
    B Reason clause: for it is not done thus in Israel.
    A' Restatement of the prohibition: Do not do this foolish thing.
34. On meanings of the term *nĕbālāh* (foolish thing), see Anthony Phillips, *"Nebalah*—a term for serious disorderly and unruly conduct," *VT* 25 (1975): 237–41. For sexual references, cf. Gen. 34:7; Deut. 22:21; Judg. 19:23–24. For this word and others, Carlson notes an associative basis in Judges 19–21; see Carlson's *David, the Chosen King,* 165–67. . . .
35. On the legality of a marriage between Tamar and Amnon, see Conroy, *Absalom Absalom!,* 17–18, notes 3 and 4; also Phillips, *"Nebalah,"* 239.
36. Hagan calls her "the real wise one in the story"; see "Deception as Motif and Theme," 310.
37. Rape, not incest, is Amnon's crime; see Conroy, *Absalom Absalom!,* 18 n. 4; Fokkelman, *King David,* 103–4. *Contra* James W. Flanagan, "Court History or Succession Document? A Study of 2 Samuel 9–20 and 1 Kings 1–2," *JBL* 91(1972): 180; and, apparently, Long, "Wounded Beginnings," 27. My use of the phrase "against her will" comes from Susan Brownmiller's study of rape: *Against Our Will* (New York: Simon & Schuster, 1975), 18.

38. On the three levels of violence, see Fokkelman, *King David,* 106–7.
39. On the pilgrimage of the verb *škb,* see ibid., 104–5.
40. See Ridout, "The Rape of Tamar," 83. Fokkelman's pairing of *mĕʾōd* and *kî* is not altogether convincing *(King David,* 107). Though these two words fit the concentric structure, they, unlike the other pairs, are not repetitions.
41. Thus far, *desire* and *hate* are evenly matched with four appearances each (13:1, 4, 15). But the imbalance in the center of the story (13:15) shows hatred overtaking the ambiguity of desire; in the end, it will surpass (see 13:22).
42. *Contra* Fokkelman, *King David,* 108, the halves of this chiasmus of command do not "precisely match up with each other." The point is that rape has destroyed the perfect symmetry of form, content, and characters.
43. Though the Hebrew text of 13:16 is unclear, the fraternal vocative is not there (see ASV, NEB, NJV). Those translations in which "my brother" appears follow the Lucian recension of the Greek Bible (e.g., RSV, JB, and NAB; see S. R. Driver, *Notes on the Hebrew Text and the Topography of the Books of Samuel* [Oxford: At the Clarendon Press, 1960], 298–99). Ridout observes that the Lucian reading provides an exact parallel to the vocative in 13:12, thereby enhancing the overall symmetry of 13:11–14a and 13:15b–16; see "The Rape of Tamar," 82–83. Fokkelman agrees; see *King David,* 108. But the omission of the vocative in Hebrew fits well the flawed symmetry that characterizes the entire unit. Again, rape disturbs form and content as it alters the characters.
44. Note the absence of Tamar's name in the introduction to her words. "But she said to him" (13:16) contrasts with "And Amnon said to her" (13:15c). See the comments above on 13:12–13.
45. In calling Tamar a wise woman (*ʾiššâ ḥăkāmâ*), I employ terminology that is not in the text. Yet the designation fits. Speaking with the authority of custom, Tamar reasons and counsels with Amnon. Her use of the word *fool* (*nbl*) is characteristic of sapiential speech (13:12–13). Cf. Claudia V. Camp, "The Wise Women of 2 Samuel: A Role Model for Women in Early Israel?" *CBQ* 43 (1981): 14–29.
46. Perhaps this expansion compensates in length for the missing segment in the flawed chiasmus, where c' and b' merge (13:15c–16). Note that the alternative structure proposed by Ridout separates the command of 13:17 from its response in 13:18b. Further, by making 13:18–19 a unit, this proposed structure mixes action within Amnon's house (13:18) with action outside (13:19) and also fails to see the unit present in 13:19–20. See "The Rape of Tamar," 81.
47. Fokkelman observes that "the servants and Tamar form a chiastic pattern of motion [13:8–9 and 13:17–18] about the centre, the horrible *tête-à-tête* of Amnon and Tamar in vv. 10–16"; see *King David,* 102.
48. E.g., ASV, RSV, NEB, and NJV; cf. NAB.
49. Only here does the word *daughter* (*bat*) appear in the story. Note that the use is generic, not specific. On the textual problem in this verse (Hebrew *mĕʿîlîm*), see Driver, *Notes on the Hebrew Text,* 299–300; Gunn, *The Story of King David,* 32–33.

50. Structurally, the unit combines chiasmus and alternation; see H. Van Dyke Parunak, "Oral Typesetting: Some Uses of Biblical Structure," *Biblica* 62 (1981): 153–68.
51. On the artistry of this sentence, see Fokkelman, *King David,* 109–10.
52. See Conroy, *Absalom Absalom!,* 34.
53. Cf. Esther 4:1 and 2 Kings 5:8.
54. Conroy fails to acknowledge these possibilities. Too easily he describes Absalom's words as "consolation," embracing a "gentle command" and a "mild prohibition" to "convey a tone of tenderness." See *Absalom Absalom!,* 34–35.
55. Elsewhere in scripture the imperative, "be quiet" (*ḥrš,* Hiphil), is a warning (Judg. 18:19), sometimes that the speaker wishes to be heard (Job 13:13; Isa. 41:1). Fokkelman interprets this command juridically: "Don't involve yourself actively in this matter." See *King David,* 110–11. Similarly, cf. J. Hoftijzer, "Absalom and Tamar: A Case of Fratriarchy?" in *Schrift en uitleg: W. H. Gispen Festschrift,* ed. Dirk Attema et al. (Kampen: J. H. Kok, 1970), 60, note 18.
56. As Amnon's power wanes behind the bolted door, Absalom's rises on the public scene. See the aftermath of this story, leading to Absalom's challenge to David for the throne (13:23–15:18).
57. The repetitions of the phrase, "house (*byt*) of . . . brother (*ʾḥ*)" in 13:7, 8, and 20b accent further the fraternal contrast. On the concentric structure of space ringed by the word *house,* see Fokkelman, *King David,* 102–3.
58. See also Isa. 54:1. The verb *šmm* is often applied to land that is plundered, raped, and destroyed (e.g., Isa. 49:8; Ezek. 33:28). Utterly inadequate to convey the meaning here is the translation "sad and lonely" (2 Sam. 13:20c in the *Good News Bible*).
59. See Fokkelman, *King David,* 111–12, who follows Bar-Efrat. Cf. also the circular compositions of 13:1, 2, 15a.
60. By a skillful use of vocabulary, the opening clause of this sentence connects the monarch to each of his sons: "When the king David heard all these deeds. . . ." The verb *hear* (*šmʿ*) recalls Amnon's refusal to hear Tamar (13:14, 16), and the object *deeds* (*dbr*) employs Absalom's own allusion to the rape (13:20). In the father the sons compete. Yet the episode in its entirety resolves the tension to contrast David with Absalom and identify him with Amnon.
61. See McCarter, "'Plots, True or False,'" 366, especially note 20.
62. Amnon's rape of Tamar recalls David's adultery with Bathsheba (2 Samuel 11); father and son are enmeshed in sensual sin. For a comparison of these events, see Gunn, *The Story of King David,* 98–100; see also Kenneth R. R. Gros Louis, "The Difficulty of Ruling Well: King David of Israel," in *Semeia* 8, ed. Robert W. Funk (Missoula, Mont.: Scholars Press, 1977), 30.
63. Cf. the rapes of the concubine and others "in those days when there was no king in Israel" (Judges 19–21). . . .
64. Fokkelman shows the concentric arrangement formed in Hebrew by the root *dbr* enclosing the two occurrences of the pair Absalom/Amnon as subject and object; see *King David,* 112. Through exclusion, this arrangement highlights

the rape of Tamar; it receives the end-stress of the sentence. On end-stress, see Axel Olrik, "Epic Laws of Folk Narrative," in *The Study of Folklore,* ed. Alan Dundas (Englewood Cliffs, N.J.: Prentice-Hall, 1965), 136–37. On the translation, "but *(kî)* Absalom hated Amnon . . ." see Hoftijzer, "Absalom and Tamar: A Case of Fratriarchy?" 55–56.

65. On the importance of a narrator's explicit notice of silence, see Alter, *The Art of Biblical Narrative,* p. 79. Other interpretations of the phrase "did not speak . . . evil or good" include (a) the failure to take legal action (W. Malcolm Clark, "A Legal Background to the Yahwist's Use of 'Good and Evil' in Genesis 2–3," *JBL* 88 [1969]: 269); (b) the lack of hostile treatment (Fokkelman, *King David,* 112).
66. Before the crime, *desire* occurs twice (13:1, 4). At the crime, *desire* again occurs twice, here in parallelism to *hatred;* the word *hatred* itself appears four times (13:15a). In all these instances, Amnon is the subject of the verbs and Tamar the object. Moreover, the two words *desire* and *hatred* appear the same number of times. After the crime, however, *desire* disappears, but *hatred* continues, with Absalom as its subject and Amnon its object (13:22). Altogether, hatred (five occurrences) surpasses desire (four occurrences). Lust fulfilled increases into hatred.
67. As commentators note (e.g., Hertzberg, *I & II Samuel,* 326), Absalom may also be motivated by a desire for the throne. This interpretation, however, is extrinsic to the story; see Conroy, *Absalom Absalom!,* 36, note 75.
68. On thematic connections between the story and its surroundings, see Hertzberg, *I & II Samuel,* 322, 326–28; Whybray, *The Succession Narrative,* 22; Long, "Wounded Beginnings," 27, 30–34. On literary connections, see Gunn, *The Story of King David,* 98–100; Flanagan, "Court History or Succession Document?" 180; Gros Louis, "The Difficulty of Ruling Well," 15–33; Fokkelman, *King David,* 101, 114–25. On Absalom's story, see Zvi Adar, *The Biblical Narrative* (Jerusalem: Department of Education and Culture of the World Zionist Organisation, 1959), 142–97; Jacob Licht, *Storytelling in the Bible* (Jerusalem: Magnes Press, 1978), 12–13; 41–48.
69. See Hagan, "Deception as Motif and Theme," 310–11.
70. In having Amnon murdered, Absalom reflects David who had Uriah murdered (2 Sam. 11:6–21). The father lives in the son.
71. See Hoftijzer, "Absalom and Tamar: A Case of Fratriarchy?" 55–61.
72. Though the reference to David's mourning "for his son" might appropriately refer to Amnon, who has just been murdered, the immediate antecedent (13:37) is Absalom.
73. A modern novel based on this story is Dan Jacobson, *The Rape of Tamar* (Middlesex, England: Penguin Books, 1973).
74. See Whybray, *The Succession Narrative,* pp. 65–66; cf. James L. Crenshaw, *Old Testament Wisdom* (Atlanta: John Knox Press, 1981), 27–36.
75. To choose a title for the female personification of wisdom is difficult. Such designations as "Lady Wisdom" and "Dame Wisdom" do convey the elitism that

marks this figure in Proverbs. From a feminist perspective, the portrayal is ambivalent. Although these texts seemingly honor woman, wisdom is woman on a pedestal who is used to attract men.

76. See William McKane, *Proverbs* (Philadelphia: Westminster Press, 1970), 284–87 and *passim;* Crenshaw, *Old Testament Wisdom,* 96–99.
77. See McKane, *Proverbs,* 334.
78. In using this verse from Proverbs, I am not proposing any intentional links between it and our story in the manner, e.g., of Whybray, *The Succession Narrative,* 71–75, 78–95. Cf. J. L. Crenshaw, “Method in Determining Wisdom Influence upon ‘Historical’ Literature,” *JBL* 88 (1969): 137–40.

[16]

Men on Rape

Timothy Beneke

RAPE MAY BE America's fastest growing violent crime; no one can be certain because it is not clear whether more rapes are being committed or reported. It *is* clear that violence against women is widespread and fundamentally alters the meaning of life for women; that sexual violence is encouraged in a variety of ways in American culture; and that women are often blamed for rape.

Consider some statistics:

- In a random sample of 930 women, sociologist Diana Russell found that 44 percent had survived either rape or attempted rape. Rape was defined as sexual intercourse physically forced upon the woman, or coerced by threat of bodily harm, or forced upon the woman when she was helpless (asleep, for example). The survey included rape and attempted rape in marriage in its calculations. (Personal communication.)
- In a September 1980 survey conducted by *Cosmopolitan* magazine to which over 106,000 women anonymously responded, 24 percent had been raped at least once. Of these, 51 percent had been raped by friends, 37 percent by strangers, 18 percent by relatives, and 3 percent

SOURCE: From Timothy Beneke, *Men on Rape* (New York: St. Martin's Press, 1982).

by husbands. Ten percent of the women in the survey had been victims of incest. Seventy-five percent of the women had been "bullied into making love." Writer Linda Wolfe, who reported on the survey, wrote in reference to such bullying: "Though such harassment stops short of rape, readers reported that it was nearly as distressing."

- An estimated 2–3 percent of all men who rape outside of marriage go to prison for their crimes.[1]
- The F.B.I. estimates that if current trends continue, one woman in four will be sexually assaulted in her lifetime.[2]
- An estimated 1.8 million women are battered by their spouses each year.[3] In extensive interviews with 430 battered women, clinical psychologist Lenore Walker, author of *The Battered Woman,* found that 59.9 percent had also been raped (defined as above) by their spouses. Given the difficulties many women had in admitting they had been raped, Walker estimates the figure may well be as high as 80 or 85 percent. (Personal communication.) If 59.9 percent of the 1.8 million women battered each year are also raped, then a million women may be raped in marriage each year. And a significant number are raped in marriage without being battered.
- Between one in two and one in ten of all rapes are reported to the police.[4]
- Between 300,000 and 500,000 women are raped each year outside of marriage.[5]

What is often missed when people contemplate statistics on rape is the effect of the *threat* of sexual violence on women. I have asked women repeatedly, "How would your life be different if rape were suddenly to end?" (Men may learn a lot by asking this question of women to whom they are close.) The threat of rape is an assault upon the meaning of the world; it alters the feel of the human condition. Surely any attempt to comprehend the lives of women that fails to take issues of violence against women into account is misguided.

Through talking to women, I learned: *The threat of rape alters the meaning and feel of the night.* Observe how your body feels, how the night feels, when you're in fear. The constriction in your chest, the vigilance in your eyes, the rubber in your legs. What do the stars look like? How does the moon present itself? What is the difference between walking late at night in the dangerous part of a city and walking late at night in the country, or safe suburbs? When I try to imagine what the threat of rape must do to the night, I think of the stalked, adrenalated feeling I get walking late at night in parts of certain American cities. Only, I remind myself, it is a fear different from any I have known, a fear of being raped.

It is night half the time. If the threat of rape alters the meaning of the night, it must alter the meaning and pace of the day, one's relation to the passing and organization of time itself. For some women, the threat of rape at night turns their cars into armored tanks, their solitude into isolation. And what must the space inside a car or an apartment feel like if the space outside is menacing?

I was running late one night with a close woman friend through a path in the woods on the outskirts of a small university town. We had run several miles and were feeling a warm, energized serenity.

"How would you feel if you were alone?" I asked.

"Terrified!" she said instantly.

"Terrified that there might be a man out there?" I asked, pointing to the surrounding moonlit forest, which had suddenly been transformed into a source of terror.

"Yes."

Another woman said, "I know what I can't do and I've completely internalized what I can't do. I've built a viable life that basically involves never leaving my apartment at night unless I'm directly going some place to meet somebody. It's unconsciously built into what it occurs to women to do." When one is raised without freedom, one may not recognize its absence.

The threat of rape alters the meaning and feel of nature. Everyone has felt the psychic nurturance of nature. Many women are being deprived of that nurturance, especially in wooded areas near cities. They are deprived either because they cannot experience nature in solitude because of threat, or because, when they do choose solitude in nature, they must cope with a certain subtle but nettlesome fear.

Women need more money because of rape and the threat of rape makes it harder for women to earn money. It's simple: if you don't feel safe walking at night, or riding public transportation, you need a car. And it is less practicable to live in cheaper, less secure, and thus more dangerous neighborhoods if the ordinary threat of violence that men experience, being mugged, say, is compounded by the threat of rape. By limiting mobility at night, the threat of rape limits where and when one is able to work, thus making it more difficult to earn money. An obvious bind: women need more money because of rape, and have fewer job opportunities because of it.

The threat of rape makes women more dependent on men (or other women). One woman said: "If there were no rape I wouldn't have to play games with men for their protection." The threat of rape falsifies, mystifies, and confuses relations between men and women. If there were no rape, women would simply not need men as much, wouldn't need them to go places with at night, to feel safe in their homes, for protection in nature.

The threat of rape makes solitude less possible for women. Solitude, drawing strength from being alone, is difficult if being alone means being afraid. To be afraid is to be in need, to experience a lack; the threat of rape creates a lack. Solitude requires relaxation; if you're afraid, you can't relax.

The threat of rape inhibits a woman's expressiveness. "If there were no rape," said one woman, "I could dress the way I wanted and walk the way I wanted and not feel self-conscious about the responses of men. I could be friendly to people. I wouldn't have to wish I was ugly. I wouldn't have to make myself small when I got on the bus. I wouldn't have to respond to verbal abuse from men by remaining silent. I could respond in kind."

If a woman's basic expressiveness is inhibited, her sexuality, creativity, and delight in life must surely be diminished.

The threat of rape inhibits the freedom of the eye. I know a married couple who live in Manhattan. They are both artists, both acutely sensitive and responsive to the visual world. When they walk separately in the city, he has more freedom to look than she does. She must control her eye movements lest they inadvertently meet the glare of some importunate man. What, who, and how she sees are restricted by the threat of rape.

The following exercise is recommended for men.

> Walk down a city street. Pay a lot of attention to your clothing; make sure your pants are zipped, shirt tucked in, buttons done. Look straight ahead. Every time a man walks past you, avert your eyes and make your face expressionless. Most women learn to go through this act each time we leave our houses. It's a way to avoid at least some of the encounters we've all had with strange men who decided we looked available.[6]

To relate aesthetically to the visual world involves a certain playfulness, spirit of spontaneous exploration. The tense vigilance that accompanies fear inhibits that spontaneity. The world is no longer yours to look at when you're afraid.

I am aware that all culture is, in part, restriction, that there are places in America where hardly anyone is safe (though men are safer than women virtually everywhere), that there are many ways to enjoy life, that some women may not be so restricted, that there exist havens, whether psychic, geographical, economic, or class. But they are *havens,* and as such, defined by threat.

Above all, I trust my experience: no woman could have lived the life I've lived the last few years. If suddenly I were restricted by the threat of rape, I would feel a deep, inexorable depression. And it's not just rape; it's harassment, battery, Peeping Toms, anonymous phone calls, exhibitionism, intrusive stares, fondlings—all contributing to an atmosphere of intimidation in women's lives. And I have only scratched the surface; it would take many carefully crafted short stories to begin to express what I have only hinted at in the last few pages. I have not even touched upon what it might mean for a woman to be sexually assaulted. Only women can speak to that. Nor have I suggested how the threat of rape affects marriage.

Rape and the threat of rape pervades the lives of women, as reflected in some popular images of our culture.

"She Asked for It"—Blaming the Victim[7]

Many things may be happening when a man blames a woman for rape.

First, in all cases where a woman is said to have asked for it, her appearance and behavior are taken as a form of speech. "Actions speak louder than words" is a widely held belief; the woman's actions—her appearance may be taken as action—are given greater emphasis than her words; an interpretation alien to the woman's intentions is given to her actions. A logical extension of "she asked for it" is the idea that she wanted what happened to happen; if she wanted it to happen, she *deserved* for it to happen. Therefore, the man is not to be blamed. "She asked for it" can mean either that she was consenting to have sex and was not really raped, or that she was in fact raped but somehow she really deserved it. "If you ask for it, you deserve it," is a widely held notion. If I ask you to beat me up and you beat me up, I still don't deserve to be beaten up. So even if the notion that women asked to be raped had some basis in reality, which it doesn't, on its own terms it makes no sense.

Second. a mentality exists that says: a woman who assumes freedoms normally restricted to a man (like going out alone at night) and is raped is doing the same thing as a woman who goes out in the rain without an umbrella and catches a cold. Both are considered responsible for what happens to them. That men will rape is taken to be a legitimized given, part of nature, like rain or snow. The view reflects a massive abdication of responsibility for rape on the part of men. It is so much easier to think of rape as natural than to acknowledge one's part in it. So long as rape is regarded as natural, women will be blamed for rape.

A third point. The view that it is natural for men to rape is closely connected to the view of women as commodities. If a woman's body is regarded as a valued commodity by men, then of course, if you leave a valued commodity where it can be taken, it's just human nature for men to take it. If you left your stereo out on the sidewalk, you'd be asking for it to get stolen. Someone will just take it. (And how often men speak of rape as "going out and *taking* it.") If a woman walks the streets at night, she's leaving a valued commodity, her body, where it can be taken. So long as women are regarded as commodities, they will be blamed for rape.

Which brings us to a fourth point. "She asked for it" is inseparable from a more general "psychology of the dupe." If I use bad judgment and fail to read the small print in a contract and later get taken advantage of, "screwed" (or "fucked over"), then I deserve what I get; bad judgment makes me liable. Analogously, if a woman trusts a man and goes to his apartment, or accepts a ride hitchhiking, or goes out on a date and is raped, she's a dupe and deserves what she gets. "He didn't *really* rape her" goes the mentality—"he merely took advantage of her." And in America it's okay for people to take advantage of each other, even expected and praised. In fact, you're considered dumb and foolish if you don't take advantage of other people's bad judgment. And so, again, by treating them as dupes, rape will be blamed on women.

Fifth, if a woman who is raped is judged attractive by men, and particularly if she dresses to look attractive, then the mentality exists that she attacked him with her weapon so, of course, he counter-attacked with his. The preview to a popular movie states: "She was the victim of her own *provocative beauty.*" Provocation: "There is a line which, if crossed, will *set me off* and I will lose control and no longer be responsible for my behavior. If you punch me in the nose then, of course, I will not be responsible for what happens: you will have provoked a fight. If you dress, talk, move, or act a certain way, you will have provoked me to rape. If your appearance *stuns* me, *strikes* me, *ravishes* me, *knocks me out,* etc., then I will not be held responsible for what happens; you will have asked for it." The notion that sexual feeling makes one helpless is part of a cultural abdication of responsibility for sexuality. So long as a woman's appearance is viewed as a weapon and sexual feeling is believed to make one helpless, women will be blamed for rape.

Sixth, I have suggested that men sometimes become obsessed with images of women, that images become a substitute for sexual feeling, that sexual feeling becomes externalized and out of control and is given an undifferentiated identity in the appearance of women's bodies. It is a process of projection in which one blurs one's own desire with her imagined, projected desire. If a woman's attractiveness is taken to signify one's own lust and a woman's lust, then when an "attractive" woman is raped, some men may think she wanted sex. Since they perceive their own lust in part projected onto the woman, they disbelieve women who've been raped. So long as men project their own sexual desires onto women, they will blame women for rape.

And seventh, what are we to make of the contention that women in dating situations say "no" initially to sexual overtures from men as a kind of pose, only to give in later, thus revealing their true intentions? And that men are thus confused and incredulous when women are raped because in their sexual experience women can't be believed? I doubt that this has much to do with men's perceptions of rape. I don't know to what extent women actually "say no and mean yes"; certainly it is a common theme in male folklore. I have spoken to a couple of women who went through periods when they wanted to be sexual but were afraid to be, and often rebuffed initial sexual advances only to give in later. One point is clear: the ambivalence women may feel about having sex is closely tied to the inability of men to fully accept them as sexual beings. Women have been traditionally punished for being openly and freely sexual; men are praised for it. And if many men think of sex as achievement of possession of a valued commodity, or aggressive degradation, then women have every reason to feel and act ambivalent.

These themes are illustrated in an interview I conducted with a 23-year-old man who grew up in Pittsburgh and works as a file clerk in the financial district of San Francisco. Here's what he said:

"Where I work it's probably no different from any other major city in the U.S. The women dress up in high heels, and they wear a lot of makeup, and they just look really *hot* and really sexy, and how can somebody who has a healthy sex drive not feel lust for them when you see them? I feel lust for them, but I don't think I could find it in me to overpower someone and rape them. But I definitely get the feeling that I'd like to rape a girl. I don't know if the actual act of rape would be satisfying, but the *feeling* is satisfying.

"These women look so good, and they kiss ass of the men in the three-piece suits who are *big* in the corporation, and most of them relate to me like 'Who are *you?* Who are *you* to even *look* at?' They're snobby and they condescend to me, and I resent it. It would take me a lot longer to get to first base than it would somebody with a three-piece suit who had money. And to me a lot of the men they go out with are superficial assholes who have no real feelings or substance, and are just trying to get ahead and make a lot of money. Another thing that makes me resent these women is thinking, 'How could she want to hang out with somebody like that? What does that make her?'

"I'm a file clerk, which makes me feel like a nebbish, a nurd, like I'm not making it, I'm a failure. But I don't really believe I'm a failure because I know it's just a phase, and I'm just doing it for the money, just to make it through this phase. I catch myself feeling like a failure, but I realize that's ridiculous."

What exactly do you go through when you see these sexy, unavailable women?

"Let's say I see a woman and she looks really pretty and really clean and sexy, and she's giving off very feminine, sexy vibes. I think, 'Wow, I would love to make love to her,' but I know she's not really interested. It's a tease. A lot of times a woman knows that she's looking really good and she'll use that and flaunt it, and it makes me feel like she's laughing at me and I feel *degraded.*

"I also feel dehumanized, because when I'm being teased I just turn off, I cease to be human. Because if I go with my human emotions I'm going to want to put my arms around her and kiss her, and to do that would be unacceptable. I don't like the feeling that I'm supposed to stand there and take it, and not be able to hug her or kiss her; so I just turn off my emotions. It's a feeling of humiliation, because the woman has forced me to turn off my feelings and react in a way that I really don't want to.

"If I were actually desperate enough to rape somebody, it would be from wanting the person, but it would be a very spiteful thing, just being able to say, 'I have power over you and I can do anything I want with you,' because really I feel that *they* have power over *me* just by their presence. Just the fact that they can come up to me and just melt me and make me feel like a dummy makes me want revenge. They have power over me so I want power over them. . . .

"Society says that you have to have a lot of sex with a lot of different women to be a real man. Well, what happens if you don't? Then what are you? Are you half a man? Are you still a boy? It's ridiculous. You see a whiskey ad with a guy and two women on his arm. The implication is that real men don't have any trouble getting women."

How does it make you feel toward women to see all these sexy women in media and advertising using their looks to try to get you to buy something?

"It makes me hate them. As a man you're taught that men are more powerful than women, and that men always have the upper hand, and that it's a man's society; but then you see all these women and it makes you think 'Jesus Christ, if we have all the power how come all the beautiful women are telling us what to buy?' And to be honest, it just makes me hate beautiful women because they're using their power over me. I realize they're being used themselves, and they're doing it for money. In *Playboy* you see all these beautiful women who look so sexy and they'll be giving you all these looks like they want to have sex so bad; but then in reality you know that except for a few nymphomaniacs, they're doing it for the money; so I hate them for being used and using their bodies in that way.

"In this society, if you ever sit down and realize how manipulated you really are it makes you pissed off—it makes you want to take control. And you've been manipulated by women, and they're a very easy target because they're out walking along the streets, so you can just grab one and say, 'Listen, you're going to do what I want you to do,' and it's an act of revenge against the way you've been manipulated.

"I know a girl who was walking down the street by her house, when this guy jumped her and beat her up and raped her, and she was black and blue and had to go to the hospital. That's beyond me. I can't understand how somebody could do that. If I were going to rape a girl, I wouldn't hurt her. I might *restrain* her, but I wouldn't *hurt* her. . . .

"The whole dating game between men and women also makes me feel degraded. I hate being put in the position of having to initiate a relationship. I've been taught that if you're not aggressive with a woman, then you've blown it. She's not going to jump on *you,* so *you've* got to jump on *her.* I've heard all kinds of stories where the woman says, 'No! No! No!' and they end up making great love. I get confused as hell if a woman pushes me away. Does it mean she's trying to be a nice girl and wants to put up a good appearance, or does it mean she doesn't want anything to do with you? You don't know. Probably a lot of men think that women don't feel like real women unless a man tries to force himself on her, unless she brings out the 'real man,' so to speak, and probably too much of it goes on. It goes on in my head that you're complimenting a woman by actually staring at her or by trying to get into her pants. Lately, I'm realizing that when I stare at women lustfully, they often feel more threatened than flattered."

Notes

1. Such estimates recur in the rape literature. See Nancy Gager and Cathleen Schurr, *Sexual Assault* (Grosset & Dunlap, 1976), or Clark and Lewis, *The Price of Coercive Sexuality* (The Women's Press, 1977).
2. *Uniform Crime Reports,* 1980.
3. See Murray J. Strauss and Richard Gelles, *Behind Closed Doors* (Doubleday, 1979).
4. See Gager and Schurr (above) or virtually any book on the subject.
5. Again, see Gager and Schurr, or Carol V. Horos, *Rape,* Banbury Books, 1981.
6. From "Willamette Bridge" in Nancy Henley, *Body Politics* (Prentice-Hall, 1977), 144.
7. I would like to thank George Lakoff for this insight.

[17]

On the Nature of Rape

John H. Bogart

THE LEGAL AND SOCIAL RESPONSES to rape in the United States have been in upheaval for nearly 20 years. Despite vast changes in the criminal law and other social institutions, despite a burgeoning scholarly and popular literature, there has been comparatively little attention paid to defining rape.[1] My aim here is to provide a discussion of the nature of rape and thereby provide a sounder foundation for both analysis and reform.

The article is divided into several sections. In the first I develop and discuss four distinct conceptions of rape found in legal and other scholarly discussions of rape. I then argue for the superiority of a particular, and very powerful, conception of rape which focuses upon a person's voluntary and effective consent and not upon force or will. In the third section I consider some objections to my account of rape. I have left for another time the discussion of implications for reform of the account defended in this article.

Definitional Accounts of the Concept of Rape

There seem to me to be four major alternatives with respect to defining rape: as forcible, coerced, nonvoluntary, or nonconsensual sex.[2] In each of these

SOURCE: From John H. Bogart, "On the Nature of Rape," *Public Affairs Quarterly* 5 (1991). Used by permission of the University of Pittsburgh.

accounts, the emphasis, in the present circumstances, is on the first element. Although necessary for a complete account of rape, I will not attempt to delineate the sexual content required for an act to be rape (or attempted rape). I should also note that the following accounts are to be understood as nested, such that each successive account includes within its scope each of the previous accounts. The scope of the force account, for example, is a proper subset of the scope of the coercion account.

The first possibility for an account of rape is that it is constituted by forcible sex.[3] Sexual intercourse is forcible if procured by means of force or the threat of force against the victim. It involves violence or the threat of violence, and the force is such that it overcomes resistance on the part of the victim.

By rape we might instead mean coerced sex.[4] What this means, in addition to what is encompassed by the concept of forcible sex, is that the sex may be obtained by means of serious threats of other kinds. The threat may be directed at a third party, or may be deprivation of livelihood, or any of a number of other serious harms. Again the threat is sufficiently serious that it overcomes resistance on the part of the victim. The victim acts in a way she otherwise would not have acted, and does so only because of the threat, but the threat is not necessarily of personal bodily harm to the rape victim.[5]

Nonvoluntary sex is the third option.[6] I mean by that to include not only what falls under both forcible and coerced sex, but also to cooperation due to compelling circumstantial pressures. When resistance is possible only at the cost of serious inconvenience or substantial harm (or to harms which fall under the preceding accounts), the action may be nonvoluntary. I would be inclined to include here such things as exchanges of sex for employment, or an exchange of sex for not being abandoned in a remote location.

The fourth possibility is to understand rape as nonconsensual sex. This account is distinguished from the other three by counting as instances of rape all cases of sexual intercourse which occur without the consent of at least one of the participants. Where participation is not willing, not chosen freely, not chosen without the application or presence of external pressures, the sexual interaction will count as a form of rape.[7]

Much of the traditional discussion of rape is in terms of consent, but this is extremely misleading because in such discussions it is not consent that is actually the definitional standard. Rather, nonconsent is equated with various standards of resistance (often "utmost" resistance).[8] The nonconsent account I have set out above, however, is not properly identified with resistance standards.[9]

Grounds for Choosing among the Definitions

There are three main grounds on which to prefer one of the preceding accounts over the others. The first ground for preference is a better fit with a variety of relevant cases (standard of scope). In this case, the domain consists of a number of types or categories of events which intuitively seem to be instances of rape despite significant variation in means and context.

The second ground of preference is that one account provides a sounder basis for an explanation of the harm intrinsic to rape (harm standard). I indicate below what I believe the intrinsic harms of rape are (and for the remainder of the essay I shall speak of these four linked harms as the harm of rape). Part of the case for the harm as I have identified it lies in the discussion of the domain of rape. Part of the claim for the superiority of the nonconsent account is that what I have suggested as the nature of the harm of rape is best captured by accepting that account of the nature of rape. The arguments should be seen, therefore, as interdependent.

The third basis for preference is superiority of fit with related background theories (background theory standard). Background theories should be understood in a wide and full sense. I include among the background theories matters which are not at all in the background of the social problem of rape.

Scope

There are a number of categories of cases that belong within the (core) domain of rape. Any adequate account of the nature of rape must yield an appropriate explanation of the inclusion of such cases within the domain. The categories I will consider are these:

- Case 1: Sexual relations brought about by means of force or threat of force against the victim.
- Case 2: Sex obtained by means of threats against a third party.
- Case 3: Relations during a period in which the victim is incapacitated.
- Case 4: Sexual relations obtained by means of fraud.
- Case 5: Sex involving a child.[10]

The first thing to be noticed is that the first account of rape, forcible sex, comfortably accounts for only one of the five kinds of cases being considered, Case 1. The coercion account fares somewhat better. It does handle at least some cases beyond the reach of the force account. For example, under a coercion theory we may count as instances of rape those cases involving induced intoxication and a portion of child cases. But the coercion account is not adequate. It does not properly handle such cases as incapacity or fraud. Merely exploiting a dependency relationship is insufficient for coercion, although such cases will surely constitute some significant portion of incestuous rapes. This is plain enough in cases where the victim is too young properly to understand the events, or is otherwise incapacitated.

The choice between the two wider accounts is reflected in differences at the edges of their respective domains. The nonvoluntary account requires treating as rape all those cases in which sexual contact is nonvoluntary. Acceptable sexual contact is voluntary sexual contact. This means that in instances of Case 5 we will need separate explanatory and justificatory accounts for prohibitions on sexual contacts. While many such cases will fail to be voluntary, certainly not all can be so characterized. A six or eight year old is certainly capable of voluntary action. Indeed, children are capable of voluntary action much earlier than that. It is not, after all, necessary for an act to be voluntary that the agent understand the *full* nature of the action or the consequences of the action.[11] The action is voluntary when not coerced or compelled by external forces.

Voluntariness and consent diverge in at least two other areas important to the present topic, those involving intoxication or fraud. Suppose a woman[12] becomes quite intoxicated. Indeed, she becomes sufficiently intoxicated that she can no longer be said fully to understand her actions or to be more than dimly cognizant of her surroundings and companions. In such a state she is no longer capable of consenting to anything, although she is still able to act voluntarily. Thus she may voluntarily enter a car, or voluntarily fall into bed with someone. No one forces her to do so, and she is not acting under an impulse we would normally call irresistible. But she does not consent. She cannot consent because her understanding is too deeply impaired. In such a case, although sex may be voluntary, it is not consensual. In important ways, this sort of case stands as a bridge to the dependency case discussed above. What links the two is the incapacity to give consent. As we should not think that a seriously intoxicated person could consent to a financial contract, so she could not consent to a sexual arrangement. In the case of intoxication, the incapacity is temporary. But the incapacity may be permanent as well and in such instances too there is no consent.

Fraud provides the final sort of case which I want to use to distinguish nonvoluntary from nonconsensual sex. Among the kinds of cases to be counted under this category, are those where sexual access is gained under false pretenses. If a woman accedes to sexual requests under the mistaken belief that it is a medical treatment, it would count as a case of rape.[13] So too would cases where the victim does not realize before the fact that what she is agreeing to is sexual intercourse. Other sorts of cases would include those where there is consent to sex with one party and it is another who actually engages in sexual relations.[14] Where a person relies on a mistake as to identity to gain sexual favors, that too would be an instance under this category.[15]

The nonconsensual model of rape will cover these cases, while none of the other accounts will. In these cases, the action is voluntary, or there would be no fraud. Because the beliefs underlying the action are false, although the action itself is voluntary, there is no effective consent. Consequently, the cases may be termed instances of rape under the nonconsent model. Under the nonvoluntary model, these are cases of simple seduction.

The Harm Standard

Part of the argument in favor of the nonconsent account of rape is that it provides a better explanation of the harm of rape, and in particular the continuity and identity of harm across distinct categories of rape. On the assumption that all five cases do in fact mark distinct categories of rape, then any adequate account must display the cases as instantiating a like harm (or set of harms). That standard can be met by the nonconsent account, and it can be met by that account because of the abstract, formal nature of harm under the account.

The case which characterizes the common image of rape involves ordinary adults and the use of force to effect the rape. Consider the following sort of case (Case 1). A is accosted by B who demands that A perform sexual intercourse with B. B's demand is backed by an explicit threat of force against A in the event A does not cooperate. A performs the requested acts. This, I take it, is a paradigmatic case of rape.

With respect to the rape itself, A has suffered four kinds of harm:

1. There has been a violation of A's interest in sexual self-determination.
2. There has been a violation of A's interest in bodily integrity.
3. A's autonomy has been violated.
4. A has suffered from alienation.

It is very likely that in addition to the rape, A has been harmed in a number of other related, collateral, and consequent ways. But it is just these four kinds of harm which characterize what A suffers insofar as we consider only the rape itself.

Of course, merely asserting that certain harms capture rape is insufficient. It is also necessary to explain why that is so. We begin with a commonplace observation, valuable despite its apparent triviality. Rape involves sex.[16] The way in which it involves sex is important. It is quite common, as in the example above, for a rape to occur in the midst of a physical attack on the victim. The aggressor may rely on force, or the threat of the use of a weapon, and the attack may include other humiliating or degrading events. These aspects of the action are conceptually distinct from that which constitutes the rape. Insofar as A is the victim of a physical attack, rape is not distinct from a mugging or other beating. We need to be careful here to disentangle the many related harms suffered by a rape victim and to focus on only those which constitute the event as an instance of rape, to focus on those which are peculiar to rape.[17]

Physical assault is not peculiar to rape, however closely related in practice. By the same reasoning we can see that the harm of rape does not lie in a physical attack directed at sexual organs. A beating which included blows to sex organs would not constitute a form of rape, nor an attempt at rape. It is not rape to attack a person because of their sex, however common that may be as motivating rape.

What it means to say that rape involves sex is that rape is an attack on a person as a sexual being, it is an attack on a person through their sexuality. For that reason, in order for a rape to occur, it is necessary for there to be contact with the victim and for that contact to implicate the victim's body as sexualized, even if the contact need not take a definite and predetermined form.[18]

It is not obvious that rape is properly characterized as an abstract harm. Talk of setbacks to interests does seem to miss something rather important: the experiences of victims. Loss of autonomy is an odd way to refer to what is often a form of torture. Is there an experiential element intrinsic to rape? If there were such an element, it would matter very much to the choice of the proper account of the nature of rape.

I do not think there is an experiential element intrinsic to the harm of rape notwithstanding the factual connection between that harm and often seriously destructive experiences of victims.[19] Requiring an experiential element leads to serious problems. It requires that there in fact be *an* experience common to all cases of rape. It is clear that there is no common experience temporally extensional with the rape. A looser temporal connection will not remedy the lack. The experiences of rape victims vary significantly. Some victims are in states which preclude relevant experiences (the unconscious, for example). We should also have to exclude those cases where the victim does not have disfavored experiences.[20] Further, the experiential requirement raises serious barriers to a proper understanding of sexual oppression on a multicultural and historical basis.[21]

A focus on experience also leads to legal snares. If rape has an experiential core, then it is natural for evidentiary inquiries to permit, indeed encourage, investigation of a putative victim's experiences. The place in an inquiry into "how it felt" is then assured.[22]

Not placing an experiential element within the essential harm of rape should not be interpreted as discounting the importance of the experiences undergone in being raped. Rape can be, and often is, devastating. When we turn to the wrong of rape, we are turning, in part, to the harms as experienced. Experiences play a pivotal role in determining the moral status of cases and classes of rape, and are important in determining the appropriate assessment of the social role of rape.

A different aspect of the abstract nature of the harm of rape is that it is immune to inconsequentiality. That the victim does not suffer does not deny the rape. The harm accrues whether or not it is recognized by the victim or by others. In that sense, it is like a violation of political rights. The seriousness of the violation does not turn solely on how the violation is perceived, experienced, felt. There may be a serious violation despite a general failure of recognition or concern.

Several important things follow if victim experience is not intrinsic to rape. First, it means that we should expect that the social response to rape and to victims of rape, along with the psychology of the victims, will be variable. Second, it means that much of what makes rape, understood as social phenomena, wrong will depend on things other than the intrinsic nature of rape. In other words, the seriousness of instances of rape will vary. The background theories matter very much to how we evaluate instances and classes of cases of rape.

It may be helpful at this point to provide a fuller explanation of the nature of the four harms, and then to explain how it is they are so linked as to constitute rape.

Every person has an interest in determining for themselves, insofar as that is practically possible, certain substantive relations in and aspects of their lives. Among the relations are those concerned with sexual expression and experience. Sexuality, after all, is an important element in the formation of individual personality. In speaking of sexual self-determination, we assign to each person some substantial control over the means of and partners (if any) in that person's sexual life. Plainly in cases of rape, the interest in sexual self-determination is severely compromised.

Many will think sexual self-determination (as well as bodily integrity) no more than a partial and limited specification of the claims of autonomy. Doubtless self-determination is part of what is meant by autonomy. An autonomous agent is self-determining, but not merely. Autonomy requires the agent's choices to be consonant with and expressive of a rational and reasonable personality. An autonomous agent, for example, is not merely subject to her desires and preferences, but is able to shape those desires and preferences. Autonomy requires an active second order set of preferences.[23]

One way to understand the difference between autonomy and sexual self-determination is to notice that self-determination is consonant with (virtually) any set of sexual preferences and practices, while autonomy is not. Self-determination and autonomy need not be harmonious, and because there is the possibility of conflict, there is a need to understand separately the role each plays in rape. Sexual self-determination gives no grounds on which to question a choice to assume the role of a sexual slave, provided that the person in question in fact has the requisite set of desires and preferences. On the basis of autonomy, in contrast, there are grounds on which the legitimacy of such a choice may be doubted.

The interest in bodily integrity is, I think, relatively transparent. It is a precondition for autonomy, but is not itself a mere specification of autonomy. Alienation is the final sort of harm to be considered. In the present context, alienation takes the form of objectification, the reduction of an individual to what is only a fragment of their being.[24] The starkest form of alienation involved in such a case of rape is the treatment of the victim as a sexual body at the disposal of the aggressor. In this sort of case the victim is appropriated as a body (for a period of time), and hence reduced to a piece of property available for appropriation. There is, of course, a great deal more to be said about alienation, as there is about autonomy and sexual self-determination. But it is not necessary at this point to provide any more elaborate discussion.

These harms are inherent in rape in the sense that it is the presence of these harms which characterizes the generalizable core content of the act such that it is an instance of the class of rapes. Yet these harms are not what directly characterize the experience of rape. However, although they do not characterize the experience of rape, they lie at the conceptual basis of those experiences. The paradigmatic case of rape invokes thoughts of invasion, humiliation, degradation, loss of control. These are just the sorts of psychological results to be expected when there are serious compromises of the interests listed above. Incurring the harms is indicative of being subject to a more or less serious assault, and an assault characterized as sexual. The confluence of the harms distinguishes rape from (simple) assault, on the one side, and nonphysical sexual harassment on the other side. So the elements identified as the harms of rape are what may be thought of as abstract structural features of rape.

This account of the harm of rape is certainly congruent with the core cases of rape described earlier. The cases involving force or coercion will fall under this account without difficulty. The incomplete discussion lay in the difference between an account of rape as nonvoluntary sexual relations and as nonconsensual sexual relations. Consider again the case of intoxication. For the nonvoluntary account, rape occurs at a point much closer to unconsciousness. It is plain that much action undertaken while the agent is in the grip of strong intoxicants will count as voluntary.[25] But the action will not count as consensual. It cannot so count because the agent is unable to appreciate the nature of action or the risk of the conduct. Present capacity to reason and full appreciation of available relevant information is required for consensual activity. The difference here is in where the line is drawn.

In cases where the key factor is one of status (Case 5) the consensual model provides a better explanation of the prohibition and more accurately captures the harm involved. The important claim is that the individuals involved may all be capable of voluntary action without defeating the charge of rape. Children are not automatons who suddenly blossom at age 18 (or 14, etc.) into rational agents. They are quite capable of voluntary action at a very early age. This is reflected in a host of behavior patterns and attitudes directed at children. But the capacity for voluntary action is not the same as a capacity for consensual activity. It is also important to notice that under the approach I am suggesting we need not treat these as special cases.[26] The theoretical explanation of and justification for the treatment of these cases as cases of rape is organic and relatively straightforward. That is not so under alternative approaches.

The harm of rape is present as well in cases of fraud. The reasons for treating such cases as inconsistent with, or compromises of, the autonomy interests are somewhat different than in the preceding cases. These cases involve an agent exploiting misinformation, or purveying misinformation, with the aim of obtaining what would otherwise be unavailable. The fraud is in a certain way like inducing intoxication. In both cases the cognitive state of the victim is "impaired" in order to prevent an accurate assessment and expression of self-determination. The victim's interests are overridden for the benefit of another agent. In the case of fraud, what is gained is gained against the expected desires, intentions, wishes of the victim. The failure of effective consent is a way of expressing the determination to lodge control of these aspects of one's life in one's own hands, as far as that is possible. Clearly fraud defeats that aim. In defeating that aim, fraud conflicts with autonomy interests. Consequently we may say that such cases constitute a sort of case in which the harm of rape occurs. But this claim only follows from accepting effective consent as the guarantor of autonomy in sexual matters.

It may help to consider the differences among the accounts of rape on the basis of the protection of relevant interests: what interests are protected, and how well, by each of the accounts? Assume the four interests identified by the harms intrinsic to rape are the relevant interests (at least from the perspective of the victim). The first two accounts do afford some protection of those interests, but only rather weak protection because so narrowly circumscribed. With respect to the second two accounts, nonvoluntary and nonconsent, the choice may be framed by asking what interests the nonvoluntary account better provides for. It does not protect the interests noted in the harm discussion as well as the nonconsent account does. If it is to be recommended on this basis it would be because it better protects some *other* interests. But what might they be? An interest in obtaining sex through deception? An interest in exploiting others, or in taking advantage of naivete or vulnerability? An interest in encouraging mystification of sex and dishonesty in social relations? So not only does a nonvoluntary account afford less protection of (and hence demonstrate less concern for) the interests of victims, but does so by promoting interests of a rather dubious sort.

Background Theories Standard

A consent-based account of rape yields the best fit with relevant background theories. The relation between rape, in particular the harm of rape, and morality is discussed at some length in the next section of the paper and so has been set to one side for the moment. There are several other bases for establishing fit with background theories, and in each case a nonconsent model seems superior.

A nonconsent model of rape is consistent with two relevant aspects of legal theory and development. First, with respect to the history of Anglo-American rape law, an admittedly parochial standard, a consent-based account of rape works quite well. The development of rape law appears consistent with an interpretation of it as developing sophistication about the conditions of effective consent over sexual affairs. The shift of rape from a form of property crime to a crime against the person of the victim may be read in light of the improved legal status of women, the extension to women of full standing to control their own affairs.[27] The introduction of sex-neutral rape laws may be seen as recognition of the dependence of rape on issues of autonomy, self-determination, etc., which are themselves sex-neutral. More recent reforms with respect to limitations on defenses to charges of rape, introduction of explicit language making consent central to the crime of rape, and abandonment of the marital exemption, among others, can be understood in the same light.

Second, the emphasis on consent reflects a pervasive shift in legal doctrines.[28] In both civil and criminal law, there has been a marked shift away from a concern with effective consent in only special circumstances. Merely voluntary action no longer serves as the paradigm for action subject to legal constraint. Again, these are changes in only some legal systems, and the question of fit is limited as a result.

The consent-based account yields a reasonably good fit with the sociology of rape and important segments of the public response to issues of rape. For example, accurate surveys of the prevalence of rape (and related sexual wrongs) reflect a nonconsent conception.[29] Rape education programs not only rely explicitly on such an approach, but require it. A nonconsent standard is what is required to make sense of the need for (and effectiveness of) educating victims to the fact of victimization.

Theories of politics and social oppression, in particular as relevant to women, provide confirmation of the nonconsent account of rape.[30] A consent approach integrates effectively into a philosophical political liberalism, which places at the center of justificatory theory the autonomy of the individual.[31] Political legitimacy depends on consent of the governed, and hence the legitimacy of social institutions and practices are conditioned on the degree of effective consent the affected may be thought to have given (even if hypothetically). Assuming the interests protected are important, consensual control of sexual activities enhances autonomy. But it is not merely political liberalism that supports a nonconsent account of rape. The values which, as central parts of liberal political theory, assure fit with the suggested account of rape also play important roles in competing political theories. Marxist theory aims at the creation of a society of human flourishing and autonomy[32] which must surely place consensual standards near the center of acceptable personal relations. Similar sorts of claims legitimately may be advanced with respect to a number of other approaches to political theory.[33]

Rape, Harm, Morality

One unusual feature of the account of rape I have advanced is that there is not a straightforward identification of rape as an egregious evil. However, nothing I have said supports the inference that rape is not a very pressing social problem or the inference that normally rape is not a very serious evil. There are conceptually important reasons for identifying the nature of rape in a way which allows for the possibility described. But we cannot understand rape without attending to the relation between rape and morality, the relation between the harm which constitutes rape and a moral assessment of that harm.

There are four elements to the determination of the evil of rape. The first element concerns the assignment of answerability. The second element is the nature of the related violations of duties and commission of immoralities. The collateral duties violated in the course of the rape matter. The third element is that of felt harms. What are the psychological and physical effects of rape on the victim? The fourth element for assessing the evil of rape is the nature of systemic effects of the presence and pervasiveness of rape, and the ideological commitments which make sexual assault of particular significance. These elements require more detailed individual discussion.

Answerability

Briefly, answerability can be thought of as a measure of the degree of wrong involved in an act determined by the degree to which the wrong was intended by the agent involved. It is not that it is *only* wrong if the agent intended the act (under the description as wrong). The wrongness of the act is amplified by the degree to which the act was undertaken intentionally or deliberately. So deliberate rape shows a higher degree of moral corruption than does an accidental case. The wrong is greater because, in part, the agent displays a greater disregard for the victim and the demands of morality (as a general matter).

This is not to suggest that responsibility is simply a function of intent. The theory is that an agent may also be responsible for proceeding with risky conduct,[34] or failing to attend to context in appropriate ways.[35] But what I wish to emphasize here is just that consideration of the different ways in which we assign responsibility reflects differences in the degree of immorality. The agent may be more or less evil even where the harm is invariant.

The influence of established social norms is an important example here. It is clear that an act of rape may not violate behavioral norms; that is a contingent matter. Indeed, it may be that some norms encourage rape, at least as I have defined it. The presence of such norms will have an effect on the assessment of the particular acts related to it. Where it is not the case that women are (normally) accorded control over access to their bodies, we should have a different view of the responsibility of men for the rapes they commit than in social contexts in which women are accorded control over sexual access to their bodies.[36] The import may lie in another area, i.e., the systemic effect of rapes, their political content. In this light we may then see that social norms may both excuse (or mitigate the responsibility of) actors in particular instances of rape and yet exacerbate the problem of individual security (among other political issues).

Collateral Obligations

The second element which affects the nature of the evil of rape is the nature and degree of related obligations violated in the course of the rape. These are of various and quite distinct sorts. In some instances what is involved is the conduct by means of which the rape is effected. Obligations to refrain from attacks on others are commonly violated in the course of committing rape.

These sorts of duties are stringent, and the evil of the rape is commensurately raised with the gravity of such violations. In addition to the wrongs involved in physical attacks on others, we should also include here constraints on infliction of psychological distress or trauma. There are, of course, various ways of expressing and cataloging the host of wrongs of these sorts which may be involved. Their implications seem, in any case, fairly plain.

But there are other quite important sorts of wrongs which may occur that are not likely to be captured under the constraints on inflicting pain or serious harms. There are, for example, also duties of information. Ignorance may be culpable after all.[37] We may do wrong when we act without appropriate inquiries regarding information or risk, or when we are insufficiently attentive to the information available to us. These wrongs have an independent status. They often play a role in the creation of serious risks or serious harms. They certainly play a complicating role in the assignment of responsibility for actions and outcomes. In the present circumstance, they take the form of a duty to inquire as to consent of sexual partners, or a duty to make reasonable efforts to assess claims or information.

I am not suggesting that this is a complete list of related duties. The point is rather that the importance and stringency of related duties has an effect on the assessment of the seriousness of the rape as it is confronted in life. The degree of evil of the rape is affected by the nature of wrongs committed in the course of the commission. As more stringent duties are violated, the rape rises in seriousness. In part this is so because these sorts of issues are indicia of the degree of moral corruption of the agent. Its place in a web of wrongdoing is therefore important, and these factors help measure that.

Experience

The third factor in assessing the evil of rape is what I have termed the consequences as felt harms. This is a somewhat misleading rubric, for there are three individualizable elements considered here. The first is such things as the psychological harms of the experience of rape. The fragmentation of personality, the creation of lasting fear, anxiety, etc., are measures of the seriousness of the consequences of the rape. As the causal nexus from which these debilitating effects flow, the rape may be judged by the import of these effects. As the victim's personality is deformed, the seriousness of the rape rises. These effects are constituted by the way in which the rape is experienced by the victim. I should also point out, once again, that some of these effects flow from the rape itself and some flow from the means used to effect the rape. We need not, and cannot, separate them at this stage because the victim need not separate them as experiential elements.

The second part of this factor in the seriousness of rape concerns the harms of autonomy. I have already discussed these harms in a fashion which indicated that I did not think of them as necessarily being wrongs. I do not wish to withdraw that characterization. I want instead to supplement it. Consider for a moment the somewhat different issue of exploitation and work. Work processes inevitably involve some exploitation of those who perform the work. I think this true of all work processes presently feasible. But I need not therefore hold that work *always* involves moral wrong. Exploitation is not a proper subset of immorality. The degree of exploitation matters to an assessment of the wrongness of the work process. Where the exploitation is trivial (or perhaps relatively so), there is no wrong. Wrong comes once the level of exploitation is serious.

The third element is that of the physical costs inflicted on the victim. The bruises, contusions, broken bones, mutilation, the further complications of possible pregnancy or contraction of sexually transmitted diseases (among other sorts of infections), etc., all constitute further substantial harms of moral significance.

Systemic Effects

The final element to be discussed is that of systemic effects of rape. Up to this point the discussion has proceeded on the basis of consideration of particular instances. But patterns of conduct are important as well as the individual acts which constitute the patterns. The systemic effects of rape, and responses to rape, are quite important and play an informative and valuable role in analyses of systems of social domination, especially as related to systems of gender or sex domination. Part of the evil of rape is its political role. The question is not just how particular acts, considered in isolation, are responded to, but also the nature and extent of protection or respect accorded to individual sexual autonomy. It is a different social world when there are isolated cases of rape from the world where rape is prevalent or within accepted social norms of interaction. The patterns of treatment and action have conditioning effects on the persons in the context of consideration.

Rape, like most forms of interactions, has social content beyond the individuals involved in particular instances, and the overall pattern generates effects autonomous of the individual acts of the pattern. So women and men may be conditioned to respond to only certain sorts of cases as legitimate cases of rape, and to consider other cases of rape as acceptable forms of sexual interaction. Such patterns matter in two ways. They affect assessments of individual participants, and guide the assessment of the social system as a whole. The two levels of assessment are distinct.

It is attention to patterns of conduct in addition to the particular instances that allows us to talk sensibly about such matters as institutional racism and sexism.[38] In the present case, the pattern of rape will itself play an important part in understanding the nature and degree of sexism embedded in the organizational core of a society. Further, such patterns play a very important role in shaping responses to the problems of controlling rape and in improving responses to victims.

Thus the assessment of the evil of rape proceeds on two levels. On the one hand, we have various factors to be considered in speaking of the evil of particular cases of rape. On the other hand, we also must attend to the social context of the occurrence of rape, the systemic role and effects of practices which control or encourage rape. It is both personal and political corruption that is involved in rape, and our knowledge of the evil is similarly doubled.

Some Implications and Objections

The account of rape advanced here has a number of implications which are likely to cause resistance. The nonconsent account of rape clearly entails some disturbing descriptions of many ordinary sexual relationships. Intoxication, for example, plays a large and widely accepted part in seduction and courtship. Under the present account, where there is intoxication, the capacity to give effective consent is compromised and, consequently, we may pass over from seduction to rape.[39] Indeed, on this account, it is entirely proper to speak of mutual rape where (at least) two individuals engage in sexual relations while intoxicated.[40] I can see no way to avoid such an outcome, but neither does it seem to me particularly bothersome. In the first place, the claim is not, in such cases, that there must have been some terrible evil done.[41] These are cases of rape, but ones of much diminished significance. Indeed, it is such cases as these that illustrate the value of separating the nature of rape from the moral assessment of rape. There is no need to consider this sort of case as a candidate for legal intervention.

In the second place, it is important to see that there is a natural path that links rape to other sexual activities.[42] There is no doubt that adoption of a nonconsent view of rape opens very serious debates about acceptable conduct, excusable conduct, and the like. But is identification of risky conduct as risky really objectionable? A failure to see the continuum here complicates the task of identifying the socially systemic workings of sexual differentiations and domination. It makes seeing the connections between kinds of rape and other forms of sexual interactions far more difficult. That is an obscurity which we are only beginning to dissipate, and of which the failure to notice has perpetuated serious harms.[43]

On first look, it would also appear that in widening the scope of rape, we would be condemning a proportionately large segment of the population for committing what is usually a fairly serious wrong. The complaint is that there are too many wrongdoers. The idea behind the complaint is that we would end up condemning unduly large numbers of men and women (although mainly the former I would expect) for committing the crime of rape when they lacked the requisite intentional states for the claim of responsibility to be justified. This complaint is the result of a misunderstanding. Because the scope of instances of rape is expanded, it does not follow that the range of those fully responsible (those to be punished by law, e.g.) must also expand.

Delineating the conditions of responsibility is a difficult task, and one that is properly sensitive to a number of factors in addition to causal roles. One factor that assignments of responsibility depend on is the purpose of the assignment (we should have different concerns when the point is imprisonment of wrongdoers than when the point is verbal admonition or is statistical analysis). Another set of factors concern the evidence available about a particular case, and the reasonableness of the beliefs and actions of the relevant agents. It is worth emphasizing that answerability and responsibility are not univocal concepts, but rather matters of complex and subtle gradations and kinds.

It may also be objected that the case developed here is not for a nonconsent account of rape as much as it is a case for multiple concepts of rape. That objection might be put in the following way. Grant that the only account of rape that covers all six categories of cases is the nonconsent account. Nevertheless the nonconsent account itself has some surprising and troublesome implications (e.g., the mutual rape case discussed above). The reason for this is that the net is being cast too widely. We can do better by admitting that there are several concepts of rape. By splitting the categories of cases we may more fully and accurately account for both our present intuitions and social practices regarding rape without including the problematic implications of the nonconsent account.

The distinctiveness, according to the objector, of rape as a crime turns on its experience by victims. The experiences are most clearly captured in thinking of rape as sex occurring against the will of the victim. This "against the will" concept of rape is the fundamental concept underlying the law.[44] There are acceptable counterfactual extensions available sufficient to provide coverage of cases of incapacity. The cases left out are handled by development of a status concept, one which takes the prohibitions on sexual activities involving children (and certain others) as manifesting a distinct set of concerns—partly paternalistic, partly prohibitions on seriously exploitive conduct.

This approach misconceives the nature of rape. Placing an experiential element at the center of the concept of rape has pernicious consequences, as I have already argued. Furthermore, maintaining such an experiential element requires treating rape in an anomalous fashion. There is no similar experiential element to homicide or theft or even battery. More importantly, the experiential claim is grounded in a parochial understanding of the nature and problems of rape. It presumes a set of deeply ahistorical human reactions and psychology. It reifies present social relations and their effects.

What seems to be occurring in the effort to identify rape with how it is experienced is a conflation of cause and effect. There is no doubting that rape occasions seriously disfavored experiences on a regular basis. But those are effects of the rape in a given historical context. The significance of rape changes with the context.

Rape understood as sex against the will of the victim is a notion ambiguous in several ways. First, acts against the will fall across the distinct categories of coercion, nonvoluntary, and nonconsensual acts. In the archaic language of will, what seems to be invoked is the idea of (at least internal) resistance.[45] Indeed, the idea of the against the will account leads to standards of resistance as relevant to the question of the occurrence of a rape. It should not be necessary to detail the reasons why that is a defect.

The will account must be understood so as to provide for counterfactual cases if it is to be at all plausible. The thought is that just as there is a sense in which surgery on an unconscious or intoxicated person may be (counterfactually) against the will of the person, so too may sex. Thus many cases of rape relying on incapacity can be accommodated by the will account. However, this effort to extend the will account fails because it demonstrates a confusion at its heart. The difficulty is that the counterfactual analogies are properly formed only with respect to consent and not will. The medical cases concern questions of consent, not questions of will. The development of proxy and implied consent theories in medicine are not disguised theories of proxy will or implied will. The counterfactual analysis simply adopts that of consent, renaming it along the way. So in those cases which rely on a counterfactual analysis, the nonconsent account of rape is to be preferred on grounds of simplicity.

Insofar as rape involves compromise of interests in sexual self-determination, it is logically independent of victim will. Consider the case where the victim lacks independence. On the will account, this person cannot be raped. There is no counterfactual extension to this sort of case. It is not like intoxication cases where we may sensibly speak of what the person would have desired had she not been intoxicated. In the present example, it is susceptible to counterfactual analysis by substituting for the victim. But then, what is the sense of adhering to the language of will? What we are concerned with is the victim's consent, a matter which is free of experiential requirements. In fact, attending to the way in which the counterfactual cases must all be handled under the will account displays the degree to which it is parasitic on a nonconsent theory. The conclusion we should draw is that the language of will hinders understanding rape. It is best thought of as a stand-in for an analysis of rape as nonconsensual sex. Rape is nonconsensual sex.[46]

Notes

1. E.g., Susan Estrich, *Real Rape* (Cambridge: Harvard University Press, 1986), discusses and criticizes current legal treatment of rape, but does not offer an analysis of the nature of rape. At 8 Estrich offers a traditional common law definition which is ambiguous among force, coercion, and involuntary accounts (discussed below . . .), but at 102–3 relies on a nonconsent account. See also, e.g., Vivian Berger, "Man's Trial, Woman's Tribulation: Rape Cases in the Courtroom," *Columbia Law Review,* vol. 77 (1977): 1–104; Leigh Beinen, "Mistake," *Philosophy and Public Affairs,* vol. 7 (1978): 224–45; Leigh Beinen and Hubert Field, *Jurors and Rape* (Lexington: Lexington Books, 1980); Toni Pickard, "Culpable Mistake and Rape: Relating Mens Rea to Crime," *University of Toronto Law Journal,* vol. 30 (1980): 75–98.

   In the nonlegal literature the situation is similar. Susan Brownmiller, *Against Our Will: Men, Women and Rape* (New York: Simon & Schuster, 1975), has no explicit discussion of the topic (although she seems to have a nonconsent model in mind; pp. 8 and 301). See also Diana E. H. Russell, *The Politics of Rape* (New York: Stein & Day, 1975) and *Rape in Marriage* (New York: Macmillan, 1982), Susan Griffin, "Rape: The All-American Crime," and Pamela Foa, "What's Wrong with Rape," both in Mary Vetterling-Braggin et al. (eds.), *Feminism and Philosophy* (Totowa: Roman & Littlefield, 1977), 313–32 and 347–59 respectively.
2. The facts about enforcement of rape laws support the idea that there are those four possible accounts. See Estrich, op. cit., for an excellent discussion of current legal standards regarding rape. The traditional common law definition is "a man commits rape when he engages in intercourse . . . with a woman not his wife, by force or threat of force, against her will and without her consent." Such a definition is ambiguous among all four definitions canvassed here. As Estrich and others have shown, the operative definition is usually force, or sometimes coercion.
3. Force remains the usual definitional requirement in U.S. jurisdictions. See Leigh Beinen and Hubert Field, op. cit.

4. The Model Penal Code defines rape as sexual intercourse where a man "compels [a woman] to submit by force or threat of imminent death, serious bodily injury, extreme pain or kidnapping, to be inflicted on anyone." MPC sec. 213.1.
5. See Alan Wertheimer, *Coercion* (Princeton: Princeton University Press, 1987), and Joel Feinberg, *Harm to Self* (New York: Oxford University Press, 1986), chapters 23 and 24, for general discussions.
6. This view may lie behind the common use of "against the will" language in legal definitions of rape. See Cal. Pen. Code Section 261(1), (3), (4). See also Feinberg, *Harm to Self,* chapter 20.
7. See Cal. Pen. Code 261.6. See also Feinberg, op cit., chapter 22, for general discussion of consent in criminal law context.
8. See Estrich, op cit.
9. For examples of such substitution, see *Reidhead v. State* 31 Ariz. 70, 250 P. 366 (1926); *Salerno v. State* 162 Neb. 99, 75 N. W. 2d 362 (1956).
10. In particular the argument below assumes that instances of Case 5 concern children (up to about age 12), rather than adolescents.
11. That is not a requirement even for adults. In many cases, it is clear that normal adults act without full understanding of action and are properly held responsible for their conduct.
12. Although the account of rape I urge is sex-neutral, realism about social facts leads me to identify perpetrators as male and victims as female.
13. *State v. Ely* 114 Wash. 185, 194 N. W. 988 (1921); *Eberhardt v. State* 134 Ind. 651, 34 N. E. 637 (1893).
14. *Crosswell v. People* 13 Mich. 427 (1865); *State v. Shephard* 7 Conn. 54 (1828); *Regina v. Dee* 15 Cox C. C. 579 (1884); MPC section 213.1(2).
15. *State v. Williams* 128 N. C. 573, 37 S. E. 952 (1901).
16. See also Catharine MacKinnon, *Feminism Unmodified* (Cambridge: Harvard University Press, 1987), 87–88.
17. The other related harms are discussed . . . below.
18. I do not think a requirement of penetration is necessary for rape. See Janice Moulton, "Sexual Behavior: Another Position," in Alan Soble (ed.), *The Philosophy of Sex* (Totowa: Rowman & Littlefield, 1980), 110–18.
19. For a contrary view, see MacKinnon, op. cit., at 82.
20. Peculiarities of individual psychology should not stand as an obstacle to understanding and properly identifying whether the person has been raped. It is instructive to consider the lives of Celine and Foucault here.
21. I have in mind particularly cases of effective and extensive socialization such that, e.g., women are considered and consider themselves primarily as sexual and reproductive property, hence finding nothing objectionable in treatment amounting to systematic and continuous rape. See Paola Tabet, "Hands, Tools, Weapons." *Feminist Issues,* vol. 2 (1982): 3–62, and "Imposed Reproduction: Maimed Sexuality," *Feminist Issues,* vol. 7 (1987): 3–31; Nicole-Claude Mathieu, "Biological Paternity, Social Maternity," *Feminist Issues,* vol. 4 (1984):

63–71; Colette Guillaumin, "The Practice of Power and Belief in Nature, Part I: The Appropriation of Women," *Feminist Issues,* vol. 1 (1981): 3–28.

22. Leaving experience outside the core account of rape would not constitute a legal anomaly. After all, it is not *experience* which defines the core harms of homicide, theft, battery, slavery (peonage). Mistreatment and disfavored experiences certainly aggravate the evil of slavery, but they are not essential to the nature of slavery.
23. See John Christman, "Constructing the Inner Citadel: Recent Work on Autonomy," *Ethics,* vol. 99 (fall 1988): 109–24.
24. See Sandra Bartky, "Narcissism, Femininity, and Alienation," *Social Theory and Practice,* vol. 8 (1982): 127–44; Alison Jaggar, *Feminist Politics and Human Nature* (Totowa: Rowman & Allenheld, 1983).
25. At least that is the entrenched view in U.S., U.K., and related jurisdictions. *D.P.P. v. Majewski* 2 A11 E. R. 142 (1976); Cal. Pen. Code Section 22. See also Jerome Hall, *General Principles of Criminal Law* (Indianapolis: Bobbs-Merrill, 1960), 537; George Fletcher, *Rethinking Criminal Law* (Boston: Little, Brown, 1980), section 10.4.5; Douglas Husak, *Philosophy of Criminal Law* (Totowa: Rowman & Littlefield, 1987), 53–56.
26. See also John Crewdson, *By Silence Betrayed* (Boston: Little, Brown, 1988), on child sexual abuse. There are interesting differences in the language commonly used in describing child cases. "Rape" seems largely confined to post-pubescent (female) victim cases, and other cases are called "molestation" despite the fact that identical conduct is involved.
27. The importance of consent can also be seen by considering American laws regarding interracial sex in historical perspective. See A. Leon Higginbotham, Jr., and Barbara K. Kopytoff, "Racial Purity and Interracial Sex in the Law of Colonial and Antebellum Virginia," *The Georgetown Law Journal,* vol. 77 (1989): 2007–29.
28. See Lucinda Vandervoort, "Social Justice in the Modern Regulatory State: Duress, Necessity, and the Consensual Model in Law," *Law and Philosophy,* vol. 6 (1987): 205–25.
29. See Diana Russell, *Rape in Marriage: Secret Trauma: Incest in the Lives of Girls and Women* (New York: Basic Books, 1986), e.g., 23; *Sexual Exploitation: Rape, Child Abuse, and Workplace Harassment* (Beverly Hills: Sage Publications, 1984).
30. See, e.g., Monique Wittig, "Social Contract," *Feminist Issues,* vol. 9 (1989): 3–12.
31. See, among others, John Rawls, *A Theory of Justice* (Cambridge: Harvard University Press, 1973).
32. See Jon Elster, *Making Sense of Mars,* chapter 9; Allen Buchanan, *Marx and Justice* (Totowa: Rowman & Littlefield, 1982); Paul Hughes, *Marx and Morality* (Ph.D. dissertation, University of Illinois at Chicago, 1985).
33. See, e.g., John Finnis, *Natural Law and Natural Rights* (Oxford: Oxford University Press, 1980); David Miller, *Anarchism* (London: J. W. Dent, 1984);

John Stuart Mill, *On Liberty* (Indianapolis: Hackett Publishing Company, 1978).

34. Model Penal Code Sect. 2.02(2) (c). See George Fletcher, *Rethinking Criminal Law,* sections 4.3, 6, 6.6, and 8.3; Alan White, *Grounds of Liability* (Oxford: Clarendon Press, 1984), chapter 7 (especially 105–11, 94–99).
35. See Alan White, op. cit., chapter 7; Toni Pickard, op. cit., and "Culpable Mistake and Rape: Harsh Words on Pappajohn," *University of Toronto Law Journal,* vol. 30 (1980): 415–20; Holly Smith "Culpable Ignorance," *The Philosophical Review,* vol. 92 (1983): 543–72; Douglas Husak, op. cit., 54.
36. This does not entail claiming the rape is less important for prevalence of occurrence, but that we should assess differently the actions of particular individuals in light of prevailing social norms. I iterate that victims of rape may be of either sex, and so too the perpetrators. In fact, nevertheless, men are disproportionately perpetrators.
37. See Holly Smith, op. cit., and A. D. Woozley, "Negligence and Ignorance," *Philosophy,* vol. 53 (1978): 293–306.
38. See Richard Wasserstrom, "Racism and Sexism" and "Preferential Treatment" in *Philosophy and Social Issues* (Notre Dame: University of Notre Dame Press, 1980).
39. Where the intoxicants are used as performance enhancers, it is likely still seduction. Where the use replaces judgment we move towards rape.
40. But no odder than the possibility for mutual battery or mutual homicide, to name two.
41. An account of rape is *not* an account of bad sex. Cf. Lois Pineau, "Date Rape: A Feminist Analysis," *Law and Philosophy,* vol. 8 (1989): 217–43. I also do not think that it is psychological states of participants that determine whether or not there has been a rape. There is nothing wrong, after all, in speaking of a person as not knowing that they were raped although conscious at the relevant times.
42. A point stressed by MacKinnon, among others. See Catharine MacKinnon, "Sexuality, Pornography, and Method," *Ethics,* vol. 99 (1989): 314–46, esp. 335–41.
43. Part of the difficulties associated with intelligent discussion of child sexual abuse lies here. Freud's failure with respect to the "child seduction" theory (which is not about seduction anyway) is instructive. See J. M. Masson, *The Assault on Truth: Freud's Suppression of the Seduction Theory* (New York: Farrar, Straus & Giroux, 1984); J. Herman, *Father–Daughter Incest* (Cambridge: Harvard University Press, 1981).
44. This approach treats rape as fundamentally a violent, rather than a sexual, act. See MacKinnon, "Sexuality, Pornography, and Method," 323.
45. See *People v. Berschneider* 89 Daily Journal D.A.R. 7208, where the requirement is met by an apparently effortless movement of the victim's hand. In such cases, it is the clear lack of consent rather than anything about the victim's will that constitutes the rape.

46. I am grateful to Carola Mone for enlightening conversations and comments on earlier versions of this work. I also owe thanks to Sandra Bartky, John Christman, Jeffrey Murphy, Karen Snell, and Monique Wittig. I have benefited from comments by the audience when this material was presented at the Central Division of the APA, University of Colorado, Florida State, Indiana University, San Francisco State, UC Davis, and USC.

THE PERSONAL IS POLITICAL

[18]

No Longer a Wife: Widows in Rural North India

Susan S. Wadley

(The husband) is the main pillar of life. When he dies, then there is nothing for women. Other supports are like the small branches of a tree. These always break at will. But when the main pillar of life falls, then it is most sad.

THIS COMMENT FROM SAROJ, a Brahman widow in her fifties from the village of Karimpur in north India, captures the views of north Indian Hindu widows: to lose one's husband is to lose one's main support. Yet the branches that Saroj belittles—a woman's other kin, both natal and affinal—must exist for support and be strengthened if the new widow is to prosper. Using case studies from Karimpur, this essay explores why widows find this loss so difficult and hence why marriage is of such major concern to Hindu women. While feminists may decry the *pardā* system and the economic dependence of north Indian women, the lives of widows only reinforce the desirability of marriage for Hindu women themselves.

Widows present both ideological and economic challenges to the Hindu system. Ideologically their femaleness and their sexuality is to be controlled by

SOURCE: From Susan S. Wadley, "No Longer a Wife: Widows in Rural North India," in *From the Margins of Hindu Marriage: Essays on Gender, Religion, and Culture,* ed. Lindsey Harlan and Paul B. Courtright (New York: Oxford University Press, 1995). Used by permission.

fathers, husbands, or sons. Economically they are to be supported by male kin, through whom they gain access to resources. Whether the control of women is rooted in ideology or economics, it rests in male hands. Ideally, if a woman is widowed at all, she is widowed in old age, with a son to control and support her. But in fact that ideal is more often challenged by early death, presenting Hindu families with the ultimate paradox: how to provide symbolic control of and economic support to an often young, childless widow.

Understanding how Hindu families approach this paradox requires that we focus on wider kin relationships often obscured by our concern for the institution of marriage per se and the symbolic transfer of a woman from her natal to her affinal family. Further, we must consider the heterogeneity of female roles and statuses within India. There is no homogeneous, essential "Hindu woman"[1] but rather a multiplicity of Hindu women in different socioeconomic classes, life stages, and personal situations. Moreover, each individual woman is herself a multiple person: a daughter, wife or widow, daughter-in-law, sister-in-law, mother, et cetera. These various personae, often demanding contradictory behaviors, become foregrounded in different life contexts, necessitating behaviors and decisions that may be difficult or unwelcome to some other role held by that same woman. The most markedly different personae are those with a patrifocal orientation toward affinal relationships (wife, daughter-in-law) and those with a filiafocal orientation toward consanguineal relationships (sister, daughter).[2] Further, the concerns of a woman's affinal and natal families often come into conflict in decisions about a widow's future. Just as the two families negotiated a marriage, they must now negotiate the forced break in that marriage and agree on the new widow's future. Thus in examining widowhood I highlight not only the importance of marriage but also the immense value placed on relationships with male kin other than the husband.

Privileged Males and Nonprivileged Females

In north India, gender stratification places severe constraints upon the activities and roles of women. It results in male control of females at all ages, the exclusion of women from public venues and places through *pardā* restrictions, and the prohibition of women from participating in income-generating activities, aside from those in which they participate with their husbands or male kin.[3] It is not remarkable, then, that the widow has been considered the "most sinful of all sinful creatures," her widowhood thought to be a result of accumulated *karma,* and her life made miserable by both natal family and affines.

Within this wider picture of female dependence upon males, in a society where alternatives to such dependence are rare, widows have the theoretical potential for becoming female household heads, earning their own livelihoods, and being "independent" women. Further, the life cycle of the Indian female suggests increasing power, authority, and autonomy as a woman ages,[4] creating the possibility of a powerful older female household head. But males' privileged access to productive resources and employment stifles, except in rare cases, this potential for widows.

Moreover, this system of gender stratification interacts with a system of hierarchical relations among men, so that men of high status are able to control the men, and hence the women, of low status. These two systems of gender stratification and social stratification have both a material base by which upper-class men control economic resources, especially land, and an ideological base defining acceptable gender relations and behavior as well as proper caste relations and behavior, respectively.

The critical arena for women's subordination is the family.[5] This subordination is clearly articulated in Hindu law, which has long recognized the threat of the female in a system of ideology giving women great power yet demanding their control by men.[6] Several sections of *The Laws of Manu* are devoted to defining proper behavior for women. A woman must never be autonomous. Rather, the ideal woman, whether young or old, married or widowed, is to be controlled by men. The widow receives special attention:

> A virtuous wife who after the death of her husband constantly remains chaste, reaches heaven, though she have no son, just like those chaste men. But a woman who from a desire to have offspring violates her duty toward her (deceased) husband, brings on herself disgrace in this world, and loses her place with her husband (in heaven).[7]

Hence the ideal widow is chaste and virtuous, and the results of unacceptable behavior are daunting.

There is another model for widows, with variants, less publicized and well known. Found in a variety of law books, it allows remarriage with the husband's (younger) brother. One version, known as a *niyoga,* is found in Manu, among others.[8] *Niyoga* allows a widow to have sexual relations with a husband's brother in order to have sons. It is noteworthy that the law books were especially concerned about the woman who desired offspring, because in a male-dominated society the desire for male offspring is particularly strong; sons are seen as a channel through which women can attain power, authority, and autonomy and, as we shall see, sons do in fact alter the strategies available to widows. Moreover, these codes of conduct (and rules for reproduction) for women are written in law books composed and read by high-caste men who seek control of women.[9]

Yet while the male-authored scriptures and law books of the Brahman elite have gained a hegemonic role in Indian and Western understandings of Indian society, in fact the vast majority of castes allow widow remarriage, as defined by a permanent relationship with a man other than the first husband. The divide in the law, and in actual practice, between those who marry again and those who do not is clear. A caste group in a local area either does or does not allow widow remarriage.[10]

Hindu legal codes not only have mandated male control of women but have denied women access to resources. Even today in rural India, land is the most valuable resource. Until the 1920s, women in north India had few rights of inheritance, and land was a resource held by men and passed from father to son. Legal changes in the 1920s, 1930s, and 1950s gave daughters and widows legal rights of inheritance, in the absence of male heirs.[11] Yet since women can inherit only in the absence of male heirs, and their chances even then of actually gaining control of land are questionable, having sons is the best security.

Thus Hindu law and high-caste ideology have mandated the control of women's sexuality and denied women access to economic resources. These norms are embedded in a hierarchy of caste and class; looking at widows demonstrates the key role of caste and class concerns, as my work in Karimpur shows. Among the upper strata of Hindu society, the ultimate threat to the privileged role of males is the woman who moves into male realms, an action most probable for women who are widows.[12]

The Intersection of Gender and Class in Karimpur

Karimpur is a village located 150 miles southeast of New Delhi. In 1984 it was an agricultural community of 327 families (2,048 individuals) divided among twenty-three castes. Although Brahmans owned nearly 60 percent of the land in 1984, a second large caste of Farmers (*Kachi*)[13] owned another 17 percent. The Brahmans have one of the highest educational levels in the village and have maintained political control for several centuries.

Although some families of Karimpur are wealthy, the village is not well off. Many families in the village live on the equivalent of less than fifty cents per day. Indebtedness affects all but a few large landowners, and increasing dowry demands affect all sections of the community. Karimpur is, however, better off than in previous years: bicycles, brick houses, and synthetic saris are seen in many parts of the village. Better crops and increased irrigation have been important to its general rise in prosperity.

Brahman political and economic superiority is reflected in social superiority: village standards for proper behavior are set by the Brahman community. Social standards for women include a rigorous seclusion of young wives, a ban on women's participation in field work, and a dislike of having one's teenage daughters traveling to high school in the nearby town. Upper-caste women maintain strict *pardā;* they remain inside their family compounds while young and stay carefully veiled before a husband's older male relatives. Gradually some restrictions are eased, so that a woman in her midthirties can leave the courtyard to fetch water, make cow-dung cakes, or process grain on a veranda. Female household work is thus defined by age, with the mother-in-law having to do outside jobs, while her young daughters-in-law cook, grind, and work inside the courtyard. All these restrictions are lessened as economic status decreases. The young poor washerwoman, for example, will have to move about the village to collect clothes from her patrons.

Working in agriculture is a male activity. While women of some groups help their male kin plant certain crops (e.g., garlic), weed, harvest, or irrigate, women do not plow or prepare fields or work, with rare exceptions, for cash wages (when women earn, they earn less than men). Some income-producing activities, defined by caste and the *jajmānī* system of hereditary patron-client relationships, are solely or mainly female: sweeping houses and cleaning "latrines" (*Bhangī*), serving as midwives (*Dhānuk, Bhangī*), preparing flowers for rituals (*Mālī*), carrying water and cleaning utensils (*Kahār*), washing clothes (*Dhobī*). But income and opportunity for these jobs are sporadic, and no family can afford to rely on them for its livelihood. Women also can earn by making and selling cow-dung cakes (five cents per one hundred cakes), raising cattle and selling milk (which may involve obtaining grass daily for fodder), or, less rarely, raising chickens. Only one woman (a Brahman) in Karimpur has a regular income: in her fifties, she has been a schoolteacher for over thirty years.

The poor and landless have increasingly moved out of agricultural pursuits. Since the 1970s there has been an expansion in the incidence of nontraditional and extravillage sources of income, especially for the poor. These men drive rickshaws, carry bags of grain for mills, load brick kilns, unload trucks, work in construction, or do any other of the many labor-intensive jobs that one finds in India. As men have moved out of agriculture, women's work opportunities, given the ban on female participation in agriculture unless accompanied by male kin, have declined. Moreover, the decline of the traditional *jajmānī* system has further eliminated female employment opportunities. These changes in access to employment limit the possibilities for maintaining a livelihood for widows.

The subordination of women within the family is best seen by examining the life cycle, for the roles of women within the family in north India change as women age. In addition, a fundamental distinction must be made between richer, higher-status families, which tend to remain joint and have land, and poor, lower-status landless families, which tend to be nuclear. Class itself is fundamentally gendered, and the maintenance of social classes is built upon distinctive household roles for lower-caste/class and upper-caste/class women and men,[14] and it is the patterns of the upper-caste/class that are closest to those in Manu and other texts, and that are often emulated by the poor.

The native terminology for female life cycles in north India corresponds to the categories derived from Manu: *bacpan* (childhood; also *mā kā rāj* [mother's kingdom]), *sās kā rāj* (the mother-in-law's kingdom), and *bahū kā rāj* (the kingdom of the daughter-in-law).[15]

In childhood the girl, whose birth is rarely celebrated and whose survival chances are not equal to those of her brothers, grows under her mother's care. If wealthy or high-caste, she may attend school for five to eight years. The most important ritual for unmarried girls is *bhaiyā dūj*, Brother's Second, a day on which women worship their brothers and seek the protection that brothers are obliged to give throughout their lives. As a girl develops, her family voices continual concern about her marriage and may spend much time and money seeking the best possible husband for her, given the constraints of its ability to pay a dowry (often equivalent to the household's yearly income, an enormous sum for both the poor and the not-so-poor peasant farmer).[16] The period of marriage ceremonies is fraught with tension, as the groom's family may not accept the proffered dowry or may make other unexpected demands.

Fortunately for most girls, the transition to the groom's house is slow: five or six days at the time of the wedding (*śadī*), then a month or so when the marriage is consummated (*gaunā*), often two or three years later, and finally "the time of crying" (*ronā*), the more permanent move to the groom's house some weeks or months after the consummation.[17] As her parents are unable to accept hospitality in her affinal village, her brothers become her main links to her natal community.[18] Women's folk songs speak of the father who forced a girl out of her home and of the brother who comes yearly to take her to visit to her parents.

The toe rings put on a woman during the marriage ceremony symbolize her dual foci on natal and affinal homes, highlighting her dual status as sister and wife. Karimpur women wear two sets of toe rings on each foot, "one for the husband and one for the brother." When either a husband or a brother dies, one set is removed. Some Brahman women wear neither set if they are widowed, but poor women remove the second pair only when husband *and* brother are dead (and often not even then). If the husband's protection, symbolically and economically, is lost, then a brother's protection should replace it.[19]

Fathers seeking husbands for their daughters want a family which will not abuse the girl, in which the potential for employment and economic security is good, and in which educational and medical facilities are not too remote. Affines desire a hardworking, childbearing, "productive" daughter-in-law. Barrenness, a husband incapable of feeding his family, and widowhood are the primary threats that may send a woman back to her brother's house. Although a woman has the moral right to demand that her natal family care for her, her family's goal is to prevent her from exercising it. Folktales tell of the widowed sister who returns to her brother's house, to be welcomed by him but mistreated by her sister-in-law. It is the "unproductive" widow without a son who highlights the conflict between her two homes, as affines are unwilling to provide for her and brothers see her as an unwelcome burden. Rituals mark these two foci, as women seek their husband's long life and the protection of their brothers in several annual cycle rituals.[20]

Once married to the person of her parents' choice, a woman of a high-status family is raised by her mother-in-law in what is almost always a joint family for at least some years after marriage. The new bride is the lowest-ranking member of the family. In landowning families the woman gradually gains seniority over yet younger wives and, critically, as she gives birth to sons, her status increases. A woman with no sons is taunted, and threats, often acted on, of a second marriage for her husband are common.

The rural landowner's wife reaches her maximum potential as a matriarch of a joint household (she gains control of the house and its environs, not of family estates or public activities), where she can exercise authority over sons, daughters-in-law, and grandchildren. By now her own mother-in-law is dead or feeble, and she has separated from her husband's brothers' families.[21] It is as senior female of a joint family that the Hindu woman attains her greatest power, authority, and autonomy. Daily household decisions are hers: what minor purchases to make, what and how much to cook, whether to send a child to the doctor, and so forth. Moreover, she is rightfully invested with the authority to make these decisions. I have seen older women asked how to cook such and such a dish, not because the younger women did not know but because the olders' authority to know and to tell must be acknowledged. Younger women sometimes wield power in joint families but are also criticized for doing so.

If belonging to a landed or farming family, lower-caste women may join their husbands in planting or weeding fields. In all cases this work is done in conjunction with male household members. *Khetī kā kām* (field work) is considered degrading, and women in the wealthier or Brahman families will not do it. Yet even high-caste richer women are significant contributors to household activities involving the production of agricultural goods, especially postharvest processing such as winnowing and threshing lentils or fennel. These are labeled *ghar kā kām,* (household work), however, and take place on verandas or hidden by the walls of their courtyards.

Older women, preferably past menopause, of all social groups have autonomy. The older woman need not ask others for permission to visit neighbors, to go to town, or to stay with relatives. With age comes a lessening of *pardā* restrictions. Most upper-caste village women retain the outer symbols such as a sari pulled over the head and a shawl when outside the house—but their faces are mostly uncovered and their mobility less restricted. This status and authority come with motherhood—having sons and daughters-in-law to dominate. Being a wife does not give status: the older barren wife may well share in decision making with her husband, but she has no one over whom she has authority. The woman, then, from ages forty to sixty, after which old age begins to take its toll and daughters-in-law gain power, is often a significant authority figure in her household.

The north Indian widow is no longer barred from auspicious religious ceremonies. Head shaving has rarely existed in the north. But the widow should wear white, break her glass bangles that symbolize auspicious marital status, and remove her toe rings, given in the marriage ceremony itself.[22] She should lead a simple life, one of chaste asceticism and religious devotion. But this ideal is seldom achieved, as women struggle to feed their families, find money for children's schooling, repair a house, or negotiate children's marriages with the aid of more distant male kin. Further, this is the time of the *bahū kā rāj* (the rule of the daughter-in-law), as the widow is unable to retain the power that she had while her husband lived.[23]

Several features of this familial picture need elaborating. First, it is critical that there are no options: rural women are expected to marry, to bear children, to aid in household production, and to become mothers-in-law. Given the lack of alternatives, women benefit by adhering to the norms defined by the male-dominated system. If wealthy, they will eventually attain the rewards of the authority and autonomy of the mother-in-law. Second, the powers and autonomy of the north Indian wife are less than those of women elsewhere in India.[24] The north Indian wife rarely retains control of her dowry: she does control household decisions, but these are often trite, with husbands making the major purchases. A women can only hope to influence decisions about educating children,[25] marriages, fields, and so forth.

Third, the situation of poor women in north India is fundamentally different from that of wealthier women. The poorer woman has little hope of ever attaining the power that comes with ruling a joint household. She is married earlier and has little or no education. Often separated from her in-laws by the time of her first child, she will have a daughter-in-law for an equally short period of time.[26] Though family ties remain very close in separated families, the constant struggle for survival forces each family unit to be self-sufficient, especially if no land or agricultural implements are shared. Without a mother-in-law a woman quickly achieves power over her own family (children), authority, and autonomy. But domestic power is of a different order of meaning when defined not by "How much must I cook?" but by "Do I have enough food to cook today?," not by "Shall I take my baby to the doctor?" but by "We have no money. He/she will have to stay sick." Poor women of any age may have domestic power, but they lack the access to resources to utilize this power. Suffering from their low rank in both gender and class systems of stratification, poor women are doubly burdened.

Poor women are unable to keep strict *pardā,* lacking the means to enclose a courtyard and by necessity having to move in public space.[27] The poor woman may be involved with her husband in *jajmānī* duties or agriculture. The widows wear whatever clothes they can get, while never removing their bangles and toe rings. This denial of the outward attributes of widowhood reflects their vulnerability as poor women without male support: if no "widow" signs are given, they have a greater chance of avoiding abuse. Those forced to be economically independent must leave *pardā,* and the protection of male kin, to work as laborers with strangers.

Let me now examine the life situations of widows in Karimpur.[28] Given the diverse roles of women, we must seek to understand which become dominant when the role of wife is lost. Some widows are seen as primarily daughters or sisters; others as mothers or sisters-in-law. Caste, age, economic class, and sons are key components in the decision about the widow's future role, as is the personality of the individual woman. Male kin play critical roles: as affines or parents they decide on new marriage partners; as sons they determine the likelihood of remarriage; and as close relatives, they can help the widow survive by acting for her in public places. Often the desires of natal and affinal kin are in conflict and must be negotiated. The upper-class widow who is able to retain the power, authority, and autonomy that she may have gained as the senior female in a joint household is rare. Instead, widowhood marks the transference of that power to a new generation. The poor, often younger, widow becomes the female head of a subnuclear household where resources are minimal and survival dependent upon her ability to feed herself. Independence is not valued, and women state a clear preference to be a subordinate wife in a joint household.

. . .

Notes

1. For a discussion of the inessential woman, see Elizabeth V. Spellman, *The Inessential Woman: Problems of Exclusion in Feminist Thought* (Boston: Beacon Press, 1988).
2. See Lynn Bennett, *Dangerous Wives and Sacred Sisters: Social and Symbolic Roles of High-Caste Women in Nepal* (New York: Columbia University Press, 1983).
3. Unlike south Indian women, those residing in the Gangetic plain are not regularly hired as independent agricultural laborers, instead working most often with husbands on their own or sharecropped fields. (See Jean Dreze, "Social Insecurity in India," paper presented at the Workshop on Social Insecurity in Developing Countries, London School of Economics, 1988.) Women whose families worked in traditional *jajmānī* service occupations also share chores with their husbands but are not considered as contributing to family income. "North" and "northern" are used in this essay to mean the Gangetic plain, the largely Hindi-speaking area of northern India.
4. See Sylvia Vatuk, "The Aging Woman in India: Self-Perceptions and Changing Roles," in *Women in Contemporary India and South Asia,* ed. A. deSouza (New Delhi: Manohar Books, 1980), 287–309.
5. Gail Omvedt's work on female subordination is critical here. See especially "Patriarchy: The Analysis of Women's Oppression," *Insurgent Sociologist* 13 (1986): 30–50.
6. My earlier article on women and Hinduism considers this point in detail. See Susan S. Wadley, "Women and the Hindu Tradition," in *Women in India: Two Perspectives,* Susan S. Wadley and Doranne Jacobson (New Delhi: Manohar Books, 1977), 111–36.
7. *The Laws of Manu* (1886), trans. Georg Bühler, Sacred Books of the East, vol. 25 (Delhi: Motilal Banarsidass, 1964), 160–65.
8. Ibid., Book IX:190. See also Wendy Doniger, "Begetting on Margin: Adultery and Pseudomarriage in Hinduism," in *From the Margins of Hindu Marriage: Essays on Gender, Religion, and Culture,* ed. Lindsey Harlan and Paul B. Courtright (New York: Oxford University Press, 1995).
9. In joint families in north India, a woman's reproduction is often controlled by the mother-in-law, who arranges sleeping quarters, watches after her son's health, and verbally condemns unapproved behavior. For a discussion of patriarchy and fertility, see Michael A. Koenig and Gillian H. C. Foo, "Patriarchy and High Fertility in Rural North India," paper presented at the Rockefeller Foundation Workshop on Women's Status and Fertility, Mt. Kisco, N.Y., June 1985. These law books are minimally concerned with the behavior of poor, low-caste widows, and specific prescriptions are directed at the higher castes only.
10. Pauline Kolenda vividly demonstrated the actuality of widow remarriage among Sweepers in a village north of Delhi. She also found a series of caste rules about better or worse remarriage options. See her "Widowhood Among

'Untouchable' Chuhras," in *Concepts of Person: Kinship, Caste, and Marriage in India,* ed. A. Östör, Lina Fruzetti, and Steve Barnett (Cambridge, Mass.: Harvard University Press, 1982), 172–220. N. K. Walli has data showing a switch in caste codes in Maharashtra from allowing remarriage to forbidding it in the early years of British rule (personal communication).

11. Bina Agrawal, "Women, Poverty and Agricultural Growth in India," *Journal of Peasant Studies* 13 (1986): 165–220.
12. Mary Hancock, "The Dilemmas of Domesticity: Possession and Devotional Experience among Urban Smārta Women," in *From the Margins of Hindu Marriage,* illuminates the threat of economic independence on male kin.
13. Except for Brahmans, I have translated caste names, giving the Hindi at the first occurrence. Caste names in English are marked by a capital letter (as in Farmer).
14. See Rayna Rapp, "Family and Class in Contemporary America: Notes toward an Understanding of Ideology," in *Rethinking the Family: Some Feminist Questions,* ed. Barrie Thorne with Marilyn Yalom (New York: Longman, 1982), 168–87.
15. Note that here the control is seen as coming from other women, not from men.
16. Hindu families in most of India look for a husband for their daughters: to have to seek a bride for a son brings much dishonor to the family.
17. As the average age of marriage has increased from eleven to sixteen. these periods have been condensed, and for brides over fifteen, *gaunā* may occur at the time of the *śadī,* although the visit is still short.
18. Upper-caste families are particularly strict, and parents are forbidden even water in their daughter's married village. These strictures ease as caste and class status lessens.
19. Bennett reports that a widow should receive her saris from her brother, again marking the importance of this key natal relative *(Dangerous Wives and Sacred Sisters,* 244).
20. For more details on the worship of male kin, see Susan S. Wadley, "Brothers, Husbands and Sometimes Sons: Kinsmen in North Indian Ritual," *Eastern Anthropologist* 29 (1976): 149–70.
21. My understanding of separation is defined by the Hindi term current in Karimpur—*nyāre. Nyāre* means, in practice, separate eating and cooking facilities and, when possible, separate living quarters. Most families prefer separate farming as well. In reality, separation is a drawn-out process, with the separation of farming, religious activities, and decision making not occurring for years in some instances.
22. Recently, even the white sari and no-bangle rules are easily broken: even Brahman widows regularly wear plastic bangles (giving the appearance of glass), and only the oldest widows wear white.
23. In one joint household the father has essentially deserted his family, though he sometimes lives with them. His oldest son is the effective head of household, and his mother has far less voice than his wife in household decisions.

24. Tim Dyson and Mick Moore, "On Kinship Structure, Female Autonomy, and Demographic Behavior in India," *Population and Development Review* 9 (1983): 35–60.
25. Women whose desires with regard to the education of children are thwarted by their husbands will often turn to their own natal families for aid, and it is not unusual to learn of a son studying at his mother's natal village.
26. David Mandelbaum documents a series of cases where lower-caste and/or non-landowning castes had larger percentages of nuclear families. See David Mandelbaum, *Society in India: Continuity and Change* (Berkeley: University of California Press, 1970). In Karimpur 38 percent of rich families are nuclear and 38 percent are joint (with the remainder primarily in supplemented nuclear households). Among the poorest, 60 percent are nuclear and 10 percent are joint, with the remainder evenly split between subnuclear and supplemented nuclear households. See Susan S. Wadley and Bruce W. Derr, "Karimpur Families over 60 Years," *South Asian Anthropologist* 9 (1988): 119–32.
27. Women who are poor do not threaten male privilege by being in public spaces because, like poor men, they already lack access to economic and political power.
28. Data from 1925 derive from the census records collected by William Wiser. Later data were collected by William Wiser. Later data were collected during three research periods in Karimpur: in 1967–69 with funding from the National Science Foundation; in 1974–75 with funding from the American Institute of Indian Studies; and in 1983–84 with funding from Faculty Research Abroad, U.S. Dept. of Education and the Smithsonian Institution. Bruce W. Derr is due many thanks for aiding in collecting these data and for the analysis of census data. This paper is in memory of Ant Ram Kahar, who painstakingly transcribed pages of life histories and whose widow provides data for this analysis.

[19]

Hunger

Naomi Wolf

. . .

HOW WOULD AMERICA REACT to the mass self-immolation by hunger of its favorite sons? How would Western Europe absorb the export of such a disease? One would expect an emergency response: crisis task forces convened in congressional hearing rooms, unscheduled alumni meetings, the best experts money can hire, cover stories in newsmagazines, a flurry of editorials, blame and counterblame, bulletins, warnings, symptoms, updates; an epidemic blazoned in boldface red. The sons of privilege *are* the future; the future is committing suicide.

Of course, this is actually happening right now, only with a gender difference. The institutions that shelter and promote these diseases are hibernating. The public conscience is fast asleep. Young women are dying from institutional catatonia: four hundred dollars a term from the college endowment for the women's center to teach "self-help"; fifty to buy a noontime talk from a visiting clinician. The world is not coming to an end because the cherished child in five who "chooses" to die slowly is a girl. And she is merely doing too well what she is expected to do very well in the best of times.

Up to one tenth of all young American women, up to one fifth of women

SOURCE: From Naomi Wolf, *The Beauty Myth* (New York: William Morrow & Co., 1991).

students in the United States, are locked into one-woman hunger camps. When they fall, there are no memorial services, no intervention through awareness programs, no formal message from their schools and colleges that the society prefers its young women to eat and thrive rather than sicken and die. Flags are not lowered in recognition of the fact that in every black-robed ceremonial marches a fifth column of death's-heads.

Virginia Woolf in *A Room of One's Own* had a vision that someday young women would have access to the rich forbidden libraries of the men's colleges, their sunken lawns, their vellum, the claret light. She believed that would give young women a mental freedom that must have seemed all the sweeter from where she imagined it: the wrong side of the beadle's staff that had driven her away from the library because she was female. Now young women have pushed past the staff that barred Woolf's way. Striding across the grassy quadrangles that she could only write about, they are halted by an immaterial barrier she did not foresee. Their minds are proving well able; their bodies self-destruct.

When she envisaged a future for young women in the universities, Woolf's prescience faltered only from insufficient cynicism. Without it one could hardly conceive of the modern solution of the recently all-male schools and colleges to the problem of women: They admitted their minds, and let their bodies go. Young women learned that they could not live inside those gates and also inside their bodies.

The weight-loss cult recruits women from an early age, and eating diseases are the cult's bequest. Anorexia and bulimia are female maladies: From 90 to 95 percent of anorexics and bulimics are women. America, which has the greatest number of women who have made it into the male sphere, also leads the world with female anorexia. Women's magazines report that there are up to a million American anorexics, but the American Anorexia and Bulimia Association states that anorexia and bulimia strike a million American women *every year;* 30,000, it reports, also become emetic abusers.

Each year, according to the association, 150,000 American women die of anorexia. If so, every twelve months there are 17,024 more deaths in the United States alone than the total number of deaths from AIDS tabulated by the World Health Organization in 177 countries and territories from the beginning of the epidemic until the end of 1988; if so, more die of anorexia in the United States each year than died in ten years of civil war in Beirut. Beirut has long been front-page news. As criminally neglectful as media coverage of the AIDS epidemic has been, it still dwarfs that of anorexia; so it appears that the bedrock question—why must Western women go hungry—is one too dangerous to ask even in the face of a death toll such as this.

Joan Jacobs Brumberg in *Fasting Girls: The Emergence of Anorexia Nervosa as a Modern Disease* puts the number of anorexics at 5 to 10 percent of all American girls and women. On some college campuses, she believes, one woman student in five is anorexic. The number of women with the disease has increased dramatically throughout the Western world starting twenty years ago. Dr. Charles A. Murkovsky of Gracie Square Hospital in New York City, an eating diseases specialist, says that 20 percent of American college women binge and purge on a regular basis. Kim Chernin in *The Hungry Self* suggests that at least half the women on campuses in the United States suffer at some time from bulimia or anorexia. Roberta Pollack Seid in *Never Too Thin* agrees with the 5 to 10 percent figure for anorexia among young American women, adding that up to six times that figure on campuses are bulimic. If we take the high end of the figures, it means that of ten young American women in college, two will be anorexic and six will be bulimic; only two will be well. The norm, then, for young, middle-class American women, is to be a sufferer from some form of the eating disease.

The disease is a deadly one. Brumberg reports that 5 to 15 percent of hospitalized anorexics die in treatment, giving the disease one of the highest fatality rates for a mental illness. The *New York Times* cites the same fatality rate. Researcher L. K. G. Hsu gives a death rate of up to 19 percent. Forty to 50 percent of anorexics never recover completely, a worse rate of recovery from starvation than the 66 percent recovery rate for famine victims hospitalized in the war-torn Netherlands in 1944–45.

The medical effects of anorexia include hypothermia, edema, hypotension, bradycardia (impaired heartbeat), lanugo (growth of body hair), infertility, and death. The medical effects of bulimia include dehydration, electrolyte imbalance, epileptic seizure, abnormal heart rhythm, and death. When the two are combined, they can result in tooth erosion, hiatal hernia, abraded esophagus, kidney failure, osteoporosis, and death. Medical literature is starting to report that babies and children underfed by weight-conscious mothers are suffering from stunted growth, delayed puberty, and failure to thrive.

It is spreading to other industrialized nations: The United Kingdom now has 3.5 million anorexics or bulimics (95 percent of them female), with 6,000 new cases yearly. Another study of adolescent British girls alone shows that 1 percent are now anorexic. According to the women's press, at least 50 percent of British women suffer from disordered eating. Hilde Bruch states that in the last generation, larger patient groups have been reported in publications in Russia, Australia, Sweden, and Italy as well as Great Britain and the United States. Sweden's rate is now 1 to 2 percent of teenage girls, with the same percentage of women over sixteen being bulimic. The rate for the Netherlands is 1 to 2 percent; of Italian teenagers also, 1 percent suffer from anorexia or bulimia (95 percent of them female), a rise of 400 percent in ten years. That is just the beginning for Western Europe and Japan, since the figures resemble numbers for the United States ten years ago, and since the rate is rising, as it did in America, exponentially. The anorexic patient herself is *thinner* now than were previous generations of patients. Anorexia followed the familiar beauty myth pattern of movement: It began as a middle-class disease in the United States and has spread eastward as well as down the social ladder.

Some women's magazines report that 60 percent of American women have serious trouble eating. The majority of middle-class women in the United States, it appears, suffer a version of anorexia or bulimia; but if anorexia is defined as a compulsive fear of and fixation upon food, perhaps most Western women can be called, twenty years into the backlash, mental anorexics.

What happened? Why now? The first obvious clue is the progressive chiseling away of the Iron Maiden's body over this century of female emancipation, in reaction to it. Until seventy-five years ago in the male artistic tradition of the West, women's natural amplitude was their beauty; representations of the female nude reveled in women's lush fertility. Various distributions of sexual fat were emphasized according to fashion—big, ripe bellies from the fifteenth to the seventeenth centuries, plump faces and shoulders in the early nineteenth, progressively generous dimpled buttocks and thighs until the twentieth—but never, until women's emancipation entered law, this absolute negation of the female state that fashion historian Ann Hollander in *Seeing Through Clothes* characterizes, from the point of view of any age but our own, as "the look of sickness, the look of poverty, and the look of nervous exhaustion."

Dieting and thinness began to be female preoccupations when Western women received the vote around 1920; between 1918 and 1925, "the rapidity with which the new, linear form replaced the more curvaceous one is startling." In the regressive 1950s, women's natural fullness could be briefly enjoyed once more because their minds were occupied in domestic seclusion. But when women came en masse into male spheres, that pleasure had to be overridden by an urgent social expedient that would make women's bodies into the prisons that their homes no longer were.

A generation ago, the average model weighed 8 percent less than the average American woman, whereas today she weighs 23 percent less. Twiggy appeared in the pages of *Vogue* in 1965, simultaneous with the advent of the Pill, to cancel out its most radical implications. Like many beauty-myth symbols, she was double-edged, suggesting to women the freedom from the constraint of reproduction of earlier generations (since female fat is categorically understood by the subconscious as fertile sexuality), while reassuring men with her suggestion of female weakness, asexuality, and hunger. Her thinness, now commonplace, was shocking at the time; even *Vogue* introduced the model with anxiety: "'Twiggy' is called Twiggy because she looks as though a strong gale would snap her in two and dash her to the ground. . . . Twiggy is of such a meagre constitution that other models stare at her. Her legs look as though she has not had enough milk as a baby and her face has that expression one feels Londoners wore in the blitz." The fashion writer's language is revealing: Undernurtured, subject to being overpowered by a strong wind, her expression the daze of the besieged, what better symbol to reassure an establishment faced with women who were soon to march tens of thousands strong down Fifth Avenue?

In the twenty years after the start of the second wave of the women's movement, the weight of Miss Americas plummeted, and the average weight of Playboy Playmates dropped from 11 percent below the national average in 1970 to 17 percent below it in eight years. Model Aimee Liu in her autobiography claims that many models are anorexic; she herself continued to model as an anorexic. Of dancers, 38 percent show anorexic behavior. The average model, dancer, or actress is thinner than 95 percent of the female population. The Iron Maiden put the shape of a near skeleton and the texture of men's musculature where the shape and feel of a woman used to be, and the small elite corps of women whose bodies are used to reproduce the Iron Maiden often become diseased themselves in order to do so.

As a result, a 1985 survey says, 90 percent of respondents think they weigh too much. On any day, 25 percent of women are on diets, with 50 percent finishing, breaking, or starting one. This self-hatred was generated rapidly, coinciding with the women's movement: Between 1966 and 1969, two studies showed, the number of high school girls who thought they were too fat had risen from 50 to 80 percent. Though heiresses to the gains of the women's movement, their daughters are, in terms of this distress, no better off: In a recent study of high school girls, 53 percent were unhappy with their bodies by age thirteen; by age eighteen and over, 78 percent were dissatisfied. The hunger cult has won a major victory against women's fight for equality if the evidence of the 1984 *Glamour* survey of thirty-three thousand women is representative: 75 percent of those aged eighteen to thirty-five believed they were fat, while only 25 percent were medically overweight (the same percentage as men); 45 percent of the *underweight* women thought they were too fat. But more heartbreaking in terms of the way in which the myth is running to ground hopes for women's advancement and gratification, the *Glamour* respondents chose losing ten to fifteen pounds above success in work or in love as their most desired goal.

Those ten to fifteen pounds, which have become a fulcrum, if these figures are indicative, of most Western women's sense of self, are the medium of what I call the One Stone Solution. One stone, the British measurement of fourteen pounds, is roughly what stands between the 50 percent of women who are not overweight who believe they are and their ideal self. That one stone, once lost, puts these women well below the weight that is natural to them, and beautiful, if we saw with eyes unconstrained by the Iron Maiden. But the body quickly restores itself, and the cycle of gain and loss begins, with its train of torment and its risk of disease, becoming a fixation of the woman's consciousness. The inevitable cycles of failure ensured by the One Stone Solution create and continually reinforce in women our uniquely modern neurosis. This great weight-shift bestowed on women, just when we were free to begin to forget them, new versions of low self-esteem, loss of control, and sexual shame. It is a genuinely elegant fulfillment of a collective wish: By simply dropping the official weight one stone below most women's natural level, and redefining a woman's womanly shape as by definition "too fat," a wave of self-hatred swept over First World women, a reactionary psychology was perfected, and a major industry was born. It suavely countered the historical groundswell of female success with a mass conviction of female failure, a failure defined as implicit in womanhood itself.

The proof that the One Stone Solution is political lies in what women feel when they eat "too much": guilt. Why should guilt be the operative emotion, and female fat be a moral issue articulated with words like good and bad? If our culture's fixation on female fatness or thinness were about sex, it would be a private issue between a woman and her lover; if it were about health, between a woman and herself. Public debate would be far more hysterically focused on male fat than on female, since more men (40 percent) are medically overweight than women (32 percent) and too much fat is far more dangerous for men than for women. In fact, "there is very little evidence to support the claim that fatness causes poor health among women. . . . The results of recent studies have suggested that women may in fact live longer and be generally healthier if they weigh ten to fifteen percent *above* the life-insurance figures *and* they refrain from dieting," asserts *Radiance;* when poor health is correlated to fatness in women, it is due to chronic dieting and the emotional stress of self-hatred. The National Institutes of Health studies that linked obesity to heart disease and stroke were based on male subjects; when a study of females was finally published in 1990, it showed that weight made only a fraction of the difference for women that it made for men. The film *The Famine Within* cites a sixteen-country study that fails to correlate fatness to ill health. Female fat is not in itself unhealthy.

But female fat is the subject of public passion, and women feel guilty about female fat, because we implicitly recognize that under the myth, women's bodies are not our own but society's, and that thinness is not a private aesthetic, but hunger a social concession exacted by the community. A cultural fixation on female thinness is not an obsession about female beauty but an obsession about female obedience. Women's dieting has become what Yale psychologist Judith Rodin calls a "normative obsession, a never-ending passion play given international coverage out of all proportion to the health risks associated with obesity, and using emotive language that does not figure even in discussions of alcohol or tobacco abuse. The nations seize with compulsive attention on this melodrama because women and men understand that it is not about cholesterol or heart rate or the disruption of a line of tailoring, but about how much social freedom women are going to get away with or concede. The media's convulsive analysis of the endless saga of female fat and the battle to vanquish it are actually bulletins of the sex war: what women are gaining or losing in it, and how fast.

The great weight shift must be understood as one of the major historical developments of the century, a direct solution to the dangers posed by the women's movement and economic and reproductive freedom. Dieting is the most potent political sedative in women's history; a quietly mad population is a tractable one. Researchers S. C. Wooley and O. W. Wooley confirmed what most women know too well—that concern with weight leads to "a virtual collapse of self-esteem and sense of effectiveness." Researchers J. Polivy and C. P. Herman found that "prolonged and periodic caloric restriction" resulted in a distinctive personality whose traits are "passivity, anxiety and emotionality."

It is those traits, and not thinness for its own sake, that the dominant culture wants to create in the private sense of self of recently liberated women in order to cancel out the dangers of their liberation.

Women's advances had begun to give them the opposite traits—high self-esteem, a sense of effectiveness, activity, courage, and clarity of mind. "Prolonged and periodic caloric restriction" is a means to take the teeth out of this revolution. The great weight shift and its One Stone Solution followed the rebirth of feminism so that women just reaching for power would become weak, preoccupied, and, as it evolved, mentally ill in useful ways and in astonishing proportions. To understand how the gaunt toughness of the Iron Maiden has managed spectacularly to roll back women's advances toward equality, we have to see that what is really at stake is not fashion or beauty or sex, but a struggle over political hegemony that has become—for women, who are often unaware of the real issues behind our predicament—one of life and death.

Theories abound to explain anorexia, bulimia, and the modern thinning of the feminine. Ann Hollander proposes that the shift from portraiture to moving images made thinness suggestive of motion and speed. Susie Orbach in *Fat Is a Feminist Issue* "reads" women's fat as a statement to the mother about separation and dependence; she sees in the mother "a terrible ambivalence about feeding and nurturing" her daughter. Kim Chernin in the *The Obsession* gives a psychoanalytic reading of fear of fat as based on infantile rage against the all-powerful mother, and sees food as the primordial breast, the "lost world" of female abundance that we must recover "if we are to understand the heartland of our obsession with the female body. . . . We can understand how," Chernin writes, "in a frenzy of terror and dread, [a man] might be tempted to spin out fashionable images of [a woman] that tell her implicitly that she is unacceptable . . . when she is large." In *The Hungry Self,* Chernin interprets bulimia as a religious rite of passage. Joan Jacobs Brumberg sees food as a symbolic language, anorexia as a cry of confusion in a world of too many choices, and "the appetite as voice": "young women searching for an idiom in which to say things about themselves focused on food and styles of eating." Rudolph Bell in *Holy Anorexia* relates the disease to the religious impulses of medieval nuns, seeing starvation as purification.

Theories such as these are enlightening within a private context; but they do not go far enough. Women do not eat or starve only in a succession of private relationships, but within a public social order that has a material vested interest in their troubles with eating. Individual men don't "spin out fashionable images" (indeed, research keeps proving that they are warm to women's real shapes and unmoved by the Iron Maiden); multinational corporations do that. The many theories about women's food crises have stressed private psychology *to the neglect of* public policy, looking at women's shapes to see how they express a conflict about their society rather than looking at how their society makes use of a manufactured conflict with women's shapes. Many other theories have focused on women's reaction to the thin ideal, but have not asserted that the thin ideal is *proactive,* a preemptive strike.

We need to reexamine all the terms again, then, in the light of a public agenda. What, first, is food? Certainly, within the context of the intimate family, food is love, and memory, and language. But in the public realm, food is status and honor.

Food is the primal symbol of social worth. Whom a society values, it feeds well. The piled plate, the choicest cut, say: We think you're worth this much of the tribe's resources. Samoan women, who are held in high esteem, exaggerate how much they eat on feast days. Publicly apportioning food is about determining power relations, and sharing it is about cementing social equality: When men break bread together, or toast the queen, or slaughter for one another the fatted calf, they've become equals and then allies. The word *companion* comes from the Latin for "with" and "bread"—those who break bread together.

But under the beauty myth, now that all women's eating is a public issue, our portions testify to and reinforce our sense of social inferiority. If women cannot eat the same food as men, we cannot experience equal status in the community. As long as women are asked to bring a self-denying mentality to the communal table, it will never be round, men and women seated together, but the same traditional hierarchical dais, with a folding table for women at the foot.

In the current epidemic of rich Western women who cannot "choose" to eat, we see the continuation of an older, poorer tradition of women's relation to food. Modern Western female dieting descends from a long history. Women have always had to eat differently from men: less and worse. In Hellenistic Rome, reports classicist Sarah B. Pomeroy, boys were rationed sixteen measures of meal to twelve measures allotted to girls. In medieval France, according to historian John Boswell, women received two thirds of the grain allocated to men. Throughout history, when there is only so much to eat, women get little, or none: A common explanation among anthropologists for female infanticide is that food shortage provokes it. According to UN publications, where hunger goes, women meet it first: In Bangladesh and Botswana, female infants die more frequently than male, and girls are more often malnourished, because they are given smaller portions. In Turkey, India, Pakistan, North Africa, and the Middle East, men get the lion's share of what food there is, regardless of women's caloric needs. "It is not the caloric value of work which is represented in the patterns of food consumption" of men in relation to women in North Africa, "nor is it a question of physiological needs. . . . Rather these patterns tend to guarantee priority rights to the 'important' members of society, that is, adult men." In Morocco, if women are guests, "they will swear they have eaten already" or that they are not hungry. "Small girls soon learn to offer their share to visitors, to refuse meat and deny hunger." A North African woman described by anthropologist Vanessa Mahler assured her fellow diners that "she preferred bones to meat." Men, however, Mahler reports, "are supposed to be exempt from facing scarcity which is shared out among women and children."

"Third World countries provide examples of undernourished female and well-nourished male children, where what food there is goes to the boys of the family," a UN report testifies. Two thirds of women in Asia, half of all women in Africa, and a sixth of Latin American women are anemic—through lack of food. Fifty percent more Nepali women than men go blind from lack of food. Cross-culturally, men receive hot meals, more protein, and the first helpings of a dish, while women eat the cooling leftovers, often having to use deceit and cunning to get enough to eat. "Moreover, what food they do receive is consistently less nutritious."

This pattern is not restricted to the Third World: Most Western women alive today can recall versions of it at their mothers' or grandmothers' table:

British miners' wives eating the grease-soaked bread left over after their husbands had eaten the meat; Italian and Jewish wives taking the part of the bird no one else would want.

These patterns of behavior are standard in the affluent West today, perpetuated by the culture of female caloric self-deprivation. A generation ago, the justification for this traditional apportioning shifted: Women still went without, ate leftovers, hoarded food, used deceit to get it—but blamed themselves. Our mothers still exiled themselves from the family circle that was eating cake with silver cutlery off Wedgwood china, and we would come upon them in the kitchen, furtively devouring the remains. The traditional pattern was cloaked in modern shame, but otherwise changed little. Weight control became its rationale once natural inferiority went out of fashion.

The affluent West is merely carrying on this traditional apportioning. Researchers found that parents in the United States urged boys to eat, regardless of their weight, while they did so with daughters only if they were relatively thin. In a sample of babies of both sexes, 99 percent of the boys were breast-fed, but only 66 percent of the girls, who were given 50 percent less time to feed. "Thus," writes Susie Orbach, "daughters are often fed less well, less attentively and less sensitively than they need." Women do not feel entitled to enough food because they have been taught to go with less than they need since birth, in a tradition passed down through an endless line of mothers; the public role of "honored guest" is new to us, and the culture is telling us through the ideology of caloric restriction that we are not welcome finally to occupy it.

. . .

Editor's note: The notes for this article have been omitted. The interested reader should refer to the original text, *The Beauty Myth* (New York: William Morrow & Co., 1991).

[20]

Heterosexuality and Feminist Theory

Christine Overall

HETEROSEXUALITY, which I define as a romantic and sexual orientation toward persons not of one's own sex, is apparently a very general, though not entirely universal, characteristic of the human condition. In fact, it is so ubiquitous a part of human interactions and relations as to be almost invisible, and so natural-seeming as to appear unquestionable. Indeed, the 1970 edition of *The Shorter Oxford English Dictionary* defines "heterosexual" as "pertaining to or characterized by the *normal* relation of the sexes."[1]

In this respect heterosexuality is strikingly different from the romantic and sexual orientation toward persons of one's own sex, or what I shall call, for the sake of brevity, non-heterosexuality.[2] I caution that the use of the term "non-heterosexuality" could be misleading, since it falsely suggests a uniformity among other sexual orientations comparable to that of heterosexuality. There are many significant differences among lesbianism, male homosexuality, and both male and female bisexuality. But what I am concerned with is not those differences, significant and far-ranging as they are, but rather the general contrast they collectively provide to heterosexuality.

Historically, for example, there has been a tendency to investigate the causes of forms of non-heterosexuality, but not of heterosexuality; to consider

SOURCE: From Christine Overall, "Heterosexuality and Feminist Theory," *Canadian Journal of Philosophy* 20, no. 1 (March 1990). Used by permission.

whether non-heterosexuality, but not heterosexuality, can be spread through a sort of contagion effect;[3] to ask whether non-heterosexuality is unnatural, but not to contemplate whether heterosexuality in any sense could be. If we make any assumption about a person's sexual orientation, it is almost always the assumption that the person is heterosexual. Ordinarily most parents seldom wonder whether their offspring will grow up to be heterosexual, and, compared to the ubiquitous depictions of heterosexual relations, there are very few widely available cultural images of non-heterosexuality. If one is not heterosexual, one may have the choice to pass as heterosexual; one may, that is, attempt for purposes of self-protection to assimilate into the dominant culture. But except within the context of the very specific non-heterosexual culture, we would not usually speak of someone as passing as non-heterosexual. To be a sexual being, in our culture, is just to be heterosexual. Moreover, heterosexual sexual expression is defined as *real* sex; in particular, sexual intercourse is the standard of "having sex" by reference to which all other sexual stages and activities—e.g., "virginity," "foreplay," etc.—are defined.

This is, then, the first of what I shall refer to as the paradoxes of heterosexuality: As an expected, supposedly normal characteristic of adult and even pre-adult life, it is so pervasive that it melts into our individual lives; its invisibility as a social condition makes it seem to be just a matter of what is personal, private, and inevitable. Heterosexuality is simultaneously the only "real" form of sexuality, and yet (for that very reason) very difficult to perceive. Heterosexuality is transparent, in the way that a piece of plastic wrap is transparent. Yet, like plastic wrap, it has the ability to hold things in place, to keep things down, and to provide a barrier to prevent other things from coming in contact with that which it seems to be protecting.

I. The Institution of Heterosexuality

It is this transparent, virtually invisible, yet very powerful condition that I wish to subject to examination. But I am not primarily concerned with *individual* heterosexual relationships: who loves whom, who is attracted to or turned on by whom, or who does what to whom. Although, of course, what happens in those individual heterosexual relationships is not at all irrelevant to the understanding of heterosexuality, nevertheless it is not individual practices in and of themselves which interest me here. Instead, it is heterosexuality as an *institution* of contemporary Western culture which is the focus of my examination. Although this institution is not the only cultural influence upon human sexuality, it is one of the most significant. By the institution of heterosexuality, or what I shall call for short the heterosexual institution, what I mean is the systematized set of social standards, customs, and expected practices which both regulate and restrict romantic and sexual relationships between persons of different sexes in late twentieth-century Western culture.

The heterosexual institution by definition involves both men and women. But, given the constraints imposed by patriarchal society, in which oppression for the fact of being female is often both accepted and promoted, it cannot be expected that the heterosexual institution will say and do the same things to women as it does to men, or that it will be experienced in the same way by women and by men. As Marilyn Frye points out, "institutions *are* humanly designed patterns of access—access to persons and their services."[4] It is important to be aware of the ways in which access is patterned differently for women and for men. As a feminist, what I therefore want to discuss is the reality of the heterosexual institution *for women:* that is, its effects on women, its meanings for women, what it says to and about women. I shall first describe some main features of the heterosexual institution, and then turn to a discussion of the place of heterosexuality in women's lives and its interpretation by feminist theory. I cannot accomplish any of this without saying a fair amount about men, but I think that an examination of the heterosexual institution as it is experienced by men would be an endeavor quite different from this one.[5]

In referring to heterosexuality as an institution, I am rejecting an essentialist or reified view of sexual orientations. Human sexuality is culturally constructed, that is, it is "a social, not [only] a biological phenomenon."[6] There is no reason to suppose that sexual activity and expression are more immune to the effects of enculturation than are other apparently "natural" human activities such as caring for children, or eating. Of course, the fact that sexuality is culturally constructed does not entirely preclude the possibility that some form of sexual expression is innate or "natural," or that we have "biological inclinations" toward some form of sexual activity. But it does imply both that the evidence for such a natural sexuality will be virtually impossible to detect, and that the stronger hypothesis is that there is no such natural sexuality. One cannot even refer to primordial feelings or irresistible passions as natural, since enculturation processes, including the heterosexual institution, help to define what feelings we do and do not, or ought and ought not to have.

I shall therefore assume that there is no "fixed sexual 'essence' or 'nature' that lies buried beneath layers of social ordering"[7] in any of us. In particular, I deny that most human beings are "naturally" or innately heterosexual; if sexual desire and activity are socially constructed, then one sort of orientation is no more natural, innate, or inevitable than another. Nor do I make the somewhat more fashionable (these days) assumption that human beings are "naturally" bisexual. Bisexual is no more what we *really* are than is heterosexual.[8] In other words, if the heterosexual institution somehow did not exist, I see no more (and no less) reason to suppose that individuals would therefore be romantically and sexually oriented to persons of both sexes than to suppose that individuals would be romantically and sexually oriented to persons of only one sex or the other. Neither of these seems to be more natural or inevitable than the other. In fact, the only useful interpretation of the claim some have made that we are "really" bisexual is just that we all have the physical capacity for sexual interactions with members of both sexes. And no one would dispute that, for the reason that it is not a very interesting or controversial claim; and it certainly tells us nothing whatsoever about a person's "real" or "natural" sexual orientation.

But, for the purposes of this paper, nothing much depends upon the assertion that no sexual orientation is innate. For, whatever our inherent proclivities may or may not be, there is undeniably tremendous social pressure toward heterosexuality. This pressure is a part of the heterosexual institution. Indeed, I wonder why, if heterosexuality is innate, there are so many social voices telling us, ad nauseum, that that is what we should be. These voices include the ideology that surrounds heterosexual romance, "dating," and marriage; the mythology of falling in (and out of) heterosexual love, of flings, crushes, affairs, passions, and helpless attractions; the cultural apparatus that purports to assist women to be heterosexually attractive, to be coy, alluring, "sexy," and flirtatious, in order to "find true love" or to "catch a man," and then to maintain his interest once he's caught; the psychotherapies and medical treatments, together with literature ranging from self-help manuals to scholarly treatises, that claim to prescribe the nature and forms of and adjustment to healthy female heterosexuality and the cures or panaceas for its disfunctions; the cultural images, in popular music, paintings, dance crazes, novels, stories, advice columns, films, videos, plays, and advertising, that interpret human sexuality and love exclusively in terms of two by two heterosexual pairing; and the predominant instruments of Western social life—the bars, dances, parties, clubs—that recognize only the heterosexual couple. Why is there so much insistence, via these intensive socialization mechanisms, that all women *be* heterosexual and *learn* to be heterosexual, if that is what we are all naturally inclined to be anyway? So the presence of that strong social insistence upon heterosexuality is, to my mind, one very large piece of evidence that heterosexuality is not innate. But, whether it is or it is not, it is the heterosexual institution that is the subject of discussion in this paper.

II. The Politics of Heterosexuality

To examine the heterosexual institution is to raise questions not only about sex but about the nature of love, passion, loyalty, and trust between men and women. These are, at least at first glance, moral questions, about human responsibility, obligation, and commitment. But, since the heterosexual institution involves connections between unequals, they are also political questions, concerned with the uneven distribution of power between members of two groups which have been socially constructed to be very different. Hence, a feminist discussion of heterosexuality requires the consideration of questions about allegiances and affiliations, about separatism, and about political choices and strategies.

To arrive at a better understanding of the political nature of the heterosexual institution, it is helpful to consider one aspect of the dictionary definition of "institution." The *Shorter Oxford English Dictionary* defines "institution" as "an establishment, organization, or association instituted for the *promotion of some object,* especially one of public utility, religious, charitable, educational, etc."[9] This definition raises the question, what object is promoted by the heterosexual institution?

In asking about the object of the heterosexual institution, I am not of course assuming that there is any consciously chosen goal of heterosexuality. No person or power, no god or father nature, created the heterosexual institution, and I am not asking a teleological question here. The easy answer, that the object of the heterosexual institution is the facilitation of human reproduction, seems not to be the whole story, for it overlooks the institution's historically variant features. Although there is undeniably some connection between heterosexual behavior and reproduction, that connection is becoming more tenuous, with the availability of contraception on the one hand and new reproductive technologies on the other.

In fact, a number of observations count against the claim that the object of the heterosexual institution is reproduction. First, not all heterosexual activity, even when unconstrained by deliberate use of contraception and abortion, results in procreation—consider the case of heterosexually active individuals who are too young or too old to reproduce, or who are, for other reasons, infertile, or who engage in non-reproductive sexual behavior. Such persons may be just as interested in heterosexual activity as those who do wish to reproduce, and that interest is fostered by the heterosexual institution quite independently of their willingness or ability to reproduce. Second, it is remarkable that women who are celibate, whether by choice or through force of circumstance, are usually still thought of as being heterosexual; the presumption of heterosexuality operates in the absence of reproductive activity. Third, heterosexual desire is not at all the same as the desire to reproduce; one may have either one without the other[10] and there is no longer much pressure in Western culture to promote or to evaluate heterosexual desire by reference to reproductive goals. Fourth, the heterosexual institution continues to operate at full force even in places where, one would think, the needs of reproduction are already amply or even excessively filled. Finally, seeing reproduction as the object of the heterosexual institution simply "portrays men and women as the dupes of their own physiology and considers eroticism as a mere cover-up for Nature's reproductive aims."[11] Hence, although heterosexual activity and reproduction are sometimes causally connected, the latter is not the object, or at least not the only object, of the former. The heterosexual institution does not exist merely to further procreation; it has some other important function or functions.

My question about the object of the heterosexual institution is akin to questions about the object of other institutions such as the state, the family, the educational system, or religion. And one way of starting to answer such questions is by looking to see what individuals or groups of individuals benefit from the institution, what the benefits are, how those benefits are created and distributed, and at whose cost the benefits are acquired.

For the past two decades, radical feminists have offered disturbing answers to these questions. They have argued, first, that the heterosexual institution primarily benefits men, not women; and that it affords men easy sexual gratification and material possession of women, as well as reproduction of themselves and their offspring. Second, these benefits are created and distributed through what Adrienne Rich and others have described as the compulsory nature of heterosexuality: female heterosexual desire and activity must be enforced and coerced, through a myriad of social practices in the family, in culture, in religion, education, and law.[12] This process has been described as the deliberate recruitment of women into active participation in heterosexuality.[13] Mariana Valverde states,

> [G]iven the enormous social weight of heterosexism, one cannot accurately describe heterosexuality as merely a personal preference, as though there were not countless social forces pushing one to be heterosexual. People do not generally choose heterosexuality out of a number of equally valid, equally respected lifestyles. . . . As long as certain choices are punished while others are presented as natural, as the norm, it is naive to describe the complicated process of the construction of conformity and/or deviance by reference to a consumer-type notion of personal preference.[14]

Third, whatever its rewards may be (and they are more than amply celebrated in romantic fiction, films, songs, and everyday mythology), the costs for women of providing the benefits of female heterosexuality for men are of two types: First, violence, degradation, and exploitation of women's bodies and women's sexuality, through such practices as prostitution, rape and other forms of sexual assault, woman battering, pornography, and incest; and second, the deliberately cultivated separation of women from their allies, each other. The operation of the heterosexual institution is a very successful demonstration of the political maxim that to keep a subject group down, it is important to keep its members divided, to prevent them from developing loyalties to each other, and to direct their trust and commitment to members of the oppressor group. In short, the heterosexual institution is the strongest arm and most powerful manifestation of patriarchy; and therefore one of its most important objects is the oppression of women.

As an agent of patriarchal oppression, the heterosexual institution generates a second paradox in heterosexuality: the conjunction of heterosexual privilege and heterosexism. On the one hand, the heterosexual institution grants a certain privilege to heterosexual women that is not possessed by non-heterosexual women. A heterosexual woman is validated for having (or at least wanting) men in her life: the presence of a boyfriend or husband—or even the search for a male partner—confirms that the woman is a "real woman"; that (some) men (sometimes) find her attractive; that, whatever else she might be or feel or think, she is not (so the assumption goes) a "manhater" and therefore beyond the moral pale (even though woman hating is considered a fairly normal part of human civilization). A woman's heterosexuality, visibly demonstrated, shields her from the vicious attacks reserved for non-heterosexual women.

At the same time, heterosexual privilege is coupled with heterosexism, that is, discrimination on grounds of non-heterosexual orientation. Hence, heterosexual privilege has its price: strict conformity to the standards and requirements of heterosexual behavior and appearance. On the one hand, deviations, even apparent ones, are usually noticed and punished, through verbal and even physical violence, ostracism, and the threatened loss of employment, reputation, peace and safety, home, children, or financial security. In many instances to be a feminist (regardless of one's sexual activities) is to invite heterosexist vituperation; many people, including some feminists as well as non-feminists, are inclined to regard the word "lesbian" as a dangerous term whose application to oneself undermines one's credibility and acceptability. Yet on the other hand, successful conformity to heterosexual standards of behavior and appearance may also be painful, and necessitate contortions, self-abasement, and continual self observation in order to regulate one's feelings, speech, and behavior to fit the image of the heterosexual woman.

Hence, not only are there tremendous costs for the person who is non-heterosexual, but also the heterosexual woman is in a classic double-bind situation: to avoid the damages of non-conformity, she must incur the damages of conformity.

III. Heterosexuality and Choice

In one of my favorite cartoons, a young woman asks her tough and savvy feminist mother, "Ma, can I be a feminist and still like men?" "Sure," replies the mother, "Just like you can be a vegetarian and like fried chicken." When I recounted this joke in an introduction to feminism course, my young female students were disturbed rather than amused. And this is not surprising. To some, the mother's reply may seem to be a reductio ad absurdum of combining feminism and heterosexuality. A good vegetarian, one might think, just does not like fried chicken; or she certainly *ought* not to like it. And if, in a moment of weakness, she does consume fried chicken, then she is either not a good, moral, consistent vegetarian, or, worse still, she is not a vegetarian at all. So also with the feminist. While many of my students hoped that it would be both logically and empirically possible to be a feminist and still like men, or even to love them, they also saw considerable tension in being both heterosexual and feminist. Some feminists who love men have expressed both doubt and guilt about the legitimacy of their lives, and some non-heterosexual feminists have encouraged those feelings. For some women, for example,

> feminism has made them sharply aware of how male power is used, abused and reproduced in personal relationships, to the point where they despair of ever achieving equality. They begin to question their attachment to men and wonder if it is really men's bodies they desire, or if they are merely addicted to their power. . . . [To be heterosexual seems like a weakness, like a] chink in [one's] feminist armour.[15]

Is, then, a "feminist heterosexuality" possible?[16] To answer that question, it is necessary first to consider the nature of choice. If, as some feminists have argued, heterosexuality in women is coerced, it would seem that no woman chooses to be heterosexual. When there are not several recognized and legitimate options, when there are so many pressures to be heterosexual, and when failure to conform is so heavily punished, it is difficult to regard heterosexuality as the genuine expression of a preference. In fact, as one (heterosexual) woman remarked to me, given the damning indictment of heterosexuality which has been presented by some feminists, it might seem that any woman would be heterosexual only if it were *not* a choice.

But this is not all that can be said about the possibility of choosing heterosexuality. For, first, a single-minded focus on the coercive aspects of the heterosexual institution absolves heterosexual women of any responsibility for their sexual practice in a way that seems inappropriate, at least in the case of feminist women, who have had some opportunities to reflect upon the role of heterosexuality in patriarchal oppression. The idea that all heterosexual women (unlike non-heterosexual women) just can't help themselves and are somehow doomed to love and be attracted to men gives too much weight to the view of women as victims, and too little credit to the idea that women can act and make decisions on their own behalf. Moreover, it implicitly imputes to all heterosexual women a sort of false consciousness. Most such women will not see themselves as victims of coercion. Although they may not think of heterosexual practice as a choice they have made, they also do not necessarily feel like helpless victims of the heterosexual institution. But if no woman can choose to be heterosexual, then all heterosexual women either fail to correctly understand their own sexuality, or they can correctly understand their sexuality only by seeing themselves as helpless victims.

On the contrary, I would argue, it is a mistake to summarily dismiss *all* heterosexual women's experience as a failure to understand their own sexuality. Indeed, it is possible that some such women may

> have actively chosen, rather than fallen into, a life of heterosexual marriage and children . . . and that in their heterosexual relationships, they have control over their own sexuality and share equally in the enjoyment of and participation in their sexual relationships.[17]

I am not saying here only that some heterosexual women may lead exceptional lives in the sense that their relationship with their man (or men) is experienced as egalitarian and uncoercive; I am saying that there is an important sense in which a woman can genuinely and even sanely choose to be heterosexual, although the conditions and opportunities for that choice may be fairly rare. Beyond the claim that heterosexuality is innate (which seems to be an insufficiently grounded essentialist claim) and the claim that heterosexuality is coerced (which seems true in regard to the heterosexual institution as a whole) there is a third possibility: that heterosexuality is or can be chosen, even—or especially!—by feminists.

If it is possible to choose *not* to be heterosexual—and most radical feminists have argued that it is—then it is possible to actively choose to be heterosexual. To some degree, each of us is able to make ourselves into the kinds of sexual beings we are, through a process of interpretation and reinterpretation of our past and present experiences and of our feelings and emotions, and through active interaction with other persons, not just passive receptivity to their influence. By choosing one's heterosexuality I mean not merely acquiescing in it, or benefiting from heterosexual privilege, but actively taking responsibility for being heterosexual. Admittedly, most apparently heterosexual women never make, and never have an opportunity to make, such an active conscious choice. In what cases, then, might it be correct to say that a woman has genuinely chosen her heterosexuality? The following remark by Charlotte Bunch provides a crucial insight into the paradoxical answer to that question:

> Basically, heterosexuality means men first. That's what it's all about. It assumes that every woman is heterosexual; that every woman is defined by and is the property of men. Her body, her services, her children belong to men. If you don't accept that definition, you're a queer—no matter who you sleep with. . . .[18]

For a heterosexual woman, to start to understand the institution of heterosexuality and the ideology of heterosexism is already to start to leave standard heterosexuality behind. For part of what is customarily meant by the ascription of heterosexuality is its unconscious "perfectly natural" character. Persons who are non-heterosexual never have the luxury of accepting their sexuality in this way. As Mariana Valverde has pointed out, even those non-heterosexuals who feel driven by their sexual needs and desires, and compelled to seek sexual partners of the same sex,

> are forced at some point to define themselves, and ask how and why they have come to have such desires. . . . Since we all "naturally" grow up to be heterosexual, it is only the deviations that call out for an explanation; the norm appears as natural, and few heterosexual people ever wonder whatever caused them to be heterosexual.[19]

Anne Wilson Schaef claims that in general, women do not view the world in sexual terms:

> First, we do not categorize individuals and situations according to their sexuality. Second, we do not assume that each and every relationship must be sexual, nor do we view everything we do and everyone we meet as having some sexual significance. In fact, women do not define the world in sexual terms.[20]

Sometimes, however, instead of being enlightened, as Schaef seems to assume, this refusal or inability to categorize in sexual terms may be a form of blindness. Marilyn Frye has pointed out that in discussions of sexual prejudice and discrimination one may often hear a statement such as "I don't think of myself as heterosexual"—presumably said by a person who engages in heterosexual activity.[21] Heterosexuals ordinarily extend to others the somewhat dubious privilege of assuming that everyone is like them; since to be sexual is to be *heterosexual,* "[t]he question often must be *made* to arise, blatantly and explicitly, before the heterosexual person will consider the thought that one is lesbian or homosexual."[22] On the other hand, such persons often perceive non-heterosexuals as being unnecessarily preoccupied with their sexuality, unable to stop talking about it and "flaunting" it to the world. But, Frye suggests,

> Heterosexual critics of queers' "role-playing" ought to look at themselves in the mirror on their way out for a night on the town to see who's in drag. The answer is, everybody is. Perhaps the main difference between heterosexuals and queers is that when queers go forth in drag, they know they are engaged in theater—they are playing and they know they are playing. Heterosexuals usually are taking it all perfectly seriously, thinking they are in the real world, thinking they are the real world.[23]

The person whose sexual practice is heterosexual and who honestly and innocently states that she does not think of herself as heterosexual shows herself most clearly to be heterosexual in the standard sense. Paradoxically, then, for a woman to firmly and unambiguously affirm her heterosexuality may already be to begin to leave it behind, that is, to cease to be heterosexual in the unthinking unconscious way she once was: She ceases to participate wholeheartedly in the heterosexual institution, and begins the process of disaffiliation from it.[24] When that sort of reflection takes place, I believe, the woman is beginning genuinely to choose her heterosexuality; and she is choosing heterosexual practice without a concomitant endorsement of the heterosexual institution.

Of course, for such a woman, heterosexuality is still something which is enforced, in Rich's sense; that is, persistent cultural pressures strive to ensure her conformity, and deviance from heterosexuality is penalized, often severely. No amount of awareness of the heterosexual institution can, by itself, change the compulsory nature of heterosexuality, and disaffiliation by one woman will not rock the institution.

Nevertheless, that awareness can make a difference, for the previously unawarely heterosexual woman, in the dimensions of her own sexuality: She can begin the process of shaping her own sexuality, by making decisions and choices based upon an understanding of the power and the limits of the heterosexual institution. For she can explore her own personal history and determine how and when her sense of the erotic became separated from women and connected to men.[25] In so doing, she can no longer regard her heterosexual orientation as something over which she has no power or control, as something which just dominates her sexual feelings and practices. Instead, she can distinguish between sexual passion and attraction, on the one hand, and dependence, need, fear, and insecurity on the other. She can become aware of her feelings about women's and men's bodies, and discover whether and/or to what degree she has internalized a socially validated revulsion toward the female body. She can genuinely ask herself whether sexual activity with men is something she wants, or merely something in which she engages. (For, of course, we cannot assume that all women whose sexual practice is heterosexual also enjoy their sexual activities.)

If the answer is no, it is not something she wants, she then has the prospect of choosing to be non-heterosexual. On the other hand, if the answer is yes, she can, in a way, begin to come out as a heterosexual: not in the heterosexist fashion by which almost all heterosexuals, male and female, ordinarily mark their heterosexuality, but rather in terms of an informed and self-aware feminist evaluation of her life as a heterosexual,[26] renouncing as far as possible the privilege accorded by heterosexuality,[27] and recognizing both the different varieties of oppression non-heterosexuals undergo and also the affinities she shares with non-heterosexual women. She can support non-heterosexual women, validate their relationships, and refuse any longer to be complicitous in the erasures they often undergo. She thereby chooses to be heterosexual as a matter of sexual practice, but not as a matter of the exclusive heterosexist alignment or orientation of her life.

Nevertheless, although it may now seem that heterosexuality can be genuinely chosen by women, for some feminists the question may still remain whether it *ought* to be chosen, whether it is ever a good choice, a choice a feminist could responsibly make. Although some heterosexual feminists pride themselves on their "exceptional" heterosexual relationships, relationships which are, apparently, non-oppressive and egalitarian, still, whatever the particular relationship is like, it nonetheless remains *possible* for the man to take advantage of his potential power. All that stands in the way of his using that power is his own good will, while he is not similarly dependent on the woman's good will. And he still benefits, however indirectly, from male hegemony, and "even the advantages that he is in a position to refuse are waiting for him if he changes his mind."[28]

> [C]hanging our expectations will [not] by itself change the unequal power relationship. It does not, for instance, change the expectations and behaviour of the man. Neither does it remove the institutional power vested in the male in heterosexual relationships.[29]

Moreover, the woman in such a relationship is still giving her energies very largely to a man, consorting intimately with a member of an oppressor group, and hence, indirectly withholding her energies from a woman. For any woman, heterosexual orientation seems to mean putting men, or at least a man, first. And even while rejecting the heterosexual institution, such a woman also still benefits from heterosexual privilege. Thus, no matter how idyllic her relationship, it seems to fail of its very nature to challenge the status quo, and to reinforce the apparent exclusive loyalty of a woman to her man. Together, the two persons in the relationship still appear to participate in and contribute to the perpetuation of an institution which is oppressive of women, particularly of non-heterosexual women and unattached women of any orientation, as well as of heterosexual women in abusive relationships.[30] And of course having an exceptional relationship does not in any way spare a woman from the worst excesses of the heterosexual institution as they may be visited upon her by men other than her immediate sexual partner(s).

The foregoing observations appear to call into question the *legitimacy* of a woman's deliberately deciding to be heterosexual, and I have only very tentative responses to them. The first involves taking seriously the distinction between the institution of heterosexuality on the one hand, and on the other hand, specific heterosexual relations and the persons who become involved in them. This is the same sort of distinction made by Adrienne Rich in her discussion of motherhood. Rich has urged us to recognize that while motherhood itself is an oppressive institution, mothering particular children may be a delightful, worthwhile, valuable human activity.[31] Similarly, while heterosexuality is an oppressive institution, not all heterosexual relationships are valueless as a result. Glimpsing this possibility might also encourage feminists to make a distinction between what could be called the *institution* of manhood, on the one hand, and individual men on the other. It must have been some such distinction that I had implicitly in mind years ago when I complained to a male friend at some length about masculine behavior. After he mildly pointed out that he was a man (and therefore, presumably, a counterexample to some of the generalizations I was inclined to make), I spontaneously patted his hand and replied, "But Bob, I don't think of you as a man!"

In regard to this distinction between being male and being "a man," or masculine, Marilyn Frye writes,

> I have enjoined males of my acquaintance to set themselves against masculinity. I have asked them to think about how they can stop being men, and I was not recommending a sexchange operation.[32]

This answer, by itself, has of course all the weaknesses of any "individual solution" to problems of oppression. For it depends upon a commitment of the man in the relationship not to avail himself of the power of his position. And so, it must be said, for a woman to actively choose to be heterosexual is an act of faith—faith first of all in the fundamental humanity of the men whom she chooses to love. By actively choosing to be heterosexual, a feminist woman is rejecting the view that male sexuality is inevitably and innately violent and exploitive, and that men are hopelessly fated to engage only in aggressive and oppressive relationships. Although members of the two sexes acquire very different roles, men just as much as women learn to participate in the heterosexual institution. And it is a lesson which men can reject. The heterosexual institution is a social artifact that can be changed, and men themselves may be the allies of women in changing it.

A woman who deliberately chooses to be heterosexual is also expressing her faith in her own individual power and strengths, her belief that a woman in a heterosexual relationship can be something far more than a helpless victim. She is rejecting the invidious all-or-nothing fallacies that restrict what she is and can be. She is recognizing that she is not, or need not be, only a sexual being; that she is not, or need not be, only heterosexual. Joanna Russ points out that in the late nineteenth century the new focus on sexuality as an indicator of the "health" of one's personality led to the invention of a new kind of person: "The Homosexual."[33] Similarly, I think, some recent feminist theory has resulted in the invention of "The Heterosexual," seen as a woman entirely defined by her sexual orientation to men. Both moves, though they originate from very different sources and agendas, hypothesize the existence of an entire personality and political affiliation on the basis of a species of sexual activity. But while we can easily recognize the power and ubiquity of the heterosexual institution, we need not thereby conclude that that institution subsumes entire personalities. To describe a woman as heterosexual (or as not heterosexual) in no way provides an exhaustive description of that woman's activities, beliefs, values, attitudes, or temperament.

There are, moreover, degrees of heterosexuality. Heterosexual orientation need not mean the exclusion of loyalty to, attraction toward, and love for women. Women who are heterosexual can develop intimate relationships with women, and value them at least as much as they value their relationships with men. Adrienne Rich has spoken movingly of what she calls "the lesbian continuum." She defines it as

> [the full] range—through each woman's life and throughout history—of [women-identified] experience; not simply the fact that a woman has had or consciously desired genital sexual experience with another woman. [The lesbian continuum] embrace[s] many more forms of primary intensity between and among women, including the sharing of a rich inner life, the bonding against male tyranny, [and] the giving and receiving of practical and political support. . . .[34]

Sometimes, unfortunately, the concept of the lesbian continuum is appealed to by some feminists rather prematurely as a way of foreclosing on confrontation and acrimony between heterosexual and non-heterosexual women. Nevertheless, provided the differences between heterosexual and non-heterosexual women in culture, experience, oppression, and privilege are not glossed over, the concept of the lesbian continuum is a powerful source of insight for women who have chosen to be heterosexual, and a reminder that they are not or need not be only heterosexual. So far, under patriarchal conditions, what women's sexuality is and can be has scarcely been explored; but in a non-patriarchal society there would be no limitations on life-promoting human relationships.

Notes

An earlier version of this paper was first presented at the Queen's University Philosophy Department Colloquium, and I am grateful for the suggestions which I received. I am particularly indebted to Michael Fox for his detailed and thoughtful commentary.

1. *Shorter Oxford English Dictionary,* Addenda (1970), my emphasis.
2. Frances Giberson has pointed out to me that celibacy could also be thought of as a type of non-heterosexuality, indeed, a rejection of the heterosexual institution. In men, the absence of heterosexual behavior is usually taken as prima facie evidence of homosexuality; whereas in women, the absence of heterosexual behavior is often taken to mean the woman is celibate. Unfortunately, there is not space in this paper to explore further the important issues connected with celibacy.
3. See Christine Overall, "Sexuality, Parenting, and Reproductive Choices," *Resources for Feminist Research/Documentation sur la recherche feministe* 16 (September 1987): 44.
4. Marilyn Frye, "Some Reflections on Separatism and Power," in her *The Politics of Reality: Essays in Feminist Theory* (Trumansburg, N.Y.: The Crossing Press, 1983), 106–7, Frye's emphasis.
5. And it has been done. See, for example, Howard Buchbinder's "Male Heterosexuality: The Socialized Penis Revisited," in Howard Buchbinder et al., eds., *Who's On Top? The Politics of Heterosexuality* (Toronto: Garamond Press, 1987), 63–82.
6. Carole S. Vance and Ann Barr Snitow, "Toward a Conversation about Sex in Feminism: A Modest Proposal," *Signs* 10 (1984): 127.
7. Ruth Bleier, *Science and Gender: A Critique of Biology and Its Theories on Women* (New York: Pergamon Press, 1984), 166.
8. Mariana Valverde, *Sex, Power, and Pleasure* (Toronto: Women's Press, 1985), 113–14.
9. *Shorter Oxford English Dictionary,* my emphasis.

10. Alan Soble, "Preface: Changing Conceptions of Human Sexuality," in Earl E. Shelp, ed., *Sexuality and Medicine: Conceptual Roots* (Boston: D. Reidel, 1987), xiii.
11. Valverde, 50.
12. Adrienne Rich, "Compulsory Heterosexuality and Lesbian Existence," in Catharine R. Stimpson and Ethel Spector Person, eds., *Women: Sex and Sexuality* (Chicago: University of Chicago Press, 1980), 62–91.
13. Beatrix Campbell, "A Feminist Sexual Politics: Now You See It, Now You Don't," in The Feminist Review, ed., *Sexuality: A Reader* (London: Virago Press, 1987), 23.
14. Valverde, 114.
15. Ibid., 62–63.
16. The question is taken from the title of Angela Hamblin's article, "Is a Feminist Heterosexuality Possible?," in Sue Cartledge and Joanna Ryan, eds., *Sex and Love: New Thoughts on Old Contradictions* (London: The Women's Press, 1983), 105–23.
17. Bleier, 182–83. Cf. Ann Ferguson, "Patriarchy, Sexual Identity, and the Sexual Revolution," in Nannerl O. Keohane, Michelle Z. Rosaldo, and Barbara C. Gelpi, eds., *Feminist Theory: A Critique of Ideology* (Chicago: University of Chicago Press, 1982), 159.
18. Charlotte Bunch, "Not For Lesbians Only," in Charlotte Bunch et al., eds., *Building Feminist Theory: Essays from Quest* (New York: Longman, 1981), 69.
19. Valverde, 114–15.
20. Anne Wilson Schaef, *Women's Reality: An Emerging Female System in a White Male Society* (Minneapolis: Winston Press, 1985), 47.
21. Marilyn Frye, "Lesbian Feminism and the Gay Rights Movement: Another View of Male Supremacy, Another Separatism," in *The Politics of Reality,* 147. Michael Ramberg has pointed out to me that to say "I don't think of myself as heterosexual" could also mean "I am not *only* heterosexual" or "I will not always be heterosexual."
22. Marilyn Frye, "On Being White: Toward A Feminist Understanding of Race and Race Supremacy," in *The Politics of Reality,* 116, her emphasis.
23. Marilyn Frye, "Sexism," in *The Politics of Reality,* 29, her emphasis.
24. Frye, "On Being White," 127.
25. Marilyn Frye, "A Lesbian Perspective on Women's Studies," in Margaret Cruikshank, ed., *Lesbian Studies: Present and Future* (Old Westbury, N.Y.: The Feminist Press, 1982), 197.
26. See Katherine Arnup, "Lesbian Feminist Theory," *Resources for Feminist Research/Documentation sur la recherche feministe* 12 (March 1983): 55.
27. Amy Gottlieb, "Mothers, Sisters, Lovers, Listen," in Maureen Fitzgerald, Connie Guberman, and Margie Wolfe, eds., *Still Ain't Satisfied! Canadian Feminism Today* (Toronto: Women's Press, 1982), 238–39.
28. Sara Ann Ketchum and Christine Pierce, "Separatism and Sexual Relationships," in Sharon Bishop and Marjorie Weinzweig, eds., *Philosophy and Women* (Belmont, Calif.: Wadsworth, 1979), 167, 168.

29. Hamblin, 117.
30. See Leeds Revolutionary Feminist Group, "Political Lesbianism: The Case Against Heterosexuality," in *Love Your Enemy? The Debate between Heterosexual Feminism and Political Lesbianism* (London: Onlywomen Press, 1981), 5–10.
31. Adrienne Rich, *Of Woman Born: Motherhood as Experience and Institution* (New York: Bantam Books, 1976).
32. Frye, "On Being White," 127.
33. Joanna Russ, *Magic Mommas, Trembling Sisters, Puritans and Perverts* (Trumansburg, N.Y.: The Crossing Press, 1985), 67.
34. Rich, "Compulsory Heterosexuality and Lesbian Existence," 81.

[21]

Erotic Justice

Marvin M. Ellison

FOR THE MOST PART, religious communities have responded with neither creativity nor compassion to the cultural crisis in sexuality. In fact, when it comes to sex, many religious people (and institutions) are at their worst. On the one hand, they are fearful about sex; on the other hand, they become fixated on the forbidden and repressed. This interlocking dynamic of fear and fixation makes it exceedingly difficult to keep sexuality in perspective. Concerning this important, but far from consuming dimension of human life, people vacillate between making too much ("It's everything") or too little ("It means nothing") of it. As a result, moral thinking becomes skewed.

Most cultural discourse about sexuality is fear-based, but religious discourse is often the most blatantly negative. Sexuality and erotic desire are viewed stereotypically as powerful and dangerous, requiring strong externally imposed controls. Morality is reduced to "private" matters or to a punitive code restricting sexual conduct. Religious communities, by communicating explicitly negative, often shaming messages about sexuality, attempt to control people and coerce them into compliance with moral convention. However, shaming serves only to alienate people further from religious traditions.

SOURCE: From Marvin M. Ellison, *Erotic Justice: A Liberating Ethic of Sexuality* (Louisville, Ky.: Westminster John Knox Press, 1996).

Although secularized sources may appear to be more open about sexuality, sex is widely commodified as a means to drive consumption and, therefore, equally alienated. Consumerism plays off people's lack of self-esteem in this culture and their fears that "being more" requires "having more." The Radical Right capitalizes on this fear, which can easily be manipulated and exteriorized as stigmatizing projections onto less powerful social groups. The Right speaks relentlessly about the body's insatiability, (feminist) women's "inordinate" desires for power, and the corrupting promiscuity of (urban, white) gay male sexuality. The Right deliberately uses erotophobia to mobilize and also distract people from criticizing the capitalist economic system. Contrary to conservative polemics, however, it is neither sexual freedom nor widespread nonconformity to traditional family patterns that is undermining community, but rather late capitalism's massive global restructuring that is creating severe dislocations and moral upheaval.

In contrast, theological liberalism communicates more positively about sexuality. Its perspective, however, is also deficient. The criticism I offer here about liberalism I offer with reluctance, for several reasons. First, theological liberalism has nurtured my own moral development. As someone who came of age in the 1960s era of the civil rights and antiwar movements, I was then, and am still now, excited, unnerved, and constantly inspired by a theological tradition that insists on the centrality of justice for any credible view of God and the world.[1] Second, liberalism has become unfashionable during a time of intense cultural reaction and is now constantly under siege. Because liberalism has strongly defended a critically informed humanism and advocated human rights, I have no desire to give legitimacy to right-wing attacks on liberalism. Whatever the deficiencies of the liberal tradition, its strengths should be preserved in any theological or ethical reconstruction. After all, liberalism is the moral tradition that has most willingly valued sexuality as an essential dimension of human dignity.

Liberalism's strength is its placement of human freedom at the core of its theological vision. Responsible moral agency to recreate the world is the primary mark of faithfulness to God. Rethinking moral meaning is encouraged as an ongoing historical task, including searching for more adequate institutional forms of love and justice. We become human by our open participation in equalizing social power relations. However, liberalism has limitations that have to date prevented the development of an adequate social ethic of sexuality. First, liberal social theory splits public from private life. Justice, it says, belongs to the public ordering of social, political, and economic power relations. Love, politically ineffectual and reduced to an affective sentiment, is restricted to private matters among intimates in a separate, autonomous interpersonal sphere. The private is sealed off from the public, the personal from the social. Moreover, sexuality is viewed as nonhistorical and subject, by and large, to natural determination. Liberalism's presuppositions, especially about female nature and a naturalized family structure, replicate a nineteenth-century white bourgeois worldview that divides social reality into man's (public) world and women's (private) space. The privatized zone of nonfreedom includes sexuality, reproduction, and the care of children, all matters judged inconsequential—and typically rendered invisible in liberal social theory—in relation to the "real" (read "manly") concerns of war, politics, career, and empire-building.

Second, liberalism leaves in place a patriarchal split between thinking and feeling, a gender-based dichotomy in which feeling, associated with women and things female, is devalued, while rationality and abstract reasoning, associated with men and things male, is prized. Liberals fear that passion and strong feeling of any kind will lead inexorably to confused thinking, biased by personal involvement and self-interest.[2] Self-assertion, self-interest, and nearly all self-love are consistently met with suspicion. Liberal social theory sees the self as basically nonsocial, self-preoccupied, and able to enter—or not enter—with others into community. It fails, however, to appreciate the limits of its culturally constructed view as the product of reified masculine consciousness. In contrast, feminist theory appreciates how all persons, male and female, are fundamentally relational and social beings whose personhood is constituted in the communities upon which they depend for survival, care, and ongoing development.

Although liberalism professes to value human dignity, its tendency toward individualism places self-regard and other-regard in tension, forever in opposition. Their irreconcilable conflict, liberalism conjectures, can be resolved only by a selfless altruism or, when necessary, by self-denial. However, liberalism has not shaken free of misogyny. It continues to assign self-sacrifice selectively to women (and other socially subordinate people) and rarely invokes it as a male virtue or as an obligation for the powerful. In contrast, feminist and gay liberation perspectives encourage self-love as healthy and morally good, especially among marginalized peoples. Self-love is a corrective to internalized oppression and self-hate. Contrary to liberal fears, valuing of self and valuing of others are not mutually exclusive, antagonistic options, but rather reciprocal, fully interdependent possibilities.[3] Doing justice, in liberation perspective, is a remarkable pathway for deepening love.

Finally, liberalism by and large accepts the prevailing cultural model of power as unilateral control. Such power competes with others for scarce, limited resources. Again, this contrasts with feminist theory that envisions power as power-with and power-for others and as the humanizing capacity to sustain relationship and build community through mutual regard and care.[4]

Although liberalism insists that concern for justice should lie at the heart of any ethic, liberal Christianity has discounted oppression in the so-called private sphere and has been reluctant to integrate feminist and gay liberation insight into its own perspective. Sexuality has been depoliticized and set apart from social structures and power conflicts. Liberalism's language about love often appears idealized and disconnected from people's everyday struggles and pain. Liberalism sidesteps power and conflict within interpersonal relations and is neither clear enough nor tough enough about family violence or abuse of power among intimates. In the real world, countless women, children, and sexual minorities are at risk, especially in racial/ethnic communities and among the poor. As a gay man, although I have been nurtured by liberalism, I have also become vividly aware that this tradition makes no room for receiving me or other nonnormative peoples. Liberalism sees my struggle for self-respect as a private concern, not as a matter of justice or as a problem of disordered power.

Although relatively sex-positive in outlook, liberalism also fails to value erotic power as a significant *moral* power making intimacy possible between people and their world. Not only does liberalism fail to associate intimacy with justice, it also bypasses the deficits of love without justice. The romanticizing of marriage and idealizing of family life conceal widespread abuse and human suffering. The notion that family life is private blocks recognition of how the quality of personal life is dependent on the wider social order. Many women, however, grasp these interconnections simply by taking into account differentials in earning power and how these differently impact men and women's options, within and outside of the family. Women's economic dependence on men affects power relations within the household, and it limits access to education, employment, leisure, and community life. These disparities constrict women's freedom. At the same time, most men, especially white affluent men, feel entitled to exit any relationship when they choose, and they have the power and resources available to do so. The freedom to extricate oneself from an undesired situation, however, is denied to all but the most economically privileged women. Most women lack the independent economic resources that would allow them to break free from abusive situations and leave loveless marriages.

An ethic of sexuality must realistically assess what poor women, women of color, and other disenfranchised people are up against in this culture. The fact that many women "put up with" abuse and degradation tells us volumes, if we can hear, not about any purported female desperation to seek "love" at any cost, but rather about the devastating absence of justice and well-being in most women's lives and in the lives of their children. Those lacking social power stay in dehumanizing, often life-threatening situations not because of *personal* inadequacies but because there are few, if any, *social* alternatives that justify taking the risks of leaving an abusive but familiar situation, especially because men typically escalate their violence to keep "their" women in place.[5] Liberalism's moral guidance about sex and family life will never be useful if it leaves unquestioned the power hierarchies of husband over wife, parent over child, white over black, able-bodied over disabled, and so forth, or if it naturalizes these relationships as beneficial to all parties.

"The best theorizing about justice," feminist philosopher Susan Moller Okin writes, "is not some abstract 'view from nowhere,' but proceeds from the carefully attentive consideration of *everyone's* point of view."[6] The strength of Okin's statement is that she insists that moral reason is concretely situated, but her claim, as it stands, is not strong enough to make a real difference in a stratified, conflicted world of power inequities. From a postliberal perspective, theorizing about sexual injustice must proceed by listening to—and giving priority to—those who are subjected to sexual oppression and who manage against all odds to resist its indignities. Listening can become justice-bearing only as the conversation is recentered and democratized. The voices of socially powerful, privileged people need to be heard, but their voices must no longer monopolize the discussion. Moral traditions can correct past distortions and become more humanizing, but only if we pay special attention to the voices and moral wisdom of women, gay/lesbian/bisexual people, survivors of sexual violence, and others without social status and power. By incorporating these voices from the margins, the liberal theological tradition can also be transformed. Perspectives from "the underside" enrich the ethical analysis, as well as stretch the vision of the moral good.

. . .

How is sexuality a structural problem, and what does it mean to say that eroticism becomes attached to injustice? Carter Heyward provides a useful analogy. A structure, she writes, is a "pattern of relational transactions that gives a society its particular shape." When a house has a structural problem, more is needed to fix it than new wallpaper or rearranging the furniture. Solving a structural problem requires digging down to the foundation of the edifice, uncovering any rot, and making basic repairs to put the building once again on sound footing. Then and only then, Heyward argues, "can we begin to reconstruct the house in such a way as to provide adequate, trustworthy space for all."[7] Similarly, a structural analysis of sexuality offers a critical assessment of its foundational assumptions and of the basic organization of the prevailing sexual system in order to determine the soundness of present arrangements and their adequacy for its "occupants."

The feminist insight that the personal is political makes a related claim. Personal life is shaped by social dynamics, including structured patterns of power and powerlessness. We live and love, or not, within societal arrangements. These same societal arrangements are reflected in, reinforced by, and sometimes challenged and transformed by the ways we live and love, or not. No sphere of personal life exists outside of or entirely divorced from the political, economic, and cultural forces that shape both the personal and the political. No autonomous, privatized space exists into which we can retreat and do our loving untouched by social realities. The world is with us always, including in our bedrooms. In an alienated world of injustice, sexuality itself will also be alienated. People are estranged *in their sexuality* from themselves and others, that is, not fully at home in their own bodies or in the company of other bodies.

. . .

Sexual essentialism defines sex as a natural force, a fixed and unchanging essence that exists prior to and independent of sociocultural arrangements. Sex is a property belonging to individuals. It resides in their hormones, their psyches, or their genetic structures. Sex is "what comes naturally." Biological imperatives determine the "normal" course of things, what feels right, and what fits natural mandates. From an essentialist viewpoint, "sexuality has no history and no significant social determinants."[8] After all, essentialism asks, isn't sexuality what is *most* natural about humans and *least* susceptible to change?

Essentialists posit that when all goes according to plan, biological mandates give rise to a natural expression of sexual desire. In keeping with such naturalistic assumptions, heterosexuality is seen as natural and normal because it fits nature's anatomical design for male-female sexual intercourse and because it has a biologically functional purpose in reproducing the species. By this same logic, homosexuality is unnatural and abnormal. A troubling sleight of hand takes place, however, in some subtle shifts in language from "natural" to "normal" and the implied "normative." As sociologist Michael Kimmel suggests, "That which is *normative*—constructed and enforced by society through socialization of the young and through social sanctions against deviants—begins to appear as *normal,* that which is designed by nature."[9] The normative and the normal, however, in a statistical sense, are not necessarily the same. The normative, a product of moral discernment and deliberation, reflects a communal valuing of what is good, right, and fitting. Normative judgments, including those made about sexuality, are subject to challenge and revision. What *is* may be far off from what *ought* to be.

Essentialism falsely assumes that sexuality is the same for everyone, everywhere. Sexuality, however, is a more complex reality, more fluid and more amenable to cultural molding. In some cultures, people refrain from sex during the daytime while in other cultures sex is prohibited at night. Some societies are not at all concerned about when sex takes place but rather about where. Inside the house may be acceptable as long as it is not near the food supply, or sex may be permitted only outdoors. Kissing is customary behavior in our culture, but some indigenous peoples in South America consider mouth-to-mouth kissing an offensive, even barbaric practice.[10] Therefore, what sexuality looks like and signifies varies from culture to culture. "Far from being the most natural element in social life, the most resistant to cultural moulding," [Jeffrey] Weeks argues, "[sexuality] is perhaps one of the most susceptible to organization."[11]

In contrast to essentialism, a social constructionist approach assumes that sexuality is constituted within, not apart from, society and history. Sexuality's purpose and meaning cannot be grasped by biology alone, but must be comprehended within its sociocultural context. This historical, contextualized approach puts the primary emphasis on analyzing sexuality *within* society and social relations. A significant ethical implication follows. If sexuality is socially constructed, then it is not a fixed and unalterable essence, but rather something susceptible to modification and transformation. Properly viewed, sexuality becomes a social and cultural issue as well as a personal concern. Furthermore, it makes sense to raise questions about sexuality in relation to injustice and the righting of distorted, harmful patterns of sexual interaction.

. . .

The social construction of sexuality cannot be understood apart from racism and the cultural construction of white racial supremacy. The cultural obsession with an idealized body is an obsession to maintain the normativity of (adult) white men and their right to control others. In this culture affluent white men are assigned the right of access to women, children, and nonwhite men, as well as the right to manage their bodies, including their productive and reproductive labor. Socially powerful men are expected to control the lives of social inferiors.

In this culture everyone receives moral instruction about how social domination is justified by human differences, that is, by measurable deviations from the white, affluent male norm. When human differences are ranked hierarchically and naturalized, people see differences as markers of dominant or subordinate status. They learn to fear that those with more power will harm them or that those with less power will take away their privileges. Some fear is of course warranted, especially among women and people of color, because of rape, lynchings, and other forms of social control. This fear, however, can also be exaggerated and used to discourage people from banding together across their differences to challenge abuses of power and to promote safety and mutual respect as community norms. Because difference is routinely associated with domination, a generalized fear is promoted *not of domination, but of difference itself.* This fear keeps the socially marginalized in line and all people mistrustful of efforts to alter power dynamics.[12]

Fear, suspicion, and intolerance are marks of a social order in which sexism, racism, and other injustices teach the devaluing of difference. Therefore, gaining awareness of and mounting resistance to racist patriarchal standards of superiority and inferiority is a means of transcending fear and also enlarging human loving. Race and sex/gender oppression constrict people's natural affections to a closed social circle. In a racist culture, people rarely exhibit what sociologist Patricia Hill Collins calls a "big love." Big loving depends on trust that men can love and truly value women, that whites can see blacks as fully human, and that men-loving-men and women-loving-women can be respected as dignified members of the community. In the midst of multiple oppressions, however, our affective knowledge of our common humanity becomes distorted. The capacity to identify with each other and delight in our diversity "must be distorted on the emotional level of the erotic," Collins suggests, "in order for oppressive systems to endure."[13] Our fear of others lodges in our bodies, not merely in our heads. Basic human feelings of trust, respect, and playful curiosity about diversity have been corrupted, and our fellow-feeling has been diminished.

Supremacist models of sexuality promote an ethic of alienation, possession, and control. Injustices, including sexism and racism, are eroticized, so that what stirs many people is not a passion for justice as right-relatedness and mutual regard, but rather a perverse desire to exercise power over someone else, especially someone "not their kind," or alternately, a felt need to be put down and kept in one's place of inferiority. In a culture of inequality, the sexual problematic, as Beverly Harrison contends, is fear of genuine intimacy and mutuality among social equals.[14]

Race itself is not a natural, objective category for dividing groups or assigning differentials of power and status, but rather a political and cultural category, institutionalized in systemic patterns of ownership and control of one group by another. In the words of Audre Lorde, racism institutionalizes and culturally represents "the belief in the inherent superiority of one race over all others and thereby the right to dominance."[15] In a racist society, encountering race does not mean encountering difference within social relations of equality, shared power, and mutual respect, but rather within long-standing patterns of inequality, disrespect, and fear. White supremacy has crafted a social world of permanent race inequality, justified by naturalistic assumptions that white-skinned persons differ from persons of color in those moral and physical aspects that supposedly legitimize white mastery and control. Furthermore, white supremacy is a major component of the social construction of sexuality, and racist ideology is tightly intertwined with sex-negativity. White racism assumes that sexuality differentiates Euro-Americans from African Americans. The sexuality of black people is seen as chaotic, a power outside white control, and therefore something both deviant and mesmerizing. As Cornel West points out, "Americans are obsessed with sex and fearful of black sexuality."[16]

Black sexuality is subject to relentless stereotyping and projections of white fear onto black bodies. Dominant white culture or, more accurately, white racial narcissism assigns permanent negative value to the color black. Womanist theologian Delores Williams observes that white culture "considers black frightening, dangerous and/or repulsive—especially when this is the color of human bodies."[17] As I have already noted, the human body is a powerful signifier, and amplifier, of social fears and ideological conflicts. Black bodies, something both fearful and fascinating in the dominant culture, are a highly visible, hotly contested site of ideological claims. Moreover, white fear of and suspicion toward black sexuality gives white racism an energy and its edge. This fear, Cornel West suggests, is based on the degradation of black bodies and on white determination to control them.[18] Similarly, Williams cites the exploitation of black women under slavery and the demands made that slave women surrender their bodies to their owners. Black women's sexual labor, including their nurturing capacities as mothers and as community leaders, was made available to whatever powerful white persons, male or female, demanded their submission. Black women were, therefore, "bound to a system that had no respect for their bodies, their dignities or their motherhood, except as it was put to the service of securing the well-being of ruling-class families."[19] In this culture white supremacy has been the primary obstacle to securing body right for women and men of color.

Racism and sexuality have long intersected in white Western culture. Beginning in the seventeenth century, Europeans drew on racial and sexual ideology to differentiate themselves from indigenous peoples. They justified destruction of local cultures and appropriation of their land by labeling others as sexually and morally inferior. In the nineteenth century, sexuality continued to serve as an instrument of white dominance. White people viewed themselves as rational and civilized and others, especially blacks and native peoples, as irrational and savage. As propertied white men struggled during times of economic dislocation and cultural flux, they invested in a morality of (white) female purity which forced "their" women and children into the "safe haven" of the privatized home. "Stereotypes of immoral women of other races," historians John D'Emilio and Estelle Freedman argue, only "contributed to the belief in white superiority" and to the avoidance of racial amalgamation because of the fear that "it would debase whites to the status of other races."[20] Sexual rule making rigidified as white males experienced moral panic in response to increasing cultural instability.

Throughout the United States and elsewhere, affluent white men have promulgated the moral superiority of white family practices and sexual customs. At the same time, supremacist attitudes justified their taking control of others and their sexual exploitation of women of color, including Native, Mexican, African, and African American women. The sexual ideology of "true womanhood" pedestalized (and disempowered) white women as spiritually superior to men and reduced their social role to dutiful wives and mothers. In contrast, women from subjugated groups were identified with sensuality and the body, an identification white women were not allowed to possess. Nonwhite and poor women were de-spiritualized and seen as bound to the body and animalistic. White men objectified black women and shamelessly exploited them, sexually and economically. With the abolition of slavery, protecting white women's moral superiority became the justification for white men's intimidation of the black community through rape, castration, and lynchings. Then and now, violence imposed through sex was an effective means of social control for maintaining a white supremacist social order.

Notes

1. Daniel C. Maguire, *The Moral Core of Judaism and Christianity: Reclaiming the Revolution* (Minneapolis: Fortress Press, 1993).
2. Daniel C. Maguire, "The Feminization of God and Ethics," in *The Moral Revolution: A Christian Humanist Vision* (San Francisco: Harper & Row, 1986), 105–21.
3. Beverly Harrison argues that mutual love is "love in its deepest radicality" and that "the power of love [is] the real pleasure of mutual vulnerability, the experience of truly being cared for or of actively caring for another," in Beverly Wildung Harrison, *Making the Connections: Essays in Feminist Ethics,* ed. Carol S. Robb (Boston: Beacon Press, 1985), 18. See also Christine E. Gudorf, "Parenting, Mutual Love, and Sacrifice," in *Women's Consciousness, Women's Conscience: A Reader in Feminist Ethics,* ed. Barbara Hilkert Andolsen, Christine E. Gudorf, and Mary D. Pellauer (New York: Winston Press, 1985), 175–91.
4. Bernard Loomer, "Two Conceptions of Power," *Criterion* 15, no. 1 (winter 1976): 12–29. Loomer describes control or unilateral power as alienating power, the continual use of which "breeds an insensitivity to the presence of the other—again, whether the other be a person or nature or God" (18). The alternative is mutual or relational power, which Loomer defines as "the ability both to produce and to undergo an effect. It is the capacity both to influence others

and to be influenced by others" (20). Such relational power is not weak, but in fact powerful: "Our readiness to take account of the feelings and values of another is a way of including the other within our world of meaning and concern. At its best, receiving is not unresponsive passivity; it is an active openness. Our reception of another indicates that we are or may become large enough to make room for another within ourselves: . . . The strength of our security may well mean that we do not fear the other, that the other is not an overpowering threat to our own sense of worth" (21).

5. On women's struggles to leave abusive situations, see Ginny NiCarthy, *Getting Free: You Can End Abuse and Take Back Your Life* (Seattle: Seal Press, 1982); Susan Schechter, *Women and Male Violence: The Visions and Struggles of the Battered Women's Movement* (Boston: South End Press, 1982); R. Emerson Dobash and Russell Dobash, *Violence against Wives: A Case against the Patriarchy* (New York: Free Press, 1979); and Joy M. K. Bussert, *Battered Women: From a Theology of Suffering to an Ethic of Empowerment* (New York: Division for Mission in North America, Lutheran Church in America, 1986).
6. Susan Moller Okin, *Justice, Gender, and the Family* (New York: Basic Books, 1989), 15, 22 (emphasis in original).
7. Carter Heyward, *Touching Our Strength: The Erotic as Power and the Love of God* (San Francisco: Harper & Row, 1989), 50.
8. Gayle S. Rubin, "Thinking Sex: Notes for a Radical Theory of the Politics of Sexuality," in *The Lesbian and Gay Studies Reader,* ed. Henry Abelove, Michele Aina Barale, and David M. Halperin (New York: Routledge & Kegan Paul, 1993), 9.
9. Michael S. Kimmel, "Introduction: Guilty Pleasures—Pornography in Men's Lives," in *Men Confront Pornography,* ed. Michael S. Kimmel (New York: Crown Publishers, 1990), 4 (emphasis in original).
10. Ibid., 4–5.
11. Jeffrey Weeks, *Sexuality* (New York: Routledge, Chapman & Hall, 1986), 24–25.
12. Charlotte Bunch, *Passionate Politics: Essays 1968–1986; Feminist Theory in Action* (New York: St. Martin's Press, 1987), 150–51.
13. Patricia Hill Collins, *Black Feminist Thought: Knowledge, Consciousness, and the Politics of Empowerment* (New York: Routledge & Kegan Paul, 1991), 182, 196.
14. Harrison, *Making the Connections,* 148.
15. Audre Lorde, *Sister Outsider: Essays and Speeches* (Trumansburg, N.Y.: Crossing Press, 1984), 45.
16. Cornel West, *Race Matters* (Boston: Beacon Press, 1993), 83.
17. Delores S. Williams, *Sisters of the Wilderness* (Maryknoll, N.Y.: Orbis Books, 1993), 85.
18. West, *Race Matters,* 83, 85, 86.
19. Williams, *Sisters of the Wilderness,* 71.
20. John D'Emilio and B. Estelle Freedman, *Intimate Matters: A History of Sexuality in America* (New York: Harper & Row, 1988), 86.

PART TWO

THE SEARCH FOR ETHICAL GUIDANCE

[22]

Sexuality and Christian Ethics: How to Proceed

Lisa Sowle Cahill

. . .

Both sexual ethics and ethical methodology clearly are problems, which is what makes their discussion not only interesting but urgent. One of the many reasons sex is of interest for every adult human being is that all people at least some of the time are unsure how to understand their sexuality and how to behave sexually in ways that are morally praiseworthy rather than reprehensible. Moreover, ethicists want to talk theoretically and normatively about sexuality and sex in ways that are not only praiseworthy but coherent. This ambition too is problematic, peculiarly so for the Christian ethicist. He or she has to take into account factors and perspectives that seem to lead in opposed directions. These include common wisdom; what the empirical studies, which presently command so much attention, reveal about human sexual experience and gender identity; the ways Christian authors and churches traditionally have educated the faithful to perceive male and female relations, sexuality, and sex; what the Bible says or indicates about these subjects; and even central philosophical presentations of them. Perhaps the

Source: From Lisa Sowle Cahill, *Between the Sexes: Foundations for a Christian Ethics of Sexuality* (Philadelphia: Fortress Press, 1985).

salient obligation of the moral analyst, given this state of affairs, is to muster the nerve to proceed at all.

Despite its pitfalls, the task of analysis may not be avoided. For humans, "sexuality" is "morality." It is part of our expressing, for good or ill, relationship to the material world, to other life forms, to the self, and to other persons, including God. As our point of departure we will pay attention to the experiential phenomena of sex and sexuality, for they bring home in a most pressing and universal manner the necessity of systematic reflection on the moral life.

Sexual Experience

Sex is now no more a simple matter than it ever has been, however much in the name of "sexual liberation" we claim to have demystified it. Twentieth-century Americans are no more or less obsessed with sex than our predecessors; it is only that our obsessions take different forms. Sex, despite its prosaic side, was to our grandparents' generation a hidden idol, enshrined in an aura of mystery, fascination, and danger; we glorify, pursue, and parade it to the point of banality. Sex has been connected with elemental and divine powers in certain historical periods and cultures; but our protestations that it is natural" do not conceal our own fear and even contempt of it. Why is it that sex among human beings is always so puzzling? Why are humans not able, like other animals, to come together by instinctual motives of self- and species preservation, to couple briefly, to conceive, and thereafter to part or affiliate (without problems), motivated again by instinct to do what is necessary to raise the young that result?

It seems to be precisely the animal-like compulsion of sexual yearning that most bewilders and beleaguers the human moral agent, philosopher, and theologian. Augustine of Hippo referred to "the shameful motion of the organs of generation"[1] and went so far as to suggest that in the Garden of Eden sexual intercourse between Adam and Eve would have taken place without any sexual desire at all. Apparently, it seemed to Augustine that the replacement of disorderly passion by a sheer act of the rational will would have been more in keeping with human dignity.[2] While this theory may be extreme, it does represent an influential Christian author's perception of the ambivalence of human sexual experience.[3] Humans have tended to conclude from reflection on the matter that sexual impulses either are in an essential sense anti-human because they cannot be conformed to some ideal of pure rationality and freedom, of absolute self-control; or, on the other side, are so quintessentially, immediately, and irresistibly natural that it is as futile to deny, suppress, or sublimate them as it would be the contractions of the heart muscle. Human beings have a preference for thinking in extremes; it makes matters far more simple. But simplicity in human affairs is more often than not illusory. Sexuality is no exception. Some accounts of human sexuality and its genital expressions construe them as counter-human because they are among those experiences in which humans feel least in control of themselves and most under the influence of instincts and physical responses. To the minds of some of the fathers of the Christian tradition, sexual desire is to be resisted lest it bring humanity to the level of the animals. Such interpretations miss the obvious point that "animality" is not a pejorative term and that, indeed, it is one aptly applied to the species Homo sapiens.[4] But accounts of sex that explain it as a simple, universal, and irresistibly attractive drive ignore the fact that humans are animals of a special sort. Their ability to reflect self-consciously and empathetically on their own and others' needs and interests, to discriminate cognitively and affectively among them in terms of immediate and long-range outcomes, and to act so as to rearrange priorities and redirect impulses in the interests of communities and of other persons is not unparalleled in the animal world, but it is nowhere matched.

We have, then, a certain duality in sexual experience. It is physical, urgent, and pervasive. It is also an avenue of affective and spiritual relations among persons, for good or ill. Yet the human person is not a duality. At least Western philosophical and religious traditions have learned to resist dualistic interpretations of the person, even if they have not overcome them. To cut the person into separate pieces of soul and body, psyche and physique, freedom and determinacy, is again too simple. We shall note that the Genesis creation accounts attest that the human being is one, a unity, which has two aspects but not two discrete components.

It is this duality of experience in unity of being that grounds the problem of human sexuality. Sex in humans is not understood completely if it is explained only as a physiologic species-survival mechanism, or a technique of physical enjoyment. It is also an instrument, or indeed a constituent, of the sorts of interpersonal relations that are most distinctively human. Since humans are as capable of evil, wickedness, selfishness, and manipulation in these relationships as they are of good, rectitude, self-sacrifice, and generosity, sex is a problem. And sinfulness in sex, as in other realms of human existence, often springs from just the fact that humans are slothful and cowardly and shortsighted, and thus refuse to take on the project of reconciling the troublesome human reality of what Reinhold Niebuhr called freedom and finitude, or spirit and nature.[5] The ever-mobile, dialectical relation between these poles is what makes the human situation so precarious and causes our anxiety. It is because we cannot resolve this anxiety, and refuse to endure it, that we attempt to evade it. In so doing, according to Niebuhr, we sin by denial of what it is to be human.

I fear that this beginning has had about it an air of moroseness which, I hope, does not represent adequately the sexual experiences of most people, even of most Christians. But I see it as the necessary backdrop for the project of ascertaining what the Christian religious tradition demands of humans in their sexual being and relationships and acts. It is this ambiguous, problematic quality of sex that has instigated much of the worrying and writing about it that has gone on in Christianity. No doubt, in a profound way sexuality will remain an enigma. It would be naive, ahistorical, and self-aggrandizing to think that we might achieve an unassailable or even unique formulation of the problem of sexuality and its ethical resolution. But we may come to understand it more adequately, if never completely, by recollecting and critically renewing what some of our predecessors have had to say of our common experience.

The Sources of Christian Ethics

But what are the wellsprings of this process? The interrelation and priority of the sources of Christian ethics is the major methodological theme of this chapter. This concern is another version of the "reason and revelation" question. How ought the Christian ethicist to include, interpret, and weigh religious and secular sources of moral insight? Not infrequently, Christian authors writing about sexual ethics so stress a chosen point of departure that the contributions of other sources are neglected or virtually excluded. Whether one begins with, for instance, received "natural law" teaching, certain biblical prohibitions, or scientific studies of sexual psychology and behavior, a fully "Christian" process of reflection will permit interpretation and qualification of that initial source by other complementary ones.[6] My thesis, whose lack of originality may be its strength, is that there are four complementary reference points for Christian ethics:[7] the foundational texts or "scriptures" of the faith community—the Bible; the community's "tradition" of faith, theology, and practice; philosophical accounts of essential or ideal humanity ("normative" accounts of the human[8]); and descriptions of what actually is and has been the case in human lives and societies ("descriptive" accounts of the human). While Scripture is the reference point most obviously associated with Christian theological ethics, empirical sciences recently have received most emphasis as sources of insight into human sexuality, sexual behavior, marriage, parenthood, and gender roles. Both Bible and empirical studies present particular problems for the ethicist, for they entail special, internal canons of interpretation, with which the theological ethicist may not have sophisticated familiarity. Yet both sources are indispensable for contemporary Christian ethics. Sometimes Christian theologians have rejected the adequacy for a Christian moral perspective of nonreligious definitions of the normatively human ("human nature"), but Christian ethics is never uninfluenced by secular philosophical anthropologies, even those against which it defines itself. Because it is the fundamental content for explicitly theological ethical reflection, the Christian tradition forms the "hermeneutical circle" within which Christian theology defines itself and interprets its other sources. The most distinctive source of Christian ethics, the Bible, is the product of the most primitive stage in the life history of the community founded in Christ. In a sense, the Bible is not only the basis of the Christian religious tradition, but is actually a representation of the first phases within that tradition. Although "tradition" is sometimes taken to mean dogmatic or moral propositions transmitted from the past, it is better understood as the "story" of a people, "handed on" or "transmitted" for reappropriation in each generation. It includes but is not limited to formulations of dogma and ethics derived from the faith life of the community. Specific criteria for what counts as "tradition" might include antiquity, widespread usage, consensus of the faithful, and authoritative definition. Tradition is the historical identity and self-understanding of the religious community, which is formed by the Scriptures, and which continues to inform its present and future.[9]

I contend that fidelity to these four mutually correcting sources, and success in judiciously balancing them, is a standard by which we can measure the adequacy of various positions in the tradition, including our own. Thomas Aquinas, for example, gives priority to the philosophical element in ethics. He interprets the relation of man and woman, marriage, and procreation on the basis of his understanding of what it would mean to be fully and authentically human, that is, to live in accord with the nature that God bestows in the creation. His philosophical anthropology, however, is informed in a radical way not only by that of Aristotle but also by the perspective of medieval Christianity. Although Thomas accomplishes much in terms of a reasonable account of human existence, he neglects a primary source to which Martin Luther redirects our attention: the Bible. With his radical insistence that ethics be ordered by Scripture, and *sola Scriptura,* Luther revitalizes the nature of Christian ethics as the delineation of the practical consequences of faith and life in Christ. In filling out the details and ramifications of the biblical witness for sexuality and marriage, however, Luther relies a great deal on common experience and common sense. Even the inspired Word of God in Scripture is not a sheer "datum" but an occasion of hearing and understanding the spirit of the Lord present in community.

In contemporary theology, the realization is increasing that it is no easy matter to determine how these four resources of Bible, tradition, and descriptive and normative accounts of the human should be balanced. This is especially so, given the facts that no one source is understood apart from the complementary contributions of the others; and that their perspectives on some moral issues may in the end diverge.

. . .

Toward a Christian Ethics of Sexuality

The most important biblical contribution to a Christian ethics of sexual activity and of relationship between the sexes is the placement of morality within the life of the faith community. Morality is not an interest for its own sake, but for the sake of understanding how the people of God will live and act toward one another and toward others if they are faithful. In the Hebrew Bible or Christian Old Testament, the covenant with Yahweh leads to certain religious and moral forms of existence which are an expression of covenant fidelity. In the New Testament, faith and conversion in Jesus Christ establish membership in the Spirit-filled community. The Christian bears the "fruits of the Spirit," or certain qualities of character that dispose one to act in certain ways. Sexuality receives some attention as a concrete mode of action, but certainly far less than we are inclined to give it.

In examining the biblical witness for sexual morality, we will focus on patterns of male-female relationship and sexual relations that can be referred broadly to canonical material, rather than on the specific content of isolated texts.

Both Old and New Testament resources support a view of sexuality as part of the goodness of humanity's creation, but as also subject to the corruption of sin. Humanity is essentially male and female. Man and woman are created for a physical, procreative, psychological, and social partnership, which presupposes sexual differentiation but not hierarchy. Human sexual acts fulfill cooperation and express community, but are in themselves never the focus of biblical discussions. Morality for both the Hebrew and Christian communities is one aspect of cohesive living in obedience and fidelity. While I would judge that the biblical literature points toward heterosexual, monogamous, lifelong, and procreative marriage as the normative or ideal institutionalization of sexual activity, I would not say that the biblical texts represent preoccupation with, or indeed much interest in, the justification or exclusion of other sexual expressions. It will be necessary to turn to additional resources of Christian ethics both to confirm the general scriptural views of male and female, of human sexuality, and of sexual acts; and to consider in what ways the scriptural norm can be realized or adapted in variable concrete situations. As the New Testament divorce texts show us, the process of adaptation begins already within the canon.

Christian authors do better or worse in developing a theology of human sexuality in proportion to their ability to consider, relate, and balance these sources. When the influence of one or more is ignored or minimized, the position becomes less secure. We have indicated already that Thomas Aquinas respects a philosophical perspective on human sexuality, but is not very critical of his cultural milieu and largely neglects the Bible. Luther uses the Bible to criticize received tradition, but finds it necessary to interpret the Bible in the light of concrete experience.

We too will need to complement our reading of the Bible and to respond to the mores of our own culture by attending to all the reference points of Christian ethics. Of the Christian tradition it will be asked what the community of faith consistently has affirmed about human sexuality. A response might suggest the goodness of sexuality as God's creation, male and female differentiation and union, the importance of procreation as a purpose of sexual acts, marriage and family as the institutionalization of procreation, and the social partnership of male and female. The tradition, however, also yields elements that today are regarded as less than normative: the dubious moral nature of all sex, the subordination of women, and intended procreation as the only complete justification of sexual acts. The ambiguity of the tradition, as well as of the Bible, presses us to the question of *criteria* for the elimination or appropriation of biblical and traditional meanings of sexuality and sexual activity. The standard of an adequate Christian theology and ethics of sexuality is precisely the dialectical and complementary relationship of Bible, tradition, and normative and descriptive accounts of human existence.

Since moral philosophy and philosophical anthropologies have many incarnations, it is difficult to isolate a single normative view of the human as central. . . . Thomas Aquinas will exemplify one central view of human nature. The classical, medieval, and modern worldviews entail different presuppositions about whether what is "natural" to humans can be known in any clear and final way, and about whether human "nature" may indeed change. But philosophical accounts of sexual ethics commonly presuppose that it is possible to define at least approximately some "essential" or "ideal" meaning of sexuality, despite actual historical distortions or adaptations of it in the human sexual reality, and despite the limits of the human mind seeking to discover it. Sometimes, of course, such definitions are used in the service of a religious tradition or culture and its view of sexuality, and thus transmit some of the same "values" that were defined above as inadequate components of the

Christian tradition. However, most moral philosophers today, as well as some classical ones, at least to a degree, may be understood to affirm the essential character of sex in relation to human being, the meaning of sex as expression of interpersonal relation as well as procreation, and the equal dignity of man and woman.

Descriptive accounts of what the human situation actually is like gives us a "window" onto the normative. In our century, the empirical sciences have become preeminent sources of such factual information. Another form of describing the human situation is the "personal story," which is then generalized, implicitly or explicitly, to persons in situations similar to that of the author of the account. Empirical or other descriptive resources serve as correctives to biblical, traditional, and normative accounts that simply do not correspond to the realities of human experience.

. . .

Notes

1. Augustine, *City of God* XIV. 19, 21.
2. Ibid., XIV. 23–24.
3. Although the "irresistibility" of sexual drives indeed has been a major component in Christian reflection on sexual ethics, I wonder if it is not more an element of the male experience of sex than of the female. It was precisely the involuntary movements of the male sexual organ that Augustine seemed to find so shameful and even frightening. (See David F. Kelly, "Sexuality and Concupiscence in Augustine," in *The Annual of the Society of Christian Ethics: 1983,* ed. Larry L. Rasmussen [Southern Methodist University: Society of Christian Ethics, 1983].) A complementary (not opposite) female perspective on the experience of sexuality was offered by Karen Lebacqz, who was a member of a panel that responded to my Earl Lectures at the Pacific School of Religion (February 1983). Lebacqz offered that our sexuality is an avenue of *vulnerability,* because through it we both need and are open to other persons. Lebacqz did not suggest that vulnerability is a characteristic of the woman's sexuality only, nor is the experience of an urgent physical drive only the man's. However, the male and female experiences of sexuality (which certainly differ physically and may differ psychologically and emotionally) may enable men and women to be more sensitive to its various aspects. The philosopher Sara Ruddick also comments that in the most complete sexual exchanges "vulnerability is increased for *both* sexes by the active desiring of the partners" ("Better Sex," in *Philosophy and Sex,* ed. Robert Baker and Frederick Elliston [Buffalo: Prometheus Books, 1975], 97).
4. Mary Midgley, *Beast and Man* (Ithaca, N.Y.: Cornell Univ. Press, 1978).

5. Reinhold Niebuhr, *The Nature and Destiny of Man,* vol. 1 (New York: Charles Scribner's Sons, 1964), chap. 7.
6. For a critical discussion of the use of sources in recent Christian ethics of sexuality, see my "Sexual Issues in Christian Theological Ethics: A Review of Recent Studies," *Religious Studies Review* 4/1 (1978): 1–14.
7. Several who heard the Earl Lectures pointed out the resemblance of my method to the Methodist "quadrilateral" test, inspired by John Wesley. Although this test is formulated somewhat differently, I take its similarity to confirm my conviction that the sources I name are no novelty, but substantive for Christian theology and ethics. Another discussion of the method of Christian ethics, which resembles mine in appealing to several sources but which is much more exhaustive, is provided by Robert J. Daly, *Christian Biblical Ethics: From Biblical Revelation to Contemporary Christian Praxis* (New York: Paulist Press, 1984). See especially part 1, chap. 3, "The Bible and Ethics." The book began in a task force of the Catholic Biblical Association, and incorporates chapters by members of that group, woven by Daly into a lengthy study. Daly and others raise many of the hermeneutical questions that I do, come to a consensus that Christian ethics is both a science and an art, and address issues of practice such as nonviolence, marriage, divorce, and politics.
8. "The normatively human" is a phrase borrowed from James M. Gustafson ("Genetic Engineering and a Normative View of the Human," in *Ethical Issues in Biology and Medicine,* ed. Preston N. Williams [Cambridge: Schenkman, 1972], 46–58). It indicates what is to be valued and promoted in human existence, or what is fulfilling for humanity, but is free of the connotation of the classical term "human nature" that essential human being is an ahistorical and clearly knowable entity.
9. See James Hennesey, S.J., "Grasping the Tradition: Reflections of a Church Historian," *Theological Studies* 45/1 (1984): 153–63.

TEXT

[23]

An Islamic Perspective

Riffat Hassan

The Islamic Tradition: Primary Sources and Their Interpretation

It is necessary to clarify at the outset what one means by "the Islamic tradition." This tradition—like other major religious traditions—does not consist of, or derive from, a single source. Most Muslims, if questioned about its sources, are likely to refer to more than one of the following: The Qur'an (the book of Revelation believed by Muslims to be the Word of God), the Sunnah and Hadith (the practice and sayings ascribed to Muhammad, the Prophet of Islam), Fiqh (jurisprudence) or Madahib (schools of law), and Shari'ah (the code of life which regulates all aspects of Muslim life). While all of the above "sources" have contributed to what is cumulatively referred to as "the Islamic tradition," it is important to note that they do not form a coherent or consistent body of teachings or precepts from which a universally agreed-upon set of Islamic "norms" can be derived. Many examples can be cited of inconsistency between various sources of the Islamic tradition as well as of inconsistency between various sources of the Islamic tradition and the Hadith literature. In view of this fact, it is inappropriate, particularly in a scholarly

SOURCE: From Riffat Hassan, "An Islamic Perspective," in *Women, Religion, and Sexuality,* ed. Jeanne Becher (Geneva, Switzerland: World Council of Churches, 1991).

work, to speak of "the Islamic tradition" as if it were monolithic. Its various components need to be identified and examined separately before one can attempt to make any sort of generalization on the Islamic tradition.

Since it is not possible, within the scope of this paper, to discuss the complex subject of women's sexuality and bodily functions comprehensively in the light of all of the sources of the Islamic tradition, I will focus, for the most part, on the Qur'an, which is *the* primary source of *normative* Islam. Reference will also be made to some *ahadith* (plural of hadith: a tradition ascribed to the Prophet Muhammad), which have had a formative impact on Muslim ideas and attitudes pertaining to women's sexuality. Here it may be useful to mention that, according to Islamic theory, the Qur'an has *absolute* authority since it is believed to be God's unadulterated message conveyed through the agency of Archangel Gabriel to the Prophet Muhammad, who then transmitted it to others without change or error. However, since the early days of Islam, the Hadith literature has been the lens through which the words of the Qur'an have been seen and interpreted.

It must however be pointed out that every aspect of the Hadith literature is surrounded by controversies. In particular, the question of the authenticity of particular ahadith as well as of the Hadith literature as a whole has occupied the attention of many scholars of Islam since the time of Ash-Shaft'i (died in A.D. 809). As stated by Fazlur Rahman in his book *Islam,* "A very large proportion of the Hadiths were judged to be spurious and forged by classical Muslim scholars themselves."[1] This has generated much scepticism regarding the Hadith literature in general among "moderate" Muslims. Though few of them are willing to go as far as Ghulam Ahmad Parwez (leader of the "Tulu' e Islam" or "the Dawn of Islam" movement in Pakistan), who rejects the Hadith literature virtually *in toto,* many of them are likely to be in agreement with the following observations of Moulvi Cheragh Ali, an important Indian Muslim scholar who wrote in the nineteenth century:

> The vast flood of tradition soon formed a chaotic sea. Truth, error, fact and fable mingled together in an undistinguishable confusion. Every religious, social, and political system was defended when necessary, to please a Khalif or an Ameer to serve his purpose, by an appeal to some oral traditions. The name of Mohammad was abused to support all manner of lies and absurdities or to satisfy the passion, caprice, or arbitrary will of the despots, leaving out of consideration the creation of any standards of test. . . . I am seldom inclined to quote traditions having little or no belief in their genuineness, as generally they are inauthentic, unsupported and one-sided.[2]

Though valid ground exists for regarding the Hadith literature with caution, if not scepticism, Fazlur Rahman is right in saying that "if the Hadith literature as a whole is cast away, the basis for the historicity of the Qur'an is removed with one stroke."[3] Furthermore, as pointed out by Alfred Guillaume in his book, *The Traditions of Islam:*

> The hadith literature as we now have it provides us with apostolic precept and example covering the whole duty of man: it is *the basis* of that developed system of law, theology, and custom which is Islam. . . .[4] However sceptical we are with regard to the ultimate historical value of the traditions, it is hard to overrate their importance in the formation of the life of the Islamic races throughout the centuries. If we cannot accept them at their face value, they are of inestimable value as a mirror of the events which preceded the consolidation of Islam into a system.[5]

Not only does the Hadith literature have its own autonomous character in point of law and even of doctrine,[6] it also has an emotive aspect whose importance is hard to overstate since it relates to the conscious as well as to the subconscious patterns of thought and feeling of Muslims individually and collectively. As H. A. R. Gibb has observed perceptively:

> It would be difficult to exaggerate the strength and the effects of the Muslim attitude toward Muhammad. Veneration for the Prophet was a natural and inevitable feeling, both in his own day and later, but this is more than veneration. The personal relationships of admiration and love which he inspired in his associates have echoed down the centuries, thanks to the instruments which the community created in order to evoke them afresh in each generation. The earliest of these instruments was the narration of hadith. So much has been written about the legal and theological functions of the hadith that its more personal and religious aspects have been almost overlooked. It is true, to be sure, that the necessity of finding an authoritative source which would supplement the legal and ethical prescriptions contained in the Koran led to a search for examples set by Muhammad in his daily life and practice. One could be certain that if he had said this or that, done this or that, approved this or that action, one had an absolutely reliable guide to the right course to adopt in any similar situation. And it is equally true that this search went far beyond the limits of credibility or simple rectitude, and that it was in due course theologically rationalized by the doctrine of implicit inspiration.[7]

Having underscored the importance of the Qur'an and the Hadith literature as primary sources of the Islamic tradition, it is necessary to point out that through the centuries of Muslim history, these sources have been interpreted only by Muslim men who have abrogated to themselves the task of defining the ontological, theological, sociological, and eschatological status of Muslim women. While it is encouraging that women such as Khadijah and A'ishah (wives of the Prophet Muhammad) and Rabi'a al-Basri (the outstanding woman Sufi) figure significantly in early Islam, the fact remains that the

Islamic tradition has, by and large, remained rigidly patriarchal till the present time, prohibiting the growth of scholarship among women particularly in the realm of religious thought. In view of this it is hardly surprising that until now the overwhelming majority of Muslim women have remained almost totally unaware of the extent to which their "Islamic" (in an ideal sense) rights have been violated by their male-centered and male-dominated societies which have continued to assert, glibly and tirelessly, that Islam has given women more rights than any other religious tradition. Kept for centuries in physical, mental, and emotional confinement and deprived of the opportunity to actualize their human potential, even the exercise of analyzing their personal life-experiences as Muslim women is beyond the capability of most Muslim women. Here it is pertinent to mention that while the rate of literacy is low in many Muslim countries, the rate of literacy of Muslim women—especially those who live in rural areas where the majority of the population lives—is among the lowest in the world.

In recent times, largely due to the pressure of anti-women laws which are being promulgated under the cover of "Islamization" in some parts of the Muslim world, women with some degree of education and awareness are beginning to realize that religion is being used as an instrument of oppression rather than as a means of liberation. For instance, in the face both of military dictatorship and religious autocracy, valiant efforts have been made by women's groups in Pakistan to protest against the enactment of manifestly anti-women laws and to highlight cases of gross injustice and brutality towards women. However, it it still not clearly and fully understood, even by many women activists in Pakistan and other Muslim countries, that the negative attitudes pertaining to women which prevail in Muslim societies, in general, are in general rooted in theology. Unless and until the theological foundations of the misogynistic and androcentric tendencies in the Islamic tradition are demolished, Muslim women will continue to be brutalized and discriminated against despite improvement in statistics relating to women's education, employment, social and political rights, etc.

Sexuality and the Islamic Tradition

Underlying the discussion on almost any women-related issue which is of importance in Muslim communities or societies are some widely prevalent notions concerning sexuality in general, and women's sexuality in particular. The Muslim attitude towards the former generally tends to be highly positive. The Muslim attitude towards the latter, however, is far more complex, as will become evident in this paper.

Sexuality, which in its broadest sense refers to "the quality of being sexual,"[8] is affirmed by the Islamic tradition (much as it is by the Jewish tradition) because the creation of human beings as sexual as well as sexually differentiated creatures is believed to be an integral part of God's plan for humankind. Unlike dualistic traditions, whether religious or philosophical, the Islamic tradition does not see sexuality as the opposite of spirituality, but describes it as a "sign" of God's mercy and bounty to humanity, as the following Qur'anic passage shows:

> And among His (God's) signs
> Is this, that He created
> For you mates from among
> Yourselves, that ye may
> Dwell in tranquillity with them,
> And He has put love
> And mercy between your (hearts)
> Verily in that are signs
> For those who reflect (Surah 30: *Ar-Rum:* 21).[9]

It is noteworthy that in the above passage, sexuality is not associated with animality or corporeality (as it is in some religious and philosophical traditions), but is regarded as the divine instrument for creating man woman relationships characterized by togetherness, tranquillity, love, and mercy.

It is important to note that, in the context of human creation, the Qur'an describes man and woman as each other's *zauj* or "mate." The term "zauj" is generally used to refer to one of two in a pair when reference is made, for instance, to "a pair of shoes" or "night and day." Not only are both parts necessary to complete a pair but also the proper functioning of each requires the presence of the other.[10] While the Qur'anic usage of *azwaj* (plural form of "zauj") to refer to husbands and wives is well known in Muslim societies, it is not generally known that the Qur'an uses the term *zaujain* (dual form of "zauj") for man and woman in describing the process of creation itself, as can be seen from the following passages:

> He (God) did create
> In pairs ("zaujain")—male and female,
> From a seed when lodged
> In its place[11] (Surah 53: *An-Najm:* 45–46).
> Does Man[12] think
> That he will be left
> Uncontrolled. (without purpose)?
> Was he not a drop
> Of sperm emitted

(In lowly form)?
Then did he become
A leech-like clot;
Then did (God) make
And fashion (him)
in due proportion.
And of him He made
Two sexes ("zaujain"), male
And female[13] (Surah 75: *Al-Qiyamat:* 36–39).

In other words, man and woman—two sexually differentiated human beings—created by God from a unitary source *(nafs in wahidatin*[14]) are related to each other ontologically, not merely sociologically. The creation and sexuality of one is, thus, inseparable from the creation and sexuality of the other. That man and woman, or men and women, are bound together not only by virtue of their common source but also by virtue of their interdependent (though different) sexualities seems to be implicit in a number of Qur'anic statements about human creation. These statements warrant the inference that sexual differentiation between man and woman was intended by God to create closeness, not opposition, between them. It is interesting to see how, in a sense, Muslim societies honor this intent, for besides the relationship between husbands and wives (in which "sexuality" becomes associated with "sexual intercourse") they also promote a variety of other relationships between men and women (which are not characterized by "sexual intercourse"). A strong sense of the interdependence of men and women generally pervades Islamic societies which, despite their frequently blatant patriarchalism, acknowledge the pivotal role of women in maintaining the physical, emotional, moral, and spiritual well-being of the *ummah* (community).

With regards to sexuality in the context of a heterosexual marriage, a highly affirming attitude is to be found both in sources of normative Islam as well as in actual Islamic societies. The Qur'an encourages Muslims who are able to marry a "single" or "virtuous" man or woman to do so regardless of the differences in status or wealth between them:

Marry those among you
Who are single, or
The virtuous ones among
Your slaves, male or female:
If they are in poverty
God will give them
Means out of His Grace:

For God encompasseth all,
And He knoweth all things[15] (Surah 24: *An-Nur:* 32).

Recognizing that marriage to a slave woman might put less economic strain on a man than marrying a free woman,[16] the Qur'an says:

If any of you have not
The means wherewith
To wed free believing women,
They may wed believing
Girls from among those
Whom your right hands possess:
And God hath full knowledge
About your Faith.
Ye are one from another:
Wed them with the leave
Of their owners, and give them
Their dowers, according to what
Is reasonable[17] (Surah 4: *An-Nisa':* 25).

A major reason why Muslims are encouraged, even urged, to marry is because the human need for sexual satisfaction and intimacy is considered "natural" by the Islamic tradition which regards Islam as the "Din" (religion) of nature. According to the Qur'an, monasticism, which followers of Jesus had imposed upon themselves, was not prescribed by God.[18] In other words, from the Qur'anic perspective, neither renunciation of the world nor celibacy is required of those who wish to dedicate their lives to the service of God or to spiritual (as opposed to material) pursuits. Marriage is seen by Muslims generally not as an obstacle to attaining the "higher" goals of life, but rather, as an aid to the creation of a just and moral society. It protects human beings (particularly men) from immorality and lewdness,[19] providing them with a religious framework in which their sexual and other energies can be channeled constructively.

It is of interest to note here that there are many Qur'anic prescriptions relating to the regulation of man–woman relationship in marriage. The assumption underlying these prescriptions is that if men and women can attain justice in their marital relationship which is the basis of the family—the basic unit of society—then they can also attain justice in the ummah and the world at large. The larger ramifications of marital relationships for the Muslim ummah have generally been recognized by the Islamic tradition which would appear to endorse the popular Hadith in which the prophet of Islam is reported to have said that by marrying Muslims they had fulfilled half of their "Din."[20]

That is to say, sexuality in general, particularly in the context of marital relationship, is viewed as normal and wholesome both by the primary sources of Islam and by Muslims generally. However, when one considers issues relating to women (as sexually differentiated from men) one discovers many instances when divergence is found not only between normative Islam and popular Islam but also between Qur'anic teachings and individual ahadith. There are also many cases of one Hadith contradicting another. In view of these discrepancies or inconsistencies it is not possible to give a simple answer to the question: What is Islam's view of women's sexuality and bodily functions? Even as the question is complex, so also the answer must include reference to a number of interrelated issues pertaining to significant stages and aspects of women's lives. In the account which follows, an attempt is made to answer the above-stated question in the light both of normative Islam (which represents Islamic ideals) and of Muslim practice (which represents Islamic realities), for both are part of the Islamic tradition which spans a period of over thirteen centuries.

Women and Normative Islam: Three Fundamental Theological Issues

Much of what has happened to Muslim women through the ages becomes comprehensible if one keeps one fact in mind: Muslims, in general, consider it a self-evident truth that women are not equal to men. Men are "above" women or have "a degree of advantage" over them. There is hardly anything in a Muslim woman's life which is not affected by this belief, hence it is vitally important, not only for theological reasons but also pragmatic ones, to subject it to rigorous scholarly scrutiny and attempt to identify its roots.

The roots of the belief that men are superior to women lie—in my judgment—in three theological assumptions: (a) that God's primary creation is man, not woman, since woman is believed to have been created from man's rib, hence is derivative and ontologically secondary; (b) that woman, not man, was the primary agent of what is customarily described as "Man's Fall" or man's expulsion from the Garden of Eden, hence "all daughters of Eve" are to be regarded with hatred, suspicion, and contempt; and (c) that woman was created not only *from* man, but also *for* man, which makes her existence merely instrumental and not of fundamental importance. The three theological questions to which the above assumptions may appropriately be regarded as answers are: (i) How was woman created? (ii) Was woman responsible for the "Fall" of man? and (iii) Why was woman created? While all three questions have had profound significance in the history of ideas and attitudes pertaining to women in the Islamic as well as the Jewish and Christian tradition, I consider the first one, which relates to the issue of woman's creation, to be more basic and important, philosophically and theologically, than any other in the context of man–woman equality. This is so because if man and woman have been created equal by Allah, who is the ultimate arbiter of value, then they cannot become unequal, essentially, at a subsequent time. On the other hand, if man and woman have been created unequal by Allah, then they cannot become equal, essentially, at a subsequent time.

It is not possible, within the scope of this paper, to deal exhaustively with any of the three questions. However, in the brief discussion of each question which follows, an attempt is made to highlight the way in which sources of normative Islam have been interpreted to show that women are inferior to men.

(i) How Was Woman Created?

The ordinary Muslim believes, as seriously as the ordinary Jew or Christian, that Adam was God's primary creation and that Eve was made from Adam's rib. While this myth has obvious roots in the Yahwist's account of creation in Genesis 2:18–24, it has no basis whatever in the Qur'an, which, in the context of human creation, always speaks in completely egalitarian terms. In none of the thirty or so passages which describe the creation of humanity (designated by generic terms such as "an-nas," "al-insan" and "bashar") by God in a variety of ways is there any statement which could be interpreted as asserting or suggesting that man was created prior to woman or that woman was created from man. In fact there are some passages[21] which could—from a purely grammatical/linguistic point of view—be interpreted as stating that the first creation ("nafs in wahidatin") was feminine, not masculine![22] The Qur'an notwithstanding, Muslims believe that "Hawwa" (the Hebrew/Arabic counterpart of "Eve"), who—incidentally—is never mentioned in the Qur'an, was created from the "crooked" rib of "Adam," who is believed to be the first human being created by God. Here, it needs to be mentioned that the term "Adam" is not an Arabic term but a Hebrew term meaning "of the soil" (from "adamah": the soil). The Hebrew term "Adam" functions generally as a collective noun referring to "the human" (species) rather than to a male human being.[23] In the Qur'an, also, the term "Adam" refers, in twenty-one cases out of twenty-five, to humanity. Here it is of interest to note that though the term "Adam" mostly does not refer to a particular human being, it does refer to human beings in a particular way. As pointed out by Muhammad Iqbal:

> Indeed, in the verses which deal with the origin of man as a living being, the Qur'an uses the words "Bashar" or "Insan," not "Adam," which it reserves for man in his capacity of God's viceregent on earth. The purpose of the Qur'an is further secured by the omission of proper names mentioned in the Biblical narration—Adam and Eve. The term "Adam" is retained and used more as a concept than as a name of a concrete human individual. The word is not without authority in the Qur'an itself.[24]

An analysis of the Qur'anic descriptions of human creation shows how the Qur'an evenhandedly uses both feminine and masculine terms and imagery to describe the creation of humanity from a single source. That God's original creation was undifferentiated humanity and not either man or woman (who appeared simultaneously at a subsequent time) is implicit in a number of Qur'anic passages.[25] If the Qur'an makes no distinction between the creation of man and woman—as it clearly does not—why do Muslims believe that Hawwa' was created from the rib of Adam? Although the Genesis 2 account of woman's creation is accepted virtually by all Muslims, it is difficult to believe that it entered the Islamic tradition directly, for very few Muslims ever read the Bible. It is much more likely that it became a part of Islamic heritage through its assimilation in the Hadith literature. That the Genesis 2 idea of woman being created from Adam's rib did, in fact, become incorporated in the Hadith literature is evident from a number of ahadith. These are particularly important since they appear to have had a formative impact on how Muslims have perceived women's being and sexuality (as differentiated from men's). The *matn* (content[26]) of these ahadith—one from *Sahih Al-Bukhari* and one from *Sahih Muslim*—all ascribed to the Companion known as Abu Harairah,[27] is given below:

1. Treat women nicely, for a woman is created from a rib, and the most curved portion of the rib is its upper portion, so if you should try to straighten it, it will break, but if you leave it as it is, it will remain crooked. So treat women nicely.[28]
2. Woman is like a rib. When you attempt to straighten it, you would break it. And if you leave her alone you would benefit by her, and crookedness will remain in her.[29]

I have examined these and similar ahadith elsewhere[30] and have shown them to be flawed both with regard to their formal *(isnad)* and their material *(matn)* aspects. The theology of woman implicit in these ahadith is based upon generalizations about her ontology, biology, and psychology which are contrary to the letter and spirit of the Qur'an. These ahadith ought, therefore, to have been rejected, since Muslim scholars agree on the principle that any hadith which is inconsistent with the Qur'an cannot be accepted. However, despite the fact that the ahadith in question contradict the teachings of the Qur'an, they have continued to be an important part of the ongoing Islamic tradition. Undoubtedly, one of the major reasons for this is that these ahadith come from the two most highly venerated Hadith collections by Muhammad ibn Isma'il al-Bukhari (810–870 A.D.) and Muslim bin al-Hallaj (817 or 821–875 A.D.). These two collections known together as *Sahihan* (from "sahih," meaning sound or authentic) "form an almost unassailable authority, subject indeed to criticism in details, yet deriving an indestructible influence from the *ijma* or general consent of the community in custom and belief, which it is their function to authenticate."[31] While being included in the *Sahihan* gives the ahadith in question much weight among Muslims who know about the science of Hadith, their continuing popularity among Muslims in general indicates that they articulate something deeply embedded in Muslim culture—namely, that women are derivative[32] creatures who can never be considered equal to men.

Theologically, the history of women's subjection in the Islamic (as well as the Jewish and Christian) tradition began with the story of Hawwa's creation. In my view, unless Muslim women return to the point of origin and challenge the authenticity of the ahadith which make all representatives of their sex ontologically inferior and irremediably crooked, male-centered and male-controlled Muslim societies are not likely to acknowledge the egalitarianism evident in the Qur'anic statements about human creation.

(ii) Was Woman Responsible for the Fall of Man?

Many Muslims, like many Jews and Christians, would answer this question in the affirmative, though nothing in the Qur'anic descriptions of the so-called Fall episode would warrant such an answer. Here it may be noted that whereas in Genesis 3:6, the dialogue preceding the eating of the forbidden fruit by the human pair in the Garden of Eden is between the serpent and Eve (though Adam's presence is also indicated, as contended by feminist theologians) and this has provided the basis for the popular casting of Eve into the role of tempter, deceiver, and seducer of Adam, in the Qur'an, the Shaitan (satan) has no exclusive dialogue with Adam's *jauj*. In two of the three passages which refer to this episode, namely Surah 2: *Al-Baqarah:* 35–39 and Surah 7: *Al-A'raf:* 19–25, the Shaitan is stated to have led both Adam and *jauj* astray though in the former (verse 36) no actual conversation is reported. In the remaining passage, namely, Surah 20: *Ta-Ha:* 115–124, it is Adam who is charged with forgetting his covenant with God (verse 115), who is tempted by the Shaitan (verse 120), and who disobeys God and allows himself to be seduced (verse 121). However, if one looks at all the three passages as well as the way in which the term "Adam" functions generally in the Qur'an, it becomes clear that the Qur'an regards the act of disobedience by the human pair in "al-jannah" (the Garden) as a collective rather than an individual act for which exclusive, or even primary, responsibility is not assigned to either man or woman. Even in the last passage in which "Adam" appears to be held responsible for forgetting the covenant and for allowing himself to be beguiled by the Shaitan, the act of disobedience, i.e., the eating from "the Tree," is committed jointly by Adam and zauj and not by Adam alone or in the first place.

Having said that, it is extremely important to stress the point that the Qur'an provides no basis whatever for asserting, suggesting, or implying that Hawwa', having been tempted and deceived by the Shaitan, in turn tempted and deceived Adam and led to his expulsion from "al-jannah." This fact notwithstanding, many Muslim commentators have ascribed the primary responsibility for man's Fall to woman, as may be seen from the following extract:

> In al-Tabiris *Tarikh* (1:108) the very words Satan used to tempt Eve are then used by her to tempt Adam: "Look at this tree, how sweet is its smell, how delicious is its fruit, how beautiful is its colour!" This passage is concluded by God's specifically accusing Eve of deceiving Adam. Later in the narrative (1:111–112) al-Tabari mentions a report that is also cited by other commentators, the gist of which is to say that Adam while in his full reasoning faculties, did not eat of the tree, but only succumbed to the temptation after Eve had given him wine to drink. Al-Tha'labi in citing the same report also stresses the loss of Adam's rationality through the imbibing of wine, and al-Razi (*Tafsir* 3:13) says that such a story, which he has seen in several "tafsirs," is not at all far-fetched. Implicit in this specific act, of course, is both Eve's culpability and Adam's inherent rationality. Lest any should miss the point that Eve is actively and not just innocently involved in Adam's temptation, Ibn Kathir asserts that as God surely knows best, it was Eve who ate of the tree before Adam and urged him to eat. He then quotes a saying attributed to the Prophet, "But for Banu Isra'il meat would not have spoiled (because they used to keep it for the next day), and but for Hawwa' no female would be a traitor to her husband!" (*Bidaya* 1:84).[33]

There is hardly any doubt that Muslim women have been as victimized as Jewish and Christian women by the way in which the Jewish, Christian, and Islamic traditions have generally interpreted the Fall episode. However, it needs to be pointed out that the Qur'anic account of the episode differs significantly from the biblical account, and that the Fall does not mean in the Islamic tradition what it means in the Jewish, and particularly in the Christian, tradition.

To begin with, whereas in Genesis 3 no explanation is given as to why the serpent tempts either Eve alone or both Adam and Eve, in the Qur'an the reason why the Shaitan (or "Iblis") sets out to beguile the human pair in "al-jannah" is stated clearly in a number of passages.[34] The refusal of the Shaitan to obey God's command to bow in submission to Adam follows from his belief that being a creature of fire he is elementally superior to Adam, who is a creature of clay. When condemned for his arrogance by God and ordered to depart in a state of abject disgrace, the Shaitan throws a challenge to the Almighty: he will prove to God that Adam and Adam's progeny are unworthy of the honor and favor bestowed on them by God, being—in general—ungrateful, weak, and easily lured away from "the straight path" by worldly temptations. Not attempting to hide his intentions to "come upon" human beings from all sides, the Shaitan asks for—and is granted—a reprieve until "the Day of the Appointed Time." Not only is the reprieve granted, but God also tells the Shaitan to use all his wiles and forces to "assault" human beings and see if they would follow him. A cosmic drama now begins, involving the eternal opposition between the principles of right and wrong or good and evil, which is lived out as human beings, exercising their moral autonomy, who must now choose between "the straight path" and "the crooked path."

In terms of the Qur'anic narrative, what happens to the human pair in "al-jannah" is a sequel to the interchange between God and the Shaitan. In the sequel we learn that Adam and zauj have been commanded not to go near "the Tree" lest they become *zalimin.* Seduced by the Shaitan, they disobey God. However, in Surah 7: *Al-A'raf:* 23 they acknowledge before God that they have done *zulm* to themselves and earnestly seek God's forgiveness and mercy. They are told by God to "go forth" or "descend" from "al-jannah," but in addressing them the Qur'an uses the dual form of address (referring exclusively to Adam and "jauj") only once (in Surah 18: *Ta-Ha:* 123); for the rest the plural form is used, which necessarily refers to more than two persons and is generally understood as referring to humanity as a whole.

In the framework of Qur'anic theology, the order to "go forth" from "al-jannah" given to Adam or the children of Adam cannot be considered a punishment because Adam was always meant to be God's vice-regent on earth, as stated clearly in Surah 2: *Al-Baqarah:* 30. The earth is not a place of banishment but is declared by the Qur'an to be humanity's dwelling place and a source of profit to it.[35] The "al-jannah" mentioned in the Fall story is not—as pointed out by Muhammad Iqbal—"the supersensual paradise from which man is supposed to have fallen on this earth."[36]

There is, strictly speaking, no Fall in the Qur'an, What the Qur'anic narration focuses upon is the moral choice which humanity is required to make when confronted by the alternatives presented to them by God and the Shaitan. This becomes clear if one reflects on the text of Surah 2: *Al-Baqarah:* 35

and Surah 7: *Al-A'raf:* 19, in which it is stated: "You (dual) go not near this Tree, lest you (dual) become of the 'zalimin.'" In other words, the human pair is being told that *if* they go near the Tree, *then* they will be counted among those who perpetrate "zulim." Commenting on the root ZLM, Toshihio Izutsu says:

> The primary meaning of ZLM is, in the opinion of many of the authoritative lexicologists, that of "putting in a wrong place." In the moral sphere it seems to mean primarily "to act in such a way as to transgress the proper limit and encroach upon the right of some other person." Briefly and generally speaking "zulm" is to do injustice in the sense of going beyond one's bounds and doing what one has no right to.[37]

By transgressing the limits set by God the human pair become guilty of zulm towards themselves. This zulm consists in their taking on the responsibility for choosing between good and evil. Here it is important to note that the

> Qur'anic legend of the fall has nothing to do with the first appearance of man on this planet. Its purpose is rather to indicate man's rise from a primitive state of instinctive appetite to the conscious possession of a free self, capable of doubt and disobedience. The fall does not mean any moral depravity, it is man's transition from simple consciousness to the first flash of self-consciousness, a kind of waking from the dream of nature with a throb of personal causality in one's own being. Nor does the Qur'an regard the earth as a torture hall where an elementally wicked humanity is imprisoned for an original act of sin. Man's first act of disobedience was also his first act of free choice; and that is why, according to the Qur'anic narration, Adam's first transgression was forgiven. . . . A being whose movements are wholly determined like a machine cannot produce goodness. Freedom is thus a condition of goodness. But to permit the emergence of a finite ego who has the power to choose, after considering the relative values of several courses of action open to him, is really to take a great risk; for the freedom to choose good involves also the freedom to choose what is the opposite of good. That God has taken this risk shows his immense faith in man; it is now for man to justify this faith.[38]

There is no Fall in the Qur'an, hence there is no Original Sin. Human beings are not born sinful into this world, hence do not need to be "redeemed" or "saved." This is generally accepted in the Islamic tradition. However, the association of the Fall with sexuality, which has played such a massive role in perpetuating the myth of feminine evil in the Christian tradition, also exists in the minds of many Muslims and causes untold damage to Muslim women.

It is remarkable to see that though there is no reference to sexual activity on the part of man or woman even in their post-lapsarian state of partial or complete nakedness in either Genesis 3 or the Qur'an, many Muslim scholars have jumped to the conclusion that exposure of their *sau'at* (i.e., "the external portion of the organs of generation of a man and of a woman and the anus"[39]), generally translated as "shameful parts," necessarily led the human pair to sexual activity which was "shameful" not only by virtue of being linked with their "shameful parts" but also because it was instigated by the Shaitan. The following explanation by A. A. Maududi—one of contemporary Islam's most influential scholars—represents the thinking of many, if not most, Muslims on this point:

> The sex instinct is the greatest weakness of the human race. That is why Satan selected this weak spot for his attack on the adversary and devised the scheme to strike at their modesty. Therefore the first step he took in this direction was to expose their nakedness to them so as to open the door of indecency before them and beguile them into sexuality. Even to this day. Satan and his disciples are adopting the same scheme of depriving the woman of the feelings of modesty and shyness and they cannot think of any scheme of "progress" unless they expose and exhibit the woman to all and sundry.[40]

The initial statement leaves no doubt about Maududi's negative view of "the sex instinct," which he describes as "the greatest weakness of the human race." Associating sexuality with the Shaitan's "attack on the adversary," Maududi assumes that on discovering their state of physical exposure, the human pair resorted irresistibly to an act of "indecency," i.e., sexual intercourse. However, there is nothing in the text which warrants this assumption. In fact, according to the text, the human pair's first act on discovering their exposed state was one of "decency," namely, that of covering themselves with leaves.

That Maududi—like many other Muslims, Jews, and Christians—sees women as the primary agents of sexuality which is regarded as the Shaitan's chief instrument for defeating God's plan for humanity, is clear from the way in which he shifts attention from the human pair to the woman, in the above passage. In turning his eyes away from the "nakedness" of the sons of Adam to focus on the "nakedness" of the daughters of Hawwa', he is typical of Muslim culture.

Though the branding of women as "the devil's gateway"[41] is not at all the intent of the Qur'anic narration of the Fall story—as the foregoing account has shown—Muslims, no less than Jews and Christians, have used the story to vent their misogynistic feelings. This is clear from the continuing popularity of ahadith such as the following:

Narrated Usama bin Zäid: The Prophet said, "After me I have not left any affliction more harmful to men than women" (*Shahih Al-Bukhari,* vol. VII, p. 22).[42]

Ibn Abbas reported that Allah's Messenger said: "I had a chance to look into Paradise and I found that the majority of the people were poor and I looked into the Fire and there I found the majority constituted by women" (*Sahih Muslim,* vol. IV, p. 1431).[43]

Abu Sa'id Khudri reported that Allah's Messenger said: "The world is sweet and green (alluring) and verily Allah is going to install you as vice-regent in it in order to see how you act. So avoid the allurement of women: verily, the first trial for the people of Isra'il was caused by women" (*Sahih Muslim,* vol. IV, p. 1431).

(iii) Why Was Woman Created?

The Qur'an, which does not discriminate against women in the context of the Fall episode, does not support the view—held by many Muslims, Christians, and Jews—that woman was created not only *from* man but also *for* man. That God's creation as a whole is "for just ends" (Surah 15: *Al-Hijr:* 85) and not "for idle sport" (Surah 21: *Al-Anbiya':* 16) is one of the major themes of the Qur'an, humanity, fashioned "in the best of molds" (Surah 95: *At-Tin:* 4) has been created in order to serve God (Surah 51: *Adh-Dhariyat:* 56). According to Qur'anic teaching, service to God cannot be separated from service to humankind, or—in Islamic terms—believers in God must honor both *Haquq Allah* (rights of God) and *Haquq al-'ibad* (rights of creatures). Fulfilment of one's duties to God and humankind constitutes the essence of righteousness.[44] That men and women are equally called upon by God to be righteous and will be equally rewarded for their righteousness is stated unambiguously in a number of Qur'anic passages such as the following:

The Believers, men
And women, are protectors,
One of another: they enjoin
What is just, and forbid
What is evil: they observe
Regular prayers, practice
Regular charity, and obey
God and His Apostle.
On them will God pour
His mercy: for God
Is exalted in power, Wise.
God hath promised to Believers,
Men and women, Gardens
Under which rivers flow,

To dwell therein,
And beautiful mansions
In gardens of everlasting Bliss
But the greatest bliss
Is the Good Pleasure of God:
That is the supreme felicity (Surah 9: *At-Taubah:* 71:72).[45]

Not only does the Qur'an make it clear that man and woman stand absolutely equal in the sight of God, but also that they are "members" and "protectors" of each other. In other words, the Qur'an does not create a hierarchy in which men are placed above women, nor does it pit men against women in an adversary relationship. They are created as equal creatures of a universal, just, and merciful God whose pleasure it is that they live—in harmony and in righteousness—together.

In spite of the Qur'anic affirmation of man–woman equality, Muslim societies in general have never regarded men and women as equal, particularly in the context of marriage. Fatima Mernissi's observations on the position of a Muslim woman in relation to her family in modern Morocco apply, more or less, to Muslim culture generally:

> One of the distinctive characteristics of Muslim sexuality is its territoriality, which reflects a specific division of labour and a specific conception of society and of power. The territoriality of Muslim sexuality sets ranks, tasks, and authority patterns. Spatially confined, the woman was taken care of materially by the man who possessed her, in return for her total obedience and her sexual and reproductive services. The whole system was organized so that the Muslim "ummah" was actually a society of male citizens who possessed among other things the female half of the population. Muslim men have always had more rights and privileges than Muslim women, including even the right to kill their women. . . . The man imposed on the women an artificially narrow existence, both physically and spiritually.[46]

Underlying the rejection in Muslim societies of the idea of man–woman equality is the deeply rooted belief that women—who are inferior in creation (having been made from a crooked rib) and in righteousness (having helped the Shaitan in defeating God's plan for Adam)—have been created mainly to be of use to men who are superior to them.

The alleged superiority of men to women which permeates the Islamic (as also the Jewish and Christian) tradition is grounded not only in Hadith literature but also in popular interpretations of some Qur'anic passages. Two Qur'anic passages—Surah 4: *An-Nisa':* 34 and Surah 2: *Al Baqarah:* 288—in particular, are generally cited to support the contention that men have "a degree of advantage" over women. Of these, the first reads as follows in A. A. Maududi's translation of the Arabic text:

> Men are the managers of the affairs of women because Allah has made the one superior to the other and because men spend of their wealth on women. Virtuous women are, therefore, obedient; they guard their rights carefully in their absence under the care and watch of Allah. As for those women whose defiance you have cause to fear, admonish them and keep them apart from your beds and beat them. Then, if they submit to you, do not look for excuses to punish them: note it well that there is Allah above you, Who is Supreme and Great.[47]

It is difficult to overstate the impact of the general Muslim understanding of Surah 4: *An-Nisa':* 34, which is embodied in Maududi's translation. As soon as the issue of woman's equality with man is raised by liberals, the immediate response by traditionalists is, "But don't you know that God says in the Qur'an that men are *qawwamun* in relation to women and have the right to rule over them and even to beat them?" In fact, the mere statement, *ar-rijal-o qawwamun-a 'ala an-nisa* (literally, the men are *qawwamun* in relation to the women) signifies the end of any attempt to discuss the issue of woman's equality with man in the Islamic ummah.

It is assumed by almost all who read Surah 4, verse 34, that it is addressed to husbands. The first point to be noted is that it is addressed to "ar-rijal" (the men) and to "an-nisa" (the women). In other words, it is addressed to all men and women of the Islamic community. This is further indicated by the fact that in relation to all the actions that are required to be taken, the plural and not the dual form (used when reference is made to two persons) is found. Such usage makes clear that the orders contained in this verse were not addressed to a husband or wife but to the Islamic "ummah" in general.

The key word in the first sentence of this verse is "qawwamun." This word has been translated variously as "protectors and maintainers (of women)," "in charge (of women)," "having pre-eminence (above women)," and "sovereigns or masters (over women)." Linguistically, the word "qawwamun" means "breadwinners" or "those who provide a means of support or livelihood." A point of logic that must be made here is that the first sentence is not a descriptive one stating that all men as a matter of fact are providing for women, since obviously there are at least some men who do not provide for women. What the sentence is stating, rather, is that men ought to have the capability to provide (since "ought" implies "can"). In other words, this statement, which almost all Muslim societies have taken to be an actual description of all men, is in fact a normative statement pertaining to the Islamic concept of division of labor in an ideal family or community structure. The fact that men are "qawwamun" does not mean that women cannot or should not provide for themselves, but simply that in view of the heavy burden that most women shoulder in bearing and rearing children, they should not have the additional obligation of providing the means of living at the same time.

Continuing with the analysis of the passage, we come next to the idea that God has given the one more strength than the other. Most translations make it appear that the one who has more strength, excellence, or superiority is the man. However, the Qur'anic expression does not accord superiority to men. The expression literally means "some in relation to some," so that the statement could mean either that some men are superior to some others (men and/or women) and that some women are superior to some others (men and/or women). The interpretation which seems to me to be the most appropriate contextually is that some men are more blessed with the means to be better providers that are other men.

The next part of the passage begins with a "therefore," which indicates that this part is conditional upon the first: in other words, if men fulfill their assigned function of being providers, women must fulfill their corresponding duties. Most translations describe this duty in terms of the wife being "obedient" to the husband. The word *salihat,* which is translated as "righteously obedient," is related to the word *salahiat,* which means "capability" or "potentiality," and not obedience. Women's special capability is to bear children. The word *qanitat,* which succeeds the word "salihat" and is also translated as "obedient," is related to a bag for carrying water from one place to another without spilling. Women's special function, then, according to this passage, is that like the bag in which water is transported without loss to its destination, she carries and protects the fetus in her womb until it can be safely delivered.

What is outlined in the first part of this passage is a functional division of labor necessary for maintaining balance in any society. Men who do not have to fulfill the responsibility of childbearing are assigned the functions of being breadwinners. Women are exempted from the responsibility of being breadwinners in order that they may fulfill their function as childbearers. The two functions are separate but complementary and neither is higher or lower than the other.

The three injunctions in the second part of the verse were given to the Islamic ummah in order to meet a rather extraordinary possibility: a mass rebellion on the part of women against their role as childbearers, the function assigned to them by God. If all or most of the women in a Muslim society refused to bear children without just cause as a sign of organized defiance or revolt, this would mean the end of the Muslim ummah. This situation must, therefore, be dealt with decisively. The first step to be taken is to counsel the rebels. If this step is unsuccessful, the second step to be taken is isolation of the rebellious women from others. (It is to be noted here that the prescription is "to leave the women alone in their beds." By translating this line, "keep them apart from your beds," Maududi is suggesting, if not stating, that the judging party is the husband and not the Islamic community—an assumption not warranted by the text). If the second step is also not successful then the step of confining the women for a longer period of time may be taken by the Islamic community or its representatives. Here, it is important to point out that the Arabic word that is generally translated as "beating" has numerous meanings. When used in a legal context as it is here, it means "holding in confinement," according to the authoritative lexicon *Tal-al-'Arus.*[48] (In Surah 4: *An-Nisa':* 15, unchaste women are also prescribed the punishment of being confined to their homes.)

While Muslims, through the centuries, have interpreted Surah *AnNisa':* 34 as giving them unequivocal mastery over women, a linguistically and philosophically/theologically accurate interpretation of this passage would lead to radically different conclusions. In simple words what this passage is saying is that since only women can bear children (which is not to say either that all women should bear children or that women's sole function is to bear children)—a function whose importance in the survival of any community cannot be questioned—they should not have the additional obligation of being breadwinners while they perform this function. Thus, during the period of a woman's childbearing, the function of breadwinning must be performed by men (not just husbands) in the Muslim ummah. Reflection on this Qur'anic passage shows that the division of functions mandated here is designed to ensure justice in the community as a whole. There are millions of women all over the world—and I am one of them—who are designated inaccurately as "single" parents (when, in fact, they are "double" parents) who bear and raise children singlehandedly, generally without much support from the community. This surely does not constitute a just situation. If children are the wealth and future of the ummah, the importance of protecting the function of childbearing and child raising becomes self-evident. Statistics from all over the world show that women and children left without the care and custodianship of men suffer from economic, social, psychological, and other ills. What Surah *An-Nisa':* 34 is ensuring is that this does not happen. It enjoins men in general to assume responsibility for women in general when they are performing the vitally important function of childbearing (other passages in the Qur'an extend this also to child rearing). Thus the intent of this passage, which has traditionally been used to subordinate women to men is in fact to guarantee women the material (as well as moral) security needed by them during the period of pregnancy when breadwinning can become difficult or even impossible for them.

The second passage which mentions the so-called "degree of advantage" that men have over women is Surah 2: *Al-Baqarah:* 228, which reads:

> Divorced women
> Shall wait concerning
> For three monthly periods.
> Nor is it lawful for them
> To hide what God
> Hath created in their wombs,
> If they have faith
> In God and the last Day.
> And their husbands
> Have the better right
> To take them back
> In that period, if
> They wish for reconciliation.
> And *women shall have rights*
> *Similar to the rights*
> *Against them, according*
> *To what is equitable;*
> *But men have a degree*
> *(of advantage) over them,*
> And God is Exalted in Power, Wise.[49]

As can be seen, the above-cited passage pertains to the subject of divorce. The "advantage" that men have over women in this context is that women must observe a three-month period called "iddat" before remarriage, but men are exempted from this requirement. The main reason why women are subjected to this restriction is because at the time of divorce a woman may be pregnant and this fact may not become known for some time. As men cannot become pregnant they are allowed to remarry without a waiting period.

In my judgment, the Qur'anic passages—in particular the two discussed above—on which the edifice of male superiority over women largely rests, have been misread or misinterpreted, intentionally or unintentionally, by most Muslim societies and men. A "correct" reading of these passages would not, however, make a radical or substantial difference to the existing pattern of male–female relationships in Muslim societies unless attention was also drawn to those Ahadith which have been used to make man not only superior to a woman, but virtually her god. The following hadith is particularly important:

> A man came in with his daughter and said, "This my daughter refuses to get married." The Prophet said, "Obey your father." She said, "By the name of Him Who sent you in truth, I will not marry until you inform me what is the right

> of the husband over his wife." He said . . . if it were permitted for one human being to bow down (*sajada*) to another I would have ordered the woman to bow down to her husband when he enters into her, because of God's grace on her." (The daughter) answered, "By the name of Him Who sent you, with truth, I would never marry!"[50]

A faith as rigidly monotheistic as Islam cannot conceivably permit any human being to worship anyone but God, therefore the hypothetical statement "If it were permitted . . ." in the above-cited hadith, is, *ipso facto,* an impossibility. But the way this hadith is related makes it appear that if not God's, at least it was the Prophet's will or wish to make the wife prostrate herself before her husband. Each word, act, or exhortation attributed to the Prophet is held to be sacred by most of the Muslims in the world and so this hadith (which, in my judgment seeks to legitimate *shirk:* associating anyone with God—an unforgivable sin according to the Qur'an) becomes binding on the Muslim woman. Muslims frequently criticize a religion such as Hinduism where the wife is required to worship the husband *(patipuja),* but in practice what is expected from most Muslim wives is not very different from patipuja. In India and Pakistan, for example, a Muslim woman learns almost as an article of faith that her husband is her *majazi khuda* (God in earthly form). This description, undoubtedly, constitutes "shirk."

Most ahadith dealing with the subject of married women describe a virtuous woman as one who pleases and obeys her husband at all times. Pleasing the husband can, in fact, become more important than pleasing God. Putting it differently, one can say that most Muslims believe that a woman cannot please God except through pleasing her husband. Some ahadith are cited below to illustrate this point:

> The wife of Sufwan B. Mu'attal went to the Prophet when we were with him and said, "O Messenger of God, my husband . . . beats me when I perform my devotions, and makes me eat when I fast. . . ." (The Prophet) asked Sufwan about what she had said and he replied, "O Messenger of God . . . she fasts and I am a young man and have not patience." Then the Messenger of God said, "From now on let a woman not fast except by permission of her husband" (Ibn Hanbal).[51]
>
> A woman whose husband is pleased with her at the time of her death goes straight to Paradise (Tirmidhi).[52]
>
> There are three (persons) whose prayer is not accepted nor their virtues taken above: the fugitive slave till he returns to his masters and places his hand in their hands; the woman on whom her husband remains displeased; and the drunkard, till he becomes sober (Baihaqi).[53]
>
> Hadrat Anas reported that the Holy Prophet had said: "For a woman her husband is Paradise as well as hell" (Ahmad and Nasa'i).[54]

> Hadrat Ibn Abi Aufi reported that the Holy Prophet has said: "By Allah in Whose Hand is my life, the woman who does not discharge her duties to her husband is disobedient to Allah, and the discharge of duties towards Allah depends on the discharge of duties towards the husband" (lbn Majah).[55]

Man and woman, created equal by God and standing equal in the sight of God, have become very unequal in Muslim societies. The Qur'anic description of man and woman in marriage:

> They are your garments
> And you are their garments (Surah 2: *Al-Baqarah:* 187)

implies closeness, mutuality, and equality. However, Muslim culture has reduced many, if not most, women to the position of puppets on a string, to slave-like creatures whose only purpose in life is to cater to the needs and pleasures of men. Not only this, it has also had the audacity and the arrogance to deny women direct access to God. Islam rejects the idea of redemption, of any intermediary between a believer and the Creator. It is one of Islam's cardinal beliefs that each person—man and woman—is responsible and accountable for his or her individual actions. How, then, can the husband become the wife's gateway to heaven or hell? How, then, can he become the arbiter not only of what happens to her in this world but also of her ultimate destiny? Surely such questions must arise in the minds of thoughtful Muslim men, but Muslim women are afraid to ask questions whose answers are bound to threaten the existing balance of power in the domain of family relationships in most Muslim societies.

Qur'anic Islam versus Islam in History and Issues of Women's Sexuality

The foregoing account provides much evidence to show that the Qur'an does not discriminate against women, whose sexuality is affirmed both generally and in the context of marriage. Furthermore, while making it clear that righteousness is identical in the case of man or woman, the Qur'an also provides particular safeguards for protecting women's special sexual/biological functions such as carrying, delivering, suckling, and rearing offspring.

Underlying much of the Qur'an's legislation on women-related issues is the recognition that women have been disadvantaged persons in history to whom justice needs to be done by the Islamic ummah. Unfortunately, however, the cumulative (Jewish, Christian, Hellenistic, Bedouin, and other) biases which existed in the Arab-Islamic culture of the early centuries of Islam infiltrated the Islamic tradition, largely through the Hadith literature, and undermined the intent of the Qur'an to liberate women from the status of chattels or inferior creatures and make them free and equal to men.

A review of Muslim history and culture brings to light many areas in which—Qur'anic teachings notwithstanding—women continued to be subjected to diverse forms of oppression and injustice, not infrequently in the name of Islam. However, there are also areas in which the message of the Qur'an has been heeded. For instance, in response to the Qur'an, condemnation of female[56] infanticide, which was not uncommon among pre-Islamic Arabs. Muslim Arabs abolished the practice of burying their daughters alive. This means that when Muslims say with pride that Islam gave women the right to live, they are, indeed, right. However, it needs to be added here that though Muslims do not kill their baby daughters, they do not, in general, treat them equally with boys. Generally speaking, the birth of a daughter is met with resignation and even sadness. A woman who produces only daughters is likely to be the target of harsh and abusive behavior and threatened with divorce. It will be interesting to see what change, if any, takes place in Muslim culture when the fact becomes widely known that it is not the mother but the father who determines the sex of the child!

Underlying the gruesome practice of female infanticide was the notion, prevalent among Bedouin Arabs, that the birth of a daughter meant not only additional drainage of extremely scarce means of survival, but also—and more importantly—a real hazard to their "honor." The concepts of "honor" and "shame," which have a profound significance in Bedouin culture (as also in Mediterranean societies), are linked with the idea of women's chastity or sexual behavior. Pre-Islamic nomadic Arabs, who lived in a state of constant warfare with the environment and with other tribes, had a separate word for the honor of women—*ird,* about which B. Fares observes:

> "Ird" from its etymology seems to be a partition which separates its possessor from the rest of mankind. . . . This partition is certainly fragile since it was easily destroyed. . . . (In the pre-Islamic jahiliyya period) "ird" was intense and of momentous importance; besides it was the guiding motive in the acts and deeds of all the Arabs except those of the Yemen . . . on account of its sacred nature, it was entitled to take the place of religion; the Arabs put it in the highest place and defended it arms in hand.[57]

So fearful were pre-Islamic Arabs of the possibility of having their "ird" compromised by their daughters' voluntary or involuntary loss of chastity that they were willing to kill them. Obviously, to them their honor mattered more than the lives of their infant daughters. It is important to note that the "honor" killings still go on in many Muslim societies in which a woman is killed on the slightest suspicion of what is perceived as sexual misconduct. There are also many instances of women being killed for other reasons and the murder being camouflaged as an "honor" killing in order to make it appear less heinous a crime.

The term "ird" does not appear in the Qur'an. However, just as in the case of Bedouin Arabs, most Muslim men's concept of "honor" revolves around the orbit of women's sexuality, which is seen as a male possession. Commenting on how men's honor is intertwined with women's virginity (which symbolizes their chastity) in patriarchal Muslim culture, Fatima Mernissi observes:

> virginity is a matter between men, in which women merely play the role of silent intermediaries. Like honour, virginity is the manifestation of a purely male preoccupation in societies where inequality, scarcity, and the degrading subjection of some people to others deprive the community as a whole of the only true human strength: self-confidence. The concepts of honour and virginity locate the prestige of a man between the legs of a women. It is not by subjugating nature or by conquering mountains and rivers that a man secures his status, but by controlling the movements of women related to him by blood or by marriage, and by forbidding them any contact with male strangers.[58]

Since women's sexuality is so vitally related to men's honor and the self-image in Muslim culture, it becomes vitally important in Muslim societies to subject women's bodies to external social controls. One way in which some Muslim societies (e.g., in North Africa) have sought to do so is by means of female circumcision, which ranges from cutting off the tip of the clitoris to virtual removal of the clitoris and the sealing of the mouth of the vagina except for a small passage. The extent of physical, emotional, or psychological damage done to women by the practice of female circumcision depends, among other things, upon the nature of the "operation" and how it was performed. Having heard personal testimonies from Muslim women who have experienced the horror of radical circumcision, I have no doubt at all that this practice constitutes an extreme form of cruelty towards women which must not be tolerated. Here it needs to be pointed out that though the Islamic tradition (following the Jewish tradition) requires male circumcision, it does not require female circumcision. Female circumcision practiced in countries such as Egypt, the Sudan, and Somalia is, thus, rooted in the culture of those regions and not in religion.

Another way in which Muslim societies seek to control women's bodies is by denying women access to means of birth control. Here it may be noted that though there are Qur'anic statements referring to the killing of one's living children,[59] there are no Qur'anic statements on birth control. In the

Hadith literature, examples may be found which support the practice of *azl*[60] *(coitus interruptus)* and which do not.[61] A similar ambiguity is found among Muslim jurists.[62] In view of the fact that there is no definitive statement on the subject of birth control in the major sources of the Islamic tradition, the issue—in a sense—remains open. Considering the overwhelming importance of the problem of expanding population in most Muslim countries, the subject of family planning or birth control should obviously be considered a high priority for discussion by the learned in the Muslim ummah. ("Ijma," or consensus of the community, constitutes a source of law in the Islamic tradition.) However, family planning programs have met with strong resistance in the Islamic world in general and most of this resistance appears to be rooted in religious grounds.

One Qur'anic passage commonly cited by opponents of birth control in Muslim societies is Surah 2: *Al-Baqarah:* 223, which states:

> Your wives are
> As a tilth unto you
> So approach your tilth
> When or how you will;
> But do some good beforehand,
> And fear God,
> And know that you are
> To meet Him (in the Hereafter),
> And give (these) good tidings
> To those who believe.[63]

The likening of a wife to life-containing soil has profound meaning but the average Muslim is not sensitive to the subtleties of the comparison or to the implications of the Qur'an's reminder to the husband that he should act righteously. Since wives are described as a "tilth" and permission has been given to the husbands to approach them "when or how you will," the average Muslim man believes not only that husbands have the right to have sexual intercourse with their wives whenever they choose, but also the right to impregnate them at will in order that they might yield a harvest.

Numerous ahadith attributed to the Prophet insist that a wife must never refuse to have sexual relations with her husband. For instance, Imam Muslim reports the following ahadith on the authority of Abu Huraira:

> Allah's Apostle said: "When a woman spends the night from the bed of her husband the angels curse her until morning."
>
> . . . Allah's Messenger said: "By Him in whose Hand is my Life, when a man calls his wife to his bed and she does not respond, the One who is in the heaven is displeased with her until he (her husband) is pleased with her."[64]

In view of this insistence that the husband's sexual needs be instantaneously satisfied (unless the wife is menstruating, fasting, or in some other exceptional circumstances) it is rather ironic to note that a large number of Muslim women suffer from "frigidity." Like the earth, all too often they are "cultivated" without love or proper care and never discover the wonder or joy of their own womanhood.

Undoubtedly the threat of unlimited pregnancies and childbirths with little or no health care available has made many Muslim women afraid of sex. But the manner in which Muslim societies have legislated that regardless of her own wishes a woman must always meet her husband's sexual demands as *duty* has also led to sexual intercourse becoming a mechanical performance which leaves both the man and the woman sexually unsatisfied.

A number of studies[65] conducted by social scientists indicate that Muslim societies put a high premium on female fertility. Among the reasons why this should be so is the belief, however unfounded, that birth control and abortion are morally "wrong." A second reason is a hankering for a son and then more sons. A third and more traditional reason is the desire to keep women tied to the homestead and in a state of perpetual dependency upon men.

It has been assumed by conservative Muslim scholars (who form the majority of scholars in the Muslim world) that birth control is demonic in origin and its primary purpose is to facilitate immorality. A. A. Maududi's views cited below are typical of this viewpoint.

> Co-education, employment of women in offices, mixed social gatherings, immodest female dresses, beauty parades, are now a common feature of our social life. Legal hindrances have been placed in the way of marriage and on having more than one wife, but no bar against keeping mistresses and having illicit relationships prior to the age of marriage. In such a society perhaps the last obstacle that may keep a woman from surrendering to a man's advances is fear of an illegitimate conception. Remove this obstacle too and provide to women with weak character assurance that they can safely surrender to their male friends and you will see that the society will be plagued by the tide of moral licentiousness.[66]

In this day and age it hardly needs to be argued that a woman who has no control over her own body or who is compelled by social and religious pressures to play the part of a reproductive machine becomes less than a fully autonomous human being. Furthermore, there is a definite connection between the status of women and their ability to control or determine the number and spacing of children they will have, as a recent United Nations study has shown.[67]

While the issue of birth control is of great urgency and importance to many Muslim women, the issue of segregation and veiling seems to me to affect an even larger proportion of women in Muslim culture. In recent times, the heated, ongoing discussion in a number of Muslim societies (e.g., Egyptian, Iranian, Pakistani) as well as among Muslim minority groups (e.g., in Western Europe or North America) on whether Muslim women are required to veil themselves totally or partially shows that the issue of veiling is at the heart of the greatest dilemma confronting contemporary Islam. It is necessary to understand that the most serious challenge to the world of traditional Islam is that of modernity. The caretakers of Muslim traditionalism are aware of the fact that viability in the modern world requires the adoption of the scientific or rational outlook which inevitably brings about major changes in modes of thinking and behavior. While all Muslim societies want to have "modernization" (which is largely identified with science, technology, and a better standard of living), hardly any Muslim society wants to have "Westernization" (which is largely identified with "mass" Western culture leading to moral and social laxity).

To the majority of Muslims in the world, perhaps the most undesirable symbol of "Westernization" is a woman who does not honor the boundary between "private" space (i.e., the home, which belongs to women) and "public" space (i.e., the world, which belongs to men), which they consider essential for preserving the integrity of the Islamic way of life in the face of endless onslaughts by erstwhile colonizers of the Muslim peoples. Muslims, in general, believe that it is best to keep men and women in their separate, designated spaces, and that the intrusion of women into men's territory leads to the disruption, if not the destruction, of the fundamental order of things. However, if it becomes necessary for women to intrude into men's space, they must make themselves faceless, or at least, as inconspicuous as possible. This is achieved through veiling, which is thus an extension of the idea of segregation of the sexes.

While it is beyond the scope of this paper to analyze all the Qur'anic statements which have a bearing upon the institution of *purdah* (i.e., segregation and veiling), a few observations need to be made. The Qur'an does not confine women to "private" space. In fact, in Surah 4: *An-Nisa':* 15, confinement to the home is prescribed as a punishment for unchaste women! The Qur'anic law of modesty[68]—addressed to men as well as to women—does indeed discourage exhibitionism in dress or conduct. Its underlying message—addressed particularly to women who have, since time immemorial, been reduced to sex objects by androcentric cultures—is: do not dress or act like sex objects. The purpose of the Qur'anic legislation pertaining to women's attire or behavior is not to confine them, spatially or psychologically, but to enable them to move round in "public" space without the fear of being molested.[69] Its larger aim is to transform women into *persons* who are secure and self-respecting and who do not feel that their survival depends on their ability to attract, entertain, or cajole those men who are not interested in their personality but only in their sexuality.

In evaluating the impact on Muslim women of veiling, it is necessary to clarify two points. The first is that "veiling" can be understood in a variety of ways, ranging from the wearing of a head-scarf to total covering of the body from head to foot. The second is that, in recent times, the veil has functioned not as a symbol of women's oppression but as an emblem of their political, economic, and cultural emancipation and as a means of asserting their multi-faceted identities. The "veiled" revolutions which have taken place in Iran and Egypt in the 1980s illustrate this well.

While the wearing of a head-scarf by a Muslim woman, especially if she has worn the head-scarf as an act of free choice, does not restrict her autonomy as a person, total veiling of the body, especially if it is imposed externally, certainly constitutes a serious deterrent to the full and healthy development of Muslim women. While the Qur'an has given the Muslim woman the right to work, to earn,[70] to go about her daily business without fear of sexual harassment, Muslim societies in general have imprisoned and entombed many Muslim women in oppressive veils and put them behind locked doors.

Nothing illustrates the obsession of Muslim men with women's sexuality and the desire to control it than the constant effort made by many of them to ensure that not a single hair on the head of any woman related to them is visible to a man who is not related to them! Not satisfied with "the outer garment"[71] prescribed for Muslim women in a specific cultural context, conservative Muslims seek the help of a weak hadith[72] to compel women to cover themselves from head to foot, leaving only the face and hands uncovered. Ultraconservative Muslims have gone even further, requiring that a woman also cover her face.[73] Certainly there are no Qur'anic statements which justify the rigid restrictions regarding segregation and veiling which have been imposed on Muslim women in the name of Islam. If, for instance, the Qur'an had intended for women to be completely veiled, why would it have required Muslim men to lower their gaze when looking at them?[74]

Summary

Within the Islamic tradition both negative and positive attitudes are found towards women and women's issues. The Qur'an—which to me is the primary source on which Islam is founded—consistently affirms women's equality with men and their fundamental right to actualize the human potential which they possess equally with men. Seen through a non-patriarchal lens, the Qur'an shows no sign of discrimination against women. If anything, it exhibits particular solicitude for women, much as it does for other disadvantaged persons.

The attitude of the Hadith literature towards women is a mixed one. While there are a number of ahadith which recommend an attitude of kindness towards daughters and wives, there are also others—such as the following—which reflect a number of anti-women biases characteristic of Islamic culture.

> Narrated Abu Sa'id Al-Khudri: Once Allah's Apostle went out to the Musalla (to offer the prayers) of 'Id-al-Adha or Al-Fitr prayer. Then he passed by the women and said, "O women! give alms, as I have seen that the majority of the dwellers of Hell-fire were you (women)." They asked, "Why is it so, O Allah's Apostle?" He replied, "You curse frequently and are ungrateful to your husbands. I have not seen anyone more deficient in intelligence and religion than you. A cautious, sensible man could be led astray by some of you." The women replied, "O Allah's Apostle! What is deficient in our intelligence and religion?" He said, "Is not the evidence of two women equal to the witness of one man?" They replied in the affirmative. He said, "This is the deficiency in your intelligence. Isn't it true that a woman can neither pray nor fast during her menses?" The women replied in the affirmative. "This is the deficiency in your religion."[75]

In this paper many instances have been cited in which individual ahadith conflict with the Qur'an. However, there is one area in which the Qur'an and the Hadith literature seem to be in total accord. This pertains to attitudes towards one's mother. Surah 4: *An-Nisa':* 1 commands human beings to revere God who created them, and next, to revere the wombs which bore them. There are also numerous ahadith on the subject of honoring one's mother. One of these—"Paradise lies at or under the feet of your mother"—cited by a number of Hadith collections, is probably the best-known of all ahadith in Muslim culture.

Muslims, in general, have been faithful to the Qur'anic commandment and in Muslim societies great love and respect is shown to one's mother. Here, it is of interest to note that the two most beloved names of God—Rahman and Rahim—come from the root-word "Rahm," which means "womb." Also, the word "ummah" comes from the root-word "umm," which means "mother." Hence, some of the most important symbols/images in the Islamic tradition are women-related.

But though respect for *one's own mother* is universal in the Islamic world, it must be noted that this respect is not necessarily extended to *all* mothers. In other words, though a Muslim may revere his own mother before all others, he does not consider motherhood as such to be worthy of the same respect that is given to his mother. The Qur'an, however, is concerned about all mothers and seeks to protect their rights. In Surah 2: *Al-Baqarah:* 233, for example, the Qur'an refers to the duties of a man towards his divorced wife, who is the mother of his child or children:

> Mothers shall suckle their children for two whole years: (that is) for those who wish to complete the suckling. The duty of feeding and clothing nursing mothers in a surely manner is upon the father of the child. No one should be charged beyond his capacity. *A mother should not be made to suffer because of her child, nor should he to whom the child is born be made to suffer because of the child.* And on the (father's) heir is incumbent the like of that (which was incumbent on the father) if they desire to wean the child by mutual consent and (after) consultation, it is no sin for them; and if ye wish to give your children out to nurse, it is no sin for you, provided that ye pay what is due from you in kindness. Observe your duty to Allah, and know that Allah is Seer of what ye do.[76]

This verse shows, among other things, the way in which the Qur'an ensures that no one—mother, father, or child—is exploited or unjustly treated and how even in the event of a divorce the fundamental rights and duties connected with motherhood or fatherhood must be recognized. This verse also speaks of "mutual consultation" with regard to the weaning and nursing of the child—yet another acknowledgment of the right of the mother to be a party to every important decision affecting her child.

Although the Qur'an lays down that no mother should be made to suffer on account of her child, many millions of Muslim mothers—like non-Muslim mothers—suffer indescribable ordeals and hardships if they have the misfortune to be without means and without a husband or to have a husband who is not mindful of his duties.

A point of psychological interest needs to be made regarding the importance that is given to a Muslim mother when she has a grown son. This mother is the same woman who was discriminated against in her father's household and given an inferior position in the context of her own marriage. Her chance to "get even" with the world comes when she has a son who reaches manhood. The bitterness, resentment, and frustration caused by a lifetime of repression, oppression, and deprivation tend to find rather ugly expression when, at last, the son's mother becomes a mother-in-law and begins her (generally, not-too-benign) rule over her son's household. In Muslim societies the figure of the mother-in-law is feared as much as the figure of the mother is loved. However, as Fatima Mernissi has observed in the context of Moroccan society:

> It is the structure which sets up the roles for everyone and leaves specific outlets

for the human individual's cravings and wishes. It is the structure which is vicious, not the mother-in-law.[77]

I want to end this paper with the hope and prayer that men and women—created equal by God—remembering that they are *zaujain* whose different sexualities complement each other, work together to construct that order in the home and in the world which reflects the justice and mercy, compassion and love of God towards God's creatures, and foreshadows that lasting Paradise from which the myth of feminine evil has finally been expelled.

Notes

1. Rahman, Fazlur, *Islam,* Doubleday and Company, Inc., Garden City, New York, 1968, 70.
2. Ali, Cheragh ("The Proposed Political Reforms in the Ottoman Empire and Other Muhammadan States," Bombay, 1883, XIX and 147) quoted by Alfred Guillaume, *The Traditions of Islam,* Khayats, Beirut, 1966, 97.
3. *Islam,* 73.
4. *The Traditions of Islam,* 15.
5. Ibid., 12, 13.
6. Hodgson, Marshall, G. S., *The Venture of Islam* (Conscience and History in a World Civilization), The University of Chicago Press, Chicago, 1974, vol. 1 (The Classical Age of Islam), 232.
7. Gibb, Hamilton A. R., *Studies on the Civilization of Islam,* edited by Stanford J. Shaw and William R. Polk, Beacon Press, Boston, 1962, 194.
8. *The Shorter Oxford English Dictionary* (prepared by W. Little, H. W. Fowler, and J. Coulson; revised and edited by C. T. Onions), 3d ed., Clarendon Press, Oxford, 1964, 1859.
9. Ali, A. Yusuf (translator), *The Holy Qur'an,* McGregor and Werner, Inc., USA, 1946, 1056.
10. Parwez, Ghulam A., *Tahwib ul Qur'an,* Idara Tulu' e Islam, Lahore, 1977, vol. 2, 853.
11. *The Holy Qur'an,* 1450.
12. "Mari" is the rendering of "Al Insan," which is a generic term for humanity.
13. *The Holy Qur'an,* 1653.
14. Reference is made to "nafs in wahidatin" in a number of Qur'anic verses, e.g., Surah 4: *An-Nisa':* 1; Surah 6: *Al-an'am:* 98; Surah 7: *Al-A'raf:* 189; Surah 31: *Luqman:* 28; and Surah 39: *Az-Zumar:* 6.
15. *The Holy Qur'an,* 905.
16. The Qur'an is deeply concerned about issues raised by slavery and contains many recommendations aimed at the freeing of slaves and at their gradual absorption into the society of free believers. Marriage to a slave woman could serve several ends: it would free her from slavery and give her a socially

respectable position, it would make it possible for a man with modest means to get married, it would rid society of the problems caused by illicit sex with slave women leading to illegitimate offspring who would also have the status of slaves, thus perpetuating the immoral institution of slavery. (See *Islam: A Challenge to Religion,* Idara Tulu' e Islam, Lahore, 1968, 346.)

17. *The Holy Qur'an,* 187–188.
18. Referring to the followers of Jesus, the Qur'an states in Surah 57: *Al-Hadid* 27, "The Monasticism/Which they invented/For themselves. We did not/Prescribe for them." (*The Holy Qur'an,* 1507).
19. Reference may be made in this context to the following hadith which is reported by both Bukhari and Muslim, the two most authoritative Hadith scholars of Sunni Islam: "'Abdullah b. Mas'ud reported God's Messenger as saying: 'Young men, those of you who can support a wife should marry, for it keeps you from looking at strange women and preserves you from immorality, but those who cannot, should devote themselves to fasting, for it is a means of suppressing sexual desire'" (Robson, James, translation of *Mishkat Al-Masabih,* Shaikh Muhammad Ashraf, Lahore, 1975, vol. I, 658).
20. Reference here is to the following hadith: "Anas reported God's Messenger as saying, 'When a man marries he has fulfilled half of the religion: so let him fear God regarding the remaining half.'" *(Mishkat Al-Masabith,* vol. I, 660).
21. For instance, Surah 4: *An-Nisa':* 1; Surah 7: *Al-A'raf:* 189; and Surah 39: *Az-Zumar:* 6.
22. In the aforementioned passages (as also in Surah 6: *Al-An'am:* 98 and Surah 31: *Luqman:* 28) reference is made to the creation from one source of being ("nafs in wahidatin") of all human being. Muslims, with hardly any exceptions, believe that the one original source being referred to in these passages is a man named Adam. This belief has led many translators of the Qur'an to obviously incorrect translation of simple Qur'anic passages.
23. "Adam" is used as a proper name in Surah 3: *Al. 'Imran:* 35 and 59; Surah 5: *Al-Ma'idah:* 30; and Surah 19: *Maryam:* 58.
24. Iqbal, Muhammad. *The Reconstruction of Religious Thought in Islam,* Shaikh Muhammad Ashraf, Lahore, 1962, 83.
25. For instance, in Surah: 75: *Al. Qiyamah:* 36–39. This passage reads: "Does 'al-insan' think that he will be left aimless/Was he not a drop of semen emitted? Then he became something which clings. Then He (Allah) created and shaped and made of him two mates: the male and the female."
26. Each hadith consists of two parts: "isnad" (or "sanad") and "matn." The "isnad" contains the names of persons who have handed on the substance of the hadith to one another. The "matn" is the text or actual substance of the hadith.
27. Since the early centuries of Islam, it has been axiomatic for (Sunni) Muslim masses to regard the Companions of the Prophet as being totally above the suspicion of being untrustworthy in any way least of all as transmitters of the Prophet's ahadith. Given such an attitude of absolute devotion, a critical examination of the credentials of the Companions as transmitters could hardly have

been undertaken. However, in the earliest phase of the development of Islam, a more critical attitude prevailed towards the Hadith literature and its transmitters. Here it is of interest to note that according to the well-known Muslim scholar 'Abdul Wahab Ash-Shairani, Imam Abu Hanifah, considered to be the founder of the largest school of law in Sunni Islam, did not consider Abu Hurairah to be a reliable transmitter of ahadith *(Al-Mizan al-Kubra,* Cairo edition, vol. I, 59).

28. Khan, M. M., translation with notes of *Sahih Al-Bikhari,* Kazi Publications, Lahore, 1971, vol. IV, 346.
29. Siddiqui, A. H., translation with notes of *Sahih Muslim,* Shaikh Muhammad Ashraf, Lahore, 1972, vol. II, 752.
30. See note 21.
31. *The Traditions of Islam,* 32.
32. It is interesting to observe that while in the Genesis 2 story, woman is derived from Adam's rib, there is no mention of Adam in any of the ahadith under discussion. This is a further "dehumanization" of woman since she could—in the ahadith in question—have been created from a disembodied rib which may not even have been human.
33. Smith, Jane I., and Haddad, Yvonne Y., "Eve: Islamic Image of Woman," in *Women and Islam,* edited by Azizah al-Hibri, Pergamon Press, New York, 1982, 139.
34. See Surah 15: *Al-Hijr:* 26–43; Surah 17: *Bani Isra'il:* 16–64; Surah 18: *Al-Kahf:* 50; and Surah 38: *L U:* 71–85.
35. *The Reconstruction of Religious Thought in Islam,* 84.
36. Ibid.
37. *The Structure of the Ethical Terms in the Koran,* Keio Institute of Philosophical Studies, Mita, Siba, Minatoku, Tokyo, 1959, 152–53.
38. *The Reconstruction of Religious Thought in Islam,* 85.
39. Lane, E. W., *Arabic-English Lexicon,* Williams and Norgate, London, 1863, book I, part 4, p. 1458.
40. *The Meaning of the Qur'an,* Islamic Publications Ltd., 1976, vol. IV, 16, footnote 13(2).
41. The famous expression comes from Tertullian (A.D. 160–225), a church father from North Africa who wrote: "And do you not know that you are (each) an Eve? The sentence of God on this sex of yours lives in this age; the guilt must of necessity live too. You are the devil's gateway; you are the unsealer of that (forbidden) tree; you are the first deserter of the divine law, you are she who persuaded him whom the devil was not valiant enough to attack. You destroyed so easily God's image, man. On account of your desert—that is, death—even the Son of God had to die" *(De cultu feminarum* 1.1, cited in *Biblical Affirmations of Woman,* 346).
42. Also cited in *Sahih Muslim,* vol. IV, 1431.
43. Also cited in *Sahih Al. Bukhari,* vol. IV, 305, vol. VIII, 362–63.
44. The Qur'anic understanding of "righteousness" is described in Surah 2: *Al-*

Baqarah: 177, which states: "It is not righteousness/That ye turn your faces/Towards East or West;/But it is righteousness/To believe in God/And the Last Day/And the Angels/And the Book/And the Messengers;/To spend of your substance/Out of love of Him,/For your kin/For orphans/For the wayfarer/For those/who ask/And for the ransom of slaves;/To be steadfast in prayer/And practice regular charity/To fulfil the contracts/Which ye have made/And to be firm and patient/In pain (or suffering)/And adversity/And throughout/All periods of panic/Such are the people/Of truth, the God-fearing" *(The Holy Qur'an,* 69–70).

45. *The Holy Qur'an,* 174–75.
46. *Beyond the Veil,* Schenkman Publishing Company, Inc., Cambridge, 1975, 103.
47. *The Meaning of the Qur'an,* vol. II (1971), 321.
48. Shehab, Rafi ullah, *Rights of Women in Islamic Shariah,* Indus Publishing House, Lahore, 1986, 117.
49. *The Holy Qur'an,* 89–90. The emphasis is mine.
50. Khan, Sadiq Hasan, *Husn al-Uswa,* 281.
51. *Al-Hadith,* vol. III, 80.
52. Imran, Muhammad, *Ideal Woman in Islam,* Islamic Publications Limited, Lahore, 1979, 50.
53. Ibid., 51.
54. Ibid.
55. Ibid.
56. See Surah 81: *At-Takwir:* 8 and 9; Surah 16: *An-Nahl:* 57–59; and Surah 17: *Bani Isra'il:* 31.
57. Article on "Ird," in *Supplement to the Encyclopaedia of Islam,* Brill, Leiden, 1938, 96–97.
58. "Virginity and Patriarchy," in *Women and Islam,* 183.
59. See, for instance, Surah 6: *Al-An'am:* 137, 140, 152; Surah 60: *Al-Mumpahanah:* 12; Surah 71: *Nuh:* 3.
60. See *Mishkat Al-Masabih,* vol. 2, 677–78.
61. Ibid.
62. Rauf, M. A., *Marriage in Islam,* Exposition Press, New York, 1974, 65–66.
63. *The Holy Qur'an,* 88.
64. *Sahih Muslim,* vol. II, 723.
65. For example, A. Aitken and J. Stoekel, "Muslim-Hindu Differentials in Family Planning Knowledge and Attitudes in Rural East Pakistan," in *Journal of Comparative Family Studies,* spring, 1971.
66. *Birth Control,* Islamic Publications Limited, 1974, 176.
67. *Status of Women and Family Planning,* United Nations, New York, 1975, 4.
68. See Surah 24: *An-Nur:* 30 and 31.
69. See Surah 33: *Al. Ahzab:* 59.
70. See Surah 4: *An-Nisa':* 32.
71. Reference here is to Sirah 33: *Al-Ahzab:* 59.
72. In this hadith, Ayesha reports that the Prophet Muhammad told Asma, her sis-

ter, when she appeared before him wearing thin clothes, "O Asma, when woman attains her puberty, it is not proper that any part of her body should be seen except this" and he pointed to his face and hands. (*Rights of Women in Islamic Shariah,* 4.)

73. In this context, see A. A. Maududi, *Purdah and the Status of Woman in Islam,* Islamic Publications Limited, Lahore, 1975.
74. Reference here is to Surah 24: *An-Nur:* 30.
75. *Sahih Al. Bukhari,* vol. I, 29.
76. Pickthall, Muhammad M., *The Meaning of the Glorious Qur'an,* Muslim World League—Rabita, New York, 1977, 36.
77. *Beyond the Veil,* 79.

[24]

Sexual Subversions in the Bible

David Biale

THE CONTEMPORARY DEBATE over whether Judaism liberates or represses sexuality must begin with the Hebrew Bible. This foundational document of Jewish culture, like any other such document, is subject to contradictory readings. Those who wish to portray Judaism as a this-worldly affirmation of sexuality look to the Bible, best represented on this subject by the Song of Songs, as setting the tone for all subsequent Jewish tradition. Indeed anti-Semites who hold that the Jews are hypersexual contrast the "lustful" nature of Judaism, which, they say, has its roots in the same biblical texts, with the more ascetic spirituality of Christianity. Taking the opposite position are those who believe that Judaism is sexually repressive. In their eyes, the basis for sexual repression in Western culture lies in the biblical laws of sexual purity. Feminists who hold this view argue further that the Bible is the origin of patriarchy: the male God of the Old Testament—the paragon of stern monotheism—jealously stamped out the erotic matriarchy of the pagan gods. Biblical culture, they charge, treated women as dangerous temptresses whose sexuality had to be controlled and domesticated.[1]

Each of these contradictory accounts assumes that the biblical text and bib-

SOURCE: From David Biale, *Eros and the Jews: From Biblical Israel to Contemporary America* (New York: Basic Books, 1992).

lical culture were stable and monolithic. But the Bible is less a factual history of ancient Israel than the record of a culture in conflict over its own identity, a conflict frequently represented by tensions between law and narrative and, just as often, by contradictions between different laws and different narratives. The conflicting genres and ideas within the Bible are not unlike the cultural conflicts that appear in texts from later periods of Jewish history. Thus, the Bible, itself the canonical text, includes material that foreshadows the later struggles between canon and alternative voices.

Since biblical culture was not monolithic, all of the contemporary interpretations of the Bible can find some support for their contradictory positions in the text. But as partial interpretations, they are often more misleading than helpful. The biblical legacy cannot be reduced to the harsh and repressive strictures of patriarchal custom. In addition to divinely ordained laws and patriarchal custom, the Bible also contains narratives in which these norms are suspended or undermined. Biblical culture takes on issues of sexuality with a remarkable theology of sexual subversion in which erotic brashness, often on the part of women, becomes a metaphor for the political brashness of a young, upstart nation. God is both the author of the laws and the hidden force behind their mythic subversion. Within what was undoubtedly a patriarchal legal culture, one finds surprisingly subversive alternatives that survive, not necessarily because there was external resistance to patriarchy, but because the dominant culture itself was neither monolithic nor utterly self-confident.

Sexuality was a central issue in Israel's self-conception,[2] with adultery and fidelity the dominant metaphors both for Israel's relationship to God and for national identity. The prophet Ezekiel combines the two explicitly in his accusation that Israel is whoring with her neighbors, the "well-endowed Egyptians" (16:26); Israel's depravity, he explains, derives from her origins: "You are daughters of a Hittite mother and an Amorite father" (16:45). Sexual anxiety is thus at the very heart of the struggle with this ambiguous identity. Would intermarriage with the competing nations in the land dilute a discrete Israelite identity, or was there no choice for a small, poorly defined people but to strengthen its position through such marital alliances? Intermarriage, as we shall see, was as defining and controversial an issue in biblical times as it is for Jews today.

Closely linked to problems of sexuality were deep concerns about fertility. The religion of ancient Israel is frequently seen as a refutation of the fertility cults of the Canaanites and the other peoples who lived in the area that became the land of Israel. Fertility rites are thought to be particularly characteristic of polytheists, who are said to engage in wild sexual orgies that will incite the gods and goddesses to copulate, which, in turn, is meant to bring fertility to the worshipers and their land. If it is highly doubtful that this is an accurate picture of Canaanite religion, it is equally false that Israelite religion lacked interest in fertility. On the contrary, ancient Israelite religion is not reducible to the abstract monotheism of later Jewish theology. Rather, it flourished in complex interaction with its milieu, at once adopting, transforming, and resisting Canaanite ideas and practices.

Fertility was a central component of biblical religion, a result, no doubt, of the Israelites' sense of their origins as a small, weak people.[3] As Psalms 105:12 puts it: "They were then few in number, a mere handful, sojourning there [in the land of Canaan]." Psalms 127:3–7 beautifully captures the connection between fertility and national power, represented respectively by female and male metaphors:

Sons are the provision of the Lord;
the fruit of the womb, His reward,
Like arrows in the hand of a warrior
are sons born to a man in his youth.
Happy is the man who fills his quiver with them;
they shall not be put to shame
when they contend with the enemy at the gate.

This sense that fertility was a precarious matter accompanied the ancient Israelites from the recurring stories of female infertility in Genesis to the thundering threats of the later prophetic texts:

From birth, from the womb, from conception
Ephraim's glory shall be like birds that fly away.
Even if they rear their infants, I will bereave them of men.
Give them, O Lord—give them what?
Give them a womb that miscarries
And shriveled breasts! (Hosea 9:11–12, 14)

Like intermarriage, the fear of the demographic demise of the Jewish people is an ancient theme in Jewish history, with its roots in biblical culture.

Preoccupied as it was with defining its national myth, biblical culture repeatedly situated sexuality in national and political contexts that pertained to fertility. With the exception of the Song of Songs, the Bible displays little interest in erotic desire as such. Desire was instead subordinated to communal concerns, and as long as it was expressed in its proper place, it did not pose a problem, as it would for later Jewish cultures. In this respect, the Hebrew Bible—although it is the sacred text on which all of subsequent Judaism is based—is in some ways disconnected from the later tradition. Let us therefore consider biblical culture on its own terms, as the first chapter in our history of Jewish sexuality.

Ruth: Sexual Subversion and the Origins of King David

We begin with the Book of Ruth. This ancient folktale artfully reveals many of the central themes of sexuality in ancient Judaism.[4] As the story of the journey of an Israelite family out of the land of Israel and then back again, it defines many of the boundaries—both geographic and metaphoric—that would preoccupy the Jewish people in the ancient period and, indeed, throughout the subsequent ages. Ruth addresses questions of fertility and lineage, and its iconoclastic solutions to these problems are emblematic of similarly surprising solutions found elsewhere in the biblical record.

Ruth is the story of the family of Elimelech of Bethlehem. In time of famine the family emigrates to Moab, where Elimelech's two sons marry Moabite women but fail to have children. After all the men in the family die in the foreign land, Elimelech's wife, Naomi, and her two daughters-in-law begin the journey back to Bethlehem. One of the two, Orpah, returns to Moab on the advice of Naomi, but the other, Ruth, pledges eternal loyalty to Naomi and stays with her. In Bethlehem, Naomi instructs Ruth to glean in the fields of Elimelech's distant kinsman Boaz and then to approach him at night on the threshing floor, where he has fallen asleep from drink. Boaz awakes and pledges to marry Ruth and thus redeem the inheritance of her deceased husband and father-in-law. After persuading an anonymous closer relative of Elimelech to forgo his duty as redeemer, Boaz marries Ruth, who then conceives and bears the child who will be the grandfather of the future King David. Thus, a story that begins with death and infertility ends with the birth of David's ancestor.

Eroticism, procreation, and agricultural fertility are intertwined throughout the book, as befits a tale from a predominantly agrarian society.[5] The "house of bread" (Bethlehem) has become infertile and the man, Elimelech, seeks fertility in the "fields" of Moab. Yet he and his sons die there, childless: the fields that had appeared so fertile from afar become the graveyard of Elimelech's lineage, the burial ground of his own fertility. Indeed, the Hebrew word for a barren woman, *akarah,* literally means "uprooted."[6] To leave one's land is to become infertile, and, in this story it is the foreigner, Ruth, who restores fertility.

Naomi and Ruth return to Bethlehem at the beginning of the barley harvest. The ensuing action, from Ruth's gleaning in the fields to her probable seduction of Boaz on the threshing floor, connects the harvest of grain with sexuality and reproduction. These interlocked themes may well have been taken directly from older Canaanite myths.[7] If so, however, the author of Ruth, like other biblical authors, covered up the cultic origins of the story.

The lineage of Elimelech is restored by an act of implied sexual transgression. In the charged scene of Ruth accosting the drunken, sleeping Boaz on the threshing floor, the text repeatedly uses words like "to lie down" and "to know," both of which have clear sexual connotations.[8] Ruth uncovers Boaz's legs, an occasional biblical euphemism for the genitals.[9] The text alludes to a Genesis legend here, for Noah, too, had his nakedness revealed, in his case when he lay drunk in his tent after leaving the ark (Genesis 9:21). To "uncover the genitals" is the technical term in biblical law for a sexual violation,[10] and Ruth's act alludes suggestively to the sin of Noah's son Ham.

The ancient audience would have recognized these terms as implying that Ruth actually seduced Boaz. After this delicately suggested seduction, Ruth invites Boaz to spread his "wing" (the corner of his cloak) over her, a phrase that evidently means marriage.[11] To "uncover" the genitals is a transgression, but to "cover" them by marriage makes sexual activity permissible. Thus, Ruth subverts sexual custom in order to secure her marriage to Boaz; only by bending the social norms can she win her destined mate and give fertility to the line of David.

The erotic initiative in this tale falls, significantly, to women.[12] When Ruth chooses to remain with Naomi and return to Bethlehem, the text says that she "clung to her" *(davkah bah),* just as Genesis 2:24 states that when a man leaves his father and mother, he "clings" *(davak)* to his wife. It is this "clinging" of Ruth to Naomi, the bond between these women, that guarantees the continuity of Elimelech's line. So predominant is the role of Naomi that the women of the town, who form a kind of Greek chorus, name Ruth's son after her, rather than after her deceased husband, saying "a son has been born to Naomi" (4:17). Ruth is a surrogate for the postmenopausal Naomi, much like the famous concubines of Genesis: Hagar for Sarah, Zilpah for Leah, and Bilhah for Rachel. Thus, although the story concludes with the male lineage that leads from Boaz to King David, Ruth's great-grandson, it is really Naomi whose name is perpetuated.[13]

The Book of Ruth therefore at once reinforces *and* subverts patriarchy. Women play the critical role of ensuring fertility—a role perhaps dictated by patriarchy—but they do so by subversion of sexual custom. This ostensibly antipatriarchal role is implicitly based on a view of women as erotic creatures whose sexuality could just as well be destructive.[14] We shall presently see how this projection of ambivalent sexual power onto women is repeated in other stories, some of which are explicitly connected to Ruth, as if for the biblical authors women represented the subversion of norms necessary for fertility.

The ultimate purpose of Ruth's sexual initiative is to bear the child who will be the grandfather of King David. Here too, however, the story challenges biblical norms by emphasizing Ruth's Moabite origins; no fewer than five times in this short book she is referred to as "Ruth the Moabite" or the

"Moabite girl." Readers over the centuries, including the rabbis of the talmudic period, could not fail to notice the glaring contradiction between Ruth's origins and the law of Deuteronomy 23:4: "No Ammonite or Moabite shall be admitted into the congregation of the Lord."[15] The Moabites were not only periodic enemies of the Israelites, but the Bible's own account of their origins casts doubt on their legitimacy. According to Genesis 19:30–38, the Moabites were the product of an incestuous union between Lot, Abraham's nephew, and one of his daughters. Following the destruction of Sodom and Gomorrah, from which they were saved, Lot and his daughters found refuge in a cave. Believing that they were the only people left in the world, the two women got their father drunk and had sexual relations with him. Out of this incest came two sons, Moab, the eponymous father of the Moabites, and Ben-ammi, the first of the Ammonites, precisely the two nations forbidden by Deuteronomy to enter the congregation of the Lord. As in Ruth, it is women who ensure fertility by bending or breaking with convention; and as in Ruth, the sexual ruse involves the seduction of an inebriated older relative.[16]

The story of Ruth, then, reunites the two branches of Abraham's family. Boaz represents the line of Judah, Jacob's son and Abraham's great-grandson, whereas Ruth represents Moab, the son of Lot, Abraham's nephew. King David is the eventual product of this genetic recombination, and to complete the story, the son Solomon chooses to succeed him, Rehoboam, is born of an Ammonite mother (1 Kings 14:21). According to these genealogies, the Davidic dynasty had Moabite and Ammonite, as well as Israelite, origins. These stories may have been primarily ideological in intent; since David had conquered the Moabites and Ammonites, the legend that the Judean kings shared the blood of their vassal peoples would have served the political end of helping to solidify the Davidic empire.

But there may have been a broader motive at work, as well. The biblical concept of fertility demanded the suspension of norms when it came to the birth of heroes. The crossing of boundaries, both sexual and ethnic, became a central component in the ideology of the monarchy as well as in the national ideology of the Israelite people. Ruth is doubly antinormative: a woman who takes the sexual initiative in a patriarchal culture and a Moabite who becomes the ancestor of King David, despite legal bans on intermarriage.[17]

The Politics of Sexual Subversion

The sexual deceits practiced by Ruth and by Lot's daughters are but two of many more instances in the biblical record in which subversion of sexual norms is central to the lives of heroes like David or to the survival of whole nations, including Israel itself. Both Abraham and Isaac become dangerously entangled with foreign kings by passing off their wives as their sisters (Genesis 12, 20, and 26), in clear violation of biblical law.

Sarah may actually have been Abraham's half sister, for so he claims to Abimelech in Genesis 20:12. If so, their marriage would violate the incest law of Leviticus 18:11: "The nakedness of your father's wife's daughter [that is, a half sister born of a common father but different mothers] . . . she is your sister; do not uncover her nakedness." Furthermore, Genesis 12 says that when Sarah poses as Abraham's sister in Egypt, she is taken into Pharaoh's household, implying that they have sexual relations. If so, she has committed adultery with Abraham's complicity. This is precisely the argument made by Abimelech in the case of Isaac's wife Rebecca (Genesis 26:10–11). Finally, Jacob, the eponymous father of the Israelite nation, marries two sisters, Leah and Rachel, in seeming violation of the law of Leviticus 18:18, which prohibits marrying two sisters while both are alive.

All of these stories no doubt preceded the Levitical incest laws by many centuries; what is therefore noteworthy is that they were included in the biblical text. The authors or editors who produced the text were surely aware of the flagrant contradictions between the laws and the narratives, but they must have seen those contradictions as serving an important cultural function. The creation of the Israelite nation was seen by these later authors as a result of the suspension of conventions, a sign, perhaps, of divine favor for a ragtag, ethnically mixed people. Far from a disgrace to be hidden, sexual subversion, like the repeated preference for younger over older sons, hints at the unexpected character of God's covenant with Israel.[18]

All of these themes found their most vivid expression in the stories of David's origins, his rise to power, and his reign as king of Israel and Judah. This is perhaps not surprising since the Davidic dynasty, which was to rule the Kingdom of Judah until its demise in 586 B.C.E., was the dominant political force in whose shadow and later memory most of the biblical text was composed. The royal theology became a synecdoche for Israel's national identity.

The sexual transgressions that underlie David's lineage are particularly manifest in the last chapter of Ruth. The people at the gate conclude their fertility blessing to Boaz: "And may your house be like the house of Perez whom Tamar bore to Judah—through the offspring which the Lord will give you by this young woman" (4:12). According to the genealogy appended to the end of the book, Boaz's ancestor was Perez, the son of Jacob's son Judah. The author of Ruth alludes specifically to Perez because of the striking similarities between the story of the birth of Perez, recorded in Genesis 38, and the Book of Ruth.[19]

Genesis 38 interrupts the Joseph stories to relate the following account of Jacob's son Judah.[20] Judah has three sons by his marriage with a Canaanite woman. He marries his eldest son, Er, to a woman named Tamar; when Er dies, he gives her to his second son, Onan, in order to perpetuate Er's name. Onan resists this levirate duty by spilling his seed on the ground instead of engaging in procreative intercourse. He, too, dies. Judah promises Tamar to give her his third son, Shelah, when the young boy reaches maturity, but he breaks his promise. Tamar then disguises herself as a prostitute, seduces her father-in-law, and becomes pregnant. Instead of paying the "prostitute," Judah leaves his staff and seal with her as pledges, and Tamar subsequently uses them to prove his paternity. Out of this transgressive affair come the twins Perez and Zerah.

If the author of Ruth only hints at Ruth's sexual deviousness to achieve her end, Genesis 38 is much more explicit: relations between daughter-in-law and father-in-law are forbidden as incest (Leviticus 18:15). Yet the story treats Tamar's subterfuge as thoroughly justifiable to right the failure of Judah and his sons to provide her with children. The story allows her to take matters into her own hands and violate sexual norms.

The associations between the Ruth and Tamar stories are too remarkable to be coincidental. Both stories begin with the death of two brothers (and, in the case of Ruth, their father as well). Both involve levirate (Deuteronomy 25:5–10), the custom by which the brother (or, in the case of Ruth, a more distant relative) of a man who dies childless must marry the widow in order to perpetuate the dead man's name and provide for the continuity of his inheritance.[21] In both stories, the levir, or redeemer, fails to fulfill his obligation, and the widow must take bold action, including sexual transgression, to ensure a child.

The levirate law itself is, in fact, the consummate violation of sexual boundaries for the sake of fertility. The incest laws of Leviticus 18:16 and 20:21 explicitly forbid a man from having sexual relations with his brother's wife; in the second law, the punishment for violation is childlessness. The case of the levirate is a complete reversal: the very point of allowing a man to marry his deceased brother's wife is to produce a child. The levirate and incest laws therefore appear to be conscious mirror images of one another: just as the levirate custom takes effect only if the deceased brother is childless, so relations with the wife of that brother when he is alive will result in infertility for the offender. In the first case, levirate practice suspends the normal incest laws in order to guarantee the continuity of a lineage; in the second, violation of the incest law results in the disruption of the offender's lineage. Even though the levirate served to guarantee a family's fertility, it still aroused enormous ambivalence: because there were circumstances, albeit unusual, when a brother-in-law was permitted sexually, he might have been a more tempting object of incest than other relations.[22]

It is this problem implied in the levirate law that gives the erotic charge and overtones of subversive sexuality to the threshing-floor scene in Ruth and to Tamar's seduction of Judah. The two stories cast long shadows on the legitimacy of David's lineage, from both a strictly legal and a broader cultural point of view. Neither story is presented as polemic or apology, though, which suggests that the subversion was meant to be emphasized rather than obscured.

In terms of comparative mythology, these stories reverse the pattern of many ancient myths in which the king-hero has legitimate origins that are then lost by circumstance: his parents abandon him, he is raised by peasants or animals, and through a series of adventures, he eventually returns to his parents' household and to his predestined status.[23] Thus, Oedipus murders his father and has sexual relations with the mother out of ignorance of his true, royal identity. This typology is absent in the David stories, as well as in other myths of the origins of biblical heroes. The biblical stories correspond instead to a different kind of folkloric motif: the powerless youngest son (often, as in the case of David, the seventh son) who outwits his older brothers and surprises everyone by attaining fame and fortune through cleverness and sheer good luck.[24] The hero, like Israel as a whole, is the least expected: legitimacy is not preordained, but is instead achieved by subverting the established order.

David's rise to power and his reign are no less bound up with violation of sexual boundaries than are his origins, just as his whole political career is marked by an unconventional, even scandalous path. He appropriates two mens' wives, Abigail, the wife of Nabal (1 Samuel 25), and Bathsheba, the wife of Uriah the Hittite (2 Samuel 11). In the first case, Nabal (the name itself is derogatory, meaning "boor" or "scoundrel") is said to wrong David by refusing to pay him protection money. As a reward to David for not attacking Nabal himself and as punishment for Nabal's "crime," God strikes Nabal dead, thus clearing the way for David to marry Abigail. Abigail is portrayed as God's agent in the death of her husband: he becomes like a stone and subsequently dies when she tells of David's intention to murder him. Her words, it is implied, are what actually kill him. Here is truly a lethal woman, but one whose behavior appears to be fully legitimated by God.

David's adultery with Bathsheba is the dark version of the Abigail story: the author roundly condemns David's theft of another man's wife.[25] David sleeps with Bathsheba while her husband, Uriah, is at the battlefront: the king is having fun in bed while the general is in the trenches. When Bathsheba becomes pregnant, David tries to cover up his own paternity by ordering her husband back, in hopes that he will sleep with his wife. Uriah refuses, even when David gets him drunk. Unable to hide his crime, David has Uriah killed at the front. Bathsheba then marries David, but the child born of their adulterous union dies at the hand of God.

The reference to alcohol here suggests that the story of Uriah and Bathsheba should be read against that of Nabal and Abigail. Nabal, too, becomes drunk while he is having a feast "fit for a king" (1 Samuel 25:36), ominously foreshadowing David's drunken feast with Uriah. When the effects of the wine wear off the next morning, Abigail utters her deadly words. Uriah, however, does not succumb to the effects of drink: as opposed to Nabal and David, who is now subtly equated with his late enemy, Uriah is a righteous man. Indeed, Uriah's behavior under the influence of alcohol contradicts the standard type scene in which figures like Noah, Lot, and Boaz succumb to sexual temptation while drunk.[26]

David has therefore murdered a man who was not only innocent but, we are led to understand, righteous as well. The prophet Nathan then prophesies that God will "make a calamity rise against you from within your house; I will take your wives and give them to another man before your very eyes and he will sleep with your wives under this very sun" (2 Samuel 12:11). The prophecy is fulfilled: David's adultery with Bathsheba unleashes a chain of sexual violations by his sons that sunder his house and bring civil war to Israel. Amnon rapes his half sister Tamar and Absalom, Tamar's full brother, avenges the incest by killing Amnon. Absalom flees David's wrath, and a full-fledged revolt breaks out. At a critical stage in the revolt (2 Samuel 16:20–22), Absalom fulfills Nathan's prophecy by sleeping with David's concubines, a sexual violation that, like Reuben's intercourse with Jacob's concubine (Genesis 35:22 and 49:4), signifies political and familial usurpation.[27] Absalom performs this politico-sexual ritual in public, on the rooftop "with the full knowledge of all Israel." Moreover it symbolically mirrors David's first view of Bathsheba bathing on her rooftop. Sexual betrayal thus comes full circle.

When read against each other, however, the stories of David's marriages to Abigail and Bathsheba reveal a startling reversal of moral judgment. Despite the apparent divine sanction for David's marriage to Abigail, it is not Abigail but Bathsheba, the wife acquired by adultery and murder, who gives birth to Solomon, arguably Israel's greatest king. The civil war wrought as a result of David's sexual crime has a hidden teleology: it clears the way for Solomon to become king by eliminating his competitors. Once again, erotic transgressions are covertly positive in the political fate of ancient Israel: God, it would seem, straddles both sides of the legal fence in order to advance the fortunes of his chosen people.

. . .

Sacred and Secular Fertility

Although biblical culture clearly regarded God as the hidden puppet master of Israelite history, the role played by God varies remarkably from text to text. God, so much in the foreground in the infertility stories of Genesis, is virtually absent in Ruth.[28] This is true for other transgressive stories as well, such as the story of Tamar and Judah. It is as if God must step backstage in order to make space for human actors, and particularly women, to bend social custom and law, just as the world itself contains both impurity and purity. God's absence implicitly sanctions these inversions and subversions.

Perhaps the most secular of all books of the Bible is the Song of Songs, the most erotic text in the Jewish tradition. There have been those who have argued that the Song has a Canaanite or perhaps even Indian cultic background and that many of the strange images can be explained in light of religious rites.[29] Yet, the author of the collection of poems that has come down to us suppressed any such religious overtones, if ever they existed. The Song appears to be a deliberate attempt to write a secular poem in which the Shulamit and her lover are human. Unlike Canaanite religion and unlike many other biblical texts dealing with sexuality, the Song is not directly concerned with fertility. Instead, it explores the tension between desire and fulfillment.[30] As a poetic treatment of the problem of pure desire, the Song of Songs anticipated later talmudic and medieval Jewish culture more than it resembled other books of the Bible.

What the Song does share with other biblical literature is the theme of transgressive female behavior.[31] The woman plays a sexually aggressive role; she violates boundaries by searching in the streets for her beloved; she also uses a bold, incestuous metaphor as she addresses her lover: "If only it could be as with a brother, as if you had nursed at my mother's breast: then I could kiss you when I met you in the street, and no one would despise me" (8:1). But the watchmen who find her in the street beat her, as if to control her unconventional behavior (5:7), much as her brothers force her to guard their vineyards (1:6). Perhaps the Song of Songs represents, then, a poetic rendition of the tensions between narrative subversions and legal constraints that are so essential to the Bible's treatment of sexuality elsewhere.

In its affirmation of eroticism, the Song of Songs tells us something critical about the biblical view of sexuality. For biblical culture, sexuality within its proper boundaries was not a problem, although the boundaries themselves were repeatedly contested. The sexual act itself was cultically defiling, but this was because of the divine power associated with it. The celebration of erotic desire in Song of Songs must surely be related to this dialectical theology. Because the divine was only indirectly involved in procreation, however, eroticism was properly the realm of the secular, as it is in the Song. God might intervene to guarantee fertility, but actual sexual relations take place between human beings, and the Israelite cult itself involved no ritual sexual acts, either literal or metaphoric.[32]

Later rabbinic and patristic interpretations of the Song of Songs would infuse a theological dimension into this most secular of poems: the poem, they would say, is really about the love between God and Israel or God and the Christian church. In advancing this argument, the rabbis and church fathers unwittingly resurrected the possible Canaanite cultic background of the Song. Such theological allegories also contained a radical new possibility: human love may be the model for the love of God, but love of God might come to compete with human love. The marriage metaphor of the biblical covenant demanded exclusive love between Israel and God: monotheism is the theological version of monogamy.

. . .

Notes

Abbreviations: m.=Mishnah

1. A recent example of this kind of argument can be found in Gerda Lerner, *The Creation of Patriarchy* (New York, 1986). Against this view, see Tikva Frymer-Kensky, *In the Wake of the Goddesses: Women, Culture, and the Biblical Transformation of Pagan Myth* (New York, 1992). At times, Christian feminist interpretation of the Hebrew Bible unwittingly verges on anti-Semitism. See Susannah Heschel, "Anti-Judaism in Christian Feminist Theology," *Tikkun* (May–June 1990): 25–28, 95–97; Katharina von Kellenbach, "Antisemitismus in biblischer Matriarchatsforschung?" *Berliner Theologische Zeitschrift* 3, no. 1 (1986): 144–47; and idem, "Anti-Judaism in Christian-Rooted Feminist Writings: An Analysis of Major U.S. American and West German Feminist Theologians" (Ph.D. diss. Temple University, 1990).
2. This discussion parallels and owes much to Regina Schwartz. See Schwartz, "Adultery in the House of David: The Metanarrative of Biblical Scholarship and the Narratives of the Bible," *Semeia* (forthcoming) and her forthcoming book on identity and violence in the Hebrew Bible.
3. For the connection between the theology of fertility and the social life of the ancient Israelites, see Carol Meyers, *Discovering Eve: Ancient Israelite Women in Context* (New York, 1988).
4. Without attempting to solve the still hotly debated question of when it was written, it is clear that Ruth stands at a self-reflective distance from some of the more ancient biblical traditions. It is my contention that the author wrote substantially later than the time of the composition of the Genesis stories. He or

she obviously lived *after* the period of the judges (ca. 1200–1050 B.C.E.) but sought to re-create the ambiance of that evidently distant age. For a bibliography of some of the recent scholarship on dating Ruth, see Susan Niditch, "Legends of Wise Heroes and Heroines," in Douglas A. Knight and Gene M. Tucker, eds., *The Hebrew Bible and Its Modern Interpreters* (Philadelphia, 1985), 451; and Edward F. Campbell Jr., *The Anchor Bible Ruth* (Garden City, N.Y., 1975), 23–28. Dates range from the early monarchy (ca. 950) to the late monarchy (ca. 600) to the postexilic period (500–400 B.C.E.). I assume a date during the latter part of the monarchy, probably the time of Deuteronomy (seventh century B.C.E.). It may be that the genealogy at the end of chapter 4 was appended later, but there is no reason to assign even it to a postexilic date.

5. For some acute observations on eroticism and agriculture in Ruth, see Calum Carmichael, "'Treading' in the Book of Ruth," *Zeitschrift für alttestamentliche Wissenschaft* 92 (1980): 248–66. For discussion of the connections between agricultural and human fertility in the Bible, see Howard Eilberg-Schwartz, *The Savage in Judaism: Excursions in an Anthropology of Israelite Religion and Ancient Judaism* (Bloomington, Ind., 1990), chaps. 5, 6.
6. See Ilana Pardes, *Countertraditions in the Bible: A Feminist Approach* (Cambridge, Mass., 1992), 113.
7. The threshing floor may well have been a Canaanite cultic site, and the prophet Hosea claims that it was used for acts of ritual intercourse (Hosea 9:1–2). On "threshing" or "treading" as a euphemism for sexual intercourse, see Carmichael, "'Treading,'" 249 n. 4. For the argument that the story of Ruth was originally a Canaanite cultic myth, see W. E. Staples, "The Book of Ruth," *American Journal of Semitic Literature* 53 (1936–37): 145–47; H. B. May, "Ruth's Visit to the High Place," *Journal of the Royal Asiatic Society* (1939): 75–78; S. L. Shearman and J. Biggs, "Divine-Human Conflicts in the Old Testament," *Journal of Near Eastern Studies* 28 (1969): 235 ff.; and G. R. H. Wright, "The Mother-Maid at Bethlehem," *Zeitschrift für alttestamentliche Wissenschaft* 98 (1986): 56–72.
8. See Carmichael, "'Treading'"; and idem, *Women, Law, and the Genesis Traditions* (Edinburgh, 1979), 74–93. Campbell supports this interpretation, *Anchor Bible Ruth,* 121 n. 4 and 131–32, as does, in a different vein, Mieke Bal, *Lethal Love: Feminist Literary Readings of Biblical Love Stories* (Bloomington, Ind., 1987), chap. 3. Against Carmichael, see Anthony Phillips, "The Book of Ruth: Deception and Shame," *Journal of Jewish Studies* 36 (1986): 11–13.
9. Judges 3:24, 1 Samuel 24:3, 2 Kings 18:27, Isaiah 7:20, Ezekiel 16:25.
10. See, for example, Leviticus 18:6–18.
11. See Deuteronomy 23:1, 27:20, and Ezekiel 16:8.
12. For analyses of the book along these lines, see Phyllis Trible, *God and the Rhetoric of Sexuality* (Philadelphia, 1978), 166–99; Bal, *Lethal Love,* chap. 3; and Pardes, *Countertraditions in the Bible,* chap. 6.
13. It is remarkable that Boaz, rather than Elimelech and Ruth's first husband, Mahlon, is the ancestor of David, for the point of the levirate is to perpetuate

the name of the childless deceased. In a sense, the death of Elimelech and his sons at the beginning of the book is final; instead of perpetuating their names, Boaz's redemption of Ruth creates a new family with Boaz as the patriarch and Naomi as the matriarch.

14. Bal has suggested the notion of "lethal love" to explain the role of women in many biblical stories. While this point is very persuasive, it seems to me that she makes the biblical view of women's sexuality too one-sidedly negative.
15. See also 1 Kings 11:1–2 and Nehemiah 13:23–28. For an argument that the prohibition on Moabites and Ammonites was an attack on the Davidic lineage, see Jacob Milgrom, "Religious Conversion and the Revolt Model for the Formation of Israel," *Journal of Biblical Literature* 101 (1982): 169–76. The rabbis tried to harmonize the law with Ruth by arguing that the law applied only to male Moabites and Ammonites (m. Yevamot 8.3), but since the two passages above refer specifically to women, the rabbinic exegesis is not plausible. Some have argued that by celebrating King David's Moabite origins, the Book of Ruth served as a polemic against either the laws of Deuteronomy that forbade intermarriage or Ezra's dissolution of marriages between Jews and foreigners after the return from Babylonia (ca. 440 B.C.E.). If David's own great-grandmother was a Moabite, then perhaps lesser Israelites might be equally justified in taking foreign spouses. Nevertheless, Ruth does not have the flavor of a polemic, and a more likely explanation for the contradiction is that it was written before the laws of Deuteronomy were in force.
16. For a structuralist analysis of Ruth in the context of this and other stories of sexual subversion (Genesis 38), see Harold Fisch, "Ruth and the Structure of Covenant History," *Vetus Testamentum* 32 (1982): 425–37.
17. See Pardes, *Countertraditions in the Bible,* chap. 6.
18. The Israelites were a young nation, not an old people like the Egyptians and the Sumerians. They evolved a theology of election that explained why, contrary to nature, God had chosen this weakest and youngest of nations to inherit the land. This is also the explanation for the narratives in which younger sons supplant elder sons in violation of the law of primogeniture in Deuteronomy 21:15–17. In story after story, the younger son is preferred over the older: Abel over Cain, Isaac over Ishmael, Jacob over Esau, Joseph and Benjamin over their older brothers, Perez over Zerah, Ephraim over Manasseh, David over his older brothers. Primogeniture was common practice throughout the ancient Near East. See, for example, the Middle Assyrian law that is quite close to the biblical: James B. Pritchard, ed., *Ancient Near Eastern Texts* (Princeton, N.J., 1958), 1:185. See further I. Mendelsohn, "On the Preferential Status of the Elder Son," *Bulletin of the American Schools of Oriental Study* 156 (1959): 38–40. But there are also accounts of the younger son eclipsing the older in ancient Near Eastern literature. See Pritchard, 289, 557, 603–4 (pars. 23–24).
19. For some recent analyses of the Tamar and Judah story, including its connections to Ruth, see Susan Niditch, "The Wronged Woman Righted: An Analysis of Genesis 38," *Harvard Theological Review* 72 (1979): 143–49; J. A. Emerton,

"Judah and Tamar," *Vetus Testamentum* 29 (1979): 403–15 and bibliography; Carmichael, *Women, Law, and the Genesis Traditions,* 57–73; and Fisch, "Ruth and the Structure of Covenant History."

20. Robert Alter has shown how the editor of Genesis artfully tied Genesis 38 to the Joseph cycle. See Alter, *The Art of Biblical Narrative* (New York, 1981), 3–12. For a very different analysis that also places the story in its context, see Bal, *Lethal Love,* chap. 4.

21. For a recent summary of the bibliography on levirate in Ruth compared with the levirate law of Deuteronomy 25:5ff., and Genesis 38, see Niditch, "Legends of Wise Heroes and Heroines," 452–53. See, in particular, D. R. G. Beattie, "The Book of Ruth as Evidence for Israelite Legal Practice," *Vetus Testamentum* 24 (1974): 251–67; Calum Carmichael, "A Ceremonial Crux: Removing a Man's Sandal as a Female Gesture of Contempt," *Journal of Biblical Literature* 96 (1977): 321–36; Robert Gordis, "Love, Marriage, and Business in the Book of Ruth: A Chapter in Hebrew Customary Law," in Howard Bream et al., eds., *A Light unto My Path: Old Testament Studies in Honor of Jacob M. Myers* (Philadelphia, 1974), 241–64; Baruch Levine, "In Praise of the Israelite *Mispaha:* Legal Themes in the Book of Ruth," in H. B. Huffmon et al., eds., *The Quest for the Kingdom of God: Studies in Honor of George E. Mendenhall* (Winona Lake, Ind., 1983), 95–108; and H. H. Rowley, "The Marriage of Ruth," in Rowley, *The Servant of the Lord and Other Essays on the Old Testament* (Oxford, 1965), 171–94.

22. The striking tension between sexual prohibitions and the levirate can also be deduced from a very interesting law in Deuteronomy:

> If two men get into a fight with each other, a man and his brother, and the wife of one comes up to save her husband from his antagonist and puts out her hand and seizes him by the genitals, you shall cut off her hand; show no pity. (25:11–12)

The wife is mentioned, rather than any other intervener, presumably because she is forbidden to have sexual contact with any other man. If she touches the other's genitals, even to defend her husband, she crosses a sexual boundary and causes him the shame of illegitimate exposure (the rare term *mevoshav* used for genitals is derived from "shame" [*bosh*]). The text also states, seemingly superfluously, that it is not just any two men who are fighting, but two *brothers.* This law follows immediately after the law of levirate marriage (Deuteronomy 25:5–10). As in the Levitical law prohibiting incest with a brother's wife, the legislator here is giving a warning: a woman is only allowed to touch the genitals of her brother-in-law in the exceptional circumstance when her husband dies childless; in all other cases, including a fight between the brothers, she is forbidden any sexual contact with him.

23. For a very useful collection of such myths, see Otto Rank, *The Myth of the Birth of the Hero,* ed. Philip Freund (New York, 1959), 14–64. For some interesting reflections on the Bible, with less persuasive psychoanalytic observations, see Avshalom Elitzur, *Into the Holy of Holies: Psychoanalytic Insights into the Bible and Judaism* (in Hebrew) (Tel Aviv, 1988), 173–211.

24. See Judah Goldin, "The Youngest Son or Where Does Genesis 38 Belong," *Journal of Biblical Literature* 96 (1977): 27–44. Goldin argues that this theme in the Genesis stories is a folkloristic way of turning the world upside down, a built-in correction to the abuse of the law: "The folk love such stories because they are a weapon against the powerful." This is an attractive theory and probably partly true, but it ignores the ideological function the stories fulfilled for Israelite identity.
25. See the interpretations of the Bathsheba story in Schwartz, "Adultery in the House of David"; Meir Sternberg, *The Poetics of Biblical Narrative: Ideological Literature and the Drama of Reading* (Bloomington, Ind., 1985), 190–222; Alter, *The Art of Biblical Narrative,* 75–76; and Bal, *Lethal Love,* chap. 1. None of these commentators points out the connections to the Abigail story.
26. On the theme of drunkenness in the Bible, see Hirsch H. Cohen, *The Drunkenness of Noah* (University, Ala., 1974).
27. A concubine probably had the same status as a wife with respect to the incest prohibitions. Three other instances of the same kind of behavior can be found from the period of the early monarchy (2 Samuel 3:7, 16:20–22, 1 Kings 2:28). It would appear from these passages that either marrying or having intercourse with the father's concubine may have been a symbolic way of claiming rights of inheritance or succession in the case of the monarchy. See the analysis of these incidents by Raphael Patai, *Sex and Family in the Bible and the Middle East* (Garden City, N.Y., 1959), 98–103.
28. Most of the references to the divine in Ruth are essentially formulaic: "the Lord has dealt harshly with me," "the Lord let her conceive," etc. See Campbell, *Anchor Bible Ruth,* 28–29. The Midrash implicitly recognized this theological weakness in Ruth by claiming that Ruth bore her son as a result of a miracle. See Ruth Rabbah 7.14.
29. Marvin Pope has argued that the Song reflects rituals in which eroticism and funeral rites were bound up together. See Pope, *Anchor Bible Song of Songs* (Garden City, N.Y., 1977), 210–29. For other cultic interpretations, see Pope, 145–53.
30. See Ariel and Chana Bloch, *The Song of Songs: A Translation and Commentary* (New York, forthcoming).
31. I am indebted in this analysis and in my reading of the Song of Songs as a whole to Pardes, *Countertraditions in the Bible,* chap. 7.
32. See Frymer-Kensky, *In the Wake of the Goddesses,* 97–99.

[25]

The Gender Symbolism of Kuan-yin Bodhisattva

Barbara E. Reed

All living beings are distressed
And bear unlimited pains;
Kuan-yin's profound wisdom and power
Can save the world from pain.
—from the *Lotus Sūtra*[1]

SOMEHOW DURING THE ASSIMILATION into Chinese culture Kuan-yin Bodhisattva underwent a sexual transformation. The male bodhisattva from India, Avalokiteśvara, became a beautiful white-robed Chinese woman. In addition to the sex change, the female symbolism of the bodhisattva was expanded further by the addition of *yin* symbols (for example, moon, water, vase) from the *yin-yang* polarity of Chinese thought. In a Chinese culture dominated by Confucian social values, Chinese women saw this female symbol as particularly relevant to their problems as women. Not only was Kuan-yin an object of devotion for Chinese women, she also was a popular subject for women artists from at least the Ming dynasty (1368–1644).

SOURCE: Reprinted from Barbara E. Reed, "The Gender Symbolism of Kuan-yin Bodhisattva," from *Buddhism, Sexuality, and Gender,* ed. Jose Ignacio Cabezon (Albany, N.Y.: State University of New York Press, 1992), by permission of the State University of New York Press.

This essay examines whether the female symbol of Kuan-yin Bodhisattva helped Chinese women transcend the restrictions of a Confucian-defined, male-dominated society or whether the symbol tended to reinforce those restrictions. This essay suggests that women saw the symbol of Kuan-yin Bodhisattva as clearly liberating them from the physiological suffering particular to the female *sex* (that is, those problems due to menstruation and childbirth). But the liberating symbolism of Kuan-yin is more complex in the ways it alleviates women's suffering due to culturally defined *gender* restrictions. This essay considers the ways Kuan-yin Bodhisattva has both liberated women from culturally defined roles in family and marriage and also accommodated women to those roles by alleviating some of their suffering.

The Development of Kuan-yin Bodhisattva

The earliest Buddhist texts mentioned only male buddhas and bodhisattvas; female bodhisattvas were first introduced around the late fourth century.[2] Avalokiteśvara, a male bodhisattva in India, became known as Kuan-yin in China and was viewed as female more often than male from the Sung dynasty (960–1127) to the present. Sinologists and buddhologists have produced several theories about the strange transformations of Avalokiteśvara in China: the translation of the Sanskrit name Avalokiteśvara ("the lord who looks down") into the Chinese Kuan-yin ("one who observes the sounds") and the metamorphosis of the bodhisattva into female form. Causes cited for the sexual transformation include the growing popularity of Tārā, the female consort of Avalokiteśvara; the amalgamation of Kuan-yin with Taoist goddesses such as Hsi Wang-mu, Queen Mother of the West; and the Chinese tendency to associate compassion with women because of the nature of the Chinese family.[3] I am concerned in this chapter not with the process by which Kuan-yin became female, but rather with the symbolism of the evolved female figure of Kuan-yin and her impact on the spiritual and worldly aspirations of Chinese women.

Kuan-yin's popularity grew with that of the scriptures in which her compassion was described. As the *Lotus Sūtra* became more widely read and preached, especially in Kumarajīva's translation of 406 C.E., Kuan-yin became known as the salvific being of chapter 25. According to this scripture, Kuan-yin can appear in thirty-three forms, seven of them female: nun, Buddhist laywoman, elder's wife, householder's wife, officer's wife, a Brahman woman, and a young girl.[4] Kuan-yin promises to manifest herself in whatever form is effective to save all beings in distress—from fires, robbers, drowning, and more. And she promises to grant the wishes of her worshipers: for women Kuan-yin's assent to requests for bearing good sons or daughters is especially significant. Kuan-yin as a savior from physical disaster or childlessness is portrayed vividly in the Buddhist art of China.

As the Pure Land *sūtras* gained popularity after the sixth century, Kuan-yin also became popularly known as the compassionate assistant to A-mi-t'o (Amitabha) Buddha, who created a pure buddhaland in the west in which his followers could be reborn after death. In China Kuan-yin served to link the popular, but divergent, traditions of the Pure Land *sūtras* and the *Lotus Sūtra.* At Tun-huang Kuan-yin appears as the savior of the *Lotus Sūtra* in one painting, whereas in a nearby painting from the same period she appears as the assistant of A-mi-t'o Buddha, leading people to the pure buddhaland. It is Kuan-yin who unites these artistic images and the devotional traditions which they represent.[5]

The *Hua-yen (Avataṃsaka) Sūtra* enjoyed a contemporaneous popularity with the *Lotus Sūtra* during the middle of the T'ang dynasty (618–907). In the chapter of the *Avataṃsaka Sūtra* entitled "Entering the Dharmafield" *(Ru fa-chie p'in),* Kuan-yin appears as a bodhisattva residing on top of Mount P'u-t'o (Potala), which the Chinese located as an island off the coast of Chekiang. In this form Kuan-yin was associated with the Taoist Niang-niang goddesses who act as guardians of the ocean, and she became known as the guardian of the Southern Sea.[6]

Both the male representation of Kuan-yin and his female consort Tārā became popular among the Chinese through the dissemination of tantric texts, and *dharaṇī.* In the eighth century the introduction of a tantric scripture about a white-robed female Kuan-yin inspired artists and popular religious devotion. Folk religion accepted and promulgated Kuan-yin devotion with legends about her Chinese manifestations and the magical powers of her images. Some of the legends about her may have originated from Taoist or folk traditions in China; if so, they were later linked to the popular bodhisattva imported from India. In the T'ang dynasty (618–907) Kuan-yin began appearing often in female form; by the Sung (960–1127) the bodhisattva's female representations were more common than the male images. The legends and visual images made Kuan-yin both more Chinese and more female in the Sung dynasty.

By the Ming dynasty (1368–1644), innumerable forms of Kuan-yin had appeared in legends, paintings, and sculptures. The promise of the *Lotus Sūtra,* that she would appear to living beings in whatever form could best save them, engendered acceptance and enthusiasm for the diversity of images. She appeared in radically different forms, such as the Chinese princess Miao-shan, a common fisherwoman, a goddess springing from a clam, and thousand-armed and thousand-eyed deity whose multiple arms and eyes symbolize the infinite powers of her saving compassion.

. . .

Symbol of Liberation from Women's Suffering

According to Pure Land Buddhist scriptures, Kuan-yin liberates living beings from the six realms of suffering by leading them after death to the Pure Land of A-mi-t'o Buddha, where they are assured of eventual enlightenment.[7] She also liberates them from specific sufferings within each of the realms. The sufferings from which she liberates in this world are listed in the *Lotus Sūtra;* they include incineration, imprisonment, drowning, and victimization by wild animals and robbers. These can either be interpreted objectively (literally), as in folk religion, or subjectively (psychologically), the case with Buddhist philosophical schools. The lion symbolizes pride, fire is anger, robbers are wrong views, and so on.[8]

Kuan-yin offers liberation for all suffering beings, even if they do not deserve it. As Wolfram Eberhard has shown in his study of sin and guilt in traditional China, the Chinese have maintained in their popular religious views a tension between the idea of destiny and that of individual responsibility.[9] The divine salvation represented by Kuan-yin and others breaks through both fate and karma by allowing for the possibility of liberation through the compassionate actions of an external entity. Kuan-yin can intervene to prevent suffering for which one is destined or that one creates by sinning.

Women are in special need of salvation because of the impurities and inferiority of their female forms. According to popular Chinese beliefs, the blood of both menstruation and childbirth is spiritually polluting. Kuan-yin responds compassionately to the suffering to which women are doomed merely because of their sex. In a popular tale associated with P'u-t'o Island, Kuan-yin rescues a menstruating girl in need. She and her sister-in-law had been looking forward to making a pilgrimage to P'u-t'o Island for years. After overcoming numerous difficulties the two were about to dock when the girl began menstruating. Because she was in such impure state, she had to stay alone on the boat while everyone else went ashore. When she was stranded unexpectedly on the boat because of high tides and began suffering from thirst and hunger, a beautiful woman walked across the waters to present her with food. As in most Kuan-yin tales of rescue the identity of the woman is not clear until later: the sister-in-law finally returns and reports that the bottom of the robes of the Kuan-yin statue in the temple were dripping wet.[10]

Childbirth, although providing a Chinese woman status and some hope for eventual power in her husband's family, is also an act of extreme pollution according to moralistic texts. Giving birth is a sin for which women are tortured in hell, being placed in a pond of bloody birth fluids, and it is said that through the act of giving birth women pollute even heaven and earth. According to some Chinese, women who die in childbirth are pitiful souls in hell, pinned down by a heavy stone:

> The soul groans, yes, cries out in agony. As its eyes anxiously dart all around it sees only blood. It eats only blood clots; it drinks only bloody fluid. It is not the fresh blood of animals—which in its raw state is already an abomination for the people of Tsinghai—but inevitably foul vaginal blood and fluid. The soul cannot rest in the dreadful torment that it endures. Incessantly it groans and cries, but no friendly spirit approaches to help it. All good spirits shun the soul of a woman who has died in childbed.[11]

Kuan-yin saves suffering beings in all the Buddhist realms of existence, including these women in hell. In some versions of the Princess Miao-shan legend Kuan-yin descends to hell and disrupts it completely by her powerful compassion. Kuan-yin Bodhisattva saves women from their terrible suffering, whether it arises from childlessness or childbearing.

Liberation from Marriage

In several traditional legends Kuan-yin escapes marriage or helps another woman escape. Chinese women often considered marriage as one form of suffering in the human realm. A woman who married as an adult found herself in a house of strangers—married to a man she had never met and dominated by a resentful mother-in-law. In an alternative (and probably more painful) form of marriage popular in Taiwan until the early twentieth century, infant daughters were adopted by families to become the eventual wives of their sons. A woman often found the sexual demands of marriage to a man she viewed as a brother impossible to bear.[12] Moreover, marriage provided little security because a man could take a second wife or concubine. A woman's only hope was to bear a son and hope for his loyalty and generosity.

Biographies of virtuous women have been a popular means of teaching morality to Chinese women. Some were used to inculcate Confucian virtues, such as *Lieh nü chuan,* written by Liu Hsiang,[13] which was influential into the early Ming dynasty. Other biographies have served to spread Buddhist morality and the popular devotion to Kuan-yin. These are biographies of those to whom she appears and of those women in whose form she manifests herself.

The values taught in these stories differ greatly from those Confucian biographies extolling the Confucian virtues of *li* (propriety) and *hsiao* (filial piety). In the Buddhist biographies parents are to be honored, but only in a higher way. Parents may be spiritually liberated by their children, but after perhaps blatant rejection of their parents' stated worldly desires.

The most important biographical tale about Kuan-yin Bodhisattva is the legend of Princess Miao-shan, which provides her with a Chinese origin. There are several versions of this legend, but the most popular is the twelfth century one attributed to Pu-ming.[14] Miao-shan was the youngest of three daughters of King Miao-chuang. As the monarch had no sons the marriage of his daughters was crucial for his kingdom. Miao-shan, in un-Confucian manner, defied her parents and refused to marry. She wanted to devote herself to following the Buddhist path. One version of the story says that after she became a Buddhist nun her father took his revenge on her and her sister nuns by trying to burn them alive: His rage left little doubt about the relative values he attached to female Buddhist devotion and Confucian filial piety. Miao-shan devoted herself to Buddhist teachings, underwent various adventures with human and supernatural characters, and eventually retired to P'u-t'o Island in meditation. This Chinese princess thus became the compassionate bodhisattva of the *Lotus Sūtra* and the bodhisattva of Mount Potala (P'u-t'o) of the *Hua-yen Sūtra.*

In the legend of Miao-shan, the princess rejected her parents' plan to follow what she saw as the higher path, that of the Buddha. But in the end she saved her father, both physically and spiritually, by choosing the higher Buddhist path. She saves him physically by cutting off her own arm to use as a magical medicine to cure his blindness. She saved him and her mother spiritually by preaching the *Dharma* to them once she had become a bodhisattva. Although counter to Confucian teaching about family relationships, this story accommodates the Confucian virtue of respect for parents by showing that it can be fulfilled only in Buddhism. This is similar to the story of Buddha's disciple Mu-lien (Maudgalyāyana), who asked permission to descend to lower realms to teach his greedy mother the saving truth of Buddhism.[15] She too opposed her child's religious commitment, but in the end was saved from suffering in hell by hearing Buddhism preached by her loving son, Mu-lien. Chinese Buddhists valued this scriptural account of the life of Mu-lien because it helped counter Confucian criticism that Buddhism was unfilial. The tension between filial piety and Buddhist devotion is common to the Miao-shan and Mu-lien legends and is resolved in such a way as to produce a rather satisfying and ingenious synthesis.

Rejection of marriage is the core of another legend of Kuan-yin's appearances in this world. The story of Mrs. Ma tells of a devout young woman who promised to marry the man who could recite the Kuan-yin chapter of the *Lotus Sūtra* by the next day.[16] On the following day twenty men succeeded in reciting this for her, so she increased the number of Buddhist verses to be memorized until at last only a Mr. Ma was left. He recited the scripture and they were wed. However, on their wedding night the devout bride died, leaving behind the firm belief that she was indeed a manifestation of Kuan-yin. It is striking that there is little display of supernatural power in this legend except for the woman's ability to die at her chosen moment and then have her corpse disappear. Her great act of compassion and salvation was merely to demand that men equal her, a humble fisherwoman, in devotion to the Buddhist path.

In a related legend Kuan-yin manifested herself as Ling Chao, a plain fisherwoman who was the daughter of a Ch'an believer.[17] This legend serves as the basis of some of the simplest and most realistic paintings of Kuan-yin. In the National Palace Museum collection, there is a large painting of Kuan-yin with a fishing basket done by Chao Meng-fu (1254–1322). She appears as a large plain woman with bags under her eyes, a strong common woman with character. Her appearance is extraordinary only because she has the long ear lobes symbolizing the perfect wisdom of the Buddha. Another representation of Kuan-yin with a fishing basket is that by Wu Pin of the Ming dynasty—also of a large, handsome fisherwoman but this time accompanied by Kuan-yin's attendant Shan-ts'ai, who appears small in comparison to Kuan-yin. Kuan-yin with a fishing basket and Kuan-yin as Mrs. Ma are often merged into a single personality because they both appear as common women.

Kuan-yin's miraculous powers not only save women from marriage (along with childbearing and often difficult sexual relations), they also save women from sexual attacks that bring physical, emotional, and social suffering. A good example of this kind of tale is from *T'ai-shang pao-fa t'u-shuo,* one of the popular morality texts used to teach values to common people:

> When a woman sacrificed in a temple, the judge-deity smiled and visited her at night, expressing the wish for sexual relations. Refusing, she ran away, finally flew and landed on top of a pagoda. When she went down, she came into a bedroom where she met the judge. Now she could not refuse him and lived with him. During the day, he went out and did his job of meting out punishment to sinners; at night he returned with food for her. In a conversation with him she learned that a person can improve his fate by reciting the Kuan-yin sutra. This she did, with the result that the judge-deity became unable to have sexual relations with her. She was miraculously returned to her own house and bed. It was found out that only her soul, not her body, had had sexual relations with the deity.[18]

Many representations and legends of Kuan-yin come straight out of Indian art and scriptures—the miracles of the *Lotus Sūtra,* the stories of the Pure Land *sūtras,* and the descriptions of tantric texts. But the legends previously described are concretely Chinese. Although some are indirectly inspired by Indian Buddhist texts, they all firmly tie Kuan-yin to Chinese people and places.

The legends of Kuan-yin, especially in her form as Miao-shan, provide an alternative path for women by giving them a model for resisting parental marriage arrangements, thereby escaping the pain of marriage and the pollution of childbirth. Because Miao-shan entered a Buddhist convent, her role as a model for Chinese women who sought to become nuns is obvious. Kuan-yin also served as a model for less traditional marriage resistance by laywomen. Marjorie Topley's study, "Marriage Resistance in Rural Kwangtung," is evidence of this function of Kuan-yin devotion from the early nineteenth to early twentieth century.[19] Financially independent young women in the silk industry banded together and formed sisterhoods to avoid marriage. Women interviewed said that they had wanted to avoid the loneliness and oppression of marriage, the lack of financial independence, or the pain and punishment of childbirth. They also valued the lay vegetarian houses of these sisterhoods because they provided freedom from marriage without the restrictions implied by being a nun.[20]

Kuan-yin served as both a model and patron goddess for these women. The women often cited the story of Kuan-yin's manifestation as the stubbornly celibate Miao-shan as a justification for their own rejection of marriage. Because most of the vegetarian houses had one room dedicated to Kuan-yin and A-mi-t'o Buddha, Kuan-yin's presence was always visible to these women. By seeing Kuan-yin Bodhisattva daily they experienced an affirmation of their own lives and choices. In one house girls joined the sisterhood by signing a statement of their commitment and burning it in front of their role model and protector, Kuan-yin.[21]

A Symbol of Coping

The most commonly observed Kuan-yin devotion by women is aimed not at escaping marriage but coping with it. The gift of a male child by Kuan-yin, promised in the *Lotus Sūtra,* was the hope of many female worshipers. In Chinese society the highest moral value was filial piety and according to Confucian tradition the worst violation of filial piety was the failure to have male descendants.[22] C. K. Yang, in his *Religion in Chinese Society,* identifies the social function of the Kuan-yin cult as the promotion of fertility for the continuation of the lineage.[23] In his survey of eight localities, he locates most Kuan-yin temples in the category of temples that serve the "integration and well-being of social organizations," specifically by supporting the kinship group through their promotion of fertility. Some Kuan-yin temples are listed as primarily serving the "general public and personal welfare" by bestowing general blessings, but these are found mainly in the north where Taoist temples dedicated to the Taoist child-giving goddesses Nai-nai or Niang-niang served the fertility function.[24]

The birth of a son to a Chinese family ensured the continuation of the male lineage by providing male descendants to carry on the family name and the ancestral rituals. For a woman the birth of a son gave her the opportunity to build a small power base for herself in a perhaps hostile family whose ideology was based on perpetuating the male lineage. Margery Wolf has identified this power base as the uterine family—the children who are tied to their mother through bonds of affection and obligation.[25] A husband provided no definite security, but if a woman could emotionally bind her son to her for life she would have comfort and peace in her later years. The patriarchal structure of the lineage or the male family gave women no power, although it needed them for its own perpetuation. But the uterine family gave women both emotional fulfillment and the hope for some power. As Yang's study shows, devotion to Kuan-yin for bearing sons perpetuated the values of the male family. However, it was also the means by which women survived in the family. It was their means of coping with the male family by creating the shelter and strength of their own uterine family.

. . .

Conclusion

From the Sung dynasty to the present, the Chinese have chosen to create and worship a female form of their most popular bodhisattva, Kuan-yin. For women this has meant a symbol of someone who would serve as their savior from all suffering, but especially from the suffering arising out of their female birth: arranged marriages, sexual attacks, the pain and stigma of both menstruation and childbirth, and the powerlessness of childlessness in a patriarchal society. A Buddhist savior from suffering, Kuan-yin sometimes is also a role model in her manifestations as women. In many traditional legends that still are propagated she serves as a model of piety and independence from family restrictions. In other traditions, particularly the image of the Kuan-yin who delivers children (Sung-tzu Kuan-yin), the symbol of the bodhisattva offers a means of coping with the pressures of a patriarchal family and thus remaining within it. These legends continue to be popular but are combined with modern advice for family life and recent testimonials to Kuan-yin's compassionate power to heal the body and support the modern family.

Although the stories of her miracles have been updated for the 1980s, her images remain virtually unchanged since the Ming dynasty. One Kuan-yin image dominates contemporary devotion: the white-robed Chinese woman holding willow branch and vase. In Taiwan this representation of Kuan-yin appears in temples, domestic altars, protective charms, operas, and even in film and television adaptations of *The Journey to the West.* She is virtually independent of the traditional schools and scriptures of elite Buddhism. She is not primarily the bodhisattva who assists A-mi-t'o Buddha of the Pure Land scriptures, the thousand-armed deity of tantric traditions, or even the saving bodhisattva of the *Lotus Sūtra.* Kuan-yin is a Chinese female bodhisattva known primarily through Chinese legends, art, novels, plays, and recent miracles. The woman who is saved in contemporary legends is a modern Chinese woman, but the woman who saves is from that indistinct and confused past of the T'ang-Ming often used as the setting for movies and television series. Two contemporary role models of devotional literature, Helen Keller and a handicapped Japanese artist, follow the traditions associated with Kuan-yin as a role model: they are extraordinary women with no apparent family obligations. Kuan-yin devotion continues to symbolically reconcile the conflicting values in women's lives: the value of independence from social demands to allow for spiritual growth and the value of nurturing the family relationships to which many women look for meaning and happiness. Individual women may not be able to realize both values due to the way gender roles have been defined by traditional and contemporary society, but the tension between the values is resolved in the images and stories of Kuan-yin, a figure who upholds both.

Notes

An earlier version of this paper was presented at the 1986 Midwest Conference on Asian Studies. The author would like to thank Ann Waltner for her comments on that earlier version and Gary M. Davison for comments on later drafts. All Chinese terms in this essay are given in Wade-Giles transliteration.

1. Translation by Diana Y. Paul, *Women in Buddhism: Images of the Feminine in Mahāyāna Tradition* (Berkeley, Calif.: Asian Humanities Press, 1979), 263; Kumarajīva's version of the *Lotus Sūtra* has been translated in its entirety by

Leon Hurvitz, *Scripture of the Lotus Blossom of the Fine Dharma* (New York: Columbia University Press, 1976).

2. Edward Conze, *Thirty Years of Buddhist Studies: Selected Essays* (Columbia: University of South Carolina, 1968), 81.
3. Various theories about these names are discussed by Marie-Thérèse de Mallman, *L'Introduction à l'étude d'Avalokiteçvara* (Paris: Presses Universitaires de France, 1967); and by C. N. Tay, "Kuan-yin: The Cult of Half Asia," *History of Religions* 16, no. 2 (1976): 147–77. For theories about the sexual transformation of Kuan-yin see Paul, *Women in Buddhism,* 250–52; and John Chamberlayne, "The Development of Kuan Yin, the Goddess of Mercy," *Numen* 9 (January 1962): 45–52.
4. Hurvitz, *Scripture of the Lotus Blossom,* 25–26, and Paul, ibid., 259; Tay discusses the concept of Kuan-yin in the *Lotus Sūtra* (and the *Sūraṃgama* and *Thousand-hand Dharaṇı Sūtras)* in "Kuan-yin."
5. Leroy Davidson, *The Lotus Sutra in Chinese Art* (New Haven, Conn.: Yale University Press, 1954), 71.
6. See Davidson, ibid., 85; and Michibata Ryōshū, "Chūgoku ni okeru minkan shinkō to Kannon," *Inḍogaku Bukkyōgaku kenkyū* 3, no. 1 (September 1954): 337–40, as cited by Alicia Matsunga, *The Buddhist Philosophy of Assimilation* (Tokyu: Charles E. Tuttle, 1969), 137.
7. Chih-yi described the six forms of Kuan-yin in the realms of hell beings, hungry ghosts, animals, *ausras,* humans, and deities in his *Chih-kuan* [T. 46, p. 156]; see Matsunaga, *Buddhist Philosophy,* 122.
8. For a good example of a psychological interpretation of physical dangers in Pure Land Buddhism, see Shan-tao's "Parable of the White Path" in *Kuan-ching shu (Taishō daizōkyō,* 37: 272–73); a partial translation can be found in Wm. Theodore de Bary, ed., *The Buddhist Tradition in India, China and Japan* (New York: Modern Library, 1969), 204–7.
9. Wolfram Eberhard, *Sin and Guilt in Traditional China* (Berkeley: University of California Press, 1967).
10. Ju Gong-wen, ed., *Puto shan* (Beijing: China Travel Publishing Society, 1982), 27–28. Chun-fang Yu documented pilgrimages to P'u-t'o Island and the Upper T'ien-chu Monastery in Hangchow in honor of Kuan-yin's birthday during 1987 in a film, *Kuan-yin Pilgrimage,* distributed by R. G. Video.
11. Johannes Frick, "Mutter und Kind bei Chinesen in Tsinghai, I: Die Sozialreligiose Unreinheit der Frau," *Anthropos* 50 (1955): 341–42, as cited by Emily Ahern in her excellent study, "The Power and Pollution of Chinese Women," *Women in Chinese Society* (Stanford, Calif.: Stanford University Press, 1975), 214.
12. Margery Wolf studied the relationship between marriage and suicide for Chinese women in "Women and Suicide in China," in *Women in Chinese Society,* 111–42. Arthur Wolf discusses the sexual aversion and lower fertility rates of

the marriages of sons and adopted daughters in "The Women of Hai-shan: A Demographic Portrait," ibid., 89–110.

13. Joanna Handlin, "Lü K'un's New Audience: The Influence of Women's Literacy on Sixteenth Century Thought," ibid., 16.
14. *Kuan-shih-yin p'u-sa chuan* [Biography of Kuan-shih-yin Bodhisattva], author unknown (Taichung, 1985), is the popular version today and the source for the stories cited here; for an English translation of the Miao-shan story see Glen Dudbridge, *The Legend of Miao-shan* (London: Ithica Press, 1978).
15. For a translation of a Tun-huang manuscript of this story, see Arthur Waley, *Ballads and Stories from Tun-huang* (London: George Allen & Unwin, 1960), 216–35.
16. *Kuan-shih-yin p'u-sa chuan,* pp. 150–55; for an English summary of this legend see Henry Dore, *Researches into Chinese Superstitions,* vol. 6 (Taipei: Chengwen Publishing Co., 1966), 213–14.
17. See Matsunaga, *Buddhist Philosophy,* 131.
18. Eberhard, *Sin and Guilt,* 114.
19. Marjorie Topley, "Marriage Resistance in Rural Kwangtung," *Women in Chinese Society,* 67–88.
20. Ibid., 79.
21. Marjorie Topley, "Women's Vegetarian Houses in Singapore," *Journal of the Malayan Branch of the Royal Asiatic Society* 27, no. 1 (1954): 51–67; references are found on 59 and 62.
22. According to Mencius, "There are three things which are unfilial, and to have no posterity is the greatest of them." See *Mencius* 4A:26; trans. James Legge, *The Four Books: Confucian Analects, The Great Learning, The Doctrine of the Mean, and The Works of Mencius* (New York, 1966), 725.
23. C. K. Yang, *Religion in Chinese Society* (Berkeley: University of California, 1961), 6–11.
24. Ibid., 7–11.
25. Margery Wolf, *Women and the Family in Rural Taiwan* (Stanford, Calif.: Stanford University Press, 1972).

TRADITION

[26]

Satī, Sacrifice, and Marriage: The Modernity of Tradition

Paul B. Courtright

Satī *is the* nicoṛ *[essence] of* pativratādharma *[moral action appropriate for married women].*

Agehananda Bharati

Satī and the Problem of Interpretation

Of the many images of India that Westerners have implanted in their imaginations over the centuries of contact, the spectacle of the dutiful wife calmly taking her place on the pyre of her deceased husband has provoked both moral revulsion and voyeuristic curiosity. Westerners called such ritual immolations "suttee" (*satī* according to current transliteration practices), taking the Sanskrit term meaning a wife who possesses great virtue. The specter of a married woman walking toward the funeral pyre and joining her husband in cremation presses the interpretive process to its margins. Both traditional

Source: Paul B. Courtright, "*Satī*, Sacrifice, and Marriage: The Modernity of Tradition," in *From the Margins of Hindu Marriage: Essays on Gender, Religion, and Culture,* ed. Lindsey Harlan and Paul B. Courtright (New York: Oxford University Press, 1995).

Hindu and modern Western or Indian interpreters might well agree that such an action cuts against the grain of a universal and innate human reflex for self-preservation. At the same time it raises the question of the *satī*'s agency: did she choose this act of self-annihilation freely, and if so, what is the context for such a "free" choice?

Two conclusions might be drawn from the spectacle of the *satī* immolation. Either she is not human, or she is not acting out of her own free will.[1] Traditional Hinduism has tended to take the former interpretation, stressing the ways in which the *satī*, particularly during her final moments prior to immolation, behaves in ways that make her indistinguishable from a goddess. She distributes gifts, confers blessings, inflicts curses, and acts as if the pain of her immanent fiery death and the social and physical world of *saṃsāra* were an illusion. Within the fire itself she does not exhibit the involuntary reflexes of pain that one would expect of a human being. Western and modern Indian interpretations, beginning with the late eighteenth century, have often argued that the *satī* was coerced into her actions either directly through the use of opium or other drugs that left her stupefied or, more subtly, by the patriarchal ideology that convinced her that her self-annihilation was her duty or opportunity. With either of these broad interpretations the agency of the *satī* as a woman becomes erased, toward divinity in one case and toward coercion in the other. Consequently the issue of *satī* as an interpretive issue in cross-cultural studies has far outweighed the relative importance that *satī* as an actual event has played in the long history of Hindu culture. The increased attention being paid in recent years to issues of gender and power has added new emphasis to the fact that it is only women who become *satīs*, and the sacrifice of women in a religious or pseudoreligious context connects issues of gender, power, religion, and violence in compelling ways.

Historical evidence suggests that before the British colonial period incidents of such immolations were rare, confined largely to politically elite and martial classes, especially Rajputs, along India's border regions with the largely Islamic cultures of western Asia.[2] Since the sixteenth century Western travelers to India have frequently included purported eyewitness accounts of such events, frequently with lengthy descriptions of ritual details and comments about their own moral horror at Hindus' apparent callous disregard for the woman undergoing such a death along with deep admiration for her (misguided) devotion to her late husband. In the imagined India of Western experience and interpretation, *satī* came to stand for the whole of Hinduism as an irrational, perverse, and heroic religious orientation to life.

By the turn of the nineteenth century, as Britain was establishing its sovereignty over much of India, incidents of *satī* became more common in Bengal in districts under its jurisdiction. A lengthy debate took place over how *satī* was to be understood. Consensus emerged among colonial authorities and some Hindu reformists that *satī* was not an integral part of Hinduism but a medieval perversion of its core values. The principal beneficiaries of these religiously glossed murders of women were Brahman priests who collected fees for performing the rituals and family members who stood to benefit from inheritances that otherwise might have come to the surviving widow. Consequently the British authorities and their client Hindu states banned the practice.[3] A similar policy has been followed by the government of India since 1947.

In recent years accounts of immolations of women that took place in largely isolated areas continued to be reported.[4] The issue of *satī* has emerged now as an important part of the discourse of feminist criticism of Hindu culture's patriarchal structure. From this perspective *satī* is the most egregious example of an attempt to simultaneously repress women and celebrate to the point of deification their self-annihilation in the name of religion. In both the early colonial period and the contemporary moment Hindu traditionalists have argued that *satī,* when properly understood and undertaken, is a sacred religious act that only the most extraordinary women who have a highly evolved moral vision and discipline are capable of performing. In those rare cases, it is argued, such women should not be impeded by the state from carrying out their religious destinies. For both critics and admirers of *satī* there is a shared sense that it fits into the total system of Hinduism as an emblem of its moral bankruptcy or its noble heritage. In the contemporary debate between religious and secular visions of Indian society, *satī* has taken on renewed meaning as a contested symbol that contains contradictory interpretations.

Agehananda Bharati, the late Austrian-born anthropologist and Hindu monk, once commented that *satī* was the *nicoṛ* of *pativratādharma.*[5] His comment warrants some interpretive analysis and investigation of terms. . . . *Pativratādharma* may be interpretively translated as those morally significant actions, duties, and attitudes that are appropriate to the status of a married woman, the central focus of which is the welfare of her husband and all that adheres to him: household, reputation, kin, ancestors, descendants, deities, and life circumstances. Etymologically, the term means moral action (*dharma*) that is rooted in vows *(vrata,* from the Sanskrit root *vṛ,* "turn") undertaken for the protection and well-being of the husband or lord *(pati).* These duties, and the orientations that frame them, are presented formally in classical treatises on morality (*dharmaśāstras*) and informally through patterns of behavior and expectations regarding married life passed through generations, encoded in rituals, and celebrated in mythology and folklore.

Pativratādharma may be seen as a subset of the more generic category *dharma* (morally significant action). There are many *dharmas* according to the various classes and stages of life. Kings, priests, ascetics, students, servants, warriors, and so forth all have their particular normative codes of action appropriate to their life situations. At the center of this moral universe is the notion of service or self-subordination: priests serve gods, kings serve the well-being of the populace by maintaining order and patronizing the worship of the gods, warriors serve kings, students serve teachers, children serve parents, servants serve masters, ascetics serve the goal of renunciatory liberation *(mokṣa),* and married women serve their husbands. Within this life context of service is the notion that orientation to a single set of commitments provides the environment and discipline that enable one to be effective in the world while keeping one's sights on ultimate liberation amid the interminable repetition of life. Ideally, if everyone did their service properly, harmonious order would prevail. As with any normative moral system, the ideal of an overarching, coherent *dharma* was and continues to be subverted in various ways: warriors have rebelled against kings, priests have protested against gods, students have disobeyed their teachers, and wives have rebelled in various ways against the authority of their husbands. . . . The other term Bharati used in his comment, *nicoṛ,* also requires an etymological detour, for it contains important insights into the relationship between *satī* and the ethos of marriage. . . . *Nicoṛ* refers to the process by which the juice or essence is extracted through hard pressing or squeezing. It also refers to the product, what is left over after the wringing out has taken place: the juice, essence, money, that which is of value that is left after all the contexts that located it have been stripped away. This double significance of the act and the product of hard effort gives the word a rich semantic range.

That *satī* would occupy the place of *nicoṛ,* the process and result of the wringing out of the ethos of the wife living her life in service and devotion to her husband, requires some further comment. The ethos of *pativratādharma* places much of the power and responsibility for the husband and his social context in the hands of his wife. Through ritual acts of devotion such as prayer, fasting, and service, the wife gathers together her inherent generative power (*śakti*) and focuses it toward the well-being of her husband. In north India, when this *śakti* is focused on the goals of *pativratādharma,* it transforms itself into *sat,* the capacities of dharmic perfection.[6] In the wife's ideal moral universe, the husband functions as the point of orientation for her actions, as the king does for the warrior, the teacher for the student, the deity for the priest, and so forth. Her devotion, therefore, is not necessarily borne out of romantic affection or even friendship with her husband. Indeed, in terms of the logic of *pativratādharma,* his behavior toward her is irrelevant to her commitments to her own moral orientation; her actions have a kind of radical independence that are not derivative of his. Indeed, a neglectful or even abusive husband may be construed as a more demanding challenge for a wife's devotion, just as Kṛṣṇa's neglect of his *gopī* lovers only intensifies their devotion to him.

In the normative configuration of traditional Hinduism, in addition to being empowered and responsible for the husband's well-being, the wife is also understood to be his "half body," merged ontologically through the ritual of marriage. In the process of moving from her natal to her conjugal home, she is expected to abandon her identification with her natal kin and assimilate herself into the identities of her husband's family, ancestors, deities, moral codes, and behavioral practices. . . .

Satī: The Double Bind

In the ideal construction of *pativratādharma* the wife empties herself in service to her husband's well-being. This emptying in turn generates *sat,* which regenerates her capacity for service. The expected consequence of this pattern is that she and her husband will have a long life together. When death comes, it will come to her first, as many Hindu women pray will happen as part of their ritual practices for the protection of their husbands. In the perfect Hindu moral universe, there would be no widows. However, such a perfect moral universe does not exist within the realm of *saṃsāra.* It is the widow, more than any other person, who exemplifies the tension between the ideal version of reality and its manifestation in ordinary life. The widow is the most ideologically and ritually marginalized. She is the emblem of the culture's failure to perfect the ordinary world of experience. When the husband dies first, the wife is faced with a dilemma. As his "half body" she is, in principle, inseparable from him; but as a person in a social world she is alive and he is dead. Traditional Hindu culture regards the widow as one who is dead in life, and many of the avoidances and perceived contaminations associated with death are transferred to the widow. . . .

The predicament of the deceased husband is one of the places in the Hindu world where the ideal construction and the existential situation facing the woman takes the form of a double bind. Her own powers of protection and generative moral force *(sat)* are insufficient to overcome the vagaries of her or her husband's *karma,* and the ripening of misdeeds of previous lives has now come to take its toll. She is confronted with the limits of the protective powers her culture presumes her to have. Because the husband's and wife's lives are religiously construed to be indivisible, she faces a crisis of interpretation of the meaning of her own life. If the moral force of *pativratādharma* is "real," and the world of *saṃsāra* is "illusion," as Hindu philosophy teaches, and if the wife has generated the moral capacities (*sat*) from years of service and devotion to the well-being of her husband, then she may wish to go with him in death as she did in life. While she has not been successful in keeping him alive, she retains the capacity to decide whether she should remain alive as a survivor and keep her connections with him in place through continued ritual veneration, or whether she should go with him in a single and spectacular display of violent self-annihilating devotion. The Sanskrit term for the rite of immolation with the deceased husband, *sahagamana* (going with), carries this sense of what is taking place. Such a "going with" confirms the priority of the religious construction of reality over the existential situation of the "natural" fear of death, let alone burning alive. From the religious perspective, the death of the body does not take place until the indissoluble spirit *(āt-man)* is released through the purification of the cremation fire. The wife does not become a widow until her husband is cremated. By joining him on the pyre she dies together with him as his "half body," bypassing the status of widowhood and avoiding the ritual contamination and social marginality it would bring on her and those around her. This display of devotion releases a surplus of religious merit, which the *satī* distributes to her kin and community at the time of her death and afterward in the form of her continuing presence as a beneficent ancestress to her lineage. Subsequent generations of her lineage appeal to her for protection, as she had protected her husband in the transition from one cosmological plane to another. This, I think, is what Bharati had in mind when he called *satī* the *nicoṛ* of *pativratādharma.* It is the place where the double bind of the Hindu construction of marriage, body, and *dharma* wrings itself out. And it is the wife, the *satī,* who becomes the vehicle for it. She is the field of battle for this internal conflict of the tradition. She is the *nicoṛ:* the substance and the wringing. From the perspective of the logic of Hinduism as a system, the perfection of *pativratādharma,* the *satī* is its embodied substance. She is the context or form in which the normative religious world and the existential moment converge in an act that is at one and the same time one of annihilation and deification. Hence, she takes on a supernatural persona. She walks calmly to the pyre, whereas ordinary people would shrink in terror. She dispenses blessing on those who venerate her and invokes curses on those who resist her. From the perspective of her as a person, she is the victim, the one wrung out of the system, the one who is backed into the corner of choosing between a death of life in the fire or a life of social and ritual death as a widow. This double bind, or *nicoṛ,* is what gives *satī* its religious character, its emotive power, and its moral dissonance. As a sacrificial act it carries within it the burden of the validity of the religious world from which it takes its definition. A religious interpretation, which foregrounds the normative world of *pativratādharma* and existence as *saṃsāra,* could account for what might be going through the mind of a wife when facing the choice of going with her husband in the fire or staying behind as a widow. Once the religious frame of reference is removed, as the colonial and secular state ideologies and practices have done, then what is left or wrung out is some form of suicide or murder, both of which are criminal actions under the law. Religion moves to the margin as the "mystification" appealed to in hiding the actual criminal act of the murder of a woman. The *satī* becomes a victim, and the devotees become accomplices in her destruction.

Satī and the Modernity of Tradition: The Story of Bālāsatīmātā

Nearly two centuries of colonial and secular governance have undermined *satī* as an uncomplicated act of religious heroism, removed it from its religious context altogether as far as the legal system is concerned, and relegated it to the category of the criminal. Anyone attempting to become a *satī,* assisting a *satī,* or displaying one's regard for a *satī* as a deity in rituals of veneration faces the threat of severe criminal penalties. Yet the underlying religious values that *satī* embodied have not disappeared in contemporary India, especially in the rural areas in the northern and northwestern parts of the country. In addition to the occasional cases of actual immolations that frequently receive considerable media attention, there are other, quieter expressions of the continuity of the religious importance of *satī* and its underlying moral and religious values, which have adapted themselves to changing circumstances.

In the state of Rajasthan in the northwestern part of India, there is a tradition of religious devotion to women who are called *jīvit satīmātā* (living *satī*-mothers). These are women who sought to be *satīs* when their husbands died but were prevented from carrying out their objective by their kinsmen, who feared criminal prosecution for assisting them. Consequently, they turned to saintly lives of ascetic surrender, no longer eating, drinking, or sleeping. Because they declared their intention to become *satīs,* they have retained much of the aura associated with wives who completed the sacrifice. I first learned of this tradition from Lindsey Harlan, who had been conducting research on high-caste women's religious traditions. According to Harlan, the living *satīmātā* tradition appears to be quite recent, probably emerging only after the criminalization of the actual ritual immolations of wives in Rajasthan in the mid-nineteenth century.[7] While there are not many of these women, as indeed there were not many *satīs,* their personal charisma attracts followers, predominantly women, and stories of their miraculous powers circulate through the regions in which they live. So far as I know, this *satīmātā* tradition is not found outside of Rajasthan and parts of Gujarat that border on it.

. . .

Notes

This essay is dedicated to the memory of Agehananda Bharati. I have benefited greatly from his ideas, perspectives, and critiques at earlier stages of my research on *satī.* I would also like to thank Lindsey Harlan, Wendy Doniger, Joyce Burkhalter Flueckiger, Bhoju Ram Gujar, Tony Stewart, Dharma Chandra, and Philip Lutgendorf for their help at various stages of my research.

1. I am grateful to Richard Schweder's insights in formulating the issue in this way.
2. Romila Thapar, "Death and the Hero," in *Mortality and Immortality: The Anthropology and Archaeology of Death,* ed. S. C. Humphreys and Helen King (London: Academic Press, 1981), 293–315.
3. Lata Mani, "The Production of Official Discourse on *Satī* in Early Nineteenth-Century India," *Economic and Political Weekly* 21 (1986): 32–40.
4. Kumkum Sangari and Sudesh Vaid, "*Satī* in Modern India," *Economic and Political Weekly* 25 (1990): 1464–75, 1531–52.
5. Personal communication, November 20, 1988.
6. For a discussion of *sat,* see Lindsey Harlan, *Religion and Rajput Women: The Ethic of Protection in Contemporary Narratives* (Berkeley: University of California Press, 1992), 124–33.
7. Ibid., 179.

[27]

Jewish Attitudes toward Divorce

Blu Greenberg

Traditional Jewish divorce law suggests two things: how much change has occurred throughout history and how much more change needs to occur so that the law may serve women nondiscriminately.[1] The evolutionary process begins with biblical law:

> A man takes a wife and possesses her. She fails to please him because he finds something obnoxious (*ervat davar*) about her, and he writes her a bill of divorcement, hands it to her, and sends her away from his house. (Deut. 24:1)

Both physical and psychological uprooting were in store for the woman who overly displeased her husband. She had no power to prevent or refuse the divorce, nor was there provision for her to divorce him if she wanted out of the marriage and he didn't. Divorce was the absolute right of the husband, not an illogical consequence of a patriarchal society.

The Bible itself, however, begins the process of modification of these absolute rights. First, the fact that the husband had to write a bill of divorce and present it to his wife served as protection for her (Isa. 50:1; Jer. 3:8). It was a delaying tactic; he could not, in a fit of anger, simply pronounce with

Source: From Blu Greenberg, *On Women and Judaism: A View from Tradition* (Philadelphia: Jewish Publication Society, 1981). Used by permission.

finality the formal declaration of divorce. (Irreversible oral divorce was the alternative in ancient Eastern cultures.) Second, a man was required to pay a penalty upon divorce. This is learned from the biblical law of accusation, in which a husband, as grounds for divorce, publicly accuses his wife of premarital sex and of coming to him without her virginity (Deut. 22:13–21). Why would he bother to accuse her publicly, antagonize her family, and humiliate himself in the process when he could have simply divorced her quietly and at will? Because if the charge was upheld, he was released from paying the standard penalty. Third, the Bible describes two instances in which the absolute prohibition against divorce applies: if the husband falsely accused his wife of having had premarital sex; or if a man raped a woman whom he was obligated to marry (providing, of course, she would accept him), he could not thereafter divorce her (Deut. 22:28–29). (This "law of the rapist" may appear crude and rather cruel. In reality, however, it was designed to protect the woman; having lost her virginity through no fault of her own, she would have been otherwise unmarriageable.) Both of these restrictions must be understood in the broader context—the community's prerogative to set limits on a man's absolute, private right of divorce.

The biblical law on divorce comes almost as an aside, as a wrinkle in the law that forbids a man to remarry his ex-wife in the event that she had, in the interim, married another man. This, too, was an encroachment on a man's virtual control over divorce. Moreover, the Bible teaches that there was an alternative to divorce. Polygamy, in a strange sort of way, protected a woman, for a man did not have to divorce one wife in order to take another.

Biblical narrative portrays a different situation altogether. Polygamous marriages were quite rare, yet divorce was also very rare. Women were not driven out wholesale. Even in those isolated instances where a woman was sent away, it was traumatic for the husband as well (Gen. 21:11–12; 1 Sam. 3:14–16). The social sanctions of the community against divorce must have been very strong.

One more word about contexts. Biblical divorce law seems to reflect less an ancient bias of the Hebrew religion concerning women than it does the general Near Eastern male-oriented culture in which biblical law was grounded contextually. Parallel cultures, such as the Sumerian and Hittite, have equivalent divorce rites. The Code of Hammurabi, in force in Mesopotamia during the time of the Patriarchs, records laws on marriage and divorce that are almost identical to biblical law.[2]

Nevertheless, one cannot dismiss biblical divorce law simply as ancient culture-bound mores or sociological axioms of patriarchy. For Jews, biblical law is revelation and thus the basis of all Halakhah that follows. The rabbis of the Talmud were not insensitive to inequities in biblical divorce law. Little by little, the imbalance was tempered by numerous rabbinic measures that, on the whole, gave women greater protection. Still, the basic principle of man's rights was always there, limiting how far the tradition could go in creating a better distribution of power in family law.

One method by which the rabbis reinforced this principle of absolute right was the selective weighting of scriptural phrases. "And he writes her a bill of divorcement, hands it to her, and sends her away from his house" was interpreted as a sweeping divine principle of the male prerogative. The Mishnah teaches, "The man who divorces is not like the woman who is divorced, because the woman is divorced with her consent or against her will, while the man divorces only with his own free will" (Yevamot 14:1). Only a man can write a bill of divorcement (Gittin 20a; Bava Batra 168a).

On the other hand, the phrase "hands it to her" was not interpreted as divine principle requiring the wife's acceptance or consent; rather, it was explained as procedure. Even as procedure, there was a good deal of leeway: a man may throw the get (bill of divorcement) into her lap or workbasket or date dish or onto the parapet where she might be standing (Gittin 8:1, 77a–79a). Only in some very limited situations is the phrase "hands it to her" used as a principle (Yevamot 113b).

In an early rabbinic dispute between the schools of Hillel and Shammai, a pattern emerges that characterizes much of rabbinic action for centuries to come. Shammai, the strict constructionist of biblical law, maintained that the scriptural words *ervat davar* (Deut. 24:1–4) literally and exclusively meant adultery. Thus, a woman's infidelity was the only legitimate grounds for divorce. (The Catholic Church reinforced this strict constructionist view and has wrestled with a most untenable position on divorce ever since.)

Hillel, who generally interpreted the scriptures broadly, understood *ervat davar* as anything offensive to the husband, even burning his food. As in most disputes, rabbinic law followed Hillel (Gittin 9:10).[3]

For the next few centuries, major talmudists reiterated the principle of the unrestricted right of the husband to divorce. The opposing view was not ignored entirely, however. It made itself felt in two ways: in the growing number of halakhic curbs on a man's absolute right and in the moral dicta of the Talmud, such as "he who divorces his wife is hated by God" (Gittin 90b).

Thus, throughout much of rabbinic history, three forces operated in tension: the theory of man's absolute right, the biblical precedents that qualified these rights, and the earliest layer of rabbinic sources that interpreted biblical laws broadly or narrowly. These three constructs could be weighted in every rabbinic decision, depending on one's teacher's views, the climate of the times, or one's inclinations and the particular divorce case at hand.

Rabbinic modification took several forms: increasing the number of cases in which the absolute prohibition against divorce applies, embellishing and encumbering the divorce proceedings, expanding the financial responsibilities of the husband, and enlarging the wife's opportunity to assent or dissent, giving her some mastery over her own fate as a married woman.

1. *Increasing the number of cases.* Two new cases were added beyond the two prohibitions of biblical origin: a man could not divorce a wife who had become insane and thus would have been unable to take care of herself (Yevamot 14:1, 113b), nor could a man divorce a wife who had been taken captive.[4] Another kind of prohibited divorce involved a child bride, not uncommon in oriental Jewish communities.

2. *Embellishing the proceedings.* The complex rules attending actual divorce were spelled out in the Talmud and were further refined in post-talmudic rabbinic literature.[5] These rules apply today just as they did throughout the entire medieval world.

A get must be handwritten by a scribe at the specific instruction of the husband. The language is Aramaic, following the talmudic textual form, with the details of the particular case filled in at the appropriate places. The central part of the get is the husband's declaration: "I will release and set aside you, my wife, in order that you may have authority over yourself to marry any man you desire. . . . You are permitted to every man. . . . This shall be for you a bill of dismissal, a letter of release, a get of freedom" (Gittin 9:1–3; *Mishneh Torah,* Hilkhot Gerushin 4:12).

Great care is taken in the process of writing the get. The scribe has to make a formal gift to the husband of all the writing materials he will use. A get may be declared invalid if the writing, signing, and delivery are misdated. Two male witnesses must sign the get. The husband must present the get to the wife, again in the presence of witnesses (usually the same two men). If this is impossible or impractical, he may appoint an agent of delivery, as may the wife for receipt of the get; the laws concerning agency, however, are even more complicated.

Upon receipt, the wife hands the get over to the bet din (rabbinic court), consisting of three men. They make a tear in the document, signifying the tearing asunder of the relationship as well as the conclusion of the legal transaction of divorce. The bet din files the get for safekeeping and gives a *shtar piturin* (document of release attesting that the wife has received a valid get).

The standard procedures in a divorce are so exact, so detailed, that those in attendance must be experts at it. In many medieval communities, as in modern ones, often there was only one rabbi sufficiently qualified to handle gittin (religious divorce proceedings). The real function of the myriad of laws was to bring the couple into contact with the bet din, whose members understood their role as more than scribes or legal experts. Long before the get was actually drawn, they would try to use their offices to effect a reconciliation. Only after all else failed would they monitor and supervise the final act. This whole process ultimately served to undermine the notion of absolute right. In theory, the husband still had a private and absolute right, but in practice as well as in the popular mind he now had to look to the bet din for sanction.

3. *Expanding the husband's financial responsibilities.* The ketubah (marriage contract) states that the wife is entitled to a return of her dowry and any other properties she had brought with her into the marriage, plus support for her until she remarries. It thus discouraged divorce by levying economic sanctions. If it failed to prevent divorce, however, at least the woman was provided with some measure of security. The ketubah also protected her interests during marriage. The husband was obliged to provide for her according to her station in life, to pay her medical and dental bills, to ransom her if she were taken captive, and to bury her decently (Ketubbot 4:4–9, 5a; *Mishneh Torah,* Even ha-Ezer, Hilkhot Ishut, 12:2).

The Talmud did not formalize the standard ketubah text but did establish a basic minimum level of recompense. Beyond that, it allowed many variations. Thus, in medieval times, tailor-made ketubot were written where a wife stipulated the conditions under which her husband must grant her a divorce and still pay the ketubah (say, if he took a concubine).

4. *Wife's opportunity to assent or dissent.* In practice, the theoretical right of the husband to put away his wife was eroded continually throughout rabbinic times. Finally, in the eleventh century, Rabbenu Gershom of Mainz formally decreed, by means of a takkanah (rabbinic directive), that a woman could not be divorced without her consent. Woman's will now carried legal force. Although no one would call it by that name, Rabbenu Gershom's decree formally set aside the principle of man's absolute right of divorce.

What the rabbis really were trying to do was protect a woman from being divorced. The end of the tractate on divorce closes with a quote from the prophet Malachi, which summarizes the ethical and moral values that seem to have informed the rabbinic deliberations throughout:

> If a man divorces his first wife, even the altar sheds tears . . . because the Lord has been witness between you and the wife of your youth, against whom you have dealt treacherously, even though she has been your companion and the wife of your covenant. (Gittin 90b)

What about the right of the wife to sue for divorce? The germ of such a notion existed in biblical law, for if a man didn't live up to his contractual obligations, his wife was entitled to bring suit:

> When a man sells his daughter as a slave, . . . if she proves to be displeasing to her master, who designated her for himself, he must let her be redeemed. . . . If he marries another, he must not withhold from this one her food, her clothing, or her conjugal rights. If he fails her in these three ways, she shall go free, without payment. (Exod. 21:7–11)

In other words, this Jewish bondswoman could go out, free of debts, without a financial settlement but with a bill of divorcement in hand (Mekilta, Mishpatim, sec. 3; Arakhin 5:6; Yevamot 14:1; Gittin 9:8). Because bondswomen probably had very little clout, tradition assumes that the bill of divorcement was mandated by some others with power—the court perhaps, or the city elders (Bava Batra 48a; Yevamot 106a). It was reasonable to assume that if a mere bondswoman was protected by contractual rights, certainly would a wife be who entered the marriage as a free woman.

In rabbinic times the contractual obligations of the husband were expanded and elaborated. Many of the grounds that entitled the wife to divorce reflected great sensitivity to women's needs. Sexual satisfaction, a condition legislated in the Bible, was given real definition by the rabbis. They even legislated the minimum number of times for intercourse, which varied according to the husband's occupation: a sailor had to come ashore at least once every six months, a scholar had to satisfy his wife at least once a week. If a husband refused to meet his wife's conjugal rights, she could exercise her option for divorce through the bet din. If she chose not to exercise this right, her husband could be fined, week by week (Ketubbot 61b–62b).

Impotence also was legitimate grounds for divorce, deriving from an older rabbinic law that actually permitted a woman to make such a charge without bringing proof. A late mishnaic law permitted the husband to contest the accusation but left the burden of proof upon him (Yevamot 65a–b).

If a wife vowed not to have intercourse with her husband and he did not take pains to annul such a vow, she was entitled to sue for divorce (Ketubbot 5:8–9). If she wanted to live in the Holy Land or move from one Palestinian city to Jerusalem and he refused to follow her or to remain there with her (Ketubbot 110b); if he had a serious disease or a continual bad odor from his occupation, like carrying dung or tanning hides (Ketubbot 7:9); if he did not support her in the style to which she had been accustomed or, if he was wealthy, in the style proper for one of his means (Ketubbot 5:8–9); or if he failed to live up to anything in the ketubah, the wife was entitled to sue for divorce. The medieval rabbis added two more grounds for divorce: if he beat her or if he visited prostitutes (*Shulhan Arukh,* Even ha-Ezer, Hilkhot Gittin 154:3, commentary of Rama).[6]

Contractual rights worked as follows: if a husband did not meet his responsibilities to his wife she could go to the bet din, present her case, and obtain a subpoena compelling him to appear to answer the charges. The court would first press him to fulfill his obligations. If he failed to do so, the court could coerce him into granting the divorce by levying economic and social sanctions against him. The law maintained, however, that he was taking this action "of his own free will"; the talmudic phrase is "We use coercion until he says, 'I want to'" (Yevamot 106a). By such legal fiction, the old theory of a man's initiative was retained intact, all the while that, in real life, the woman's rights increased.

A pattern thus emerges. For the husband, the original right to divorce was unchallenged and private, but the historical development of the law served continually to limit it. In the case of the wife, her initial rights were limited, but as Halakhah expanded through the post-biblical generation, these were broadened and formalized. This unmistakable pattern refutes the simple-minded charges that rabbis seized every opportunity to keep women powerless. Quite the reverse is true, considering the rabbinic capacity for interpreting the law, as well as the transfer of male authority from one generation to the next—there is an impressive degree of sensitivity and benevolence in the unfolding of the law. A growing set of obligations of husband to wife and the increasing formalization of her rights to redress through the bet din are clear indications of an attitude of concern toward the woman.

Still, we are left with some large and serious problems. Instead of grappling directly with the sexist principle that only a man had the right to divorce (i.e., write and transfer the get), the rabbis used various legal maneuvers to subvert the original principle. The exclusive right as derived from the Bible was never formally challenged; it was simply chiseled away, bit by bit. As a result, rabbinic authorities in any given generation could revert back to the original notion of a man's power over his wife.

An example of this is found in Rabbenu Gershom's decree that a man could not take more than one wife or divorce his wife against her will *(Shulhan Arukh,* Even ha-Ezer 1:10, 119:6, Rama). This was a significant breakthrough. But a minor qualification was appended to the end of this takkanah: if a recalcitrant wife refused a divorce or was physically unable to accept, a husband could deposit the get with the rabbinic court, announce his intention to divorce, receive the approval of a hundred rabbis, and then would be free to take another wife. Thus here, as in other instances, the more egalitarian decision concerning a woman's right of consent could be reversed or tempered in certain situations on the theory that the husband's legal right could not be abrogated. Somehow, in special-need cases, the Halakhah managed to find a way round the biblical and talmudic requirement that the husband hand her a get. One need not wonder why the Halakhah did not find a parallel—and equally necessary—loophole to allow a wife release from a similar situation.

This brings us to the second and more formidable problem: a woman could not and can not present her husband with a get and thereby divorce him, although she can do the actual writing of it. The theory is that the husband is the one who created the bond and therefore he must be the one to sever it (Kiddushin 56:9b). Nor is there any provision in Jewish law by which a get is granted judicially in the absence of or without the consent of the husband. Only the husband can grant a get.

This can give rise to the agunah, the anchored wife, anchored to an absentee husband.[7] There are two types of agunot: a woman whose husband either has deserted, is insane, or is missing and presumed dead but whose death has not been verified by two witnesses; and a woman who is the wife of a recalcitrant husband who refuses the get for ignoble reasons. This latter type of agunah points up the potential for real abuse in Jewish divorce law. Indeed, in every generation there have been sinister tales of spite, blackmail, extortion, and delay until the wife has met her recalcitrant husband's price.

Throughout the centuries rabbis have tried continually to alleviate the plight of the agunah. In talmudic times the bet din accepted her own testimony as sufficient proof of the husband's death, a sharp reversal of Halakhah, which required two male witnesses in all matters that come before the rabbinic courts; this is to protect her from the possibility that she might become forever anchored to an absentee husband (Gittin 3a). In talmudic law, a man was not permitted to leave the community without guaranteeing an agreement to divorce if he did not plan to return within a specified time (Gittin 6:5, 6; Ketubbot 11b). This was a regular feature of medieval Jewish society, where husbands had to leave for extended periods of time in order to earn a livelihood.[8]

In this era, contemporary rabbis expended great effort to release the agunot of the Holocaust. The Israeli rabbinate, too, has adapted Halakhah to Israel's current precarious reality. In a broad move, it required all married male soldiers to deposit a conditional writ of divorce with the bet din before going to the front lines. This was based on ancient precedent (Ketubbot 9b). Moreover, after the Yom Kippur War, in a single religious enactment, over a thousand young women were released from what otherwise would have been extended agunah proceedings.

Still, there remain many cases of agunot in Jewish communities around the world. Some cases are too hard to crack, some take years to settle, some women find they must pursue and beg. Despite the compassion of the many rabbis who resolve individual cases, women testify to a certain humiliating quality inherent in the basic notion of agunah, in her status in the community, and in the very process of release from this state.

Ironically, an open society has worked to the disadvantage of the Jewish woman who wants to bring suit for divorce. In the closed, relatively autonomous Jewish communities of the past, religious authorities could level sanctions against a recalcitrant husband; in modern societies, however, the rabbinic courts (outside of Israel) have authority only over those people who voluntarily submit themselves to its dictates. Contemporary batei din, trying to function in a secular society, have a low rate of success in their power of subpoena. Even in Israel there are men who have chosen to remain in jails to which the bet din remanded them rather than free their wives with a get.

Thus, in the attempt to reduce the disparity between man's power and woman's powerlessness in divorce, the rabbis tried hard—perhaps not hard enough. It would have taken little more collective responsibility to close the gap altogether, to create a situation of real equality under the law. The rabbis assumed wide powers of interpretation of divine law, and even of innovation, in situations where the general needs of the community called for accommodation to reality rather than rationalization of an unwieldy status quo. That the rabbis did not go the final step in equalizing divorce law indicates that they were guided in their interpretations by principles of paternalism and hierarchy rather than of equality of male and female. For this they cannot be faulted, given the almost universal nature of the sexual hierarchy. Failure of some contemporary rabbis, however, to use precedents that do exist and failure to acknowledge that past improvements in divorce law are but part of a continuing process leads one to conclude that many of them prefer to maintain the principle of absolute right, apologetic platitudes notwithstanding.

Several solutions have been formulated in modern times. Reform Judaism understood the Halakhah to be indefensible in terms of the ethical and social categories central to Reform, so it simply dropped gittin and said civil divorce will do. If one is concerned more for equality than for tradition, that solution meets the test. If, however, one's commitment is to both more equality and greater Jewish observance in every sphere of life, then that is no solution at all. In fairness, it should be added that Reform is asking of itself different questions today; it is searching for ways to make Jewish law altogether more encompassing. The time seems ripe for Reform to rethink its stance on gittin. Meanwhile, it has no operative Jewish divorce law.

Reconstructionism has formulated a solution that lies somewhere between the two ends of the spectrum—or, more correctly, at the two ends of the spectrum. The Reconstructionist rabbinate uses the traditional get and all of the attendant procedures. When a previously divorced woman wants to remarry but has been unable to secure a get from her former husband, the Reconstructionist bet din simply will give her a *shtar piturin,* a document that declares her free to remarry, even though she has no get, nor has her marriage been annulled.

For the last three decades, Conservative Judaism has gone through three stages of emendation in an attempt to eliminate potential abuse yet remain faithful to inherited tradition.[9] These changes are instructive, for they give some idea of the possibilities, the problems, and the processes involved.

The Lieberman ketubah was used first in 1954. By means of a takkanah, Rabbi Saul Lieberman appended a t'nai (conditional clause) to the standard ketubah: if the marriage ends in civil divorce, either party may invoke the authority of the bet din to determine the Jewish course of action, the transfer of a get. If either party refuses the get, he or she becomes liable to suit in civil court. Presumably the court will enforce the bet din's decision. Although this ketubah generally is no longer used for the purposes of resolving cases of a recalcitrant spouse, it is used widely in marriages performed by Conservative rabbis. (One of the problems with this ketubah was that it didn't cover divorce cases where the ketubah had not been used originally. Moreover, the credibility of its threat depended on its enforceability in a civil court, and this remains in doubt. The Lieberman clause was rejected by the Orthodox as being halakhically invalid because of its indeterminate nature. First, the damages [*knas,* fine] were not spelled out and, therefore, one would not sign such a contract making oneself liable to an undetermined penalty. The Lieberman ketubah, however, does use the word *pitzuim,* damages, a term often employed in contracts and one that is halakhically valid; this is about as specific as one would want to be at the time of a marriage ceremony. Second, the pledge the groom was making was considered an *asmakhta*—a pledge to pay a fine for a situation that he was not really expecting would come to pass.)

The second stage was adoption of the Berkovits t'nai in 1968, which differs from the Lieberman solution in that it attached conditions to the act of marriage itself. Rabbi Eliezer Berkovits based his work on two elements: the principle that a marriage could be nullified by the rabbinic authorities, and the precedent in Jewish law of establishing specific conditions for a marriage. Unmet, such conditions would enable a bet din to determine that the marriage was voided retroactively and never legally constituted. This precedent had also been used by the rabbis of Paris in the late nineteenth century. The Berkovits conditions were that the couple not be separated for an undue amount of time, that neither refuses (or becomes unable) to give or accept a divorce, and that the wife does not conceive out of adulterous union. The Conservative law committee modified this, and Rabbi Edward Gershfield worked out a text to this effect: if our marriage should end in a civil divorce and within six months thereafter I give you a get, our marriage will remain valid and binding; if, however, six months have passed and I do not give you a get, then our marriage will have been null and void. This was not appended to the ketubah; it was signed as a separate prenuptial agreement. In this instance there was no need to turn to the civil courts to enforce the get. On the other hand, its being a separate document was also its weakness; couples were reluctant to sign it at such a happy moment in their lives. (This proposal was rejected by the Orthodox on the grounds that marriage is an unconditional commitment and conditional marriages and divorces thereby are rendered invalid by consummation of the marriage.[10])

The third-stage solution, widely operative in Conservative Judaism today in problem divorce cases, is a broader application of *havkha'at kiddushin* (the power of the rabbis to annul marriages ab initio) (Bava Batra 48b; Gittin 33a; Kiddushin 3a). It is based on the talmudic principle that all who marry within the Jewish community do so with the implied consent of and under the conditions laid down by the rabbis. (The phrase "according to the laws of Moses and Israel" is in the ketubah and is also a central part of the ring ceremony.) Thus, a man's act of marrying a woman is validated by the rabbis' sanction of that act. Just as they give sanction, so can they remove sanction; the marriage continues to exist only as long as the rabbis agree to its existence. If the rabbis remove their sanction because of certain conditions no longer operating, the original act of kiddushin (betrothal) is voided. Retroactively, it becomes simply an act of giving a gift, such as a ring. And what about a marriage that was consummated? Even there, the rabbis could declare the sexual liaison to have been a non-marital act (i.e., an act of prostitution).

How does it work today in Conservative Judaism? In the case of a recalcitrant husband, the wife first goes to her own rabbi for help. If he cannot compel the husband (ex-husband by civil law) to grant a get, the wife then appears before a special bet din established by the Conservative rabbinate. She produces her civil divorce as well as proof of previous good-faith attempts to secure a get. If the bet din is satisfied, it will issue a document retroactively declaring the marriage null and void, and she is then free to remarry. This differs from the Berkovits t'nai in that no additional conditions are attached to the marriage and no special agreement needs to be signed. This, too, was rejected by many Orthodox rabbis, on the grounds that the power to annul marriages was used only in limited instances and in post-talmudic times the power to annul marriages has been constricted.

What has been done by the Orthodox community? Beyond rejecting the strides taken by Conservative Judaism there has been little movement. Meanwhile, increasing numbers of traditional women who have sued for divorce face the threat of blackmail for a get.

The winds of change are in the air, however. In 1967, when Berkovits published his book, *T'nai be-nisuin u-ve-get* (Conditional clause in marriage and divorce agreements), he intended it not for Conservative Judaism but for the Orthodox community of which he is a member. Initially he had the approval of his teacher, the eminent *posek* Harav Yechiel Yaakov Weinberg. With increasing pressure from the right, the ailing Weinberg withdrew his approval, and the vocal elements in the Orthodox rabbinate utterly rejected Berkovits's proposal. There was quiet support for Berkovits, but quiet support doesn't help much.

In the early 1970s, Ze'ev Falk, an Orthodox professor at the Hebrew University, updated the facts.[11] He gave a generous survey of all previous solutions offered, stating that the recalcitrant husband situation is more widespread in Israel than in the United States, with cases often taking up to ten years to resolve through the religious courts, ten years during which a woman cannot remarry. In 1977, Irwin Haut[12] traced the history of an ancient takkanah enacted by the geonim and used by them for over three hundred years: if, after twelve months, the wife does not relent in her pursuit of a get, the husband can be forced by the bet din to give one to her. This takkanah was enacted long ago to put an end to the practice of Jewish women hiring gentile strong-arm men "to force him until he says I want to." Haut calls for the Israeli rabbinate, as a centralized authority, to enact a new takkanah, along the lines of the geonic one that long since has expired. It would compel a man who lives outside Israel and who has been granted a civil divorce to give his wife a get; if a man so enjoined by the bet din, whether in the diaspora or in Israel, still refuses, then the bet din shall declare the marriage annulled or dissolved. The difference between this solution and the Conservative one today is the use of a takkanah and the centralization of authority in the Israeli rabbinate.

In *Jewish Women in Jewish Law,* widely read in Orthodox circles, Moshe Meiselman acknowledges the problem of recalcitrant husbands.[13] In his unswerving desire not to touch the halakhic status quo, he calls on the secular courts for a solution: the civil court should enforce the decision of the bet din when it recommends a get and none is forthcoming. Meiselman doesn't deal with the First Amendment issue; moreover, although he acknowledges the very sporadic success in civil courts thus far, he waves that problem aside with the unfounded optimism that the problems will be solved by better education of civil judges.[14] But he does call for repair.

At its annual convention in 1978, the Rabbinical Council of America devoted a major session to the contemporary problems in gittin. Rabbi Meir Feldblum, a noted halakhic authority, raised the issues and several solutions. At Bar Ilan University's Conference on Jewish Women in 1978, the president, Rabbi Emanuel Rackman, an acknowledged leader of modern Orthodoxy, opened the deliberations with a halakhic history of *havka'at kiddushin.* He forthrightly called for its use by the rabbinate. Several months later he repeated this call in print; his message was picked up on the front page of several American Jewish weeklies.

Finally, there have been the efforts of women, in smaller and larger communities. A group of Orthodox women in a Canadian city simply announced that none of them would go to the mikveh until a friend of theirs received a free get from her ex-husband, who was holding out for twenty-five thousand dollars. The woman received her get in no time. In 1980, an organization called G.E.T. was formed by traditional women who intend to apply pressure until women Get Equal Treatment in Jewish divorce proceedings.

Nevertheless, the problems of inequity remain, with an increasing number of women—the traditional women—paying a steep price for their adherence to Halakhah. What is more, an altogether new problem exists, unprecedented in Jewish history: a community operating by four different sets of divorce law, as if we were four different communities.

What remains to be done, then, is to formulate a solution that would solve both problems: eliminate any potential for abuse of women and unite all branches of Judaism in its universal acceptance. To achieve both means that all Jews will have to accept that there is something distinctive about being a Jew and living under Jewish law. It means that we will all have a heightened sense of awareness that marriage and divorce and every other sweep of our lives should be experienced properly within the framework of a holy community.

Like most of our rituals, divinely mandated and contoured by several millennia of Jewish living, a Jewish divorce is about as finely tuned to the human need of the moment as one could anticipate. Unlike the final moment in a civil divorce, a Jewish divorce is not an adversary situation. There is no litigation, no grounds, no recriminations, no attempts at reconciliation, no high drama. In fact, there is almost no conversation. All of that, whatever there was of it, took place at another time. The divorce itself is an unadorned legal procedure, performed at the last stage, an act that lends a profound sense of finality and closure to the relationship. This is no small feat, for as social scientists increasingly report, a sense of closure is one of the most difficult stages for one to reach in the throes of a divorce.

But it is not its worthiness as a therapeutic tool on which the strength of Jewish divorce rests. A Jewish divorce, like a Jewish marriage, a Jewish birth, or a Jewish death, is, quite simply, the way a Jew lives. This is how Jews have done these things for several millennia; this is the manner in which one marks oneself as a Jew today.

Thus leaders of all of the branches of Judaism will have to come together and talk to each other in order to work out a mutually acceptable solution, each recognizing the other as part of *klal Yisrael,* the total Jewish community. Smug, isolationist positions will have to fall away.

To help that process along, women will have to increase their efforts. Given the current nature of entrenched interests and institutional hard lines, Jewish women of every political and religious shade must attempt to bring together the dissonant ends and to fill the vacuum created by loss of initiative of current religious leaders. Who can know the impact of a thousand women protesting to the leaders of Reform Judaism for restoration of a halakhic Jewish divorce law? Who can know the effect of a thousand Jews calling on the bet din of the Rabbinical Council of America to reexamine the current injustices in halakhic divorce? (Surely the rabbinic authorities would approach their storehouse of halakhic precedents and principles with a different sense of urgency, in much the same way they have done in so many individual cases of agunot.) Who knows but that the pressure on Conservative leadership will spur them to seek greater cooperation with all strata of the Jewish religious community?

It is hard to project what the optimal form of revision ultimately will be. Perhaps it will be along the lines of *havka'at kiddushin,* used by the Conservative bet din and recommended by numerous Orthodox scholars. Perhaps it will be a conditional clause added to the ketubah. Perhaps the diaspora rabbinate will place it in the hands of the Israeli rabbinate, where the centralization of authority in family law lends itself more easily to global rather than individual solutions.

Perhaps, with a new sense of equality of women, the revision will take the form of a takkanah that will empower a woman to transfer a get. If, as halakhists defensively point out, marriage is a change of status rather than unilateral acquisition of woman by man, if a woman is a mutually active and reciprocal partner in all of these transactions, if divorce is a more halakhically correct way of ending a marriage than annulment, then having a woman deliver the get where a man refuses may be a better halakhic solution all around. A usable precedent may be one that circumvents the law requiring a husband to pay for the writing of the get. When a man refused to pay the scribal fee, the court required the woman to pay so that the husband would not cause her delay in securing her freedom (Bava Batra 168a).

All of this brings us to the question of tradition and change. In view of the fact that the unfolding Halakhah on divorce reflects an unmistakable pattern of limiting the husband's and expanding the wife's rights, the rabbis of today no longer can say they can not "work it out." To say their hands are tied, or to say they can resolve an individual problem but not find a global solution, is to deny their collective responsibility. Worse, it bespeaks a lack of rabbinic will to find a halakhic way. What they are really saying is they are not worthy of the authority vested in them, for well they know that the only person whose hands are tied is the woman whose family must pay blackmail.

If there were no abuses in the area of divorce, I would not mind the male prerogative preserved and this law untouched. A one-sided kiddushin harbors no real injustice and ought to be appreciated for what it is: an ancient rabbinic tradition, the Jewish way men and women have married for thousands of years. In that alone there is great value and sentiment.

But given the opposite condition today—increasing abuse—halakhists ought to commit themselves not only to alleviation of individual distress here and there but to the notion of a just law. For alleviation of an individual is not justice for an entire system. If halakhists do not put their minds and energies to this problem, then I suspect that we will see what we have seen in the past—the regulation of one more area of human relations shrinking in the hands of the interpreters of Jewish law, as growing numbers of Jews solve their problems elsewhere.[15]

Broadscale resolution of the inequity would serve another advantage. It would eliminate the enormous cost in rabbinic time and energy now spent in trying to procure a get from a recalcitrant husband. Religious leaders would then be free to attend to the real problem: the factors behind the rising rate of divorce, the unreal expectations of marriage, the ideology of "me first," the impatience men and women have when it comes to working steadily at a relationship.

Some years ago, when I first began to research the subject, I felt a great ambivalence, even a sense of dread, as I spoke of fundamental change of the biblical principle of absolute right. Part of that dread grows out of my spiritual rootedness in a community that, at most, allows itself to speak in hushed tones about gradual changes over a period of two millennia. Nor am I unmindful of the fact that the divinity of the Torah has remained so strong throughout the ages, precisely because the rabbis were so careful not to forbid what was permitted and permit what was forbidden. By nature and education, then, I have always preferred solutions that involved least change in the basic structure of Halakhah.

Nevertheless, I must stop and ask whether halfway steps would be doing a disservice to Jewish women, say, ten generations from now. Has that not happened to women in this generation of Jewish living in an open society? Moreover, with increased understanding of law and process I must question whether the principle is truly principle. Perhaps the essence of biblical law is the delivery of the get, a formal document that gives proper legal and psychological closure to a relationship. Perhaps the male prerogative—man giving the get to woman—is but form and not essence. Perhaps it was an accident of history that a pervasive notion of hierarchy of the sexes enabled procedure to be hardened into principle, thereby blocking out other more important principles such as *tikkun olam,* improvement of the social order, equality for all members of the covenanted community.

Inevitably, there will always be injustice and imbalances in every divorce situation; that, sadly, is the nature of the dissolution of a human relationship. But the law should not discriminate against one sex. And if there is one woman in each generation who suffers unnecessarily as a result of the law, then the law is biased against all women.

If, as I believe, Judaism is the most ethical, most sensitive of all religions, if since revelation Judaism has moved toward its own best values, a reinterpretation that would bring about greater equality should be articulated not in categories of change/no change but rather as part of the organic growth of a holy people as it moves through history.

Notes

1. I recommend four excellent sources on this topic, two in English and two in Hebrew: David Werner Amram, *The Jewish Law of Divorce in the Bible and Talmud* (New York: Hermon, 1968); Ze'ev Falk, *Divorce Action by the Wife in the Middle Ages* (Jerusalem: Hebrew University, 1973); Benzion Schereschewsky, *Dinei mishpahah* [Family law] (Jerusalem: R. Mass, 1967); Eliezer Berkovits, *T'nai be-nisuin u-ve-get* [Conditional clause in the marriage and divorce agreements] (Jerusalem: Mossad Harav Kuk, 1967).
2. See James B. Pritchard, ed., *Ancient Near Eastern Texts* (Princeton: Princeton University Press, 1969), 137–40; Roland de Vaux, *Ancient Israel: Its Life and Institutions* (New York: McGraw-Hill, 1965), ch. 2.
3. Rabbi Akiba extended this further: it was within the rights of the husband to discard his wife if he found another he liked better; he based his interpretation on the phrase "if she found no favor in his eyes." See Meyer S. Feldblum, *Talmudic Law and Literature* (New York: Yeshiva University, 1969), 221–23.
4. Since this was an abrogation of the biblical right of the husband, the rabbis saw fit to explain their action. They forbade it because they understood the consequences, that the woman would become destitute and helpless and an easy prey. But they "covered" their humane tracks with a legal rationale. Since the Torah required the get be given "into her hand," it must have been meant that she be capable of receiving it (i.e., in possession of her full faculties; this was one instance where "into her hand" was applied as principle and not merely as procedure). Further, the Torah described a divorcée as "one who is cast away from his house and, therefore, will not return. But an insane person, you send her away and she keeps coming back" (Yevamot 113b). This is an example of that profound rabbinic process, of making rabbinic law "continuous" with the

Torah. Interestingly, when Maimonides describes this ruling, he cites only the humane reason and not the legally continuous one *(Mishneh Torah,* Hilkhot Gerushin 10:23). Tracing the process a step further, in medieval times, after the ban on polygamy was enacted, the rabbis occasionally granted dispensation to the husband of an insane woman to take another wife. This was permitted, however, only when the insanity was deemed incurable and the husband provided adequately for her care, a rather humane solution all around. Maimonides' formulation is a bit harsher: the husband sets her aside, takes another wife, and when she becomes well he then divorces her. In other words, there is no condition of incurability here. Moreover, the husband is not required to provide shelter, medical care, nor ransom money *(Mishneh Torah,* Hilkhot Gerushin 10:23). Obviously, Maimonides applied neither Rabbenu Gershom's ban against forcible divorce nor exceptions to it. On the other hand, Maimonides went further than Rabbenu Gershom in certain respects.

5. The *Shulhan Arukh* lists 101 steps in the rules of procedure attending divorce. The Rama adds several notes and refinements to that list. See Amram, *Jewish Law of Divorce,* 192–204. Another work used by those who deal regularly with gittin is the *Kav Naki,* the seventeenth-century comprehensive manual of divorce procedures.
6. There was even a Spanish tradition that required no grounds at all: "If she says, 'I despise him,' in my opinion we compel him to divorce her immediately, for she isn't like a captive that she must have intercourse with someone who is hateful to her" *(Mishneh Torah,* Hilkhot Ishut 14:8).
7. See Chaim Grade's novel, *The Agunah* (Boston: Twayne, 1974).
8. See Israel Abrahams, *Jewish Life in the Middle Ages* (New York: Atheneum, 1969), 90.
9. See Seymour Siegel, "The Living Halakhah: Conservative Judaism and Jewish Law," *United Synagogue Review* (winter 1979).
10. See Moshe Meiselman, *Jewish Women and Jewish Law* (New York: Ktav, 1978), 103–8.
11. Ze'ev Falk, *The Divorce Action by the Wife in Jewish Law* (Jerusalem: ILRCL, 1973).
12. Irwin Haut, "A Problem in Jewish Divorce Law: An Analysis and Some Suggestions," *Tradition* 16 (spring 1977): 29–49.
13. Meiselman, *Jewish Women,* ch. 14.
14. Several scholars and legal historians have shown the inherent fallacy of relying on the civil courts in this matter. See, for example, A. Leo Levin and Mayer Kramer, *New Provisions in the Ketubah: A Legal Opinion* (New York: Yeshiva University, 1955).
15. See Stephen Beiner, "Israeli Divorce Proceedings: A Comparative Study" (unpublished).

[28]

Casti Connubii, Humanae Vitae, and *Familiaris Consortio*

Pope Pius XI, Pope Paul VI, and Pope John Paul II

Casti Connubii (1930)

Contraception

53. Turning now, Venerable Brethren, to treat in detail the vices which are contrary to each of the blessings of matrimony, we must begin with the consideration of offspring, which many nowadays have the effrontery to call a troublesome burden of wedlock—a burden which they urge married folk carefully to avoid, not by means of a virtuous continence (which is permissible even in marriage with the consent of both parties) but by vitiating the act of nature. This criminal abuse is claimed as a right by some on the ground that they cannot endure children, but want to satisfy their carnal desire without incurring any responsibility. Others plead that they can neither observe continence nor, for personal reasons or for reasons affecting the mother, or on account of economic difficulties, can they consent to have children.

Source: From Pope Pius XI, *Casti Connubii,* 1930; from Pope Paul VI, *Humanae Vitae,* 1968; from Pope John Paul II, *Familiaris Consortio,* 1981;

54. But no reason whatever, even the gravest, can make what is intrinsically against nature become conformable with nature and morally good. The conjugal act is of its very nature designed for the procreation of offspring; and therefore those who in performing it deliberately deprive it of its natural power and efficacy, act against nature and do something which is shameful and intrinsically immoral.

55. We cannot wonder, then, if we find evidence in the Sacred Scriptures that the Divine Majesty detests this unspeakable crime with the deepest hatred and has sometimes punished it with death, as St. Augustine observes: "Sexual intercourse even with a lawful wife is unlawful and shameful if the conception of offspring is prevented. This is what Onan, the son of Judah, did, and on that account God put him to death."

A Renewed Condemnation

56. Wherefore, since there are some who, openly departing from the Christian teaching which has been handed down uninterruptedly from the beginning, have in recent times thought fit solemnly to preach another doctrine concerning this practice, the Catholic Church, to whom God has committed the task of teaching and preserving morals and right conduct in their integrity, standing erect amidst this moral devastation, raises her voice in sign of her divine mission to keep the chastity of the marriage contract unsullied by this ugly stain, and through Our mouth proclaims anew: that any use of matrimony whatsoever in the exercise of which the act is deprived, by human interference, of its natural power to procreate life, is an offense against the law of God and of nature, and that those who commit it are guilty of a grave sin.

Humanae Vitae (1968)

Unlawful Ways of Regulating Birth

14. Therefore we base our words on the first principles of a human and Christian doctrine of marriage when we are obliged once more to declare that the direct interruption of the generative process already begun and, above all, direct abortion, even for therapeutic reasons, are to be absolutely excluded as lawful means of controlling the birth of children.[1]

Equally to be condemned, as the Magisterium of the Church has affirmed on various occasions, is direct sterilization, whether of the man or of the woman, whether permanent or temporary.[2]

Similarly excluded is any action, which either before, at the moment of, or after sexual intercourse, is specifically intended to prevent procreation—whether as an end or as a means.[3]

Neither is it valid to argue, as a justification for sexual intercourse which is deliberately contraceptive, that a lesser evil is to be preferred to a greater one, or that such intercourse would merge with the normal relations of past and future to form a single entity, and so be qualified by exactly the same moral goodness as these. Though it is true that sometimes it is lawful to tolerate a lesser moral evil in order to avoid a greater or in order to promote a greater good,[4] it is never lawful, even for the gravest reasons, to do evil that good may come of it[5]—in other words, to intend positively something which intrinsically contradicts the moral order, and which must therefore be judged unworthy of man, even though the intention is to protect or promote the welfare of an individual, of a family or of society in general. Consequently it is a serious error to think that a whole married life of otherwise normal relations can justify sexual intercourse which is deliberately contraceptive and so intrinsically wrong.

Lawfulness of Therapeutic Means

15. But the Church in no way regards as unlawful therapeutic means considered necessary to cure organic diseases, even though they also have a contraceptive effect, and this is foreseen—provided that this contraceptive effect is not directly intended for any motive whatsoever.[6]

Lawfulness of Recourse to Infertile Periods

16. However, as We noted earlier (n. 3), some people today raise the objection against this particular doctrine of the Church concerning the moral laws governing marriage, that human intelligence has both the right and the responsibility to control those forces of irrational nature which come within its ambit and to direct them towards ends beneficial to man. Others ask on the same point whether it is not reasonable in so many cases to use artificial birth control if by so doing the harmony and peace of a family are better served and more suitable conditions are provided for the education of children already born. To this question we must give a clear reply. The Church is the first to praise and commend the application of human intelligence to an activity in which a rational creature such as man is so closely associated with his Creator. But she affirms that this must be done within the limits of the order of reality established by God.

If therefore there are reasonable grounds for spacing births, arising from the physical or psychological condition of husband or wife, or from external circumstances, the Church teaches that then married people may take advantage of the natural cycles immanent in the reproductive system and use their marriage at precisely those times that are infertile, and in this way control birth, a way which does not in the least offend the moral principles which we have just explained.[7]

Neither the Church nor her doctrine is inconsistent when she considers it lawful for married people to take advantage of the infertile period but condemns as always unlawful the use of means which directly exclude conception, even when the reasons given for the latter practice are neither trivial nor immoral. In reality, these two cases are completely different. In the former married couples rightly use a facility provided them by nature. In the latter they obstruct the natural development of the generative process. It cannot be denied that in each case married couples, for acceptable reasons, are both perfectly clear in their intention to avoid children and mean to make sure that none will be born. But it is equally true that it is exclusively in the former case that husband and wife are ready to abstain from intercourse during the fertile period as often as for reasonable motives the birth of another child is not desirable. And when the infertile period recurs, they use their married intimacy to express their mutual love and safeguard their fidelity towards one another. In doing this they certainly give proof of a true and authentic love.

Grave Consequences of Artificial Birth Control

17. Responsible men can become more deeply convinced of the truth of the doctrine laid down by the Church on this issue if they reflect on the consequences of methods and plans for the artificial restriction of increases in the birthrate. Let them first consider how easily this course of action can lead to the way being wide open to marital infidelity and a general lowering of moral standards. Not much experience is needed to be fully aware of human weakness and to understand that men—and especially the young, who are so exposed to temptation—need incentives to keep the moral law, and it is an evil thing to make it easy for them to break that law. Another effect that gives cause for alarm is that a man who grows accustomed to the use of contraceptive methods may forget the reverence due to a woman, and, disregarding her physical and emotional equilibrium, reduce her to being a mere instrument for the satisfaction of his own desires, no longer considering her as his partner whom he should surround with care and affection.

Finally, grave consideration should be given to the danger of this power passing into the hands of those public authorities who care little for the precepts of the moral law. Who will blame a Government which in its attempt to resolve the problems affecting an entire country resorts to the same measures as are regarded as lawful by married people in the solution of a particular family difficulty? Who will prevent public authorities from favoring those contraceptive methods which they consider more effective? Should they regard this as necessary, they may even impose their use on everyone. It could well happen, therefore, that when people, either individually or in family or social life, experience the inherent difficulties of the divine law and are determined to avoid them, they may be giving into the hands of public authorities the power to intervene in the most personal and intimate responsibility of husband and wife.

Consequently, unless we are willing that the responsibility of procreating life should be left to the arbitrary decision of men, we must accept that there are certain limits, beyond which it is wrong to go, to the power of man over his own body and its natural functions—limits, let it be said, which no one, whether as a private individual or as a public authority, can lawfully exceed. These limits are expressly imposed because of the reverence due to the whole human organism and its natural functions, in the light of the principles, which we stated earlier, and according to a correct understanding of the so-called "principle of totality," enunciated by Our Predecessor, Pope Pius XII.[8]

The Church, Guarantor of True Human Values

18. It is to be anticipated that not everyone perhaps will easily accept this particular teaching. There is too much clamorous outcry against the voice of the Church, and this is intensified by modern means of communication. It should cause no surprise that the Church, any less than her divine Founder, is destined to be a "sign of contradiction."[9] She does not, because of this, evade the duty imposed on her of proclaiming humbly but firmly the entire moral law, both natural and evangelical.

Since the Church did not make either of these laws, she cannot be their arbiter—only their guardian and interpreter. It can never be right for her to declare lawful what is in fact unlawful, because this, by its very nature, is always opposed to the true good of man.

By vindicating the integrity of the moral law of marriage, the Church is convinced that she is contributing to the creation of a truly human civilization. She urges man not to betray his personal responsibilities by putting all his faith in technical expedients. In this way she defends the dignity of husband and wife. This course of action shows that the Church, loyal to the example and teaching of the divine Savior, is sincere and unselfish in her regard for men whom she strives to help even now during this earthly pilgrimage "to share as sons in the life of the living God, the Father of all men."[10]

Familiaris Consortio (1981)

28. With the creation of man and woman in his own image and likeness, God crowns and brings to perfection the work of his hands: he calls them to a special sharing in his love and in his power as Creator and Father, through their free and responsible cooperation in transmitting the gift of human life: "God blessed them, and God said to them, 'Be fruitful and multiply, and fill the earth and subdue it.'"[11]

Thus the fundamental task of the family is to serve life, to actualize in history the original blessing of the Creator—that of transmitting by procreation the divine image from person to person.[12]

Fecundity is the fruit and the sign of conjugal love, the living testimony of the full reciprocal self-giving of the spouses: "While not making the other purposes of matrimony of less account, the true practice of conjugal love, and the whole meaning of the family life which results from it, have this aim: that the couple be ready with stout hearts to cooperate with the love of the Creator and the Savior, who through them will enlarge and enrich his own family day by day."[13]

However, the fruitfulness of conjugal love is not restricted solely to the procreation of children, even understood in its specifically human dimension: it is enlarged and enriched by all those fruits of moral, spiritual, and supernatural life which the father and mother are called to hand on to their children, and through the children to the Church and to the world.

29. Precisely because the love of husband and wife is a unique participation in the mystery of life and of the love of God himself, the Church knows that she has received the special mission of guarding and protecting the lofty dignity of marriage and the most serious responsibility of the transmission of human life.

Thus, in continuity with the living tradition of the ecclesial community throughout history, the recent Second Vatican Council and the magisterium of my predecessor Paul VI, expressed above all in the Encyclical *Humanae Vitae,* have handed on to our times a truly prophetic proclamation, which reaffirms and reproposes with clarity the Church's teaching and norm, always old yet always new, regarding marriage and regarding the transmission of human life.

For this reason the Synod Fathers made the following declaration at their last assembly: "This Sacred Synod, gathered together with the Successor of Peter in the unity of faith, firmly holds what has been set forth in the Second Vatican Council (cf. *Gaudium et Spes,* 50) and afterwards in the Encyclical *Humanae Vitae,* particularly that love between husband and wife must be fully human, exclusive, and open to new life (*Humanae Vitae,* 11; cf. 9, 12)."[14]

30. The teaching of the Church in our day is placed in a social and cultural context which renders it more difficult to understand and yet more urgent and irreplaceable for promoting the true good of men and women.

Scientific and technical progress, which contemporary man is continually expanding in his dominion over nature, not only offers the hope of creating a new and better humanity, but also causes ever greater anxiety regarding the future. Some ask themselves if it is a good thing to be alive or if it would be better never to have been born; they doubt therefore if it is right to bring others into life when perhaps they will curse their existence in a cruel world with unforeseeable terrors. Others consider themselves to be the only ones for whom the advantages of technology are intended and they exclude others by imposing on them contraceptives or even worse means. Still others, imprisoned in a consumer mentality and whose sole concern is to bring about a continual growth of material goods, finish by ceasing to understand, and thus by refusing, the spiritual riches of a new human life. The ultimate reason for these mentalities is the absence in people's hearts of God, whose love alone is stronger than all the world's fears and can conquer them.

Thus an anti-life mentality is born, as can be seen in many current issues: one thinks, for example, of a certain panic deriving from the studies of ecologists and futurologists on population growth, which sometimes exaggerate the danger of demographic increase to the quality of life.

But the Church firmly believes that human life, even if weak and suffering, is always a splendid gift of God's goodness. Against the pessimism and selfishness which cast a shadow over the world, the Church stands for life: in each human life she sees the splendor of that "Yes," that "Amen," who is Christ himself.[15] To the "No" which assails and afflicts the world, she replies with this living "Yes," thus defending the human person and the world from all who plot against and harm life.

The Church is called upon to manifest anew to everyone, with clear and stronger conviction, her will to promote human life by every means and to defend it against all attacks, in whatever condition or state of development it is found.

Thus the Church condemns as a grave offense against human dignity and justice all those activities of governments or other public authorities which attempt to limit in any way the freedom of couples in deciding about children. Consequently any violence applied by such authorities in favor of contraception or, still worse, of sterilization and procured abortion, must be altogether condemned and forcefully rejected. Likewise to be denounced as gravely unjust are cases where, in international relations, economic help given for the advancement of peoples is made conditional on programs of contraception, sterilization, and procured abortion.[16]

31. The Church is certainly aware of the many complex problems which couples in many countries face today in their task of transmitting life in a responsible way. She also recognizes the serious problem of population growth in the form it has taken in many parts of the world and its moral implications.

However, she holds that consideration in depth of all the aspects of these problems offers a new and stronger confirmation of the importance of the authentic teaching on birth regulation reproposed in the Second Vatican Council and in the Encyclical *Humanae Vitae.*

For this reason, together with the Synod Fathers I feel it is my duty to extend a pressing invitation to theologians, asking them to unite their efforts in order to collaborate with the hierarchical Magisterium and to commit themselves to the task of illustrating ever more clearly the biblical foundations, the ethical grounds, and the personalistic reasons behind this doctrine. Thus it will be possible, in the context of an organic exposition, to render the teaching of the Church on this fundamental question truly accessible to all people of good will, fostering a daily more enlightened and profound understanding of it: in this way God's plan will be ever more completely fulfilled for the salvation of humanity and for the glory of the Creator.

A united effort by theologians in this regard, inspired by a convinced adherence to the Magisterium, which is the one authentic guide for the People of God, is particularly urgent for reasons that include the close link between Catholic teaching on this matter and the view of the human person that the Church proposes: doubt or error in the field of marriage or the family involves obscuring to a serious extent the integral truth about the human person, in a cultural situation that is already so often confused and contradictory. In fulfillment of their specific role, theologians are called upon to provide enlightenment and a deeper understanding, and their contribution is of incomparable value and represents a unique and highly meritorious service to the family and humanity.

32. In the context of a culture which seriously distorts or entirely misinterprets the true meaning of human sexuality, because it separates it from its essential reference to the person, the Church more urgently feels how irreplaceable is her mission of presenting sexuality as a value and task of the whole person, created male and female in the image of God.

In this perspective the Second Vatican Council clearly affirmed that "when there is a question of harmonizing conjugal love with the responsible transmission of life, the moral aspect of any procedure does not depend solely on sincere intentions or on an evaluation of motives. It must be determined by *objective standards.* These, *based on the nature of the human person and his or her acts,* preserve the full sense of mutual self-giving and human procreation in the context of true love. Such a goal cannot be achieved unless the virtue of conjugal chastity is sincerely practiced."[17]

It is precisely by moving from "an integral vision of man and of his vocation, not only his natural and earthly, but also his supernatural and eternal vocation,"[18] that Paul VI affirmed that the teaching of the Church "is founded upon the inseparable connection, willed by God and unable to be broken by man on his own initiative, between the two meanings of the conjugal act: the unitive meaning and the procreative meaning."[19] And he concluded by re-emphasizing that there must be excluded as intrinsically immoral "every action which, either in anticipation of the conjugal act, or in its accomplishment, or in the development of its natural consequences, proposes, whether as an end or as a means, to render procreation impossible."[20]

When couples, by means of recourse to contraception, separate these two meanings that God the Creator has inscribed in the being of man and woman and in the dynamism of their sexual communion, they act as "arbiters" of the divine plan and they "manipulate" and degrade human sexuality—and with it themselves and their married partner—by altering its value of "total" self-giving. Thus the innate language that expresses the total reciprocal self-giving of husband and wife is overlaid, through contraception, by an objectively contradictory language, namely, that of not giving oneself totally to the other. This leads not only to a positive refusal to be open to life but also to a falsification of the inner truth of conjugal love, which is called upon to give itself in personal totality.

When, instead, by means of recourse to periods of infertility, the couple respect the inseparable connection between the unitive and procreative meanings of human sexuality, they are acting as "ministers" of God's plan and they "benefit from" their sexuality according to the original dynamism of "total" self-giving, without manipulation or altercation.[21]

In the light of the experience of many couples and of the data provided by the different human sciences, theological reflection is able to perceive and is called to study further *the difference, both anthropological and moral,* between contraception and recourse to the rhythm of the cycle: it is a difference which is much wider and deeper than is usually thought, one which involves in the final analysis two irreconcilable concepts of the human person and of human sexuality. The choice of the natural rhythms involves accepting the cycle of the person, that is the woman, and thereby accepting dialogue, reciprocal respect, shared responsibility, and self-control. To accept the cycle and to enter into dialogue means to recognize both the spiritual and corporal character of conjugal communion, and to live personal love with its requirement of fidelity. In this context the couple comes to experience how conjugal communion is enriched with those values of tenderness and affection which constitute the inner soul of human sexuality, in its physical dimension also. In this way sexuality is respected and promoted in its truly and fully human dimension, and is never "used" as an "object" that, by breaking the personal unity of soul and body, strikes at God's creation itself at the level of the deepest interaction of nature and person.

Notes

1. Cf. Council of Trent Roman Catechism, Part II, ch. 8; Pius XI, Encycl. *Casti Connubii,* AAS 22 (1930), 562–64 (C.T.S. translation, nn. 62–66); Pius XII, Address to the Medico-Biological Union of St Luke, *Discorsi e Radiomessaggi,* VI, 191–92; Address to Midwives, AAS 43 (1951), 842–43 (C.T.S. translation, nn. 20–26); Address to the "Family Campaign" and other Family Associations, AAS 43 (1951), 857–59 (C.T.S. translation, nn. 6–15); John XXIII, Encycl. *Pacem in terris,* AAS 55 (1963), 259–60 (C.T.S. translation, nn. 8–13); Vatican Council II, Pastoral Constitution on the Church in the World of Today *Gaudium et spes,* n. 51, AAS 58 (1966), 1072.
2. Cf. Pius XI, Encycl. *Casti Connubii,* AAS 22 (1930), 565 (C.T.S. translation, nn. 67–70); Decree of the Holy Office, 22 Feb. 1940, AAS 32 (1940), 73; Pius XII, Address to Midwives, AAS 43 (1951), 843–44 (C.T.S. translation, nn. 24–28); to the Society of Haematology, AAS 50 (1958), 734–35.
3. Cf. Council of Trent Roman Catechism, Part II, ch. 8; Pius XI, Encycl. *Casti Connubii,* AAS 22 (1930), 559–61 (C.T.S. translation, nn. 53–57); Pius XII, Address to Midwives, AAS 43 (1951), 843 (C.T.S. translation, n. 24); to the Society of Haematology, AAS 50 (1958), 734–35; John XXIII, Encycl. *Mater et Magistra,* AAS 53 (1961), 447 (C.T.S. translation, n. 193).
4. Cf. Pius XII, Address to the National Congress of the Italian Society of the Union of Catholic Jurists, AAS 45 (1953), 798–99.
5. Cf. Rom 3:8.
6. Cf. Pius XII, Address to the twenty-sixth Congress of the Italian Association of Urology, AAS 45 (1953), 674–75; to the Society of Haematology, AAS 50 (1958), 734–35.
7. Cf. Pius XII, Address to Midwives, AAS 43 (1951), 846 (C.T.S. translation, n. 36).
8. Cf. Pius XII, Address to the Association of Urology, AAS 45 (1953), 674–75; to Leaders and Members of the Italian Association of "corneae" donors and the Italian Association of the Blind, AAS 48 (1956), 461–62.
9. Lk 2:34.
10. Cf. Paul VI, Encycl. *Populorum Progressio,* AAS 59 (1967), 268 (C.T.S. translation, n. 21).
11. Gen 1:28.
12. Cf. Gen 5:1–3.

13. Second Vatican Ecumenical Council, Pastoral Constitution on the Church in the Modern World *Gaudium et Spes,* 50.
14. *Propositio* 21. Section 11 of the Encyclical *Humanae Vitae* ends with the statement: "The Church, calling people back to the observance of the norms of the natural law, as interpreted by her constant doctrine, teaches that each and every marriage act must remain open to the transmission of life (*ut quilibet matrimonii usus ad vitam humanam procreandam per se destinatus permaneat*)": AAS 60 (1968), 488.
15. Cf. 2 Cor 1:19; Rev 3:14.
16. Cf. the Sixth Synod of Bishops' Message to Christian Families in the Modern World (24 October 1980), 5.
17. Pastoral Constitution on the Church in the Modern World *Gaudium et Spes,* 51.
18. Encyclical *Humanae Vitae,* 7: AAS 60 (1968), 485.
19. Ibid., 12: loc. cit., 488–89.
20. Ibid., 14: loc. cit., 490.
21. Ibid., 13: loc. cit., 489.

REASON

[29]

Sexual Perversion

Thomas Nagel

THERE IS SOMETHING to be learned about sex from the fact that we possess a concept of sexual perversion. I wish to examine the concept, defending it against the charge of unintelligibility and trying to say exactly what about human sexuality qualifies it to admit of perversions. But let me make some preliminary comments about the problem before embarking on its solution.

Some people do not believe that the notion of sexual perversion makes sense, and even those who do, disagree over its application. Nevertheless, I think it will be widely conceded that if the concept is viable at all, it must meet certain general conditions. First, if there are any sexual perversions, they will have to be sexual desires or practices that can be plausibly described as in some sense unnatural, though the explanation of this natural/unnatural distinction is, of course, the main problem. Second, certain practices, such as shoe fetishism, bestiality, and sadism will be perversions if anything is; other practices, such as unadorned sexual intercourse, will not be; and about still others there is controversy. Third, if there are perversions, they will be unnatural sexual *inclinations* rather than merely unnatural practices adopted not from inclination but for other reasons. I realize that this is at variance with the view, maintained by some Roman Catholics, that contraception is a sexual

SOURCE: From Thomas Nagel, "Sexual Perversion," *Journal of Philosophy* 66, no. 1 (1969). Used by permission.

perversion. But although contraception may qualify as a deliberate perversion of the sexual and reproductive functions, it cannot be significantly described as a *sexual* perversion. A sexual perversion must reveal itself in conduct that expresses an unnatural *sexual* preference. And although there might be a form of fetishism focused on the employment of contraceptive devices, that is not the usual explanation for their use.

I wish to declare at the outset my belief that the connection between sex and reproduction has no bearing on sexual perversion. The latter is a concept of psychological, not physiological, interest, and it is a concept that we do not apply to the lower animals, let alone to plants, all of which have reproductive functions that can go astray in various ways (think, for example, of seedless oranges). Insofar as we are prepared to regard higher animals as perverted, it is because of their psychological, not their anatomical, similarity to humans. Furthermore, we do not regard as a perversion every deviation from the reproductive function of sex in humans: sterility, miscarriage, contraception, abortion.

Another matter that I believe has no bearing on the concept of sexual perversion is social disapprobation or custom. Anyone inclined to think that in each society the perversions are those sexual practices of which the community disapproves should consider all of the societies that have frowned upon adultery and fornication. These have not been regarded as unnatural practices, but have been thought objectionable in other ways. What is regarded as unnatural admittedly varies from culture to culture, but the classification is not a pure expression of disapproval or distaste. In fact it is often regarded as a *ground* for disapproval, and that suggests that the classification has an independent content.

I am going to attempt a psychological account of sexual perversion, which will depend on a specific psychological theory of sexual desire and human sexual interactions. To approach this solution I wish first to consider a contrary position, one that provides a basis for skepticism about the existence of any sexual perversions at all, and perhaps about the very significance of the term. The skeptical argument runs as follows:

Sexual desire is simply one of the appetites, like hunger and thirst. As such it may have various objects, some more common than others perhaps, but none in any sense "natural." An appetite is identified as sexual by means of the organs and erogenous zones in which its satisfaction can be to some extent localized, and the special sensory pleasures that form the core of that satisfaction. This enables us to recognize widely divergent goals, activities, and desires as sexual, since it is conceivable in principle that anything should produce sexual pleasure and that a nondeliberate, sexually charged desire for it should arise (as a result of conditioning, if nothing else). We may fail to empathize with some of these desires, and some of them, like sadism, may be objectionable on extraneous grounds, but once we have observed that they meet criteria for being sexual, there is nothing more to be said on *that* score. Either they are sexual or they are not: sexuality does not admit of imperfection, or perversion, or any other such qualification—it is not that sort of affection.

This is probably the received radical position. It suggests that the cost of defending a psychological account may be to deny that sexual desire is an appetite. But insofar as that line of defense is plausible, it should make us suspicious of the simple picture of appetites on which the skepticism depends. Perhaps the standard appetites, like hunger, cannot be classed as pure appetites in that sense either, at least in their human versions.

Let us approach the matter by asking whether we can imagine anything that would qualify as a gastronomical perversion. Hunger and eating are importantly like sex in that they serve a biological function and also play a significant role in our inner lives. It is noteworthy that there is little temptation to describe as perverted an appetite for substances that are not nourishing. We should probably not consider someone's appetites as perverted if he liked to eat paper, sand, wood, or cotton. Those are merely rather odd and very unhealthy tastes: they lack the psychological complexity that we expect of perversions. (Coprophilia, being already a sexual perversion, may be disregarded.) If, on the other hand, someone liked to eat cookbooks or magazines with pictures of food in them, and preferred these to ordinary food—or if when hungry he sought satisfaction by fondling a napkin or ashtray from his favorite restaurant—then the concept of perversion might seem appropriate (in fact it would be natural to describe this as a case of gastronomical fetishism). It would be natural to describe as gastronomically perverted someone who could eat only by having food forced down his throat through a funnel, or only if the meal were a living animal. What helps in such cases is the peculiarity of the desire itself, rather than the inappropriateness of its object to the biological function that the desire serves. Even an appetite, it would seem, can have perversions if in addition to its biological function it has a significant psychological structure.

In the case of hunger, psychological complexity is provided by the activities that give it expression. Hunger is not merely a disturbing sensation that can be quelled by eating; it is an attitude toward edible portions of the external world, a desire to relate to them in rather special ways. The method of ingestion—chewing, savoring, swallowing, appreciating the texture and smell—is an important component of the relation, as is the passivity and controllability of the food (the only animals we eat live are helpless mollusks). Our relation to food depends also on our size: we do not live upon it or burrow into it like aphids or worms. Some of these features are more central than others, but any adequate phenomenology of eating would have to treat it as a relation to the external world and a way of appropriating bits of that world, with characteristic affection. Displacements or serious restrictions of the desire to eat could then be described as perversions, if they undermined the direct relation between man and food that is the natural expression of hunger. This explains why it is easy to imagine gastronomical fetishism, voyeurism, exhibitionism, or even gastronomical sadism and masochism. Indeed, some of these perversions are fairly common.

If we can imagine perversions of an appetite like hunger, it should be possible to make sense of the concept of sexual perversion. I do not wish to imply that sexual desire is an appetite—only that being an appetite is no bar to admitting of perversions. Like hunger, sexual desire has as its characteristic object a certain relation with something in the external world; only in this case it is usually a person rather than an omelet, and the relation is considerably more complicated. This added complication allows scope for correspondingly complicated perversions.

The fact that sexual desire is a feeling about other persons may tempt us to take a pious view of its psychological content. There are those who believe that sexual desire is properly the expression of some other attitude, like love, and that when it occurs by itself it is incomplete and unhealthy—or at any rate subhuman. (The extreme Platonic version of such a view is that sexual practices are all vain attempts to express something they cannot in principle achieve: this makes them all perversions, in a sense.) I do not believe that any such view is correct. Sexual desire is complicated enough without having to be linked to anything else as a condition for phenomenological analysis. It cannot be denied that sex may serve various functions—economic, social, altruistic—but it also has its own content as a relation between persons, and it is only by analyzing that relation that we can understand the conditions of sexual perversion.

It is very important that the object of sexual attraction is a particular individual, who transcends the properties that make him attractive. When different persons are attracted to a single person for different reasons—eyes, hair, figure, laugh, intelligence—we feel that the object of their desire is nevertheless the same, namely, that person. There is even an inclination to feel that this is so if the lovers have different sexual aims, if they include both men and women, for example. Different specific attractive characteristics seem to provide enabling conditions for the operation of a single basic feeling, and the different aims all provide expressions of it. We approach the sexual attitude toward the person through the features that we find attractive, but these features are not the objects of that attitude.

This is very different from the case of an omelet. Various people may desire it for different reasons, one for its fluffiness, another for its mushrooms, another for its unique combination of aroma and visual aspect; yet we do not enshrine the transcendental omelet as the true common object of their affections. Instead we might say that several desires have accidentally converged on the same object: any omelet with the crucial characteristics would do as well. It is not similarly true that any person with the same flesh distribution and way of smoking can be substituted as object for a particular sexual desire that has been elicited by those characteristics. It may be that they will arouse attraction whenever they recur, but it will be a new sexual attraction with a new particular object, not merely a transfer of the old desire to someone else. (I believe this is true even in cases where the new object is unconsciously identified with a former one.)

The importance of this point will emerge when we see how complex a psychological interchange constitutes the natural development of sexual attraction. This would be incomprehensible if its object were not a particular person, but rather a person of a certain *kind*. Attraction is only the beginning, and fulfillment does not consist merely of behavior and contact expressing this attraction, but involves much more.

The best discussion of these matters that I have seen is in part three of Sartre's *Being and Nothingness.*[1] Since it has influenced my own views, I shall say a few things about it now. Sartre's treatment of sexual desire and of love, hate, sadism, masochism, and further attitudes toward others depends on a general theory of consciousness and the body that we can neither expound nor assume here. He does not discuss perversion, partly because he regards sexual desire as one form of the perpetual attempt of an embodied consciousness to come to terms with the existence of others, an attempt that is as doomed to fail in this form as it is in any of the others, which include sadism and masochism (if not certain of the more impersonal deviations) as well as several nonsexual attitudes. According to Sartre, all attempts to incorporate the other into my world as another subject, that is, to apprehend him as at once an object for me and a subject for whom I am an object, are unstable and doomed to collapse into one or the other of the two aspects. Either I reduce him entirely to an object, in which case his subjectivity escapes the possession or appropriation I can extend to that object; or I become merely an object for him, in which case I am no longer in a position to appropriate his subjectivity. Moreover, neither of these aspects is stable: each is continually in danger of giving way to the other. This has the consequence that there can be no such thing as a successful sexual relation, since the deep aim of sexual desire cannot in principle be accomplished. It seems likely, therefore, that this view will not permit a basic distinction between successful, or complete, and unsuccessful, or incomplete, sex and therefore cannot admit the concept of perversion.

I do not adopt this aspect of the theory, nor many of its metaphysical underpinnings. What interests me is Sartre's picture of the attempt. He says that the type of possession that is the object of sexual desire is carried out by "a double reciprocal incarnation" and that this is accomplished, typically in the form of a caress, in the following way: "I make myself flesh in order to impel the Other to realize *for herself* and *for me* her own flesh, and my caresses cause my flesh to be born for me in so far as it is for the Other *flesh causing her to be born as flesh.*"[2] The incarnation in question is described variously as a clogging or troubling of consciousness, which is inundated by the flesh in which it is embodied.

The view I am going to suggest—I hope in less obscure language—is related to Sartre's, but differs in allowing sexuality to achieve its goal on occasion and thus in providing the concept of perversion with a foothold.

Sexual desire involves a kind of perception, but not merely a single perception of its object, for in the paradigm case of mutual desire there is a complex system of superimposed mutual perceptions—not only perceptions of the sexual object, but perceptions of oneself. Moreover, sexual awareness of another involves considerable self-awareness to begin with—more than is involved in ordinary sensory perception. The experience is felt as an assault on oneself by the view (or touch, or whatever) of the sexual object.

Let us consider a case in which the elements can be separated. For clarity we will restrict ourselves initially to the somewhat artificial case of desire at a distance. Suppose a man and a woman, whom we may call Romeo and Juliet, are at opposite ends of a cocktail lounge with many mirrors on its walls, permitting unobserved observation and even mutual unobserved observation. Each of them is sipping a martini and studying other people in the mirrors. At some point Romeo notices Juliet. He is moved, somehow, by the softness of her hair and the diffidence with which she sips her martini, and this arouses him sexually. Let us say that X *senses* Y whenever X regards Y with sexual desire. (Y need not be a person, and X's apprehension of Y can be visual, tactile, olfactory, and so on, or purely imaginary. In the present example we shall concentrate on vision.) So Romeo senses Juliet, rather than merely noticing her. At this stage he is aroused by an unaroused object; so he is more in the sexual grip of his body than she of hers.

Let us suppose, however, that Juliet now senses Romeo in another mirror on the opposite wall, though neither of them yet knows that he is seen by the other (the mirror angles provide three-quarter views). Romeo then begins to notice in Juliet the subtle signs of sexual arousal: heavy-lidded stare, dilating pupils, a faint flush. This of course renders her much more bodily, and he not only notices but senses this as well. His arousal is nevertheless still solitary. But now, cleverly calculating the line of her stare without actually looking her in the eyes, he realizes that it is directed at him through the mirror on the opposite wall. That is, he notices, and moreover senses, Juliet sensing him. This is definitely a new development, for it gives him a sense of embodiment, not only through his own reactions, but also through the eyes and reactions of another. Moreover, it is separable from the initial sensing of Juliet, for sexual arousal might begin with a person's sensing that he is sensed and being assailed by the perception of the other person's desire rather than merely by the perception of the person.

But there is a further step. Let us suppose that Juliet, who is a little slower than Romeo, now senses that he senses her. This puts Romeo in a position to notice, and be aroused by, her arousal at being sensed by him. He senses that she senses that he senses her. This is still another level of arousal, for he becomes conscious of his sexuality through his awareness of its effect on her and of her awareness that this effect is due to him. Once she takes the same step and senses that he senses her sensing him, it becomes difficult to state, let alone imagine, further iterations, though they may be logically distinct. If both are alone, they will presumably turn to look at each other directly, and the proceedings will continue on another plane. Physical contact and intercourse are perfectly natural extensions of this complicated visual exchange, and mutual touch can involve all the complexities of awareness present in the visual case, but with a far greater range of subtlety and acuteness.

Ordinarily, of course, things happen in a less orderly fashion—sometimes in a great rush—but I believe that some version of this overlapping system of distinct sexual perceptions and interactions is the basic framework of any full-fledged sexual relation and that relations involving only part of the complex are significantly incomplete. The account is only schematic, as it must be to achieve generality. Every real sexual act will be psychologically far more specific and detailed, in ways that depend not only on the physical techniques employed and on anatomical details but also on countless features of the participants' conceptions of themselves and of each other, which become embodied in the act. (It is a familiar enough fact, for example, that people often take social roles and the social roles of their partners to bed with them.)

The general schema is important, however, and the proliferation of levels of mutual awareness it involves is an example of a type of complexity that typifies human interactions. Consider aggression, for example. If I am angry with someone, I want to make him feel it, either to produce self-reproach by getting him to see himself through the eyes of my anger and to dislike what he sees, or to produce reciprocal anger or fear by getting him to perceive my anger as a threat or attack. What I want will depend on the details of my anger, but in either case it will involve a desire that the object of that anger be aroused. This accomplishment constitutes the fulfillment of my emotion through domination of the object's feelings.

Another example of such reflexive mutual recognition is to be found in the phenomenon of meaning, which appears to involve an intention to produce a belief or other effect in another by bringing about his recognition of one's intention to produce that effect. (That result is due to H. P. Grice,[3] whose position I shall not attempt to reproduce in detail.) Sex has a related structure: it involves a desire that one's partner be aroused by the recognition of one's desire that he or she be aroused.

It is not easy to define the basic types of awareness and arousal of which these complexes are composed, and that remains a lacuna in this discussion. I believe that the object of awareness is the same in one's own case as it is in one's sexual awareness of another, although the two awarenesses will not be the same, the difference being as great as that between feeling angry and experiencing the anger of another. All stages of sexual perception are varieties of identification of a person with his body. What is perceived is one's own or another's *subjection* to or *immersion* in his body, a phenomenon that has been recognized with loathing by St. Paul and St. Augustine, both of whom regarded "the law of sin which is in my members" as a grave threat to the dominion of the holy will.[4] In sexual desire and its expression the blending of involuntary response with deliberate control is extremely important. For Augustine, the revolution launched against him by his body is symbolized by erection and the other involuntary physical components of arousal. Sartre too stresses the fact that the penis is not a prehensile organ. But mere involuntariness characterizes other bodily processes as well. In sexual desire the involuntary responses are combined with submission to spontaneous impulses: not only one's pulse and secretions but one's actions are taken over by the body; ideally, deliberate control is needed only to guide the expression of those impulses. This is to some extent also true of an appetite like hunger, but the takeover there is more localized, less pervasive, less extreme. One's whole body does not become saturated with hunger as it can with desire. But the most characteristic feature of a specifically sexual immersion in the body is its ability to fit into the complex of mutual perceptions that we have described. Hunger leads to spontaneous interactions with food; sexual desire leads to spontaneous interactions with the other persons, whose bodies are asserting their sovereignty in the same way, producing involuntary reactions and spontaneous impulses in *them.* These reactions are perceived, and the perception of them is perceived, and that perception is in turn perceived; at each step the domination of the person by his body is reinforced, and the sexual partner becomes more possessible by physical contact, penetration, and envelopment.

Desire is therefore not merely the perception of a preexisting embodiment that in turn enhances the original subject's sense of himself. This explains why it is important that the partner be aroused, and not merely aroused, but aroused by the awareness of one's desire. It also explains the sense in which desire has unity and possession as its object: physical possession must eventuate in creation of the sexual object in the image of one's desire, and not merely in the object's recognition of that desire or in his or her own private arousal. (This may reveal a male bias. I shall say something about that later.)

To return, finally, to the topic of perversion: I believe that various familiar deviations constitute truncated or incomplete versions of the complete configuration and may therefore be regarded as perversions of the central impulse.

In particular, narcissistic practices and intercourse with animals, infants, and inanimate objects seem to be stuck at some primitive version of the first stage. If the object is not alive, the experience is reduced entirely to an awareness of one's own sexual embodiment. Small children and animals permit awareness of the embodiment of the other, but present obstacles to reciprocity, to the recognition by the sexual object of the subject's desire as the source of his (the object's) sexual self-awareness.

Sadism concentrates on the evocation of passive self-awareness in others, but the sadist's engagement is itself active and requires a retention of deliberate control that impedes awareness of himself as a bodily subject of passion in the required sense. The victim must recognize him as the source of his own sexual passivity, but only as the active source. De Sade claimed that the object of sexual desire was to evoke involuntary responses from one's partner, especially audible ones. The infliction of pain is no doubt the most efficient way to accomplish this, but it requires a certain abrogation of one's own exposed spontaneity. All this, incidentally, helps to explain why it is tempting to regard as sadistic an excessive preoccupation with sexual technique, which does not permit one to abandon the role of agent at any stage of the sexual act. Ideally one should be able to surmount one's technique at some point.

A masochist on the other hand imposes the same disability on his partner as the sadist imposes on himself. The masochist cannot find a satisfactory embodiment as the object of another's sexual desire but only as the object of his control. He is passive not in relation to his partner's passion but in relation to his nonpassive agency. In addition, the subjection to one's body characteristic of pain and physical restraints is of a very different kind from that of sexual excitement: pain causes people to contract rather than dissolve.

Both of these disorders have to do with the second stage, which involves the awareness of oneself as an object of desire. In straightforward sadism and masochism other attentions are substituted for desire as a source of the object's self-awareness. But it is also possible for nothing of that sort to be substituted, as in the case of a masochist who is satisfied with self-inflicted pain or of a sadist who does not insist on playing a role in the suffering that arouses him. Greater difficulties of classification are presented by three other categories of sexual activity: elaborations of the sexual act, intercourse of more than two persons, and homosexuality.

If we apply our model to the various forms that may be taken by two-party heterosexual intercourse, none of them seem clearly to qualify as perversions. Hardly anyone can be found these days to inveigh against oral–genital contact, and the merits of buggery are urged by such respectable figures as D. H. Lawrence and Norman Mailer. There may be something vaguely sadistic about the latter technique (in Mailer's writings it seems to be a method of introducing an element of rape), but it is not obvious that this has to be so. In general, it would appear that any bodily contact between a man and a woman that gives them sexual pleasure is a possible vehicle for the system of multilevel interpersonal awareness that I have claimed is the basic psychological content of sexual interaction. Thus a liberal platitude about sex is upheld.

About multiple combinations the least that can be said is that they are bound to be complicated. If one considers how difficult it is to carry on two conversations simultaneously, one may appreciate the problems of multiple simultaneous interpersonal perception that can arise in even a small-scale orgy. It may be inevitable that some of the component relations should degenerate into mutual epidermal stimulation by participants otherwise isolated from each other. There may also be a tendency toward voyeurism and exhibitionism, both of which are incomplete relations. The exhibitionist wishes to display his desire without needing to be desired in return; he may even fear the sexual attentions of others. A voyeur, on the other hand, need not require any recognition at all by his object, certainly not a recognition of the voyeur's arousal.

It is not clear whether homosexuality is a perversion if that is measured by the standard of the described configuration, but it seems unlikely. For such a classification would have to depend on the possibility of extracting from the system a distinction between male and female sexuality; and much that has been said so far applies equally to men and women. Moreover, it would have to be maintained that there was a natural tie between the type of sexuality and the sex of the body and that two sexualities of the same type could not interact properly.

Certainly there is much support for an aggressive-passive distinction between male and female sexuality. In our culture the male's arousal tends to initiate the perceptual exchange; he usually makes the sexual approach, largely controls the course of the act, and of course penetrates whereas the woman receives. When two men or two women engage in intercourse they cannot both adhere to these sexual roles. The question is how essential the roles are to an adequate sexual relation. One relevant observation is that a good deal of deviation from these roles occurs in heterosexual intercourse. Women can be sexually aggressive and men passive, and temporary reversals of role are not uncommon in heterosexual exchanges of reasonable length. If such conditions are set aside, it may be urged that there is something irreducibly perverted in attraction to a body anatomically like one's own. But alarming as some people in our culture may find such attraction, it remains psychologically unilluminating to class it as perverted. Certainly if homosexuality is a perversion, it is so in a very different sense from that in which shoe-fetishism is a perversion, for some version of the full range of interpersonal perceptions seems perfectly possible between two persons of the same sex.

In any case, even if the proposed model is correct, it remains implausible to describe as perverted every deviation from it. For example, if the partners in heterosexual intercourse indulge in private heterosexual fantasies, that obscures the recognition of the real partner and so, on the theory, constitutes a defective sexual relation. It is not, however, generally regarded as a perversion. Such examples suggest that a simple dichotomy between perverted and unperverted sex is too crude to organize the phenomena adequately.

I shall close with some remarks about the relation of perversion to good, bad, and morality. The concept of perversion can hardly fail to be evaluative in some sense, for it appears to involve the notion of an ideal or at least adequate sexuality that the perversions in some way fail to achieve. So, if the concept is viable, the judgment that a person or practice or desire is perverted will constitute a sexual evaluation, implying that better sex, or a better specimen of sex, is possible. This in itself is a very weak claim since the evaluation might be in a dimension that is of little interest to us. (Though, if my account is correct, that will not be true.)

Whether it is a moral evaluation, however, is another question entirely, one whose answer would require more understanding of both morality and perversion than can be deployed here. Moral evaluation of acts and of persons is a rather special and very complicated matter and by no means are all of our evaluations of persons and their activities moral evaluations. We make judgments about people's beauty or health or intelligence that are evaluative without being moral. Assessments of their sexuality may be similar in that respect.

Furthermore, moral issues aside, it is not clear that unperverted sex is necessarily *preferable* to the perversions. It may be that sex that receives the highest marks for perfection *as sex* is less enjoyable than certain perversions, and if enjoyment is considered very important, that might outweigh considerations of sexual perfection in determining rational preference.

That raises the question of the relation between the evaluative content of judgments of perversion and the rather common *general* distinction between good and bad sex. The latter distinction is usually confined to sexual acts, and it would seem, within limits, to cut across the other: even someone who believed, for example, that homosexuality was a perversion could admit a distinction between better and worse homosexual sex, and might even allow that good homosexual sex could be better *sex* than not very good unperverted sex. If this is correct, it supports the position—if judgments of perversion are viable at all—that they represent only one aspect of the possible evaluation of sex, even *qua sex.* Moreover it is not the only important aspect: certainly sexual deficiencies that evidently do not constitute perversions can be the object of great concern.

Finally, even if perverted sex is to that extent not so good as it might be, bad sex is generally better than none at all. This should not be controversial: it seems to hold for other important matters, like food, music, literature, and society. In the end, one must choose from among the available alternatives, whether their availability depends on the environment or on one's own constitution. And the alternatives have to be fairly grim before it becomes rational to opt for nothing.

Notes

1. Trans. Hazel E. Barnes (New York: Philosophical Library, 1956).
2. Ibid., 391. Sartre's italics.
3. "Meaning," *Philosophical Review* 66, no. 3 (July 1957): 377–88.
4. See Romans 7:23, and the *Confessions,* Book 8, v.

[30]

Lesbian Ethics

Sarah Lucia Hoagland

. . .

TYPICALLY, WHEN WE REACH for ethics, we want rules or standards or principles. We want to know what is the "right" thing to do in a given situation; that is, we want to get through a situation safely and without making mistakes. Alternatively, we appeal to ethics because we want a tool we can use to make others behave; that is, we want to get them to do what we think they should do. These are traditional uses of ethics, and I think they are both a mistake.

Professional philosophers will argue that if there are no general principles to which we can appeal as the foundation of moral choice—to determine right and wrong—then ethics is impossible.[1] And lesbian desire for principles is equally strong. We tend to feel that if we have no ultimate principles with which to judge ourselves and each other right or wrong, then ethics has no meaning.

But there are several problems with appeals to rules or principles. Principles cannot guarantee good behavior; they are of no use if individuals are not already acting with integrity. At most they serve as guides for those who already can act with integrity. Thus, for example, we have fairly intricate strategies for fair fighting or conflict resolution, and yet we can use them to sabotage mediation and to undermine integrity.[2]

SOURCE: From Sarah Lucia Hoagland, *Lesbian Ethics: Toward New Value* (Chicago: Institute of Lesbian Studies, 1988). Used by permission.

Secondly, rules or principles don't tell us how to apply them. When making a moral decision, we must first decide which principles apply in a given situation and how. For example, suppose that we agree we should always be honest with each other. What counts as being honest, especially if, as Adrienne Rich has pointed out, silences can be lies too?[3] Should I interrupt absolutely anything you are doing to tell you how I feel? If I don't, am I being dishonest by withholding information? While the questions may sound silly, we have done the former and accused each other of the latter. Or, if you don't want to address something and always change the subject when I bring it up, perhaps breaking down in tears, am I lying to you if I do not force the issue? It is not always clear what counts as being honest.

Thirdly, when two lesbians seriously disagree, often we will also disagree about which principles we think apply. Alternatively, lesbians will be focused on different principles—"she's being racist" versus "she's applying double standards"—each riveted on the fact that the other is not adhering to the principle she's concerned with. Ironically, principles only work when they really aren't needed.

Our own attraction to rules and principles comes in part from a desire to be certain and secure. If someone will only tell us a rule we can follow, we won't have to be in doubt about what we are choosing—we won't have to worry about being mistaken. Or if someone will only set down the rules, then everyone will have to conform. (This, of course, is simply false. Refusal to conform is part of what makes us lesbians.)

Our desire for certainty also involves a desire to make judgments regardless of particular circumstances and regardless of individual intentions. If we have a principle or rule, then we can hold another accountable for her actions without having to investigate the particulars involved in her choice. We set up principles and codes, and we begin to cease considering the transformations we go through in our lives as a result of our choices; we ignore a great deal. Acting from principle interferes with rather than enhances our ability to make judgments.

I am not suggesting that we never articulate or use principles or that we abandon strategies and rules of thumb, such as fair fighting, being honest, or antiracism. We have begun developing fairly intricate strategies for interacting.[4] I am merely suggesting that what *counts* as an application of a given principle depends on the circumstances of our lives. And when appeal to principles works, it is because we are already acting with integrity.[a]

---

a. For example, as Denslow Brown points out, in conflict resolution the least honest lesbian will set the tone and pace of the proceedings. Conflict resolution will work only if, beyond their anger and pain, those involved want it to work.[5]

To apply principles, we must have an ability to make judgments, and we must be able to gain and assess information about a given situation; we must be adept at making judgments. With that ability and that information, acting from principle becomes superfluous. Principles are not something we can appeal to when all else fails.[6]

And yet this is exactly the illusion traditional ethics fosters. So I find myself drawn to examining the *function* of moral rules and principles designed to help us judge what we ought or ought not do in order to be good. For much of what is called ethics in our culture involves, not the integrity and moral capability of an individual, but rather the extent to which she participates in the structural hierarchy of a social group or organization by adhering to its rules. The ethical virtues as we know them are master/slave virtues. Even in its most subtle form, traditional, normative (everyday) ethics involves principles or rules of obligation to those higher in the hierarchy (including gods) and principles or rules of responsibility for those lower in the hierarchy, often "for their own good." (Current discussions in medical ethics are illustrative.) I find that the function of traditional ethics involves promoting social organization and control at the expense of individual integrity and agency.

And this leads me to consider the basic value of traditional ethics. I am concerned with value, though not so much in the usual sense of determining which acts are right or wrong, nor in the more philosophical sense of considering theoretical principles we can appeal to in order to justify particular moral principles or rules. My concern lies with value inherent in our perceptions of reality, value presupposed by the way we address the world. What I am talking about is not value we deliberate about or think we ought to choose, but a deeper value, the value we give life to by virtue of our choices. And the value I find at the heart of traditional ethics is dominance and subordination.

My thesis about traditional ethics is this: (1) The focus and direction of traditional ethics, indeed its function, has not been individual integrity and agency (ability to make choices and act) but rather social organization and social control. (2) The values around which traditional ethics revolve are antagonistic, the values of dominance and subordination. As a result, (3) traditional ethics undermines rather than promotes individual moral ability and agency. And (4) these aspects of traditional ethics combine to legitimize oppression by redefining it as social organization. Appeal to rules and principles is at the heart of this endeavor.

When I think about ethics, I think about individuals making choices, that is, making judgments and acting. I think about our ability to interact, to connect, to be intimate, to respond. I think about our ability to perceive and judge, our ability to gain and attend information. I think about constraints on our choices, limits on our options. I think about transformations we undergo as a result of our choices—how we grow and change. I think about our ability to create lesbian meaning. When I think about ethics, I think about choice under oppression, and I think about lesbian moral agency.

What I am calling Lesbian Ethics focuses on enabling and developing individual integrity and agency in relation to others. I mean to invoke a self who is both separate and related, a self which is neither autonomous nor dissolved: a self in community who is one among many, what I call *autokoenony* (ô′ to kēn o′ nē).

In stressing a focus on choice and moral agency, I do not mean to deny that factors affect us which we do not control. Rather I mean to defy a masculine myth that says we must be in control of a situation to make choices. A moral or political theory useful to anyone under oppression must not convince the oppressed that we are total victims. While we don't control situations, we do affect them. In focusing on choice and moral agency, I mean to invoke lesbian ability to engage, to act in situations—that we move here now makes a difference. And I mean to suggest that whatever limits we face, our power—ability and agency—lies in choice.

What I need and what I hope to have developed in this essay, among other things, is a notion of moral agency under oppression. This includes developing ability within a situation without claiming responsibility for the situation. It involves resisting de-moralization under oppression. And it involves resisting the belief that if we can't control a situation, our actions make no difference and we are powerless. Moral agency involves the ability to go on under oppression: to continue to make choices, to act within the oppressive structure of our society and challenge oppression, to create meaning through our living.

Thus, what I am calling Lesbian Ethics is not a set of rules of right behavior, a list of do's and don't's aimed at guaranteeing happiness and success or freedom from pain or mistakes. I am interested, not in principles to guide and direct our behavior, but rather in the function of our ethical judgments, the central value of ethical judgments, and our lesbian moral agency.

. . . Ethics starts with our interactions and with the values we spin and weave through those interactions. I am interested in weaving new values through our choices: values which develop lesbian agency and be-ing, preserve our integrity, and make us less susceptible to oppressive values. This is what concerns me when I think about ethics.

Language

I work with language and concepts because I am a philosopher. While I am formally trained in the profession, since childhood I have pondered philosophical questions (including some designated as philosophical by professors of the discipline). I am prone to mulling things over; figuring things out and articulating them make me feel alive. Sometimes when I put pen to paper, I reach an altered state of consciousness.

More importantly, I work with language and concepts because language is involved in any transformation of consciousness as well as in resistance to such transformation. Yet many lesbians feel that attending to language is a waste of time. Indeed, some have argued that to focus on language is classist.

Language, of course, is not the only source of oppression nor the only tool of domination. But the use of language in structuring reality and trapping us in oppression is not separate and distinct from the manipulation of the material conditions of our existence to structure reality and trap us in oppression.[7] For example, the process of colonization includes sending in christian missionaries to write down and categorize the language of colonized peoples. The missionaries set up schools where the children are forced to learn their "native" language through christian and colonial categories (for example, deities assume a masculine gender; "ownership" replaces "sharing") and then produce for the sake of those categories.

Language is a tool of oppression, for we remain trapped in oppression when we perceive only what the oppressors perceive, when we are restricted to their values and categories. Language interests me because of its insidiousness as a means of maintaining a political perspective, and because of its susceptibility to change. However, language use has a contradictory dynamic for those under oppression—it is a matter both of agreement and of coercion: in using language we participate in a consensus, often unwittingly; but our participation is also coerced.[8]

In the first place, the values embedded in language are a matter of agreement, of consensus. That is, no matter what laws (rules) are passed, the values embedded in our use of language persist or change because of a general consensus in our usage and in our perceptual judgment. I do not mean that we get together and reach agreement about these matters; I mean that we don't disagree, we don't argue about them. We *agree* in that we continue to use certain concepts without question.[9] "Femininity" (in dualistic opposition to masculinity) is such a conceptual value: no matter what kind of research scientists do in connection with so-called feminine behavior, and no matter what kind of qualifications feminists and lesbians include when appealing to the feminine, through these activities we all participate in the consensus that femininity is a fundamental category of understanding.

Language and perceptual judgment are a matter of consensus in that certain judgments go unquestioned, held in place by all that surrounds them, from research to gossip. This core has no justification, and it does not justify. Rather, our knowledge holds in place what is central to it.

This is not our understanding of the foundation of knowledge from philosophy and science. Traditionally, the foundation of knowledge has been conceived of as a bedrock—holding up, supporting, justifying everything else.[10] Ludwig Wittgenstein suggests a different metaphor: a foundation is like an axis, held in place by what revolves or spins around it.[11] In this respect, a "foundation" does not justify our everyday or scientific judgments, nor is it justified by anything else; rather, the "foundation" determines the limits of what we recognize as justification. It is what goes unquestioned—held in place by what surrounds it. Should someone bring this core into question and challenge it or even try to justify it, its status as a "foundation" would be threatened.[12]

For example, the concept of "woman" is not based on a bedrock of female behavior. Rather, the concept of "woman" determines what counts as normal female behavior. And the concept is held in place by, for example, the kind of research scientists do, advertisements directed at women and also at men, the sorts of things news media report and the details reported, the ways females are portrayed for men's sexual entertainment or religious edification or medical experimentation or military inspiration. The category "woman" is not a reflection of fact but instead tells us how to determine fact. And it is a matter of agreement in that those engaged in such social activities do not disagree about how they perceive women.[b]

Thus, while the core of our knowledge is held in place by what revolves around it, it also limits and focuses our perception and judgment: Although the concept of "woman" appears to be a descriptive category, it determines for the unquestioning perceiver what would count as a woman. It determines our perception of normal female behavior. A particularly tidy illustration of this comes in the form of a well-known riddle: A father and his son were driving when they had a bad accident. They were rushed to the nearest hospital, and the surgeon on duty was called. The surgeon entered the son's room and exclaimed, "Oh my god, that's my son." How can this be?

The solution to the riddle, of course, is that the surgeon is the son's mother. However, those lodged in masculinist thought will miss it; and while they will come up with creative answers—the surgeon was a priest, he was a grandfather, he was the stepfather—their imagination will be limited to male categories. Through her linguistic research, Julia Penelope [Stanley] has found

---

b. In this respect one can understand how lesbians threaten the foundation of heterosexualism.

that words in english denoting powerful and prestigious positions like "surgeon" carry with them a value marking of "male" and "white": we presume surgeons to be male and white unless told otherwise.[13] Our judgment, our perception, is directed by the values embedded in the language we use, setting limits to what we might imagine. If language did not focus and limit thought this way, the surgeon riddle would not be a riddle.

. . .

Understanding sexism involves analyzing how institutional power is in the hands of men, how men discriminate against women, how society classifies men as the norm and women as passive and inferior, how male institutions objectify women, how society excludes women from participation as full human beings, and how what has been perceived as normal male behavior is also violence against women. In other words, to analyze sexism is to understand primarily how women are victims of institutional and ordinary male behavior.

Understanding heterosexism, as well as homophobia,[c] involves analyzing, not just women's victimization, but also how women are defined in terms of men or not at all, how lesbians and gay men are treated—indeed scapegoated—as deviants, how choices of intimate partners for both women and men are restricted or denied through taboos to maintain a certain social order. (For example, if sexual relations between men were openly allowed, then men could do to men what men do to women[15] and, further, [some] men could become what women are. This is verboten. In addition, if love between women were openly explored, women might simply walk away from men, becoming "not-women." This, too, is verboten.) Focusing on heterosexism challenges heterosexuality as an institution, but it can also lead lesbians to regard as a political goal our acceptance, even assimilation, into heterosexual society: we try to assure heterosexuals we are normal people (that is, just like them), that they are being unjust in stigmatizing us, that ours is a mere sexual preference.

In her groundbreaking work on compulsory heterosexuality, Adrienne Rich challenges us to address heterosexuality as a political institution which ensures male right of physical, economical, and emotional access to women.[16] Jan Raymond develops a theory of hetero-reality and argues: "While I agree that we are living in a heterosexist society, I think the wider problem is that we live

---

c. Celia Kitzinger suggests we stop using "homophobia" altogether. She argues that the term did not emerge from within the women's liberation movement but rather from the academic discipline of psychology. She questions characterizing heteropatriarchal fear of lesbians as irrational, she challenges the psychological (rather than political) orientation of "phobia," and she notes that within psychology, the only alternative to "homophobia" is liberal humanism.[14]

in a hetero-relational society where most of women's personal, social, political, professional, and economic relations are defined by the ideology that woman is for man."[17] I go a bit further.

Understanding heterosexualism involves analyzing the relationship between men and women in which both men and women have a part. Heterosexualism is men dominating and de-skilling women in any of a number of forms, from outright attack to paternalistic care, and women devaluing (of necessity) female bonding as well as finding inherent conflicts between commitment and autonomy and consequently valuing an ethics of dependence. Heterosexualism is a way of living (which actual practitioners exhibit to a greater or lesser degree) that normalizes the dominance of one person in a relationship and the subordination of another. As a result, it undermines female agency.

What I am calling "heterosexualism" is not simply a matter of males having procreative sex with females.[18] It is an entire way of living which involves a delicate, though at times indelicate, balance between masculine predation upon and masculine protection of a feminine object of masculine attention.[d] Heterosexualism is a particular economic, political, and emotional relationship between men and women: men must dominate women and women must subordinate themselves to men in any of a number of ways.[e] As a result, men presume access to women while women remain riveted on men and are unable to sustain a community of women.

In the u.s., women cannot appear publicly without some men advancing on them, presuming access to them. In fact, many women will think something is wrong if this doesn't happen. A woman simply is someone toward whom such behavior is appropriate. When a woman is accompanied by a man, however, she is usually no longer considered fair game. As a result, men close to individual women—fathers, boyfriends, husbands, brothers, escorts, colleagues—become protectors (theoretically), staving off advances from other men.

---

d. I think the main model for personal interaction for women and lesbians has been heterosexual. However, for men in the anglo-european tradition there has also been a model of male homosexual interaction—a form of male bonding, even though sex between men has come to be persecuted. And while it is not my intention here to analyze the model, I will suggest that it revolves around an axis of dominance and submission, and that heterosexualism is basically a refined male homosexual model.[19]

e. Julien S. Murphy writes: "Heterosexuality is better termed heteroeconomics, for it pertains to the language of barter, exchange, bargain, auction, buy and sell. . . . Heterosexuality is the economics of exchange in which a gender-based power structure continually reinstates itself through the appropriation of the devalued party in a duo-gendered system. Such reinstatement happens through each instance of 'striking a deal' in the market of sex."[20]

The value of special protection for women is prevalent in this society. Protectors interact with women in ways that promote the image of women as helpless: men open doors, pull out chairs, expect women to dress in ways that interfere with their own self-protection.[21] And women accept this as attentive, complimentary behavior and perceive themselves as persons who need special attention and protection.[f]

What a woman faces in a man is either a protector or a predator, and men gain identity through one or another of these roles.[22] This has at least five consequences. First, there can be no protectors unless there is a danger. A man cannot identify himself in the role of protector unless there is something which needs protection. So it is in the interest of protectors that there be predators. Secondly, to be protected, women must be in danger. In portraying women as helpless and defenseless, men portray women as victims . . . and therefore as targets.

Thirdly, a woman (or girl) is viewed as the object of male passion and thereby its cause. This is most obvious in the case of rape: she must have done something to tempt him—helpless hormonal bundle that he is. Thus if women are beings who by nature are endangered, then, obviously, they are thereby beings who by nature are seductive—they actively attract predators. Fourthly, to be protected, women must agree to act as men say women should: to appear feminine, prove they are not threatening, stay at home, remain only with the protector, devalue their connections with other women, and so on.

Finally, when women step out of the feminine role, thereby becoming active and "guilty,"[g] it is a mere matter of logic that men will depict women as evil and step up overt physical violence against them in order to reaffirm women's victim status. For example, as the demand for women's rights in the u.s. became publicly perceptible, the depiction of lone women as "sluts" invit-

---

f. In questioning the value of special protection for women, I am not saying that women should never ask for help. That's just foolish. I am talking about the ideal of women as needing sheltering. The concept of children needing special protection is prevalent and I challenge that concept when it is used to abrogate their integrity "for their own good." But at least protection for children theoretically involves ensuring that (male) children can grow up and learn to take care of themselves. That is, (male) children are protected until they have grown and developed skills and abilities they need to get on in this world. No such expectation is included in the ideal of special protection for women: the ideal of special protection of women does not include the expectation that women will ever be in a position to take care of themselves (grow up).

g. In her analysis of fairy tales, Andrea Dworkin points out that an active woman is portrayed as evil (the stepmother) and a good woman is generally asleep or dead (snow white, sleeping beauty).[23]

ing attack also became prevalent. A lone female hitchhiker was perceived, not as someone to protect, but as someone who had given up her right to protection and thus as someone who was a target for attack. The rampant increase in pornography—entertainment by and for men about women—is men's general response to the u.s. women's liberation movement's demand of integrity, autonomy, and dignity for women.

What radical feminists have exposed through all the work on incest (daughter rape) and wife-beating is that protectors are also predators. Of course, not all men are wife- or girlfriend-beaters, but over half who live with women are. And a significant number of u.s. family homes shelter an "incestuous" male.[24]

Although men may exhibit concern over womanabuse, they have a different relationship to it than women; their concerns are not women's concerns. For example, very often men become irate at the fact that a woman has been raped or beaten by another man. But this is either a man warming to his role of protector—it rarely, if ever, occurs to him to teach her self-defense—or a man deeply affected by damage done to his "property" by another man. And while some men feel contempt for men who batter or rape, Marilyn Frye suggests it is quite possible their contempt arises, not from the fact that womanabuse is happening, but from the fact that the batterer or rapist must accomplish by force what they themselves can accomplish more subtly by arrogance.[25]

The current willingness of men in power to pass laws restricting pornography is a matter of men trying to reestablish the asexual, virginal image of (some) women whom they can then protect in their homes. And they are using as their excuse right-wing women as well as feminists who appear to be asking for protection, like proper women, rather than demanding liberation. Men use violence when women don't pay attention to them. Then, when women ask for protection, men can find meaning by turning on the predators—particularly ones of a different race or class.

In other words, the logic of protection is essentially the same as the logic of predation. Through predation, men do things to women and against women all of which violate women and undermine women's integrity. Yet protection objectifies just as much as predation. To protect women, men do things to women and against women; acting "for a woman's own good," they violate her integrity and undermine her agency.

. . .

Complementing the protector/predator function of men is the concept of "woman," particularly as it functions in mainstream u.s. society. Consider what the concept lacks. It lacks (1) a sense of female power, (2) any hint that women as a group have been the targets of male violence, (3) any hint either of collective or individual female resistance to male domination and control, and (4) any sense of lesbian connection.

The concept of "woman" includes no real sense of female power. Certainly, it includes no sense of women as conquering and dominating forces. More significantly, it includes no sense of strength and competence. I am not denying that there are many strong women. And where women encourage each other in defiance of the dominant valuation, significant images appear. But over time, under heterosexualism, these images tend to be modified by appeals to femininity or are used against women. Without sufficient deference to men, women will find "castrating bitch" or "dyke" or comparable concepts used to keep them in line.

Men of a given group will partially modify "femininity" in order to emphasize female competence and skill when they absolutely need extra help: during wars—Rosie the riveter, for example—or on small nebraska farms or in revolutionary movements or in kibbutzim when the state is unstable or in a community deeply split under oppression. But once their domain is more firmly established, men drag up the feminine stereotype (while nevertheless expecting women to do most of the work with none of the benefits).

In her essay for black women in the cities, Pat Robinson connects the loss of a people's self-awareness and power with the loss of their deities. She states, "When a group must be controlled, you always take away from them their gods, their very reflections of themselves and their inner being."[26] Where we find reference to goddesses of any culture in dominant anglo-european scholarship, they are being kidnapped or raped, and/or they are mothers.[h] Significantly, the one female figure present in anglo-european thought is the virgin Mary, remnant of an ancient goddess transformed into a model rape victim, reputed to have said to a god, "Do unto me as thou wiliest."

. . . A second notable lack in the concept of "woman" is a sense that force is ever used against women as a group. Feminist literature has appeared about the massacre of european witches. But the vast majority of u.s. women today remain unaware of the witch burnings. One might wonder how mass destruction could be eradicated from consciousness. Perhaps it was simply suppressed. But when a social order requires the extermination of a particular

h. There were many more goddesses than fertility and mother goddesses. There were goddesses of the hunt, of weaving, of wisdom, of change, of winter, of the forest, of the land, of the dead, of justice, of love, of food, of the sun, of fire, of writing, of the dawn, of revenge, of menarche, of the moon, of the sea, of volcanoes, and of witches and magic—to name but a few.[27] Further, there is reason to believe that fat goddesses, such as the venus of willendorf, represented not mothering but power: the rolls of fat were rolls of power.[28]

group and that extermination virtually succeeds, subsequent memory of the process can be eradicated by renaming. The massacre of witches in europe over a three-hundred-fifty-year period has endured just such a renaming. The caricature of witches assaults us annually in the form of a u.s. mass-media event: halloween.

. . .

Because there is no sense that violence has ever been directed at women as a group, it is difficult to gain a perspective on the magnitude of the force used against women now. While u.s. women may be horrified at the specter of african genital mutilation and indian dowry deaths, african (particularly nigerian) and indian students in my classes are no less horrified at the incidence of rape and the amount of pornography which form a daily part of u.s. women's lives. Except for radical feminists, no one in the united states perceives the phenomenal rate of incest (daughter rape), wife beating, rape, forced prostitution, and the ideology of pornography—depicted not only in men's magazines but on television, billboards, in grocery stores, in schools, and in general in every public and private sector a woman goes—as any kind of concerted assault on women. There is no general sense that, as Sonia Johnson points out, men have declared war on women;[29] rather this assault—because men are paying attention to women—is called "attraction," even "admiration."

Thirdly, the concept of "woman" includes no sense of female resistance—either collective or individual—to male domination. While there is evidence that amazons once lived in north africa, in china, in anatolia (turkey), and between the black and the caspian seas,[i] amazons are repeatedly treated as a joke or buried.

. . .

Because there is no mythological, much less historical, memory of *female* resistance to male domination, isolated and individual acts of female resistance are also rendered imperceptible as resistance, particularly, as I argue below, through the concept of "femininity." A "woman" is one whose identity comes through her alliance with a man to such an extent that any woman who resists male violence, male advances, and male access is not a real woman.

The value of "woman," thus, excludes a sense of female presence, skill, and power, an awareness that violence has been and is perpetrated against women

---

i. In 1979, the *Chicago Sun-Times,* for example, reported the finding of the remains of an amazon tribe that lived twenty-five hundred years ago in the soviet republic of moldavia. Soviet archaeologists found a "woman warrior, her war-horse, a spear, gold earrings and other adornments" in a burial site near the village of balabany in the southwestern soviet union.[30]

as a group, and a sense of female resistance to male domination. It also excludes a sense of lesbian connection. Adrienne Rich took on the task of addressing (1) the bias "through which lesbian experience is perceived on a scale ranging from deviant to abhorrent, or simply rendered invisible;" (2) "how and why women's choice of women as passionate comrades, life partners, co-workers, lovers, tribe, has been crushed, invalidated, forced into hiding and disguise"; and (3) "the virtual or total neglect of lesbian existence in a wide range of writings, including feminist scholarship."[31]

. . .

A "woman," thus, is a sex object essentially submissive to and dependent on men, one whose function is to perpetuate the race (while protectors and predators engage in their project of destroying it). No, one is not born a woman.

I want a moral revolution.

. . .

While many claim that there is a feminine principle which must exert itself to counterbalance masculinism pervading world cultures, what they seem to ignore is that the feminine has its origin in masculinist ideology and does not represent a break from it.[j] Further, the counterbalancing works both ways. Because of the non-discriminatory nature of feminine receptivity, that is, a lack of evaluating or judging what the feminine responds to, the feminine requires the masculine to protect it from foreign invasion.

Within lesbian community, many lesbians embrace a feminine principle and suggest that self-sacrifice and vulnerability, as well as a romantic ideal of mothering and all-embracing nurturing, are desirable ethical norms in our relationships. I want to challenge this.

---

j. This dualism is related to the manichean good/evil dualism and the taoist yin/yang dualism. The manichean approach holds the two opposites in constant conflict, each attempting to dominate and vanquish the other. The taoist approach embraces the conflict but strives for harmony and balance of the two opposites. And while the taoist ideal involves harmony and balance, the nature of the opposites is significant: yin/yang, female/male, dark/light, black/white, cold/heat, weakness/strength. The one is the opposite of the other because it is the absence of it. Thus, strength is the absence of weakness as weakness is the absence of strength. Further, one of the pair is the absence of the other because it is a void. While there are two opposites, in the long run, there is only one essence. The dualism is actually a monism.[32]

In discussing the new spiritualism, Susan Leigh Star argues that the new mystics have managed to mask male identity beneath the guise of androgyny. Further, she points out, "Amidst the escalation, it is vital for us to understand that the new mysticism has to do with the control of women; that it may be seen as a sexual as well as a spiritual phenomenon; that it represents a subtler form of oppression, not a form of liberation."[33]

"Selfishness" and "Self-Sacrifice"

Consider, first, the use of the label "selfish." Those who are judged to be selfish are often those who do not respond to demands from others: the question of selfishness is a question of whether a person thinks only of herself. This consideration often develops into a complaint that the person deemed selfish does not act in ways that contribute to a social structure such as the nation, the family, the synagogue or church, the corporation, the sewing circle, or the collective. Significantly, when a person goes along with the group, even if she is only thinking of herself—being "selfish"— she may well be considered ethical for doing the "right" thing. Further, somcone who is perceived as selflessly opposing the group nevertheless often is judged immoral and unethical. Thus someone can be "selfish" and yet "good"—as well as "unselfish" and yet "bad."

Apparently, the relevant factor in judging a person to be selfish is not whether she considers herself first, but whether or not she goes along with the group (or conforms to a higher order) in one of a number of prescribed ways.[k] It seems that selfishness is not of prime concern; rather, the label is used as an excuse to manipulate our participation toward someone else's end.

Secondly, masculinist ideology suggests that true female nature affirms itself through self-sacrifice. Mary Daly defines "self-sacrifice" as the handing over of our identity and energy to individuals or institutions.[34] This ethical value encourages a woman to give up pursuit of her needs and interests in order to dedicate her efforts to pursuing others' needs and interests, usually those of her husband and children.

Self-sacrifice appears to be a sacrifice of self-interest. Yet women face limited options: men limit women's options through conceptual, physical, and economic coercion. As a result, when a woman engages in self-denial, acquiesces to male authority, and apparently sacrifices her own interests to those of a man in conformity with the dictates of the feminine stereotype, she may actually be acting from self-interest, doing what she deems necessary to her own survival.

Drawing upon Kathleen Barry's analysis of the strategy men use in female sexual slavery, Marilyn Frye suggests that when women who are trapped in actual conditions of female sexual slavery, or who are caught up in masculinist

---

k. As a result, we find that there is really no room for anyone who finds the group, the social structure, or the higher order unacceptable and does not wish to go along in any of the prescribed ways. If she separates from the group or the structure or the order, she is judged unethical and ostracized by those caught up in the structure. Such judgment can come from those who would bring change through reform as well as from those who would retain the status quo.

arrogant perception, apparently sacrifice their own needs and interests by aligning their resources in support of a man, they nevertheless are not acting selflessly or unselfishly. She argues, rather, that women facing such conditions are intently involved in acting in their own self-interest:

> The slave, the battered wife, the not-so-battered wife, is constantly in jeopardy. She is in a situation where she cannot, or reasonably believes she cannot, survive without the other's provision and protection, and where experience has made it credible to her that the other may kill her or abandon her if and when she displeases him. . . . [W]hat she does "for the other" is ultimately done "for herself" more consistently and more profoundly than could ever be the case in voluntary association.[35]

The point is that because of coercion under patriarchy, the woman realigns her choices to focus on the man. While she is not working on her own projects, nevertheless she is intensely involved in acting in her own self-interest.

One consequence is that, except perhaps in extreme cases of female sexual slavery, when a woman is in a situation in which she is expected to shift her identity to that of a man or a child, the stage is set for her to work to control the arena wherein her identity is located. She has not sacrificed her self: by altruistically adopting another's interests, she has transferred that self, or rather it has been arrogated by the man.[36] And while she may have given up pursuit of her own unique interests and needs in favor of those of her husband (and to a lesser extent those of her children), she will pursue their interests and needs as her own.

. . . I want to suggest that revaluing choice is central to Lesbian Ethics.

Now, if we decide to regard choice as a creation, not a sacrifice, situations requiring difficult decisions will still arise between us. However, we can regard our ability to make choices as a source of power, an enabling power, rather than a source of sacrifice or compromise. Thus by revaluing choice we begin to revalue female agency: female agency begins to be, not essentially a matter of sacrifice and manipulation, but rather a process of engagement and creation. (And the prerequisite for this is self-understanding.)

Understanding choice as creation, not sacrifice, helps us better understand choices we make typically considered "altruistic." We often are drawn to helping others. That's one reason so many are drawn to healing, to teaching, to volunteering to work at shelters, to practicing therapy, to working at community centers or in political campaigns, to going to nicaragua—to all kinds of political work. In doing such work, we feel we are creating something, that we are participating in something; we engage and we make a difference.

However, there remains the danger that we treat choice and engagement as "handing our identity over to individuals or institutions," or even as "acting as though in my own behalf, but in behalf of the other." To choose and engage, we are both separate and related. In heteropatriarchy, engagement and creation for women amounts to mothering. Mothering, perhaps, most clearly embodies the feminine virtues, is itself a feminine virtue. And appealing once again to the "feminine," we tend to romanticize "mothering" as women's function and regard it as unconditional loving, as a matter of selflessly protecting and nurturing all life.

In the first place, mothering is women's *function* only given the values of heterosexualism. Church fathers (inspired by Thomas Aquinas among others) and state fathers (such as Hitler and Mussolini) argue that the function of a woman is to bear and raise children. They thereby conclude that women ought to bear and raise children.

Certainly it is true that some women have borne and raised children, many women are capable of it. Nevertheless, we cannot conclude that something a woman is capable of is women's function or that women ought to do it unless we add a premise to the effect that women ought to do what they're capable of. Now, women are capable of many things, and women actually do many things—kill battering husbands, for example, or avenge the rape of daughters. Yet christian fathers are not prepared to assert that women ought to do all they're capable of, they are not prepared to add any such premise. As a result, what appears to be a factual statement about women's function is actually a disguised value statement in that men have picked one of the many things women do and decided to call *that* women's function.[37]

If I were to pick one thing and claim it is women's function these days, I would suggest it is amazoning. Some women do it, and many women are capable of it. And, in my opinion, it is far more necessary than mothering. While some might focus on mothering, the vast majority might answer the call to amazon. Further, they would accomplish through amazoning what they keep trying to accomplish through mothering—appropriate atmosphere for children, self-esteem for girls, caring, room to grow and flourish.

Other fathers in patriarchy, scientific fathers, claim that women's function is to bear and raise children because, they claim, the species will not survive otherwise.[1] As a result they target women who cannot or who do not bear children as "abnormal" women. Given the population, we can only conclude that these fathers are actually thinking of maintaining dominance of their race (which they equate with its survival) and—to touch on finer points—mainte-

1. Not surprisingly, from sociobiology comes the idea that rape and infanticide are an ethical necessity for preserving the species.[38] Indeed, rape and infanticide have been called altruistic.[39] It simply warms the heart to realize men have been altruistic all along.

nance of their class. Concomitantly, white men institute programs of forced sterilization against women of color. Further, as Marilyn Frye writes:

> In the all white or mostly white environments I have usually lived and worked in, when the women start talking up feminism and lesbian feminism, we are very commonly challenged with the claim that if we had our way, the species would die out. (The assumption our critics make here is that if women had a choice, we would never have intercourse and never bear children. This reveals a lot about the critics' own assessment of the joys of sex, pregnancy, birthing and motherhood.) They say the species would die out. What I suspect is that the critics confuse the white race with the human species. . . . What the critics are saying, once it is decoded, is that the white race might die out. The demand that white women make white babies to keep the race afloat has not been overt. . . . [White] women have generally interpreted our connections with these men solely in terms of gender, sexism, and male dominance. We have to figure their desire for racial dominance in their equations.[40]

Men stress women's breeding function when they want cannon fodder or a larger pool of unemployed through which they can drive wages down and exploit the labor force. Women may find that the species will survive only if women refuse to bear and raise children, particularly when under pressure from men to breed. Certainly, as Sally Gearhart convincingly argues,[41] the survival of the species may depend on women reducing drastically the number of male children they bear.[m] It is not at all clear that the survival of the species depends on women bearing and raising children. As Elsa Gidlow writes, "Ask no man pardon."[43]

---

m. Many feminists are caught up with the nature/nurture debate. I consider it a ruse. It may be that men do what they do because of a genetic deformity. Alternatively, the society they control may well have conditioned and produced them. But for purposes of feminist choices, it is irrelevant which view, if either, is accurate. On the one hand, just because something is genetic does not mean it is unchangeable; we treat asthma, for example. On the other hand, just because something is conditioned doesn't mean it can be changed or that it can be changed quickly or even in a lifetime. We are aware of how long it takes to unravel aspects of our own conditioning. In fact, whatever battle wounds we have will remain with us during our lifetimes, at the very least as scars. So whichever leaning we have in the nature/nurture debate, change involves time, a long time, and what we have to deal with is what there is now. If men ever decide to change their behavior, it is possible that they will succeed; but even if they do make such a decision, they will be acting the way we understand them to act for a long time. And our choices must take that into account.[42]

(One may wonder whether it is conceivable that men could change in such a way as to be able to function in the framework of lesbianism. I think it is possible. For example, if men changed themselves to become like dolphins—playful, intelligent, non-intrusive creatures—they could well fit.)

The idea that mothering is women's function also appears in women's spirituality, which is rushing to claim the "feminine." Women's spirituality embraces mothering as nurturing and as an ideal for all women.[n] Mothering, for many, is the paradigm of women's creativity and power, whether mothering takes the form of nurturing children (boys or girls or men) or saving the world and being the buttress of civilization.[o] As one author writes:

> Women's power is the power to give birth whether we are birthing children or ideas. Our power is the power to nurture, to nourish, to take care and protect all life.[46]

The idea that all women are or should be mothers in one way or another is not only not challenged, it is pursued.

To begin with, actual mothering is not simply a matter of protecting and nurturing all life. The choice to feed children is the choice to interrupt the life process of something or someone else (whether or not that action is with its consent). The choice to mother is also a choice to protect one's own against others when necessary. The choice to mother can involve the choice to destroy destructive forces, from bacteria to batterers: a mother, like others, may have to kill to survive. Mothering may also involve the choice not to bring a child into the world so long as society won't let a lesbian be the kind of mother she chooses to be.[47] The choice to mother can involve the choice to abort.

---

n. Billie Potts asked me to distinguish between lesbian spirituality and women's spirituality, pointing out that lesbian spirituality has been almost wholly coopted and that we have participated in the cooptation, for example, by calling our spirituality "womanspirit." By referring to lesbian spirituality, I do not mean to suggest there has been a well-defined tradition, though Z. Budapest and others such as Jean and Ruth Mountaingrove and Billie Potts worked to define a womon-centered tradition during the early u.s. women's liberation movement.[44] Much of what is called "women's spirituality" comes from the craft of europe and went underground during the burning times. And while that tradition has a history of oppression and persecution, it nevertheless adheres to the dualism I'm challenging and which much of early lesbian spirituality challenged.

Several elements are involved in the dissolving of lesbian spirituality. One is the embracing of the "eternally feminine." A second is accepting a christian influence and setting up churches and highly structured institutions. A third involves embracing the light/dark dualism. A fourth involves letting go of a political analysis of the context we live in when pursuing the idea that we choose what happens to us. Fifthly, women's spirituality embraces a mothering metaphor of creativity, as if the goal of this living is or could be all-nurturing and all-embracing. Finally, women's spirituality itself is dissolving into humanism.

o. Marilyn Frye notes that as a result of the anglo-european and u.s. women activists of the nineteenth century, women's anger on behalf of great moral causes became tolerated in the public realm. However, she notes, this represents an historical and logical extension of women's "right" to mother: permitting women's anger only in behalf of others.[45]

I think mothers can claim both the power (enabling) of life and the power (enabling) of death. Many feminists, for example, attempt to deny the depth of the choice to abort by claiming that a zygote is nothing but a clump of cells or that, while a fetus may be a potential person, it is not morally significant. I think this an error. The choice to abort a fetus is morally significant. To legitimize the choice we need not deny its moral import. As a moral agent, a mother who makes such a choice is making a choice about what is possible.

Mothering is one way of embracing and developing one ability to make a difference in this living; it is creating a quality of life through choice. As such, it does not always involve protecting living things, nor is the energy involved only nurturing energy. More significantly, we must challenge the concept of mothering as it is institutionalized in heteropatriarchy.[48]

. . .

I will add here some thoughts about the word "sex"; there are problems as well with using it to talk about our desire. The word "sex" comes from the latin *sexus,* akin to *secus,* derivative of *secāre,* "to cut, divide," as in "section," and itself suggests fragmenting or severing. As a result, Mariel Rae suggests that "sex" is a term which erases lesbian desire, sensuality, and orgasm.[49]

In discussing the meaning of "sex," Claudia Card asks whether sex is a purely biological phenomenon like eating and drinking and sleeping, or whether it is something whose meaning emerges through an institutional context, as is the case with breakfasting, dining, or going to potluck dinners. She suggests that if we regard sex as a purely biological phenomenon, then "when one tries to abandon a phallocentric conception of sex, it is no longer clear what counts as sexual and what does not."[50] She suggests that the only preinstitutional sense of sex she can make out is a biological one that refers in one way or another "to reproductive capacities of members of a species that reproduce sexually rather than asexually." In this respect, of course, the clitoris is not a sexual organ:

> In short, I do not see how it is possible to give an account of what it means to call . . . clitoral pleasure . . . *sexual* without reference to the institution of sexuality. If there is such a thing as "plain sex," which does not mean simply "femaleness or maleness" but which is ordinarily pleasurable and had only intermittently and is independent of the institution of sexuality (logically prior to it), it seems also to be a purely androcentric phenomenon.[51]

In other words, if one refers to "sex" as a purely biological phenomenon, such as eating, rather than an institutional phenomenon, such as potlucking, then clitoral pleasure is not part of sex.

Thus, understanding sexuality is not just understanding a "drive" but understanding the context, indeed the institutions, which gives our urges and responses depth of meaning. Now, in evaluating the patriarchal institution of sex, Claudia Card notes that it sanctions hatred and domination—they are integral rather than peripheral to it. Further, the institution of sex, even imagined outside a patriarchal context, remains essentially a male phenomenon. As Marilyn Frye has pointed out, sex is a phenomenon which requires having one or more male sexual organs present such that penetration of almost anything counts as having sex.[52]

In considering the Philip Blumstein, Pepper Schwartz survey on sex,[53] Marilyn Frye notes that it was brought to her attention that what 85 percent of long-term heterosexual married couples do more than once a month (which lesbians, according to the studies, do far less frequently) takes, on the average, eight minutes to do.[54] She goes on:

> I know from my own experience and from the reports of a few other lesbians in long-term relationships, that what we do that, on the average, we do considerably less frequently, takes on the average, considerably more than 8 minutes to do. It takes about 30 minutes, at the least. Sometimes maybe an hour. And it is not uncommon that among these relatively uncommon occurrences, an entire afternoon or evening is given over to activities organized around "doing it." The suspicion arises that what 85% of heterosexual married couples are doing more than once a month and what 47% of lesbian couples are doing less than once a month is not the same thing.[55]

Marilyn Frye wonders what violence lesbians do to our experience when answering the same questions heterosexuals answer, as though they have the same meaning for us. She notes that in her experience and reading of the culture, heterosexuals count what they report in these surveys according to the man's orgasm and ejaculation. And she suggests that the attempt to encode our lustyness and lustfulness in the words "sex" and "sexuality" has backfired: "Instead of losing their phallocentricity, these words have imported the phallocentric meanings into and onto experience which is not in any way phallocentric."[56] For example, the joy lesbians can feel in swirling a lover's vagina and in having our vaginas swirled as a potter swirls a pot has nothing to do with banging and penetration, and the male organ is inadequate to the task.[57] I want to try to leave behind the word "sex" and focus instead on "desire."

Our attraction to each other and our desire take many forms. Yet the institution of sexuality portrays all desire as leading to orgasm, and that, too, is inadequate for us. The point of desire is not necessarily orgasm. As JoAnn Loulan writes:

> Even those of us who usually have orgasms find ourselves tyrannized by this supposed goal of sex. When we constantly work towards having an orgasm, we are unable to experience each sexual encounter for the pleasure it can give us.

> Our preoccupation with this particular muscle spasm echoes our general approach in a consumer-oriented society: striving for a goal, while disregarding the pleasure (or lack thereof) that we experience in the process. For women who never reach that goal, there often may be little reason to have sex.[58]

The institution of sexuality portrays all sensuality as "foreplay," as simply part of the trek on toward orgasm.[59] This diminishes all our sensual abilities. I mean to suggest that orgasm, along with all other aspects of our sensuality and desire, ceases to be powerful when we work to make it conform to homo- and heterosexual meaning: we will remain fragmented so long as we regard orgasm as the focus and point of all lesbian desire and sensuality while everything else remains mere excuses.

Claudia Card reminds us that the language of what she calls eroticism is different from the language of sex. She distinguishes what she calls eroticism from sexuality, suggesting it is an emotional, not a biological category. She notes that the patriarchal institution of sexuality presents the erotic as sexual "by construing erotic play . . . as a sexual invitation."[60] Pointing out that the "erotic" may or may not be "sexual," Claudia Card suggests that it is a way of touching, one which does not succeed unless the other is also touching. In other words, it is interactive. Further, "erotic" interchange "can work like superglue—just a little bit can have one hooked for years." This is not true of sexual activity in general."[61]

We need new language and new meaning to develop our lesbian desire, especially as we explore and develop what draws us, where our attraction comes from, what we want to keep, what we want to change and why, how our attractions vary, how our desires change over time, and so on.[62] And this is an interactive, not an introspective matter. We need a lot more discussion and exploration among ourselves in something like consciousness-raising groups, certainly among intimates—lovers and friends—to develop the meaning of lesbian desire, and to heal our fragmentation.

Notes

1. T. Z. Lavine, *From Socrates to Sartre: The Philosophic Quest* (New York: Bantam Books, 1984), 373.
2. Note, for example, Susan Krieger, *Mirror Dance: Identity in a Women's Community* (Philadelphia: Temple University Press, 1983), chapter 5, especially 46.
3. Adrienne Rich, *Women and Honor.*
4. Note, for example, Donna Hawxhurst and Sue Morrow, *Living Our Visions: Building Feminist Community* (Fourth World, 110 W. Geneva Drive, Tempe,

AZ 85282, 1984); Tia Cross, Freada Klein, Barbara Smith, and Beverly Smith, "Face-to-Face, Day-to-Day—Racism CR," in *All the Women Are White, All the Blacks Are Men, But Some of Us Are Brave: Black Women's Studies,* ed. Gloria T. Hull, Patricia Bell Scott, and Barbara Smith (Old Westbury, N.Y.: Feminist Press, 1982); also Phyllis Jean kinheart Athey and Mary Jo kinheart Osterman, *The Lesbian Relationship Handbook* (Kinheart, 2214 Ridge Ave., Evanston, IL 60201).

5. Denslow Brown, workshop on conflict resolution, Michigan Womyn's Music Festival, August 1982.
6. For further discussion of the problem of appealing to principles, note Nel Noddings, *Caring: A Feminine Approach to Ethics & Moral Education* (Berkeley: University of California Press, 1984).
7. Conversation, Jeffner Allen.
8. Note Susan Leigh Star, "The Politics of Wholeness II: Lesbian Feminism as an Altered State of Consciousness," *Sinister Wisdom* 5 (winter 1978): 82–102; note also Barbara Starrett, "I Dream in Female: The Metaphors of Evolution," in *The Lesbian Reader,* 105–21.
9. Ludwig Wittgenstein, *Philosophical Investigations,* 3d ed., trans. G. E. M. Anscombe (New York: Macmillan Co., 1968), remark 24, for example.
10. For a critique of the empiricist/positivist tradition in science, note Sandra Harding, *The Science Question in Feminism* (Ithaca, N.Y.: Cornell University Press, 1986).
11. Ludwig Wittgenstein, *On Certainty,* ed. G. E. M. Anscombe and B. H. von Wright, trans. Denis Paul and G. E. M. Anscombe (Oxford: Basil Blackwell, 1969), remark 152.
12. For a fuller development of these ideas, note Sarah Lucia Hoagland, "The Status of Common Sense, G. E. Moore and L. Wittgenstein: A Comparative Study" (Ph.D. diss., University of Cincinnati, 1975).
13. Julia P. Stanley, "Generics, Gender, and Common Nouns in English: Usage and Reference," published as "Gender-marking in American English," in *Sexism and Language,* ed. Alleen Pace Nilsen et al. (Urbana, Ill.: National Council of Teachers of English, 1977), 43–47; note also Julia Penelope [Stanley] and Susan W. Robbins, "Sex-Marked Predicates in English," in *Papers in Linguistics* 11, 3–4 (fall–winter 1978): 487–516, and Julia P. Stanley, "Sexist Grammar," in *College English* (March 1978): 800–11.
14. Celia Kitzinger, "Heteropatriarchal Language: The Case against 'Homophobia,'" *Gossip* 5: 15–20.
15. Conversation, Marilyn Frye. Note Andrea Dworkin, *Pornography: Men Possessing Women* (New York: G. P. Putnam's Sons, 1979), 61.
16. Adrienne Rich, "Compulsory Heterosexuality and Lesbian Existence," *Signs* 5, no. 4 (summer 1980): 647; reprinted in *Women-Identified-Women,* ed. Trudy Darty and Sandee Potter (Palo Alto, Calif.: Mayfield Publishing Co., 1984), 133.

17. Janice G. Raymond, *A Passion for Friends: Toward a Philosophy of Female Affection* (Boston: Beacon Press, 1986), 11.
18. Conversation, Ariane Brunet.
19. Note, e.g., Andrea Dworkin, *Pornography,* 61–62.
20. Julien S. Murphy, "Silence and Speech in Lesbian Space," paper presented at Mountain Moving Coffeehouse, Chicago, Ill., 1984.
21. For further development of this point, note Marilyn Frye, "Oppression," in *The Politics of Reality: Essays in Feminist Theory* (Trumansburg, N.Y.: The Crossing Press, 1983, now in Freedom, Calif.), 5–6.
22. Note Susan Griffin, "Rape: The All-American Crime," in *Feminism and Philosophy,* ed. Mary Vetterling-Braggin, Frederick A. Elliston, and Jane English (Totowa, N.J.: Littlefield, Adams & Co., 1977), especially 320.
23. Andrea Dworkin, *Woman Hating* (New York: E. P. Dutton & Co., 1974), 29–49.
24. Sonia Johnson, presidential campaign speech, Chicago, Ill., 1984; conversation, Pauline Bart. The figure on wife-beating comes from the "Uniform Crime Reports of 1982," federal reports on incidences of domestic crime. According to a fact sheet from the Illinois Coalition on Domestic Violence, "National Domestic Violence Statistics, 1/84," 10 to 20 percent of American children are abused. Another fact sheet, "Verified Domestic Statistics," researched and compiled by the Western Center on Domestic Violence (San Francisco, Calif.), cites estimates of Maria Roy, *The Abusive Partner* (New York: Van Nostrand Rernhold, 1982), as indicating that violence against wives will occur at least once in two-thirds of all marriages. Another fact sheet, "Wife Abuse: The Facts" (Center for Woman Policy Studies, 2000 P. Street N.W., Washington, D.C. 20036), cites Murray Straus, Richard Gelles, and Suzanne Steinmetz, *Beyond Closed Doors: Violence in the American Family* (Garden City, N.Y.: Doubleday, 1980), as saying that 25 percent of wives are severely beaten during their marriage. There are many more statistics . . . you get the idea. Bette S. Tallen was extremely helpful in obtaining some of this information. Note also Del Martin, *Battered Wives,* revised and updated (Volcano Press, Inc., 330 Ellis St., #518, Dept. B, San Francisco, CA 94102, 1976, 1981); Leonore Walker, *The Battered Woman* (New York: Harper & Row, 1979); Florence Rush, *The Best Kept Secret: The Sexual Abuse of Children* (Englewood Cliffs, N.J.: Prentice-Hall, Inc., 1980); Diana E. H. Russell, *Sexual Exploitation: Rape, Child Sexual Abuse, and Workplace Harassment* (Beverly Hills, Calif.: Sage Publications, 1984); and Elizabeth A. Stanko, *Intimate Intrusions: Women's Experience of Male Violence* (Boston, Mass.: Routledge & Kegan Paul, 1985), among others.
25. Marilyn Frye, "In and Out of Harm's Way: Arrogance and Love," *The Politics of Reality,* 72.
26. Pat Robinson and Group, "A Historical and Critical Essay for Black Women in the Cities," in *The Black Woman,* ed. Toni Cade [Bambara] (New York: New American Library, 1970), 202.

27. Merlin Stone, *Ancient Mirrors of Womanhood: Our Goddess and Heroine Heritage,* 2 vols. (New York: New Sibylline Books, 1979).
28. Carol Moorefield, talk presented at Women and Children First Bookstore, Chicago, Ill., October 1982.
29. Sonia Johnson, presidential campaign speech, Chicago, Ill., 1984; also *Going Out of Our Minds,* 244.
30. *Sunday Sun-Times* (Chicago, Ill.), 9 September 1979.
31. Adrienne Rich, "Compulsory Heterosexuality and Lesbian Existence," 632 or 119–20.
32. Conversation, Marilyn Frye.
33. [Susan] Leigh Star, "The Politics of Wholeness: Feminism and the New Spirituality," *Sinister Wisdom* 3 (spring 1977): 39.
34. Mary Daly, *Gyn/Ecology: The Metaethics of Radical Feminism* (Boston: Beacon Press, 1990), 374–75.
35. Marilyn Frye, "In and Out of Harm's Way: Arrogance and Love," in *The Politics of Reality,* 73.
36. Ibid., 66–72.
37. This function argument comes from the work of Jim Kimble, University of Colorado.
38. Rid Brown, "The Monkeys Who Kill Their Young," *Mother Jones* 2, no. 1, (1977): 322–39.
39. Richard Dawkins, *The Selfish Gene* (New York: Oxford University Press, 1976).
40. Marilyn Frye, "On Being White: Toward a Feminist Understanding of Race and Race Supremacy," in *The Politics of Reality,* 124.
41. Sally Gearhart,"The Future—If There Is One—Is Female," *in Reweaving the Web of Life: Feminism and Nonviolence,* ed. Pam McAllister (Philadelphia: New Society Publishers, 1982), 266–84.
42. For a more in-depth discussion of the nature/nurture dichotomy, note Nancy Tuana, "Re-fusing Nature/Nurture," *Women's Studies International Forum* 6, no. 6 (special issue featuring *Hypatia,* 1983): 621–32.
43. Elsa Gidlow, *Ask No Man Pardon: The Philosophical Significance of Being a Lesbian* (Druid Heights Books, 685 Camino del Canyon, Mill Valley, CA 94941).
44. Note, for example, Z. Budapest, *The Feminist Book of Lights and Shadows;* and Billie Potts and River Lightwomoon, *Amazon Tarot* and *New Amazon Tarot* (Bearsville, N.Y.: Hecuba's Daughters, n.d.); for information, write Billie Potts, 18 Elm Street, Albany, NY 12202. Jean and Ruth Mountaingrove edited *Womanspirit* from 1974 to 1984.
45. Marilyn Frye, "A Note on Anger," in *The Politics of Reality,* 92.
46. Diane Mariechild, "Interview on 'Womanpower,'" *Woman of Power: A Magazine of Feminism, Spirituality, and Politics* (spring 1984): 18–21.
47. Conversation, Florencia Carolina.
48. Note, for example, Adrienne Rich, *Of Woman Born: Motherhood as Experience and Institution* (New York: W. W. Norton & Co., Inc., 1976).
49. Conversation, Mariel Rae.

50. Claudia Card, "The Symbolic Significance of Sex and the Institution of Sexuality," paper presented to the Society of Sex and Love at the Eastern Division meeting of the American Philosophical Association, New York City, December 28, 1984. A revised version of this paper was published as *Intimacy and Responsibility: What Lesbians Do,* Series 2, Institute for Legal Studies, Working Papers, University of Wisconsin-Madison, Law School, October 1987.
51. Ibid.
52. Marilyn Frye, "To See and Be Seen: The Politics of Reality," in *The Politics of Reality,* 157.
53. Philip Blumstein and Pepper Schwartz, *American Couples* (New York: William Morrow and Company, 1983).
54. Marilyn Frye cites Dotty Calabrese, who presented this information in a workshop on long-term lesbian relationships at the Michigan Womyn's Music Festival, 1987.
55. Marilyn Frye, "Lesbian 'Sex,'" *Sinister Wisdom* 35 (summer/fall 1988): 46–54.
56. Ibid.
57. Conversation, Harriet Ellenberger.
58. JoAnn Loulan, *Lesbian Sex* (San Francisco: Spinsters Ink, 1984, now Spinsters/Aunt Lute), 71; note also Sidney Spinster, "Orgasms and the Lesbian Touch," *Lesbian Inciter* 13 (July 1984): 17, 18, 19.
59. JoAnn Loulan, *Lesbian Sex,* 73.
60. Claudia Card, "Symbolic Significance of Sex," 10–11.
61. Ibid., 11.
62. For fun, note Tee Corinne, *Cunt Coloring Book* (San Francisco: Pearlchild Productions, 1975, subsequently published as *Labia Flowers* (Tallahassee, Fla.: The Naiad Press), and forthcoming as *Cunt Coloring Book* (Last Gasp, 2180 Bryant St., San Francisco, CA 94107).

EXPERIENCE

[31]

Human Experience and Women's Experience: Resources for Catholic Ethics

Susan L. Secker

A FREQUENT QUESTION I encounter among contemporary North American Catholics is something like the following: "I consider myself to be a good Catholic, but how can I follow my church's teachings when they do not speak to my experience?" While this question is asked by women and men alike, in more recent years it has become a constant refrain among Catholic women—as the initial draft of the United States bishops' pastoral letter on women's concerns attests.[1] Many women claim that they simply cannot connect their own experience with many of the official teachings of the Roman Catholic Church concerning sexual and biomedical ethics. Sociological studies corroborate this anecdotal evidence of a considerable and growing discrepancy between the "moral sense" of thoughtful lay Catholics and the moral teachings of the magisterium.[2]

Among American Catholic ethicists there has been a parallel tendency to accord experience a more central role in moral reflection, and ecclesial events suggest that the effort by scholars to be attentive to experience in their ethics

SOURCE: From Susan L. Secker, "Human Experience and Women's Experience: Resources for Catholic Ethics," *The Annual* (Boston: Society of Christian Ethics, 1991). Used by permission.

produces ecclesiastical ramifications. For example, one thinks of the meeting in Rome between the pope and representative American bishops during which a curial official identified the influence of "radical feminism" as an area of Vatican concern regarding the health of the American Church.[3] Another example is the censure of Milwaukee's archbishop apparently because of his listening sessions to women's experience on abortion.[4] One has to wonder whether the fate of the U.S. bishops' pastoral on women's concerns resulted from its willingness to take seriously women's experience.[5] Appeals to human experience, especially as descriptive of women's experience, constitute a double-edged challenge to Catholic ethics: one substantive and the other procedural. From the perspective of those Catholic ethicists focusing their scrutiny on the function of human experience as an ethical resource, the challenge is a substantive one. That is, the end result of their scholarship lies in articulating with greater precisions what can be known about human existence and how this knowledge ought to function in defining moral agency and in constructing ethical norms. On the other side, the Vatican response views the challenge as one questioning the authoritative teaching role of the magisterium. Thus, the significance of the research of these ethicists is reduced to the differing ethical positions their arguments produce rather than to their substantive contributions to Catholic moral wisdom.

Why is there such a gap between what American Catholics mean when they appeal to experience and its meaning in hierarchical ethics? Why have the efforts of American Catholic ethicists to close this gap precipitated not only theoretical resistance but ecclesiastical censure? This is puzzling in an ethical tradition which has consistently maintained that the human reality is a preeminent source from within which to construct normative ethical frameworks. One expects from that tradition continued efforts accurately to describe the salient features of the human reality and adequately to prescribe its normative character.

The purpose of this essay is to explore these questions. What do American Catholic ethicists mean when they appeal to human experience as a source for ethics? Derivatively, what do Catholic feminists mean when they appeal to women's experience as an ethical source? What is its methodological function? Finally, what conclusions can be drawn in suggesting implications for Catholic moral reasoning?

In what follows I will pursue these questions by turning to the work of Lisa Sowle Cahill and Margaret A. Farley, two Catholic ethicists whose writings on sexual and biomedical ethics emphasize the role of human experience in general, and of women's experience in particular.[6] I will begin by providing a conceptual framework from within which to clarify the function of human experience. Second, I will show that Cahill and Farley appeal to experience in ways that illustrate different ethical functions. Finally, in drawing conclusions from their use of human experience, I will sketch some implications for the reformulation of Catholic ethics.

Human Experience: Descriptive Accuracy and Normative Adequacy

Since the term *human experience* is employed ambiguously in the ethical literature, the following distinctions may prove helpful. The appeal to human experience functions in two different ways in ethical reflection. *First,* one finds empirically based descriptions of the way things are. To appeal to human experience in this way is to attempt to achieve complete and reliable information about human persons and societies as a foundation for moral judgment. For example, an ethical evaluation of homosexuality first requires a comprehensive and unbiased examination of the fullest possible factual evidences (i.e., the psychosocial and biological features of homosexual human reality). In developing a full understanding of the situation, the ethicist may appeal to one or both of two different sources of information about experience: (1) knowledge which is public and consensual such as that provided by the human, natural, and social sciences, and (2) personal reports of individuals concerning the situation in which they find themselves and about which they can provide firsthand reflection; this is often referred to as "lived experience" or "personal story." The ethicist uses information from these sources to establish factually accurate characterizations of human persons and of their sociocultural and politico-economic contexts, clarifying "what is." Once this kind of descriptive accuracy is achieved, sound ethical judgments can be made.

There is in the ethical literature a *second* and entirely different appeal to human experience. In usages of the second type, claims about experience are not introduced in order to clarify the factual aspects of the human situation about which an ethical evaluation is to be made. Rather, appeals to human experience are introduced to provide normative criteria according to which judgments can be made about situations once they are accurately and fully understood. In this form of ethical appeal, the ethicist attempts to conceptualize the very meaning of the human person as an aspect of human experience. The ethicist seeks to identify features of the human which are so fundamental that normative ethical arguments cannot ignore them. Experience in this sense (or some particular way of construing experience) functions as an ethical authority, i.e., as a type of truth claim.

Traditionally, this sort of ethical appeal characterized a kind of natural law reasoning. At the heart of that system was a presumption that there is a certain agreed-upon conception of the essential nature of the human person and of human experience which can be universalized. In the light of that normative conception, ethical positions are developed and ethical judgments are made. Indeed, in past centuries, those employing a normative concept of the nature of the human person or of human experience did not inquire from whence their conception arose; they took it to be self-evident truth. As Charles Curran has argued, such a classical worldview is no longer satisfactory to contemporary persons.[7] Critical studies and cross-cultural research have produced a quite different consciousness of reality. We are much more likely to develop our conceptions of the human person and human experience from within particular and identifiable sets of experiences and from within a particular cultural and communal tradition. The appeal to experience as a normative authority is therefore more problematic and often more contested. What it requires is more careful attentiveness to the particularity of the nature of human persons and human experience prior to normative universal claims.

In appealing to human experience as a norm governing moral judgments, the ethicist may employ one or both of two distinct knowledge sources: (1) authoritative claims arising from various philosophical and theological anthropologies, and (2) the collective wisdom of ordinary people based on commonalities discovered in their shared experience from which normative notions about the human reality are developed. This notion that moral weight should be given to the untutored moral reasoning of ordinary particular people is new and controversial. While this might appear to mistakenly legitimize idiosyncratic, egocentric, or subjectivist claims as normative, the force of this appeal to experience is actually quite different. In attending to the actual moral judgments people make about themselves and their experience, the ethicist is attending to a form of wisdom that is socially influenced and communally generated and that is thus shaped by the values of a religious and philosophical tradition.[8] At the same time, it constitutes a way of knowing human existence which has not been adequately captured by either philosophical or theological anthropologies. That is, it captures features of the normatively human which spring from attentiveness to particularities (i.e., of culture, race, gender, class, and sexual orientation). This type argues that patterns of meaning can be constructed from the collective reflections on their experience of groups whose perspectives have been previously absent from both theological and philosophical anthropologies.[9] Thus, the claim is that reflections of women, of persons from African, Hispanic, and Asian heritage, and of gay and lesbian persons, must be included within a conception of the normatively human.

Those who utilize human experience in this way are not content with correcting our understanding of the situation in which right action must be defined; the point of this usage is to correct the criteria and rules that guide moral judgment and define moral agency by refining them in light of an adequate conception of normative human reality. Further, since the historically received conception of the normatively human was formed by Western, celibate, highly educated, and affluent men on the basis of men's experience, these thinkers insist that it now has to be adjusted. Within this generalized framework I now proceed to its illustration in the thought of Cahill and Farley.

The Function of Experience in the Work of Cahill and Farley

First, I will examine the empirical function of appeals to human experience, showing that both Cahill and Farley have not only adjusted their ethics to take account of the findings of the human sciences but have also developed methods of moral analysis that require taking account of the concrete context of particular moral agents. Following that, I will explore the normative function of appeals to experience, concentrating on the special importance of attending to women's experience. This criterio-logical use of human experience (especially women's experience), which is present in Farley's ethics and absent from Cahill's writings, constitutes the most critical challenge to Catholic ethics. When taken seriously, it seems to put in question the possibility of a universalized notion of the normatively human in ways that the descriptive use does not.

Understanding the empirical usage of human experience requires locating it within Cahill's and Farley's ethical methodologies. Cahill's distinctive methodological contribution lies in the extent to which the four traditional Catholic sources (the Bible, tradition, philosophical accounts of the ideal or essential humanity, and descriptive accounts of the empirical sciences) critically correlate in a mutually corrective manner. Indeed, she contends that the standard of adequacy for Catholic ethics lies in "fidelity to these four mutually correcting sources, and success in judiciously balancing them."[10] According to Cahill, problems commonly arise when ethical argument exhibits (1) reliance on only one or two sources or (2) failure to place the sources in dialogue.[11] This does not preclude historical and cultural particularities from requiring an emphasis on one or two sources in order to correct past neglect or partial consideration. In fact, she argues that today "experience"—that is, descriptive empirical accounts—is the source requiring emphasis, especially in regard to sexual ethics.[12]

The distinguishing feature of Farley's sexual ethics is the importance which she attaches to the constitutive features of *concrete* human reality. Epistemological questions are in the forefront of her ethical contribution, whereas the focus of Cahill's writings is methodological. According to Farley, the way humans come to know the moral depends upon the way we define and circumscribe the human reality in which the moral becomes intelligible. Differences in ethical positions are thus importantly dependent upon what factors are understood accurately to describe and adequately to prescribe human reality. Such concrete factors as personal, relational, socioeconomic, and cultural contexts, as well as the way these are embedded structurally in thought and institutions, constitute its proper delineation.[13] Failure to take into account the fullness and complexity of experience that these factors represent is the major weakness of Catholic sexual ethics in particular, but of ethical discourse in general. For Farley, the standard of adequacy is met in Catholic ethics when the traditional sources are interpreted in accord with fidelity to human reality, concretely defined.[14]

Describing "What Is": Empirical Evidences on the Context of Choice

To take experience seriously as an ethical source means, for both thinkers, incorporating empirically accurate information about "what is" into moral reasoning about "what ought to be." The importance of this strategy and its impact on their way of thinking about moral problems only becomes clear, however, when we notice what sort of factual knowledge they are determined to take into account: knowledge about the systemic pressures, organizational structures, and social patterns that create the unchosen context within which individual agents struggle to make moral choices. Some illustrations will make this clear.

The use of information about human experience derived from the natural, human, and social sciences can be seen in Farley's critique of the narrow scope of the ethical discourse surrounding abortion.[15] She argues that the debate neglects precisely those elements of concrete reality which often encompass the moral situation, i.e., the socioeconomic and institutional dimensions. The choice for or against an abortion confronts women not in abstraction, but in a social and relational context which itself is a component part of the full moral description. The object of ethical analysis cannot be limited to the choice itself, independent of contextual characteristics. With respect to the ethics of abortion, Farley's emphasis upon the "concrete" character of human reality means that what must be assessed in the moral calculus includes (1) the ambiguity of fetal status; (2) the socioeconomic, cultural, and religious influences both on views of human sexuality and marriage, and also on views of the nature of women; (3) the complex and intimate nature of women's experience of pregnancy; and (4) the larger social reality within which pregnancies occur.[16]

Vigilance regarding these features of experience leads Farley to the conclusion that the entire discussion needs to be recast. She develops a "beyond abortion" position, arguing for values and structures which transform relational definitions for both women and men and which are conducive to mutuality in child rearing. Critical to Farley's argument is the formative influence upon moral agency of the way in which dimensions of the social context are interstructured.[17] Taking experience seriously therefore broadens the context within which moral imperatives emerge.[18] Further, it widens the scope of moral scrutiny. Thus, if contemporary Catholic ethics is to be in continuity with the tradition's emphasis on discernment of the natural law, recognizing the concrete character of the complex situation within which a woman weighs the morality of abortion (i.e., accurate information about the personal *and* social dimensions of human reality) has implications for prescriptive judgments.[19]

Farley highlights for Catholic ethics the consequences of appealing to human experience abstractly instead of contextually. In her essay "The Church and the Family," she examines the notion of family life advanced by John Paul II in *Familiaris consortio,* using it to provide an example of the problems which result from abstract conceptions of human realities. In her view he misses the mark in his description of the problems which challenge contemporary families. A concrete accounting of contemporary family life necessitates an emphasis on socioeconomic and sociological evidences. For example, there are embedded in official Catholic ethics certain presumptions about parenting, family, and sexual love within a married relationship that are often irrelevant to "the questions and struggles which characterize the lives of individuals and families."[20] The real challenge to family morality may not be, as John Paul II asserts, a "contraceptive mentality." Careful attention to concrete particularities may rather reveal "a real powerlessness before vast economic and social forces outside the family" (51). In addition, he neglects to give due weight to such factors as the implications for family morality of sexism and the mounting evidences of domestic violence against women. The church document is flawed to the extent that it does not take these features of experience into account. The ethical effect is that solutions are proposed which strike many Catholic families as addressing another reality (66–71).

Cahill's thought reveals a similar descriptive function for human experience. "Experience" is not accurately accounted for without data describing the interpersonal and social contexts of choice.[21] For instance, an accurate moral delineation of marriage, and of women's role in marriage, necessitates examining the sociocultural factors which bear upon presuppositions about how marriage and women are defined. Official ethical positions which leave unexamined the undergirding patriarchal worldviews no longer reflect the reality for Western women.[22]

Describing "What Is": The Voice of the Moral Agent

In striving to establish a complete and reliable appreciation of the situation that requires moral action, both Cahill and Farley appeal to another dimension of experience: reflections of persons on their actual lived realities, i.e., Cahill's "personal story" and Farley's "contemporary human experience."[23] It is important to stress that neither thinker means to give ethical credibility to subjective whims and desires.[24] Rather, they mean to take seriously particular experiential reports which are representative of a generalized reality. Though less systematic than scientific knowledge, this type of knowledge nonetheless functions in Farley's and Cahill's methodologies as empirical characterization of "what is." Several examples will serve to illustrate this function.

Cahill insists that marital experience (especially the reflections by women on their personal experience) must become an operative dialogical component in re-thinking Catholic ethical teaching. Her rationale is that the experience of married women (and men) relative to the role of children within their married relationship, and with respect to the place of the conjugal act within their sexual lives, simply does not match the "romanticized" presuppositions about married life that ground the official teachings of the church. The presumptions about married life on the basis of which the church constructs its ethical norms diverges disturbingly from the presumptions on the basis of which married persons themselves proceed to ethical considerations. This is especially the case for women. As an illustration, Cahill points to the Vatican document on reproductive ethics. She contents that the instruction appeals to a consensus on the meaning of marriage, sex, and parenthood which does not exist. Its argumentation is not persuasive because its underlying assumptions about married experience are inaccurate portrayals of reality. Indeed, she claims that the instruction's notion of married reality seems "almost naive."[25]

Similarly, Farley argues that Catholic family ethics would be more adequate if the actual stories of married persons served as sources in defining the moral questions which need attention. In fact, Farley argues that such problematic realities as family violence, tensions between partners, alienation of children and elderly, have ethical significance. This experience demonstrates that the family is a place where questions of justice are integral to notions of human dignity. It is imperative that Catholic ethical norms reflect an accurate account of the contemporary experience of family living.[26]

In summary, both Cahill and Farley appeal to empirical knowledge about human experience as they stress descriptive accuracy in analyzing the concrete case preliminary to the task of constructing prescriptive judgments. As Cahill argues, experience in this empirical sense constitutes a "window onto the normative."[27] Methodologically, its chief ethical function lies in its stress upon factual accuracy concerning the human reality under moral scrutiny. However, this methodological move has implications that extend beyond its value in sharpening the skill and wisdom with which we reason practically about particular cases. The work of both women is distinctive in the attention and emphasis given to the way in which the larger socioeconomic and cultural contexts shape moral agency. This gives their work a critical edge in relation to existing Catholic moral teachings. What their work makes clear is the fact that an agent's range of moral choices is impacted by social factors in ways that official Catholic ethics has not yet fully recognized. To the degree that Catholic ethics is not cognizant of this fact, Catholic ethics is impaired in its ability accurately to describe contemporary moral situations in Western culture. Moreover, Cahill and Farley make it plain that a person's self-understanding and worth—especially a woman's self-understanding and worth—are formed by these contextual factors in morally significant ways. For example, motherhood and a woman's moral obligations as a married partner have been importantly shaped by society and culture within worldviews which are now subject to critical scrutiny. For this reason, empirical examination of contemporary human experience (perhaps especially women's experience) can be expected to qualify the ethical role of biblical and theological texts which were themselves products of sociocultural presuppositions. As I will argue in the next section, Farley gives this second implication a normative significance relative to the meaning of human dignity that Cahill does not.

Women's Experience and the Normatively Human

Going beyond the empirical function of human experience, Farley's ethics exemplifies a second and entirely different use of human experience. Unlike the previous form, this usage is specifically exemplified by appeals to women's experience. Farley argues that features of women's experience, if taken seriously, would alter the very moral norms that are being brought to bear in particular judgments. Women's experience brings into view a dimension of personhood which the theological tradition has ignored, distorted, or falsely characterized in its construal of the normatively human.[28] Here the appeal to experience grounds constitutive claims about human reality which differ materially and structurally from the role appeals to experience play in correcting empirical description. There are basic convictions persons have about their concrete reality, about their personhood (e.g., convictions women have about what it means to be a woman and fully human), which are so integral to our self-understanding that to deny them is tantamount to contradicting our own truth. These convictions spring from intrinsic values rooted in fundamental understandings of personhood. They reflect our understanding of the human *qua* human. Ethical appeals based on a notion of personhood which violates women's intrinsic self-understanding—i.e., our "experience" in this normative sense—cannot be legitimately claimed to have authority, even if such appeals are grounded in Scripture or theological tradition.[29]

Farley's argument here is consistent with natural law reasoning. An adequate notion of human reality must be concretely formed; abstract conceptions are deficient. Hence women's reality, adequately conceived, must accord with basic convictions women come to about ourselves in the context of sharing our life narratives.[30] As such, women's experience must have an authoritative function in interpreting biblical and theological sources, a function which she claims is in continuity with that of human experience within the Bible itself and throughout the development of the theological tradition.[31] The result is that Farley suggests a twofold hermeneutical function for women's experience. Negatively, borrowing from Rosemary Radford Ruether, she claims that "whatever diminishes or denies the full humanity of women must be presumed not to reflect the divine or an authentic relation to the divine, or to reflect the authentic nature of things, or to be the message or work of an authentic redeemer or a community of redemption."[32] Positively, she calls for an objective construal of the normatively human which is inclusive of women's understanding of women's personhood as a component part of human personhood.

Women's experience in this sense has critical implications for official Catholic ethical teachings. It brings into sharp relief the partiality of its universalist presuppositions about the human and calls into question the normative standards built on these presuppositions.[33] Put simply, Farley argues that Catholic natural law principles were developed by men, built upon men's experience, and designed in large part to guide men's behavior. Refusal to recognize the limited character of such claims violates an adequate notion of women's humanity and perpetuates an objective conception of human reality which is distorted.

With this in mind, Farley outlines the distinctive features of a different

Catholic ethics. Biblical images (such as the *imago Dei* and the New Testament love command) and the theological concepts which ground the Catholic notion of human dignity are rejected when they legitimate notions about women's concrete reality which diminish or deny this sense of women's experience. They are retrieved when they can be reformulated as positive ideals for a more comprehensive notion of humanity, i.e., when they incorporate this sense of women's self-understanding.[34] For example, ethical interpretations of human sexuality have employed these symbols so as to distort conceptions of women's nature and our gender roles. Such distortions demand conscious correction. Further, theological doctrines have supported notions of evil which identified women with defilement and sin. Within internal ecclesiastical practices these have grounded policies which exclude women from leadership roles and thus from full ecclesial participation.[35]

Farley asserts that women's lived experience—that is, knowledge gained from living as women—provides a perspective upon human reality which is itself a source for moral truth.[36] Women's experience in this sense supports and compels a critique of the philosophical principles defining the meaning of human dignity. For example, modern liberal philosophy's principles of equality and autonomy require corrective modification from the vantage point of women's concrete reality. This means that definitions of persons as autonomous agents must be qualified through the addition of principles of human embodiedness and relationality. Human sociality implies modes of relationality which must be refined by principles of basic equality and mutuality.

On the other hand, this sense of women's experience requires that social theories which emphasize organic notions of society and human relationality be modified by the inclusion of principles of autonomy and worth which transcend gender roles. Finally, insistence on basic human equality must be further specified by a principle of equitable sharing, so that equality is construed to demand more than the protection of individual rights to freedom. It requires a positive right to participation in an equitable share of the world's goods and in human solidarity.[37]

Farley's central thesis is that these normative philosophical principles, when corrected in light of the concrete character of women's reality, constitute *in combination* the normative content of full human dignity. These principles function negatively to qualify or reject past normative formulations when such formulations represent women's personhood as derivative of or complementary to that of men, and thus only partially included in the universal claims about the meaning of human personhood.[38] Positively, women's realization of the disparity between our own experience and the claims of past theological and ethical teachings inspires efforts to reformulate the content of the teachings.[39] These efforts have produced a more adequate (meaning inclusive) view of the normatively human.

Human reality is *accurately defined* by the inclusion of comprehensive empirical evidence; it is *adequately defined* by developing philosophical notions of personhood which reflect the fullness of human experience, as opposed to partial or mistaken claims about intrinsic human dignity and worth. Arriving at ethical norms for human reality thus requires attentiveness to what can be factually known about human existence *and* to what can be argued as intrinsic to it. For Farley, therefore, the concrete character of human existence means ethical norms must give justice to, or be fitting in regard to, human reality concretely depicted.[40] Women's experience illustrates this second type of normative sense for human experience thus constituting the more radical challenge to Catholic ethics.

Implications for Catholic Ethics

What implications for Catholic ethics can be drawn from the arguments that more attention must be paid to human experience in defining moral issues and that the distinctive experience of women not only must be taken seriously but also will require significant adjustments in the normative criteria that church teachings have traditionally employed? Several methodological implications emerge. First, in regard to the descriptive type of appeals, attentiveness to the empirically accurate means greater appreciation for the role of the particular in the process of constructing the ethically normative. Empirically based descriptions which include an assessment of socioeconomic and cultural particularity must be the starting point from which to proceed to dialogue with the Bible, the theological content of the tradition, and normative philosophical views. Both Cahill and Farley argue that factual accuracy in describing human experience is instrumental in correcting distorted conceptions of situations to which moral principles are then applied. Human experience in this sense must be embraced as a necessary component in the Catholic ethical process; as such, it functions in a corrective role providing reliable evidences in relation to which biblical, theological, and philosophical views can then proceed to moral assessment. Treating empirical accounts dialectically prevents Catholic ethics from embracing absolute norms. In some instances, it justifies judging some human situations as only capable of limited realizations of the ethically ideal. Thus, this type of appeal has an important function at the level of specifying the normative ideal. Empirical data, for example, back an ethical norm which recognizes that the best possible realization of committed sexual relationships may involve for some fidelity to part of that norm.[41]

Further, in its evidence gathering, an adequate Catholic ethics must take into account more than the *personal* circumstances of an action. Ethics must attend to the *contextual features,* i.e., not only the relational factors of person's lives, but also the socioeconomic and cultural factors which function in formative ways to circumscribe a notion of moral agency. The proper focus of evaluation is thus very considerably broadened. Human experience as empirically defined is not in and of itself ethically determinative; rather, the empirical description functions as a corrective element or as the imperative *concrete* starting point in the ethical reflection process. Catholic ethical teachings which do not consider in serious ways accurate scientific information and commonly held wisdom are inadequate because their evidence base is inaccurate.

A final implication of this descriptive type of appeal is an ecclesiological one. Attention to *what* is claimed about human reality requires a concomitant attentiveness to *who* does the claiming. Who names human experience? According to what criteria? By whom is experience interpreted? These questions are importantly connected to the ethical principles which result. Thus, whose voice has access and influence in the formulation of moral teachings has decisive impact on the content of those teachings. It is therefore imperative for Catholic ethics that the means by which official ethical teachings are developed and revised be critically examined.[42]

Farley has pointed out the inadequacies of official Catholic ethics in its normative anthropological moorings. The way women's experience functions in her ethics rivets our intellectual scrutiny on a central claim of Catholic natural law methodology. Such a method claims that there are features of being human which are universally shared and which can be appealed to as a common ground basis from which to construct objective standards. What Farley's appeal to women's experience highlights is the necessity of first clarifying the constitutive features of human diversity in its *concrete* historicality and culturally conditioned particularity *before* moving to claims about what is universally shared.

Such an argument for a truly inclusive construal of the normatively human is buttressed by considerable social-scientific research. For example, Carol Gilligan's work has shown how women experience a self-consciousness which differs from men's in that it is a product of social and relational formation in quite gender-specific ways.[43] Mary Field Belenky and her research associates have demonstrated how economic and cultural factors are interstructured in such a way that they block even a minimal sense of moral agency in some women.[44] Their work has confirmed that relationality and connected knowing are characteristic for many women of our moral development processes and, hence, of our way of arriving at moral truth.

Further, this insight is supported by many contemporary theologians who make analogous appeals to this normative and authoritative sense for women's experience. For example, Susan Brooks Thistlethwaite terms it "truth-in-action," by which she means truth which emerges in the context of a communitarian practice but which does not too quickly move to harmonize the differences of race and class.[45] Indeed, Thistlethwaite, Bell Hooks, Katie Geneva Cannon, and Ada Maria Isasi-Diaz caution against the danger of making universal claims for all women when such claims may properly be characteristic of only white, middle-class, educated women.[46]

My final observation about the import of Farley's use of women's experience for Catholic ethics relates to the Catholic women whose claims about finding their own moral reflections absent in their church's teachings prompted this essay. It is clarified in reference to a recent report of the International Theological Commission in Rome. The commission asserts that a key component of feminist thought consists in a shift in the hermeneutical center. According to them, feminism shifts the center from the truth of revelation (the truth of being) to the particularity of experience.[47] This claim is superficially plausible but untrue; what contemporary Catholic women are asserting when we claim church teaching does not resonate with our experience is more nuanced than the report recognizes. Our claim is that women's experience must be a component part of the theological locus within which the content of revelation is discovered. Because past interpretations of revelation have not taken this source into account and have indeed constructed theological claims on what were only erroneously presumed to be universal features of human reality, these interpretations now require redefinition and rearticulation. Therefore, in our view, the hermeneutical center has not shifted in our arguments. Its meaning has rather been expanded upon and deepened. Appeals to women's experience call for redefinitions which broaden the perspective on the intrinsically human and underscore the component voices which an inclusive conception must represent. In other words, to use the report's language, the constitutive features of "being" require the richness of particularity in the process of capturing the commonalities which must undergird any universal claims. The focus must therefore be precisely upon those aspects of revelation which heretofore have either ignored, or falsely characterized, what can be claimed to be true about the human, and by analogy, the divine.

For Catholic ethics to attend with care to the experience of women does not necessarily imply the impossibility of objective standards. Nor is it fair to construe our claims as "radical," if by this is meant that they are dangerous threats to our common faith. On the contrary, incorporating the particularity of women's experience as an ingredient element of human experience outlines the conditions for the possibility of an objective standard and hence for the truth claims of Catholic tradition. The women whose lives and reflections on experience initially motivated my reflections are far from being "radical" Catholics. What forces women to the margins is a hierarchical unwillingness of church leadership to heed our wisdom regarding the content of Catholic ethics and to incorporate our voices and perspectives into the process of its formulation. The fact is that women's experience in this authoritative sense constitutes for the church a locus of truth about features of the normatively human which our heightened consciousness of our own integrity will not permit us to deny.

Notes

1. United States Conference of Catholic Bishops, "Partners in the Mystery of Redemption: A Pastoral Response to Women's Concerns for Church and Society," *Origins* 17/45 (April 21, 1988): 757–88; and "One in Christ Jesus: A Pastoral Response to the Concerns of Women for Church and Society," *Origins* 19/44 (April 5, 1990): 717–40.
2. See Andrew Greeley's interpretation of the General Social Survey Data as gathered by the National Opinion Research Center at the University of Chicago in *American Catholics since the Council: An Unauthorized Report* (Chicago: Thomas More, 1985); Joseph Gremillion and Jim Castelli's summary of the data gathered by the Notre Dame Study of Catholic Parish Life in *The Emerging Parish: The Notre Dame Study of Catholic Life since Vatican II* (San Francisco: Harper & Row, 1987; George Gallup Jr. and Jim Castelli, *The American Catholic People: Their Beliefs, Practices and Values* (New York: Doubleday, 1987).
3. See *Origins* 18/41 (March 23, 1989): 678–96, and *Origins* 18/42 (March 30, 1989): 697–728.
4. See "Listening Sessions on Abortion: A Response," *Origins* 20/3 (May 31, 1990): 34–39; Peter Steinfels, "Vatican Bars Swiss University from Honoring Archbishop of Milwaukee," *New York Times*, November 11, 1990, 12.
5. See "Vote on Women's Pastoral Delayed," *Origins* 20/10 (September 27, 1990): 250–51.
6. The question of whether or not there is a difference in appeals thinkers make in regard to human experience and women's experience is an important one for ethics. I argue that its importance hinges on whether the appeals function descriptively or normatively. If thinkers tend to use experience descriptively in the sense of providing reliable factual information about human reality, then the terms can be employed interchangeably. If, however, a thinker uses the term

to express a normative claim about the intrinsic features of human persons, then the distinction between women's experience and men's experience is pivotal to their arguments.

7. Charles E. Curran, *Directions in Fundamental Moral Theology* (Notre Dame: University of Notre Dame Press, 1985), 169–70.
8. See James M. Gustafson, *Ethics from a Theocentric Perspective,* vol. 1, *Theology and Ethics* (Chicago: University of Chicago Press, 1981), 129.
9. 1 am indebted to Marilyn Frye's method of pattern perception as a way to capture new webs of meaning from the diversity which constitutes women's experience. See Marilyn Frye, "The Possibility of Feminist Theory," in *Theoretical Perspectives on Sexual Difference,* ed. Deborah L. Rhode (New Haven: Yale University Press, 1990), 174–84.
10. Lisa Sowle Cahill, *Between the Sexes: Foundations for a Christian Ethics of Sexuality* (Philadelphia: Fortress Press, 1985), 6. See also Thomas A. Shannon and Lisa Sowle Cahill, *Religion and Artificial Reproduction: An Inquiry into the Vatican "Instruction on Respect for Human Life"* (New York: Crossroad, 1988), 25.
11. As an example of the too narrow approach, Cahill cites the 1975 Vatican *Declaration on Certain Questions Concerning Sexual Ethics;* see Lisa Sowle Cahill, "Moral Methodology: A Case Study," in *A Challenge to Love: Gay and Lesbian Catholics in the Church,* ed. Robert Nugent (New York: Crossroad, 1986), 79. For a discussion of the failure to place the sources in dialogue, see Cahill, *Between the Sexes,* 5.
12. Lisa Sowle Cahill, "Community and Couple: Parameters of Marital Commitment in Catholic Tradition," in *Commitment to Partnership: Explorations of the Theology of Marriage,* ed. William P. Roberts (New York: Paulist Press, 1987), 82–83.
13. Margaret A. Farley, *Personal Commitments: Making, Keeping, Breaking* (San Francisco: Harper & Row, 1986), 82.
14. Margaret A. Farley, "An Ethic for Same-Sex Relations," in *A Challenge to Love: Gay and Lesbian Catholics in the Church,* ed. Robert Nugent (New York: Crossroad, 1986), 99; and Farley, *Personal Commitments,* 82.
15. Margaret A. Farley, "Liberation, Abortion, and Responsibility," in *On Moral Medicine: Theological Perspectives in Medical Ethics,* ed. Stephen E. Lammers and Allen Verhey (Grand Rapids, Mich.: William B. Eerdmans, 1987), 434–38. For similar examples of this empirical type of claim, see Margaret A. Farley, "Sources of Sexual Inequality in the History of Christian Thought," *Journal of Religion* 56 (April 1976): 162–76; Margaret A. Farley, "New Patterns of Relationship: Beginnings of a Moral Revolution," *Theological Studies* 36/4 (1975): 627–46; Margaret A. Farley, "The Church and Family: An Ethical Task" *Horizons* 10/1 (1983): 50–71; Margaret A. Farley, "An Ethic for Same-Sex Relations," in *A Challenge to Love,* 93–106.
16. Farley, "Liberation, Abortion, and Responsibility," in *On Moral Medicine,* 436–37.

17. Anne Carr develops this in "Women, Justice and the Church," *Horizons* 17/2 (fall 1990): 269–79.
18. Margaret A. Farley, "Moral Discourse in the Public Arena," in *Vatican Authority and American Catholic Dissent,* ed. William W. May (New York: Crossroad, 1987), 174.
19. Farley, "An Ethic for Same-Sex Relations," 98.
20. Farley, "The Church and Family," 51. For an English translation of *Familiaris consortio,* see John Paul II, *Apostolic Exhortation on the Family* (Washington, D.C.: United States Catholic Conference, 1982).
21. Along with other revisionists, Cahill argues that a disjunction in Catholic ethical methodology between personal and social ethics challenges not only its adequacy but its credibility. See Lisa Sowle Cahill, "Current Teaching on Sexual Ethics," *Studies* 76 (spring 1987): 20, 28.
22. Cahill, "Community and Couple," in *Commitment to Partnership,* ed. Roberts, 81–99. The methodological import of cultural differences can be seen in Lisa Sowle Cahill, "Moral Theology and the World Church," *Catholic Theological Society of America Proceedings* 39 (1984): 35–51.
23. Cahill, *Between the Sexes,* 10; Farley, "An Ethic for Same-Sex Relations," 99.
24. Cahill, "Community and Couple," in *Commitment to Partnership,* 95.
25. Shannon and Cahill, *Religion and Artificial Reproduction,* 114. She is commenting on Congregation for the Doctrine of the Faith, *Instruction on Respect for Human Life in Its Origin and on the Dignity of Procreation* (Washington, D.C.: United States Catholic Conference, 1987).
26. Farley, "The Church and Family," 70.
27. Cahill, *Between the Sexes,* 10.
28. Margaret A. Farley, "Moral Imperatives for the Ordination of Women," in *Women and Catholic Priesthood: An Expanded Vision,* ed. Anne Marie Gardiner (New York: Paulist Press, 1976), 42.
29. Margaret A. Farley, "Feminist Consciousness and Scripture," in *Feminist Interpretation of the Bible,* ed. Letty M. Russell (Philadelphia: Westminster Press, 1985), 42–43.
30. Farley, "New Patterns of Relationship," 630.
31. Current historical and exegetical research demonstrates that Scripture and the theological tradition are themselves products of an interaction with human experience. See Farley, "An Ethic for Same-Sex Relations," 97–98.
32. Margaret A. Farley, "Feminist Theology and Bioethics," in *Women's Consciousness, Women's Conscience: A Reader in Feminist Ethics,* ed. Barbara Hilkert Andolsen, Christine E. Gudorf, and Mary D. Pellauer (Minneapolis: Winston Press, 1985), 296.
33. John Mahoney reasons similarly about the role of concrete reality in the articulation of church positions on ethical matters. "But if there is a historical shift, through improvement in scholarship or knowledge, or through an entry of society into a significantly different age, then what that same fidelity requires of

the Church is that it respond to the historical shift, such that it might be not only mistaken but also unfaithful in declining to do so." John Mahoney, *The Making of Moral Theology: A Study of the Roman Catholic Tradition* (Oxford: Clarendon Press, 1987), 327. Farley's claim is that such historical shifts have occurred in both knowledge and scholarship relative to the concrete reality of women persons.

34. Farley, "New Patterns of Relationship," 631; "Feminist Consciousness and Scripture," 50.
35. Ancient myths, cultural suspicions of human bodiliness, and philosophical dualisms have all influenced Christian Scripture and theology in such a way that, not only are women rendered inferior, but doctrines of God and of the church, as well as notions of women's nature and role, have been affected by sexist influence. The way to reconstruct these notions lies in building upon Paul Ricoeur's distinction between the mythological level of pre-ethical symbolism and the ethical level of relationships and choice. Farley's point is that sin is a matter of choosing to rupture a covenant bond, i.e., a relationship. Thus the ethics governing sexuality ought to be consistent with those which regulate human behavior in general. They must accord with notions of justice and love. See Farley, "Sources of Sexual Inequality," 166–67, 169; see also Paul Ricoeur, *The Symbolism of Evil,* trans. E. Buchanan (New York: Harper & Row, 1967), 29.
36. According to Mahoney, many of the developments in post-Vatican II moral theology concern themselves with re-evaluating the traditional objective/subjective distinction in Catholic ethics; see Mahoney, *The Making of Moral Theology,* 329–30.
37. Margaret A. Farley, "Feminist Ethics," in *Westminster Dictionary of Christian Ethics,* ed. James F. Childress and John Macquarrie (Philadelphia: Westminster Press, 1986), 230–31; "Feminist Theology and Bioethics," 290.
38. Farley, "New Patterns of Relationship," 633 ff.
39. Farley, "Feminist Theology and Bioethics," 295.
40. Farley, *Personal Commitments,* 82.
41. Examples include "remarriage after divorce; committed but premarital ('preceremonial') sex; the avoidance of conception in conjugal sexual relations; and even the committed homosexual relationship." In these situations, strict adherence to the norm of procreative, heterosexual monogamy is either inappropriate, difficult, or impossible. See Cahill, *Between the Sexes,* 148–49.
42. Lisa Sowle Cahill, "Catholic Sexual Teaching: Context, Function, and Authority," in *Vatican Authority and American Catholic Dissent,* 199; in the same volume, see Farley, "Moral Discourse in the Public Arena," 175 ff. Catholic theologians and pastoral ministers who signed the *New York Times* ad (October 7, 1984) were making the same point; they called church leadership to dialogue on an ethical issue which continues to have special significance for women. See "Statement on Pluralism and Abortion," *Origins* 14 (December 6, 1984): 414. I have written on this subject elsewhere. See Susan L. Secker, "The Crisis

within Official Catholic Sexual and Biomedical Ethics and American Revisionist Moral Theology: The Relationship between Selected Methodological and Ecclesiological Aspects" (Ph.D. diss., University of Chicago, 1989); and Susan L. Secker, "Catholic Ethics: Whose Experience Counts? Which Church Do You Mean?" *New Theology Review,* 1993.

43. Carol Gilligan, *In a Different Voice: Psychological Theory and Women's Development* (Cambridge: Harvard University Press, 1982); Carol Gilligan, Janie Victoria Ward, and Jill McLean Taylor, eds., with Betty Bardige, *Mapping the Moral Domain: A Contribution of Women's Thinking to Psychology and Education* (Cambridge: Harvard University Press, 1988); Carol Gilligan, Nona P. Lyons, and Trudy J. Hanmer, eds., *Making Connections: The Relational Worlds of Adolescent Girls at Emma Willard School* (Cambridge: Harvard University Press, 1990).
44. Mary Field Belenky, Blythe McVicker Clinchy, Nancy Rule Goldberger, and Jill Mattuck Tarule, *Women's Ways of Knowing: The Development of Self, Voice, and Mind* (New York: Basic Books, 1986).
45. Susan Brooks Thistlethwaite, *Sex, Race, and God: Christian Feminism in Black and White* (New York: Crossroad, 1989), 24–26.
46. Bell Hooks, *Feminist Theory: From Margin to Center* (Boston: South End Press, 1984); Katie G. Cannon, *Black Womanist Ethics* (Atlanta: Scholars Press, 1988); Ada Maria Isasi-Diaz, "Toward an Understanding of *Feminismo Hispano* in the U.S.A.," in *Women's Consciousness, Women's Conscience,* ed. Barbara Hilkert Andolsen, Christine Gudorf, and Mary D. Pellauer (Minneapolis: Winston Press, 1985), 51–61; Ada Maria Isasi-Diaz, "The Bible and *Mujerista* Theology," in *Lift Every Voice: Constructing Christian Theologies from the Underside,* ed. Susan Brooks Thistlethwaite and Mary Potter Engel (San Francisco: Harper & Row, 1990), 261–69.
47. The International Theological Commission, "On the Interpretation of Dogmas," *Origins* 20/1 (May 17, 1990): 5.

[32]

Locating My Theology in Sacred Places

Bill Smith

THE BLUES IS NOT JUST a music that sings a sad song. The Blues is a culture, a tradition, a people. The Blues is seeing and facing pain critically, with truth. The Blues is finally having to face and live with the reality of the consequences of history. The Blues is living in the Here. The Blues is yesterday today trying to be tomorrow. Many Queer/Gay men of color come out of the Blues tradition (if not the music, then the life) and intrinsically understand the Blues.

The Blues is a way of living, walking, talking, crawling, fighting through the anger and pain caused by the conditions of living, without trying to mask them or hide from them. The Blues is a way of consciously living through the reality of your history with whatever tools of transcendence are at your disposal. The Blues is a way of naming the devilment you be going through. The Blues is a gate to Immanuel, a gate to transcendence and transformation.

I am spiritually and existentially drawn to the Blues, drawn to juke joints, drawn to liberated gay urban spaces for my spiritual ecstatic encounters with the Holy. I am drawn to the fundamentally, literally forbidden; drawn to the impure; drawn to the most viscerally human for my expressions of communion, for the loss of and rebirth of my self in Spirit. When the band goes

---

SOURCE: From Bill Smith, "Locating My Theology in Sacred Places," in *New Visions for the Americas: Religious Engagement and Social Transformation,* ed. David Batstone (Minneapolis: Fortress Press, 1993).

home, when the last call comes, when it's time to catch the cab home, it is then Blues Time. Blues Time is the time of the Cross, the time spent in struggle with whatever would prevent Spirit from concrete realization.

I am drawn to spiritual and theological reflection when the feelings of freedom, relationship, celebration of life, unrestricted physical and aesthetic creativity experienced in the world of ecstasy are denied, repressed, and restricted. I am drawn to relationship, for witness and companionship in the struggle to reclaim the "Rule" of the Holy for every moment of my waking life. This be the "grist for the mill" of the Blues.

I am drawn to work with words in my efforts to live in Blues Time, to understand why I always have to leave Eden to enter the world that is organized systematically to exploit and exhaust the strength, the intelligence, the feelings, and the spirit of the poor in behalf of the rich. Blues Time is the residence of the human condition.

The human condition is the struggle against the forces that would deny us life. These forces themselves are products of previous struggles for life free of oppression. These forces arise out of the fear of and resistance to the change and the difference that is rooted in habituation and addiction to the familiar. These forces have many names; among them are domination, oppression, repression, subjection, despotism, imperialism, sexism, racism, heterosexism, suppression. These forces employ many strategies: murder, theft, control, appropriation, exploitation, lying, cheating, manipulation, coercion, "conventional wisdom." These forces act through every institution of culture and society.

Blues Time makes the human condition personal, real personal, unescapedly personal, unanswerably personal. From the position of the oppressed, oppression often appears to be ontological, essential, a fact of being. It is with the development of critical awareness that other responses occur.

Confession and Location

No!

I was not there when the foundations of the earth were laid, nor do I know who fixed its dimensions, nor who stretched the measuring line, nor can I command the morning to come, nor do I know the depth of the deepest reaches of the sea. This cooling rock of many rocks floating in space with all its mysteries, including the development of my human being—it is quite beyond my capacity to fathom the origin of its genesis. What I can do is study this human being responding to Here and the history of that responding.

No!

I did not create this Here. This Here is a product of many forces beyond my understanding. But this Here is what I've got to respond to. I've tried wishing it away/praying it away/planning it away/designing it away/writing it away/working in every which way for it to go away, and it still is here with all its misery and despair. I cannot stop my awareness of the exponential increasing of not only human suffering but also that of other life forms.

I cannot stop babies from shooting up/beating/killing/making babies. I cannot stop police/soldiers/presidents/businessmen from butchering/maiming/raping/torturing children/older adults/the innocent. I cannot stop the pain/"dis-ease"/horror/terror I feel every day I walk out the door/drive up streets/go to work/talk to friends/make love. I cannot stop this Here from going on. I see the genesis of its tomorrow.

No longer do the false hopes of democracy/revolution/development/consumption let me off the hook. I am really Here and it doesn't go away. I cannot dream it away/sleep it away/cry it away/smoke it away/ drink it away/eat it away/buy it away/love it away. I cannot even forget it away because it is Here, and Here is the progeny of the fathers and it will not fade away. And I do not know why Here was made this way but as long as I live Here, to be truly alive, I have to accept and acknowledge all of this pain and despair that makes Here Here. This is the "awe-full-ness" of my freedom. Here is where I must confront the reality of my being and all that which would deny me the awareness of the task or the means to accomplish it.

No!

I cannot see happiness as synonymous with freedom, although sometimes there is a convergence, nor can I see the struggle to claim one's freedom as particularly heroic, although there are heroic moments. Nor can I see freedom as a task everyone chooses to accept; Esau sold his birthright for gruel, and things seem to have turned out alright for him in Edom. Nor can I see attempting to escape the realities of Here as becoming any less costly. Being Here costs. It costs our lives, and we cannot escape that truth; trying to escape exacts greater costs. It costs us our innocence; Eden taught us that. The price for escaping from the struggle of Here/Right Now always is our freedom, because all freedom is the struggle for truth, empowerment, relationship, and transcendence Here/Right Now.

The feeling of having escaped Here/Right Now is always temporary. We always come back Here. The only exit is our death, and the peace of that death is not contained in slavery. Slavery is a living death where any moment you might be brought back and have to face yourself Here. The costs of accepting slavery are increasing, and the costs of freedom are the painful acceptance of the costs of Here. I accept the fact, hence the responsibility, of my freedom, which demands I confront Here and all that which would deny me an awareness of my birthright, freedom, and task.

No!

I don't have many tools, only where I have been/what has happened to me/what I have learned/where I am now/what is happening to me/what I am learning. I must use these tools to discover what is Here and how this Here came about. I must deconstruct the fact and how of my Here here. I must stare into the desperation of my feelings of abandonment/rejection/molestation/rape/my color/my sexual identity/my difference/my alcoholic, crazy family/my own craziness/my alienation/my crimes of commission/omission/my desertions of traditional duty/my drug and sexual attempted escapes from Here/my refusals of love/my denials of my and others' need/my failures of imagination/my spiritual doubting/my acceptance of guilt/my too easy acceptance of ideological explanations of what might be called the "Holy."

I must deconstruct these, feel each element of these histories, learning that this Here is a shared construction not only of the fathers but of myself also. And in this deconstruction, I realize that our sins are the primary constructive building blocks of the world, that the Blues/Cross are the means, the how of how I can get to the truth of the despairing genesis of our Here. In fact, we must embrace the Blues/Cross to begin to realize the fullness of freedom. It is out of the dreck of yesterday that today and tomorrow are created. No matter whose good dream we follow we break someone's heart.

The Nature of "God"

Who is this "God" of whom it is claimed creation came? Can this be the same "God" from whom it is also claimed my comfort, my support comes? Like Job I am confused.

Who and what is this "God" that the Church has historically placed at the service of the State and the rich, this "God" who would have the dispossessed and oppressed bow themselves in humility and obedience, in collaboration and complicity, in fear and in ignorance to systems of exploitation and degradation? Is this the same "God" who was discovered and encountered by African slaves, who had been kidnapped to make Europeans rich and prosperous in the New Jerusalem, the "God" that inspired these Africans to resist, to endure, to escape, and to rebel? What is this "God" that is claimed for purposes of both domination and liberation?

As a Gaymale of mixed heritage, a person of color, reared in African American culture, an orphan, working class, with a memory of childhood incest and peer rape, and a future of HIV infection, a Queer, I am drawn to resolve this spiritual contradiction that feeds my Blues Time. And I am not an exception in my community.

Even were I not to name myself as a Christian, the contradictions of these conflicting ideas of who and what "God" is shape my life in the most intimate and most political ways. My health, my civil rights, my economic well-being are, to a large extent, all shaped by the collective understanding of who and what this "God" is and what this "God" considers appropriate human behavior.

As I understand Christian history, the contradictions between a "God" who demands sacrifice for the sake of the ruling classes, the Temple Priests, owners of the means of production and the State, a source of fear and awe, and a "God" who is an indwelling spirit that comforts, inspires, and sustains one in the midst of despair, a cause for joy, are part of the nexus of Christianity's beginnings in the Hebrew Torah. This struggle is archetypally represented in the Gospels' Jesus stories, with the balance of the New Testament a midrash on the outcome of that struggle. This Hebraic-Christian archetypal struggle over conflicting ideas of what a "God" is, as well as the attempts to reconcile the inescapable contradictions, are a primary core of the Christian biblical "story"; in fact, it is also the reason for its writing. Further, this struggle serves as a metaphor for the uses of the "holy" or "spirit" in the struggles between the oppressed and the oppressor.

The ruling classes claim that "God" authorizes the distinctions between purity and impurity, sin and sinlessness, obedience and sacrifice, favor and disfavor. They justify their rule through the Church, the First Estate, by means of that authorization. Those who struggle for empowerment reclaim "God's" presence and power on their behalf and attempt to rename the distinctions of the ruling classes.

The biblical metaphor of the struggle between the "God" of the oppressor and the "God" of the oppressed is useful as a base for the development of a common language between myself and other Christians struggling against oppression and for the development of relationships that create spiritual bonds in that struggle. However, the biblical metaphor of the patriarchal "God" as authority must be recast to be of use Here to my community. Beverly Harrison speaks of "God" as "our passion for justice."[1] Carter Heyward speaks of "God" in terms of "mutual relationship."[2] I accept Matthew's Immanuel, "God with us" (Matt. 1:23), as the embodied incarnational source of our individual and collective ability to transform reality; it is this same representation of "God's" presence that is celebrated by Mary in the Magnificat (Luke 1:46–55).

The Task and Methodology of This Local Theology and Presence of the Holy Spirit

My experiences and my relationships mark my spiritual journey. I find this is not unusual in the communities from which I come. It is from these sources that the tasks for my theology are drawn. It is in answer to collective community needs felt personally that I experience call. It is in the struggle to realize materially and in everyday life what is experienced in the spiritual ecstasy of the dance, music, sex in the liberated spaces of the emerging Gay/Lesbian/Queer community.

We are an emerging community, created out of the ongoing, dynamic social construction of sexuality and the evolution of industrialism. Our community and identity come from relationships born of struggle: struggle with ourselves, struggle with our families, struggle with the Church, struggle with the State, struggle with the health care system, struggle with death. Our community is bonded from these struggles. Our community, like the Jesus community, creates family out of these struggles, creates culture from these struggles, creates love from these struggles, creates truth from these struggles, creates and discovers healing in these struggles.

Our community is a people who were born out of the oppression and repression of our sexuality, our ways of talking, walking, being in relationship. We were born out of the denial of our existence as legitimate human beings. Our sexual and behavioral individualities were made into a psychological and criminal category. Out of that category we emerged as a people fighting for liberation. Emerging as a people, we created communities.

The first order of theological business for our emerging community is critical analysis of the spiritual and concrete conditions of our oppression. Once these conditions are understood and named, once we have faced our Here, our yesterday turned into today, our Blues, the task then turns to employing the technologies of the sacred, the fields and avenues of the transcendent—in Christian terms, the sacraments—to transform our today into the resurrection of tomorrow. The Blues, another word for Crossroads, for the Cross, is the place where the struggle for liberation takes place. Blues Time is when the struggle takes place. Blues Time is when revelation occurs.

Immanence and transcendence are the existential experience of the Holy Spirit, the desire for transformation of the Here of oppression, emerging from the concrete experience of suffering, and reaching into the not Here yet of liberating imagination, to inspire, shape, change this Blues of yesterday today into the hope of tomorrow. This communally experienced feeling is a spirit born of the crucifixion of the pain of daily life of the oppressed. It is Immanent and is called "Immanuel." Its reaching into the Not Yet Become with the intention of transforming the Already Here is a hope in the liberating power of Transcendence.

Church and Sacred Space

For this Queer, like many other Gaymen of color, Church is not my only place of spiritual renewal and celebration. Being a Christian is only part of the process I employ in my struggle to extend liberated space and time. It is the lessons and means of the Blues, the full-get-down-funky feeling of the Blues, the mean-sweaty-holler-stomp dance of the Blues, the echoes of African spiritual tradition where sexual ecstasy brings you into the communion with deepest spirituality that is the Blues.

It was one of my foster fathers who called me into the Blues; he was a musician. He called me into the music of W. C. Handy and his "St. Louis Blues." And it is the Blues that taught me how to explore Gay/Queer holy space and discover more than a promise of full liberation. It is the Blues that brought me to the door of resurrection and rebirth. The Blues is the dissonance that remembered the sexuality, sensuality, fecundity, the rebelliousness of African spirituality that the African American church, with its stress on purity, tried to forget. The Blues and its institutions became the refuge of those called impure by the African American church, those called criminal, those called sinful, those called slothful, the sexual but unmarried.

It is the Blues, with its tradition of sanctuary for the impure, those whose sexuality fell outside of the church door, that serves as my inspiration and model. Gay/Queer dance spaces are liberated spaces, spiritual playgrounds for a community in transformation. Like the Jesus community in its formative stages, like the Blues People of the "juke joints," we are refugees of the purity codes of the Temple/Church, seeking liberation from life-denying restrictions. These liberated spaces are where the immanent becomes the transcendent, and they are defined by our denied spiritual/sexual needs. They are primordial spaces created as sanctuary from the ever-encroaching tentacles of "civilizing society," tentacles that seek to domesticate all human experience. They are shadow spaces transformed into a place of revolt against that domestication; a place of exploration of the nonrational; a place to release and eroticize the brokenness of spirit, of heart; a place of psychic renewal; a place of nonsocial hierarchy; a place where all of it gets played out; a place requiring serious initiation and training in order to survive; a place not for the innocent, the naive; a place of phantoms, demons, and angels; a place where the denied spirits have play. They are playgrounds where the spiritual power of sexuality is both immanent and transcendent; where reality is deconstructed to serve the needs of the erotic imagination; where social roles are exchanged, magnified, or reversed.

Because everyday social identities act as barriers for entering this space and sense of transcendence, identities become categories of consciousness. Rituals, tools, and agents of transformation of consciousness, like different forms of "drag," dancing, cruising, and sexual conversation are gateways to the other side of this sexually repressive domain and into our liberated underground territory. The Blues tradition would recognize these spaces as kindred. They are kindred as are the spaces of the Jesus community (early Christian churches), kindred to people breaking class, cultural, sexual, gender boundaries and seeking spiritual liberation.

Spiritual liberation is necessary for and the base of the imagination for material liberation. In these spaces, the technologies of the sacred, art, music, oral and written literature all express the needs and struggles of the community seeking the transformation of oppressive conditions. A Gay/Queer positive ministry would be a ministry that expresses, respects, and utilizes the experience and witness of these forms, a ministry that empowers and helps in the enabling of the community to use the insights and gifts of these spaces to create freedom-making activity in the Blues Time of the concrete jungle world we live in.

The Biblical Metaphor

My cultural background called me into being a Christian, that same African American background which had come to claim the European "God" as its own protector and liberator. Malcolm X called me into a critical evaluation and awareness of the African American, "colored" churches' self-hatred of Blackness. James Baldwin called me into awareness of the awesome price that the church's hatred of homosexuality exacted.

It is in the critical examination and evaluation of our experiences and in the context of struggle for mutuality in relationship that an understanding of how the Bible's texts and our relationships within the church can shed light on our struggle for liberation. Part of a *Gay/Queer of color* Christian theology, a theology of particularity, is the sharing of critical biblical hermeneutical skills and resources, which include sociohistorical, anthropological and literary, and politico-economic analytic tools with the community. Critical biblical analysis is necessary to relativize the text so that the concretely useful liberative information may be revealed. Because we are not included in the Bible, like African American womanists, we must also reopen the canon to include our presence and our struggle, to include our Blues, the written and oral accounts of our experiences in struggle.

The Church, its Scriptures, and its Traditions make up what may be called the biblical metaphor. In the struggle against oppression, the question must be asked: Is the biblical metaphor of the struggle between the oppressed and the oppressor for power over human organic creative energy a useful tool in the struggle to create liberated space and time? If it is, in what way(s) would it be most useful? These questions must be asked because the Bible and Tradition have been a primary source of my oppression as a Queer Christian of color. They have been a tool the Church employs to continue its campaign of dehumanizing and demonizing the sexuality and even the very lives of Gay people. Furthermore, except in a few denominations, we are not welcome as whole human beings in Christian churches. For this reason, many of us see the Church, along with its Scriptures and Traditions, as a primary enemy and oppressor and have found spiritual support elsewhere.

For those who remain we must determine why. Many Gaymen have accepted the metaphor as real and reside in the metaphor. That is, they see, in some way, the biblical metaphor as the authoritative description of the "Truth." In many cases it was because they entered into the metaphor at an early age through the efforts of parents or caretakers and were taught to believe in the biblical story as the Truth through their formative years. This teaching was reinforced in every part of their socialization process, in one way or another, even by people who were themselves unchurched.

For these Gaymen, seeing themselves as the oppressed, identifying themselves with the oppressed of the Bible and with the "God" of the oppressed, has liberating possibilities. Christian Gaymen are engaged in writing liberating theologies and stretching the biblical metaphor to include us in the biblical story. Others of us, whose experiences and critical examination have placed us outside the biblical metaphor and do not see it as the "Truth" but still identify ourselves as Christian, must come to terms with why we remain Christians.

My resistance to authority and the Bible's property and purity codes prevent me from entering into the metaphor. I see its world and spiritual view as relative, not universal. The biblical metaphor has the proclivity to co-opt struggle, to pacify the oppressed. The biblical metaphor—Church, Scripture, and Tradition—does not see itself as participating in the social construction of oppression of gay people and, hence, is not self-critical or repentant. Its program of liberation is partial and not determinative because the metaphor calls for obedience to spiritual authority and the hierarchy of the nonrational, not for critical thinking and integration of the nonrational with the rest of the personality.

On the other hand, the biblical metaphor's value as a tool against the spiritual encroachment and exploitation by the ruling class has been historically proven. Its sacraments and rituals have the power to open us to sacred space, to the imagination. Even with its limitations, it provides hope, comfort, and healing for the oppressed. The task of uncovering and utilizing that value is a collective task that must be undertaken critically with a respect for the traditional and experiential background of the participant in this theological liberative process.

The Blues, Jesus, the Cross, Resurrection, and Christ

Jesus was a man of color who loved men. The Jesus stories tell us that Jesus prayed, fasted, partied, and hung out with his friends, his men friends, and he loved them. This Asian-born, loving man, whose ancestors had a long, shared history with Africa, this loving man of color, loved men and showed it and talked about it and encouraged it. Jesus, like myself, and the community of my ministry, was a man of color, whose ministry, we are told by the stories, healed them. Jesus died on a cross.

The Blues are part of a continuum of African traditional religion. The story of Jesus and his Cross is a Blues story as well, a Legba story: Legba, Ellegua, the Orisha is the Spirit of the Crossroads. Legba, a God of the African Diaspora, is the Spirit behind the Blues. The Cross/Blues is told as a time of struggle, crises, and opportunity for transformation, for liberation; Blues Time, Cross Time, time for hope born of struggle; getting through the yesterday today time of Here, through the birth channel of hope into tomorrow, into the spirit of resurrection. Resurrection is the time of emergence from yesterday's struggle with renewed strength, vision, and hope for today's and tomorrow's. Gay/Queer affirmative ministry is a midwife to the birthing.

Christ, the early church's attempt to universalize the Jesus story, became the means by which Jesus' spiritual-political message for the poor and oppressed was co-opted by privileged classes and transformed into a spiritual system that excluded the egalitarian message taught by Jesus. To reclaim Christ we must see the Christ as the creative energy available to us through our passion for justice and mutual relation, another name for Immanuel.

Liberation, Salvation, and Grace

My neighborhood childhood peers, in the process of raping me, called me into awareness of my sexual difference, called me into the beginnings of my awareness and questionings of my sexual identity. It was because I was other that I was raped. I did not know what that otherness meant. The fact of the rapings called me to question the why of this childhood exile.

It was my working at jobs from the age of five that gave me the awareness of my working-class status and its connection with my color and cultural background. I was not the boss. The boss paid for my time, and everything I created in the time I worked for him belonged to him. I was never to rest in the time I worked for him.

I have resisted external authority from early childhood. This resistance is a product of my early rebellion against the racism in public schools and at work. I was positively reinforced by my foster families in my efforts toward independence. From childhood, then, spiritual struggles reflected the material struggles for liberation. They were from the same piece of cloth. The most vital and important parts of me were to be suppressed in the name of some outside authority. These are the doors I have had to walk through first to understand "God," sin, salvation, Jesus, Christ, the Resurrection.

No!

I was not here when the mountains crested out of the oceans, nor when the sun sent the planets spinning in their orbits, nor when the first critters emerged from the muck. I was not present when the first horrors of creation occurred. I did not create this pattern of coming into being. However, my "being-ness" brings the consciousness of the feeling of pain and horror into the world. I am not able to withstand the "awe-some awe-full-ness" of the creation's face without struggling to change it. My innocence is shattered in the comprehension of the full face of reality.

How can I stand in acknowledgment of my birthright of freedom? First I must find my will to freedom, my volitional acknowledgment and learning of Here and how Here came to be. I must first accept the gift of courage born of the struggle to be Here in Freedom. In this acceptance, I must submit to the reality of my frailty/my incompleteness in my aloneness and admit to the need of community.

"Freedom's just another word for nothing left to lose." It is only when nothing works to keep the wolf from devouring your soul and you've tried everything else that you reach for the hem of the garment/that you climb the tree/that you pay for the pearl of great price. That payment/that climb/that reach is the Confession of the recognized fragility, the realized limitation of our individuality, the recognition of the need for community in conscious critical struggle for transformation and liberation. The activity that comes out of this witness/testimony/confession, this recognized need for community relationship is concrete living prayer, informed struggle for liberated space, time to hope, envision, to imagine the possibility of freedom, a time of meditation. This meditation is an invitation for Grace, the gift of the experience of resurrection.

The process of liberation is an historical one. It is inexorable. It is not an event of a few months, a few years. Oppression is a result of long-term historical forces, human responses to natural and social environmental conditions. Africans became slaves not out of some divine plan, but rather as a result of geographical location, planetary resource distribution, different technologies, and social organization. The African American liberation from slavery was a 240-year process, a process of learning, critical awareness, and seizing historic opportunities. African American womanists speak of the "everyday-ness" of the liberation struggle, the weaving of small gains into major actions. Rosa Parks's bus ride was such an event, made of centuries of learnings, decades of labor and church organizing, all coming together at an historic opportunity. The community was prepared for the opportunity.

Maintaining the spirit of the struggle over the time necessary to learn the skills and tools necessary for liberation is a theological task. The gospel story of Jesus suggests to me that he had an image of the historical process of liberation. He came from a culture that had a millennium of resistance practice.

The purpose of a Queer/Gay affirmative theology of healing is to participate fully and mutually in the process of struggle for liberation through the sharing of creation's gifts. But liberation itself is no tea party, not the end of struggle. For the oppressed, it is only through struggle for justice and liberation, through the development of ever-increasing critical awareness, that the gift of Grace and Hope occurs. It is this process of intentional critical action that reveals the permanent necessity for the liberative struggle against any organization, system, action, and behavior that might evolve into oppressive social and personal structures.

Jesus reminded us of the difficulty of the rich, the privileged, the self-righteous in finding Grace. His reminder was not a moralism but the accurate critical analysis of a Mediterranean peasant who knew the reality of struggle and created a liberative praxis. In doing so, he rigorously employed an awareness of the power of creative energy, the power of the Transcendence, on behalf of liberation and thereby demonstrated the truth of his observations. A theology that serves Queers/Gaymen of color, and especially those who live with AIDS/HIV, can benefit from the Blues Story of the Judean peasant on the Cross. Jesus did not do it once and for all or else the material conditions for oppression would no longer exist. Jesus did it for then. We have to do it now.

Notes

1. See Beverly Wildung Harrison, *Making the Connections: Essays in Feminist Social Ethics,* ed. Carol S. Robb (Boston: Beacon Press, 1985).
2. See Carter Heyward, *The Redemption of God: A Theology of Mutual Relation* (Washington, D.C.: University Press of America, 1982).

CONTEMPORARY PROPOSALS

[33]

New Testament Sexual Ethics and Today's World

L. William Countryman

A CLOSE READING of the New Testament, as we have discovered, shows how alien its sexual ethics are to the world of today. They are framed in terms of purity and property systems that no longer prevail among us. Although we have grown accustomed to reading the Bible as if it pertained directly to our own experience, such a reading ignores much that is important in the texts themselves and is, for the most part, incapable of dealing with them literally—that is, in terms of their simplest, least adapted sense. The reader may therefore be tempted to conclude that the sexual ethics of the New Testament are now irrelevant, even for Christians, and that we must begin from the beginning to construct some kind of sexual ethic suitable to our own era. I believe this conclusion would be mistaken.

As I have argued elsewhere, one of the primary contributions which Scripture makes to the work of the Spirit in the life of the Christian community is that it stands outside our present and therefore prevents us from treating our contemporary world as an inevitability. The antiquity of the biblical writings means that they give Christians other models of social life to stand alongside

SOURCE: From L. William Countryman, *Dirt, Greed, and Sex* (Philadelphia: Fortress Press, 1988).

those we know directly. These models come from the past and are therefore in some sense irretrievable. Every culture, including that of the first-century Mediterranean world, is a whole and not recoverable in isolated pieces; even when isolated pieces survive or are consciously revived, they will no longer mean the same thing in their new contexts. The first-century Mediterranean world—or its sexual ethics or any other single aspect of its culture—is not, then, of the substance of the gospel. To suggest that it is would be to place the gospel forever beyond our reach. The spiritual function of the Bible's antiquity is rather to relativize the present, to rule out in advance the notion that things can be only as they are. We cannot return to the past, and we do not know what shape the future will take. What we can do is seek, with the help of the past, to understand the present in its own terms and proclaim the gospel in ways pertinent to it.[1]

In sexual matters, as elsewhere, this is the goal of Christian theology. The dominance of dogmatic or systematic theology in Western Christianity since the Scholastic period has created the unfortunate illusion that the gospel is a system of ideas which can be fully comprehended by any person of adequate intelligence quite apart from any necessity of personal transformation. Nothing could be further from the teaching of Jesus, as presented in the New Testament Gospels. This teaching is unsystematic in form; but, what is more important, it is devoted to the transformation *(metanoia,* conversion) of the hearer rather than to the creation of a theological system. In the earlier eras of Christianity, the "theologian" was preeminently one whose encounter with God shaped the person with such power that he or she could speak of God with the authority of grace.

Such speech was more often "occasional" than systematic; that is to say, it responded to occasions of immediate concern, seeking to explicate them in terms of grace and making no pretense to a complete or exhaustive knowledge of God. Thus, Paul wrote to the Corinthians in order to speak to conflicts and problems raised in the life of their congregation, not to explicate the whole of his gospel. Dogmatic theology has sometimes pretended to a complete and perfect knowledge of things sacred, and it has suggested such pretensions to the unreflective even when it has known better than to take them seriously itself. The idea that an ordinary human being could, through a form of intellectual endeavor, be fully in command of the mysteries of the gospel or that anyone could progress toward knowledge of God faster than one was in fact being transformed by that knowledge is fundamentally alien to early Christianity.

Theology in the older, presystematic sense assumes that we live in our own moment, our own historical and cultural context. We meet, in that context, God's grace as definitively made known through the ministry, death, and resurrection of Jesus. We experience grace as transforming our life; and we proclaim the power of grace as we have known it. This is not to say that all theology must always take the form of personal testimony. In most cases, this would prove boring—for the very good reason that one person's experience becomes relevant to another only insofar as the one can show the other how they belong to the same world and share the reality or possibility of intimately comparable experience. What this means, rather, is that all theology must be true to the speaker's living, not spun out as the logical consequence of an objectivized intellectual system, but cohering with an experience of grace in the world we actively share. If this theology is to be, moreover, Christian theology, then it must meet the further criterion of continuity with the experience of grace expressed in the New Testament.

This brings us to the other side of the New Testament's relevance today. If Scripture is important partly because it is alien to and therefore relativizes our own historical-cultural situation, it is even more important in that it can show, by reference to the way the grace of God broke into the self-sufficiency of another culture, how it breaks into our own as well. The New Testament writers did not try to construct a new sexual ethic from the ground up. They took over the existing cultural patterns and refocused them, pushing some elements from the center to the periphery, altering the balance of powers allotted to various members of society, and, most important, relativizing the familiar life of this world by subordinating it to the reign of God. The result was that Christians could, in many ways, continue to conform to familiar cultural mores while, at the same time, understanding these familiar institutions in ways which undermined their absolute claims.

This suggests a pattern worth applying to the present situation. Ideally, it would invite us to comprehend the nature of sexual institutions in our own time and culture, and then to subject them to the same kind of critique on behalf of the gospel of God's grace. This will prove difficult. The difficulties arise both from the side of the modern world and from that of the gospel. Our world has been (and perhaps still is) passing through an era of great changes, making it difficult for us to know what in fact our social structure provides in the way of sexual institutions. The world of the first century was probably more fixed and settled in this regard. At the same time, the demands of the gospel of grace are being constantly renewed and fitted to new situations by the Spirit who animates the church. There is no simple list of them that can be lifted out of Scripture or the church's past experience and reflection and applied without further ado to the present.

This is not a task for one theologian, but for the church. It will require insights from many perspectives, both on the modern world and on the Bible, brought together in what I suspect will be a long conversation. I am not so foolish as to propose, in one essay, to resolve all the relevant questions or even to raise them. I hope rather to show that the major emphases of the New Testament, if applied with appropriate sensitivity to our cultural and historical distance from the first-century Mediterranean world, will yield the outlines of a sexual ethic that is both intelligible and practicable in our world and also coherent with the gospel of grace. . . .

In the following pages, I shall first put forward a series of principles. . . . I call these principles "generative" because I believe that, when applied, they will give rise to explicit ethical guidelines, such as I have sketched in the latter part of this essay. These, in turn, I present not as invariable rules, but as a kind of alarm system whose violation signals a very high probability (amounting in some cases to a practical certainty) that the principles behind them are being violated. Throughout the present chapter, I am writing as a Christian for Christians. In the present confused state of our culture, I presume that any coherent statement of a sexual ethic will hold some interest for a larger public, but I do not propose what follows as a universally applicable ethic, for it is directly dependent on the message of the gospel.

Generative Principles

. . . Six principles . . . must enter into the formation of any Christian sexual ethic today. Most of them are drawn directly from the New Testament; one of them (the third) speaks rather of the distance of the first-century world from our own time. These are not "first principles," for they are themselves dependent on more fundamental assertions about God, God's grace, and humanity under God's grace. The oneness of God, which implies a oneness of this created world and of humanity in it; the absolute priority of God's action over our own, both in creation and in subsequent acts of grace; the sinfulness of humanity which becomes most destructive in the form of claims to righteousness; God's presence in flesh through the incarnation; the call to *metanoia* (repentance, conversion, transformation) and the demands made on us in this world by our citizenship in the age to come; the equality of all human beings under grace and the priority of love over all other virtues—all these are prior to the principles enunciated here. The links which lead from the ones to the others can, in fact, be made explicit, but this is not the place to do so. At present, it is enough to have shown that these generative principles are those which the New Testament itself lays down for dealing with the questions of sexual ethics or which the change of cultures compels us to take into account.

1. *Membership in the Christian community is in no way limited by purity codes.* Individual Christians may continue to observe the purity code of their culture, but they may not demand that other Christians do so. If one wishes to assert that any given proscription is a part of Christian sexual ethics, one must justify that claim by showing that the act in question infringes some principle other than purity. Any claim that a given sexual act is wrong in and of itself will be found ultimately to represent either a lack of ethical analysis or a hidden purity claim.

2. *Christians must respect the sexual property of others and practice detachment from their own.* There are two points to be made here. The first is that the New Testament interests itself in property not so much in order to defend me against my neighbor as to defend my neighbor against me. Paul, for example, wrote to the Corinthians that it would be preferable for them to suffer injustice and deprivation at one another's hands rather than take their cases to the public courts where they would themselves probably be seeking to commit injustice (1 Cor. 6:7–8). The second is that property also had value, for the New Testament writers, as an extension of the self; in this respect, the essential question was not "How shall I maintain what is mine?" but "How shall I dispose it in obedience to the reign of God?" The self is not something to be preserved and enhanced at all costs, but rather a means by which we become compatible with and enter the world to come.

3. *Where, in late antiquity, sexual property belonged to the family through the agency of the male householder, in our own era it belongs to the individual.* The difference between the ancient and modern worlds in this respect is one of focus. The ancient householder could say "mine": the modern individual is usually still implicated, to some degree, in the restrictions and pressures of a family. "Family" and "individuality" are the poles of a continuum, with life taking place in the area of tension between. Nonetheless, the brief treatment of family-oriented society provided in the preceding chapters should be enough to show the distance between a world in which the individual is the primary arbiter of his or her sexual acts and one in which these were functions of the life of a family. If the New Testament's critique of sexual property is to be illuminative in our present world, we must take into account that the type of "owner" has changed; and such a change in ownership will always imply a change in the character and understanding of what is owned.

4. *The gospel can discern no inequality between men and women as they stand before God's grace.* The New Testament writers came to accept a good deal of inequality between the sexes in day-to-day life; but this represented an accommodation to existing patterns, not the working out of the gospel principle. Perhaps this principle could never have been worked out very effectively in a

family-oriented society, since it implied the destruction of the existing family order. The early Christians, in general, found it achievable only in the context of celibacy. It remained, however, a principle of basic importance.

5. *Marriage creates a union of flesh, normally indissoluble except by death.* This principle brought sexual union into the family in a new way which rivaled the existing family structure; indeed, had not Paul and some later New Testament writers reaffirmed the subordination of women, it would have dissolved the ancient family. In a society which defines the individual as the basic social unit rather than the family, the meaning of "one flesh" must necessarily go through some redefinition if this principle is still to be challenging, intelligible, and useful.

6. *The Christian's sexual life and property are always subordinate to the reign of God.* This is not a rejection of the values of sexual life, but rather a focus on God's calling of each person under particular circumstances, which may demand sacrifice of lesser to greater good. Since Christ "owns" all believers, their lives must cohere with this reality—not by some show of pietism, transforming each aspect of life into a kind of religious show, but by the clear linking of what is more peripheral to what is more central.

To say how these principles give rise to a sexual morality in our own time calls for an exercise of judgment in relating them to the facts of our sexual life. Grace calls us not to leave this world, but to live in it, wherever God calls us to be, as citizens of God's reign. This calls for ethical discernment of the problems and possibilities implicit in our milieu in order to see what God asks us to do in this context.

Derived Guidelines

Rejection of the Requirements of Physical Purity

When the New Testament rejected the imposition of the purity codes of the Torah on Gentile Christians, it was not in order that a new, distinctively Christian purity code might take their place. Except for hints of such developments in Jude and Revelation, the New Testament did not justify any sexual rule by appeal to physical purity. Indeed, it exhibited a strong concern that purity, as a distinction dividing human societies from one another, should give way before a massive awareness of the grace of God, extended impartially to all human beings. The creation of its own purity code has been one of several ways in which the church has at times allowed itself to become a barrier to the gospel of God's grace. A Christian sexual ethic that remains true to its New Testament roots will have to discard its insistence on physical purity.

The great difficulty of this demand is that it excises what has become, at least for many Americans, the very heart of Christian sexual morality. It therefore places the churches under a great test—essentially the same test as that which confronted the pious among the Jewish people during Jesus' own ministry and the circumcision party within the earliest Christian church at the time of Paul's Gentile mission. Will the churches hang onto their own self-defined purity and so hold themselves aloof from those excluded by it, or will they proclaim the grace of God which plays no favorites? Will they make their existing purity codes conditions of salvation, or will they acknowledge that they have no right to limit what God gives?

To be specific, the gospel allows no rule against the following, in and of themselves: masturbation, nonvaginal heterosexual intercourse, bestiality,[2] polygamy, homosexual acts, or erotic art and literature. The Christian is free to be repelled by any or all of these and may continue to practice her or his own purity code in relation to them. What we are not free to do is impose our codes on others. Like all sexual acts, these may be genuinely wrong where they also involve an offense against the property of another, denial of the equality of women and men, or an idolatrous substitution of sex for the reign of God as the goal of human existence.

Christians have increasingly accepted that masturbation or even nonvaginal heterosexual intercourse, in and of themselves, are not wrong. Bestiality, where it is the casual recourse of the young or of people isolated over long periods of time from other humans, should occasion little concern. It is probably too isolated a phenomenon to justify strong feelings. More difficulty may attach to the other issues in the list. They therefore call for a somewhat more detailed discussion.

Polygamy is more likely to be a serious issue in the Third World than in the modern West. Nowhere, however, does the Bible make monogamy a clear and explicit standard for all Christian marriage. Our usage in this matter must derive from the Greco-Roman milieu in which the church spent its formative early centuries. This does not mean that the modern church should seek to reinstitute polygamy where there is no cultural demand for it; but it does mean that, in cultures which have hitherto been polygamous, monogamy as such should not be made a condition of grace. The church, however, should concern itself with the question of the equality of women and men, particularly with regard to the way marital patterns affect the status of women. Monogamy offers no guarantee of equality; but the relative benefits of monogamy and polygamy in this respect should be the principal point at issue wherever the church must make such decisions.

Homosexual orientation has been increasingly recognized in our time as a given of human sexuality. While most people feel some sexual attraction to members of both the same and the opposite sex and, in the majority of these, attraction to the opposite sex dominates, there is a sizeable minority for whom sexual attraction to persons of the same sex is a decisive shaping factor of their sexual lives. It appears that this orientation is normally inalterable and that there is no strong internal reason for the homosexual person to wish to alter it. To deny an entire class of human beings the right peaceably and without harming others to pursue the kind of sexuality that corresponds to their nature is a perversion of the gospel. Like the insistence of some on the circumcising of Gentile converts, it makes the keeping of purity rules a condition of grace. It is sometimes suggested that homosexual persons be told to become celibate. While celibacy is a venerable Christian tradition and may even, as Paul suggested, be called for under certain circumstances, it is also a *charisma* (gift) and can never be demanded of those to whom such a gift has not been given. Paul indicated that the presence of this gift is known by the ability of the celibate person to deal with ungratified sexual desires without being dominated by them. For those without this gift, Paul considered the satisfaction of their desires, so long as it was within the boundaries of the property ethic, entirely appropriate. Any insistence on celibacy for homosexuals as such is, accordingly, contrary to the New Testament witness.

Erotic literature and art (commonly called "pornography")[3] form a widespread and diverse phenomenon which may at times be contrary to Christian ethics, particularly when they set up idolatrous ethical standards which treat the self and its sexual gratification as the final goal of all existence or when they present as acceptable the degradation of adults (usually women, in our society) or abuse of children. Explicit verbal and pictorial representations of sexual acts are not forbidden by the gospel—apart from such considerations which may render one or another particular item ethically obnoxious. By the traditional standards of Western Christianity, however, whatever is sexually explicit is impure. Although we tend to think of the issue of pornography as limited to newsstands, so-called "adult" bookstores, and theaters, actually it permeates our whole society, as attested, for example, by our lack of an ordinary vocabulary in English (as distinct from a medical or an obscene one) for the discussion of sexuality. Anxiety about the erotic is, most importantly, the thing which prevents the clear and open sexual education of our young. We are currently reaping the consequences of this purity rule in the form of widespread pregnancies among teenagers who are neither capable of nor very interested in the rearing of children. And we shall be very lucky indeed if we do not promote the rapid spread of AIDS by our unwillingness to speak explicitly to children in the educational process. The pleasure attached to explicit sexual portrayals, in words or pictures, should be accepted as the powerful ally of any effort to teach the responsible use of so beautiful a thing. We cannot, however, expect to forbid sexually explicit representations in most respects and still make good use of them in one narrowly permitted area, namely, education.

The New Testament, of course, does not demand that those Christians whose consciences are committed to some purity law give up the practice of it. No one should be required to take an interest in erotica or to indulge in sexual practices which, however permissible, seem to that person a violation of conscience. For that person, they would indeed be wrong actions. Conscience, of course, is not fixed in its final form, and one must expect that it will mature along with our comprehension of other aspects of God, the world, and the gospel. It remains true, however, that every Christian is responsible to his or her own present understanding. Those whose confidence in grace is great enough to free them from purity codes (the "strong," as Paul called them) may not force their position on others; but neither may those who observe such codes (the "weak") refuse the strong the right to follow their consciences. Since neither group has any right to deprive others of what properly belongs to them, it follows that the weak should not attempt to prevent open sexual education, outlaw erotic art and literature, or keep homosexual persons out of the church and ministry. The strong, on the other hand, must not make their standard of conduct a prerequisite of grace any more than the purity rules are. Paul urged the strong to avoid occasions of public offense to the weak. This is good, so long as the weak also commit themselves to a clear recognition that the strong have a part in the church; it would be a betrayal of the gospel, however, if the needs of the weak were made an excuse for the reinstitution of purity law as a condition of grace.

There has been a tendency, over the past century or so, to reinstitute purity law under the guise of mental health, by claiming that deviations from it are a kind of sickness. Our society, having made a religion of medicine and a priesthood of physicians, is tempted to invoke the word "sickness" as a mere synonym of "impurity" without imparting any definite meaning to it. This sham was long used to threaten children who masturbated with such dire consequences as insanity; but the most obvious and shameful use of it has been against homosexuals, who have been labeled as sick merely because they differed from the majority. Even though intelligent and truly comparable studies have now shown that there was never any foundation for such claims, there are those who, on dogmatic grounds (nothing else being available), still make them.

The identification of sickness and impurity has become even more apparent in the irrational anxieties focused recently on people with AIDS. These anxieties have induced many to seek a radical separation from carriers and potential carriers of the virus, even though competent authorities have repeatedly assured the public that the virus is communicated only in quite specific ways. The irrationality and intensity of such responses testify to the enormous power that the purity ethic can still have for us. It is not death which is the primary source of these fears, for the advocate of quarantines may well be willing to take much greater risks, day by day, in driving metropolitan freeways. The great fear is of contracting a disease as "dirty" to many in the modern world as leprosy was in antiquity.

Those who wish to rescue our society's purity rules by designating everyone who deviates from them as "sick" are merely renaming purity; they are not telling us anything new or illuminating. In many cases, they have even been uttering falsehoods; and, in the process, they have harmed many generations of the young who were forced to fear that masturbation or homosexual attractions were signs of insanity.

Respect for the Property of Others

Where statutory law concerns itself with property mainly in order to conserve what already belongs to me from seizure by another, the great Jewish religious teachers of antiquity were concerned primarily to protect my neighbor from me. This was not unique to the Christian tradition, but is found also in the Mishnah's well-known definition of the four types of human beings: the "type of Sodom," who says, "What is mine is mine and what is yours is yours"; the evil person, who says, "What is yours is mine, and what is mine is mine"; the ignorant person, who says, "What is mine is yours, and what is yours is mine"; and the saintly person, who says, "What is mine is yours and what is yours is yours."[4] We have already examined the way adultery or incest infringed on the property of others in the ancient family system. These were so intimately involved, however, in that family system that we shall have to reevaluate their meaning, below, in the context of the shift to the individual as the basic social unit.

Under the present heading, I should like to do something simpler, but equally important—suggest what property meant, in a positive vein, for the New Testament writers and relate this to what I believe to be its most significant violation in our era. For the New Testament, property represents a certain personal realm in which one can act in obedience to the reign of God; it is, as in the etymology of our English term, all that pertains or "is proper to" each person. As such, it is something which may be trusted in and hoarded to the soul's detriment, or something to be given in alms or even surrendered entirely if the claims of discipleship require it. It generates claims and counterclaims; but it is better to suffer loss than to take one's brother or sister to court. In every case, including sexual property, one must administer and care for one's property with a view to sanctification, that is, one's transformation into a citizen of the reign of God. Property, in other words, is the wherewithal of being human in this age—which can also become, by grace, the wherewithal of becoming a fit citizen of the age to come.

The wherewithal of being human must include, at the very minimum, sustenance, space, the means to grow, the community of other humans, and some freedom of choice. Theft of sustenance or space is the most obvious kind of violation of property; yet, violations of that trust which is the foundation of human community or of the freedom of choice are at least as grave. If in antiquity, given the existing concept of family, adultery was the characteristic violation of sexual property; in our own age, it has become rape.[5] When committed by a stranger, it violates the victim's freedom of choice; when committed by a family member or presumed friend, it violates the bonds of human community as well. The metaphorical space which surrounds each of us and which we characterize as "mine" is of the essence of our being human. It offers some protection for the freedom to develop and become what God is calling us to be, which is the principal goal of being human. When it is opened voluntarily to another, it is also a means of community. But when it is broken into by violence, the very possibility of being human is at least momentarily being denied to us. As there is nothing more precious to us than our humanness, there is no sexual sin more serious than rape.

Rape, as property violation, includes not only the use of physical violence to gain sexual access to another, but also the use of social, emotional, and psychological violence. This takes the form of sexual harassment in workplaces, of sexual impositions by trusted authorities upon their clients, and of manipulative pressures in intimate relationships. Our contemporary culture, with its constant glorification of sex, largely for commercial ends, creates a climate in which this sort of violence flourishes. It offers leverage for the unscrupulous to press inexperienced or unwilling persons into acts which they have not freely chosen. Even within marriage or other established sexual relationships, both physical violence and these other forms of rape are by no means unknown.

An ethic consistent with the gospel will condemn not only individual acts of rape, but also those in which whole groups attack other groups to deny them the property necessary to their humanness. Assaults on women or homosexual people, whether as individual attacks or as political and legal campaigns to deny them equality as citizens and human beings, are the most obvious cases in point. This kind of communal violence may also be based on differences other than sexual, especially on racial, ethnic, and economic ones. Even here, however, sexual elements are often entangled in the violence. For example, in the United States, white men have often justified their violence against black men by accusing them of having sexual designs on white women, while reserving to themselves the right to make sometimes violent use of black women. What is more, violence may be done to others' freedom not only through direct assault, but also through patronizing the less powerful, making them dependencies and therefore properties of the more powerful. Both kinds of violence have been characteristic of the relations of men with women and of rich with poor in our culture.

All these kinds of violence have sunk their roots deep in our culture, and it is difficult to imagine their complete eradication. The Christian, however, has an obligation to name them and struggle against them inwardly, in personal relationships, and in the larger society. In this respect, it is disturbing that some Christian denominations seem to have taken the side of violence themselves. Their condemnations of homosexual people, for example, are accompanied, at the very best, by only the mildest of rebukes to those who persecute them; some denominations, such as the Roman Catholic and Southern Baptist, even encourage denial of their legal rights. Some who call themselves "Evangelical," "Charismatic," or "Pentecostal" also oppose equal freedom for women and call for complete subservience even on the part of battered wives. Until this changes, it is unlikely that our society will begin to treat rape of all kinds with the revulsion that it deserves, for to some extent such violence will always appear to be at least a quasi-legitimate reaffirmation of the dominance of men over women, of heterosexuals over homosexuals, and, indeed, of the powerful generally over the weak.

Sexual Property as Individual Property

When the owner of property changes, the nature of the property changes also. To take a nonsexual example, a piece of farmland that is underlain by coal deposits suitable for surface mining will appear to be various things to various possible owners. If the owner of the coal is a mining company which may not own the surface of the land but has the right to remove it in order to gain access to the coal, the farmland itself will appear to be incidental to the property that matters. In many cases, such a company is not part of the local community and has no bond to either the human or the natural ecosystem in which the farmland participates, but exists only to make a certain profit through the mining of coal. The coal is therefore purely a capital investment, and the company will make decisions about it in the extremely narrow context of profit and loss—unless, of course, the larger community of state or nation forces a greater measure of social responsibility on the company. At the other extreme, if a resident farmer owns both the farmland and the coal under it, the coal is only one aspect of the larger whole to which she relates. It has an economic value, but the owner will balance that value against her self-understanding as farmer rather than miner, against her identity as part of the local community where she lives and farms, against any sense of spiritual connection she may have to the land, and so forth. These do not predetermine her choice whether to mine the coal or not; but they do create a certain distinctive context for the making of that choice. If, to create a third case, the owner is an absentee landlord with at most a remote family connection to the land, both the arable surface and the underlying coal may still be of interest. Yet, with the withdrawal of the landlord from the local human and natural community, the property comes to be identified mainly with its economic value. Such an owner is likely to make decisions based primarily on economic considerations but is not likely to be quite so narrowly focused as a coal company.

Many readers will recognize the above as a sketch of varieties of ownership in parts of the Appalachian region in the United States. The point is that, even if the property remains, physically, the same object, its relationship to various owners can constitute it as, in effect, several different objects. The same is true of sexual property. In the ancient world, where it pertained primarily to the family and secondarily to the male householder as representative of the family, it meant one thing; in the modern world, where it can pertain only to the individual, it means another. It will be useful to say here a few words about the nature of this transition. The individualization of modern American society is a social fact, an aspect of the environment in which we make ethical decisions, not an ethical principle itself. As such, it is neither good nor bad. It represents some losses as against earlier, family-structured eras and also some gains. If the human being now lacks the kind of inevitable links with a social continuum that the earlier society afforded, that loss must be balanced against the fact that individualization has gone hand in hand with—and is probably the condition for—what progress this century has made toward genuine equality of races, nationalities, and the sexes. The ability of modern people to choose for themselves with regard to education, work, living place, life partner, religion, or politics became conceivable only as the family ceased to be the basic unit of society and was replaced by the individual.

Individuality can become an ethical principle in two ways. Philosophically speaking, it may become so by a recognition that my individuality is intelligible only as an expression of the principle which renders every other human being an individual, too. This principle was already being expressed in late antiquity in the Golden Rule; respect for my individuality implies respect for that of others. As such, it enters into Christian ethics, but it is by no means the crowning element in them. It could not, for example, have generated the sacrifice of Jesus on the cross or the witness of the martyrs, which require the further principles of love, faith, and hope for their understanding. On the other hand, individuality can also become an ethical principle in the form of individualism—an idolatry of the self, which treats the self as its own source and end. Such individualism has been a pervasive ethical influence in the modern West, enshrined in certain forms of capitalist ideology as the image of the "self-made" person—that is, the person who has chosen to forget the role others played in his fashioning and rise and who regards with interest only those people and things that contribute to his own aggrandizement. This individualism, like any other idolatry, is utterly inconsistent with the gospel.

The gospel does, to be sure, call for serious attention to be given to the self. Jesus held up the unjust steward, who threw caution, morality, and household loyalty to the winds in order to ensure his own future, as a model for the Christian (Luke 16:1–13). From the preaching of John the Baptist onward, belonging to the family of Abraham by physical descent no longer counts for anything in the economy of salvation (Matt. 3:9). Yet, the gospel's rejection of the idolatry of family, the social unit of the first century, implies an equally stern rejection of the idolatry of the individual in our own time. The connection between the two was clearly visible at the time of transition between them, the Industrial Revolution, when William Blake declared that the family was simply a grand excuse for selfishness.[6] This was so in several ways. Insofar as the individual is, in a family-structured society, simply an expression of the family, any claim one makes on behalf of one's family is a claim on behalf of one's self. At the same time, the diffusion of the self in the family that is thus achieved will seem to relieve one of the burden of selfishness. As society became more individualized, however, Blake's insight became more literally true; the lesser members of the family (wife, children, slaves, servants) came to be no longer expressions of the family to which they belonged, but extensions of the male individual who owned them. This modern kind of "family" has little to do with the family of late antiquity, is even more repugnant to the gospel than the ancient family, and is probably inherently unstable in its own right.

In the ancient world, the man, on behalf of his natal family, owned one or more women, either as spouses or as concubines or as slaves. The man received sexual satisfaction; the family received as goods the labor of the women involved and, in the case of the spouse, the promise of legitimate heirs. (In very rich households, of course, the number of subordinate women indicated the prominence of the family as well.) The Greco-Roman world limited a man to one wife at a time, and Western Christianity restricted this still further by rejecting the right of divorce. Even then, however, what the man still chiefly sought in marriage was a combination of sexual satisfaction, household labor, and legitimate heirs. Only the first of these was specific to him; the rest benefited the family.

What goods, by contrast, does the modern individual seek in entering upon a sexual relationship? The goods the ancients sought have not, of course, ceased to be of importance. Apart from the most individual of them (sexual satisfaction), however, they will seldom appear as the primary reasons for marriage or other sexual relationships in the mainstream of modern American society. Why do most of us marry and how do we choose our partners? We seek things that can benefit an individual. The thrill of romantic love is, of course, enormously important; and we typically hope that this will form the basis for a lasting intimacy, in which our spouse will provide friendship, encouragement, counsel, solace, and a new sense of family to supplement and eventually replace the natal family. These are, of course, interior goods—goods which cannot be given without a genuine delight in and commitment to the other; and in this respect they stand in sharp contrast to the primary goods sought in antiquity. To be sure, there are external goods involved in modern marriage as well: the expectation of security, financial support, and perhaps the desire for children. Yet, we are inclined to look askance at those who marry for money, and childbearing and rearing have become a vast and still largely unacknowledged problem for our society. For us, the heart of sexual property in marriage and in other lasting sexual liaisons lies in the interior goods.

When the nature of what is owned changes, the nature of theft necessarily changes as well. From the perspective of the Appalachian farmer, the destruction of the farm in order to mine the coal underneath it is a kind of theft; from the perspective of the mining company, refusal to allow the removal of this "overburden" would be a kind of theft. In antiquity, theft, as applied to sexual property, was easily defined, since sexual goods themselves were external and therefore easily defined. Adultery meant a man's taking the womb and family resources which belonged to another man and using them for the nourishment of his own seed. We continue, for the most part, in our society to regard adultery as wrong, but we are forced to find a quite different reason for so regarding it. We usually say that it is wrong because it is a betrayal of trust—that is, theft of an interior good. Insofar as this is in fact the case in a given situation, it gives a good account of adultery in our modern context; but it does not go far enough.

Trust is not the only interior good essential to marriage or to its equivalents, and the outsider is not the only possible thief. Since, in ancient marriage, the man owned the woman, it was not possible for the man to steal from his wife. If he committed adultery he was stealing from another man. Jesus, however, by redefining adultery, altered this internal balance and made both spouses capable of taking from one another. That is still more true under present circumstances, for partners can easily withhold from each other those interior goods which they have contracted, explicitly or implicitly, to provide; and there is in fact no way to gain them from an unwilling partner. An ancient wife need have no deep affection for her husband in order to bear his children and do her part in the running of the household. Neither partner, in the modern world, can fulfill his or her obligations in such an external, "objective" manner.

The form of adultery most characteristic, then, of our own society is not adultery with another person, but the purely self-regarding adultery which demands of the partner the full range of goods associated with sexual property but gives few or none of them in return. This is not to discard the older understanding of adultery, in which one person takes from another what belongs to a third party; this is certainly not dead. It is rather to stress the prevalence of adultery in the form of profiteering, the use of a sexual relationship for one's own physical, economic, emotional, or psychological satisfaction with minimal regard for that of the partner. In comparison, the technical act of adultery by sexual intercourse with a third person is a relatively trivial matter.

Our transition from a familial to an individual society has been particularly difficult in the matter of children and lies at the root of many modern troubles, ranging from abortion to unwanted infants to child abuse to educational uncertainties and beyond. Not that these are of a single or simple origin! The increase of child abuse, for example, is probably partly a matter of fact and partly a matter of changed perceptions, for kinds of corporal punishment which were normal parental prerogatives a few generations ago now appear to be abusive. In the familial society, after all, children were the property of the family, part of its assets, and the family's self-interest would dictate that it discipline them without harming them in a way that would damage its own investment. In the individual society, however, children have become an obligation rather than an investment.

This has brought with it the permission for—and even the necessity of—conscious decision making about the conception of children. Agricultural societies, before the advent of modern medicine, might afford the luxury of producing as many children as they could; now, more urbanized societies with lowered birthrates and greater longevity must make deliberate decisions, with the cooperation of those of childbearing age. Since both Jesus and Paul seem to have encouraged celibacy, one cannot imagine that the conceiving of children is any sort of intrinsic Christian virtue. Since it is now also the incurring of a substantial burden which can be borne successfully only out of love, no one should undertake it without due consideration. In most areas of the modern world, the use of birth control should be the norm and the conception of children should represent a deliberate and considered departure from it. (A significant exception must certainly be made for those human groups that are threatened with disappearance or with diminution to numbers too small to maintain their cultural traditions.) No existing method of birth control is inherently unacceptable, though certain ways of imposing them may certainly be.

Some particular discussion of abortion is called for. The Bible contains nothing helpful on the subject. Other early Christian literature, too, has surprisingly little, given that abortion was not uncommon in the Greco-Roman world. One must distinguish two separate issues: abortion as therapeutic for the physical, mental, or emotional health of the pregnant woman; and abortion as a means of birth control. While the ancient family ethic may have regarded the legitimate offspring as of greater importance than the mother in some cases, there can be no basis in the New Testament itself for such a judgment. To the contrary, in making the wife equal to her husband, Jesus implied that she was no longer merely an instrument of his natal family in their quest for heirs. This implies that her health is at least as important as that of an uncertain offspring.

The question of abortion as a method of birth control is more difficult. Human societies—and different voices within our own society—disagree about when the fetus should be considered a separate human being. The Greeks and Romans, who allowed exposure of the newborn if unwanted by its family, recognized this as occurring some time after birth; others have placed it at conception (a process little understood at the time of the New Testament writers), at quickening, or at the earliest moment when a premature infant might survive outside the womb. The child who has actually passed through the birth channel seems qualitatively different from one still in the womb; even the Greeks and Romans tended to expose unwanted newborns to be collected by anyone who might want them rather than killing them outright. Still, there is no compelling logic to tell us how to choose among the other three options. The principal consideration must be that the choice in relation to childbearing should always be, if at all possible, a choice *for,* not a choice *against.* No one should be obligated to bear children and, given the present threat to the world from its human population, no one should do so unless moved thereto as a specific calling and gift. Christians should not, then, place themselves in the position of having to decide repeatedly not to bear this particular fetus, but rather in the position of deciding when they are called to conceive a child.

Now as in other eras, parents conceive children for a variety of reasons, perhaps including innate biological urges as well as social pressures, sentiment, the desire for some kind of genetic immortality, a sense of social responsibility, pure carelessness, and the rest—perhaps a longer list than any one person can imagine. Yet, once born, the child is, in our age, a quite different matter from what he or she was in the first century. The ancient family had to have legitimate heirs in order to maintain its own existence. But what is the child to a society of individuals? If they are individualists, in the idolatrous sense, the child is, of course, nothing at all except an extension of the parents and insurance against their being left unattended in senility. The individual society however, is not necessarily committed to individualism of this kind, any more than a familial society is doomed to be torn apart by the grander selfishness of its families. In each, the worst case is a possibility, but not the only possibility. Ultimately, the individual society militates against individualistic megalomania on the part of parents, for the children will learn from the society itself that they, too, are expected to become individuals and will refuse to cooperate with parents who sought to use them purely for their own ends. They may, in turn, adopt the same self-defeating individualism, of course, unless something more rational and loving is offered in its place.

What sort of rational and loving alternative can one suggest? That children should be understood as individuals in preparation. They are, in other words, ultimately their own property, not that of their parents; while the parents have the role not of owners but of educators, those who prepare the child to become the best of herself or himself. The model parent will be one who seeks to discern the child's unique qualities, both good and bad, and help the child form the self-discipline to make the best of his or her resources. This is not a kind of "permissive" project, for the child is not yet a realized individual ready to be in full command; it is, rather, a loving and persistent demand that children become responsible for themselves, their choices, their relationships and community, their work, their world. Parents who understand that the child is not obligated to them to be exactly what they want will be better parents. Children who understand that they cannot evade their responsibilities either by habitually obeying or by habitually reacting against their parents are more likely to become stable, creative, and faithful adults.

Parenting is thus a gift to the child of the child's self; it is the passing on of gifts which the parents received from their own parents and from all the others who contributed to their being who they are. It is more like the work of the educator than any other model—not the educator as a communicator of a single specialized kind of information, but the educator as one who cooperates with the pupil as a kind of critic and guide in the shaping of the educated person. This must of necessity be a somewhat disinterested task. The parent who wants only an athlete for a child will be an incompetent parent to a painter. The parent who wants a substitute for adult companionship from the child, making the child a quasi spouse, will confuse the child into thinking that adulthood is a kind of mannerism and so make true adulthood, which is an inner certainty, the more difficult to identify or to achieve. Above all, the parent or other senior family member who uses the trust which that position bestows in order to make the child his or her lover thereby makes demands on the child totally inconsistent with the disinterested love of one who seeks only the other's good.

While in the familial society of antiquity it was the violation of the patriarch's status which characterized incest, in our own, individual society it is the violation of the child's individuality. The inequality between adult and child (and, to a lesser degree, between older and younger child) means that, in a sexual relationship, the needs of the child will be subordinated to the needs of the adult. What the child loses in the process is, above all, the preparatory space and time when responsible adults encourage and assist children to know themselves before assuming full adult obligations. This, in turn, renders the child's growth into real adulthood extremely difficult, creating an alienation not only from the available adult models, but from the child's very self. Adulthood comes to seem a rejection of the past instead of something that grows out of the experience of childhood.

In addition, incest also carries with it, in our culture, a strong purity taboo, often used by the perpetrator of incest to frighten the child into silence. While Christians do not make this the basis for their own objection to incest, we must recognize that some part of the harm done to the child in such cases arises not from the sexual act itself, but from the revulsion with which the society at large greets it—a revulsion which almost inevitably spills over onto the child and encourages the child in self-loathing. Christians have a responsibility to reduce their own inner involvement in this kind of purity response, so that they can deal more constructively with individuals who have experienced incest and also can, one hopes, better instruct society at large. The hiding away of this topic or its discussion only in hushed tones and ambiguous language can only work harm, not good.

Sexual abuse of children, in the context of modern society, is a kind of generalized incest. For the child, every older person is to some extent a parent. The child's growth into individual adulthood is promoted if the child has a variety of adult models and so does not identify adulthood with the characteristics of a single person. If, on the other hand, the child encounters adults as people whose only interest is to take advantage of the child for their own satisfaction, the model of adulthood that emerges is disastrous. Most abusers of children, it is said, are adult heterosexual males, frequently friends or relatives of the child's family. In their case, the disadvantage the young girl experiences may be compounded by an unexpressed wish on the man's part that all women would remain children. In any case, all such abuse contains in it the implied desire that the sexual object not grow up. Thus, it is akin to incest in the harm it does to children.

Sexually, the child must be considered his or her own property. As the child grows old enough to begin wanting to make active exploration of sexuality, the parent or other adult guide will contribute most effectively by teaching the child frankly about the realities of sex, including its dangers, and by holding the child to the necessity of making clear and responsible decisions. A stonewalling technique of refusing to discuss the issue or of presenting all discussion in the form of prohibitions denies the child's developing responsibility and status as an adult-in-becoming. As a result, it encourages either repression and much future sexual misery on the part of the quieter, more obedient child or rebellious irresponsibility on the part of the more energetic and active one. Most children will probably do well to pass through a period of experimentation, though they should not be pushed into it against their wills. They should be shown how to do this as safely as possible. Certainly no child—and probably few teenagers—is prepared to enter upon a true marriage of equal adults such as the gospel calls for.

Even among young adults, the first choice of a sexual partner is not likely to be the best, and their initial picture of themselves in a serious sexual relationship is not likely to be fully formed. If marriage is treated in the individual society simply as license to have sex, we can be quite sure that many will choose marriage partners for the most inadequate of reasons and with poor judgment. If the decision is not merely one about first sexual experience but about life partners, it will be easier for people to make it in a realistic way. Christian thinkers as diverse as Margaret Mead and Archbishop Fisher suggested some decades ago that the church should not rush to make the unions of the young permanent; but we have yet to honor the importance of their suggestions by giving them due discussion.

Finally, with regard to sexual property it is necessary to speak in our era about the value of physical health as the property of each individual and about one's obligation not to deprive another of it. Although Leviticus probably refers to gonorrhea, the author seems not to have understood that it was a communicable disease. In our own century, we have passed from a time when sexually transmitted diseases were a major threat to life and health to a time when antibiotics could combat most of them and back to a time when, first with herpes and then with AIDS, they have once again moved beyond our ability to cure. Knowingly to endanger another person with such a disease is clearly a transgression of that person's property in the sense in which I am here using the term, and is prohibited by the New Testament's sexual ethic.

Equality of Women and Men

Both Jesus and Paul laid it down as a principle that women and men are basically equal in marriage. Although Paul, in the circumstances of his own times, did not find it necessary or appropriate to carry that principle into practice in all areas of married life, the church today, with the shift from familial to individual society, no longer has any reason to delay in this process. Indeed, society has led the way in this matter, and it is entirely consistent with New Testament practice for the church to accept the emerging marital customs of the modern West as the basis for its own usage. This is not to suggest that the situation has stabilized, however, or that the acceptance of equality will be easy either for men or for women.

What is called for is something more than the revision of household rules and the alternation of household roles. It involves new understandings of manliness and womanliness that can come about only with some pain and anxiety as well as some sense of liberation and joy. If the husband gives up the image of himself as sole ruler of the household, waited on by wife and children, his whim the family's law, he must also give up its spiritual equivalent—the image of himself as the family's unique sacrificial sustainer, isolated in his moral strength and grandeur. If the wife gives up being the servant of all, with no life of her own except in responding to the needs of others, she must also give up the spiritual vision of herself as the one who gives all for others' good. Men cannot give up their responsibilities as sole wage earner and still claim the benefits of that position by demanding an uneven distribution of labor and services; women cannot claim equality and still reserve the right to be dependent if equality does not yield what they want. None of this will be easy but the survival of marriage in our society surely depends on it.

Spouses in heterosexual marriages will have much to learn in this process from partners in stable, long-term homosexual relationships. They have long experienced the difficulties of maintaining enduring relationships in a society which is even less supportive of them than of heterosexual couples; and they have had to do it without socially prescribed divisions of roles and labor. If there are useful models to be had, they will probably be found among them.

On a deeper level, the re-understanding of womanliness and manliness in our changed circumstances will make headway only if the conversation leading toward it includes both heterosexuals and homosexuals. One interesting feature of recent times is the importance of serious, nonsexual friendships between men and women where the man involved is homosexual; perhaps the absence of a sexual factor facilitates this. If heterosexual men were more open to friendships with women, they might find, for the same reason, that they formed them most readily and deeply with lesbian women. While heterosexual men and women begin with the greater attraction toward each other, it does not always lead to real personal knowledge or respect. In a time when the old definitions are no longer serviceable, we shall need the variety of perspective that male and female, homosexual and heterosexual, can offer on one another in order to reach new models of the properties of either sex.

Marriage as Union of Flesh

When the author of Genesis 2 described marriage as making man and woman "one flesh," he was describing their bond as equivalent in power and importance to that of the natal family. Jesus used the phrase as the foundation of his prohibition of divorce. Paul, however, applied it to every act of sexual intercourse, without thereby suggesting that every such act formed an indissoluble union. The image thus raises a number of questions for us to deal with: When is a marriage a marriage? What can the phrase "one flesh" mean in a nonfamilial society? To what extent is the institution of marriage, as transformed by our very different context, still to be understood as indissoluble? What is the role of the church in relation to marriages? To what degree is nonmarital or casual sex permitted or forbidden?

These are difficult questions, but reference to the property aspects of marriage as discussed above may help illuminate them. To begin with, the nature of the property desired in modern marriage, being largely interior and therefore more complex and more difficult to convey successfully, implies that marriage is in itself more difficult to consummate. In the familial world, the first act of sexual intercourse, with its accompanying proof of the bride's virginity, was sufficient, since it showed that the new wife was indeed the property which the husband's family had intended to acquire. Jesus, at least according to Matthew, acknowledged that some marriages were not real marriages, and I have suggested above that he was probably referring to those where the bride was found not to be a virgin.

Is there any sensible way to apply a measure of this kind to contemporary marriages, where the purity of the family line is no longer the primary desideratum? The virginity of either spouse is no longer a primary issue, for the goods sought in connection with marriage in an individual society are goods which can best be offered only by a mature person, and such a person will more often than not have acquired some sexual experience. What is still more difficult, the goods are not simply brought to the marriage, but must be developed within it in the form of the relationship between the spouses. Thus, it is very difficult to specify a date, even in the most successful of marriages, when it became clear that the property transactions involved were indeed in good order. Certainly it could not be known at once. Once the initial romantic enthusiasm wears thin, it may become apparent that one or both spouses is unable or unwilling to give anything of importance to the other. Clearly, one should not and seldom would enter upon marriage knowing that to be the case; but the transition from romance to the business of marital living will always be a somewhat risky undertaking, if only because the romantic face is but one aspect of the other person and sometimes a misleading one at that.

Paul did not count every act of sexual intercourse as constituting an indissoluble bond of marriage. We should not do so, either. This means that not every external marriage in our own experience constitutes a real marriage in the more interior sense demanded in our society. We must therefore be prepared to consider the possibility that what some divorces—perhaps a large percentage of them—do is not to end an existing marriage but to announce that, despite whatever efforts were made and ceremonies performed, no marriage has in fact taken place. This insistence on the property involved in constituting a marriage may appear crass to some readers. Yet it is precisely analogous to what was assumed by the biblical writers, and I venture to argue that it is a far more realistic approach to the ethical issues. To characterize Christian marriage, as some would do, as an idealistic commitment to eternal loyalty without any regard for what one receives in return is ultimately destructive of the whole institution. It encourages abused spouses, female and male alike, to remain with those who profit from them in various ways and give nothing in return. In the process, not only does the abused person suffer to no end, but the abusive spouse is seldom effectively confronted with any realization of what he or she is doing. A sound marriage is not, of course, a dispassionate business arrangement, but it ought to be based on perception of mutual benefit arising from mutual devotion and affection.

One part of our present difficulty arises from the church's custom of blessing marriages. Marriage, in the milieu of the New Testament, was typically the celebration of a secular contract. Since, under the ancient circumstances, the property aspects of the marriage were readily and efficiently verifiable, there was no appreciable delay in ascertaining that the contract had been fulfilled. Only in the Middle Ages, it seems, did the church begin to take a part in solemnizing the occasion; but it was an intelligible step, since all the necessities of the case could be verified. At present, however, when the great majority of church people are married with church ceremonies, the rites give an impression of definiteness to the marriage which cannot in fact be verified at once and perhaps not for many years to come.

At the present time, the church would perhaps be better advised not to solemnize marriages at the inception of the relationship itself, but to wait a period of some years before adding its blessing. When it does so, it may as easily bless homosexual as heterosexual unions, for the new definition of the goods making up sexual property, which has already come informally to prevail in our society, makes no distinction between the two. Two persons of the same sex cannot engender children and could not therefore have contracted a full-fledged marriage in the familial milieu of the New Testament itself; they are, however, fully capable of giving one another the interior goods demanded by marriage in our time. Even after the blessing of a union, the failure of a marriage and consequent divorce probably cannot be ruled out altogether. The church should, however, discourage it. It can rightly ask its members not to proceed to divorce without having done all that they could do to compromise their differences, and it can also insist on the exercise of a high degree of responsibility in the contracting of a further marriage. For an unblessed union, that is, one that has not progressed to the point of mutual stability that would justify the church's blessing it, the church might reserve judgment.

Since the solution I have suggested blurs the distinction between marriage and nonmarital sexual liaisons—a blurring demanded by the actual nature of marriage in our times—we must also ask whether all sexual activities of however casual a nature and however little personal involvement are to be permitted. Jesus did not speak to the matter, but Paul clearly would have said no. Sexuality, as an essential aspect of the self, cannot be treated as if it were either trivial or peripheral. Every sexual act does constitute some kind of bond with the partner, and that bond must, at the very least, be free of falsehood and violence toward the partner and in some way be compatible with the Christian person's relationship with Christ. Paul reproved men in Corinth who visited prostitutes though they had open to them the options of either celibacy or marriage. He did not, however, have occasion to address the situation of the person for whom neither option existed—the sailor, to create an example, who did not have the gift of celibacy but whose exceedingly mobile occupation also did not permit permanent cohabitation with a wife.

We might also add, in our own age, the examples of the homosexual person, for whom no marital forms are provided in our society, the young person of either sexual orientation for whom marriage would be premature but who does not have the gift of celibacy, the single person of whatever age who has not met the appropriate person to contract marriage with, or the widowed person for whom a new legal marriage would create financial stringency or unnecessary confusions about inheritance. At one extreme, one cannot defend the promiscuous person who desires only personal gratification at whatever expense to others. At the other, two widowed persons who wish to contract a faithful and giving relationship without benefit of legal marriage seem to create a problem of words more than of things. Between these extremes, there lies a large area of difficult individual decisions. People will have to wend their way through such decisions, however, for the gift of celibacy is not given to all and the property demands of modern marriage are such that one cannot, even if one wishes, enter upon it lightly.

Some nonmarital liaisons may in fact prove to be preparatory to marriage in the stricter sense. Others may serve to meet legitimate needs in the absence of genuine alternatives. Still others may be abusive and exploitative. Only the last are to be condemned. Prostitution appears to belong most often in the last of these three categories, though perhaps at times it may belong in the second. I think, for example, of abnormal conditions where there is a vast disproportion of the members of one sex; in such cases, those who have no other access to sexual gratification are not to be condemned for resorting to prostitutes, though I am not willing to encourage them in it. The person who prefers prostitutes, however, to a sexual relationship which would make greater demands on him or her must be asked whether this is not an avoidance of deeper relationships in general and therefore also an effort to treat one's sexuality as peripheral or irrelevant to one's humanity.

The same question must be put to the prostitute, provided that one is such of one's own will. In antiquity many prostitutes were slaves and had no freedom of choice as to the use to which they would be put. Jesus' abolition of purity requirements gave these people renewed access to God, which must not be taken away from any legitimate successors they may have. In our own day, this would include at least those street children whose only alternatives are return to an intolerable home situation or starvation. If those prostitutes, however, who are such by choice—whether because they make a good living or because of attachment to another person who is abusing them—should wish to be fully active participants in the church, the church would legitimately urge them to accept some other occupation and, if need be, assist them to do so, so that they may honor themselves as sexual beings under the reign of God.

Sex and the Reign of God

Although we have said a great deal thus far about what the New Testament sexual ethic forbids and not much about what it advocates, that is largely a function of the style in which the Bible speaks about sexual matters. This study has worked throughout with specifically moral texts—that is, texts which define acceptable and, more often, unacceptable behavior. Some might feel it preferable to begin with texts speaking to the nature of sexuality rather than defining its limits. There are several difficulties with that approach, however. One is that such texts are few and far between in Scripture. The Bible takes sex more or less for granted and does not explicitly lay out a theological or philosophical understanding of it. The few pertinent verses in Genesis 1 and 2, for example, are brief and allusive in their language, which leaves them open to a variety of speculative interpretations. In order to form a well-founded understanding of a viewpoint alien to our own, we have had to find and study a corpus of materials sufficiently rich that we can test our speculations and see where they do or do not account for all the details. This quality, which is lacking in the theological materials on sex, is abundantly present in the moral ones.

The resulting negative bias, however, is misleading insofar as it suggests that the New Testament writers were negative toward sexuality as such. The results of the present study confirm that that was by no means the case. We have seen that Jesus, for example, attacked the institutions of the family rather than sexuality itself and that Paul specifically acknowledged the satisfaction of sexual desire as a valid reason for marriage. In order to locate the New Testament's positive ethic of sexuality, however, one must refocus from the boundary lines marked out by negative pronouncements to the area that they enclose and give shape to. The New Testament's positive account of sex is that it is an integral part of the human person, particularly as joining us to one another, and therefore has a right to be included in the spiritual transformation which follows upon our hearing of the gospel.

The gospel, as it permeates every aspect of life, will and must permeate sexuality as well. If Christian teaching appears to flinch from sex as something dirty or suspect, it is falsely Christian. This does not mean that sexuality, for the Christian, is to be saturated in a kind of pietism, that the bedroom should become a chapel, or that sex should be submerged in prayer. It means rather that sexuality, like every other important aspect of human life, should be clearly related to the center and goal of that life, the reign of God. The life of the world to come, characterized by a joyful reverence and love, is already the standard by which our growth in faith and hope is measured in this life. Sex, therefore, is to be received with delight and thankfulness. It is a gift of God in creation which also reflects for us the joy of God's self-giving in grace and the perfect openness of true human life in the age to come.

If the reign of God is central, to be sure, other things can no longer make that claim. Sex, in other words, is *not* central—nor is knowledge, wisdom, money, power, success, security, one's job or family or marriage, even oneself. None of these things is wrong, in and of itself. They become wrong only at the moment when they become ultimate goals for us. As long as we can name something which is, for us, a condition of God's reign—as long as we find that we must say, "I am ready for God's reign only if it includes this or excludes that"—then we are still placing idols at the center and goal of life alongside God. Yet, insofar as we are ready to hand back whatever God asks of us, then it becomes, to that degree, innocent for us.

Sex is one of the rich blessings of creation, to be received with delight and thanksgiving. At the point when one's actions no longer express that truth, they become wrong. If I grab something for myself that belongs rightfully to another, whether through direct violence or through manipulation or any other means, I acknowledge what I have grabbed as a good, but I no longer confess it as a part of the whole richness of creation—a richness which includes all goods, including myself and the neighbor whom I have robbed as well. If I make satisfaction of sexual desire the overarching goal of my life, I have put the part in place of the whole and thereby lost perspective on its real value. These considerations are what make libertinism wrong, for they condemn any pursuit of sexual pleasure which is based on megalomania and idolatry. What is less commonly observed is that they also make prudery, legalism, and addiction to respectability wrong. For just as sex is not the final goal of the creation, neither is works-righteousness, the fulfillment of the law, or the sense of comfort that comes from having fulfilled the expectations of my neighbors. The world begins in God's free act of creation and concludes in God's free act of grace—or rather in the rejoicing to which it gives rise. Prudery, narrowness, self-confident respectability will be no preparation for the life of the age of rejoicing. It is not surprising that Jesus alienated those who practiced such "virtues."

This is not to suggest that the path to the age to come is all one of ease and pleasure. Its difficulties, however, are not self-induced. We do not have to make the Christian life difficult with the constant recitation and amplification of rules, for there are real challenges, arising both from our own selfish idolatry and also from our times. As Paul stressed the need for a certain kind of preparedness in the face of what he believed would be an imminent eschaton, we, too, must undertake to be prepared in terms of the needs of our own time. As marriage and family could not be a final goal for the first-century Christian, sexuality and self cannot be today. The Christian will find it very difficult to live in an intimate relation with one who does not understand or accept the kind of demands which God's calling makes. While it is not impossible to live in such a relationship with a nonbeliever, the partner must at least be one who respects commitments that may seem unworldly and which do not place self or sexual partner first. The Christian must also retain a certain freedom to respond to God's call loyally in critical times. While we cannot make any confident predictions about the timing of the eschaton, we live in times when great demands are being made of us in relation to justice, peace, and the survival of the world. If relations of dependency prevent us from responding to those demands, we shall have something to answer for.

Finally, the gospel, the news of God's grace in Jesus and the inbreaking of God's reign, has not yet finished transforming us—and will not this side of the grave. If we look at the great exemplars of its work, in the New Testament and afterward, from Jesus to Martin Luther King, Jr., we shall find that it does not normally act to make us more respectable—to produce conventional, predictable husbands and wives, devoted to nothing more than one another's happiness. For that matter, Jesus himself excepted, the gospel does not even work to produce perfect people. The gospel works rather to express the power of God's love, which rejects our rejections and breaches our best defenses and draws us out of our fortifications toward a goal that we can as yet barely imagine. The measure of a sexuality that accords with the New Testament is simply this: the degree to which it rejoices in the whole creation, in what is given to others as well as to each of us, while enabling us always to leave the final word to God, who is the Beginning and End of all things.

Notes

1. Countryman, *Biblical Authority or Biblical Tyranny: Scripture and the Christian Pilgrimage* (Boston: Cowley, 1994), 77–93.
2. I use this term in its common sense of intercourse with an animal, not the technical psychological sense in which it designates a distinctive complex of attractions and behaviors.
3. Some reserve the term "pornography" specifically for those erotic materials involving degradation of women. These, I think, are contrary to Christian sexual ethics, but not because of their erotic element. Children will not usually trust claims on which they have no independent controls whatever.
4. *Aboth* 5.14. Need one observe that this is yet another piece of evidence to show

that the ancients did not typically identify the sin of Sodom as homosexual intercourse?

5. The difference between the cultures in this respect is vividly apparent in Philo, who argued that the law of Moses specified no punishment for the forcible violation of a widow or divorced woman because that was, in effect, only half the crime that adultery was (*Special Laws* 3.64). So, too, in ancient Athens, rape was considered a less grave offense than seduction (Pomeroy, *Goddesses,* 86–87).
6. At least, I believe it was Blake. The statement stuck in my mind more than twenty years ago, but I have not been able to locate it again.

[34]

Toward a Theology of Human Sexuality

Anthony Kosnik et al.

RECENT YEARS have made it increasingly evident . . . that there is a growing gap between what the Catholic Church officially teaches in matters sexual and what the faithful have come to believe and practice. One would be shortsighted to believe that the differences are restricted to the debate between the magisterium and theologians regarding the morality of contraception. Repeated surveys, statements, and writings clearly indicate that the differences are more fundamental and pervasive of almost every area of church teaching on sexuality.

One of the explanations offered for this diversity is the increased awareness of, and respect for, sociological and cultural factors, which always exert a subtle but powerful impact on the sexual mores of people. Another influence that Christians should never lose sight of is the reality of sin and the role it plays in keeping persons from both appreciating and realizing the ideal in their lives. A third factor contributing to this dilemma is an inadequate theology, one which fails to formulate the Christian ideal in a manner faithful to fundamental values yet also responsive to the changing historical, sociological, and cultural conditions in which this ideal must be realized.

Our aim at this point is to address this third factor. Our purpose is to pre-

---

SOURCE: From Anthony Kosnik, William Carroll, Agnes Cunningham, Ronald Modras, and James Schulte, *Human Sexuality: New Directions in Catholic Thought* (Louisville, Ky.: The Catholic Theological Society of America, 1977). Used by permission.

sent a theological approach that provides a more adequate orientation and general framework for dealing with particular questions that will follow in the area of human sexuality.

At the outset, three important considerations seem in order. The first concerns moral methodology today. Note should be made of the following admonition given by the Fathers of Vatican II in this regard:

> For recent studies and findings of science, history, and philosophy raise new questions which influence life and demand new theological investigations.
>
> Furthermore, while adhering to the methods and requirements proper to theology, theologians are invited to seek continually for more suitable ways of communicating doctrine to the men of their times.
>
> May the faithful, therefore, live in very close union with the men of their time. Let them strive to understand perfectly their way of thinking and feeling, as expressed in their culture. Let them blend modern science and its theories and the understanding of the most recent discoveries with Christian morality and doctrine. Thus their religious practice and morality can keep pace with their scientific knowledge and with an ever advancing technology. Thus too, they will be able to test and interpret all things in a truly Christian spirit.[1]

Moral theology today has the task, therefore, to collaborate with other sciences in the light of our times. Thus we have endeavored to place this study in touch with the empirical data concerning sexuality.

Second, we need to take note of the more dynamic view of human nature expressed at Vatican Council II,[2] for it departs so markedly from the earlier, more static view within our tradition. Concerning human dignity, and significant for our purpose, the same conciliar document states:

> God did not create man as a solitary. For from the beginning, "male and female he created them" (Gen 1:17). Their companionship produces the primary form of interpersonal communion. For by his innermost nature man is a social being, and unless he relates himself to others he can neither live nor develop his potential.[3]

The Council Fathers call attention to the idea of human nature as dynamic and relational, and this in accord with our modern self-understanding.

Third, moral theological speculation is necessarily and properly enculturated. . . . We see it reaffirmed in the reflections of Vatican II, when it acknowledges that the Church too is an "historical reality." As such, and "with the help of the Holy Spirit, it is the task of the entire people of God, especially pastors and theologians, to hear, distinguish and interpret the many voices of our era, and to judge them in the light of the Divine Word."[4]

Given these considerations, contemporary moral theology is challenged to attempt to articulate a theology of sexuality that is both consistent with Catholic tradition and yet sensitive to modern data.

Problem

The significant and critical questions raised by recent scientific and theological developments in sexual morality can be reduced to three general areas:

(1) the definition of sexuality,
(2) the principle of integration for the various purposes of sexuality,
(3) the moral evaluation of sexual conduct.

Definition of Sexuality

Moral textbooks and treatises of the past have generally regarded human sexuality as an experience proper only to married people. The following excerpt from a widely used moral textbook of the 1930s reflects an attitude and approach that has prevailed in moral writings for centuries:

> The rational motive of the virtue of chastity is the reasonableness of controlling sexual appetite in the married and of excluding it in the unmarried, as also of seeking and expressing it in marriage in a rational way, unless the exercise of some higher virtue or more pressing duty justify complete continence, temporary or perpetual, without prejudice to the rights of others. Chastity is a virtue for every state of life. There is a chastity of the married and of the unmarried. Perfect chastity is abstinence from all expressions of the sexual appetite, both in the external act and internal thought, desire and complacency. This virtue connotes a great victory over an imperious appetite. Few persons of adult age are immune from the incitement and allurement of this appetite. The practice of the virtue is usually arduous, is highly meritorious, gives man a great mastery over himself in this respect, and is pleasing to God. Divines have a good reason, therefore, for assigning a special aureola to virgins, as they do to martyrs and preachers.[5]

According to such a view, children, the severely handicapped, the unmarried, the celibate, the divorced and widowed are not to be sexual beings. The moral ideal for such persons consists in eradicating every sexual impulse and desire. Thus it is not surprising that the same author, together with most of his contemporaries, concludes that "it is grievously sinful in the unmarried deliberately to procure or accept even the smallest degree of true venereal pleasure; secondly, that it is equally sinful to think, say, or do anything with the intention of arousing even the smallest degree of this pleasure."[6]

The reason advanced for these conclusions is that venereal pleasure has no purpose other than to lead to legitimate sexual intercourse and the possibility of procreation. It was argued that to use what was designed for the good of the human race to serve the good of the individual constitutes a substantial inversion of an essential order or relation. Such an approach reflects an understanding of sexuality that is predominantly genital and generative even though it was acknowledged that in the context of married life sexuality could also bring about greater mutual fulfillment of the spouses.

The experience of people today supported by contemporary behavioral and theological sciences understands sexuality much more broadly. Sex is seen as a force that permeates, influences, and affects every act of a person's being at every moment of existence. It is not operative in one restricted area of life but is rather at the core and center of our total life response. As the recent Vatican *Declaration on Certain Questions Concerning Sexual Ethics* maintains: "It is from sex that the human person receives the characteristics which, on the biological, psychological and spiritual levels, make that person a man or a woman, and thereby largely condition his or her progress towards maturity and insertion into society."[7]

Given the wholistic view of person expressed in the documents of Vatican II, . . . we suggest that human sexuality must be more broadly understood than it was in much of our earlier tradition. We would, therefore, define human sexuality simply as the way of being in, and relating to, the world as a *male* or *female* person. Men and women, at every moment of life and in every aspect of living, experience themselves, others, and indeed the entire world in a distinctly male or female way. Sexuality then is the mode or manner by which humans experience and express both the incompleteness of their individualities as well as their relatedness to each other as male and female. The book of Genesis reminds us that male and female together reflect the image and likeness of God.[8] To complete this mission, to which every human being is called by the very invitation to life, man must strive to be fully man, a woman to be fully woman, and each must relate to the other. This definition broadens the meaning of sexuality beyond the merely genital and generative and is so to be understood in all that follows.

Human sexuality is the concrete manifestation of the divine call to completion, a call extended to every person in the very act of creation and rooted in the very core of his or her being. From the first moment of existence it summons us incessantly to both intrapersonal and interpersonal growth. Intrapersonally, it propels each person toward the task of creating the male or female each was destined to be. Interpersonally, it calls each to reach out to the other without whom full integration can never be achieved. Thus sexuality like every other aspect of humanness is destined to serve human relationships, not subjugate them. Sexuality is not just an isolated biological or physical phenomenon accidental to human beings but an integral part of their personal self-expression and of their mission of self-communication to others.

From this point of view, sexuality is not elevated into a good in itself nor repressed as somehow tainted with guilt. Sex is rather to be accepted as all other characteristics of humanness and used to facilitate human growth to full maturity. For Christian men and women, this call to full maturity takes on an added dimension inasmuch as we see ourselves as called to growth in Christ, our model. Jesus realized himself fully as a human person and spent his life reaching out to others. His disciples then model their lives after him, "building up the body of Christ, until we all attain to the unity of the faith and of the knowledge of the Son of God, to mature manhood, to the measure of the stature of the fullness of Christ" (Eph 4:12–13). This growth, both intrapersonal and interpersonal, takes place in a sexual person, incomplete in self but reaching toward "fullness" in Christ. It is from this distinctly Christian anthropological perspective that we define and approach the entire question of human sexuality.

Personhood—The Principle of Integration for the Various Purposes of Sexuality

Sexuality is a pervasive and constitutive factor in the structure of human existence. . . . Implicit in this view is the realization that we *are* our bodies. Our fleshly reality fashions our perception of everything. All levels of consciousness are touched by our embodied presence in the world. The body's way of knowing and tending is there before we reflect upon it. The body asserts its wisdom whether or not we choose to advert to it or even whether we desire to turn from it and deny it.

Within this embodied view of human existence, sexuality is seen as that aspect of our fleshly being-in-the-world whereby we are present and open to that which is not ourselves, to that which is "other." The "other" may be objects or other subjects, persons. Preeminently, it is the mode whereby an isolated subjectivity reaches out to communion with another subject. Embodied subjectivity reaches out to another body-subject in order to banish loneliness and to experience the fullness of being-with-another in the human project. The human being needs another to realize the potential for sharing subjectivity.

Copulation and orgasm are obviously satisfying tension reducing experiences on all levels of animality. At the level of human existence, an other-directed orientation pervades what otherwise might be considered a blind drive toward biochemical equilibrium. For us humans, the teleology of the pleasure bond is an intercoursing of subjectivities.

Subjectivity is embodied in either a male or a female body. Does this make a difference? The view of human sexuality thus far elucidated gives no reason not to anticipate that intersubjective encounter could be realized as much in the homosexual mode as the heterosexual. The kiss and embrace between close friends of the same biological gender are common enough, at least in some cultures. Moreover, in the view here presented these are indeed sexual expressions. The genital union and that which prepares for it, however, is a different phenomenon—a phenomenon in which the biological difference in gender is significant.

Our understanding of bodily existence requires that the specific structure of one's body colors the manner in which oneself and the world are experienced. A person born with unusually acute hearing or an unusually acute sense of smell perceives the world and himself differently than one differently endowed. A person born with a broad, stubby hand experiences the outside world differently than another born with a small, delicate hand. Anatomy and physiognomy modify the manner in which the world is perceived and form a basis for relationships with that world.

It follows that one who experiences existence in a female body structure perceives reality differently than one born in a male body structure. To what extent anatomical, physiological, and biochemical differences between body structures affect the way in which the genders perceive themselves and the world, independently of cultural manipulation, is currently a much discussed and debated issue. Research thus far reported on the subject is inconclusive for the most part. . . . We are of the opinion that the two sexes experience existence in subtly different ways by reason of their differences in bodily structure.

However that may be, it is apparent that the genital impulse is predisposed in favor of heterosexual union. The incidence of homosexuality remains small. While human sexuality is much more than the impulse to genital union, it hardly excludes this impulse and its urgency. The impulse, biologically tied to procreation and a "given" in each one's existence, assures that the reaching out to a genital encounter will be biased in the direction of heterosexuality. It is in the genital union that the intertwining of subjectivities, of human existences, has the potential for fullest realization.

There exists, then, a sexual atmosphere whenever two human beings meet. This is especially true when the relationship is male-female. The possibility of shared existence, indeed of intimacy and union, emerges on the horizon of movement toward the other. There is a call, an invitation that goes forth from bodily existence to bodily existence. It colors every transaction between the sexes, adding interest and delight, promising mystery and disclosure and delivery from loneliness. At one and the same time it realizes the self and enriches the other.

In view of this understanding of sexuality,[9] it can be said that sexuality serves the development of human persons by calling them to constant creativity, that is, to full openness to being, to the realization of every potential within the personality, to a continued discovery and expression of authentic selfhood. Procreation is one form of this call to creativity but by no means is it the only reason for sexual expression. Sexuality further serves the development of genuine personhood by calling people to a clearer recognition of their relational nature, of their absolute need to reach out and embrace others to achieve personal fulfillment. Sexuality is the Creator's ingenious way of calling people constantly out of themselves into relationship with others.

Throughout much of Catholic history, at least from the patristic period onward, the general thrust of the Church's teaching on sexual morality is fairly accurately summarized in the formulation of canon law: "the primary purpose of marriage is the procreation and education of children. The secondary purpose is mutual support and a remedy for concupiscence."[10] Vatican II took a major step forward when it deliberately rejected this priority of the procreative over the unitive end of marriage.[11] It insisted on the inseparable connection between these two purposes of sexuality and suggested the consideration of the human person as the integrating principle that could harmonize them.[12] It also recognized the tremendous role conjugal love plays in calling marriage partners to continuing personal and mutual growth. The 1975 Vatican declaration on sexual ethics further extended this development by identifying human sexuality even in the unmarried as the source of a person's most fundamental characteristics and as a crucial element leading to personal maturity and integration into society.[13] We think it appropriate, therefore, to broaden the traditional formulation of the purpose of sexuality from *procreative and unitive* to *creative and integrative.*

Wholesome human sexuality is that which fosters a *creative growth toward integration.* Destructive sexuality results in personal frustration and interpersonal alienation. In the light of this deeper insight into the meaning of human sexuality, it is our conviction that creativity and integration or, more precisely, "creative growth toward integration" better expresses the basic finality of sexuality. We further believe that this formulation while being essentially rooted in the traditional expression of the procreative and unitive purposes of sexuality moves beyond the limitations inherent in this formula. Without excluding the former purposes, creative growth toward integration helps to unfold the fuller dimensions implied in asserting that "the nature of the human person and his acts" constitutes the harmonizing principle of human sexuality. As such, it represents a development of, rather than a departure from, the traditional formulation. We maintain that this newer terminology better expresses the purpose of sexuality for the following reasons:

(1) It is faithful to the essential insights of the biblical understanding of human nature . . . ; consistent with the fundamental values upheld throughout the Christian tradition . . . ; and more compatible with the data provided by the empirical sciences. . . .

(2) It better articulates the modern insight into what makes life truly human, enhances human dignity, and thereby constitutes our moral task. This view of the purpose of sexuality is consistent with the proposition that whatever humanizes people is commensurate with their vocation to be and become the image of God. We maintain that creative growth toward integration—intrapersonally and interpersonally—is the essence of the human and Christian vocation.[14]

(3) Given today's insight into the fact that sexuality is at the core of each person's being, we further suggest that this view of the purpose of sexuality is more properly addressed to modern men and women in terms of "their way of thinking and feeling as expressed in their culture." It blends "modern science and its theories and the understanding of most recent discoveries with Christian morality and doctrine," as called for by Vatican II.[15]

(4) Finally, this terminology seems to reflect more accurately the profound and radical understanding of human sexuality expressed in the church's more recent documents. Vatican II's dynamic concept of personhood, springing as it does from a renewed and de-stoicized Christian anthropology, provides the basis for this new approach further extended in the 1975 *Declaration on Certain Questions Concerning Sexual Ethics.* Creative growth and integration, grounded in this more dynamic vision of human nature, provide a more total and inclusive way of expressing the whole finality of human sexuality. Given this new concept of Christian personhood and proclaiming "the nature of the human person and his acts" as the harmonizing principle, it is our contention that the older expression of procreative and unitive is too static and limiting to be of value in guiding the development of a theology of human sexuality. Such a formulation too narrowly restricts the meaning of sexuality to the context of marriage as has been the case throughout much of our tradition.

In appreciating human sexuality as a call to creative and integrative growth, Christians will be further helped in their understanding by keeping in mind the example and command of Jesus: "Love one another as I have loved you" (Jn 15:12). Jesus' demand, illustrated by his selfless life and death, calls for a level of concern for others ("unto death on the cross") that has perhaps been realized only seldom in Christian history, although it remains an ideal for all.

The extent of concern for the other, demanded and exemplified by this fundamental Christian law, provides a basis for human living that is at the core of the gospel message and at the same time at the apex of the Christian ideal for the fullness of growth and integration "in Christ." True, sexuality is temporal and passing. But when caught up in this Christian motivation, it transcends the temporal and becomes sacramental. The Gospel invitation to celibacy "for the sake of the Kingdom" and to fidelity in a tragic marital situation "for the sake of the Kingdom" are important reminders that transcendent values must influence a Christian evaluation of the meaning of human sexuality.

The Moral Evaluation of Sexual Conduct

Catholic tradition, in evaluating moral behavior, has placed a heavy emphasis in recent centuries on the objective moral nature of the given act itself. Particularly with regard to sexuality, it was believed that there is a meaning intrinsic to the very nature of the act itself—a meaning that is absolutely unchangeable and in no way modifiable by extenuating circumstances or special context. Thus, masturbation, any premarital sexual pleasure, adultery, fornication, homosexuality, sodomy, and bestiality were considered intrinsically evil acts, seriously immoral, and under no circumstances justifiable. This approach was influenced to a great extent by an oversimplification of the natural law theory of St. Thomas, the negative sin-oriented approach of the moral manuals, and a strong desire for clear, precise, absolute norms to govern moral conduct.

Biblical, historical, and empirical evidence raises serious questions regarding such an approach. Both the Old and New Testament are far more person-oriented than act-oriented in their evaluation of human sexuality. The multiple moral distinctions with regard to the same physical expression of sexuality found in the medieval penitentials indicate a similar appreciation that there is more to the evaluation of human sexual behavior than the act itself. In the empirical data, acts of masturbation are found to be helpful, indifferent, or harmful to the growth and development of the person as a result of circumstances apart from the act itself. Current studies have likewise revealed a significant difference in the human value of sexual activity occurring in a context of caring commitment and that same activity occurring in a casual or loveless context.

It is not surprising then that recent developments in moral theology have called into serious doubt the impersonalism, legalism, and minimalism that often result from such an act-oriented approach. Focusing on the isolated act and assigning it an inviolable moral value in the abstract left little room for consideration of the personal and interpersonal values that are central to genuine morality. Modern trends, returning to some of the emphases observed in

Sacred Scripture, in the Middle Ages, and in the theology of St. Thomas, prefer to give greater importance to attitude over act, to pattern or habit over the isolated instance, and to the intersubjective and social over the abstract and individual.[16]

The process of moral evaluation becomes especially difficult in actions that involve both good and evil effects. In the past these decisions were usually made on the principle of double effect interpreted with a "narrowly behavioral or physical understanding of human activity."[17] Contemporary theologians are once again insisting that any attempt to evaluate the moral object of an action apart from motive and circumstances is necessarily incomplete and inadequate. It is the whole action including circumstances and intention that constitutes the basis for ethical judgment. This is not to say that the concrete act is not an important consideration. It is simply to insist that the genuine moral meaning of particular individual acts is most accurately discerned not solely from an abstract analysis of the biology of the act but necessarily including the circumstances as well as intention that surround the action.[18]

Vatican II called for a renewal of moral theology in which morality is seen as a vocation, a way of life, a total response to God's invitation lived out from the depths of a person's being. Morality must never allow itself to be reduced to a simple external conformity to prejudged and prespecified patterns of behavior. For this reason, we find it woefully inadequate to return to a method of evaluating human sexual behavior based on an abstract absolute predetermination of any sexual expressions as intrinsically evil and always immoral.

One alternative to this exaggerated objective approach to moral evaluation is the position that there is no intrinsic objective significance at all to sexual behavior. All sexual behavior draws its meaning and significance from the intention or motive of the person or persons involved. To be sure, the motive must be directed by Christ's command of love, which is regarded as the one and only ultimate norm of morality, but there are no prescriptive rules or norms that necessarily must guide such a response.[19]

To our mind, such a view of sexual morality falls into the danger of being completely subjective, totally relative, and easily mutable according to individual tastes, preferences, and dispositions. Moral rules in such an approach reflect nothing more than the collective choices of different human individuals and societies.

Although we recognize the personal element as indispensable to any moral evaluation, we regard this latter position as too narrow in its restriction of morality to love-motivation, particularly for its neglect of the social and communal implications of sexual behavior. Therefore, we view approaches along these lines to the moral evaluation of sexual behavior as inadequate.

A sound approach to the moral evaluation of sexual behavior must do justice to several extremely complex factors:

(1) It must recognize both the objective and the subjective aspects of human behavior as indispensable to any genuine moral judgment. To ignore either aspect results either in a rigid moral externalism or self-serving moral subjectivism.
(2) It must acknowledge the radical complexity and unity of the human person's sexual nature and avoid any attempt to establish a hierarchy of creativity over integration or vice versa.
(3) It must demand a constant awareness of the delicate, interpersonal dimension of this experience which constitutes an integral part of any moral standard or judgment.

In view of these considerations we heartily endorse the recommendation of Vatican II that "the nature of the human person and his acts" provides a basic principle from which to evaluate the morality of sexual behavior. A broader definition of human sexuality has led us to suggest that the traditional "procreative and unitive" purposes of sexuality may be more aptly and accurately described as "creative and integrative." It is in the very nature of the human person that these quite distinct dimensions (intrapersonal and interpersonal) are harmonized and integrated.

Traditionally the question of evaluating the morality of sexual behavior has been approached by asking the simple, direct question: "Is this act moral or immoral?" Such an approach is flawed in two highly significant ways.

First, it does a disservice to the complexity of the human moral enterprise. It implies that morality can occur apart from personal intention and human decision and that moral evaluation can be made of specific acts viewed in this isolated way. Morality, however, is a reality that involves not only the specific objective act but also relevant circumstances and the mystery of human intention. Therefore, from the point of view of ethical methodology, the question should be formulated: Is this act, in and of itself, predictably an appropriate and productive means of expressing human sexuality? Can it constitute, from a perspective that is broadly humanistic and deeply influenced by the gospel, an objective value or disvalue?

But even in this more precise expression, the above question remains flawed. For, in the second place, it implies a greatly oversimplified understanding of sexuality. That any specific act can be measured and evaluated in a way totally adequate to the intricate manifold of human experience is dubious at best. Human sexuality is simply too complex, too mysterious, too sacred a human experience for such categorization. Tentativity is inevitable in the attempt to discern the objective significance of such a mysterious and many-splendored reality.

Yet the human spirit must ask such questions. It is a human inevitability. It is also a clear moral challenge flowing from the gospel call to authentic and genuine living. Hence we suggest that it is both possible and quite necessary to articulate some of the values which sexuality ought to preserve and promote, to indicate some of the functions which sexuality serves in the human Christian community, and thereby to sketch, at least in a tentative way, a series of criteria in terms of which the great variety of sexual behavior may be honestly evaluated.

In short, we maintain that it is appropriate to ask whether specific sexual behavior realizes certain values that are conducive to creative growth and integration of the human person. Among these values we would single out the following as particularly significant:

(1) *Self-liberating:* Human sexuality flows freely and spontaneously from the depth of a person's being. It is neither fearful nor anxious but rather genuinely expressive of one's authentic self. It begets self-assurance, thereby enhancing the full development of a person's potential for growth and self-expression. There is a legitimate self-interest and self-fulfillment that sexual expression is meant to serve and satisfy. To deny this is unrealistic and a contradiction of universal human experience. Too frequently in theological literature sexual union is seen as a sign and expression of the total gift of self to another. Little attention is given to the element of wholesome self-interest that must be part of authentic human sexual expression. This characteristic underscores the importance of sexuality as a source and means of personal growth toward maturity and rejects as unacceptable sexual expression that is self-enslaving. For this reason, it is a serious distortion to speak of the sexual relationship exclusively in terms of expressing a totally altruistic giving of self to another.[20]

(2) *Other-enriching:* Human sexuality gives expression to a generous interest and concern for the well-being of the other. It is sensitive, considerate, thoughtful, compassionate, understanding, and supportive. It forgives and heals and constantly calls forth the best from the other without being demeaning or domineering. This quality calls for more than mere non-manipulation or non-exploitation of others against their will. It insists that wholesome sexuality must contribute positively to the growth process of the other.[21]

(3) *Honest:* Human sexuality expresses openly and candidly and as truthfully as possible the depth of the relationship that exists between people.

It avoids pretense, evasion, and deception in every form as a betrayal of the mutual trust that any sexual expression should imply if it is truly creative and integrative. Many writers call attention to the difficulty in maintaining honesty in a sexual relationship. The force of passion, the psychological differences in the male and female natures, and the diversity in cultural background, education, and personal sensitivities all tend to make this a very difficult quality to maintain. The prudent counsel and advice given in this area deserves special hearing.[22]

(4) *Faithful:* Human sexuality is characterized by a consistent pattern of interest and concern that can grow ever deeper and richer. Fidelity facilitates the development of stable relationships, strengthening them against threatening challenges. In marriage, this fidelity is called to a perfection unmatched at any other level and establishing a very special, distinct, and particular relationship. Even this unique relationship, however, should not be understood as totally isolating a spouse from all other relationships, thereby opening the way to jealousy, distrust, and crippling possessiveness.[23]

(5) *Socially responsible:* Wholesome human sexuality gives expression not only to individual relationships but in a way also reflects the relationship and responsibility of the individuals to the larger community (family, nation, world). Since human beings are by nature social beings, it is only fitting that the creative and integrative force of human sexuality be exercised in the best interest of the larger community as well. The precise implications of this responsibility may vary considerably with time, place, and culture, but a genuinely responsible exercise of human sexuality cannot ignore this dimension. Both the historical and empirical data indicate that every society has found it necessary to give direction and impose restrictions on the expression of human sexuality in the interests of the common good. This characteristic, however, goes far beyond what is required for the good order of society. One may observe the law of a given society and still be far from leading a moral life. Law cannot be expected to legislate personal morality. What is required here is that people use their sexuality in a way that reveals an awareness of the societal implications of their behavior and in a manner that truly builds the human community. At times, this may mean a willingness to forego personal benefit and growth in order to preserve or promote the greater good of society.[24]

(6) *Life-serving:* Every expression of human sexuality must respect the intimate relationship between the "creative" and "integrative" aspects.[25] And every lifestyle provides means for giving expression to this life-

serving quality. For the celibate and the unmarried, human sexuality may find expression in a life of dedicated service to people through church or society. For the married, this life-serving purpose will generally be expressed through the loving procreation and education of children.

Persons giving themselves totally to each other should realize that, from the beginning, the Creator has chosen the complete intimate union of man and woman to be both a special sign of their commitment to one another and the normal means of transmitting life for the continuation of the human race. Precisely in this total giving of themselves to one another are they able to express their sexual creativity and to move toward their personal integration. A genuine openness and sincere readiness to become responsible "interpreters of God's will"[26] in this regard should underlie such total expressions of human sexuality. In most cases, this openness and readiness will lead marriage partners to become generous cooperators with God in the task of responsibly transmitting life. In some instances, however, this value could mean that a responsible interpretation of God's will leads to a life-serving decision not to beget children. In both instances, the "creative" and "integrative" aspects of human sexuality will be harmonized in the overriding life-serving orientation of the sexual expression. Full sexual expression with an accompanying abortive intent should procreation ensue would be a clear contradiction of this life-serving quality of human sexuality.[27]

(7) *Joyous:* Wholesome sexual expression should give witness to exuberant appreciation of the gift of life and mystery of love. It must never become a mere passive submission to duty or a heartless conformity to expectation. The importance of the erotic element, that is, instinctual desire for pleasure and gratification, deserves to be affirmed and encouraged. Human sexual expression is meant to be enjoyed without feelings of guilt or remorse.[28] It should reflect the passionate celebration of life, which it calls forth.

Where such qualities prevail, one can be reasonably sure that the sexual behavior that has brought them forth is wholesome and moral. On the contrary, where sexual conduct becomes personally frustrating and self-destructive, manipulative and enslaving of others, deceitful and dishonest, inconsistent and unstable, indiscriminate and promiscuous, irresponsible and non-life-serving, burdensome and repugnant, ungenerous and un-Christlike, it is clear that God's ingenious gift for calling us to creative and integrative growth has been seriously abused. By focusing on the many-splendored values of wholesome sexuality and avoiding absolute categorizations of isolated, individual sexual actions, one can arrive at a much more sensitive and responsible method of evaluating the morality of sexual patterns and expressions.

Again let it be recalled that all of these values must be enlightened and permeated by the core principle of Christian conduct, the gospel law of love. It is in the light of the life of the Lord that each of these values or qualities is illuminated by a unique Christian dimension or motivation. In the light of the life of the Lord the Christian has the potential to take each of these values and transcend the temporal to contribute thereby to the coming of the kingdom to give to human living a Christic dimension.

Sexuality then can be elevated to its potential sacramental meaning. The Old Testament saw sexuality as symbolic of the covenant reality of the love of God for his people. St. Paul spoke of it in marriage as the sign of the union of Christ and his church. Only when it has been humanized and Christianized by the law of love can sex reach this full potential of significance in the lives of those men and women who would use it according to the example of the Lord as a source of their fullest growth and integration as Christian people of God.

At this point, it might be helpful to recall several levels of moral evaluation as one moves from abstract principle to concrete decision. The first level is that of universal principle. We have accepted Vatican II's recommendation that the nature of the person and his acts be the fundamental criterion for evaluating wholesome sexual behavior.[29] The implications of this basic evaluative norm for the area of human sexuality are brought out more explicitly by expressing it in terms of creativity and integration. This principle of creative growth toward integration, which encompasses the Christian meaning of person, reflects an unfolding of Christ's ultimate commandment of love into the sphere of human sexuality. It expresses in a very general but fundamental manner the way in which sexuality is to serve the human person and be consonant with human dignity. In its abstract formulation as a principle, it is absolute and universal providing an overall direction or thrust toward which all wholesome sexual activity ought to tend.

At a second level, the identification of the more particular values associated with human sexuality—self-liberation, other-enrichment, honesty, fidelity, service to life, social responsibility, joy—serves to further unfold the meaning of the basic principle of creative growth toward integration. Note that these values are not expressed in terms of concrete, physical actions. Nor is it likely that each of these values will be equally served or protected in any specific sexual expression. They are not meant to serve as a checklist, the full and complete presence of which will guarantee wholesome sexual expression. This would be an unreal expectation and contradictory to human experience.

Humans are finite beings who cannot possibly realize all human values fully at every moment of their existence.

In applying these values to reach a moral decision regarding specific sexual behavior, one must beware not to lose sight of the fundamental principle of creative growth toward integration. This principle provides a framework in the light of which the significance and interrelatedness of these various individual values are to be appreciated and interpreted. Though each value may not be equally served in any particular sexual expression, the substantial violation of any of these values should raise serious questions about the ability of that sexual expression to enhance creative and integrative growth of the human person.

The third level of moral evaluation consists of more concrete norms, rules, precepts, or guidelines. These formulations attempt to distill from the experience of the Christian community the most practical and effective way that the desired values may be realized. They serve to enlighten the Christian conscience as to which particular patterns or forms of sexual behavior have proven generally to be conducive to or destructive of creativity and integration. To the extent that they refer to concrete, physical actions (e.g., masturbation, sterilization, contraception, premarital sex) without specifying particular circumstances or intention, to that extent they cannot be regarded as universal and absolute moral norms.

These norms indicate what Christian experience has proven to occur generally *(ut in pluribus)*. If the formulation is adequate, it constitutes a presumption that is usually valid and serves as a helpful guide in reaching a responsible moral decision, especially in doubtful situations. Exceptions may occur, but in these instances the burden of the proof that departure from the norm will nonetheless be creative and integrative not only for the individuals involved but for the larger community as well rests with those who choose to make the exception. Because such norms are not universal moral absolutes, we have chosen to refer to these more concrete formulations as "guidelines." . . . It is hoped that this terminology will caution against an oversimplistic and absolute application of such criteria in forming moral judgments. The direction of contemporary moral theology (Janssens, Fuchs, Knauer, Schuller, et al.)[30] and the aspirations of the Christian conscience seem to require this.

The final level of moral evaluation is the individual concrete decision. It is here that personal conscience finds its sphere of competence and must be respected. Christian moral life may not be looked upon solely from the viewpoint of conformity to predetermined rules or standards. Such an approach would deny that God-given freedom of response essential to human dignity and lying at the core of Christian morality.

The well-formed Christian conscience will be well aware of the fundamental principle of creative growth toward integration that ought to guide all sexual activity. It will be open and responsive to the complexity of values involved in this many-splendored gift of human sexual expression. It will be attentive to the more concrete guidelines which reflect the wisdom of the Christian experience and which surface considerations that should be part of every serious moral decision. But it knows that such guidelines must be read and understood not as commands imposed from without but as demands of the inner dynamism of human and Christian life. Their application to a particular decision will usually entail a great deal of prudence and wisdom. This is the place where personal conscience must exercise its responsibility.

In the last analysis, guidelines will serve to enlighten the judgment of conscience; they cannot replace it.[31] The well-formed individual conscience responsive to principles, values, and guidelines remains the ultimate subjective source for evaluating the morality of particular sexual expressions.

Notes

1. Walter Abbott and Joseph Gallagher, "Pastoral Constitution on the Church in the Modern World," *The Documents of Vatican II* (New York: Association Press, 1966), no. 62.
2. Ibid.
3. Ibid., no. 12.
4. Ibid., no. 44.
5. Henry Davis, S.J., *Moral and Pastoral Theology* (London: Sheed and Ward, 1936), 2:173.
6. Ibid., 182.
7. *Declaration on Certain Questions Concerning Sexual Ethics,* no. 1.
8. Cf. Gen 2:17, as interpreted by Karl Barth, *Church Dogmatics* (Edinburgh: T. and T. Clark, 1961), III/1, 184–87; III/4, 116–18.
9. *Church in the Modern World,* no. 51.
10. *Canon* 1013, no. 1.
11. Cf. Herbert Vorgrimler, *Commentary on the Documents of Vatican II* (New York: Herder, 1969) 5:239 ff.
12. *Church in the Modern World,* no. 51.
13. *Declaration on Certain Questions Concerning Sexual Ethics,* no. 1.
14. Ibid., no. 12.
15. Ibid., no. 62.
16. Bernard Haring, *The Law of Christ,* trans. E. G. Kaiser (Westminster, Md.: Newman Press, 1963), 1:35–53.
17. Richard McCormick, "Ambiguity in Moral Choice" (Washington, D.C.: Kennedy Center for Bioethics, Georgetown University, 1973), 65.

18. Joseph Fuchs, S.J., "The Absoluteness of Moral Terms," *Gregorianum* 52 (1971): 415–58. For a good evaluation of the recent literature and developments in this direction consult McCormick's comments on the "Understanding of Moral Norms," in *Theological Studies* 36 (March 1975): 85–100.
19. John A. Robinson, *Honest to God* (London: SCM Press, 1963), 115; Joseph Fletcher, *Situation Ethics: The New Morality* (Philadelphia: Westminster Press, 1966), 18 ff.; A. Heron, ed., *Towards a Quaker View of Sex* (London: Friends Home Service Committee, 1963), are representative of such an approach. Cf. Gene Outka and Paul Ramsey, *Norm and Context in Christian Ethics* (New York: Scribner, 1968), 3 ff. for a fuller discussion of this matter.
20. Sources which have contributed to a renewed appreciation of this point include *Declaration on Certain Questions Concerning Sexual Ethics,* no. 1; Peter Bertocci, *Sex, Love, and the Person* (Mission, Kans.: Sheed and Ward, 1969): John Milhaven, "Conjugal Sexual Love," *Theological Studies* 35 (December 1974): 692–710; Michael Valente, *Sex: The Radical View of a Catholic Theologian* (New York: Bruce, 1970), especially 132 ff.: E. Kennedy, *What a Modern Catholic Believes about Sex* (Chicago, Ill.: Thomas More Press, 1971), 25 ff.; Jerome Hayden, O.S.B., "Theological and Psychological Aspects of Habitual Sin," *Proceedings of CTSA* (1956): 130–63.
21. The Vatican Constitution on *The Church in the Modern World* (no. 49) speaks eloquently on this characteristic of human love in the context of marriage, and the more recent Vatican *Declaration on Certain Questions Concerning Sexual Ethics* implies the same for non-marital sexuality (no. 1).
22. Cf. *Sex and Morality: A Report Presented to the British Council of Churches* (Philadelphia: Fortress Press, October 1966), 29–30; Matthias Neuman, O.S.B., "Friendship between Men and Women in Religious Life," *Sisters Today* 46 (October 1974): 89–92.
23. Richard Roach, S.J., "Sex in Christian Morality," *Way* 11 (1971): 148–61, 235–42.
24. The report of the British Council of Churches reflects this kind of concern when it suggests with regard to the rules of abstinence before marriage and fidelity within it that "even if such rules do not completely coincide with the rights and wrongs of each case taken in isolation, yet they do prescribe what is normally good for our society. In this case we may have a duty to uphold the rule even at some sacrifice of personal liberty." *Sex and Morality,* 27.
25. The Christian Catholic tradition has generally maintained that the procreative and unitive aspects of human sexuality are in some sense inseparable. In what precise manner the relationship between the two elements is to be understood and harmonized is far from agreed upon. See Chapter V of Anthony Kosnik et al., *Human Sexuality: New Directions in Catholic Thought* (Louisville, Ky.: Catholic Theological Society of America, 1977), for more complete discussion of this problem.
26. *Church in the Modern World,* no. 50.

27. The final report of the Papal Commission studying the problem of birth control and responsible parenthood treats this aspect of human sexuality especially well. Cf. Robert Hoyt, ed., *The Birth Control Debate* (Kansas City, Mo.: National Catholic Reporter, 1968), 83 ff.
28. The important role of the erotic element in human sexuality has received increased attention in the writings of recent authors on the subject. Milhaven and Greeley especially have made important contributions in this area. Cf. John Milhaven, 692–710; Andrew Greeley, *Sexual Intimacy* (Chicago, Ill.: Thomas More Press, 1973); Andrew Greeley, *Love and Play* (Chicago, Ill.: Thomas More Press, 1975).
29. *Church in the Modern World,* no. 51.
30. Richard McCormick, "Notes on Moral Theology," *Theological Studies* 36 (March 1975): 85–100.
31. Cf. 1970 edition of the *Medico-Moral Guide* preamble approved by the Canadian Catholic Conference.

[35]

Sexual Morality in Five Tiers

Raymond A. Belliotti

A PERSUASIVE AND COMPREHENSIVE framework for sexual morality must . . . understand the lingering power of mainstream positions on sexual ethics while at once recognizing the intellectual currency of contemporary radical critiques. Thus, a remodeled theory of sexual ethics emerges from the attempt to mediate the seemingly irreconcilable tensions between politically centrist analysts of morality and their leftist critics. I call my preferred version of sexual ethics, reimagined and remade, "sexual morality in five tiers."

The ideology to which I subscribe is fueled by my ambition to mediate the tensions between mainstream Western morality and its leftist and feminist critics. If these efforts are judged successful, readers will perceive the ideology of sexual morality in five tiers as a sensible synthesis of several traditions, each of which captures an important dimension of sexual morality, but none of which adequately explains and justifies our sexual theory and practice. If these efforts are judged unsuccessful, readers will perceive the ideology of sexual morality in five tiers as the flaccid eclecticism of a hopelessly conflicted academic.

SOURCE: From Raymond A. Belliotti, *Good Sex: Perspectives on Sexual Ethics* (Lawrence, Kans.: University of Kansas Press, 1993).

Tier 1: Libertarian Agreement

. . . [L]ibertarians insist that the paramount values are individual freedom and autonomy. Thus it is tyranny to insist on a particular kind of sexual interaction or to prescribe a specific domain for acceptable sex. The test of morally permissible sex is simple: Have the parties, possessing the basic capacities necessary for autonomous choice, voluntarily agreed to a particular sexual interaction without force, fraud, and explicit duress? Accordingly, sex is impermissible if one or both parties lack the capacities for informed consent (e.g., underage, significantly mentally impaired, or nonhuman); or if there is explicit duress (threats or extortion), force (coercion), or fraud (one party deceives the other as to the nature of the act or the extent of his or her feelings as a way of luring the other to accepting the liaison).

The strength of libertarianism lies in its clear and uncompromising pinpointing of moral defects that adulterate sexual acts. To the extent that libertarianism affirms sound social values such as freedom and autonomous consent and celebrates the requirement of informed choice, it provides an undeniable service.

The fragility of this perception, however, manifests itself in the corollary libertarian proposition that the presence of the prescribed agreement between the parties is sufficient to establish the moral permissibility of their sexual act. The most glaring weakness of this position is that it ignores numerous moral distortions that occur in the realm of contract: radically unequal bargaining power, prominent differences in psychological vulnerability, the oppression of destitute circumstances, or the treatment of important attributes constitutive of human personality as if they were mere commodities subject to barter. Such distortions call into question whether a particular contract is truly morally permissible. Accordingly, the existence of a contract based on the presence of libertarian agreement is not morally self-validating. Once we know that a contract, arrived at through "voluntary consent," exists, there remains the further question: Are the terms of that contract morally permissible? The libertarian corollary can succeed only if voluntary contractual interaction comprises the totality of morality. But it does not.

The antidote to these deficiencies is supplied when we moderate libertarianism and accept only one of its central claims: informed agreement is a necessary condition for morally permissible sexual interaction. Thus, sexual morality in five tiers rejects the libertarian corollary that informed agreement is a sufficient condition for morally permissible sex.

Some readers, however, might recoil at even this moderate version of libertarianism. They might argue that making informed agreement a necessary condition for moral sex is still too strong. They would conjure hypothetical cases where the consequences of failing to initiate nonconsensual sex were so disastrous that truculent adherence to informed agreement as a necessary condition for moral sex seemed irrational.

For example, suppose that only by raping someone could ten other people's lives be saved. Is it morally wrong under such circumstances to rape? Would the rape be permissible even though the victim, fully aware of the operative facts, refused? If one failed to rape under such circumstances, what would be said to the ten people about to die and their families?

We could, of course, raise the stakes even higher. Suppose the rape would save one thousand people? ten thousand? ten million? the entire world population? Surely, a critic might argue, an absolutist interpretation of informed agreement as a necessary condition for moral sex is irrational if it could lead to the destruction of the entire world.

Moreover, we could alter the example even further. Suppose that only by raping someone could ten other *rapes* be prevented. Now we are no longer trading a rape for other lives, but a rape to prevent other rapes. Thus, those who take rape to be an unspeakable horror, perhaps more noxious in magnitude even than death, are effectively muted: as terrible as rape is, the critic could underscore, it is axiomatic that ten rapes are much worse than one rape of the same sort.

What response is available to these examples? One temptation is to stigmatize all such illustrations as fanciful, radically hypothetical, and unhelpful in real world moral analysis. Here we might refashion the adage "hard cases make for bad law" into "unrealistic, bizarre cases make for bad moral analysis."

This approach, however, evades confrontation by dismissing troubling counterexamples straightaway. This strategy is too easy and ultimately unsatisfying. The force of the counterexamples is not in their specificity, but in the general point they illustrate: Are there not times when the consequences of nonconsensual sex invalidate an absolutist rendering of the libertarian agreement principle? Are there not times when the ends do justify the means?

Hence, undermining the plausibility of the specific examples leaves the general point unscathed. With sufficient ingenuity and care, critics could conjure counterexamples much "closer to home"—cases that did not trade on seemingly farfetched circumstances or unbelievable contexts. Such counterexamples could not be brushed off so easily. Accordingly, sexual morality in five tiers resists the temptation to dismiss cravenly such cases by mocking their bizarre terms and invoking the need for realism.

A second approach to parrying the threat of unsettling counterexamples is a "lesser of two evils" analysis. Under this view, nonconsensual sex is still immoral, but its initiation is excused because it prevents even worse evil or facilitates an otherwise unobtainable good. Given the contexts conjured earlier, it is plausible to argue that, while libertarian agreement remains a necessary condition for moral permissibility, under the relevant circumstances an immoral sexual action may be the lesser of two evils when we confront an unappealing and inescapable moral dilemma. Engaging in the sexual act under such circumstances does not remove its stigma, but does supply the act's initiator with an excuse: "I know the act was morally wrong, but because of the circumstances, I cannot be held morally culpable."

At first blush, this approach offers an appealing compromise between those who aspire to an absolutist rendering of the libertarian agreement principle and those who yearn to prove that informed agreement cannot be a necessary condition of sexual interaction. But the compromise is unstable and unsatisfying at its core. First, those critics who would offer counterexamples such as those outlined above do so to show that the ends sometimes justify, and not merely excuse, the means needed to secure them. They want to argue that nonconsensual sex can be the morally right thing to do in certain situations, not merely that such sex is always morally wrong but sometimes excusable: "I know that nonconsensual sex is almost always wrong, but because of the circumstances in this case, such sex is not only morally permissible but perhaps morally obligatory." Thus, such critics would be unfulfilled by any lesser-of-two-evils approach that concludes that nonconsensual sex is always morally wrong but sometimes excusable.

Second, those who hold that libertarian agreement is a necessary condition of morally permissible sex would also be disturbed by the proffered compromise. They would want to hold that any sexual activity that violates the informed agreement principle renders itself morally wrong. To say in the instant cases that nonconsensual sex is wrong but excusable as the lesser of two evils holds the libertarian agreement principle hostage to the exigencies of the moment and to recurring aggregations of overall benefit. This would lead, it may be argued, to a crude instrumentalism in which there are no necessary conditions for moral interactions. This, in turn, implies that we have only constant situational calculations of right and wrong, or fragile prima facie moral principles that are themselves hostage to their ability to produce generally optimal outcomes.

The advocates of the libertarian agreement principle contend that nonconsensual sex is immoral and inexcusable. Their critics offer counterexamples that allegedly manifest how nonconsensual sex can be morally justified in certain extreme situations. The lesser-of-two-evils approach concludes that nonconsensual sex is always immoral but sometimes excusable. As such, this approach will satisfy neither the advocates of the libertarian agreement principle nor their critics. Accordingly, it should be clear that the lesser-of-two-evils approach achieves its compromise by slyly recasting the positions of the two protagonists.

In the face of all this, sexual morality in five tiers bites the bullet and affirms the libertarian agreement principle despite the critics' counterexamples. Thus, this theory subscribes to the inviolability of persons in certain important respects, one of which is sexual access. We cannot deny others their status as freely choosing, rationally valuing people with moral personality. The value of personhood is not determined by choice, but is, instead, presupposed in the very notion of informed choice. There must be some moral constraints on what can be done to individuals against their will in the name of advancing the collective good. Whether we call this limit "inviolability," "human dignity," "human rights," "taking seriously the differences between persons," or any similar slogan is less important than that we recognize at least some necessary moral constraints on using people against their will for the benefit of others. This recognition blocks a social appeal to aggregate consequences in justifying violations of these constraints. Instrumentalism, at least in its cruder forms, eviscerates the constitutive attributes of personhood by permitting their adjustment according to the dictates of the optimal calculus of the moment. As such, crude instrumentalism is anathema to sexual morality in five tiers, because the former portrays all constitutive human attributes as contingent while the latter embraces (a few) necessary, nonconsequentialist moral constraints.

As already noted, however, sexual morality in five tiers moderates libertarianism's gushing and boundless veneration of human choice. The theory urged here takes libertarian agreement to be a necessary, but not sufficient, condition of morally permissible sex.

What moral coinage, then, does Tier 1 analysis mint? At this stage of analysis we are not concerned with addressing moral subtleties such as exploitation, commodification, unequal bargaining power, and destitute circumstances. We ask only the basic libertarian question: Have the parties, possessing the basic capacities necessary for autonomous choice, voluntarily agreed to a particular sexual interaction without force, fraud, and explicit duress? If the answer is negative then we need go no further: the sexual act is morally impermissible. If the answer is affirmative then the sexual act must meet the requirements of the other four tiers if it is to gain the honorific title of "morally permissible."

A critic might claim that my argument assumes that we can evaluate the consensual properties of particular sexual acts independently of their historical and cultural contexts. This may suggest that sexual morality in five tiers falls prey at the outset to errors identified previously: essentialism and universalism.

Such a reading is based on a misunderstanding. The perceptions of the properties of libertarian agreement are themselves culturally and historically shaped. That is why sexual morality in five tiers necessarily provides only a framework for analysis rather than concrete, timeless, universal, substantive conclusions. The distinction here is between an analysis, such as my own, that argues only that libertarian agreement must be present for morally permissible sex and an analysis that specifies the precise properties which constitute libertarian agreement at all times and places. The latter analysis would be fairly subject to charges of essentialism and universalism, while the former is not. In sum, Tier 1 analysis tells us only that libertarian agreement is a necessary but not sufficient condition of morally permissible sex; it does not claim that we can evaluate consensual properties of particular sex acts ahistorically.

Tier 2: General Moral Considerations

Although I am presenting the theory in discrete levels of analysis, sexual morality in five tiers is not so easily categorized. Often the questions implicated at one level of analysis replicate themselves at another level or require answers supplied at least partly from analyses at other levels. These facts are clearest in Tier 2.

Here we look to general considerations which are applicable when evaluating all moral decision making. There are a number of prima facie principles of morality acknowledged in our culture: keep promises; tell the truth; return favors; aid others in distress when doing so involves no serious danger or sacrifice to oneself or innocent third parties; make reparation for harm to others that is one's own fault; oppose injustices when doing so involves no great cost or sacrifice to oneself; promote just institutions and facilitate their continuation and refinement; assume one's fair share of societal burdens and thus avoid being a "free rider"; avoid causing pain or suffering to others; avoid inexcusable killing of others; and avoid stealing or otherwise depriving others of their property.[1]

This is not an exhaustive litany of our moral duties, but it does constitute the general framework from which we derive other specific obligations. Accordingly, Tier 2 analysis encompasses all of those relevant considerations that must be consulted when assessing morally any human interaction. The principles listed above are prima facie, not absolute. Their respective imperatives often conflict, and thus it is often impossible to fulfill all of their dictates in every moral context. Moreover, appeals to consequences and the real effects of actions will often compel the overriding of a prima facie moral principle.

In Tier 2 we cannot ask simply, "Has a lie been told?" and conclude that if the answer is affirmative then the surrounding sex act is automatically immoral. Although I have claimed that libertarian agreement is a necessary condition for morally permissible sex, I also recognize the quite obvious truth that transgressions of one or more of the prima facie principles listed above are often morally justified.[2]

At this tier we must also confront the motives and intentions of the parties engaging in sex. Further, we must evaluate ancillary issues such as abuse of one's institutional role and social power and the foreseen and actual consequences of the sexual acts in question. Although the primary focus in Tier 2 is on the interacting parties themselves, full evaluation of the justifiability of transgressions of prima facie moral principles will often require an inquiry into issues described in Tiers 4 and 5. It is thus impossible to separate plausibly the five tiers into fully autonomous layers of analysis. We probably come the closest in Tier 1, but even there we must ponder questions of fraud, force, and deception which implicate and overlap issues in other tiers.

Tier 3: Sexual Exploitation

Interpersonal exploitation, in its morally pejorative sense, is characterized by the following: One party (E) takes advantage of another party's (V) attributes or situation to exact gain for E and/or E's compatriots.[3] The various types of exploitation display various degrees of coercion. Joel Feinberg points out that "exploiters are typically opportunists; they extract advantage from situations that are not of their own making. Coercers, on the other hand, are typically makers rather than mere discoverers and users of opportunities."[4]

At times, exploitation is explicitly coercive, which destroys the possibility of mutually informed consent and libertarian agreement. At other times, exploitation is subtly coercive: E may capitalize on V's relatively inferior bargaining power or special vulnerabilities. At still other times, exploitation may not seem coercive at all: V may render fully informed libertarian agreement to V's misuse by E.

In noncoercive exploitation, V's consent is relevant to, but not dispositive of, moral assessment. That Jones renders fully informed consent to Smith's mutilation of Jones's body, for example, does not entail that Smith's act is morally permissible. Thus, V's consent may prevent V from lodging a credible claim that V has been personally wronged by E's opportunism, but it does not by itself exonerate E from charges of wrongful exploitation: "What we must mean by (unfair) exploitation is 'profitable utilization of another person that is either on balance unfair to him, or which in virtue of its other unfairness-producing characteristics would be unfair on balance to him but for his voluntary consent to it.'"[5]

At the heart of exploitation is the profit extracted by E from E's use of V: "We must employ an admittedly extended sense of 'gain' including both gain in the strict sense and fulfillment of one's aims, purposes, or desires, including altruistic and conscientious ones. The 'gain' in question, moreover, need not be a *net* gain if there should happen also to be attendant losses."[6] E's profit is procured at V's expense: V either suffers an overall setback to V's interests, or no gain, or a disproportionately meager gain. All this yields the flavor of exploitation as one person "using another as a mere means" for her own ends. The images here are those of V being regarded as less than V is: not as an equal subject of experience, but as a mere instrument for the advance of E's purposes and profits.

Explicitly coercive exploitation is of little interest to Tier 3 analysis because such actions necessarily vitiate the possibility of libertarian agreement. Thus, Tier 1 would dismiss such cases straightaway. Instead, subtly coercive exploitation and consensual exploitation are of greater interest here.

Unsurprisingly, it is much easier to provide a general framework for exploitation than to detail a mechanical method of identifying specific cases. Tier 3 analysis, however, assumes the following: as a result of socially created and other historical conditions, sexual contracts are different from nonsexual exchanges of goods and services; the relative situation of men and women, taken as classes, differ historically, as does the relative situation of heterosexuals vis à vis homosexuals; and when evaluating the presence of exploitation, attention must be given to the particular circumstances, vulnerabilities, prior entitlements, relative bargaining power and social status, and wants/needs of the parties.

In this vein, the paradigm of subtly coercive exploitation consists of an E with relatively strong socioeconomic bargaining power; a V with special vulnerabilities, needs, or deep wants; and a proposition, initiated by E and formulated for E's advantage and at V's loss or disproportionately small gain, that has the effect of narrowing or closing V's overall opportunities.[7] Such exploitation is "subtly coercive" because the force used to secure "consent" is not so obvious as to trigger a violation of libertarian agreement, yet not so benign as to translate clearly to fully informed, mutual consent.

However, we cannot be mystified by our paradigms of exploitation into thinking dogmatically that only men are sexual exploiters and only women are the victims of exploitation. Academics, under the spell of the prodigious amount of contemporary literature sympathetic to feminist concerns, sometimes stumble into believing that our paradigms—for example, a socially powerful, lecherous male misusing his advantages to coerce overtly or subtly a relatively less powerful woman to engage in sexual acts she otherwise detests—constitute the whole of sexual exploitation. While it is undeniable that our society has an inglorious historical record with regard to women's full enfranchisement in the public sphere and that our society, indeed, embodies numerous patriarchal vices, it is also true that in the sexual microcontexts that men and women create, either party can be exploited. Virginia Held, a feminist philosopher, captures this well:

> In their dealings with one another, man and woman discover not only that man can overpower woman . . . and woman can overpower man—that is, at the level of *sexual* power, as opposed to muscular and other power, they really *are* equal. What human beings also discover is that in this relation, mutual respect is only possible when neither overpowers the other, and coercion of any kind, including the use of sexual power in coercive ways, is transcended.[8]

That brings us to the special problems raised by the third type of exploitation, consensual exploitation. Here V renders fully informed consent to V's misuse by E. One might be tempted to argue that so long as V consented, it is presumptuous of others to deem the interaction a "misuse." For who is a better judge of V's interests and preferences than V?

But . . . a person's perceptions of her best interests and what would advance them are not incorrigibly correct. Moreover, there are moral limits to what we may do to others even with their consent. Feinberg tells us:

> exploitation of another's rashness or foolishness is *wrong,* even when because of prior voluntary consent it does not violate the other's right. . . . It is wrong because the actor believes on good evidence that it will probably set back [the victim's] interest, and deliberately choosing to be an instrument of another's "harm" (setback to interest) for one's own gain is often something we ought not to do, even though the other can have no [personal] grievance against us when we do.[9]

The key here is to distinguish different sorts of risks that others are willing to take, but that we would refuse. When is consent to an uncommon action "rash and foolish" and thus likely to "set back" V's interests? When is it mere risk taking that reveals nothing more than V's adventuresome and unrepressed nature? The answers are found when we assess the prospects of V's gain relative to E: Will E realize significant "profit," as defined earlier, while V suffers loss, no gain, or disproportionately paltry gain? Does V's consent betray V's vulnerabilities, negative self-image, misfortune and destitute circumstances, or human weaknesses? Has E manipulated V by appealing to such vulnerabilities, circumstances, and weaknesses? Has E thus pandered to the worst aspects of V? It becomes clearer that to establish "exploitation," we must attend not merely to the foreseeable effects on V's interests but also to E's motives, intentions, and expected gain.

Accordingly, the totality of circumstances surrounding V's consent is paramount. Who initiated the proposition which formed the basis of possible exploitation is especially relevant. For example, E may have won V's consent through subtle manipulation which traded on V's known weaknesses through "seductive luring, beguiling, tempting, bribing, coaxing, imploring, whimpering, flattering, and the like, short of deceptive innuendo, threats, or coercive offers."[10] Such manipulation is more probative of exploitation then straightforward offers and explicit propositions. There are, of course, numerous other ways E might initiate the proposition:

> Less likely to be unfair are fishing expeditions in which [E] merely hangs his lure within range of vulnerable [V], attracting his voluntary agreement to a scheme that is in fact likely to promote [E's] gain at [V's] expense. [E] may initiate the process by making a proposal to [V] which [V] after due contemplation, but no manipulative persuasion, readily accepts. Least likely of all to be unfair to [V] are those agreements which [V] himself initially proposes and to which [E] reluctantly responds.[11]

I must underscore, however, that the circumstances surrounding the initiation of the proposition are one, but only one, source of evidence where we evaluate the possibility of wrongful exploitation. The reason that V's initiation of the proposition makes exploitation less likely is that it manifests V's antecedent willingness to participate in the acts constituting the proposition and precludes the possibility that V complied because of overt threats. But, although V's initiation of a proposition is less likely to trigger exploitation than is E's coercive, manipulative, and straightforward offerings, it is still possible for V to initiate a proposition that results in V's wrongful exploitation by E. Once again, the keys are V's special vulnerabilities, circumstances, and relative bargaining power, the fashion in which these were used in the acts constituting the proposition, and the distribution of gains and setbacks to interests as between E and V.

Tier 4: Third Party Effects

Sexual acts can be immoral despite the presence of libertarian agreement, the absence of exploitation, and compliance with general moral considerations vis à vis the consenting parties.

For example, we can imagine a married couple who mutually agree to have sexual relations with other parties. Suppose further that within the confines of the acts performed by these other parties and the married couple all general moral considerations are honored, no exploitation occurs, and full libertarian agreement is present. However, the children of the married couple suffer greatly as a result of their parents' sexual profligacy. Without detailing the precise nature of that suffering, we can hypothesize that it is caused directly by the parents' sexual experimentation and is serious enough to constitute clear harm. (We must concede that harm to children because of their parents' sexual excesses does not necessarily imply a failure of parental moral duty—we can summon cases where we would be more sympathetic, from a moral perspective, to the parents than to their suffering children—but stipulate here that the instant case is no such aberration.)

In such a situation it is reasonable to declare the married couple's actions morally impermissible. Invoking the presence of libertarian agreement among the sexually involved parties, the absence of exploitation, and the parties' mutual fulfillment of prima facie moral requirements via à vis one another would be insufficient to redeem morally the sexual acts in question.

Accordingly, third party effects become an important tier of analysis for sexual ethics. We are concerned here mainly with the reasonably foreseeable and actual consequences of the sexual acts in question on the immediate circle of people affected by the acts. The wider social effects of the sexual acts are more appropriately analyzed in Tier 5.

I must underscore, however, that the mere presence of harmful or offensive effects to others by a sexual act is insufficient to establish that the act in question is morally flawed when judged by Tier 4. Consider the following example: Jones and Smith are a racially mixed couple who enjoy taking walks on the main street of a small town. Biggs and Boggs are deeply offended by these walks because the two men are vehemently opposed to miscegenation. The reader can use his or her imagination and summon the details, but stipulate that Biggs and Boggs suffer gravely as a result of the racially mixed couple's strolls. Obviously, Jones and Smith are not guilty of immoral actions simply because the two bystanders are deeply offended.

Consider another example: Jackson and Johnson have dated for three years. After a period of discontent, Jackson informs Johnson that she wishes to stop dating him. Shortly thereafter, Jackson begins dating Russo. Johnson, who still pines for Jackson, perceives Russo as an intruder. He accuses Russo of "cutting my grass." Are Jackson and/or Russo immoral simply because Johnson suffers as a result of their liaisons? Certainly not under the illustration as it is sketched here.

In both of the examples above, and in innumerable others we might construct, the "victims" have not been wronged by the facts that lead to their suffering: their rights have not been violated nor have their interests been transgressed unjustifiably. In that important sense, they have not been harmed. Instead, their suffering is the result of the offense they take at the actions of others. This observation does not lessen the extent of that suffering, but it does tend to exonerate morally the people whose fully permissible actions led to that suffering. Negative third party effects are most compelling, from a moral perspective, where they result from unjustified harming. They are much less commanding where they result from offense taken by bystanders.

The fact that people are offended by certain actions is relevant in moral assessment, but only some cases of rendering offense are morally culpable. To determine whether offensive conduct translates into moral culpability, Joel Feinberg recommends that we balance the seriousness of the offense caused by an act against the reasonableness of the act.[12] The seriousness of the offense caused by the act is calculated by the following: (1) the magnitude of the offense as measured by its intensity, duration, and extent; (2) the extent to which the offense was reasonably avoidable; (3) whether the offended party voluntarily assumed the risk of experiencing the offensive act; and (4) whether the offended party had an abnormal susceptibility to offense. The reasonableness of the act is calculated by the following: (1) the importance of the offending conduct to the actors; (2) the social value of the act; (3) whether the act is a case of free expression; (4) the availability of alternative opportunities for the actors to engage in the act; (5) whether the animating motive of the act was malicious or spiteful; and (6) whether the act was performed in locales where it is common and expected, or in locales where it is rare and unexpected.[13]

In sum, Tier 4 focuses on the way sexual activity affects the interests of the immediate circle of third parties. Specifically, it asks the following questions: Have these third parties been unjustifiably harmed? Has the sexual conduct at issue rendered wrongful offense?

Tier 5: Wider Social Context

There are times when sexual activity accompanied by libertarian agreement nevertheless has detrimental social effects. Such acts might reflect and reinforce oppressive social roles, contribute to continued social inequality, gestate new forms of gender oppression, or otherwise add to the contamination of the wider social and political context surrounding sexual activity.

Although liberal-centrists venerate personal choice and private morality, doing so often marginalizes the wider social background and effects attending sex and illustrates a subtle form of the error of isolationism. Marxists and feminists are most diligent in pressing this point: sex acts are not always merely discrete interactions between consenting parties.

In this vein, the self-described "Lesbian-Feminist" Coletta Reid argues that "[Sex] is not private; it is a political matter of oppression, domination, and power."[14] Moreover, "In a world devoid of male power and, therefore, sex roles, who you lived with, loved, slept with, and were committed to would be irrelevant. All of us would be equal and have equal determination over the society and how it met our needs. Until this happens, how [women] use our sexuality and our bodies is just as relevant to our liberation as how we use our minds and our time."[15]

For example, numerous feminists insist that the depiction of women in books and movies as sexual playthings and sexually submissive entertainers of men demeans women generally. Regardless of the fully informed consent of those women who participate in such ventures, feminists claim that all women share the attributes at issue and thus women generally are degraded by the demeaning portrayals of the consenting models.[16] Such observations lead numerous feminists to conclude that "the personal is *always* political" and that heterosexual acts *must* reinforce a social structure that is antecedently and irredeemably flawed. Marxists could make a parallel claim that particular occasions of bourgeois heterosexuality necessarily reflect and reinforce the socially incapacitating imperatives of capitalism. As such, both perspectives could argue that conventionally accepted sex within a corrupt social setting is necessarily wrong because of its subsidizing effects.

Sexual morality in five tiers, subscribing as it does to the possibility of heterosexual couples creating salutary microcontexts even within an otherwise unhealthy social structure, cannot endorse this leftist prescription in its unregenerative form. However, sexual morality in five tiers does not thereby reinstate the liberal-centrist axiom that sex is securely within the domain of personal choice and private morality. The challenge, then, is to avoid the Scylla of leftist necessitarianism and the Charybdis of liberal-centrist isolationism.

This challenge, however, is more easily raised than fulfilled. In their respective ways, leftist necessitarianism and liberal-centrist isolationism both embody the virtue of easy applicability: each generates moral conclusions quickly and clearly. On the other hand, perspectives such as sexual morality in five tiers, which aspire to chart courses less traveled, require careful attention to specific cases and resist inflexible characterizations. Moreover, this fifth tier raises issues of widespread social effects that invite speculation and evaluation that are unsusceptible to easy verification.

Accordingly, users of sexual morality in five tiers must attend carefully to the specifics of each case and answer questions such as the following: Does this sex act contribute in a specific and articulable way to the general oppression of women (or any other disadvantaged class) by men (or any other advantaged class)? Does this act facilitate intermediate institutions (such as prostitution) which reflect and reinforce social oppression? Does this act hinder in a specific way the establishment of intermediate institutions which might rectify social oppression? Is this act public enough to affect directly the social roles of disadvantaged and advantaged classes?

Quantifying the Five Tiers

Moral analysis evades mathematical precision. But, often, we can roughly quantify a theory to illustrate more clearly its underlying commitments and aspirations. In this vein, we can take the five tiers—libertarian agreement (LA), general moral considerations (MC), sexual exploitation (SE), third party effects (TP), and wider social context (SC)—and sketch a formula or test for sexual morality:

Sexual Morality Quotient = LA x (MC + SE + TP + 1/2 SC)

We could use this formula in the following way when evaluating a sexual interaction: Libertarian agreement is assigned a score of either 1, if it is present, or 0, if it is absent. Libertarian agreement is a necessary condition of morally permissible sex. Thus if it is lacking in the instant case then the action is morally wrong. By assigning "LA" as 0 in such cases we ensure that the act's morality quotient is 0 (as 0 times any number is 0).

The other four elements—general moral considerations (MC), sexual exploitation (SE), third party effects (TP), and wider social context (SC)—are assigned scores of 0 to 100. These scores represent the range from the thoroughly depraved and morally irredeemable (0) to the morally permissible but mundane (80) to the morally supererogatory and ideal (100). The score that is assigned the fifth tier, wider social context, is multiplied by 0.5 to reflect the difficulty and speculation necessarily involved in evaluating the issues raised by this tier. These problems militate that fifth tier analysis should count less than the analyses of the other tiers.

A perfect cumulative score is 350. This represents morally ideal sex, whatever that may be. We cannot fully describe this type of sex, but we can say generally that it goes above and beyond the call of moral duty. It is sex that is not merely morally permissible, but morally exemplary. It would involve some extraordinary moral benefits to others not attainable in merely morally permissible sex. I am hesitant to describe it further because such an exercise requires extensive delineation of our moral duties and how we might exceed them. My more pressing concern is adumbrating morally permissible, not morally ideal, sex. Hence this work is pitched to the morally conscientious, not the saintly.

A cumulative score of 280 represents morally permissible sex. Such sex does not violate our moral duties, but it is not so praiseworthy as to rise to the level of a supererogatory act. A cumulative score below 280 represents morally impermissible sex. Such sex violates our moral duties. But, of course, not all such acts are equally wrong. The formula permits users to conclude not simply that a sex act is wrong, but also the degree of its moral deficiencies, ranging from the utterly depraved (0–50) to the thoroughly defiled (51–100) to the clearly contemptible (101–240) to the somewhat contaminated (241–265) to the mere peccadillo (266–279).

Moreover, for those sex acts that violate the requirement of libertarian agreement and automatically earn a 0, users can still complete the rest of the formula to determine which of two such impermissible acts is morally worse: the act that scores higher on assessment of the remaining four tiers is less wrong to that degree than the other act. Finally, we have the case of two morally impermissible acts of the following sort: the first fails the test of libertarian consent but, should we continue the analysis, scores reasonably well on the tests of other four tiers; the second passes the test of libertarian consent but scores woefully on the tests of the other four tiers. The former might be represented by [0 x (80 + 80 + 80 + 40)], while the latter might be represented by [1 x (40 + 60 + 60 + 30)]. Given its scores, the former would have been judged morally permissible if and only if it had passed the test of libertarian agreement, while the latter is clearly contemptible despite the fact that it did pass the test of libertarian agreement. Which of the two is, all things considered, morally worse? I am inclined to view the first act as morally worse than the second act. While there may be extraordinary cases where we would want to conclude otherwise, in most such comparisons my inclination would remain, due to the primacy I place on libertarian agreement as a necessary condition of morally permissible sex.

Some readers will recoil at this entire effort at quantification. They may wonder whether I have fallen prey to one of the very analytic traps I have already disparaged: rigidity. Has the apostle of flexibility and the shameless shill of continuums suddenly been exposed as just another anal-retentive bean counter? Perhaps—but I must resist such harsh characterization. The horizontal line joining the two poles of the thoroughly depraved and morally irredeemable (0) and the morally supererogatory and ideal (350) remains a continuum. But in moral theory we must draw at least one other vertical line to distinguish the morally permissible from the morally impermissible. There comes a time, at the end of moral analysis, when inquiring minds demand to know: Is the act morally right or wrong?

Readers may also scoff at assigning scores to each tier of the analysis. How does one quantify a lie, a broken promise, or a laudatory third party effect? How does an 80 represent anything? The answer here is that we make comparative judgments of this sort all the time. We judge of two morally impermissible acts that one is worse than the other. We declare actions morally right and morally wrong. We decide that certain morally permissible actions are of higher moral quality than other morally permissible actions. And so on. Perhaps we do not literally assign exact scores to such judgments, but we surely make relative comparisons in a figurative fashion. Such comparisons may not require a slide rule or computer, but they do demand, among other things, relative weighing of moral principles, careful consideration of context, and aggregation of numerous, often competing, factors. Although moral reasoning is not susceptible to mathematical precision, it necessarily requires quantification in some form to some extent.

Accordingly, the sexual morality quotient urged here is neither self-executing nor rigid. Instead, it merely provides a theoretical framework into which substance must be supplied by general moral theory. The explanation and justification of a full-blown moral theory is necessarily beyond the scope of this work, but I can provide many of the commitments and presuppositions that animate the conclusions to specific cases that will follow.

. . .

Case 5

Bonnie Hughes is a widow with three small children. Stud Wallace is a well-known playboy who has wished for a long time to add Bonnie to his extensive list of sexual conquests. Stud has often made his desires known to Bonnie, but Bonnie has always spurned Stud's entreaties as the "evil conjurings of a loathsome man." Upon hearing this phrase, Stud has always sneered, laughed, and insisted that one day Bonnie would relent. Stud has often added that her constant refusals only make Bonnie more desirable to him. Bonnie's disgust with Stud has intensified over time.

But events soon conspire in Stud's behalf. Bonnie and her family suffer horrible financial setbacks. They are forced to sell most of their personal possessions and, eventually, find it exceedingly difficult to honor their mortgage payments. The holder of the mortgage threatens to foreclose. Bonnie can find no alternative to losing her family's home.

Stud Wallace, a consummate opportunist, offers to make Bonnie's mortgage payments on a continuing basis if and only if Bonnie agrees to accompany Stud for two weeks of sex and sun at Stud's favorite resort in Perkinsville, New Mexico. Bonnie, although horrified by this exchange, grudgingly accepts Stud's proposal.

This is, of course, a classic case of exploitation, an illustration chronicled in numerous movies and cartoons from the days of silent pictures to the present. Stud Wallace has taken advantage of Bonnie's desperate situation, overwhelming need, lack of bargaining power, and absence of viable alternatives to secure what he could not otherwise win. Accordingly, Stud's actions clearly violate Tier 3 analysis, and, depending on fuller details, may well transgress other tiers as well.

One sidebar is appropriate here. It must be clear that when we conclude a sexual act is "morally wrong," we do not thereby necessarily hold each of the participants morally culpable. For example, in the instant case we would hold the exploiter, Stud Wallace, morally culpable, but many of us would fully excuse the participation of his victim. Here we recognize a well-known distinction between the morality of an action and the morality of the agent who performs or participates in it: an action can be morally right, but if the agent who performs it does so from ersatz motives and intentions, we would hold her culpable to some degree; an action can be morally wrong, but if its agent is guided by proper motives and intentions, we could excuse or even justify her conduct in at least some cases; an action can be morally wrong, yet we may hold one party fully culpable, while excusing or justifying the conduct of the other party; an action can be morally wrong and we may hold all parties jointly and severally culpable, and so on.

Notes

1. Joel Feinberg, "Civil Disobedience in the Modern World," in *Philosophy of Law,* ed. Joel Feinberg and Hyman Gross (Belmont, Calif.: Wadsworth Publishers, 1986), 134.
2. "Insofar as a given act is an instance of one of the [prima facie moral principles], that is a moral reason in favor of doing it, and if it is not, at the same time, a negative instance of one of the other categories on the list, then it is a decisive reason. If it is a positive instance of one type and a negative instance of another, say a promise that can only be kept by telling a lie, then one's actual duty will be to perform the [prima facie obligation] which is the more stringent in the circumstances. That is all a moralist can say in the abstract with any degree of certainty" (ibid.).
3. The best analysis of "exploitation" that I have read is advanced by Joel Feinberg, *Harmless Wrongdoing* (New York: Oxford University Press, 1988), 176–210.
4. Ibid., 184.

5. Ibid., 200.
6. Ibid., 193.
7. Ibid., 178–179.
8. Virginia Held, "Marx, Sex, and the Transformation of Society," *Philosophical Forum* 5 (1973): 175.
9. Feinberg, *Harmless Wrongdoing,* 181.
10. Ibid., 201.
11. Ibid., 202.
12. Joel Feinberg, *Offense to Others* (New York: Oxford University Press, 1985), 25–43.
13. Ibid., 44. It should be obvious that the following factors militate in favor of exonerating the actors from moral culpability: relatively meager offense that was reasonably avoidable by the offended party; assumption of risk by the offended party; usual susceptibility of the offended party; an act that bore social value and special importance to the participating parties; a lack of alternative opportunities to engage in the act; performance of the act in a place where acts of its type are common and expected. The converses of these descriptions would, of course, militate in favor of holding the actors morally culpable.
14. Coletta Reid, "Coming Out in the Women's Movement," in *Lesbianism and the Women's Movement,* ed. Nancy Myron and Charlotte Bunch (Baltimore: Diana Press, 1975), 103.
15. Ibid.
16. "[Nude] centerfolds contribute to an environment in which more direct and familiar types of exploitation of women by men is encouraged, and it does this by spreading the image of women as sexual playthings. The pictures then have a direct causal influence on the way the woman's role is conceptualized in society and that in turn makes certain kinds of exploitation posssible" (Feinberg, *Harmless Wrongdoing,* 191).

[36]

Making Love as Making Justice: Towards a New Jewish Ethic of Sexuality

Yoel H. Kahn

1.

The contemporary question "What does Judaism say about homosexuality?" does not lend itself to a simple answer. In accordance with Jewish tradition, I can best answer this question with another question or two: Which Judaism do you mean—biblical, rabbinic, medieval, pre-modern, or modern? How can ancient sources speak to us about a category of meaning unconceptualized in their language and culture?[1] And if many contemporary Jews do not endorse the historical Jewish condemnation of male homosexual behavior, which, to be sure, is the unequivocal voice of the received tradition, what is our relation to the rest of historical Jewish teaching on human sexuality? How do we describe the logarithm of change which permits us simultaneously to dissent radically from received teaching while claiming to stand in and even represent the tradition from which it comes?

The full exploration of these questions is beyond the scope of this essay. I

Source: From Yoel H. Kahn, "Making Love as Making Justice: Towards a New Jewish Ethic of Sexuality," in *Gay Affirmative Ethics,* ed. L. Stemmler and J. Michael Clark (Las Colinas, Tx.: Monument Press, 1993). Used by permission.

begin with these questions, though, in order to locate this essay within its larger context. This essay has its roots in an inquiry about Judaism and homosexuality[2] and in turn led to research on what liberal Judaism has had to say about human sexuality in general.[3] Ultimately, this inquiry led to an exploration of the theological self-understanding of how we mediate between the conflicting values of our received religious tradition and the contemporary society, a society of which we are both a part and have helped create. In this essay, a précis of a longer work in process, I shall outline how such a process might proceed by applying a methodology of liberal Jewish decision making to sexuality in general.[4]

2.

The starting place for any Jewish discussion of contemporary standards is historical Jewish teaching, as codified in the *halachah,* traditional Jewish law. Rooted in the Hebrew Bible and formulated in the Talmud, halachah has continued to evolve over the generations. The halachah about human sexuality is expressed in the context of the ancient rabbis' understanding of anthropology and physiology, and reflects their ideas about subjects as varied as authority, "natural law," and revelation as expressed through the Torah. Nonetheless, we can posit five specific organizing values of sexuality within rabbinic culture. Although not always recognized by the rabbis, these organizing values give shape to—and account for much of—the halachah which defines appropriate sexual expression. These five values are: the economy of seed, the procreative purpose of sex, the role of women, *onah* (conjugal duty), and the concern for ritual purity.[5] The application of these values, within the wider context of the rabbinic worldview and its concretization in the halachic system as a whole, generate the rules which regulate when and how sexual relations can occur. These rules are codified as *mitzvot*—sacred obligations. All the individual mitzvot are fulfilled out of the Jew's commitment to the covenant between God and Israel. The proper expression of sexual relations, as codified in the relevant mitzvot, is a significant aspect of a life of holiness in the covenant. We begin with a brief look at these five organizing rabbinic values and how they shaped sexual behavior.

The biblical and rabbinic traditions express abhorrence at the "destruction" of semen. In the ancient Near East, semen was considered a "life force," akin to blood.[6] Apparently, people believed that there was a finite quantity of semen, which could not be wasted. Further, as a "life force" fluid, it had to be properly cared for and disposed of; and only acceptable repository for semen was inside a woman's vagina during intercourse. This concern for the quantity and disposition of seed is the primary basis for the later halachic prohibitions on male masturbation,[7] non-vaginal intercourse and coitus interruptus,[8] and the use of condoms[9] or diaphragms.[10]

Although pleasure and intimacy are known and legitimate aspects of rabbinic sexuality, the halachah has an overwhelming bias towards procreation.[11] Procreation is an affirmative mitzvah for men and, according to Talmudic law, a woman who is barren after ten years can be divorced by her husband.[12]

On the other hand, the halachah permits marriages and sexual relations which are known in advance to be infertile. The symbolic bias towards procreation is reflected in the halachah's permission of sexual intimacy with an infertile woman as long as the particular sexual act would be potentially procreative were the wife not infertile.[13] In general, the halachah only considers sexual acts which are *presumably* procreative licit.[14]

The wife's sexual role is determined in part by her second-class legal status in the halachah. The organizing premise of the halachah on marital relations is that a woman's sexual and reproductive capacities are the property of her husband.[15] Thus, there is a general rabbinic principle that "the husband may do as he pleases" with his wife. This value is in conflict with the rabbinic understanding of women's sexual needs and the husband's conjugal obligation. This conflict is a source of tension throughout the generations.

A husband is obligated to have sexual relations with his wife at regular times. The biblical term *onah* (Exodus 21:11) is understood to mean conjugal rights. The second-century code the Mishnah specifies the frequency with which onah must be provided; later commentators differ as to whether these times constitute a minimum or maximum requirement. The rabbis expand the mitzvah to encompass the husband's obligation to provide sexual satisfaction to his wife.[16] The man's own sexual pleasure is not recognized by the halachah as a legitimate goal; the ancient rabbis saw men's sexual energy as boundless and in need of "control" while women's is more subdued and therefore must be aroused.[17] The regulation of sexual behavior is extended by some of the ancient rabbis to include approved and discouraged positions.

Finally, according to the halachah, sexual relations are forbidden during times of ritual impurity. A women is ritually unclean for up to fifteen days of each menstrual cycle,[18] during mourning, and on other days on the personal and communal calendar.

The above organizing values underlie the halachic norms for licit sexuality. Summarizing these values and the behavioral norms they generate, the halachah teaches that sexual relations are licit and sacred when they occur

1. between opposite sex-partners[19]
2. in the context of marriage[20]

3. through vaginal intercourse
   a. preferably in the missionary position
4. at permitted times according to the religious calendar
5. at permitted times during the women's menstrual
6. with attention to the women's satisfaction and pleasure[21]
7. with the expectation that the act will be procreative[22]

3.

The above criteria reflect the halachah's specific understanding of sexuality on the micro level, and, on the macro level, are consistent with the entirety of the halacha's worldview. Our modern response properly begins, therefore, with an acknowledgment that our organizing values are different than those of our ancestors, reflecting our changed priorities and premises. These values are grounded in our contemporary understanding of the meaning of God, Torah, and Israel. They emerge out of our ongoing dialogue with God, out of historical Jewish teaching, and out of the lived experience of the Jewish people, men and women, gay and non-gay, as the embodiment of contemporary Jewish culture, itself embedded in liberal Western culture. Before turning to the specific question of sexuality, let's first note some of the organizing values of contemporary liberal Judaism and point out how they shape a modern Jewish ethic of sexuality.

The Torah teaches us that each person—as person—is created in the divine image. We first part from previous generations when we place particular emphasis on the ultimate dignity of the person and the individual's autonomy as part of the blessing of being made in the divine image. Accordingly, we explicitly reject Judaism's historical distinction between men and women and insist upon complete equality for all individuals. Second, we lift up the human capacity for relationship as an especially significant aspect of humanity's creation in the divine image. Martin Buber is our primary teacher of this value.

Our sexual lives and sexual relationships should not be separated from the rest of our lives and relationships, but part of a continuum with them. Applying our organizing values of personal dignity, equality, and relationship to the realm of sexuality, we believe that sexuality, at its core, is a yearning for connectedness, intimacy, and relationship. Sexual intimacy, an expression of intimate human meeting, can be a route to and expression of "knowing" another, to borrow from Hosea, "in justice, in truth and in faithfulness."[23] It can therefore be a primary mode of both spirituality—knowing God, as Carter Heyward has taught, and of justice-making—making God known.[24]

Sexual intimacy is one place along an "intimacy continuum," and intimacy is a section of the "relationship continuum." The route to knowing God, says Buber, is through our relationships. If the route to knowing God is through knowing others, than our yearning for another and the seeking after intimacy, connectedness and relationship is a God-seeking act. The experience of knowing another with sexual intimacy can bring us closer to God. Just as our worship can be misdirected and result in idolatry, so can this yearning for intimacy and connection be misdirected in idolatrous ways.[25]

Our commitment to the equality, dignity, and autonomy of each person as an individual is unprecedented in our tradition. We should not be surprised, therefore, that the halachah's categories which strictly regulate permitted and forbidden acts do not satisfy our desire to affirm as much individual autonomy as possible. In general, we turn away from the halachah's concern for the acceptability of discrete acts and instead emphasize the quality of the relationship in which the actions occur. We consider the possibility that any sexual acts—whether previously permitted or forbidden—can be a means to the realization of sanctified human relationship through sexual intimacy. Our most intimate relationships should be the place of our primary and greatest expression of covenantal justice. Our sexual lives are a significant opportunity for and important place of transformation of the ordinary and instinctual into the sacred.[26] Accordingly, our religious interpretation of sexuality is measured not according to whether acts are permitted or forbidden, nor ritually pure or impure, but whether the relationship as a whole and its specific expression is just or unjust, contributing to or diminishing from holiness.

Sexual relationship can be an expression of and seeking after covenantal relationship. Covenantal commitment is lived out over time and as part of a community. Our sexual relationships, when lived as aspects of covenantal living, are properly respectful of both of these commitments. Accordingly, we must consider the long-term impact and possible consequences of our actions. Made in God's image, we need to consider our own selves. As part of our covenantal relationships, we should be equally concerned for our partners. Covenant living occurs within a community. Responsible sexual expression, therefore, occurs with attention to and respect for the existing commitments of both partners, whether these are commitments to themselves or to others.[27]

4.

How then do we understand received Jewish teaching on sexuality? We reconsider the organizing values—and their consequent embodiment in specific mitzvot—in light of our own organizing values and total worldview. We begin with a bias towards affirming historical Jewish practice unless the organizing value or its application conflict with our contemporary organizing values. In order to affirm a primary value, it is sometimes necessary to modify, reinterpret, or even reject a historical value and the mitzvot it generated. Let's return to the five organizing values of the rabbinic teaching on sexuality and consider them in light of our organizing values.

We begin with the ban on spilling seed. The physiological concerns for not wasting semen have been long answered by modern science. We no longer consider ourselves bound by the biblical and rabbinic prohibitions concerning the other life-force fluid, blood; is there any enduring spiritual value in maintaining in some form the ban on wasting semen? We do not think so; in fact, we consider acts which were formerly forbidden on this basis (e.g., masturbation) to be otherwise perfectly acceptable, and, in proper circumstances, even desirable.

Two, if the secondary status of women is a basic premise of the halachah, a central value for Reform Jews is the legal, covenantal, and personal equality of women and men. This emerges from our valuation of every human being as a reflection of the divine image and our internalization of what we value in Western culture. A consequence of this organizing value is our rejection of any aspect of the tradition which discriminates between persons on the basis of gender.[28]

We affirm the traditional value of sexuality as a means of procreation, but we no longer accept procreation as the primary paradigm around which sexuality is organized. Instead, we will propose that covenantal relationship is the paradigm of sexual activity. If procreation is no longer the ontological paradigm, heterosexuality need no longer be the ideal mode of sexual expression.

In the halachic system, responsibility for another's sexual pleasure as a mitzvah is limited to the husband's obligations to his wife. Most halachic authorities hold that a married couple is permitted whatever sexual acts the husband desires regardless of the procreative potential of the act. Combining this traditional norm with our modern commitment to equality between persons, we expand the mitzvah of onah to include obligations of both partners to seek to satisfy the sexual needs of the other. We cannot accept the principle that "a man can do what he wishes" regardless of the woman's desires because it denies the woman's equality and autonomy. We transvalue this rabbinic teaching, and invoking our value of equality and mutuality in relationship, conclude that mutually desired sexual acts between two persons are acceptable, so long as the individual acts and the relationship as a whole meet the ethical criteria for right relationship and right action, as explained below.

The fifth value, the question of ritual purity, is so bound up with other aspects of the rabbinic system of daily life, that a full discussion is beyond the scope of this essay. Let us merely note that we treat the system of ritual purity as another potential route to spirituality whose demand can properly only be taken on by an individual and can no longer be imposed from without.

Earlier, we listed the criteria for licit sexual expression according to the halachah. The comparable list in our system begins in our understanding of sexual expression as a dimension of our covenantal relationship with God, in the context of and contributing to right relation. We believe that this is possible when sexuality is expressed

1. between equals—people who are peers in maturity, independence, and personal and physical power
2. who share mutual respect and affection
3. who assume equal responsibility for the possible consequences of their sexual activity[29]
4. with concern for one another's pleasure
5. with concern for one another's physical and emotional health and well-being
6. in the context of open communication and truth telling
7. with respect for one another's body right and bodily integrity
8. in the context of and with attention to each person's existing personal and communal covenantal obligations to others

The above superficially dualistic presentation, between a modern focus on the context and relationship, in contrast to the tradition's emphasis on the specifics and circumstances of actions, distorts the nuances of both systems. Nonetheless we are indeed proposing a radical break with our tradition's teaching.

5.

Up to this point, we have not explicitly spoken about homosexuality. Male homosexual acts are forbidden by explicit biblical command and are condemned as violations of the prohibitions against spilling seed and non-procreative intercourse. In so far as these historical concerns are no longer in force as criteria for heterosexual behavior,[30] the continued application of them as a reason to condemn homosexual acts can only be considered homophobic. We do explicitly reject the biblical prohibition on homosexual acts, applying in its place our contemporary standard of covenant relationship, in which acts and actors are measured not in accordance of who and what they are but how they live.

6.

Some liberal Jewish teachers have cautioned against rejecting traditional values in favor of the prevailing cultural values of the society in which we live. It is appropriate, therefore, to explicitly note some of the ways in which our new Jewish ethic dissents from the prevailing cultural ethos which surrounds us. Although our new ethic is fundamentally a departure of Jewish tradition as seen through the prism of the organizing values of this generation of liberal Jews, it is also a corrective of the culture from which it emerges. We part from the mainstream of American culture in three notable ways: the focus on pleasure, the use of sexuality as an instrument of power, and the genital focus of sexual expression.

American culture treats sexuality primarily as a form of personal pleasure. We consider pleasure desirable, as does the Jewish tradition. However, the excessive focus on personal pleasure and private ego-needs opens the door to the exploitation and abuse of others. Our concern with mutuality excludes a sexual ethic which ends with the self.[31]

The Jewish tradition, through the prophetic tradition, has always been concerned about the abuse of power. By and large, our concern has been with the use and abuse of power in the wider social and political realm. Feminism has taught us to consider the place of power in interpersonal relationships as well. Just sexual relationships cannot occur when sexuality is used as an instrument of control or power. Nor is justice consistent with the use of power or its threat to coerce or force another into sexual intimacy.

Susan Brownmiller argues persuasively that in our culture violence is erotic and passion is associated with having power over another or being overpowered by another.[32] This attitude is supported by the cultural definition of sexual relations as "conquest." Our ethic of sexuality therefore includes the transformation of culture so that mutuality is erotic, personal empowerment is desirable, and passion is linked to both strength and tenderness.[33] The understanding of sexual relations as an act of conquest, along with the historical emphasis on procreation, has led to the focus on genital sexuality. Contemporary cultural images of sexuality, whether in advertising or pornography, gay and straight, continue to equate sexual pleasure with genital contact. In contrast, when sexuality is an instrument of intimacy and relationship, than the total person and the total act will be eroticized. Such sexual expression changes the focus of the act from the goal (orgasm) towards the experience of mutual intimacy.

7.

If, as Buber taught, we come to know God through our I-Thou relationships with others, then our most intimate relationships with others are a unique place for sacred living. The I-Thou relationship demands that we see another not as an object but as a wholistic person in the divine image. Because we are so vulnerable in these private relationships, we are uniquely challenged to practice ethical living and covenant respect in our sexual lives. Through learning to live and act justly in this private sphere, and through the enhancement of our own person which emerges from true relationship, we are strengthened and encouraged to channel passion and action towards justice in wider, more public spheres. The realization of our most intimate yearnings is not a closed circle which in turn leads us back to our partner; rather, the Jewish dialectic of personal and communal obligation turns us outward from the most intimate sphere to return and reengage in the labor of restoring and healing the world.

Notes

This paper is the product of a lengthy collaboration with my colleague, Rabbi Margaret Moers Wenig of Hebrew Union College-Jewish Institute of Religion, New York, who began this research and contributed the title, the structure and many of the ideas.

1. Even if we limited our discussion to the contemporary Reform movement, the primary liberal wing of American Judaism, we would immediately discover a vast range of positions.
2. Yoel H. Kahn, "Judaism and Homosexuality: The Traditional/Progressive Debate," *Journal of Homosexuality* 18:3–4 (1989/90), 47–82; this essay appears in a slightly different form in *Homosexuality, the Rabbinate, and Liberal Judaism* (New York, N.Y.: Central Conference of American Rabbis, 1989).
3. The answer is "not much." The paucity of discussion illustrates, in my opinion, the uncomfortableness of the contemporary Jewish community with sexuality and confronting the chasm between the values of the halachah and those of this culture.
4. See Kahn, 1989; Yoel H. Kahn, "The *Kedushah* of Homosexual Relationships," *CCAR Yearbook XCIX* (New York, N.Y.: Central Conference of American Rabbis, 1989), 136–41.
5. The discussion which follows is based in large part on David Feldman's exhaustive research in *Marital Relations, Birth Control, and Abortion in Jewish Law* (New York, N.Y.: Schocken, 1974). The conclusions are, of course, my own.

6. In the biblical world, blood and semen both ritually polluted those who came in contact with them. The force of the later rabbinic prohibition was greatly strengthened when the 13th-century mystical book, the *Zohar,* declared the violation of this law "greater than all other transgressions." *(Zohar,* Va'yeshev, 188a). The Zohar's statement was codified in the later codes, including the very influential 16th-century work, the *Shulchan Aruch* (E. H. 23). See Feldman, chap. 6. *passim,* esp. p. 115, n. 37 ff.
7. Talmud, Niddah 13a; Moses Maimonides, *Mishnah Torah,* "Issurei Bi'ah (Laws of Forbidden Intercourse)" 21:18: *"K'ilu harag nefesh."*
8. See Feldman, 152–54. On non-vaginal intercourse, see 155 ff. and below.
9. See "Hashhatat Zerah," *Encyclopedia talmudit* (Jerusalem, Israel: Talmudic Encyclopedia Institute, 1965) vol. 11, col. 141, n. 179, and Feldman, 229–30.
10. See Feldman, part IV, esp. 227 ff. According to the stringent *poskim* (decisors), the concern for *sheflchat zerah* prohibits all non-procreative sexual activity, including intercourse in which the semen is not directly deposited in the vagina. See the responsum of the Asheri, *Teshuvot ha-Rosh,* Klal 33, no. 3, cited in Feldman, 153, and the discussion which follows, esp. 155, n. 60.
11. This principle is articulated in the tannaitic statement "If a man married a woman and remained with her for ten years and she has not yet given birth, he is not allowed to neglect further the duty of procreation." Talmud, Yevamot 64a and parallels. See Feldman, 37–45. The rabbis did not require the husband to divorce his wife in practice; see the responsum cited in Feldman, 40, n. 104.
12. Current halachah does not require a man to divorce an infertile wife.
13. What is permitted to a fertile couple is permitted to an infertile couple and what is not permitted a fertile couple is likewise not permitted to an infertile couple. Feldman quotes *Nimmukei Yosef,* the 15th-century commentary to Al-Fasi's code:

    > *Intercourse* with a woman incapable at all of childbearing is permissible, and the prohibition of *hashhatat zerah* is not involved so long as the intercourse is in the manner of procreation; for the rabbis have in every case permitted *marriage* with women too young or too old for childbearing. No prohibition is involved with a barren or sterile woman, except that the mitzvah of procreation is not thus being fulfilled (Feldman, 68; emphasis in original).

14. According to Feldman, 66, it is not particular non-procreative acts but "consciously fruitless marriage" that "so violates the very spirit of Judaism." According to the rabbis, the "natural" sexual act, is intercourse in the missionary position. Some authorities permit "unnatural acts" (woman on top, rear entry, anal intercourse), basing themselves on the talmudic passage: "A man may do with his wife as he will." Feldman, 155, n. 63. See Talmud, Nedarim 20b, Sanhedrin 58b, and Moshe Feinstein, *Igrot Moshe,* E. H., 63–64, cited in Feldman, 165. Feldman comments: "Here we have an example of an act which, while sanctioned by law, was a source of embarrassment to the many moralists who could not bring themselves to accept so liberal a ruling even in theory. Unnatural positions are prohibited either on the basis of immorality *(Shulchan aruch,*

O.H. 240:5), or because they interfere with procreation (E.H. 25:2)." Many *poskim* who were inclined to permit "unnatural acts" on this basis felt constrained by the force of the Zohar's prohibition on *hash-hatat zerah* and its later codification. See *Encyclopedia talmudit,* esp. n. 139, which quotes a later commentator about a permissive ruling: "If he had seen what the Zohar says about the punishment of . . . this [transgression], since it is greater than all of the other transgressions, then he would never have written what he did."

15. The husband [*ba'al*] "acquires" her from her father. This premise begins the mishnaic discussion of marriage: "A woman is acquired in one of three ways . . . (Mishnah, Ketubot 1:1). The talmudic discussion of this passage explores how marriage is both like and unlike property. See Rachel Biale, *Women and Jewish law* (New York, N.Y.: Schocken, 1984), 46–49. The term *kedushah* in the context of marriage means "set aside" or "reserved" (see Biale, 48; Abraham Ibn-Shoshan, *Ha-Milon he-chadash* (Jerusalem, Israel: Kiryat Sefer, 1979), vol. 6, col. 2292, def. 2). In a divorce, the "setting aside" of the woman is reversed, as she moves from the special status of "reserved for a particular man" ("*mekudeshet li*") to the general "permitted to any man" ("*mooteret le kol adam*"). Adultery therefore is intercourse between a man and another man's wife. (Deut. 22:22; Talmud, Kiddushin 80b–81b; Biale, 183–84; Epstein, *Sex laws and customs in Judaism* (New York, N.Y.: Ktav, 1967), 196–99. Rape is considered a crime against property whose penalty was the monetary reimbursement of the value of the raped woman by the rapist to the woman's father (Deut. 21:28–29; Biale, 243).
16. Including, according to Moses Nachmanides, "physical intimacy, appropriate surroundings and regularity." Nachmanides on Ex. 21:11, cited in Biale, 129.
17. Biale, 121–46 *passim,* esp. 137. Biale also discusses the rabbis' understanding of male and female sexual desire, which shaped their norms of acceptable behavior.
18. The biblical basis for the laws of *niddah* is Leviticus 15:19–33. Their application was greatly expanded by the rabbis. A couples' freedom to enjoy sex and physical intimacy together is greatly restricted by the requirements of *niddah.* For a full discussion, see Biale, 147–74.
19. The biblical and rabbinic world has no concept of "homosexuality." Male homosexual behavior is strictly forbidden in Leviticus 18. Lesbianism is also prohibited by the halachah but considered a less severe crime. See Maimonides, "Issurei Bi'ah," 1:14, 21:8, and Biale, 192–94.
20. Intercourse between a man and a woman not forbidden to each other effected a marriage between them; such "marriages" were prohibited by the later authorities.
21. See Feldman, 72–74, and esp. notes 78–82 there.
22. See Feldman, 65–70.
23. Hosea 2:21.
24. Beverly Wildung Harrison, *Making the Connections: Essays in Feminist Social*

Ethics, ed. Carol. S. Robb (Boston: Beacon, 1985), 149, quoted in Carter C. Heyward, *Touching Our Strength: The Erotic as Power and the Love of God* (San Francisco; Harper and Row, 1989), 55.

25. We consider the exploitation of sexuality and the treatment of people as sexual objects as primary forms of contemporary idolatry. We are aware of the vast potential for evil and abuse in the realm of sexuality and sexual power. While sexuality is not the only or exclusive route to intimacy and connectedness, its special place in the order of human need cannot be ignored or denied.
26. This is our understanding of *kiddushin*—a sanctified relationship.
27. Adultery, therefore, is properly understood as the violation of covenantal trust between two people.
28. See, for example, the rejection of the ceremony for *pidyon ha-ben,* redemption of the first born son, in Simeon J. Maslin, ed., *Gates of Mitzvah* (New York: Central Conference of American Rabbis, 1979), 72, n. 19.
29. I.e., assume mutual responsibility for contraception, safer sex, emotional and material support for abortion, pregnancy, childbirth or offspring.
30. If this were not so, then Jews would practice birth control in accordance with halachic, rather than Western, standards.
31. This is a central theme in Borowitz, *Choosing a Sex Ethic* (New York: Schocken, 1968). We particularly reject the mass cultural portrayal of casual sexual activity without attention or concern for either consequences or continuity.
32. Susan Brownmiller, *Against Our Will: Men, Women, and Rape* (New York: Simon and Schuster, 1975), chap. 4.
33. Carter Heyward and Beverly Harrison in a discussion at "Conference on What Women Theologians Are Thinking," Union Seminary, New York, N.Y., October 1987.

Bibliography

Belliotti, Raymond A. *Good Sex: Perspectives on Sexual Ethics.* Lawrence, Kans.: University Press of Kansas, 1993.

Beneke, Tim. *Men on Rape.* New York: St. Martin's Press, 1982.

Biale, David. *Eros and the Jews: From Biblical Israel to Contemporary America.* New York: Basic Books, 1992.

Biale, Rachel. *Women and Jewish Law.* New York: Schocken Books, 1984.

Bogart, John H. "On the Nature of Rape." *Public Affairs Quarterly* 5 (1991): 117–36.

Borowitz, Eugene B. "The Jewish Self." In *Contemporary Jewish Ethics and Morality: A Reader,* edited by Elliott N. Dorff and Louis E. Newman. New York: Oxford University Press, 1995.

Cahill, Lisa Sowle. *Between the Sexes: Foundations for a Christian Ethics of Sexuality.* Philadelphia: Fortress Press, 1985.

Countryman, L. William. *Dirt, Greed and Sex.* Philadelphia: Fortress Press, 1988.

Courtright, Paul B. "*Satī,* Sacrifice, and Marriage: The Modernity of Tradition." In *From the Margins of Hindu Marriage: Essays on Gender, Religion, and Culture,* edited by Lindsey Harlan and Paul B. Courtright. New York: Oxford University Press, 1995.

Crawford, June, Susan Kippax, and Catherine Waldby. "Women's Sex Talk and Men's Sex Talk: Different Worlds." *Feminism and Psychology* 4, no. 4: 571–87.

D'Emilio, John. "Capitalism and Gay Identity." In *Making Trouble: Essays on Gay History, Politics, and the University.* New York: Routledge, 1992.

Ellison, Marvin M. *Erotic Justice: A Liberating Ethic of Sexuality.* Louisville, Ky.: Westminster John Knox Press, 1996.

Greenberg, Blu. *On Women and Judaism: A View from Tradition.* Philadelphia: Jewish Publication Society, 1981.

Grey, Mary. "Claiming Power-in-Relation: Exploring the Ethics of Connection." In *Christian Perspectives on Sexuality and Gender,* edited by Elizabeth Stuart and Adrian Thatcher. Grand Rapids, Mich.: Wm. B. Eerdmans, 1996.

Hassan, Riffat. "An Islamic Perspective." In *Women, Religion and Sexuality,* edited by Jeanne Becher. Philadelphia: Trinity Press International, 1991.

Hoagland, Sarah Lucia. *Lesbian Ethics: Toward New Value.* Chicago: Institute of Lesbian Studies, 1988.

John Paul II. *Familiaris Consortio.* 1981.

Kahn, Yoel H. "Making Love as Making Justice: Towards a New Jewish Ethic of Sexuality." In *Gay Affirmative Ethics,* edited by Michael L. Stemmler and J. Michael Clark. Las Colinas, Tex.: Monument Press, 1993.

Kilmartin, Christopher T. *The Masculine Self.* New York: Macmillan/Maxwell, 1994.

Kosnik, Anthony, William Carroll, Agnes Cunningham, Ronald Modras, and James Schulte. *Human Sexuality: New Directions in American Catholic Thought.* New York: Paulist Press, 1977.

Lebacqz, Karen. "Appropriate Vulnerability: A Sexual Ethic for Singles." *The Christian Century,* May 6, 1987, 435–38.

Morgan, Kathyrn Pauly. "Women and the Knife: Cosmetic Surgery and the Colonization of Women's Bodies." In *Living with Contradictions: Controversies in Feminist Social Ethics,* edited by Alison M. Jagger. Boulder, Colo.: Westview Press, 1994.

Nagel, Thomas. "Sexual Perversion." *Journal of Philosophy* 66, no. 1 (1969): 5–17.

Nelson, James. *The Intimate Connection: Male Sexuality, Masculine Spirituality.* Philadelphia: Westminster Press, 1988.

Overall, Christine. "Heterosexuality and Feminist Theory." *Canadian Journal of Philosophy* 20, no. 1 (March 1990): 1–17.

Parker, Rebecca. "Making Love as a Means of Grace: Women's Reflections." *Open Hands* 3, no. 3 (winter 1988): 8–12.

Paul VI. *Humanae Vitae.* 1968.

Pellauer, Mary D. "The Moral Significance of Female Orgasm." *Journal of Feminist Studies in Religion* 9, no. 1–2 (spring/fall 1993): 161–82.

Pius XI. *Casti Connubii.* 1930.

Reed, Barbara E. "The Gender Symbolism of Kuan-yin Bodhisattva." In

Buddhism, Sexuality, and Gender, edited by Jose Ignacio Cabezon. Albany, N.Y.: State University of New York Press, 1992.

Secker, Susan L. "Human Experience and Women's Experience: Resources for Catholic Ethics." In *The Annual.* Boston: Society of Christian Ethics, 1991.

Smith, Bill. "Locating My Theology in Sacred Places." In *New Visions for the Americas: Religious Engagement and Social Transformation*, edited by David Batstone. Minneapolis: Fortress Press, 1993.

Tachibana, Shundo. *The Ethics of Buddhism.* Surrey, England: Curzon Press, 1992.

Tiefer, Leonore. *Sex Is Not a Natural Act and Other Essays.* Boulder, Colo.: Westview Press, 1995.

Trible, Phyllis. *Texts of Terror.* Philadelphia: Fortress Press, 1984.

Wadley, Susan S. "No Longer a Wife: Widows in Rural North India." In *From the Margins of Hindu Marriage: Essays on Gender, Religion, and Culture,* edited by Lindsey Harlan and Paul B. Courtright. New York: Oxford University Press, 1995.

Wawrytko, Sandra A. "Sexism in the Early *Saṅgha:* Its Social Basis and Philosophical Dissolution." In *Buddhist Behavioral Codes and the Modern World,* edited by Charles Wei-hsun Fu and Sandra A. Wawrytko. Westport, Conn.: Greenwood Press, 1994.

Wolf, Naomi. *The Beauty Myth.* New York: William Morrow & Co., 1991.